SMALL

BUSINESS

MANAGEMENT

SMALL

BUSINESS

MANAGEMENT

SIXTH EDITION

Nicholas Siropolis

Cuyahoga Community College

HOUGHTON MIFFLIN COMPANY   **Boston**   **New York**

Sponsoring Editor: Jennifer B. Speer
Senior Associate Editor: Susan M. Kahn
Assistant Editor: Yuka Sugiura
Senior Project Editor: Charline Lake
Senior Production/Design Coordinator: Sarah Ambrose
Senior Manufacturing Coordinator: Priscilla J. Bailey
Marketing Manager: Michael B. Mercier

Cover design: Darci Mehall, Aureo Design
Cover photographs: © Image Club Graphics Inc.

Credits: Page 8: © Rob Crandall/The Image Works; pages 29, 220, 323, 348, 441, 525, 527, 552, and 583: Photograph copyright by Karabinus & Associates, Inc. Reprinted by permission of Joseph Karabinus.; page 38: © Frank Siteman/PhotoEdit; page 65: © Michael Siluk/The Image Works; pages 97, 193, 301, and 398: © Michael Newman/PhotoEdit; pages 135 and 254: © James L. Shaffer; page 143: *The Business Review,* formerly *The Western Reserve Business Review;* pages 155 and 356: © Jeff Greenberg/Unicorn Stock Photos; pages 178 and 181: Photographs reprinted by permission of Arthur Treacher's, Inc.; page 228: © John Griffin/The Image Works; page 278: Kathie Hirko, Riverbed Studio, Cleveland, Ohio; page 339: © PhotoEdit; page 423: © Myrleen Ferguson Cate/PhotoEdit; page 453: Copyright © 1995 Houghton Mifflin Company. All Rights Reserved. Reprinted by permission.; page 497: Copyright, Pittsburgh Post-Gazette. Reprinted with permission.; page 511: © Jim Pickerell/The Image Works; page 534: © Paul Conklin/PhotoEdit; page 560: © Jean Higgins/Unicorn Stock Photos; page 589: © Jim Mahoney/The Image Works.

Dedicated to my father, Constantine,
and to my mother, Penelope—
both of whom
were entrepreneurs.

CONTENTS

Entrepreneurship currently is riding the crest of a tidal wave of popularity. Record numbers of men and women alike are embracing entrepreneurship as a lifestyle. Students, in particular, find entrepreneurship appealing, mostly because it offers them a vibrant vision of the ways in which they may fulfill their highest potential.

It is the richness of this vision that infuses our textbook. Though the inspiration of an idea coupled with the passion to make it on one's own provide the catalyst, entrepreneurship is really much more than that. Much more. To succeed, entrepreneurs must know, for example, how to write a business plan, research markets, raise money, analyze accounting records, and use information technology.

This textbook covers these subjects as well as numerous others across the spectrum of entrepreneurship. This coverage will help students in every walk of life gain insights into what drives entrepreneurial behavior and tools for coping with their roles as entrepreneurs. Turning to the chapter guide on the next page, note the full list of topics:

▶ Chapters 1–3 offer an overview of entrepreneurship, covering topics such as the state of small business, the global challenge, cultural diversity, as well as ethics and social responsibility.

▶ Chapters 4–10 discuss the aspects of launching a venture, focusing on topics such as the business plan, franchises, legal aspects, and financing.

▶ Chapters 11–20 explore the topics connected with managing an ongoing venture, such as marketing, financial analysis, human relations, and information technology.

Following are some of the features of our textbook:

▶ Focus on cases. Each chapter has three cases: one comprehensive case and two short cases. The comprehensive cases describe how the entrepreneurs began their ventures, how they progressed with them, and the direction in which they are moving. These cases also have financial statements, including ones that show how entrepreneurs financed their ventures at the start. Such in-depth accounts of entrepreneurs let students know what it is *really* like to be in business for themselves.

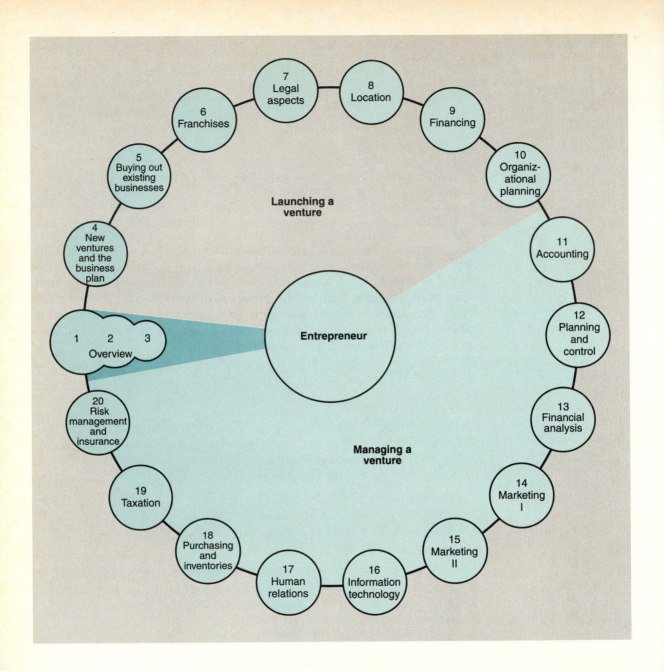

The diagram shows a circular arrangement of topics around a central "Entrepreneur" hub, divided into "Launching a venture" (top) and "Managing a venture" (bottom).

- 1, 2, 3 Overview
- 4 New ventures and the business plan
- 5 Buying out existing businesses
- 6 Franchises
- 7 Legal aspects
- 8 Location
- 9 Financing
- 10 Organizational planning
- 11 Accounting
- 12 Planning and control
- 13 Financial analysis
- 14 Marketing I
- 15 Marketing II
- 16 Information technology
- 17 Human relations
- 18 Purchasing and inventories
- 19 Taxation
- 20 Risk management and insurance

▶ Building a business plan. New to this edition, this feature, which is included in every chapter, serves as a step-by-step guide for students to follow successfully when creating a business plan in the real world. A sample business plan at the end of the book provides a model for further understanding.

▶ Extremely readable text. Virtually free of jargon, our textbook is written in a lively, enthusiastic style that invites students to learn about entrepreneurship, its opportunities and its promise.

- Real-world examples coupled with business principles and concepts. Throughout the text, examples from the world of entrepreneurship clarify key concepts, such as the business plan and the marketing mix.

- A systematic approach to the study of entrepreneurship. Students' first exposure to entrepreneurship may easily be confusing or overwhelming, if only because of the many concepts, procedures, and regulations that must be learned. Our sequencing of subjects is a logical and orderly approach to mastering our textbook's body of knowledge.

- An emphasis on social responsibility and ethical behavior. In fact, an entire chapter at the beginning of the text (Chapter 3) is devoted to those subjects. Our cases also reflect the need for entrepreneurs to behave ethically and be socially responsible.

Specific Changes from Prior Editions

This edition of our textbook differs in many ways from prior editions. Informed by a vision of what entrepreneurship should be and could be, this edition's changes reflect the latest wisdom and thought about what it takes to make good as an entrepreneur. Specifically, this edition has, among other changes:

- Added an appendix featuring a sample business plan keyed to subject matter in the chapters, as mentioned earlier

- Included twenty cases new to this edition and continued our tradition of celebrating the cultural diversity of entrepreneurship through the case method of instruction

- Reinforced the cardinal importance of ethics and social responsibility by moving coverage forward to Chapter 3 and by expanding coverage

- Added numerous real-world examples of small businesses and entrepreneurs

- Updated and refined the content of every chapter

- Reflected the latest thought on information technology, the Internet in particular

- Expanded coverage of the global challenge

- Added coverage of home-based businesses

- Reinforced coverage of women-owned businesses

- Emphasized the role that entrepreneurs play as innovators

- Expanded coverage of legal aspects to include limited liability companies (LLCs)

- Added an employee bill of rights to our discussion of human relations

- Expanded coverage of intellectual property to include copyrights and trademarks

- Added the latest thought on how best to apply the principles of total quality management (TQM)

- Expanded coverage of pricing

▶ Refined the coverage of cultural diversity, emphasizing its promise and its opportunities

There are, however, things about *Small Business Management* that we have not changed. As in earlier editions, we have tried to write a textbook that reflects the letter and spirit of the entrepreneurial tradition, a textbook that is teachable and readable, content-rich and stimulating. And, as always, we have tried to convey the conviction that entrepreneurship is a vital, dynamic, and rewarding endeavor.

Features of the Package

▶ **For Instructors**

Instructor's Resource Manual features for every chapter: a discussion of the purpose of the chapter, tips on using the chapter, learning objectives, a chapter outline, and answers to the discussion and review questions. Also included are answers to the case discussion questions, which provide detailed analysis of all cases. A transition guide has been added, telling instructors in one spot how this edition differs from the prior edition.

Test Bank contains true-or-false, multiple choice, and essay questions for each chapter, for a total of more than 1,300 items.

Computerized Test Bank is a computerized testing program with all items from the printed test bank in a powerful, easy-to-use format. It has the flexibility and sophistication to adapt to all your needs and experiences.

Transparency Package contains seventy-seven acetates of all important exhibits from the text.

▶ **For Students**

Computerized Business Plan is a computerized version of the textbook's Building a Business Plan feature.

Entrepreneur: A Simulation concerns the takeover and operation of a retail clothing store. Students consider the variables involved in business decision making.

Opening a Business guides students through the process of gathering and analyzing data on key areas of business ownership, then asks them to complete summary sheets based on that information.

Acknowledgments

This textbook is by no means the work of one person. Many have contributed to its development. Let me mention just a few:

▶ The entrepreneurs who gave so freely of their time and energies to supply me with the case material.

▶ The faculty and staff at Cuyahoga Community College, who enabled me to create an accredited curriculum devoted to entrepreneurship. I am especially indebted to Darl Ault, Elizabeth Boyer, Mildred Brown, John Coleman, Walter Johnson, Kenneth Killen, Kermit Lidstrom, Joseph Malone, Robert Parilla, George Plavac, Robert Sexton, Richard Shapiro, Booker Tall, and Lowell Watkins.

- ▶ The Greater Cleveland Growth Association, where I first got the idea to create an entrepreneurship curriculum. In particular, I am indebted to Melvin Roebuck, with whom I have had a long professional relationship.

- ▶ The U.S. Small Business Administration, which never failed me in my numerous requests for help.

- ▶ Glenn Owen, University of California at Santa Barbara, for his assistance in revising the information technology chapter.

- ▶ Robert J. Hughes, Dallas County Community College, for his assistance in preparing business plan material.

- ▶ Thomas Lloyd, Westmoreland County Community College, for his assistance in revising the Test Bank.

- ▶ Reviewers whose suggestions and comments were helpful in creating this and previous editions:

David V. Aiken
Hocking Technical College

Barry Ashmen
Bucks County Community College

Richard Bevans
Kodiak College

Robert E. Bidwell
University of Dayton

Ernest H. Brass, III
Lake Erie College

John J. Buckley
Orange County Community College

John Carpenter
Corpus Christi State

Bonnie Chavez
Santa Barbara City College

James Christensen
Delta College

Edward Hamburg
Gloucester County College

Gene Hastings
Portland Community College

Richard Hilliard
Nichols College

Ronald Jones
Laney College

William J. Jordan
Community College of Allegheny
County—Boyce Campus

Richard E. LaBarre
Ferris State University

Jack K. Mandel
Nassau Community College

Paul D. Maxwell
Bridgewater State College

Timothy S. Mescon
Kennesaw State College

Ken Millner
College of the Redwoods

Joan Nichols
Emporia State University

David O'Dell
McPherson College

Diana Pappin
Indiana Vocational Technical College

Michael Pitts
Virginia Commonwealth University

Kevin J. Roth
Clarion University of Pennsylvania

Joseph Stasio
Merrimack College

A. Keith Strasser
Moorpark College

Gary Strom
Minneapolis Technical College

William Syvertsen
Fresno City College

John Tate
Montclair State University

Bernard W. Weinrich
St. Louis Community College
at Forest Park

▶ Members of the North American Case Research Association for their permission to use two of their cases.

To all of these men and women and their organizations, my heartfelt thanks.

NICHOLAS SIROPOLIS

Small Business in a Global Economy

- to define small business
- to explore and identify the strengths and weaknesses of small business
- to summarize the role that small business plays in both the U.S. and the global economy
- to explain the need for cultural diversity in small business
- to outline some of the long-term trends expected for small business

When I look into the future, it's so bright it burns my eyes.

—Oprah Winfrey

Small business enjoys a tradition of infinite variety and solid achievement. It thrives everywhere, from New York to Saginaw in the United States, to Tokyo and Kinshasa (Zaire) overseas. So vital is small business that few, if any, parts of the global economy could go on without its products and services. Small business is also a civilizing influence, rising above dollars and cents to enrich the lives of men and women the world over.

The Place of Small Business in History

Small business has played a role in history since practically the beginning of recorded time. The first known piece of writing on small business, describing how bankers loaned money at interest, appeared more than 4,000 years ago.[1] Since then, small businesspersons have spent countless hours creating products and services to benefit the consumer.

Small business flourished in almost all ancient cultures. The Arabs, Babylonians, Egyptians, Jews, Greeks, Phoenicians, and Romans excelled at it. Their products and services, however, were frequently shoddy and slipshod. Consumers were often cheated and defrauded. The result was that small businesses became objects of scorn.

Into this controversy stepped Hammurabi, King of Babylon. In 2100 B.C., he drafted a code of 300 laws to protect consumers and small businesspersons, especially against fraud. Carved on marble columns 8 feet high, the original code—much of it now erased by time—resides at the Louvre Museum in Paris. A sampling of Hammurabi's laws follows:

> If outlaws hatch a conspiracy in the house of a wineseller and she does not arrest them and bring them to the palace, that wineseller shall be put to death.

If a builder has built a house for a man and does not make his work perfect; and the house which he has built has fallen down and so caused the death of the householders, that builder shall be put to death.[2]

These two laws underscore the truth of the saying that "the more things change, the more they stay the same." Indeed, the need to protect consumers is as vital today as in Hammurabi's time.

It was largely through small business that civilization was spread to all four corners of the then known world. Small businesses brought to the have-nots such things as Babylonian astronomy, Greek philosophy, the Jewish calendar, and Roman law.

▶ **The Rising Status of Small Business**

During the 1980s and early 1990s, small business began to enjoy more esteem and prestige than ever before, no small thanks to its ability to invent new products and to create new jobs, as is explained later in this chapter. Even as a recession gripped the nation in the late 1980s and early 1990s, the number of small businesses rose. As job security eroded and became a thing of the past, more men and women opted to start their own businesses and take their chances on success or failure. As a result, educators, journalists, and politicians alike now herald the achievements and opportunities, promise, and problems of small businesses.

One measure of small business's new prestige is the dozens of publications devoted to small business today. Until the late 1970s, there were hardly any, and certainly none were popular. Today, one of the most successful is *Inc.* magazine. Its total paid circulation was 300,000 just 3 years after its birth in 1979. It took *Fortune* and *Business Week,* two of the nation's leading business magazines, roughly 25 years to reach that level of paid circulation.

Small business's current prestige is well-deserved. Indeed, its dynamism has aroused the envy of nations throughout the world. If U.S. small business were in fact a nation, it would rank third among the world's economies. In the words of *Inc.* magazine:

> The world has changed, in short, and small business along with it. Where once it was a sleepy appendage to the corporate sector, it now stands alongside it—and in some cases well out in front of it.
>
> Small companies themselves rarely look the way they once did, even if they're in traditional industries. They use state-of-the-art technology to deliver sophisticated goods and services. They push aggressively into niches that would once have been dominated by the *Fortune 500.** They don't shrink from international, even world-wide, markets.[3]

Definitions of Small Business

Small business defies easy definition. Typically, we apply the term *small business* to so-called mom-and-pop stores, such as neighborhood groceries and restaurants, and the term *big business* to such giants as IBM and General

---

*A yearly listing by *Fortune* magazine of the 500 largest U.S. manufacturers in terms of sales revenues.

Motors. But nearly all U.S. businesses fall between these two extremes. They are viewed as big or small depending on the yardstick and cutoff point used. And there are a number of common yardsticks:

▶ **Total assets** The total cash, inventory, land, machinery, and other resources a business holds.

▶ **Owners' equity** The total investment made by investors, often referred to as capital. In a corporation, investors are generally the shareholders who buy stock; creditors are generally those who either lend money or supply credit.

▶ **Yearly sales revenues**

▶ **Number of employees**

Each yardstick has points in its favor, but *number of employees* has more than any of the others. Among other things, this yardstick is:

▶ **Inflation-proof** It is not affected by changes in the dollar's purchasing power.

▶ **Transparent** It is easy to see and understand.

▶ **Comparable** It allows good comparisons of size among businesses in the same industry.

▶ **Available** It is easy to get from businesses.

If we accept number of employees as the yardstick of size, what should the cutoff point be? The U.S. Department of Commerce recommends 500, which is also the figure widely used by chambers of commerce. Accordingly, in this textbook we call a business small if it employs fewer than 500 persons, unless noted otherwise.

Almost all definitions require some qualifications, and ours is no exception. To qualify as small, a business should employ fewer than 500 persons and should not be part of another business. In short, it must be independently owned and managed. This second qualification rules out many franchises. For, an investor who buys a franchise must often live up to numerous contractual obligations, such as keeping certain store hours, paying monthly fees to the franchisor, and preparing monthly performance reports. In these cases, the true boss is the franchisor, not the franchisee.

▶ **The SBA's Definitions**

Let us now look at some other definitions of small business, namely those made by the U.S. Small Business Administration (SBA). Congress created this federal agency in 1953 to help small business thrive. To meet this goal, the SBA offers programs to help small businesses upgrade their managerial skills and borrow money.

For businesses seeking loans, the SBA has drawn up definitions of smallness to fit virtually every industry. Each definition depends on the industry average. For example, the SBA's definition of smallness for computer manufacturers is fewer than 1,000 employees. A business with 600 or 800 employees may not seem small, but the industry average is high, reflecting the size of giant computer manufacturers like IBM.

EXHIBIT 1.1

SBA's definitions of smallness for selected industries (made in 1987 and still in effect in 1996).

▶ **Manufacturers**	**Employing Fewer Than**
Petroleum refining	1,500 persons
Electronic computers	1,000
Macaroni and spaghetti	500
▶ **Wholesalers**	**Employing Fewer Than**
Sporting goods	500 persons
Furniture	500
Paints and varnishes	500
▶ **Retailers**	**Earning Sales of Less Than**
Groceries	$13.5 million a year
Automobile dealerships	11.5
Restaurants	10.0
▶ **Services**	**Earning Sales of Less Than**
Computer	$12.5 million a year
Accounting	4.0
Television repair	3.5

Source: "U.S. Small Business Administration: Small Business Size Standards." *Federal Register,* Vol. 49, No. 28 (Washington, D.C.: U.S. Government Printing Office, January 6, 1987).

Exhibit 1.1 lists the SBA's definitions for selected industries, and Exhibit 1.2 condenses these definitions into broad industry groups. Notice that many of the SBA's definitions really cover medium-sized businesses. For example, a manufacturer employing 1,000 people probably has sales revenues in excess of $50 million a year. Few laypeople would consider such a business small.

The Strengths of Small Business

Returning to our earlier, simpler definition of a small business as one that employs fewer than 500 persons, let us place this number in focus. How many businesses are that small? How many people does a small business employ?

As shown in Exhibit 1.3, in 1995 more than 99 percent of the nation's 21.5 million nonfarm businesses were small—even if we define a small business as one that employs fewer than 100 persons rather than 500. By no means does the total of 21.5 million businesses, based as it is on tax returns, measure the total number of full-time businesses in our economy. For, many tax filers are part-time businesspeople or hobbyists; as such, they have little sales revenues and, in turn, have little or no profit.

EXHIBIT 1.2

SBA's definitions of smallness by major industry group (as of 1996).

Major Industry Group	Maximum Number of Employees	Maximum Yearly Sales Revenues (in millions)
Manufacturing	250 to 1,500*	—
Wholesaling	500	—
Retailing	—	$3.5 to $13.5*
Services	—	$3.5 to $14.5*

*Varies by industry.

EXHIBIT 1.3

Small business as a percentage of U.S. nonfarm businesses.

Number of Employees Fewer than	Percentage of Businesses
10	88.9%
20	91.3
100	99.1
500	99.7

Source: U.S. Small Business Administration, *The State of Small Business: A Report of the President* (Washington, D.C.: U.S. Government Printing Office, 1995), p. 34; Ibid., (1991), p. xv.

A better measure of the total number of full-time businesses is the number of businesses with full-time employees. By law, such businesses must report their employment tax liability to their state employment agencies. This information is then reported to the U.S. Department of Labor. At the end of 1994, this federal agency found that, of the total number of businesses filing tax returns, only 5.8 million—or 27 percent of the total—had employees.

Clearly, small business is a vital force in the American economy. Further evidence of its vitality is the fact that small business employs roughly half of the nation's workforce and generates 54 percent of the sales revenues and 40 percent of the gross national product. "Thus, a great deal of our nation's economic activity comes from the record number of entrepreneurs living the American Dream."[4]

▶ Financial Performance

In terms of sheer numbers, then, small business far outstrips big business. But how well are small businesses doing in terms of dollars? Are they falling behind, keeping pace with, or moving ahead of big business? These questions are hard to answer with precision, but the evidence suggests that small business outearns big business. Some proof appears in Exhibit 1.4.

On the average, small manufacturers earn a higher return on owners' equity than large manufacturers do. In other words, for each dollar they put in, small-business investors earn more than do big-business investors. Although we lack hard data showing why small manufacturers do better, we can offer two reasons:

▶ In many industries, small businesses can respond more quickly and at less cost than big businesses to the quickening rate of change in products and services, processes and markets.

▶ Small business has become more attractive to talented, individualistic men and women.

Although we lack similar data to compare the performance of small and big businesses in nonmanufacturing industries such as retailing, services, and wholesaling, it appears that, for these same reasons, small businesses in these industries are also doing well.

▶ Innovation

Small businesspeople tend to be mavericks, and it is often the mavericks who extend the frontiers of knowledge. Ideas are their stock in trade. In fact, study after study shows that significant innovations are as likely to come from small businesses or from individuals as from big businesses.

EXHIBIT 1.4
Comparative return on owners' equity of small and big business. Since 1980, small manufacturers have outperformed big manufacturers.

Source: Federal Trade Commission, *Quarterly Financial Reports for Manufacturing Corporations* (Washington, D.C.: U.S. Government Printing Office, 1995), Table E.

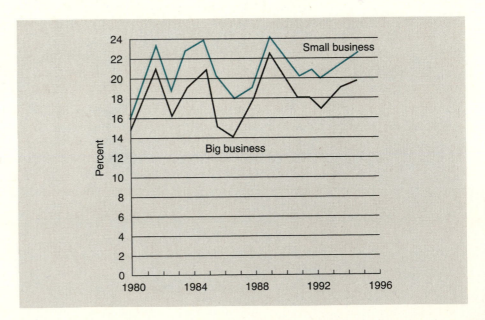

Significant innovations by small business in the twentieth century are wide-ranging; air conditioning, FM radio, overnight mail delivery, the personal computer, and xerography are just a few examples. The beneficial impact on society of such innovations is all but incalculable. Benefits include not only lower prices and better product quality for consumers but also a better quality of life—for example, cleaner air.

Perhaps no better measure of small business's vitality is its ability, innovatively, to outdo big business. In fact, according to studies by the SBA, small business gives birth to more than *twice* as many significant innovations per employee as big business, as depicted in Exhibit 1.5. The SBA offers the following reasons for so stellar a performance:

▸ The incentives to innovate are greater, mostly because small business has the potential to create or capture an entire industry, while big business often stands pat, protecting its market niche.

▸ The motivation to innovate is greater, not only because of the prospect of generous financial rewards but also because of the small business's creative drive and the need for peer recognition as an overachiever.[5]

EXHIBIT 1.5

Significant innovations per employee by small business compared with big business.

Source: Office of Advocacy of the U.S. Small Business Administration, *The State of Small Business: A Report of the President* (Washington, D.C.: U.S. Government Printing Office, 1995), p. 114.

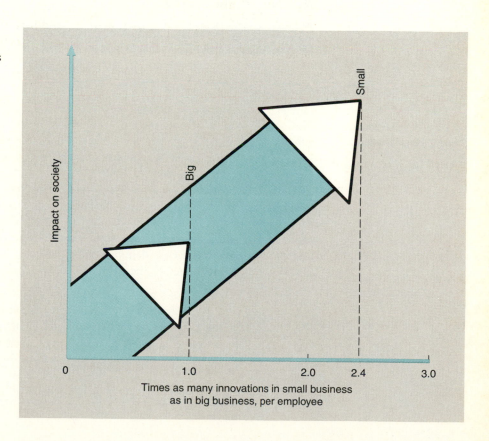

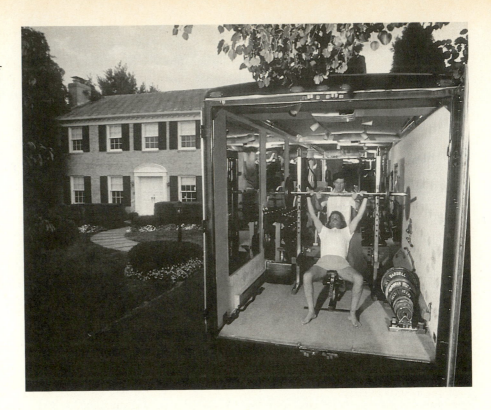

The landscape of small-business opportunities spreads far and wide, as evidenced by this example of a mobile fitness center that comes to a customer's home for workouts.

▶ **The Dependence of Big Business on Small Business**

Our economy depends on small business for much more than invention and innovation. Small businesses employ tens of millions of men and women. They also sell most of the products made by big manufacturers to consumers. In addition, they provide big businesses with many of the services, supplies, and raw materials they need.

General Motors, for example, buys from more than 10,000 suppliers, most of whom are small. Why? Because big businesses cannot supply products and services as cheaply as do small businesses. Among the kinds of products and services that small businesses can supply more cheaply are those whose sales volume is small, those that demand close personal contact with customers, and those that must meet each customer's unique needs.

▶ **Creation of New Jobs**

Moreover, small businesses are major creators of new jobs. In fact, since 1990, the greatest job growth nationally has taken place in such quick-expanding industries as health care and computer software—with small business accounting for the lion's share. In 1993, for example, industries dominated by small business added 1.1 million jobs, while industries dominated by big business lost 700,000 jobs.

Here, it would be simplistic to assume that all small business is a job engine. According to Dr. David Birch of The Massachusetts Institute of Technology:

"The stereotype is that Main Street America is doing this. That's not true. It's not the local florist, bowling alley, or drugstore. Rather, it's the businesses that start small but grow quickly through marketing or technology that are creating jobs. Examples include such household names as Apple and Wal-Mart."[6]

Still another measure of small-business vitality is the increasing number of businesses formed each year since 1960. New business incorporations crossed the 700,000 mark for the first time in 1993.[7] This number is roughly four times the number in the early 1960s. However, the total also includes mature businesses that began as either sole proprietorships or partnerships and then incorporated later.

The Weaknesses of Small Business

Financial performance and innovation, responsiveness and job creation are the bright side of the small-business picture. In contrast, the dark side reflects problems unique to small business and thus defies analysis. For one thing, myths about the rate of small-business failure abound. To justify government help for small business, students and researchers of the small-business scene often pointed to what they perceived to be the "precarious state of small business." One of their most deeply held "truths" was that half of all new businesses died within 18 months after birth, in their infancy.

This "truth" was false, as researchers have just recently found. In an exhaustive study of the federal government's Small Business Data Base, two researchers—Bruce Phillips of the SBA and Bruce Kirchhoff of the New Jersey Institute of Technology—found that:

▶ Forty percent of new businesses lasted at least six years, thus laying to rest the myth of widespread failure at infancy.

▶ New manufacturers enjoyed a longer life than did new retailers.

▶ Businesses that have never added a single employee had a shorter life than others that have added employees.[8]

This study was unavoidably flawed, however. Its Small Business Data Base lacked the records of the tiniest businesses, ones that never make it into any database. There is no way to tell how long these businesses, which tend to be highly at risk, survive.

Healthy debate about small-business failure is likely to continue unabated, because related databases will always be incomplete and imprecise. In the words of Professor Albert Shapero, who taught at Ohio State University and who was a pioneer in the study of small business:

The fact is that no one knows the startup rate or the failure rate. In fact, we don't even know what "failure" means. Do we mean bankruptcy? But many people go out of business without declaring bankruptcy, working like hell to settle every debt even though they have to close the doors of their business.

Others close because their owners reach retirement age and have no one to turn the company over to. Still others shut down because they're bored. Are these business failures?

And is failure really failure? Many heroes of business failed at least once. Henry Ford failed twice. Maybe trying and failing is a better business education than going to a business school that has little concern with small business and entrepreneurship.[9]

▶ Reasons for Failure

Why do some small businesses fail? Perhaps the chief reason is ease of entry. In fact, it is often easier for men and women to go into business for themselves than to find employers. No law stops them from choosing to be their own bosses. And they can choose almost any line of business they like. They may have 20 years of experience in that line or none at all. They may do a textbook job of researching their markets or plunge in with no information at all. They may be millionaires or penniless. Yet, regardless of their qualifications, freedom of opportunity guarantees them the right to launch their own ventures.

But, as economists often point out, freedom of opportunity means not only the freedom to succeed but also the freedom to fail. Failure to see this reality often causes untold stress, trauma, and tragedy.

Should we somehow screen would-be small businesspersons before the marketplace does its own screening? No. The right to make wrong choices lies at the heart of our economic system. Without this right, initiative and incentive would soon dry up, and our free enterprise system would cease to be free.

What are some of the reasons why some fledgling businesses die? Besides ease of entry, researchers point to several *specific* reasons why fledgling businesses fail; some of these are listed in Exhibit 1.6. Note that this exhibit suggests that the difference between success and failure rests mostly on preparation and readiness. For example, a college education linked with managerial experience is likely to lessen the chance of failure and, conversely, boost the chance of success. According to the *Journal of Small Business Strategy:*

> The pivotal role of small business suggests that understanding why businesses succeed or fail is crucial to our economy's health and stability. Thus, lists like the one in Exhibit 1.6 can only serve to benefit the would-be entrepreneur in the effort to better assess his or her chance of success.[10]

It bears mention, however, that there is no widely accepted list of reasons distinguishing success from failure—nor is there likely to be, given the complexity and character of small business.

Which are the safest and riskiest industries dominated by small business? To find out, the SBA studied the question and came up with some startling findings. They found that failure rates vary widely, as shown in Exhibit 1.7. Note the contrast between the failure rate for private education services (13 per 10,000 businesses) and that for amusement and recreational services (578 per 10,000).

▶ Lack of Managerial Expertise

Often small businesses fail because management is not prepared to handle increased demands on its skills and knowledge. It is one thing, for example, to manage a shop of 10 employees and quite another to manage a shop of 100.

EXHIBIT 1.6

List of reasons why small businesses succeed or fail.

▶ *Age.* Younger people who start a business have a greater chance of failure than older people do.

▶ *Capital.* Businesses that start with too little investment by owners have a greater chance of failure than businesses with adequate investment by owners.

▶ *Economic Timing.* Businesses that start during a recession have a greater chance of failure than businesses that start during prosperity.

▶ *Education.* People with no college education who start a business have a greater chance of failure than people with one or more years of college education.

▶ *Experience.* Businesses run by people without prior *industry* experience have a greater chance of failure than businesses run by people with prior industry experience. Similarly, businesses run by people without prior *managerial* experience have a greater chance of failure than businesses run by people with prior managerial experience.

▶ *Marketing.* Business owners without marketing skills have a greater chance of failure than others with marketing skills.

▶ *Parents.* Business owners whose parents did not own a business have a greater chance of failure than owners whose parents did own a business.

▶ *Partners.* A business started by one person has a greater chance of failure than a business started by more than one person.

▶ *Planning.* Businesses that do not prepare business plans have a greater chance of failure than businesses that do.

Source: Robert N. Lussier and Joel Corman, "There Are Few Differences between Successful and Failed Small Businesses," *Journal of Small Business Strategy* (May 1995), p. 21. Adapted by permission.

EXHIBIT 1.7

The safest and riskiest industries for small business.

Source: Bruce Phillips, The Office of Advocacy of the U.S. Small Business Administration. Reported by "The State of Small Business." *Inc.* (1995), p. 20.

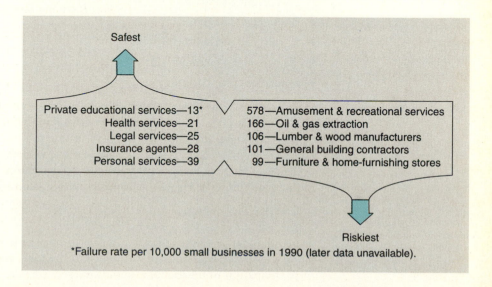

Safest

Private educational services—13*	578—Amusement & recreational services
Health services—21	166—Oil & gas extraction
Legal services—25	106—Lumber & wood manufacturers
Insurance agents—28	101—General building contractors
Personal services—39	99—Furniture & home-furnishing stores

Riskiest

*Failure rate per 10,000 small businesses in 1990 (later data unavailable).

With only 10 employees, small businesspersons generally have visual control over everyone and everything under them. But once their business grows to, say, 100 employees, small businesspersons must rely on more sophisticated ways to plan and control their business. Unfortunately, they often lack the managerial skills to recognize, hire, and tap the talents they need to survive and grow.

In contrast, presidents of billion-dollar corporations are more likely to be professional managers. Skillful in the best and latest managerial tools, they orchestrate the talents of dozens of knowledgeable workers to solve problems and pursue opportunities.

The Global Economy and Cultural Diversity

With the rise of new technology, each year the world is becoming a smaller place. What affects one nation often affects the entire world. In no area is this more true than in business. As we move toward the 21st century, we increasingly find that our problems are our neighbors' problems as well, and that only by working together can we solve them.

Noted futurist Alexander King predicts a world in which "a few countries shelter 20 percent of the population, the rich elite, favored by birth, using the tools of science and technology to benefit themselves and surrounded by the remaining 80 percent of the people, young, hungry, poor, and shut out."[11]

This pessimistic view is already under siege. The prestigious British publication, *The Economist,* surveyed the global economy in 1995 and learned that the rich countries are finding unprecedented opportunity in improving the lot of underdeveloped countries like those in Africa and Central America. The following list shows the percent of exports that the underdeveloped countries account for:

▶ 49 percent of Japan's
▶ 42 percent of the United States'
▶ 25 percent of Italy's
▶ 23 percent of France's
▶ 23 percent of Germany's
▶ 20 percent of Great Britain's
▶ 8 percent of Canada's

Export trade of this size can only help bridge the gap between the haves and the have-nots. Not only will it help relieve poverty in underdeveloped countries, it may also provide them with marvelous business opportunities. For there is little question that to achieve some measure of prosperity at home, underdeveloped countries must first participate fully in the global economy. In the words of Peter F. Drucker, the noted author, lecturer, and consultant:

> The one unambiguous lesson of the last forty years is that increased participation in the global economy has become the key to domestic economic growth and prosperity. There is a *one-to-one* correlation between a country's domestic economic performance in the forty years since 1950 and its participation in the global economy.[12]

Supporting evidence may be found in the examples of Japan and Korea, whose domestic economies have grown the fastest in the global economy since 1950. On the other hand, the countries that have retreated from the global economy—Great Britain among them—have fared the worst domestically.

A qualifying word is in order about the export numbers given in the previous list. These numbers, official though they may be, fail to tell the whole story. They cover only the export of *products*, such as tools and trucks that we can touch and see. Missing from the official numbers, and all but impossible to measure with precision, is the export of *services*, which we cannot touch and see—for example, those services generated by:

▶ Royalties on books, videos, and software

▶ Management consulting firms

▶ Royalties on technology

▶ Financial services

▶ Higher education

▶ Law firms

▶ Hollywood

Note that most of these services have to do with exporting *knowledge*. In rich countries like the United States, the export of knowledge may equal, if not exceed, the value of the export of products.

▶ **Global Change and Small Business**

As the world moves, however haltingly, toward a global economy, the barriers among nations will gradually dissolve. And small business is likely to play a pivotal role in that scenario.

Indeed, freedom of opportunity, or what economists often refer to as *free enterprise*, is a basic freedom, one of the pillars of liberty. So it follows that with the winds of change sweeping across lands like the former Soviet Union, small business is likely to emerge as an agent of creativity.

For, it is the genius of small business to offer the greatest hope for the greatest number of people. Now accepted by virtually every nation is the thought that something basic has happened to change forever the way our global economy works. In the words of Merrill Lynch, the nation's largest investment banking firm:

> Today's global marketplace offers new opportunities for investors to expand their borders beyond national borders. Technology is erasing traditional barriers. Thanks to the computer, we can send billions of dollars overseas and back again in a second.[13]

Some idea of just how vital the global economy is to U.S. small business may be gleaned from Exhibit 1.8. Note that from 1992 to 1995, the percentage of exports by small business more than doubled. Here again the numbers may be in question, mostly because service exports are so hard to track.

▶ **Cultural Diversity, Globally and at Home**

According to Professor Ray Browne of Bowling Green State University, culture can be defined as the "arts, beliefs, customs, institutions, and all other products of human work and thought created by a people or group at a particular time."[14]

EXHIBIT 1.8

Growth of exports by U.S. small business (1992–1995).

Source: Survey by the National Small Business and Arthur Andersen's Enterprise Group. Reported by Janean Chun, "Global Vision." *Entrepreneur* (November 1995), p. 86.

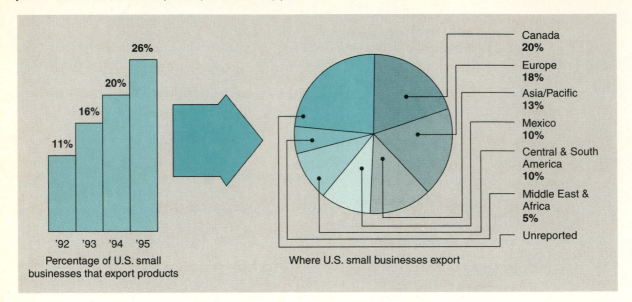

Percentage of U.S. small businesses that export products

Where U.S. small businesses export

- Canada **20%**
- Europe **18%**
- Asia/Pacific **13%**
- Mexico **10%**
- Central & South America **10%**
- Middle East & Africa **5%**
- Unreported

Browne, who coined the phrase *popular culture*, says that "one swims in culture as a fish swims in water. It's all around us."[15]

Now that the cold war is in ashes, cultural change, along with global trade, is engulfing the globe. A new world is rising, one that urgently calls for new, global thinking. More than ever before, our prosperity at home is linked to that of the global economy.

This is the message of a report by the Carnegie Endowment for International Peace called "Changing Our Ways: America and the New World." The report emphasizes that economic power has replaced military might as the source of any nation's influence and suggests that:

▶ A free flow of ideas, products, and investment can enrich every nation.

▶ A go-it-alone attitude can only doom a nation to economic decline.[16]

"An America that lacks economic strength *and* social cohesion will lose respect abroad," warns the Carnegie report. This means America's economic strength can be renewed only if it embraces social change, cultural diversity in particular, not only globally but at home as well.

▶ **Growth of Minorities**

In the words of Mayor Michael White of Cleveland, Ohio: "As we look toward a new century and new global challenges, the United States is well-positioned to draw upon its diverse strengths to be a beacon into the future where racial harmony and multiculturalism are not luxuries but essential keys for understanding, progress, and peace."[17]

To small business, the challenges and opportunities of cultural diversity are plain. For support, one need look no further than the 1990 U.S. Census, which underscores the explosive growth of minorities. For example:

▶ Asians are America's fastest-growing minority. In fact, the Asian population had doubled since the 1980 census, to 7 million in 1990.

▶ The Hispanic population is also growing rapidly, followed by the black population. In fact, the black population grew by 13.2 percent during the 1980s, compared to the national average of 9.8 percent.[18]

Clearly, both big and small businesses face a choice between ignoring the growing number of minorities in the workforce and recognizing this diversity as an advantage in the marketplace. And if they make diversity a top priority—if they resist the natural tendency to surround themselves only with people like themselves—small businesspeople can also fulfill their social responsibilities to their communities.

As we look to the future, we cannot help but see the need for open-mindedness and togetherness as the key to a fruitful tomorrow. America's growing cultural diversity offers challenges to blend minorities into the workplace and marketplace, as well as opportunities to embrace and encourage a more culturally diverse workforce and a demand for products and services expanded by the needs of a multicultural society.

A Look at the Future

What will tomorrow be like? What products and services will consumers want 10 or 20 years from now? Which industries will lend themselves to entrepreneurial adventure?

Looking into the future is high art. Knowledge is now exploding so quickly that industry leaders must look five, ten, or twenty years ahead just to keep up. In fact, our store of knowledge is doubling every 5 years, or several hundred times faster than in the 1920s. By contrast, in the Stone Age, human knowledge doubled every 100,000 years.[19]

Futurists foresee a world far different from today's. For example, the magical year 2000 is likely to see a breakthrough in entrepreneurship education. The federal government is already committed to promoting "entrepreneurial education in the free enterprise system" in high schools as well as in colleges.[20]

Each year, the renowned World Future Society selects what it deems the most stimulating forecasts made by esteemed futurists. These forecasts are also plausible, based as they are on what is known about current trends. A sampling appears in Exhibit 1.9.

Forecasts such as these hint at answers to the key question: In what industries lie the best opportunities for entrepreneurial adventure in the future? There is no way to answer this question with precision. We can only guess. But it seems that entrepreneurs will be drawn to those industries prepared for strong upward trends in service individualism and technology.

EXHIBIT 1.9
Sampling of forecasts made by futurists affecting the U.S. economy.

▶ Business firms will continue to stay slim by assigning functions to subcontractors. This will make it easier for corporations to adapt to the constantly changing realities of the marketplace.

▶ Today's computer nerds and cyberpunks will be the business lions of tomorrow. Future entrepreneurs are now becoming seasoned travelers on the information superhighway, learning to create virtual enterprises quickly and efficiently. This key skill will give them an edge over traditional, monolithic businesses.

▶ Half of today's retail stores will disappear by the year 2000, as more customers flock to the "Meta-Mart"—the commercial lanes of the information superhighway. As communications technologies become more sophisticated and interactive, viewers will be able to feel the fabric of the suit they're buying just by touching the TV screens.

▶ As more people shop at home instead of at stores, some communities may fall on hard times. Suburbs will lose real estate and sales taxes, and traditional summer jobs and lower-paying retail jobs will dry up. Rural areas could see a population boom as people decide they don't need the "convenience" of living near shopping areas.

▶ Interactive multimedia will become the new tool of education. For the students of tomorrow, the traditional blackboard will be replaced by text, graphics, sound, animation, full-motion video, and other formats.

▶ Computer programming will become irrelevant as conversational, natural-language software allows voice interaction with computers. Computer hackers will be replaced by "yackers."

▶ The concept of the job is fading from the working landscape. In the future, workers will possess a variety of skills and responsibilities, rather than being confined to the parameters of a traditional job description.

Source: Edward Cornish, Editor, "Outlook '96." *The Futurist* (Bethesda, Maryland: World Future Society, 1995), pp. 1–7.

▶ **Hierarchy of Technology**

One area that will continue to grow dramatically is high-technology entrepreneurship. The U.S. Department of Labor defines a high-technology venture as any company that spends twice as much for research and development as the average for all manufacturing companies, or counts among its employees at least 5 percent who have four-year college degrees in either the engineering sciences, such as chemical and electrical engineering; or the basic sciences, such as chemistry and physics.

In the public mind, high technology generally conjures up images of such emerging industries as robotics, biotechnology, and telecommunications. It is these industries, marked by rapid and sometimes dizzying change, that have dominated the news and captured the public's attention. Yet, of the 800,000

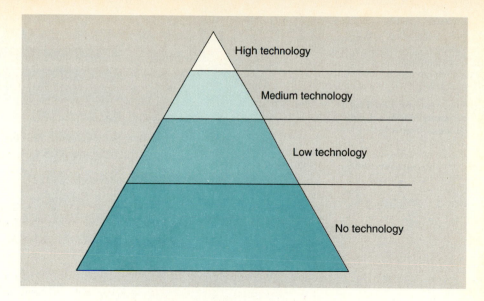

new ventures being founded yearly, no more than 1.5 percent—about 12,000 a year—are high-technology companies. The remaining new ventures include:

▸ Medium-technology companies, such as makers of surgical instruments or small robotized foundries for special-purpose castings.

▸ Low-technology companies, such as financial service firms or toy makers.

▸ No-technology companies, such as ethnic restaurants or garbage pickup and disposal services.[21]

In short, high technology may be the mountaintop in our economy as the creator of tomorrow's jobs. To succeed, however, it must be supported by the growing workforce in the medium-, low-, and no-technology companies, as suggested in Exhibit 1.10. These lower levels of technology are as vital to our economy as high technology, and they abound with entrepreneurial opportunities.

▸ **General Outlook**

From now until the year 2000 and beyond, more entrepreneurial opportunities than ever before can be expected. Competition surely will be keener, but it will be so healthy as to stimulate the birth of new ventures, especially those in such knowledge-rooted industries as software and management consulting, chemicals and electronics.

In fact, even older industries, usually viewed as backward, offer entrepreneurial opportunities. Two such industries are textiles and insurance. Both are changing so rapidly that they are now part of the high-technology revolution. For example, in the textile industry, cloth is being cut by laser beams and looms are driven by computers programmed to duplicate the irregularities of hand weaving. And insurance firms now offer a wide variety of policies that would have been impossible before the arrival of computers.[22]

EXHIBIT 1.11

SBA's forecast of the fastest-growing small-business-dominated industries* (between 1992 and 2005).

Source: Adapted by the Office of Advocacy of the U.S. Small Business Administration from data prepared by the U.S. Bureau of Labor Statistics, *Employment and Earnings* (Washington, D.C.: U.S. Government Printing Office, February 1994), Table B-2.

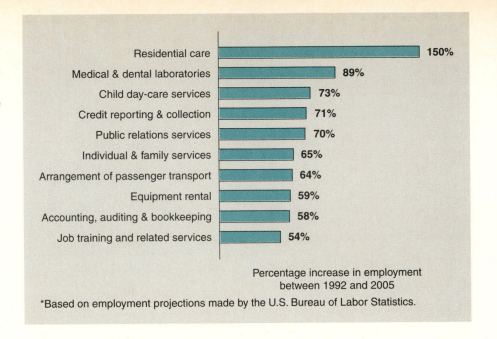

Residential care — 150%
Medical & dental laboratories — 89%
Child day-care services — 73%
Credit reporting & collection — 71%
Public relations services — 70%
Individual & family services — 65%
Arrangement of passenger transport — 64%
Equipment rental — 59%
Accounting, auditing & bookkeeping — 58%
Job training and related services — 54%

Percentage increase in employment between 1992 and 2005

*Based on employment projections made by the U.S. Bureau of Labor Statistics.

Which industries, in particular those traditionally dominated by small business, promise to grow the fastest? Which industries are likely to be the trendsetters? According to the SBA, the small-business industries poised for growth through the year 2005 reside wholly in services, as shown in Exhibit 1.11. This forecast reflects the growth trends in the economy at large, as services have outpaced manufacturing in job growth since the early 1980s, according to the U.S. Bureau of Labor Statistics.

SUMMARY

The different definitions of small business are based on common yardsticks, among them total assets, owners' equity, yearly sales revenues, and number of employees. The definition we use in this textbook states that to qualify as small, a business must have fewer than 500 employees and should be independently owned and managed.

Whatever our specific definition of small business, there is no question that small business has certain strengths and weaknesses. Its strengths include financial performance (small manufacturers, on the average, earn a higher return on their investment than do large manufacturers) and innovation (small businesspeople tend to be mavericks whose ideas are their stock in trade). Also, our economy depends on small business to employ tens of millions of men and women, to sell most of the products made by large manufacturers, and to create new jobs. Its weaknesses include failure, chiefly due to ease of entry and lack of managerial expertise.

Clearly, small business plays a major role in the U.S. economy. But it also has a critical role in the developing global economy. Small-business interactions between nations are an important factor in the move toward a global economy; and the global marketplace offers small businesspeople the opportunity to expand their businesses beyond traditional borders.

One by-product of the global economy is an increasing awareness of cultural diversity, a cultural diversity that is very much a part of the American experience as well. To succeed, both at home and in the global marketplace, small business must accommodate cultural diversity in the workplace. But the ends here are more than financial as the cohesion of our society depends on our tolerance and understanding of all races and cultures.

Life in the future will differ sharply from life today. Two areas where significant change is expected are individualism and technology. And it is in the industries that respond to that change where we expect to see the greatest growth and success of small business.

Discussion and Review Questions

1. Write a short paragraph indicating what you believe you are likely to get out of a course in small business management.
2. Does small business dominate the business world? Why or why not?
3. Cite at least two examples of the rising status of small business.
4. Define these terms: *small business, return on owners' equity, invention, innovation, total assets, freedom of opportunity,* and *culture.*
5. What guarantees the continued existence of small business?
6. Why did Congress create the U.S. Small Business Administration?
7. How does the definition of small business used in this textbook differ from the SBA's definitions? How did you define a small business before you read this chapter?
8. Why, on the average, are small manufacturers more profitable than big manufacturers?
9. What are the major strengths and weaknesses of small business?
10. Should people be screened before they go into business for themselves? Why or why not?
11. Why do some small businesses fail in the first few years of their existence? Explain fully.
12. What are some ways that big business can help small business?
13. Why is cultural diversity so vital to the success of small business?
14. What are some of the long-term trends expected for small business in the future?
15. Why does high technology depend for its survival on the existence of medium-, low-, and no-technology businesses?

Introduction

The future looks bright for entrepreneurs who possess the skills and experience needed for the challenges of business ownership. But make no mistake, successfully operating a small business is no accident. As you might guess, it takes a great deal of planning, a lot of hard work, and even a pinch of luck.

To help you complete the planning that leads to success, we have included material on constructing a business plan at the end of each chapter. A *business plan* is a carefully constructed guide for the person starting a business. It also serves as a concise document that potential investors and lenders can examine to see if they will provide the additional financing a small business owner may need. Here's what you can expect in this section of our textbook.

▶ Explanations, instructions, and examples of the type of information that should be included in a practical business plan

▶ Specific questions that will help guide the preparation of your own business plan

Building a Business Plan has been designed so that you can develop a notebook of worksheets from which to prepare a business plan. In your notebook, you should enter your responses to the questions and guidelines in each Business Plan segment. You can then add to or modify your responses so your notebook serves as an active record of data, ideas, and goals for your business.

A Word of Caution

One word of caution before you begin to build your business plan. Any business plan is only as good as the information it contains. When answering the questions at the end of each chapter, dig deep, look hard, and try to use the best information available. The quality of your business plan depends on it.

Instructions for Worksheet 1

Planning is important to any business, large or small, and should never be overlooked or taken lightly. To help begin the planning process that leads to an effective business plan, you should

▶ Define a specific business that you would like to start, in part 1.

▶ Describe potential problem areas that could affect your business, in part 2.

▶ Explain how you would avoid potential problem areas in your business, in part 3.

Part 1—Definition for Your Business

The experts suggest that one of the most important steps for would-be entrepreneurs is to answer the question, "What business should I be in?"

1. In your own words, define the business that you would like to start.

2. What specific products or services would your business provide?

3. Who is your potential customer for your products or services?

Part 2—Potential Problem Areas That Could Affect Your Business

A number of problem areas that affect small businesses are summarized on pages 9 to 12 in your text.

4. Based on the information in the text, what do *you* think are the most important reasons for small business failures?

5. How could the reasons for failure that you included in your answer to question 4 affect the business that you want to start?

6. Are there other problem areas that could reduce your chances of success?

Part 3—Ways to Avoid the Problem Areas Described in Part 2

While it is important to identify possible problem areas that could affect your small business, it is more important to determine methods that can be used to either eliminate or at least minimize the problem areas.

7. Describe how you would "handle" the problem areas described in part 2.

The author is grateful to Bob Hughes, Dallas County Community Colleges, for his work on the Building a Business Plan feature and Sample Business Plan.

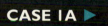 **CASE 1A** ▶ *Academy Specialties, Inc.*

Each year since its birth, Academy Specialties, a furniture reupholstery company, has increased both its sales revenues and its after-tax profits. Five years after its startup, its after-tax profits were $18,100 on sales revenues of $128,500. Founders Shirley Bosko and Dorothy Werblow are now wondering whether to expand sales by diversifying into related fields. Werblow recently was chosen by the U.S. Small Business Administration (SBA) as its Small Businessperson of the Year.

Background

Bosko and Werblow first thought about running their own small business while they were working for a franchising company that sewed vinyl restaurant tablecovers and sold them to franchisees. Bosko was the company's office manager and Werblow its plant manager.

Despite what Werblow describes as a "fabulous product," the franchising company fell victim to its own success—it expanded so rapidly that it

EXHIBIT 1A.1

Academy Specialties, Inc.: Beginning balance sheet.

Assets		Equities	
Cash	$ 700	Liabilities	$ 0
Inventory	200	Owners' equity	1,800
Sewing machine	500		
Cutting table	200		
Other	200		
Total	$1,800	Total	$1,800

overextended itself financially. The result was bankruptcy, and both women were left without jobs.

Their joblessness was short-lived. Discovering that their former employer had left dozens of orders for tablecovers unfilled, they decided to invest $900 each for shop space, a sewing machine, a vendor's license, and other assets to start their own business. They named their company Academy Specialties, Inc. Why? "Because it got at the top of the Yellow Pages and off to a good start," says Werblow. The business's beginning balance sheet appears in Exhibit 1A.1.

As they expected, when they filled the backlog of orders, they found themselves with few repeat orders. It was clear that most of the franchisees had found local producers of tablecovers. "Some franchisees were awful to us," says Werblow. "They thought we were naive, although we produced a high-quality tablecover, on time."

A Crucial Product Decision

With orders for tablecovers dwindling, the two women had to make a major operating decision. They both wanted to continue running their own business. As Bosko says, "The thought of looking for a job depressed us deeply. We dreaded inflexible work schedules, ornery bosses, and office politics. . . . It was a real gutsy thing. We

were scared to death. Neither of us had any other means of support, so we were determined to make a go of it."

They needed to develop another product— something else to do with their cutting table and sewing machine. They both wanted to continue working with fabric, but not to make tablecovers, because as Werblow says, "making tablecovers is both boring and repetitive."

It was Bosko who first suggested that their company specialize in furniture reupholstery. "We started by brainstorming a little to figure out just where our skills might best be used," says Bosko. "We soon realized that a lot of offices out there would have bruised or damaged chairs that needed refurbishing and fixing."

First, however, the two women had to overcome a major obstacle—neither one knew much about reupholstery. They both enrolled in night classes at a local high school to learn all they could about reupholstery and then practiced what they learned on an antique chair at their shop.

Their Niche in the Marketplace

They were aware that no upholsterer in town was aggressive in filling the need that most offices had for furniture repair. "They were order takers, waiting for decorators to call them," says Werblow. "If that was so, then we were sure we could take that business away from them by simply going after it aggressively. Office reupholstery was a completely untapped market."

The two women decided to test their convictions by canvassing every business in the city's bustling downtown district. "To our delight," says Werblow, "we discovered that businesses were indeed happy to find someone willing to replace just the damaged part of their chairs, thereby restoring their value." Bosko visited such major corporations as Eastman Kodak, General Electric, IBM, McDonald's, and U.S. Steel with few turning her away.

Her visits had several purposes. First, she wanted to make office managers aware they had the need for furniture reupholstery. Second, she informed them that Academy Specialties was prepared to fill that need. "Our sales pitch was that replacing furniture is a capital expenditure like a typewriter," says Werblow. "We pointed out that redoing their chairs comes out of the maintenance budget. Our service is as consumable as the typewriter ribbon." Finally, she added that Academy Specialties would gladly do the smallest of jobs. "We told them that we are *the* shop to which they should give all their business," says Werblow.

A Difficult Beginning

All the while, the two women were barely scraping by financially. "We starved the first year," says Werblow. "So much so that I even began doubting myself. I even asked myself, 'Did this nonsense make sense?' I almost gave it all up. Without Shirley to pick me up when I was down, I'm not sure I would have persevered."

For some time, the two women worried that they would not be able to pay the rent; so, in the hope that it would lead to a larger, continuous use of their services, they accepted repair jobs as small as armrests. Cash flow was so slow that they did not have $50 to buy a stapler; so they used only tacks in their repairs. They also had to

overcome the anger and frustration at being robbed four times, twice losing all of their hand tools and office equipment. "Even with all these headaches," says Bosko, "I was not about to trade my lot for a plush sales manager's job with an established company marketing a glamorous product. I'd rather be in my own business, not under somebody else's thumb. I like knowing that all the benefits and pats on the back are for Dorothy and me."

A Momentous Decision

With sales limping along the first year, the two women made what they believe to be their most important operating decision. They had been working in tandem, both sharing the production and the marketing aspects of their business. After their first year, their duties would be separate.

▶ Bosko would market the company's services. Her duties would range from making sales calls to making pick-ups and deliveries in her Chevette hatchback. She would also help the customers select fabrics. Her only advertising piece would be a bright pink card, because "hot pink doesn't get lost in the shuffle."

▶ Werblow, on the other hand, would "get out the work." She would run the shop, doing all of the furniture reupholstering. "I'm not suited to selling," she says. "My personality is such that I seek solitary environments. I'm a perfectionist at heart, so I'm better suited to production and doing high-quality work than I am at knocking on office doors to get orders."

This organizational decision worked. By the end of the first year, sales revenues had increased sharply and each woman was able to draw a salary of $100 a week, roughly the federal minimum wage at the time. Their organizational chart, unchanged since then, appears in Exhibit 1A.2.

EXHIBIT 1A.2

Academy Specialties, Inc.: Organizational chart.

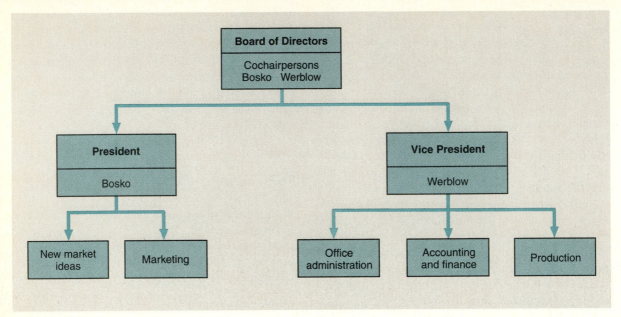

Marketing Style

Although both women had studied business administration in college, they did not use a traditional, textbook marketing approach. In their eagerness to land clients, they shunned both advertising and sales promotion. Instead, they focused their energies almost entirely on personal selling and, later, on public relations.

The two women purposely developed a reputation for uniqueness. In addition to invading the "male-dominated world of business," they are willing to do any task, however menial, that is necessary to complete a job.

They never let a customer down. They answer telephones in the middle of the night, and even work round the clock to meet clients' deadlines. An especially tough job came from a restaurateur who wanted twelve new banquette seats and backs upholstered for the grand opening of his new restaurant—the *next* day. Bosko and Werblow quickly determined a strategy for the job, instructed the carpenter to order the materials, and came to the restaurant to complete the upholstering overnight. "The carpenter was building the seats at the very same time as we were working," says Bosko. "He took one look at us and couldn't believe that we were upholstering faster than he could do the carpentry work."

Occasionally, sexism complicates their efforts to land new clients. Once an attorney agreed to meet with Bosko, just so he could ask her for a tennis date. "All it takes is one off-color comment that I don't laugh at, and they know we mean business," says Bosko. Some men also try what Bosko calls the "cutesy-pie approach." "We don't go for that either," says Bosko. "Some of them are thinking, 'Boy, the audacity of those women.' They really wonder, 'Can two middle-class suburban women really pull this off?' Yes, we sure can."

Financial Performance

The two partners are proud of their business's performance. Sales revenues and after-tax profits

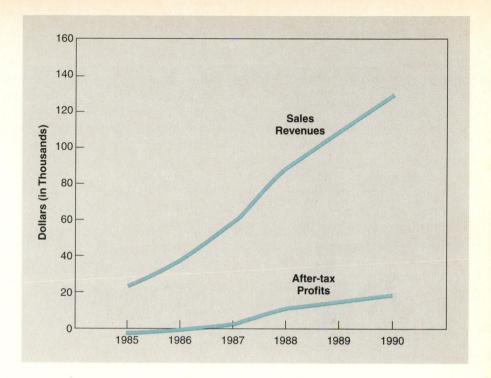

EXHIBIT 1A.3
Academy Specialties, Inc.: Financial performance.

have both gone up every year since they founded the business. Their yearly financial performance is summarized here and graphed in Exhibit 1A.3.

Year	Sales Revenues	After-Tax Profits
1985	$23,100	$(2,700)
1986	37,300	700
1987	58,700	3,300
1988	88,300	9,700
1989	107,600	14,400
1990	128,500	18,100

They are especially pleased that profits have increased yearly, along with sales. "We make every effort to be financially productive," says Werblow. "I keep exact records of materials, labor, and time so that I can see whether we make a profit on each job."

Indeed, as the partner who runs the office, Werblow has tried "at all times to bring big-business methods to our little shop." She keeps detailed cost records, cash flow charts, and inventory controls; and she reads magazines for small businesses, such as *Inc.,* to find the latest ideas, methods, and management tips that she can apply in the business.

So cost-conscious is Werblow that she does all her own bookkeeping to save on accountant's fees. She now employs three women in production, two of whom she hired because they were receiving benefits from the federal program, Aid for Dependent Children (AFDC). "By hiring AFDC mothers," says Werblow, "I also earn tax credits."

She knows at all times how much customers owe the business as well as how old each bill is. Similarly, she knows to the penny how much the business owes to suppliers. "If my accounts payable are less than my accounts receivable, then I'm making a profit," says Werblow.

EXHIBIT 1A.4

Academy Specialties, Inc.: Three-year income statements.

	1988	1989	1990
Sales revenues	$88,300	$107,600	$128,500
Cost of sales	22,900	25,800	31,500
Gross profit	$65,400	$ 81,800	$ 97,000
Operating expenses:			
Wages	$19,400	$ 26,000	$ 30,500
Insurance	4,600	5,400	6,000
Automobile	3,900	4,600	6,000
Utilities	5,000	5,200	5,400
Payroll taxes	2,800	3,800	4,400
Depreciation	2,300	2,300	4,300
Office	3,000	2,900	3,800
Rent	3,600	3,600	3,600
Supplies	2,100	2,200	2,500
Repairs and maintenance	1,600	1,800	1,900
Sales promotion	1,300	1,700	1,900
Bank fees	1,000	1,300	1,800
Advertising	1,100	1,300	1,700
Employee welfare	1,000	1,200	1,600
Legal and accounting	900	1,000	1,100
Licenses	200	200	200
Total operating expenses	$53,800	$ 64,500	$ 76,700
Profit before taxes	$11,600	$ 17,300	$ 20,300
Federal income taxes	1,900	2,900	2,200
Profit after taxes	$ 9,700	$ 14,400	$ 18,100

Although she does the bookkeeping herself, she pays a certified public accountant to prepare the business's tax returns. Recently, from the detailed books kept by Werblow, the accountant prepared income statements, as shown in Exhibit 1A.4, and balance sheets, as shown in Exhibit 1A.5, for the past three years.

Volunteer Activities

Although she regularly logs a 60-hour workweek and rarely takes a vacation, Werblow nevertheless finds time to volunteer her services and talents for causes that she "strongly believes in." She has embraced the promotion of entrepreneurship among

EXHIBIT 1A.5

Academy Specialties, Inc.: Three-year balance sheets.

	Year-end		
Assets	**1988**	**1989**	**1990**
Current assets			
Cash in bank	$ 2,200	$ 4,000	$ 7,300
Accounts receivable	1,100	3,400	9,700
Inventory	2,300	3,500	8,800
Total current assets	$ 5,600	$10,900	$25,800
Fixed assets			
Furniture and fixtures	$12,600	$12,600	$22,600
Automobiles	15,500	15,500	15,500
Less: Accum. depreciation	(6,800)	(9,000)	(13,300)
Total fixed assets	$21,300	$19,100	$24,800
Total assets	$26,900	$30,000	$50,600
Equities			
Current liabilities			
Accounts payable	$ 700	$ 200	$ 1,000
Taxes payable	1,400	700	1,800
Notes payable, shareholders	10,300	200	800
Total current liabilities	$12,400	$ 1,100	$ 3,600
Owners' equity			
Common stock	$ 1,000	$ 1,000	$ 1,000
Retained earnings	13,500	27,900	46,000
Total owners' equity	$14,500	$28,900	$47,000
Total equities	$26,900	$30,000	$50,600

women almost single-mindedly, never turning down an opportunity to speak about the need for women to become independent through entrepreneurship.

It was Werblow's belief in this cause that led her and several other women entrepreneurs to form the Women's Business Ownership Association (WBOA) in her city. Now boasting more than 150 members, the WBOA has become the most active women's business group in the city. Werblow goes one step further and calls the WBOA "the *only* entrepreneurial group in town. Sure, there are other entrepreneurial groups, mostly male-dominated, but they are not truly entrepreneurial. By that I mean their membership includes big law firms, big CPA firms, and big family-owned businesses. Are they entrepreneurial? I don't believe so."

Currently its vice president, she also sees the WBOA as a vehicle for "renewing" herself. Monthly meetings are devoted almost exclusively to networking and to education. Seminars and workshops focus on such topics as:

▶ How to approach your banker for a loan

▶ How to motivate your employees

▶ How to succeed

Of her many activities, Werblow is proudest of the Women's Business Ownership Educational Conference. Held yearly, this conference attracts more than 500 women, most of them "eager to find out what it takes to become a successful entrepreneur." At a recent conference, two of the workshops were conducted by Bosko and Werblow:

▶ Bosko's workshop was *Selling Your Product or Service: Sell Hard, Keep It Light, and Close the Sale.*

▶ Werblow's workshop was *Do-It-Yourself Marketing Research: What Is It and How Can It Help You? It's for Everyone.*

The entire conference is organized, staffed, and carried out by women. "We believe that successful women entrepreneurs offer the best role models for aspiring women entrepreneurs," says Werblow.

Small Businessperson of the Year

Each year, the regional office of the SBA selects a Small Businessperson of the Year. Recently, Werblow was chosen. "I can't begin to tell you how thrilled I was," says Werblow. "It was one of the most exciting things that ever happened to me, to be recognized like that."

In screening candidates for the Small Businessperson of the Year Award, the SBA applies a set of strict standards, including:

▶ **Staying power**   Several years as an established and profitable business.

▶ **Increase in sales revenues**   An indication of continued growth.

▶ **Innovativeness of product or service offered** Illustrations of creativity and imagination.

▶ **Response to adversity**   Examples of problems faced by the business and the solutions used by the entrepreneur.

▶ **Contributions to community-oriented projects** Evidence that the small businessperson has volunteered personal resources to help improve a community's quality of life.

▶ **Growth in number of employees**   The impact of the business on the community's job market.

Werblow won the award, despite competition with many other small businesspersons with businesses much larger than hers. Submitted by the WBOA, hers was the only presentation packet that the SBA judges rated "exceptional."

Looking to the Future

Academy Specialties, Inc., is in no hurry to grow. As shown earlier, in Exhibit 1A.3, both its sales revenues and after-tax profits have grown steadily since its beginning. "I prefer to grow slowly," says Werblow. "Making a lot of money is not a big thing with me or Shirley. I would rather visit the Grand Canyon. Nor are we building the business to leave it to somebody."

Their idea of slow and controlled growth is to double sales revenues and after-tax profits every five years. "That means it would take us 15 years to reach that magical sales level of a million dollars," says Werblow. "We don't know exactly how we're going to accomplish that little feat, but we'll find a way, Shirley and I."

Recently, Academy Specialties received a special order from a steel manufacturer to make covers for microcomputers. The unexpected order ignited Werblow's imagination. "Hundreds of thousands of microcomputers are sold every year," says Werblow. "What an enormous market that is, and with no competition." She charged the steel manufacturer $28 a cover, although material costs were only $3 a cover. "Like light bulbs, I charge what the traffic will bear," says Werblow.

Academy Specialties, Inc.: Dorothy Werblow and Shirley Bosko in their shop.

The company has just begun providing services such as drapery cleaning, window treatments, and carpet cleaning. "These services are logical extensions of what we do now," says Werblow. "But we must be careful not to overextend ourselves. We must never lose sight of the fact that reupholstery is the core of our business."

Nor do the partners plan to move out of their high-crime location, even if growth justifies their moving to a safer part of town. "We're going to be part of this area's renaissance," says Werblow. A view of Bosko and Werblow in their shop appears in Exhibit 1A.6.

Questions

1. What are the company's prospects?
2. What are the key elements in the success of this kind of business?
3. Comment on the entrepreneurial qualities of Shirley Bosko and Dorothy Werblow.
4. Analyze the company's financial performance.
5. Comment on Bosko's and Werblow's plans for the future.

The Paradox of Our Times

Never before have so many lived so well so far behind—or so it may seem. In the 1990s, "it is the paradox of our time that we are feeling bad about doing well," intoned *Newsweek* in a cover story on the state of our economy.[1] Consider for a moment these paradoxical aspects of today's economy:

▶ Undeniably, we have achieved both unprecedented prosperity and personal freedom. On the whole, we are healthier, work at less exhausting jobs, and live longer than ever. Moreover, many discriminations—especially those having to do with race, sex, or religion— have diminished sharply. In short, America has become a better place to live.

▶ Yet, at the same time, we have serious misgivings about the future and our place in it. Voices of gloom, doom, and despair cry out that something has gone deeply wrong with our economy.

So much so that *The New York Times* ran a six-day series of page-one articles headlined: "On the Battlefields of Business, Millions of Casualties." The theme of these articles was "workers fall as business rises."[2]

Indeed, in the 1990s, announcements of layoffs by giant corporations, most of whom were highly profitable, sent shock waves through the economy. For example, between 1992 and 1996, these familiar corporations, among many others, announced drastic cuts:

Corporation	Jobs Cut	Share of Work Force
AT&T	123,000	30%
IBM	122,000	35%
General Motors	99,000	29%
Sears	50,000	15%

An Overriding Question

In a time of unprecedented prosperity and personal freedom, what is happening to our jobs? That is the question. Today's so-called Information Age is displacing millions of workers, blue-collar and white-collar alike, causing untold stress, if not pain. We worry that, as computers keep making us more productive, we will need fewer and fewer workers.

And the rub is that the quality of jobs has already changed forever. This means that there are, and likely will continue to be, fewer and fewer good jobs—if we loosely define a good job as one that "pays enough for a reasonably comfortable lifestyle."[3] Especially troubling is the plight of 18- to 24-year-old workers, only *half* of whom held full-time jobs in 1995 that paid more than a poverty wage.

Without question, we are experiencing the dawning of a new economic order, one seemingly empty of job stability and humanizing sensitivity. Small wonder, then, that so many adults and young people believe their prospects for the future are bleak. For example:

In 1996, three-fourths of all adults surveyed by the Harris Poll and two-thirds of all high-school seniors surveyed by *Scholastic* magazine said they believed the "United States will be a worse place 10 years from now than it is today."[4]

In the words of *Business Week*, "So far, most Americans have tended to blame Big Government for their economic woes. But now this anger may be shifting in some measure toward Big Business. The role of the corporation in society is being challenged. Only the foolish would ignore the signs."[5]

Questions

1. Describe the paradox at work in the U.S. economy today. How does today's economy differ from yesterday's? Who is affected more by layoffs: white-collar or blue-collar employees? Why?

2. In today's corporate world, to whom do entrepreneurs and other executives owe more loyalty: their employees or their shareholders? Explain.

3. In your judgment, what changes are called for in the way businesses operate? Why?

4. Given the paradoxical reality of today's economy, how has your desire to strike off on your own and become your very own boss been affected? Explain.

Sources:
1. "Cover Story: Great Expectations," *Newsweek* (January 8, 1996), p. 24.
2. Louis Uchitelle and N. R. Kleinfield, "On the Battlefields of Business, Millions of Casualties," *The New York Times* (March 3, 1996), p. 1.
4. Ibid., p. 11.
5. "Editorial: The Backlash Building Against Business," *Business Week* (February 19, 1996), p. 102.

 **CASE IC ▶** *Marvelous Meals*

David and Carol Williams first met when they were both college students studying elementary education. They found that they shared many interests. Upon graduation, they both became nursery school teachers.

One of their shared interests was cooking and eating only naturally grown organic foods. They created several original recipes, which they served at their wedding.

The wedding menu was so popular with their guests that they soon opened a small restaurant—Marvelous Meals—near the campus of Whitehall Community College. It offered mostly take-out food and had seating for only sixteen persons. With both Williams teaching, the restaurant was open only for dinner. Starting with just $3,500, they were only able to afford second-hand equipment and occasional part-time help.

Within the first six months of operation, however, sales revenues more than doubled; Mr. Williams left his teaching position to work full time at the restaurant. They now were open for both lunch and dinner, and they expanded their take-out service. Ms. Williams kept her teaching position as insurance in case the new business failed.

The restaurant soon became one of the most popular near campus, capitalizing on the trend toward healthy dieting and non-chemically treated foods.

Repositioning of the Business

Their cousin, a business professor at a large community college, later visited them and became impressed with the success of their operation. He spent two months with the Williams. Together, they prepared a business plan to reposition Marvelous Meals from a restaurant to a manufacturer of organic foods.

The restaurant was sold, and the proceeds used to purchase processing and packaging equipment and to rent manufacturing space.

The business plan included extensive marketing research, financial projections, and marketing strategy. It was decided to sell the line of food products to distributors only, as the company could only afford a one-person sales force—Mr. Williams. They were able to hire and train several of their restaurant employees to assume production positions, as Ms. Williams managed the manufacturing process and Mr. Williams called on natural food distributors across the country.

In its first years, the company had only three natural, organically grown food products, which were sold to national distributors. Marvelous Meals entered one of these products—a soyburger mix—in a natural food competition sponsored by *Good Housekeeping* magazine. It won first place and brought recognition to Marvelous Meals.

Since those early years, the company has added eight more organically grown, natural food products, which are widely distributed in the United States, Canada, and several countries in Europe and South America. The Williams still run the organization, along with help from two of their original employees, who have been promoted to managerial positions.

For 1995, the company posted sales revenues of $1.6 million and earned before-tax profits of 17 percent on sales.

Questions

1. Identify the key factors that made Marvelous Meals a successful venture.
2. What personal factors made David and Carol Williams a successful entrepreneurial team?
3. Identify some possible areas for future expansion and diversification.

Source: Adapted from a case prepared by Professor Richard W. Shapiro of Cuyahoga Community College. Used with permission.

Diversity and the Entrepreneur

Effort must exceed opportunity in order for there to be change.

—Jesse Jackson

Successful men and women come from such diverse backgrounds that it is impossible to explain exactly what it takes to create a successful business. And, as shown in Exhibit 2.1, they get their ideas for businesses from a wide variety of sources, including prior job experience, personal passion, chance, and friends and relatives. Experts often try to pinpoint those traits that favor success and those that do not. But most have only been able to conclude that good businesspersons succeed and bad ones fail.

What kinds of men and women are likely to found successful businesses? We don't have a definitive answer. But research does show that successful entrepreneurs share certain traits.

Defining the Entrepreneur

Today, we take for granted the meaning of the word *entrepreneur*. It suggests spirit, zeal, ideas, diversity. But we tend to apply the word loosely to describe anyone who runs a business—for example, the person who presides over General Electric or owns a corner fruit stand, who owns a Pizza Hut franchise or hawks magazine subscriptions from a home telephone.

In the past, the word *entrepreneur* enjoyed a purer, more precise meaning. It described only those who created their own business. In fact, the *American Heritage Dictionary* defines an entrepreneur as "a person who organizes, operates, and assumes the risk for a business venture," as did two pioneers of the computer world, Sandra Kurtzig and Bill Gates.*

---

*Copyright © 1996 by Houghton Mifflin Company. Adapted and reprinted by permission from *The American Heritage Dictionary of the English Language, Third Edition.*

EXHIBIT 2.1
Where the ideas are likely
to come from to start
a business.

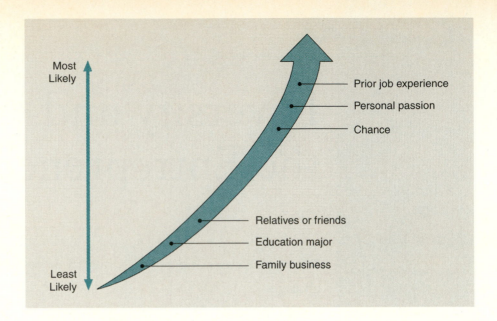

Most
Likely

Prior job experience

Personal passion

Chance

Relatives or friends

Education major

Family business

Least
Likely

▶ **Sandra Kurtzig, Entrepreneur**

The example of Sandra Kurtzig offers dramatic proof that entrepreneurship transcends gender. On a shoestring of just $2,000, and working out of the comfort of a spare bedroom, she nourished her hunger for entrepreneurship to become one of the pioneers of the computer industry. She named her fledgling business the ASK Computer Systems Corporation.

In short order, and giving her talent and vision full rein, she created the country's fastest-growing software business, with sales revenues reaching $400 million a year. It also became the largest business founded and run by a woman.

Kurtzig's achievements soon drew praise from virtually every quarter of the computer world—so much so that, when she became the first woman to take a high-technology business like hers public, the stock offering sold out overnight, even though Wall Street was in the throes of a deep slump.

In her widely-acclaimed book, *CEO: Building a $400 Million Company from the Ground Up,* she offers aspiring entrepreneurs this advice:

▶ My first advice to the aspiring entrepreneur is to think about what you like to do—a hobby, for example, that you can turn into a business—since whatever business you *do* go into, you'll have to give it the time, dedication, and nurturing it will demand.

  Also, don't go into business with the idea of getting rich quick. Keep in mind that the reason that instant success stories make headlines is precisely because they are so rare. More than likely, your success will be some time in coming.

▶ In the good old days, you'd grow a business primarily by doing more of what you are already doing. Nowadays, growth is more a factor of *changing* what you're doing, of being sensitive to your market and altering your course in response.

> Keep in mind, too, that in most businesses a sale is more than a transaction. It's a partnership. This is true whether you're selling a $250,000 software package that's going to require years of support or a $6.00 movie ticket that requires you to keep your theater clean and quiet and your feature film running on schedule.
>
> Buying into the partnership notion becomes even more important if you're seeking return business. It is also a good idea to keep tabs on what is happening in your company at the all-important sales level by remaining involved in the sales process. For [my software company], this may mean going on sales calls; for the theater owner, working a shift in the ticket booth.[1]

> **Bill Gates, Entrepreneur**

Not unlike trail-blazing entrepreneurs such as Henry Ford and Apple's Steven Jobs, Bill Gates has uncorked a whole new industry that is remodeling our economy and changing our lives dramatically, as did the Model T Ford and the Apple II personal computer. Imbued with entrepreneurial dynamism, Gates dropped out of Harvard University in 1975 at the tender age of 19 to strike off on his own to create software for personal computers—which at the time were in their infancy. He named his business the Microsoft Corporation.

By 1995, just 20 years later, Microsoft had become the world's most powerful software business. And, in turn, Gates had become the world's richest executive, worth more than $10 billion. Often called the software wizard, Gates oversees a business that is deceptively small if compared with computer *makers* like IBM and Apple. For example, in 1994:

> Microsoft posted sales revenues half that of Apple and one-fourteenth that of IBM; yet—

> Microsoft earned a 25 percent profit on every dollar of sales revenues compared to just 3 percent for Apple.

Gates's springboard to such phenomenal success was his mastery of the fly-speck detail of software design. It was largely this mastery that had inspired his co-workers to create software that, in 1995, ruled the market for such universal applications as electronic spreadsheets, word processing, scheduling, and filing.

The best measure of Microsoft's power over the computer industry may be the fact that 8 out of 10 of the world's personal computers could not boot up—that is to say, start—without Microsoft's software. Not even IBM wielded such power in its heyday.

A visionary, Gates is not at all content with his success and his celebrity. He knows the information revolution has only just begun. In fact, virtually every-thing—from education to dating, from medicine to chemistry—has already been radically changed by the computer, which, by the way, was invented a scant 50 years ago by Howard Aiken at Harvard University. No question about it, the information revolution is here, and Gates intends to continue being heralded as its torch bearer.

Gates's grand vision is to make the coming information highway into a giant electronic shopping mall for *consumers*—one complete with banks, boutiques, brokerages, department stores, libraries, movie theaters, newsstands, post offices, ticket vendors, and travel agencies. Moreover, he envisions an even larger arena for *businesses,* focusing on such applications as:

▶ Managing factories, inventories, and databases
▶ Verifying credit cards
▶ Trading stocks

At the center, servicing all these applications, presides Gates's flagship software product called Windows, which does everything from setting the look of a personal computer's screen to overseeing its link to other personal computers.

What makes Bill Gates tick? What is he really like? Often posed, these questions defy a ready answer. We all know about his single-mindedness to be the very best at what he does, to learn all he can about emerging technologies, such as biotechnology, in the belief that such knowledge would surely hone his competitive edge in the future. Yet, in the eyes of the media, he is something of an enigma, a bundle of contradictions. As *Fortune* magazine put it:

▶ To his family, he's still the precocious kid with big ideas.
▶ To his friends, he's a pesky debating partner.
▶ To Microsoft's employees, he's the franchise.
▶ To high-tech entrepreneurs, he's the ultimate role model.
▶ To Microsoft investors, he's the sugar daddy.
▶ To television's Robin Leach, he's a video segment.
▶ And to competitors, he is Attila the Hun.

Perhaps more than anything, Gates is all-curious. Never has he lost his childlike sense of wonder about the world around him—a world spiced with entrepreneurial dynamism. And by the way, his motto is: "A computer on every desk and in every home, *all running Microsoft software."*[2]

▶ **Pure Entrepreneurs**

In this textbook, we define *pure entrepreneurs* as men and women who create a venture from the raw materials of their own ideas and hard work. Like Sandra Kurtzig and Bill Gates, pure entrepreneurs launch their own ventures from scratch. They nurse them into successful businesses with their instinct for opportunity and sense of timing, their hard work and idea-producing ability. Pure entrepreneurs quicken the development of our economy, and they seem motivated not merely by profit but also by the "desire to found a private dynasty, the will to conquer in a competitive battle, and the joy of creating."[3]

As a nation, we often put pure entrepreneurs like Sandra Kurtzig and Bill Gates on a pedestal. Novelists and economists alike glorify them; and in recent years so have the media, which now treat successful entrepreneurs with the same celebrity once afforded only famous movie stars and politicians. In addition, economists credit pure entrepreneurs with pushing our economy ahead in giant steps. Others, of course, qualify as entrepreneurs, but not as pure ones. Among them are those who take over a business after the founder retires, dies, or sells out, but who continue to build and innovate—and those who run a franchise independently of the franchisor.

▶ Entrepreneurship and Management

Let us pause here to distinguish between the terms *entrepreneur* and *entrepreneurship*. Although we define entrepreneurs mostly as those who launch new ventures, entrepreneurship is far more widely practiced—in old businesses as well as new ones, and in big businesses as well as small ones. In the words of Professor Nathaniel H. Leff, "Entrepreneurship is the capacity for innovation, investment, and expansion in new markets, products, and techniques."[4]

This means that an entrepreneur is at work whenever someone takes risks and invests resources to make something new, designs a new way of making something that already exists, or creates new markets.

Entrepreneurship is not the same thing as management. The first job of the manager is to make a business perform well. The manager takes given resources—people and money, machines and materials—and orchestrates them into production. In contrast, the first job of the entrepreneur is to bring about change on purpose. As economist Irving Kristol has suggested:

> More and more, chief executives refer to themselves as "managers," sometimes even "professional managers." Well, if that indeed is what they are . . . then they are wildly overpaid. A good executive . . . is above all an energetic and shrewd entrepreneur, seeking out—no, creating—new opportunities for profitable economic transactions. It is only the possession of this talent . . . that justifies the high salaries they receive.[5]

Entrepreneurial Traits

Sandra Kurtzig and Bill Gates are not typical entrepreneurs. In fact, no two entrepreneurs are exactly alike. In the words of Peter F. Drucker, noted author-lecturer-consultant, "Some are eccentrics, others painfully correct conformists; some are fat and some are lean; some are worriers, some relaxed; some drink quite heavily, others are total abstainers; some are men of great charm and warmth, some have no more personality than a frozen mackerel."[6]

Drucker's words underline the futility of painting a word picture of the typical entrepreneur. Precious little is known about entrepreneurs, about the kinds of men and women who go into business for themselves. How do they get started? Why do they do it? Is it because, in Henry David Thoreau's phrase, they "lead lives of quiet desperation" and want something new and different? Are they society's rejects who "instead of becoming hobos, criminals, or professors make their adjustment by starting their own business?"[7]

If people decide to go into business for themselves, they usually do so for good reasons. They may prefer not to be ciphers in somebody else's business, or they may want to exploit an invention themselves. Others, however, often go into business for the wrong reasons, with outside pressures playing a strong role. They may decide to go on their own only after being demoted,

Women in record numbers are choosing to become entrepreneurs, as did these two owners of a maid service.

passed up, or fired. Not all fail. Some succeed, sometimes spectacularly, as did these two sisters:

EXAMPLE ▶

For Annette and Victoria Quintana, you might say success is relative. The sisters founded Colorado-based Excel Professional Services in 1990 with help from their father. Their venture has since mushroomed into a multi-million-dollar business.

The idea for Excel came when Annette was fired from her computer sales job after a falling-out with the owner's wife. Meanwhile, Victoria was uneasily watching the layoffs at MCI, where she was a product manager. "Think of it as an education," their father said when they approached him about starting Excel. "And ask yourself: How much are you willing to lose?"

"I had about $20,000—my life's savings," says Annette, "and our father used some real estate to help collateralize a $35,000 loan."

That was enough to get their computer consulting business off the ground; and today, the sisters offer advice to such blue-chip clients as US West and AT&T on everything from personal computers to mainframe computers.[8] ▲▼▲

Clearly, and as suggested in Exhibit 2.2 men and women become entrepreneurs for a variety of reasons. The desire for self-expression, however, appears to be a common thread and may help explain why so many men and women, as shown in Exhibit 2.3, prefer to work for themselves than for someone else.

Of all the men and women who do become entrepreneurs, why do some fail? What is it, then, that enables a business to succeed instead of fail? Can we pinpoint the key traits of successful entrepreneurs? If we could, we might predict what kinds of men and women are most likely to succeed as entrepreneurs.

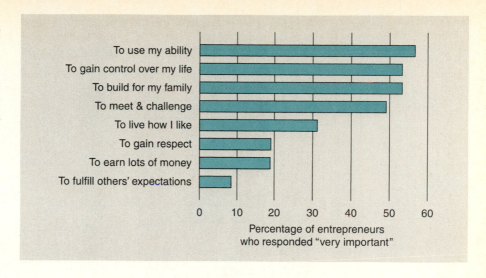

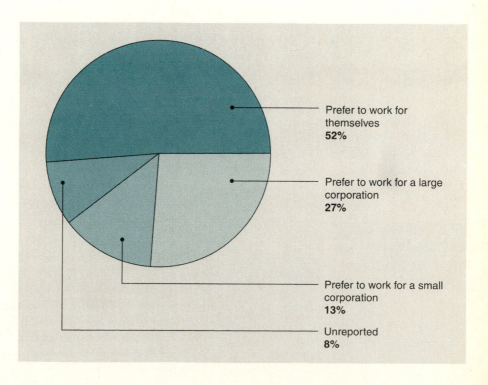

EXHIBIT 2.4
Traits generally found in
high-achieving
entrepreneurs.

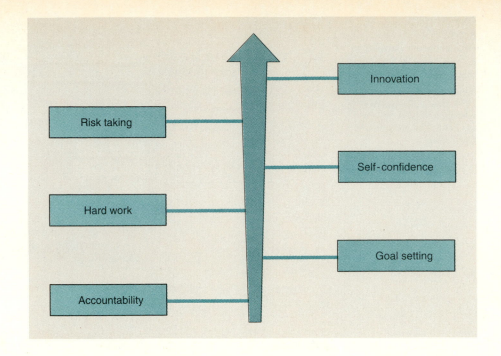

To begin with, successful entrepreneurs are likely to be overachievers. That is, like Sandra Kurtzig and Bill Gates, they burn with the desire to excel. In his landmark study of entrepreneurs, Professor David C. McClelland of Harvard University found that they are likely to do well if they also have the six traits shown in Exhibit 2.4.[9]

▶ **Innovation**

To the lay mind, innovation is generally the most distinctive entrepreneurial trait. Entrepreneurs tend to tackle the unknown; they do things in new and different ways; they weave old ideas into new patterns; they offer more solutions than excuses.

In practice, however, the role of the entrepreneur often differs from the role of the innovator. Although innovation may be vital to being entrepreneurial, it becomes entrepreneurial only when carried into production to benefit consumers, as in this example:

EXAMPLE ▶

It was Steven Jobs, cofounder of Apple Computer, more than anyone else, who kicked open the door and let the personal computer move in. But he did not start the personal computer revolution alone. He did not even make the Apple II, the machine that started the revolution and that seemed to mint money.

Steven Wozniak, Jobs's friend, created the Apple II. He worked from some preexisting technology, scaling it down radically and making it affordable to consumers as well as corporations.

"Steve [Jobs] didn't do one circuit, design, or piece of code," says Wozniak, who was widely regarded as the true technological wizard in Jobs's corporate Oz. "He's not really been into computers, and to this day he has never gone through a computer manual. But it never crossed my mind to sell computers. It was Steve who said, 'Let's hold them up in the air and sell a few.'"[10] ▲▼▲

▶ Risk Taking

Any new business poses risks for entrepreneurs. They may succeed or they may fail, and they cannot foresee which it will be. For protection, entrepreneurs are likely to shun ventures in which the odds against them are high. An example is the automobile industry. Few entrepreneurs would try to come up with a pollution-free automobile to vie with Detroit's billion-dollar automobile industry because their chances of success would approach zero.

At the same time, most entrepreneurs also shun a sure thing because the satisfaction would be too small to justify the effort. Entrepreneurs are not likely to be found performing routine chores like sorting buttons or grinding coffee. Successful entrepreneurs tend to launch ventures that fall between these two extremes, a middle ground in which the risk of failure is neither too high nor too low. This tendency suggests that they seek out venture opportunities that stretch their skills and thus offer personal fulfillment. In short, successful entrepreneurs may be like mountain climbers, who opt to test their skills and abilities against a terrain that matches yet challenges their knowledge and experience. Take this example:

EXAMPLE ▶

For years, black women have tried to conceal skin imperfections with makeup. A complete skin-care line for female consumers of color was unheard of, although hair-care products abounded. As a teenager growing up in New York City, Carol Jackson Mouyiaris was keenly aware of the problem.

"I had known for years that I wanted to do something in the cosmetics and beauty arena for the ethnic market," says Jackson Mouyiaris, who holds a master's degree in human relations from New York University and a juris doctorate from Boston University's law school.

And, indeed, she did do something by creating her very own line of skin-care products in partnership with her husband, Nikos. Today they are the owners and founders of BioCosmetic Research Labs, a New York–based maker of such popular products as Black Opal Skin Care and Black Opal for Men. By the way, their broadcast media campaign starred Warren Moon, who at the time played quarterback for the Minnesota Vikings of the National Football League.

From very nearly the first hour of its introduction in 1993, Black Opal made a big splash in the marketplace. In fact, by 1995, Black Opal had captured a 33 percent share of the ethnic skin-care market; in turn, the company's sales revenues had soared to $8 million.

This stellar performance has not been lost on such aggressive competitors as Revlon and Maybelline, who are likely to introduce their own line of ethnic skin-care products. For years, of course, these companies had offered hair-care products for women of color, all the time ignoring their need for skin care. BioCosmetic Research is well-positioned, however, to meet the challenge of its competitors, mostly through the steady introduction of new and better skin-care products.[11] ▲▼▲

Moreover, and contrary to popular belief, entrepreneurs generally avoid ventures that are pure gambles. They would rather depend on themselves than on luck. There is no way, for example, to influence the roll of a pair of dice—unless, of course, they are loaded. Entrepreneurs prefer to shape events by their own actions, to make things happen rather than let them happen.

▶ Self-Confidence

Entrepreneurs believe in themselves. They have confidence that they can outdo anyone in their field. They tend not to accept the status quo, believing instead that they can change the facts. Often, they insist the odds are better than the facts would justify.

The old New York Yankees used this strategy, and their winning habits once dazzled the world of sports. But they often won with mediocre ballplayers, prompting one sportswriter to say, "Those pinstripe uniforms convince a ballplayer that he's better than he ought to be." This description captures the essence of entrepreneurs like this one:

EXAMPLE ▶

During the 1980s, it was enough simply to call Russell Simmons the king of rap music. After all, his New York–based record label, Def Jam, was a pioneering force behind the explosion of the "street"-inspired genre.

Simmons, though, is more than that. His business—Rush Communications—is the country's second-largest black-owned entertainment company, with sales revenues of $34 million in 1993. His company includes five record labels, several management companies, a film and television branch, a radio production company, and a clothing line.

The key to Simmon's success has been his knack for packaging and selling black culture— music, comedy, and film—to mainstream America, especially to urban teenagers. Several artists on his record labels, from *Public Enemy* to *LL Cool J,* boast crossover appeal; and his latest venture, HBO's *Russell Simmons's Def Comedy Jam,* is among the cable giant's most popular programs with black and white audiences alike.

Justifiably confident in his abilities, Simmons has considered taking his media empire public to finance future growth. If Wall Street goes along, he will be one step closer to realizing his dream of building a true black powerhouse in the entertainment industry, which is as competitive as any. Even the SBA shies away from helping to finance entertainment businesses because the industry is so volatile.[12] ▲▼▲

▶ Hard Work

Few people in our society work harder than entrepreneurs, as suggested in Exhibit 2.5. Many big-business executives put in long hours, too, but entrepreneurs seem to put in even longer hours, driven by their desire to excel. Take these two examples:

EXAMPLE ▶

Although secure as the vice president of media at one of the Midwest's top public relations firms, Natalie Wester left that position to found the Wester Communications Group, based in Cleveland. Yet it was that security that fed what she calls an "entrepreneurial spirit."

"Starting my own firm was just something I had always wanted to do," she recalls. Despite the vast experience she had gained as an employee, starting her own business still involved adjustments and risks. "The biggest adjustment is probably the isolation that you experience at first, especially if you're used to working in a large corporate structure."

Wester has overcome these hurdles, however, and now has carved a strong niche for her fledgling firm as a freelance consulting practice, offering high-quality services to clients who otherwise could ill afford the fees charged by a high-ticket agency.

On the subject of her work ethic, she told a reporter that "there is no such thing as a holiday, or a weekend off, or a paid vacation. In fact, we had our first child last year and during labor, *under* anesthesia, I was on the phone to clients."[13] ▲▼▲

EXHIBIT 2.5

Results of survey of weekly hours worked by small-business owners.

Source: John B. Hinge, "Small Business, Big Numbers," *The Wall Street Journal* (November 22, 1991), p. R18. Reprinted by permission of *The Wall Street Journal,* © 1991 Dow Jones & Company, Inc. All Rights Reserved Worldwide.

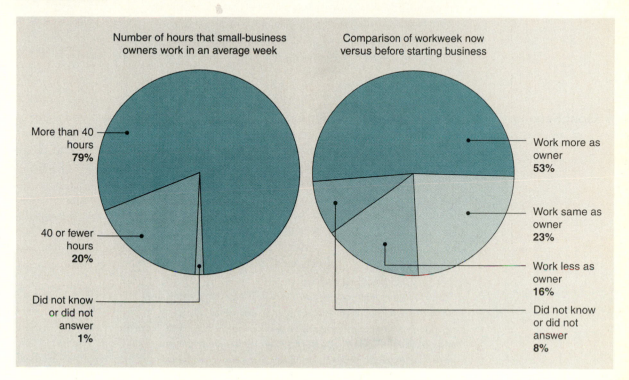

Number of hours that small-business owners work in an average week

More than 40 hours **79%**

40 or fewer hours **20%**

Did not know or did not answer **1%**

Comparison of workweek now versus before starting business

Work more as owner **53%**

Work same as owner **23%**

Work less as owner **16%**

Did not know or did not answer **8%**

EXAMPLE ▶

Perhaps the one dream that women entrepreneurs relinquish is the notion that they will have more time for themselves and their families. Wendy Wilson left her job as head of investor relations at the AMR Corporation, parent of American Airlines, after five years of working 14-hour days and weekends because "I wanted to have a life."

Now, she is working even longer hours at her own investor-relations company. And she often has trouble sleeping. But, she says, "I'm much happier because I'm in control of it."

As more women take control of their economic destinies, Wilson is not the only one staying awake nights. And with their growing visibility and clout, Wilson and other women entrepreneurs may soon feel comfortable ignoring those who ask: "Have you thought about getting a real job?"[14] ▲▼▲

Dr. Marilyn Machlowitz of Yale University has found that it is a mistake to assume that hard workers never have any leisure. "They have reversed the relationship that America has with work. It is far better to live for the 50 weeks a year that you work than for the 2 weeks you are off."[15] To Winston Churchill, hard workers were "fortune's favorite children whose work and pleasures are one."

Not that entrepreneurs always work harder. They do so only when their own skills can shape events. If a situation lacks challenge, they leave it alone.

EXHIBIT 2.6 ▶
Entrepreneurial goal
setting.

▶ Goal Setting

Psychologists often define happiness as a striving toward meaningful goals, not necessarily the achievement of those goals. This definition of happiness fits many entrepreneurs. Happiest with goals in front of and not behind them, they rarely feel that they have arrived. As shown in Exhibit 2.6, the process of setting and achieving goals repeats itself continually.

To entrepreneurs, merely choosing a new meaningful goal is self-renewing. Planning and carrying out the steps needed to reach their goal are stimulating. And the result opens a door that leads to still another goal. Moreover, each level of achievement only makes the next level on which the entrepreneur sets her sights appear that much more reachable, as in this example:

EXAMPLE ▶

James Lindsay is nibbling away at the $10 billion salty snack food industry. The 33-year-old founder of the Philadelphia-based Rap Snacks Food Company ships 360,000 bags per week and gets less than 5 percent of his product returned. From New York to Maryland, thousands of people a week are buying bags of Rap Snacks potato chips and popcorn. These snack foods include flavors like honey barbecue, hot cheese, and the triple mix (caramel, cheese, and butter).

Lindsay is a goal setter, an entrepreneur with a mission. "I want to provide a quality product to the consumer as well as address the social issues surrounding inner-city areas, and improve the image of rap music," says Lindsay. It is not surprising, then, that each one-ounce Rap Snacks bag carries a printed message, such as:

- ▶ Education is Knowledge
- ▶ Realize Your Dream
- ▶ Stop the Violence
- ▶ Stay in School

A graduate of Cheyney State University with a bachelor's degree in marketing, Lindsay is hardly daunted by the fact that the snack food industry is ruled by a few major companies, such as Pepsico's Frito-Lay and Wise Potato Chips. These companies, however, tend to ignore smaller firms like Rap Snacks that sell their products mostly to mom-and-pop shops and not to supermarkets. The advantage here is that Lindsay does not have to vie for supermarket shelf space.

So far, Lindsay's goal of marketing solely to young hip-hoppers is paying off. "We realized that kids are the main purchasers of snack foods, and we decided to do something they could relate to," says Lindsay.

Raising his sights, Lindsay's next goal is to partner with Wise Potato Chips to become a national player. For a product that the major players in the snack food industry thought would fail, Rap Snacks is slowly making its way into smaller grocery chains and proving itself to be "all that and a bag of chips."[16] ▲▼▲

> ◆ **Accountability**

Entrepreneurs generally want full credit for their success—or will assume full blame for their failure. To measure their performance, entrepreneurs may use any of several yardsticks, among them return on investment and rate of profit growth. What these yardsticks measure is profitability: It is profits that best tell entrepreneurs how well they are doing in the marketplace. However, profits really serve only as a yardstick of performance, not as a goal. In the words of Marvin Bower, a pioneer in management consulting:

> Profits are really a measure of the competitive value of a company's contribution to users, distributors, and the public. And, it is only by maximizing that contribution that a company can maximize its profits. In other words, concentrate on things that produce a profit rather than on profit itself. Perhaps using profit as a measure instead of a goal is a distinction without a difference. Maybe so. But it is a useful distinction to guide the thinking of entrepreneurs.[17]

Profits play another role, as a reward for successful risk taking. Entrepreneurs deserve some return (profits) on their investment, just as individual savers deserve some return (interest) on their savings accounts. Entrepreneurs, moreover, deserve a higher return because they risk failure, while individual savers usually do not.

Developing Entrepreneurs

Our profile of the successful entrepreneur only partially answers the question of what makes entrepreneurs tick. A more rounded answer requires a look at the social origins of entrepreneurs.

> ◆ **A Tradition of Entrepreneurship**

Psychologists say that entrepreneurs are likely to come from families in which parents set high standards for their children's performance, encourage habits of self-reliance, and avoid being strict disciplinarians. Although the need to achieve crops up in all ethnic groups, it is more likely to take an entrepreneurial form in groups with a tradition of entrepreneurship—largely because of the example set by parents and relatives.

With the exception of Asian Americans, learning experiences like these are rare among minorities. As a result, most minorities tend to channel their energies into businesses not as employers, but as employees. Blacks and Hispanics have fewer entrepreneurial role models among close relatives than do either Asian Americans or whites. Asian Americans rely more than other groups on relatives or friends for business startup loans.[18]

Still another reason is bias, as minorities have long been denied equal access to entrepreneurial opportunities. These barriers are dissolving, however. Just as there have been dramatic changes in women's role in the entrepreneurial world, as discussed on the following page, so too are we likely to see equally dramatic changes among minorities in the future.

Both the federal government and the nation's educational institutions are working to boost entrepreneurship among minorities. Community colleges, in particular, have pioneered educational programs to help bring minorities into the nation's entrepreneurial mainstream. Many minorities with undergraduate or advanced degrees are more likely than ever before to leave big business for a business of their own. For example:

▶ **Robert Johnson, Entrepreneur**

An entrepreneur all the way down to his finger tips, Robert Johnson is bent on molding a major communications network that addresses the tastes and wants of millions of black consumers. Now well on the way to fulfilling his dream, Johnson's venture—Black Entertainment Television Holdings, Inc. (BET)—is the first black-owned business to win a listing on the New York Stock Exchange, and for good reason:

▶ In 1994, BET posted sales revenues of $97.5 million, up from $74.2 million in 1993—an increase of 31 percent.

▶ In 1994, BET earned a profit of $14.8 million, up from $12.6 million in 1993—an increase of 18 percent.

A graduate of Princeton University, Johnson launched his venture in 1979, backed by a $15,000 loan. This bare-bones beginning forced him to limit his programming to just two hours a week, hardly enough to keep body and soul together.

He soon found, however, that fortune favors the bold. After failing to raise additional money from commercial banks and individual investors, he boldly approached the country's biggest cable company—Telecommunications, Inc.—and persuaded them to back his vision by investing $500,000 in BET.

Buoyed by such good fortune, Johnson's business soon grew into a 24-hour cable powerhouse reaching 41 million homes. This success persuaded him to expand BET into other communications fields. As a result, BET is no longer solely a cable television network but also a host of other businesses, among them:

▶ *BET Direct*, a direct marketing arm for skin-care products.

▶ *BET Pictures*, a joint venture with the Blockbuster Entertainment Corporation to finance, produce, and distribute black, family-oriented films.

▶ *Emerge Magazine*, a news magazine aimed at the black community.

▶ *United Image Entertainment*, a joint production venture with actor Tim Reid.

▶ *YSB Magazine*, a lifestyle magazine aimed at the black community.

With so many diverse businesses under one corporate umbrella, it would seem that Johnson would relax his sights. Not so. In fact, he has already laid plans to launch a 24-hour home-shopping channel by 1997. He is convinced it would help leverage his company's name among black viewers, such that BET would become a household name, like CBS or NBC. His goal is for viewers to think of BET as, in his words, "the preeminent provider of information, entertainment, and direct marketing services to the black community."

Though fraught with risk, Johnson's foray into home shopping makes eminent sense, he believes. For one thing, there surely is a niche for home products that appeal to black consumers. And he plans to pursue that niche with gentle intensity, firm in the knowledge that black consumers spend more of their take-home pay than the average consumer on the kinds of products that shopping channels promote: apparel, electronics, and personal-care items. Also, blacks have needs and wants that are largely ignored by the mainstream marketplace; for example, there are some styles of clothing and shoes that appeal to black women but not to other women.

With a presence of 2,500 cable markets, BET now reaches 96 percent of all black cable households. With such vast exposure, Johnson is betting that many of these households will also tune in to his home-shopping channel. And with his track record, he likely will win the bet.[19]

▶ **The Emergence of Women in Small Business**

Historically, women have played a disproportionately small role in small business. But this is no longer true. In fact, women are launching small businesses at twice the rate of men. Equally impressive is the number of sole proprietorships owned by women in 1991: 5.5 million.* This number is:

▶ double that since 1981
▶ one-third the nation's total[20]

Although these gains by women are inspiring, their sales revenues are not, falling far short of those realized by their male counterparts:

▶ $54,000/year for men
▶ $19,000/year for women[21]

According to the SBA, the lower sales level for women stems from, among other reasons, their concentration in the service and retail industries and the newness of their businesses. Still, their entrepreneurial reach is striking, as shown in Exhibit 2.7. Note that, although their numbers are small, women have begun to break away from tradition and invade fields that have long been exclusively male-dominated. Take this example:

EXAMPLE ▶

The advances of women throughout corporate America have produced a new pool of talent, with experience in virtually every industry. Now as they leave large companies to strike off on their own, women are invading such longtime bastions as manufacturing and construction, as did Nancy Novinc and Hillary Sterba.

---

*Later data were unavailable as of this book's publication date.

EXHIBIT 2.7

Distribution of women-owned businesses* by industry (1990).

Source: U.S. Small Business Administration, reported by Wendy Zellner et al., "Women Entrepreneurs," *Business Week* (April 18, 1994), p. 107.

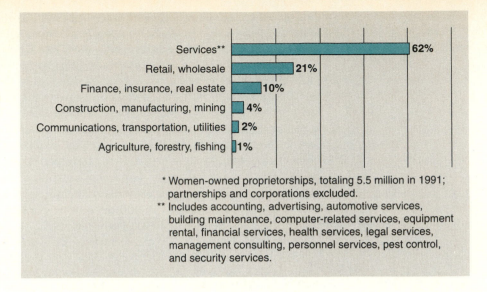

Services**	62%
Retail, wholesale	21%
Finance, insurance, real estate	10%
Construction, manufacturing, mining	4%
Communications, transportation, utilities	2%
Agriculture, forestry, fishing	1%

* Women-owned proprietorships, totaling 5.5 million in 1991; partnerships and corporations excluded.

** Includes accounting, advertising, automotive services, building maintenance, computer-related services, equipment rental, financial services, health services, legal services, management consulting, personnel services, pest control, and security services.

Economic necessity drove both women to start their own tool engineering company in 1992. They had just been laid off from the Cleveland Twist Drill Company, a manufacturer of cutting tools, when they decided to start S&N Engineering Services Corporation. "We decided if we were going to put in these long hours and work this hard, we would do it ourselves," observes Sterba.

Thus, rather than lamenting their layoff, the two women put their combined 26 years of machine-tool experience to work. Their talents and skills were a creative match, as Novinc had been the director of new products at Cleveland Twist Drill and Sterba its manager of national account services. This blend of production and marketing experience gave them lots of contacts that they could use to succeed in so male-dominated a field as machine tools.[22] ▲▼▲

▶ Education: An Influence

According to the SBA, the major reason for the emergence of women as founders of their own businesses is:

> The large influx of women entering the labor force, who later launched their own businesses. For example, during the 1980s, women made up the largest segment of new or reentering workers in the labor force, landing about two-thirds of all new jobs. This increased economic activity tends to spawn new businesses.[23]

To the SBA's explanation we can add the fact that women, in 1995, comprised 50 percent of U.S. undergraduate business students, up from 4 percent in 1970.[24] Clearly, with the explosive growth of business-educated women, it follows that, more than ever before, women would aspire to start their own ventures.

Cultural Diversity in Small Business

In the words of the SBA, "we have much to celebrate in the fact that American business ownership increasingly reflects our great national strength—our cultural diversity. The individuals who own small businesses continue to make remarkable contributions to our economy."[25]

The richness of cultural diversity is evidenced in the makeup of the U.S. business community. For example, the most recent figures from the U.S. Bureau of the Census show that:

▶ Blacks own more than 400,000 businesses, of which the 100 largest posted total sales revenues of $5.7 billion in 1992.

▶ Hispanics own more than 500,000 businesses, of which the 500 largest posted sales revenues in excess of $40 billion in 1993.

▶ Asians own more than 400,000 businesses. In California alone, 1 out of every 10 Koreans is a business owner.[26]

Just as blacks, Hispanics, and Asians can point to successes in businesses, so can Native Americans. They, too, are becoming entrepreneurs in ever-increasing numbers, although hard data measuring their progress was lacking when this textbook was prepared.

Rewards and Hazards of Entrepreneurship

In general, entrepreneurs like nothing better than the psychological satisfaction of being their own boss. Esteemed by friends and relatives alike, their self-image mirrors that esteem.

Financially, successful entrepreneurs often outdo big-business executives. Rather than save money or dabble in stocks, entrepreneurs are likely to plow profits back into their ventures to keep them growing. They often are interested more in seeing their equity in the business increase than in drawing big monthly paychecks.

These are the chief rewards of entrepreneurship. But what of the hazards? Launching a new venture always carries some risk of failure. There is no such thing as a perfectly safe investment. As a rule, the riskier the venture, the greater the potential for profit. If the entrepreneur succeeds, profits may be high; if not, life savings may be lost.

For some, failure is tragic; for others, it is an opportunity to begin anew. Henry Ford, for example, failed twice before he successfully launched the Ford Motor Company. As Ralph Waldo Emerson wrote, "Valor consists in the art of self-recovery." Even so, many men and women cannot take failure in their stride; it shatters their ego, dulls their drive, weakens their will—and with each personal tragedy, society loses also.

SUMMARY

Entrepreneurs are individuals who assume the risks and management of their own ventures. Pure entrepreneurs create a venture from the raw materials of their own ideas and hard work. Entrepreneurship is the capacity for innovation, investment, and expansion in new markets, products, and techniques. Unlike the manager, who uses given resources to operate the business, the entrepreneur creates new opportunities for success.

Although scholars have had little success defining exactly what it is that makes an entrepreneur, they have found that successful entrepreneurs share a number of traits. One common thread is the need for self-expression; another is the likelihood of being an overachiever. In addition, David McClelland suggests that high-achieving entrepreneurs tend to be innovative, to take reasonable risks, to be self-confident, to work hard, to set goals, and to hold themselves accountable.

Another element that entrepreneurs share is a tradition of entrepreneurship: They tend to be children of parents who own businesses. This may explain, in part, why minorities historically have played a disproportionately small role in small-business management and ownership. Equal access to entrepreneurial opportunities is another factor here, although in the 1990s that is changing. Today, minorities have made considerable progress in owning and running their own businesses—a dramatic indication of the power of cultural diversity in the United States. At the same time, women are also succeeding in business at a rapid rate. Armed with business educations, they are penetrating traditionally male-dominated fields.

Most entrepreneurs like nothing better than the satisfaction of being their own boss. For the successful entrepreneur, the rewards are both monetary and psychological—profits and esteem. Not surprisingly, the costs of failure are also monetary and psychological—financial ruin and a shattered ego.

Discussion and Review Questions

1. In what ways are entrepreneurs necessary to the health and growth of our economy?
2. Do you agree that a person who takes over a business from its founder is not a pure entrepreneur? Why or why not?
3. Define the terms *entrepreneur, entrepreneurship, management, innovation, risk taking,* and *accountability.*
4. How do entrepreneurs and managers differ?
5. Why do few men and women become entrepreneurs, although most say they would rather work for themselves than for someone else?
6. What are the traits of successful entrepreneurs? Which trait is most often identified with entrepreneurship? Why?
7. Are innovators necessarily also entrepreneurs? Explain, using an example.
8. Why do entrepreneurs generally prefer ventures in which the risk of failure is high but not too high? Explain, using an example.
9. Why is goal setting a self-renewing process? Explain, using an example.
10. Do you agree that profits are *not* the goal of doing business? Explain, using an example.
11. Write a paragraph on the traits of an entrepreneur you know well.
12. In light of the tradition of entrepreneurship, how can parents influence entrepreneurial behavior in their children?
13. What accounts for the emergence of women as entrepreneurs? Of minorities?

14. In your judgment, how does cultural diversity enrich a community's economic life?
15. What are the rewards and hazards of entrepreneurship? Explain fully, using community examples.

Building a Business Plan

Diversity and the Entrepreneur

According to the American Heritage Dictionary, an entrepreneur is a person who organizes, operates, and assumes the risk for a business venture. And according to many small business experts, the entrepreneur is probably the most important reason why one business is successful and another is a failure.

Instructions for Worksheet 2

Worksheet 2 requires that you complete both part 1 and part 2. In part 1, you must use your own words to define what an entrepreneur is and to evaluate the rewards and risks of entrepreneurship. In part 2, you must describe how your individual traits match up with the traits exhibited by the successful entrepreneurs described in Chapter 2.

Part 1—Definition of Entrepreneur

As pointed out in this chapter, we often take for granted the meaning of the word entrepreneur. To most everyone, the word does suggest spirit, zeal, idea, and diversity. But what does the term mean to you?

1. In your own words, define entrepreneur.
2. What do you consider to be the rewards of being an entrepreneur?
3. What do you consider to be the risks associated with being an entrepreneur?

Part 2—Traits of Successful Entrepreneurs

While no two entrepreneurs are the same, there are some common traits that seem to be a common thread among successful entrepreneurs. (HINT—Before you answer the questions below, you may want to review the material on pages 37 to 45 in the text.)

4. In your own words, describe how each of the traits listed below could be important when managing the business that you want to start.
   a. Innovation
   b. Risk taking
   c. Self-confidence
   d. Hard work
   e. Goal setting
   f. Accountability

5. Using a scale of 1 to 5 (low to high), rank yourself on each of the traits listed below.
   a. Innovation
   b. Risk taking
   c. Self-confidence
   d. Hard work
   e. Goal setting
   f. Accountability

6. After careful assessment of your answers to the above questions, do you feel that you have what it takes to be a successful entrepreneur? Justify your answer.

Teddi's Restaurants

When he came to this country from Greece, Steve Caloudis owned just the clothes on his back and spoke not a word of English. Today, he owns three restaurants that ring up sales revenues of $2.1 million a year.

His success has caught the eye of shopping center developers throughout the state. "They want me because of my record," says Caloudis. "It's a good feeling, but I'm not sure I should keep expanding. I'm happy with what I've got."

Background

To Caloudis, hard work is a way of life. "Work is a habit that I've never grown out of," he says. Indeed, he began working when he was 12, selling apricots and grapes to tourists in Greece. When he was 18, Caloudis left Greece for New York City, where he hired on as a dishwasher. He worked from 6:00 A.M. to 6:00 P.M., six days a week.

Caloudis continued to work in restaurants and bars, mostly as a waiter. His objective was to learn the restaurant business "inside out." To meet that objective, he often "did a lot of extra work for nothing." For example, he worked with the chef, the bartender, the cleaning crew—on his own time, without pay.

His appetite for work paid off. He finally became manager of one of the city's biggest downtown restaurants. That turned out to be his last promotion; Caloudis had decided to go into business for himself. He was sure he was ready, and he had saved $11,000. After looking around for a month, he zeroed in on a 40-seat coffee shop that was for sale.

His First Venture

The owner wanted $25,000 for the shop. Before he bought it, Caloudis wanted to be sure that he could make a go of the business. For a week, he stood outside the coffee shop, 12 hours a day, asking customers just one question: "What attracts you to this location?"

Although his family thought $25,000 was too much to pay for a coffee shop, Caloudis felt strongly that he was buying "clientele, not salt shakers and coffee cups." He was sure that if he upgraded the menu and gave customers "more of a variety," he could double revenues in a year. He paid the owner $25,000, making no attempt to negotiate a lower purchase price. His beginning balance sheet appears in Exhibit 2A.1.

EXHIBIT 2A.1

Ted's Restaurant, Inc.: Beginning balance sheet.

Assets		Equities	
Cash	$ 500	Bank loan	$15,000
Equipment	2,000	Owners' equity	10,500
Goodwill	23,000		
Total assets	$25,500	Total equities	$25,500

EXHIBIT 2A.2

Ted's Restaurant, Inc.: Sales revenues (1973–1977).

Year	Sales Revenues	Notes
1973	$ 35,000	Under former owner
1974	60,000	Under Caloudis
1975	110,000	
1976	190,000	Seating capacity expanded from 40 to 86 seats
1977	190,000	

To swing the $15,000 loan, Caloudis had the help of his wife, Mary, who did the banking for the advertising agency she worked for. When he applied for the loan, the Caloudis name already was familiar to the bank.

Mrs. Caloudis helped her husband in still another way. She was taking a course in business law at a local college. When she told the instructor, an attorney, about her husband's plans to go into business for himself, he offered to incorporate the business at a small fee. The attorney still counsels Caloudis on all legal matters—now, of course, at his usual fee.

The restaurant was a quick success. In fact, soon after Caloudis took over, customers began lining up outside at 11:15 A.M. for lunch. Word had spread that he had enlarged the menu, improved the service, and called each customer by name. Revenues soared, as shown in Exhibit 2A.2.

A Second Restaurant

Caloudis's success soon drew the attention of shopping center developers. Impressed by the restaurant's performance, the owner of the Southgate Shopping Center told Caloudis: "I have a place for you in Southgate. You'd be a good tenant for us."

Again his family was skeptical. After all, he was making a lot of money where he was. Why move? "My family told me I was overextending myself financially," says Caloudis.

True to form, he went ahead anyway. He estimated it would cost $120,000 just to install equipment, fixtures, and furniture. "When you go into a shopping center, all you get is four walls and a ceiling," says Caloudis. "The rest is up to you." Unwilling at the time to sell his other restaurant, he had to look elsewhere for money to finance his new venture. So he sold his house for $40,000 and borrowed $80,000 from a bank, using the market value of his other restaurant as collateral.

Unexpected Problems

When it opened, the new restaurant was not the runaway success his first restaurant had been. "I never stopped to think about who to cater to," says Caloudis. "I was too busy running the other restaurant and setting this one up. In fact, I was putting in 18-hour days."

The problem of "who to cater to" took up most of Caloudis's time. To solve the problem, he talked to customers, other businesspeople, and his wife. He found that the shopping center drew its shoppers mostly from middle-income families. So he decided to change his image:

▸ He changed the restaurant's name from Ted's to Teddi's, to erase a truck-stop image.

▸ He upgraded the quality of the menu. "People wanted home-cooked meals," says Caloudis.

EXHIBIT 2A.3

Teddi's Restaurant at Southgate: Sales revenues (1978–1983).

Year	Sales Revenues	Notes
1978	$300,000	Restaurant opened
1979	300,000	Foreign meals added
1980	310,000	Open kitchen changed to closed kitchen
1981	375,000	
1982	375,000	
1983	465,000	Cocktail lounge and party room added

Despite these changes, revenues did not go up until 1980, when Caloudis borrowed $30,000 to carpet the restaurant and enclose the kitchen. "That improved the atmosphere," says Caloudis. "You can't offer broiled shrimp and champagne to customers with an open kitchen staring them in the face." His revenues picked up immediately, as shown in Exhibit 2A.3.

Other Opportunities

Soon opportunity knocked again. This time the developer of a Parmatown shopping center asked Caloudis to become a tenant. Despite his family's opposition, Caloudis said yes, but only after the developer agreed to help finance the $200,000 cost of the new restaurant. "The only way to get ahead is to use other people's money," says Caloudis. His new restaurant was an instant success, as shown in Exhibit 2A.4.

That success moved another shopping center developer to ask Caloudis to take over a bankrupt restaurant in Richmond Mall. Its owners had gone under after just six months in business. The bankrupt owners offered Caloudis the equipment and furnishings for $25,000. After inspecting the restaurant, Caloudis estimated it would take another $175,000 to make it over to his own taste.

Again his family thought it would be a mistake for him to buy another restaurant. "You'll lose

EXHIBIT 2A.4

Teddi's Restaurants, Inc.: Sales revenues (1983–1987).

Year	Southgate	Parmatown
1983	$465,000	—
1984	510,000	—
1985	525,000	$450,000
1986	550,000	465,000
1987	610,000	510,000

everything," they told him. But Caloudis went ahead. And again he succeeded. In fact, it took just three years for this restaurant to catch up with the other two, as shown in Exhibit 2A.5.

The Secret of His Success

A newspaper reporter recently asked Caloudis for the secret of his success. The reply: "We've learned what the public wants. They like family-type, home-cooked meals—along with the right price, good service, and a clean establishment."

Caloudis knows that he probably never would have made it without his wife. "She's been by my side for 17 years," he says. Working as a team, they still put in 12-hour days. And being fully involved has paid off for both of them.

EXHIBIT 2A.5

Teddi's Restaurants, Inc.: Sales revenues: (1988–1990).

Year	Southgate	Parmatown	Richmond
1988	$635,000	$515,000	$415,000
1989	720,000	580,000	510,000
1990	760,000	705,000	660,000

Shopping center developers still beat a path to Caloudis's door, wanting him as a tenant. They always come away impressed with his grasp of details. For example, he keeps in his head these kinds of financial details:

▶ Payroll costs as a percentage of revenues, broken down by restaurant and by month for the past two years

▶ Sales revenues and before-tax profits, broken down by restaurant and by year for the past 17 years

His strong memory helps him spot trends and danger signals quickly. "That's why my restaurants have never had a losing month," says Caloudis. "I always know where I stand and where I'm going. You can't get along without figures in a business like mine."

Indeed, he is one of the most efficient restaurateurs in the state. Last year, out of every sales dollar, $0.10 was left over as profit, as shown in Exhibit 2A.6. Compared to the industry average of $0.045, it is obvious that Caloudis has excellent managerial skills.

Organization

Caloudis receives almost all the profits himself. Of the 1,500 shares of stock outstanding, he owns 1,400; his daughter, 100. Yet his business is organized as an S corporation, which allows as many as 35 shareholders.

EXHIBIT 2A.6

Teddi's Restaurants, Inc.: Breakdown per sales dollar.

Item	Breakdown	
Sales revenues		$1.00
Operating expenses		
Food	$0.42	
Overhead	0.26	
Labor	0.22	0.90
Operating profit		$0.10

In addition to this corporation, Caloudis owns four others. The S corporation serves as the management company; the others serve as operating companies, as shown in Exhibit 2A.7.

To help him run all five corporations, Caloudis relies on just three people: his wife, daughter, and son-in-law. They hold all the key positions. "It's all in the family," says Caloudis. His organizational chart appears in Exhibit 2A.8.

Altogether, Caloudis employs 190 people. "I hire the best," he says. "My turnover is low compared to other restaurants, only 12 percent a year. If I hire cheap employees, my costs are going to go up. That's why I go after the best."

Controlling Performance

Caloudis controls his employees' performance by setting standards and rewarding them if they do

EXHIBIT 2A.7
S&M Management
Company, Inc.: Corporate
structure (S&M stands for
Steve and Mary).

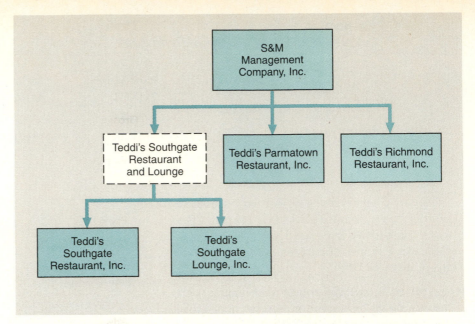

EXHIBIT 2A.8
S&M Management
Company, Inc.:
Organizational chart.

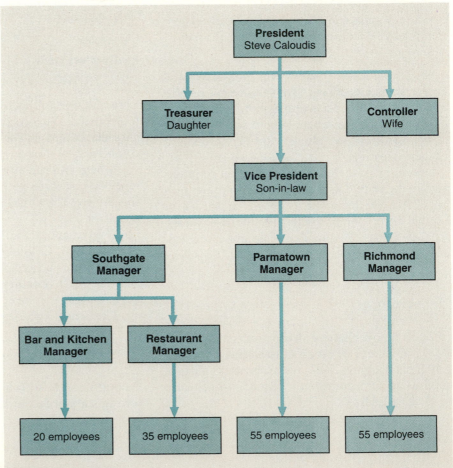

well. "Your employees have to know what you expect of them," he says, "and they appreciate knowing. Also, I pay them well." For example, he pays his dishwashers $6.00 an hour.

Caloudis also believes in treating his employees humanely. "In a capitalistic system, we have to learn to share. I even lend employees up to $300 each, without interest. And I never get mad when they make mistakes. Self-respect is important. I know every one of my 190 employees by name. They know I mean it when I say, 'How are you?' I even have a policy that my managers cannot fire an employee without first consulting me. I don't like the word *fire*. It's bad for morale." Benefits available to Caloudis's employees are a pension plan, profit sharing, medical insurance, paid vacations, and business-interruption insurance.

Caloudis is especially proud of his management team. Every manager has come up through the ranks, working at jobs ranging from dishwasher to chef. "We develop our own managers," he says. One example is his daughter: She started when she was just 12 years old; now 24, she is treasurer of the business.

Sets Goals

Looking back, Caloudis says, "I knew what I wanted to do, and I did it. My record speaks for itself. And my credit is triple-A. Nobody asks me when I'm going to pay. Instead they ask how much do I want." He has never submitted his financial statements to Dun & Bradstreet, the national credit-rating firm. "I don't need them," says Caloudis. A recent income statement appears in Exhibit 2A.9.

Looking ahead, Caloudis has set a goal of $5 million in revenues over the next four years, up from $2.1 million in 1990. To reach that goal, he may have to add two restaurants. But he has second thoughts about further expansion. For one thing, his family opposes the idea of "expansion for expansion's sake." For another, Caloudis, now 53 years old, has been training his son-in-law and daughter to take over his business.

EXHIBIT 2A.9
Teddi's Restaurants, Inc.: 1990 income statement.

Sales revenues		$2,125,000
Cost of goods sold		861,000
Gross profit		$1,264,000
Operating expenses		
Payroll	$468,000	
Office*	164,000	
Rent	119,000	
Payroll taxes	49,000	
Depreciation	47,000	
Utilities	38,000	
Interest	36,000	
Supplies	36,000	
Advertising	33,000	990,000
Operating profit		$ 274,000

*Includes accounting, entertainment, insurance, legal, office payroll, telephone, travel, and other expenses.

At the present time, Caloudis continues to feel pressures to expand. In the past month alone, two shopping center developers have asked him to set up restaurants in the centers they are currently building. One will be the largest shopping center in the state, with 260 shops.

Questions
1. If you were Steve Caloudis, would you expand again? Why or why not?
2. Comment on how Caloudis has organized his business.
3. What accounts for Caloudis's success?
4. Comment on Caloudis's attitude toward his employees.
5. Looking at Exhibit 2A.9, how would you adjust the income statement to arrive at a better estimate of profit?

Arlene Craig

For two years, Arlene Craig pursued her desire to own an ATLAS rent-a-car franchise. ATLAS has 270 franchised outlets, concentrated mostly in airports. These outlets rent passenger cars only. Craig is 39 years old. In December 1995, she received this letter from an ATLAS executive:

Dear Arlene:

We have reviewed your application. After consulting with our people, we have decided that we cannot now consider you favorably for an ATLAS franchise, although your credentials are indeed impressive.

We sincerely appreciate your interest in ATLAS, and hope you will understand that our decision was difficult to make. Arlene, let me wish you well in your career-seeking efforts.

Sincerely,
Robert Pizzuli
Franchising Manager
ATLAS, Inc.

The bad news left Craig speechless. To realize her dream of someday owning her own business, she had taken the following steps:

▶ She studied entrepreneurship and accounting at the University of Kentucky, graduating cum laude. At present, she is a certified public accountant with a pharmaceutical manufacturer, earning $52,000 a year.

▶ She moonlighted on Saturdays for two years at an ATLAS franchise, learning all she could about the rent-a-car industry.

▶ She had amassed personal assets worth $155,000 and owed no one.

"I'm really at a loss why they turned me down," says Craig. "Divorced, I'm active in my community, I teach Sunday school, and I chair a political action committee. People respect me. I know it wasn't the money, because I could've easily raised the $90,000 cash needed for a franchise."

An ATLAS brochure offers the following profile of a typical franchisee:

The entrepreneur awarded an ATLAS franchise benefits from the prestige of operating under a nationally known reputation and of receiving strong corporate support.

Our selection process focuses on matching the right place with the right person. Our franchisees enthusiastically accept the responsibility of a 20-year franchise. All are on-the-job owners. Some have an automotive background, but most come from backgrounds as diverse as law and computers, the U.S. Army and professional football.

Our franchisees are thoughtful decision makers with the ability to hire, train, and motivate the 10 to 20 full- and part-time employees that work for them.

Questions

1. What should Arlene Craig do now?
2. In your opinion, why did ATLAS turn down Craig's application for a franchise?
3. Do you believe that Craig could make a go of an ATLAS franchise? Why?

Karla Addington

Karla Addington is an entrepreneur in the truest sense. At the age of 18, she combined an idea on how to improve a service with a steely determination to succeed. The business she opened from the basement of her mother's home had two locations in Cincinnati with sales revenues that were expected to top $350,000.

Her business, Bow-Wow Boutique, Inc., is an award-winning grooming and pet supply service for the pampered dogs and cats of Cincinnati. To date, Bow-Wow Boutique's success story has been featured in numerous national trade publications, on seven television news programs, and in five radio interviews.

Entrepreneurial activity is nothing new to Karla. To promote her childhood lemonade stand, Addington said, "I would ride my bike around the neighborhood with this silly hat with lemons all over it." At the age of 14, she was honing her sales skills by selling Fuller Brush products door-to-door.

Bow-Wow Boutique had its genesis in Addington's work experience at other grooming shops. Disappointed with what she saw at other shops as a "lack of knowledge, courtesy, and cleanliness," and bothered that the "professionals" were not taking the time to educate clients on proper pet care, Addington began thinking about how she could offer a better service.

She planned to provide a clean, attractive atmosphere, and the safe, healthy, and unique gifts for pets and pet lovers alike. But the foundation of Addington's business would be superior customer service. "I knew I could do it better," she said.

To finance her business's startup, Addington worked three jobs until she had saved $1,000. "Things were definitely tight," she said. "I had absolutely no knowledge of projections, key assumptions, or business plans—but I had chutzpah. I knew I could never be happy unless I took the risk."

After opening her first shop, Addington ran headlong into one of the obstacles facing young entrepreneurs today. "Not too many people took me seriously," she said. "I was an 18-year-old female with absolutely no business knowledge. Salesmen would call on the shop, look me over, and ask for the manager."

But Addington was not about to let her lack of knowledge stop her. She took an assertiveness training course, read management books, attended management seminars, and "even started to read the business section of the *Cincinnati Enquirer*" to sharpen her business skills. Addington said, "I wasn't really sure what cash flow was, but I was going to learn!"

What makes Bow-Wow Boutique special? Besides the superior service that Addington provides, the boutique carries pet gifts that you would expect to find only in the most spoiled pet's home. Doggie tuxedos and top hats, hand-finished cherry waterbeds, and white gamma mink coats are just a few of the extravagant pet gifts found at Bow-Wow Boutique.

Do not, however, expect to find Addington resting on her past success. "Actually, I feel I've just touched the tip of what I will call personal success. I have not yet achieved my business or financial goals." Her ultimate goal? "To be the Mary Kay of the pet industry," said Addington, who is now 28 years old.

Questions

1. To what do you attribute Karla Addington's success?
2. What role did education play in Addington's success?
3. Comment on Addington's ultimate goal "to be the Mary Kay of the pet industry."

Source: U.S. Small Business Administration, *Young Entrepreneur Seminars* (Washington, D.C.: U.S. Government Printing Office, 1988), pp. 75–76.

Ethics and Social Responsibility

Always do right. This will gratify some people and astonish the rest.

—*Mark Twain*

I f this is the "age of information," it is also the age of nervousness. Many people agree there is much to be concerned about these days. They are especially nervous about what they perceive to be a deep decline in ethical behavior among Americans—a blurring of the distinction between right and wrong.

Like all of us, entrepreneurs face ethical dilemmas virtually every day of their lives. Many do not fully appreciate the depth, or even the nature, of the ethical choices they must make. How should they sort out such dilemmas? What makes for ethical behavior?

In this chapter, we discuss these questions, which go right to the heart of what troubles many entrepreneurs. We also discuss the entrepreneur's responsibility for helping to solve the host of problems plaguing society today, such as urban blight and education reform, racial bias and threats to the environment.

The Meaning of Ethics

Above all, it bears mention that ours is by no means a society empty of ethical behavior. Many of us live well and decently. Yet there is a lot less of this than there ought to be. That is why virtually every community college and university now offers courses in ethics. Novelist John Updike put it this way:

▶ The fact that . . . we still live well cannot ease the pain of feeling that we no longer live nobly.[1]

According to the *American Heritage Dictionary,* ethics are "the rules or standards governing the conduct of a person or a profession." And by extension, ethics are the rules and standards by which entrepreneurs and their employers ought to behave. It follows, then, that:

▶ Ethical, or the right, behavior lives up to the standards set by society, while—

▶ Unethical, or the wrong, behavior does not.

Let us now look at the nature of wrong behavior. How do we know *wrong* when we see it? According to Rushworth Kidder, author* and founder of the Institute for Global Ethics, and as depicted in Exhibit 3.1, there are three kinds of wrong behavior:

▶ Violation of law

▶ Departure from truth

▶ Deviation from moral rectitude[2]

Violation of Law   It is wrong, of course, to run a stoplight, take an apple without paying the grocer, or park in a space reserved for the disabled. And more severely, it is wrong to bribe politicians, pass bad checks, or batter your spouse. These examples of wrongdoing reflect the failure to live up to the letter of the law—either because we do not know the law or because we choose to break the law. Take this example of illegal and dehumanizing behavior:

EXAMPLE ▶

In August 1995, federal agents raided a garment factory in El Monte, a blue-collar district east of Los Angeles. They found dozens of immigrants from Thailand held in virtual slavery in a factory ringed with barbed wire and spiked fences.

Made to work at sewing machines for up to 17 hours a day, 7 days a week, the immigrants were paid an average of $1.60 an hour instead of the minimum $4.25 required by law. They were receiving slave wages while presumably paying off their fares to California.

The workers—mostly women in their twenties lured to California with the promise of higher wages—lived in squalor. They slept on the floor and had to pay to do their own laundry. Attempts to escape were always met with beatings and threats to their families in Thailand.

The Thai entrepreneurs who ran the factory were jailed on charges of harboring and transporting illegal immigrants. Other charges included extortion and kidnapping. Moreover, department store chains, among them Montgomery Ward, who used this sweatshop's services under contract, were held liable for the shameful violations, in accordance with California law.[3] ▲▼▲

Departure from Truth   This kind of *wrong* has to do with lying purposely. Whenever we say anything that does not fit the facts, we are lying and are engaging in wrongful behavior. Examples of this kind of wrong are: calling in sick when you are not, claiming that the oil slick in the river is not from your factory when it is, or assuring customers that a toy for toddlers is safe when in fact it is not.

---

*Author of a widely acclaimed book on ethics: *How Good People Make Tough Choices.*

EXHIBIT 3.1
Three kinds of wrong
behavior.

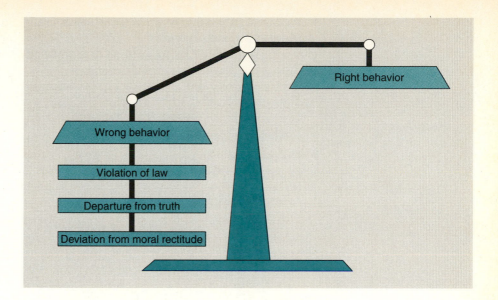

Such departures from truth are black-and-white in nature. But there are others that are gray in nature, where it may be hard to distinguish between fact and fiction, between what the parties *say* happened and what *actually* happened. Either party may then have no recourse but to seek relief from the courts, as in this example:

EXAMPLE ▶

Monday mornings during football season are anxious times for Julie Nimmons, chief executive of Schutt Sports Group located in Litchfield, Illinois, near St. Louis. That's when newspaper clipping services start delivering news of injuries to young athletes in the weekend's high-school games—a crude barometer of what lawsuits could be heading toward her company.

As one of only two surviving sports-helmet manufacturers in the country, Schutt is exposed constantly to threats of product-liability lawsuits from angry parents and their lawyers who blame helmet failures for children's athletic injuries.

"I spent seven weeks in a courtroom outside New Orleans [in 1993]," Nimmons says. "Unfortunately, a young man put his head down in a high-school football game and hit an opposing player and became quadriplegic."

Though she lamented the tragedy, Nimmons said the helmet was of sound design and workmanship and did not contribute to the injury—a view the court agreed with, ruling that the company was not liable.[4] ▲▼▲

Deviations from Moral Rectitude Differing markedly from the other two kinds of *wrong*, deviations from moral rectitude are wrong not because they dodge the facts or break the law but rather because they go against our moral fiber. We would not, for example, hesitate to call these behaviors wrong:

▶ Canceling a meeting with your employee but not bothering to call him or her

▶ Passing off as your own an idea for a new product when in fact somebody else had proposed it first

▶ Taking company tools home daily to build a patio, though returning them the next day

Here, it is our values that ought to define the difference between right and wrong—values that are shared with others in our community; among them:

▶ Honesty and fair play

▶ Decency and tolerance

▶ Hard work and service to others

▶ Civility and generosity

Core values such as these strongly influence our behavior and help us to distinguish between what is right and what is wrong. They enable us to stay the course and make hard decisions, even at the risk of rejection by our peers. William Shakespeare put it well when he wrote in *Hamlet:*

This above all—to thine ownself be true. And it must follow, as the night the day, thou canst not then be false to any man.

▶ **Ethical Decline**

As a society, how are we doing? How healthy are we ethically? Poll after poll suggests a grave decline. In 1992, for example, the Gallup Poll found that:

▶ Americans believe the United States is in decline as a nation. The decline is not military—we are still the only superpower—but economic, moral, and spiritual.[5]

Most telling of all was the Gallup Poll's finding that nearly two-thirds of the respondents believed the nation was on the wrong track ethically.[6] Who is doing things wrong? Who are the good guys and who are the bad guys? According to a *Business Week*/Harris Poll, and as shown in Exhibit 3.2, small business is trusted the most by Americans.

EXHIBIT 3.2
Results of a poll on public trust in major institutions.

Source: *Business Week*/Harris Poll, reported in "Who Do You Trust: Americans Have Faith in Entrepreneurs," *Entrepreneur* (September 1995), p. 18.

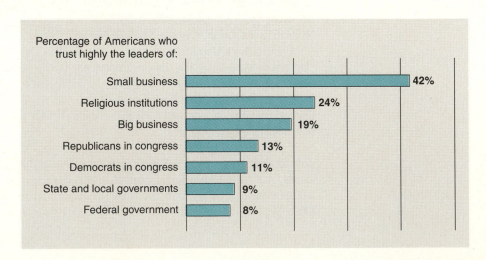

Percentage of Americans who trust highly the leaders of:

Small business	42%
Religious institutions	24%
Big business	19%
Republicans in congress	13%
Democrats in congress	11%
State and local governments	9%
Federal government	8%

The word *trust,* it bears adding, implies one's unquestioning belief in another person or in an institution. This means that, if left alone, a person or an institution like small business will always behave in your own best interests and will never knowingly do harm.

Why does small business inspire trust? According to Renée Frengut, a New York psychologist, the reason is that customers look upon entrepreneurs as their neighbors. "[Small businesses] are the people down the street, the shops you go into every day where you see [the owner] face to face," says Frengut. "And people trust their neighbors."[7]

The Meaning of Social Responsibility

In this section, we will shift our focus from ethics to social responsibility. These terms are often used interchangeably, so closely linked are they in purpose. Although ethics addresses individual and group behavior, social responsibility does that *and* more, reaching out to society, both local and at large. Social responsibility may thus be defined as:

▶ The circle of care and concern that a business has for the well-being of society.

▶ **Property Rights vs. Social Rights**

"What's good for General Motors is good for the country," said a former president of General Motors.[8] His remark sums up the sentiments of many entrepreneurs today. They sincerely believe that what is good for their ventures is likely to be good for the community in which they invest their energy

Every business, big or small, must be socially responsible in its community.

and money. They see their investments as sparking new products, new services, new jobs. Especially as their ventures prosper, do entrepreneurs see themselves as benefactors of the community.

Years ago, this narrow view generated little debate. Today, the public no longer wholeheartedly accepts it. Doubt has grown about the absolute supremacy of the ideas basic to free enterprise, such as individualism and personal property rights, unhindered competition and the limited role of government.

Today, property rights are widely seen as subject to challenge from such social rights as equal opportunity, justice, good health, clean air, survival, and a decent income. Social rights are not eliminating property rights, but their preeminence is diminishing. In the words of Professor George Cabot Lodge of the Harvard Business School:

> Your right to enjoy your property is no longer subject merely to paying your taxes and obeying the laws. It is subject as well to the needs of the people who work for you and of the entire community. . . . It's not that property rights are wiped out, it's just that they become less important.[9]

▶ Entrepreneurs' Feelings of Helplessness

Few entrepreneurs know how to overcome their sense of futility about such social problems as urban blight and education reform, racial bias and threats to the environment. They know that the giant pieces of a new order are falling into place, and they feel helpless. Why? Because the very size of each problem makes it remote from the individual entrepreneur. Each entrepreneur feels somehow connected to the problem but not to the means of solving it.

This feeling of helplessness can be overcome, however. Individual entrepreneurs may not be able to write legislation for the entire nation, but they can surely make their ideas known to those around them and take active roles to help clean the air; help make the streets safer; make their plants safer places to work; employ the disabled, the poor, and minorities; and participate in politics to help ensure the election of honest and intelligent public officials.

Clearly, entrepreneurs must act in ways that enhance the community's well-being. However great their abilities to innovate and sell, if they cannot also use their skills to work for a safer and better community, they are incomplete businesspersons. In the words of economist Irving Kristol, "Business tends to operate too narrowly within the constraints of 'economic' concern. The businessman must act within the broader contexts of the 'human' community."[10]

The implications are clear. Businesspeople, including entrepreneurs, ought to do more than they have to enhance the well-being of society, if only to meet expectations concerning *local* causes, as suggested in Exhibit 3.3. Note that "donating money to a cause rates as the most desirable way to show you care."[11] And in Exhibit 3.4, note the large percentage of consumers who said, in a study, that a business's social-responsibility practices were key in their buying decisions.

▶ Positive Action

Let us now look at the example of a global entrepreneur who is responsive to the social challenges of the times:

▶ An Uncommon Entrepreneur

Anita Roddick's life as a global entrepreneur is wrapped in the aura of an icon. Since launching her first Body Shop in a storefront in Brighton, England—selling natural beauty products only—Roddick has become known as the very

EXHIBIT 3.3
Results of a study on cause-related marketing.

Source: Cone/Coughlin Communications and Roper Starch Worldwide, reported in "Cause-Related Marketing: What Works," *Inc.* (August 1994), p. 102.

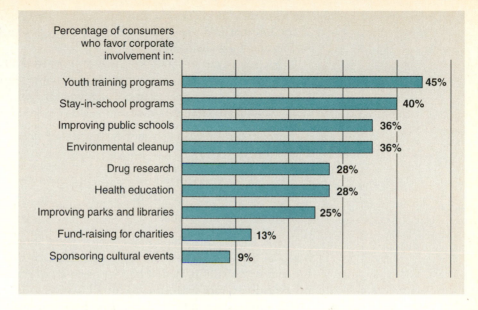

Percentage of consumers who favor corporate involvement in:

Youth training programs	45%
Stay-in-school programs	40%
Improving public schools	36%
Environmental cleanup	36%
Drug research	28%
Health education	28%
Improving parks and libraries	25%
Fund-raising for charities	13%
Sponsoring cultural events	9%

EXHIBIT 3.4
Results of a study on why consumers may refuse to buy from a business.

Reprinted with permission from Business Ethics Magazine, 52 S. 10th St. #110, Minneapolis MN 55403.

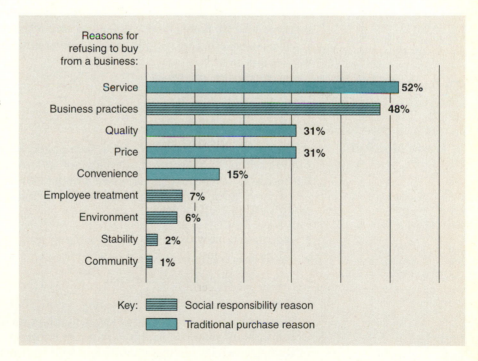

Reasons for refusing to buy from a business:

Service	52%
Business practices	48%
Quality	31%
Price	31%
Convenience	15%
Employee treatment	7%
Environment	6%
Stability	2%
Community	1%

Key:
Social responsibility reason
Traditional purchase reason

model of an ethical entrepreneur. So much so that her achievements with Body Shop, International, have merited cover stories in such prestigious magazines as *Inc.* and *Business Ethics.*

When she began in 1976, Roddick envisioned a business that would be like no other in its dogged pursuit of ethical behavior. The customary way of doing business in the cosmetics industry was not for her. Instead, she would take a radical tack and, as she stated:

▶ Make naturally-based cosmetics that would *never* be tested on animals.

▶ Fight to protect the environment.

▶ Commit herself to social causes.

▶ Shun all forms of advertising.

▶ Make no miracle claims.

It was largely this vision that enabled Body Shop to multiply, by 1995, into a global chain of more than 700 cosmetics shops in 39 countries. Valued at more than $1 billion, Body Shop has seen its profits soar 50 percent per year, on average—a rare performance for a business as large as Body Shop.

Roddick literally circles the globe in tireless pursuit of her vision. With hundreds of franchises the world over, it is, at best, a Herculean task to keep that vision alive and well. Undaunted, she keeps it alive by spending up to five months a year away from home, visiting not only a country's franchised shops but also its people—especially those in places like Ghana and the Hopi Reservation—in attempts to:

▶ Learn first-hand about their unique cultures

▶ Explore their secrets of skin care

▶ Support their economies

▶ **Trade Not Aid**

All but unheard of in business circles, such political derring-do has brought her both fame and fortune. In her autobiography, *Body and Soul,* Roddick credits her success to being "first and foremost a trader looking for a trade." Indeed, her concept of "Trade not Aid," has enabled her to sign government-blessed agreements to build:

▶ A soap-making factory in a Glasgow slum

▶ An oil-processing factory in Brazil

▶ A paper-making factory in Nepal

Counting Princess Diana and *Sting* among her boosters, Roddick also encourages each of her franchised shops to adopt local community causes. For example, Body Shop has paid for child-care experts to help orphaned children in Romania, while employees throughout the 700-shop chain raised money to help restore a down-at-the-heels orphanage. Besides local causes like this one, Body Shop also adopts causes of global appeal, among them:

▶ Banning ozone-depleting chemicals

▶ Saving the rain forest and whales

- ▶ Preventing human rights abuses
- ▶ Stopping animal testing

Blessed with seemingly boundless energy, Roddick also finds time to socialize with her franchisees and their employees. Every month, for example, she invites them, usually twenty at a time, to her home in Scotland. "We all cook together, talk, play music," says Roddick. "It's three days where we try to stay in touch with where we want to be and where we want to go."

In an interview with *Business Ethics* magazine, Roddick was asked: "How do you create and sustain . . . that passion in a company that's as large as yours is now?" Her reply:

> You create passion by taking vision that goes beyond who you are, what you own, what the company gave in terms of numbers, and you bring in something so elementary that it is even embarrassing to state: It's *service!* It's the Christian principles or the Judaic principles, or the principles of every great tradition—it's giving of yourself, making somebody's life a bit better. It's so simple, it's embarrassing even to say that. And you relate that passion in a hundred squillion ways.[12]

Such positive action is spreading to all corners of the business world, although not yet to anything like the same degree as Roddick's example would suggest. Even so, there is little doubt that, out of enlightened self-interest, entrepreneurs and other businesspersons are undertaking projects that enhance the well-being of their communities. But this is just a start. Businesspersons have some way to go before they convince a skeptical public that they have, indeed, developed a social conscience. According to a 1994 study reported in *Business Ethics*, an overwhelming number of consumers—78%—said they preferred products made by socially conscious businesses.

▶ Codes of Ethics

In their efforts to be socially responsive and to appear humane, many businesses—large ones, especially—have adopted Codes of Ethics. Of course, it is one thing to draft a set of values to live by, and quite another to act upon them. Unfortunately, lofty professions of noble intent often fall on deaf ears, gathering dust rather than sparking action.

Even so, in the hope that it will encourage entrepreneurs to draft *and* carry off their own Code of Ethics, we offer, in Exhibit 3.5, excerpts from the Global Ethics Code drafted by the Caux Round Table in Switzerland. Naturally, an entrepreneur's code would be narrower in scope and more precise than the one in the exhibit—for example, embodying such precise statements of intent as:

- ▶ Volunteering two hours a week to help high school students with reading problems
- ▶ Giving a community advance notice of a factory closing
- ▶ Paying fair wages; consistent, at the very least, with industry averages
- ▶ Donating money to local colleges for small-business scholarships benefiting inner-city students

EXHIBIT 3.5

Excerpts from the Global Ethics Code Developed by the Caux Round Table.*

Section 1. Preamble

The mobility of employment, capital, products, and technology is making business increasingly global in its transactions and its effects.

Laws and market forces are necessary but insufficient guides for conduct.

Shared values, including a commitment to shared prosperity, are as important for a global community as for communities of smaller scale.

Section 2. General Principles

Principle 1. The Responsibilities of Businesses: Beyond Shareholders Toward Stakeholders

Businesses have a role to play in improving the lives of all their customers, employees, and shareholders by sharing with them the wealth they have created. Suppliers and competitors as well should expect business to honor their obligations in a spirit of honesty and fairness.

Principle 2. The Economic and Social Impact of Business: Toward Innovation, Justice, and World Community

Businesses established in foreign countries to develop, produce, or sell should also contribute to the social advancement of those countries by creating productive employment and helping to raise the purchasing power of their citizens.

Principle 3. Business Behavior: Beyond the Letter of Law Toward a Spirit of Trust

While accepting the legitimacy of trade secrets, businesses should recognize that sincerity, candor, truthfulness, the keeping of promises, and transparency contribute not only to their own credibility and stability but also to the smoothness and efficiency of business transactions, particularly on the international level.

Principle 4. Respect for Rules

To avoid trade frictions and to promote freer trade, equal conditions for competition, and fair and equitable treatment for all participants, businesses should respect international and domestic rules.

Principle 5. Support for Multilateral Trade

Businesses should cooperate in efforts to promote the progressive and judicious liberalization of trade, and to relax those domestic measures that unreasonably hinder global commerce.

Principle 6. Respect for the Environment

A business should protect and, where possible, improve the environment, promote sustainable development, and prevent the wasteful use of natural resources.

Principle 7. Avoidance of Illicit Operations

A business should not participate in or condone bribery, money laundering, or other corrupt practices: indeed, it should seek cooperation with others to eliminate them.

Section 3. Stakeholder Principles

Customers

We believe in treating all customers with dignity, irrespective of whether they purchase our products and services directly from us or otherwise acquire them in the market. We therefore have a responsibility to:

▸ provide our customers with the highest quality products and services consistent with their requirements;

▸ treat our customers fairly in all aspects of our business transactions, including a high level of service and remedies for their dissatisfaction;

▸ make every effort to ensure that the health and safety of our customers, as well as the quality of their environment, will be sustained or enhanced by our products and services;

*A collaboration of business leaders in Europe, Japan, and the United States.

▶ respect the integrity of the culture of our customers.

Employees

We believe in the dignity of every employee and in taking employee interests seriously. We therefore have a responsibility to:

▶ provide jobs and compensation that improve workers' living conditions;

▶ provide working conditions that respect each employee's health and dignity;

▶ be honest in communications with employees and open in sharing information, limited only by legal and competitive restraints;

▶ avoid discriminatory practices and guarantee equal treatment and opportunity in areas such as gender, age, race, and religion;

▶ promote in the business itself the employment of differently abled people in places of work where they can be genuinely useful;

▶ encourage and assist employees in developing relevant and transferable skills and knowledge

Owners/Investors

We believe in honoring the trust our investors place in us. We therefore have a responsibility to:

▶ apply professional and diligent management in order to secure a fair and competitive return on our owners' investment;

▶ disclose relevant information to owner/investors subject only to legal requirements and competitive constraints;

Suppliers

Our relationship with suppliers and subcontractors must be based on mutual respect. We therefore have a responsibility to:

▶ seek fairness and truthfulness in all of our activities, including pricing, licensing, and rights to sell;

▶ ensure that our business activities are free from coercion and unnecessary litigation;

▶ seek, encourage, and prefer suppliers and subcontractors whose employment practices respect human dignity.

Competitors

We believe that fair economic competition is one of the basic requirements for increasing the wealth of nations and, ultimately, for making possible the just distribution of goods and services. We therefore have a responsibility to:

▶ foster open markets for trade and investment;

▶ promote competitive behavior that is socially and environmentally beneficial and demonstrates mutual respect among competitors;

▶ refrain from either seeking or participating in questionable payments or favors to secure competitive advantages

Communities

We believe that as global corporate citizens, we can contribute to such forces of reform and human rights as are at work in the communities in which we operate. We therefore have a responsibility in those communities to:

▶ respect human rights and democratic institutions, and promote them wherever practicable;

▶ respect the integrity of local cultures; and

▶ be a good corporate citizen through charitable donations, educational and cultural contributions, and employee participation in community and civic affairs.

Source: Reprinted with permission from Business Ethics Magazine, 52 S. 10th St. #110, Minneapolis MN 55403.

For the past ten years, an entrepreneur's small business has *anonymously* donated $7,000 per year to Cuyahoga Community College in Cleveland for scholarships to be awarded to inner-city students majoring in entrepreneurship. In 1995, forty-one scholarships were awarded.

Moreover, the entrepreneur's business has adopted a shelter for homeless women. In 1995, employees donated forty-four large bags of clothing and nearly a thousand cans of food to the shelter. And for the Thanksgiving and Easter holidays, they also donated turkey dinners benefiting 20 women.

These socially responsible acts reflect in part the entrepreneur's Code of Ethics, which all employees must follow to the letter. Such generosity surely illustrates the entrepreneur's willingness to turn his good fortune to the benefit of others.[13] ▲▼▲

Often, the law forces entrepreneurs and other businesspersons to live up to their responsibilities to society. Abuses by business were so flagrant just before the turn of the century, that public opinion pressed the federal government to impose standards of behavior on business—a movement that continues virtually unabated to this day.

As a result, business has been saddled with a complex web of federal regulations—to protect the safety, health, and well-being of all of us. Listed in Exhibit 3.6 are some of the federal agencies whose mission is to keep business

EXHIBIT 3.6
Selected federal legislation that requires the performance of socially responsible behavior.

Agencies Created by Federal Legislation	Main Activities
Consumer Product Safety Commission	Minimizes consumer complaints about product design and labeling
Environmental Protection Agency	Sets and enforces environmental standards regarding air pollution, noise, and water pollution
Equal Employment Opportunity Commission	Investigates and resolves complaints of discrimination in employment based on race or gender
Food and Drug Administration	Sets standards for certain foods and drugs and issues licenses for the manufacture and marketing of drugs
Occupational Safety and Health Administration	Sets and enforces safety and health standards
Office of Federal Contract Compliance Programs	Assures that businesses holding federal contracts practice equal employment opportunity

socially responsive—not only in the solution of problems plaguing society but also in their prevention.

One especially nagging problem has been environmental pollution. For too long, both business and government ignored the problem until it became a threat to life and health. Today, no small thanks to the work of the Environmental Protection Agency, we can expect business and government, as partners in a cause, to act swiftly to clean up the environment—*and* to keep it clean.

Civil Rights and Employment Discrimination

▶ **Minorities**

Today, most businesses claim to be equal opportunity employers. Many are, indeed, working to erase bigotry and provide full equality of opportunity by observing the spirit as well as the letter of the hiring-practices law laid down by the federal government in 1964:

> It shall be an unlawful employment practice for an employer . . to discriminate against any individual . . . because of such individual's race, color, religion, sex, or national origin.[14]

Good intentions do not, however, ensure good results. True, some progress has been made, but, to many entrepreneurs, being an equal opportunity employer means simply being willing to consider minorities for employment. Moreover, few minorities move into managerial jobs. According to Professor Robert W. Nason of the Wharton School at the University of Pennsylvania:

> A new and subtle deterrent to black mobility is institutional racism. In this case, individuals may justifiably feel they and fellow managers hold no personal prejudice against blacks, yet there are real barriers to black mobility in management.

Entrepreneurs who only pay lip service to the principles of equal opportunity are not living up to their social responsibilities. Nor are only blacks denied equal opportunities. Native Americans, Hispanics, Asians, and other minorities face similar problems. All the talk about equal opportunity cannot hide the fact that business still discriminates against minorities either openly or unconsciously.

▶ **People with Disabilities**

So far, our discussion has focused mostly on minorities. Another group that merits attention is those with disabilities. In the rush for equal opportunity, these people have been largely overlooked, yet discrimination against them is often more severe than that against minorities.

In recent years, businesses have begun to realize that people with disabilities are as dedicated and talented as any other group. Studies show that, to compensate for their disabilities, they often work harder than the able-bodied. Moreover, absenteeism among people who are disabled often approaches zero.

So, it behooves entrepreneurs to at least try hiring people who are disabled. The experience is likely to be mutually rewarding.

The Impact of Consumerism

The coming of consumerism can be traced to 1966, when Ralph Nader began making headlines with his exposés of unsafe automobiles. He has since broadened his interests and helped launch a consumer movement that now spans the continent. Thanks largely to Nader's efforts, consumers are no longer alone in the fight against dishonest businesspersons.

The main goal of the consumer movement is to end private abuses of the public interest. In essence, the consumer movement tries:

▶ To teach consumers to care.

▶ To make businesses more open, accessible, and accountable to consumers.

▶ To educate consumers about their opportunities and their responsibilities to make changes.

▶ To teach consumers how to learn what is going on, how to register complaints, and how to effect change.

Today, almost every community has a consumer group. These groups already have made their mark on businesses and even on the federal government. In response to consumerism, the Federal Trade Commission (FTC) has hired hundreds of consumer specialists to spot-check businesses for violations of FTC rules, investigate complaints about faulty products or slipshod service, and educate consumers on how to avoid being taken in by dishonest businesspersons.

Turning to Exhibit 3.7, note the types of businesses that give rise to the most pre-purchase doubt among potential customers. Credit firms top the list, according to a report by the Council of Better Business Bureaus, which analyzed 14.6 million inquiries and complaints received by 163 Better Business Bureaus in 1993.

▶ **Opposing Views of Consumerism**

Traditionally, the FTC investigated mergers and other practices that could hamper free trade. Now that the FTC has joined the consumer movement, one FTC official described the behavior of business in this way:

> Every business is involved in some sort of misrepresentation. They're not all doing it maliciously, though. Some of them are doing it because they have to keep up with the competition that is doing it.[15]

This somewhat exaggerated statement echoes the attitude of Nader and other consumer advocates. In response, some businesses now go to extreme lengths to please the consumer, while others believe that government—at all levels—has overreacted to consumerism. One entrepreneur had this to say:

> The government has been pushed and badgered and harried by consumer groups, and it has acted before making a proper study of the matter under question. Some of our politicians . . . are going around the country saying all clothing should be fire-proof without regard to how much this is going to cost the consumer.
>
> When you say, "Make all clothing flame-retardant," it gets out of control. People won't be able to afford their clothes. There would be no variety, no fashion. But to argue for it makes great politics.[16]

EXHIBIT 3.7

Ten most asked-about businesses among consumers.

	Number of Inquiries
Credit card companies	213,910
Work-at-home companies	212,500
Mortgage and escrow companies	201,840
Loan brokers and advance fee brokers	186,920
Service firms	181,110
Home remodeling contractors	174,980
Roofing and gutter service	158,360
Franchised auto dealers	118,440
Home construction and remodeling	114,110
Auto repair shops	108,580

Source: Council of Better Business Bureaus, reported in "They're Checking Up on You," *Small Business Reports* (September 1994), p. 8.

There is more than just a grain of truth in these remarks. The price of consumer protection often is a higher cost. Automobiles are a good example: Prices rose dramatically when manufacturers were required to equip each automobile with safety belts and pollution controls.

▶ Benefits of Consumerism

Despite its critics, the consumer movement has left its mark in many areas. Consumer advocates have, for example:

▶ Exposed the cozy relationship between some federal regulatory agencies and the industries they presumably watch over.

▶ Forced the Atomic Energy Commission to give verified assurances that backup systems will work reliably if an atomic reactor breaks down.

▶ Established Congress Watch, a group that promotes legislation on such matters as consumer protection and tax reform. It also follows and grades the performance of each U.S. senator and representative.

Although consumerism has struck fear in the hearts of many businesspersons, it also has encouraged tens of thousands of consumers. Remember, the only true test of a satisfactory product or service is a satisfied consumer. If that test be their guide, entrepreneurs need never worry about doing the right thing.

SUMMARY

Increasingly in society, there is more emphasis on ethics and social responsibility. Ethics are the rules or standards governing the conduct of a person or a profession. Ethical, or the right, behavior lives up to the standards set by society; unethical, or the wrong, behavior does not.

There are three kinds of wrong behavior: Violations of law, departures from truth, and deviations from moral rectitude. Among the core values that ought to define the difference between right and wrong are:

▶ Honesty and fair play

▶ Decency and tolerance

▶ Hard work and service to others

▶ Civility and generosity

Social responsibility is the circle of care that a business has for the well-being of society, especially in the solution of such severe problems as:

▶ Urban blight and education reform

▶ Racial bias and threats to the environment

In their efforts to be socially responsible, many businesses have adopted Codes of Ethics. One code that may serve as a model is the Global Ethics Code drafted by the Caux Round Table in Switzerland.

Over the years, federal legislation has created agencies to force entrepreneurs and other businesspeople to act in socially responsible ways. These agencies include the:

▶ Consumer Product Safety Commission

▶ Environmental Protection Agency

▶ Equal Employment Opportunity Commission

▶ Food and Drug Administration

▶ Occupational Safety and Health Administration

▶ Office of Federal Contract Compliance Programs

Discrimination in the workplace is not only unethical; it is illegal. In 1964, Congress passed a law that prohibits discrimination "against any individual . . . because of such individual's race, color, religion, sex, or national origin." Yet, many employers fall short in the hiring and promotion of minorities and people who are disabled. Although often well intentioned, many entrepreneurs are hamstrung by stereotyped attitudes about these groups. As a result, minorities and those with disabilities have rarely been treated equally in the workplace.

The main goal of the consumer movement is to end private abuses of the public interest. The need for consumerism is indicated by its efforts to:

▶ Teach consumers to care.

▶ Make businesses more open, accessible, and accountable to consumers.

▶ Educate consumers about their opportunities and their responsibilities to make changes.

▶ Teach consumers how to learn what is going on, how to register complaints, and how to effect change.

Discussion and Review Questions

1. What is ethical behavior? Explain fully, using examples.
2. What are the three kinds of wrong behavior? Give examples in support of your answer.
3. What are some of the values that define the difference between right and wrong? What values do you esteem most? Why?
4. In your judgment, what is today's ethical climate like? Is it improving or worsening? Why do you think so?
5. Why do small business owners tend to inspire trust in their communities? Identify a small businessperson that you know and trust; explain why you do.
6. What is social responsibility, and how does it differ from ethics?
7. What role do Codes of Ethics play? Why are they important?
8. List some federal agencies created to enforce socially responsible behavior. What areas is each agency responsible for?
9. If an entrepreneur observes the law to the letter, does it also necessarily follow that his or her behavior is ethical? Explain, giving an example.
10. How would you, as an entrepreneur, go about pursuing the principle of equal opportunity? What guidelines for hiring and promotion would you use?
11. On the basis of your own observations, do you believe that job barriers against minorities and people who are disabled have been reduced? Explain your answer.
12. Do you believe that consumerism helps or hinders the entrepreneur? Why?
13. On the basis of your own observations, do you believe that entrepreneurs in your community are living up to their social responsibilities? Why?
14. Explain how you, as an entrepreneur, would go about meeting your social responsibilities.
15. Define these terms: *property rights, social rights, equal opportunity employer, consumerism.*

Ethics and Social Responsibility

Obviously, ethical decisions and social responsibility cost money. It is perhaps not so obvious that ethical decisions and social responsibility are good business.

Why Social Responsibility Makes Sense

Customers eventually find out which firms are acting responsibly and which are not. And just as easily as they cast their dollar votes for a product produced by a company that is socially responsible, they can vote against the firm that is polluting the air or waterways.

Instructions for Worksheet 3

According to your text, entrepreneurs face ethical dilemmas virtually every day of their lives. And yet, entrepreneurs must act in ways that enhance their community well-being. However great their abilities to innovate and sell, if they cannot also use their skills to work for a safer and better community, they are incomplete business owners. In part 1 of this worksheet, you should develop a list of guidelines that encourage ethical and socially responsible behavior in your business. In part 2, you should identify potential opportunities and benefits of responsible behavior for your business.

Part 1—Ethical Guidelines

Both large and small businesses often develop a code of ethics to guide their employees and help them make socially responsible and ethical decisions. A Code of Ethics is a written guide to acceptable and ethical behavior that outlines uniform policies, standards, and punishments for violations. Such codes are perhaps the most effective way to encourage ethical behavior.

1. Develop specific guidelines that can be used to encourage socially responsible and ethical behavior in your small business.

Part 2—Promoting Opportunities for Responsible Behavior

Can business be made more ethical in the real world? The majority of the experts suggest that individuals, not business organizations, are responsible for ethical or unethical behavior.

2. Given your product or service and the community in which you will operate, how could you and your employees act in an ethical and socially responsible manner?

3. After reviewing your potential business, describe potential problem areas that could cause you or your employees to make socially irresponsible or unethical decisions.

4. In your own words, explain the benefits of ethical and socially responsible behavior.

The Hue-Man Experience Bookstore

What began in 1984 as an attempt to set up an independent business targeted to affluent African Americans was by 1992 a 3,000-square-foot retailing establishment and North Denver community landmark. The Hue-Man Experience Bookstore specialized in books, cards, jewelry, and artwork by and for people of color—hence the "Hue" in "Hue-Man."

While most patrons lived within five miles of the bookstore, the Hue-Man Experience Bookstore had gained a national reputation, attracting frequent out-of-town visitors. By 1994, Clara Villarosa was looking at expansion. The availability of the building next door kindled her dream of creating an Afrocentric retail and cultural center.

History

The Hue-Man Experience Bookstore grew out of the dream of a woman who had already made it in corporate America. Clara Villarosa started out professionally as a psychiatric social worker, working in an outpatient, nonresidential clinic in Chicago, after receiving a master's degree in social work in 1954.

Like many women of her generation, she dropped out of the workforce when her children were born. In 1968, when her daughters were 5 and 9 years old, Clara and her husband moved the family to Denver. Clara soon took a position in the department of behavioral sciences at Denver's Children's Hospital. By the time she left the hospital in 1980, she had become the director of behavioral sciences and assistant hospital administrator. After entering a doctoral program in social work and law, she started a consulting business. In her words:

I wanted to help African Americans move up the corporate ladder, and I thought I could sell that idea to large corporations. As a social worker, I had some skills, but I didn't know how to knock on doors, to get a business off the ground.

When I ran out of money, I took a temporary job at United Bank. I started out in employee relations and moved quickly up the corporate ladder, becoming the vice president of human resources within two years.

Again, I found myself in the position of being the highest paid African American on the payroll. But, as often happened in those times, I hit the glass ceiling. People were extremely resentful and angry about African Americans and affirmative action, and I received a significant backlash. So I left the bank. But left the bank with some money. I think they *wanted* me to quit.

Lessons Learned

Clara's consulting business had taught her that she wanted to sell something tangible, and at the same time, something that would relate in a positive way to the African American community. In her words:

I came up with books, because I've always been a reader. My father was a reader, and I grew up immersed in books. We, the African American community, had had a bookstore in Denver, but there wasn't one now, so my dream was to create the largest African-American bookstore in Denver.

This time, Clara researched her market and wrote a business plan, outlining the financial and marketing requirements of her ethnic bookstore concept. With the help of two friends and her severance from the bank, she got together $35,000 and secured a lease on a two-story row house in a predominantly African American area.

The Hue-Man Experience Bookstore opened in 1984. In 1986, realizing that business and friendship do not always mix well, Clara arranged to buy out her partners' shares over a two-year period by selling shares of the business to interested friends and customers.

In 1993, the Hue-Man Experience Bookstore was governed by a nine-member board of directors, elected annually by Clara, who owned 58 percent, and by 31 shareholders. Financial data for the Hue-Man Experience Bookstore for 1990–1993 are given in Exhibits 3A.1 and 3A.2.

The Bookselling Industry

In 1992, book sales in the United States exceeded $16.1 billion, according to the Association of American Publishers. The American Book Trade Directory estimated that there were about 27,000 retailers of books in the United States, 15,700 of which were privately owned independent bookstores.

The largest book retailers were bookstore chains, which had sales of $2.9 billion in 1992 from a total of 2,768 outlets. Exhibit 3A.3 contains sales information for the largest bookstore chains in 1991 and 1992.

Major chain expansion began in the late 1970s to mid-1980s. Mall outlets carrying 1,000 to 20,000 titles proliferated toward the end of the 1980s. As mall growth slowed, the focus changed to superstores, huge discounters that averaged

EXHIBIT 3A.1

The Hue-Man Experience Bookstore: Condensed income statements for 1990–1993 (Figures in dollars).

	1990	1991	1992	1993
Sales revenues				
From books	181,134	216,922	272,542	269,751
From sidelines*	79,155	85,276	85,299	55,884
Total sales revenues	260,289	302,198	357,841	325,635
Cost of sales				
For books	121,719	143,793	196,666	152,104
For sidelines	40,013	47,950	43,281	37,781
Total cost of sales	161,732	191,743	239,947	189,885
Gross margin	98,557	110,455	117,894	135,750
Administrative expenses**	111,561	113,583	122,655	127,755
Operating profit (loss)	(13,004)	(3,128)	(4,761)	7,995

*Includes sales from cards, prints, jewelry, catalogs, and tapes.

**Includes salaries, rent, telephone, utilities, advertising, depreciation, office supplies, maintenance, accounting, and legal.

EXHIBIT 3A.2

The Hue-Man Experience Bookstore: Balance sheets for 1990–1993*
(Figures in dollars).

	1990	1991	1992	1993
Assets				
Current assets				
Cash	6,401	14,675	11,891	13,787
Accounts receivable			681	1,998
Prepaid expense			1,134	
Inventory	61,153	55,536	59,583	65,579
Total current assets	67,554	70,211	73,289	81,364
Fixed assets				
Building		79,260	79,260	79,260
Equipment	16,888	21,888	23,943	25,917
Other assets	10.024	10,024	18,924	18,924
Less: accum. depreciation	(13,994)	(18,887)	(25,557)	(33,977)
Total fixed assets	12,919	92,286	96,571	90,125
Total assets	80,473	162,497	169,860	171,489
Equities				
Current liabilities				
Accounts payable	11,847	12,060	19,686	14,219
Sales tax payable	2,618	3,358	4,596	3,886
Property taxes payable		806	792	2,413
Officer loan	4,400	4,400	4,400	4,400
Interest owed officer			2,097	2,383
Other current liabilities	3,529	5,070	6,825	1,075
Total current liabilities	22,394	25,694	38,396	28,376
Long-term loan (SBA)		72,000	66,948	70,255
Stockholders' equity				
Common stock	94,004	104,184	104,184	104,184
Retained earnings	(35,925)	(39,381)	(39,668)	(31,326)
Total stockholders' equity	58,079	64,803	64,516	72,858
Total equities	80,473	162,497	169,860	171,489

*For period ending December 31.

EXHIBIT 3A.3

The Hue-Man Experience Bookstore: U.S. Sales revenues of largest bookstore chains (1991–1992).

Chain	Ownership	1992 Sales*	1991 Sales	% Change	No. Stores at Year End
Waldenbooks	K-Mart	$1,146.0	$1,139.0	.06	1260
Barnes & Noble	public (in 1993)	1,086.7	920.9	18.0	916
Crown Books	Dart Group	240.7	232.5	3.5	247
Borders Books	K-Mart	116.0	82.5	40.6	22†
Books-A-Million	public	95.1	72.8	30.6	107
Encore Books	Rite-Aid Corp.	65.2	52.3	24.7	103
Lauriat's‡	Chadwick-Miller	49.0	46.0	7.0	56
Tower Books‡	MTS Inc	33.0	29.0	13.8	15
Kroch's & Brentano's‡	Waldenbooks	30.0§	33.0	−9.0	20
Rizzoli Bookstores‡	private	24.0	21.0	14.3	11
Taylor's Inc.‡	private	20.0	17.5	14.3	11
Totals		$2,905.7	$2,646.5	9.8%	2768

*Sales in millions. Figures are for calendar 1992 or most current fiscal year.

†Store totals do not include nine Basset Books transferred to Borders at year-end.

‡Estimated sales.

§Sales estimate is a projection for year ending June 30, 1993.

Source: *Publishers Weekly*, June 14, 1993.

200,000 titles, five to ten times the number offered by specialty or mall stores.

Profit margins among the large chains were estimated at less than 1 percent, which made volume critical to this business. Exhibit 3A.4 shows estimates of financial performance of 1991 or 1992 based on *Publishers Weekly* data.

Questionable Practices

Many independent bookstore owners were concerned that the industry was going the way of hardware stores and neighborhood pharmacies. According to John Mutter of *Publishers Weekly*, there was fear that superstores were creating "a concentration of power that threatens the diversity of what gets published." The American Booksellers Association was cooperating with the Federal Trade Commission in investigating business practices and pricing policies that appeared to threaten the small independent book retailers.

While chains offered cheap prices, few could offer the personal service of independents who knew their customers. Some specialty booksellers focused on a particular subject, such as Armchair Sailor in New York, which specialized in nautical books; or Victor Kamlin in Rockville, Maryland, which specialized in Russian literature.

Some stores focused on one particular market group, such as Charis Bookstore in Atlanta, which positioned itself as a feminist bookstore; OutBooks in Fort Lauderdale, which targeted lesbians and gays; and Hue-Man Experience Bookstore in Denver, which catered to an African American clientele.

EXHIBIT 3A.4

The Hue-Man Experience Bookstore: Comparison of independent and chain bookstore expenses as a percentage of total sales revenues.*

	Chains Composite Dollars (Millions)	Chains (%)	Sample Independents Composite Dollars	— Independents (%)
Net sales	$1197.8	100	$170.5	100
Receipts from books[†]	1078.1	90	136.4	80
Receipts from sidelines[†]	119.7	10	34.1	20
Cost of goods sold	816.3	68.2	106.4	62.4
Gross profit	381.5	31.8	64.1	37.6
Operating, selling, and administrative expense	317.8	26.5	61.4	36.0
Occupancy costs			12.3	7.2
Advertising			4.9	2.9
Depreciation and amortization	27.6	2.3		
Operating profit	36.1	3.0	2.8	1.6
Interest expense	29.9	2.5	0.34	0.2
Income before tax	6.2	0.5	2.42	1.4
Income tax	5.5	0.4	0.68	0.4[†]
Net income	0.7	0.1	1.7	1.0

*Calendar year 1991 or fiscal year ending 1992. (Most independents operate on a calendar year; chains report earnings on a fiscal year basis.)

[†]Estimate from anecdotal reports.

Source: *Publishers Weekly,* October 18, 1993.

African American Surge

Bookselling and publishing by and for African Americans had surged since 1988. An increasing interest in African American culture, aided by school curriculum reforms, fueled a growth in bookstores catering to African Americans. According to Wade Hudson, who ran Just Us Books in New Jersey, "African Americans are hungry for knowledge and understanding about their experience, so they are looking for books that provide it.

Until recently, these books had been published by small independent publishing operations, or by the authors themselves, and were sold out of car trunks at book conventions. More recently, the major publishers and national distributors had entered this market, providing easier access to booksellers through mainstream distribution channels.

"Bookstores used to assume there was no market because blacks didn't come in asking for titles like these, but that's because they assumed the stores wouldn't stock them," Mr. Hudson commented. Early in 1992, Kassahun Checole, president of the Red Sea Press, the largest distributor of African American titles, told *Publishers Weekly,* "The Red

Sea Press now distributes titles from about sixty publishers, approximately half of them African American."

The Denver Market

According to the 1990 Census, Colorado had almost 3.3 million residents; nearly 2 million lived in the greater metropolitan Denver area, 460,000 of whom lived within the city limits. While only 4 percent of Colorado's population was black, the city of Denver was nearly 13 percent black; 60 percent of these lived north of downtown.

According to Scarborough Research Corporation, Denver ranked 10 percent above the national average in the popularity of reading in 1993, ranking twenty-second out of 209 surveyed metropolitan areas.

The Denver area had over one hundred independent retailers of new and used books. Specialty bookstores included Murder by the Book, which specialized in mystery fiction; Astoria Books and Prints, which specialized in rare books and artwork; Isis Metaphysical Bookstore, which specialized in books on metaphysics, crystals, and jewelry; Category Six Books, which specialized in gay and lesbian literature; and Cultural Legacy, which specialized in books in Spanish.

Hue-Man Bookstore Site

The Hue-Man Experience Bookstore was located on Park Avenue West, a well-traveled thoroughfare about a mile north of downtown, bordering the area known as Five Points, which was named for the five tramway lines that once intersected there. Five Points had once been known as a cultural center for African Americans, with more African American-owned businesses than any other place in the United States except for Harlem.

This picture began to change in 1959 with the passage of Colorado's Fair Housing Act. During the 1960s and 1970s, many of the more affluent African Americans moved to other, more integrated, neighborhoods. In 1993, the Five Points area was populated with small service and retail establishments and rundown houses. According to 1990 Census data, half of the residents in the vicinity of Five Points had an annual household income under $35,000; nearly 30 percent of the households reported an annual income under $15,000.

Walking in the vicinity of Five Points was not considered advisable, especially after dark. In 1993, this area had the third highest crime rate in Denver, with 315.2 crimes reported per 1,000 population. In 1992, Five Points had ranked second.

Hue-Man's Operations and Layout

The Hue-Man Experience Bookstore began operations in a two-story row house, one of four attached residential apartments, shown in Exhibit 3A.5. Within two years, Clara had expanded her store into the adjacent row house, convincing the landlord to do renovations to connect the two. She thought that with 4,200 titles occupying 3,000 square feet, the Hue-Man Experience was, very likely, the largest African American bookstore in the United States.

Two cash registers, or point-of-sale computer terminals, were located just inside the door. Afrocentric greeting cards and note cards were located in a separate room adjacent to the checkout area. Afrocentric art created a backdrop for the checkout area, which was surrounded by a glass case displaying ethnic jewelry. Fine art prints and ethnic artwork by local artists were displayed on the walls throughout the store and in two browsing racks. Calendars featuring African American history and African American art were also prominently displayed.

During the holiday season, two rooms upstairs were full of distinctive boxed Christmas and Kwanzaa cards. People who bought books as gifts could also purchase gift wrapping and gift bags with African designs.

Industry insiders recognized that books are often an impulse purchase, bought on a whim for

personal reasons or to be given as a gift. Both small mall boutiques and large chain stores understood the importance of lighting and displays for enticing people to walk in the door to browse. Location and name recognition were also important, especially for independent booksellers.

Employee Relations

Employees were critical to the success of independent booksellers, whose customers relied on service. Many booksellers had difficulty finding qualified employees, people who read and were knowledgeable about books, who were personable, and who were willing to work hard.

Wages in most bookstores ranged from $4.50 to $5.50 per hour, far less than most full-time employment. Despite this, and even given Denver's strong economy, booksellers such as Hue-Man Experience had had no trouble finding competent, well-educated employees who liked their work.

There were four full-time employees at the Hue-Man Experience Bookstore. Turnover was low, with employees typically staying over a year, a rarity in minimum-wage positions. The employees at the Hue-Man Experience Bookstore conveyed a sense of belonging, not only to the bookstore, but also to the cultural community.

Marketing

On the subject of marketing, Clara commented:

I started out with a marketing plan, but there were many flaws because it was based on Anglo book purchasing behavior. We were unable to anticipate the difficulty in getting African American people to buy books. I had to go back and reevaluate my marketing strategies.

Clara originally put out fliers and took out ads to publicize her store but quickly realized that she was not reaching her market. And she soon understood that the people who came into the store were not the well-to-do clientele that she had envisioned. In her words:

We found out that our market was the working class. So we had to direct our advertising to these people. Unfortunately, they don't belong to a lot of groups. They belong to churches, but marketing from churches is very difficult because pastors do not want you to come into their congregation to sell something—other than what they sell.

So we've tried to determine what our people buy and why they buy what they buy. We've studied the psycho-demographics of our population and tried to create a presence in the community. And we have tried to create a national presence. People make purchases based on prestige, so the bookstore had to develop prestige.

Clara Villarosa began telling everyone who came in the store that Hue-Man Experience was the largest African American bookstore in the country. She became an influential figure in the African American community. She did book reviews on the radio. She was appointed to the governor's council for business development and served on the board of directors of the Small Business Development Center. She was a "friend of the library."

Marketing Tools

In the ten years since the store had opened, Clara felt she had become much better at marketing. By the end of 1993, the only paid advertising was in the form of courtesy ads: ads placed in local programs or newsletters. These ads generated goodwill, but Clara did not believe that they generated new business.

Word of mouth was the main source of advertising, but it was a sophisticated type of word of mouth, cultivated through sophisticated public relations. Clara had been featured in *Ms. Magazine*, *Executive Female*, and *Publishers Weekly*. She was on the board of directors of the American Booksellers Association and was a member of the Mountains and Plains Booksellers Association.

In 1989, at the suggestion of many out-of-town customers, Clara put together a 64-page mail-order catalog. "They said, 'Send me the booklist.' They like to read it but they don't order. It's a different motivation to pick up the phone and order a book. But the catalog appears to create a feeling of connectedness, and brings them back to the store."

Public Relations

Clara also published a quarterly newsletter, highlighting author signings and community events; a sample newsletter appears in Exhibit 3A.6. Regular customers were on the mailing list; customers who spent at least $10 were added to this list. Clara had found out the hard way that sending out unsolicited newsletters was not an efficient way to bring in new customers. As she put it, regular customers were "the ones most likely to come to store-sponsored events. They pay for the newsletter." On the subject of public relations, Clara commented:

PR is critical in this business—community connections. It's interesting, because that's what we built this store on—a community presence. Local people say that we have something of value and this creates pride and ownership. And we perpetuate that image by showing them that we care about them as individual customers and that we care about their community.

We find that our customers expect to be treated well, everyone is greeted, everyone is treated warmly, nurtured. We have to recognize our history, based on segregation, discrimination.

Plans for the Future

In November 1992, with financing backed by the U.S. Small Business Administration, Clara Villarosa bought the four houses that comprised the building that contained the bookstore. She was able to buy the building for $79,000. With her track record as a successful retailer, she secured a $72,000 24-year loan on the building, which was appraised at $120,000. Her bookstore occupied two units; the other two were rented to an art gallery and an ethnic apparel retailer.

Clara viewed her business as more than a bookstore. To her, it was a cultural center. She observed, "People who come here are culturally connected." she also recognized that there was strength in

EXHIBIT 3A.6
The Hue-Man Experience Bookstore: Sample Newsletter (Front and back of flier).

More Author Signings

Mark your calendar for these book talks and author signings. For more information call 293-2665.

ALSO APPEARING . . .

Wilbur Hughes III
This book is an important look at 300 unique African-American cemeteries.

Lay Down Body
Tuesday,
May 7
5:30 - 7:00 p.m.

Joseph Marshall, Jr.
This novel details the author's efforts to help young people at risk.

Street Soldier
Wednesday,
May 22
5:30 - 7:00 p.m.

Patricia Raybon

Deuvertie tells a personal journey to relinquish her racial rage.

My First White Friend
Friday, June 21
5:30 - 7:00 p.m.

Anita Bunkley

The author of *Black Gold* and *Wild Embers* discusses her mesmerizing new novel about a young woman who explores her heritage and finds hidden secrets and love.

Starlight Passage
Friday,
June 28
5:30 - 7:00 p.m.

The Hue-Man Experience Bookstore
911 Park Avenue West
Denver, Colorado 80205

OPEN:

Monday - Friday
10:30 a.m. - 6:30 p.m.

Saturday
10:00 a.m. - 5:00 p.m.

(303) 293-2665

BULK RATE
U.S. Postage
PMD
Permit No. 904
Denver, CO

Promoting and Nurturing African-American Thought

THE HUE-MAN READER

April, 1996

Author Signings

By attending these authors' signings, you ensure our ability to continue bringing the best literary artists to your home town in the future! For more information call 293-2665.

Connie Briscoe

In her eagerly awaited second novel, author of *Sisters & Lovers*, Ms. Briscoe examines issues faced by a young woman determined to be successful both professionally and romantically.

Big Girls Don't Cry
Monday,
May 6
5:00 p.m. - 7:00 p.m.

Edwidge Danticat

The author of *Breath, Eyes, Memory* offers 9 stories that encompass both the demonic cruelties and the high ideals of Haitian life and reveal the enduring strength of women.

Krik? Krak!
Wednesday,
May 15
5:30 p.m. - 7:00 p.m.

Marsha Hunt

The true story of the author's grandmother who, despite being beautiful and gifted, was committed to an asylum in the 1920s and spent 50 years in mental institutions.

Repossessing Ernestine
Thursday,
May 16
5:30 p.m. - 7:00 p.m.

Sheneska Jackson

In her first novel, Ms. Jackson spins a gritty Romeo and Juliet tale moving from the desperate streets of L.A. to the deceptive glamour of the music industry.

Caught Up In The Rapture
Friday,
May 17
5:30 p.m. - 7:00 p.m.

"Entreat me not to leave thee, or to return from following after thee. For whither thou goest, I will go; and where thou lodgest, I will lodge. Thy people shall be my people . . . "
Ruth 1:16

At the Hue-Man Experience Bookstore, our loyalty to you is symbolized by Ruth's loyalty to her mother-in-law in the Old Testament. Similarly, your support has allowed us to build something special for our community — to "go where you go," to "lodge where you lodge." African-American businesses depend on this kind of commitment to and from customers if they are to be successful. We thank you for sticking with us and remind you of the importance of your continual support not just to our bookstore but to the entire community.

By coming to the Hue-Man Experience Bookstore more frequently, you empower African-American authors, publishers, artists and ultimately, the entire community. You show them your appreciation by attending their book signings, book readings, and art showings.

We are a relatively small percentage of the Denver population — 12%. We have one of the largest African-American book stores in the country. Therefore, it will take all of us to keep the Hue-Man Experience Bookstore in Denver. Do you want the Hue-Man Experience Bookstore here? Do you like what we do? Let us know by thinking of us first — by coming to the author signings and being a regular customer.

We'd love to know how we can serve you better. Next time you're in the store, please take a moment to set us know how you feel about the bookstore. Your input will help us build a business that is truly representative of your interests.

numbers: a larger concentration of African American businesses could serve as a catalyst for cultural connections. In her words:

> I'd like to create an Afrocentric marketplace and position it as a minimall. So I bought this building two years ago. The other rented spaces in this building are complementary product lines. One sells African clothing and cloth and accessories and the other is an art gallery. I'd eventually like to work with them to make it a coffee shop also.
>
> The rent is fixed, it's stable, so they aren't going to deal with escalating rent costs. I maintain the property but we work cooperatively. I know the bookstore is the anchor. They each have their own customer base, but we feed off of each other. We want to create a synergy that will create more traffic for everyone.

Targeted for Redevelopment

The Mayor's Office of Economic Redevelopment had targeted the Five Points area for low-interest redevelopment loans. Clara believed that there was potential for a lot of retail activity in this area, but that it would be slow in coming. A light rail transit system, connecting Five Points to downtown, was scheduled to open in October 1994. Clara commented:

> I had hoped that the catering operation around the corner would also serve food, but she just wants to cater, and my suspicion is that they're not stable tenants. The top floor of the building needs to be renovated for retail or office space. I think the purchase is still an option.

Clara Villarosa was confident that she could get financing for expansion without diluting her ownership in the business. Business loan rates were going for as low as 10 percent. But, even if she could obtain the building at less than the current asking price, she was not sure that this would be a prudent investment.

At this point in her life, Clara was particularly concerned about the income potential of any expansion effort. At the same time, she did not want to give up her dream of creating an Afrocentric marketplace with national recognition.

Questions

1. What are the competitive forces in the bookselling industry and for The Hue-Man Experience Bookstore?
2. Describe Clara Villarosa's marketing strategy. How do you think it has worked so far?
3. What are the key success factors in this industry?
4. Describe the demographic factors in the Denver area. How do they impact The Hue-Man Experience Bookstore?
5. Should Clara make an offer on the building around the corner from her store? Why or why not?
6. What recommendations would you suggest for Clara at this time?
7. To what extent is this business delivering to Clara what she wants in life?

This case was prepared by Joan Winn of the University of Denver. Distributed by the Case Research Association. All rights reserved to the authors and the Case Research Association.

Questions of Ethics

Consider each of the scenarios described below.

▶ You are a sophomore at a community college and work weekends in a pizza parlor that employs 17 persons part time. After two weeks on the job, you notice that the owner pays employees in cash but fails to withhold federal, state, and city taxes—as required by law.

Having just completed a course in ethics, you are wondering what to do about the owner's failure to pay these taxes. At present, the job market is tight, and you need the job to make ends meet while pursuing your degree in small-business management.

▶ You own a thriving home-construction business. The day before New Year's Eve, a magnum of imported champagne is hand-delivered to you with a note: "Happy New Year—I truly look forward to working with you in the New Year. Take care and enjoy." The gift is from a supplier of concrete who has bid on a contract you plan to award the very next week.

▶ You are the owner of a home-appliance store. In the past year, your sales and profits have slumped because the local economy has dipped into a recession. Moreover, many customers have fallen behind in their payments.

Cash-poor, you have little recourse but to go to the bank. To look good in the eyes of the bank, you are wondering whether to report how much of the money owed you by customers is uncollectible—so as to show some growth in profits rather than the loss your books would otherwise show. You believe the bank is much more likely to approve your loan request if you do so.

▶ You are the founder and partner of a CPA firm that serves small corporate clients exclusively. In your spare time, you help a relative prepare his personal federal tax return, and he pays you $400 in cash. Because there is no record that you did the tax work, you are now wondering whether to report the $400 on your own federal tax return.

Questions

1. Pinpoint the ethical dilemma in each scenario.
2. Identify possible courses of action for each scenario.
3. Tell what you would do in each case.

Ben & Jerry's Homemade, Inc.

Ben Greenfield and Jerry Cohen opened their first scoop shop in a converted gas station in Burlington, Vermont, in 1977, investing $12,000 in some secondhand equipment. Their rich, all-natural ice cream, full of crunchy bits of cookies and candies, soon became popular. Before long, they were packaging more and more ice cream to sell in local restaurants and grocery stores, gaining shelf space in 150 stores across the state. By 1995, Ben & Jerry's Homemade, Inc. topped $150 million in sales revenues.

Cohen and Greenfield have made it their business not only to taste sweet success but to give something back to their employees, their community, and the world at large. The company's rapid growth, however, caused several crises for the two "hippies," who had never envisioned themselves in three-piece business suits. In fact, when Cohen and Greenfield first went into business together, they vowed to write their own rules. Among these was a mission statement that called for "innovative ways to improve the quality of life of a broad community—local, national, and international."

But by the early 1980s, Cohen and Greenfield feared their company's growth was uncontrollably veering away from their 1960s values; Greenfield even dropped out of the business for a time. When Cohen then considered selling the company, a friend convinced him to reconsider and suggested that Cohen could make the company into whatever he wanted it to be. Cohen soon developed the idea of a "caring capitalism," which meant putting part of the company's profits into worthy causes as well as finding creative ways to improve the life of the company's employees and its community. Greenfield rejoined the company soon after.

Uniquely Caring

Ben & Jerry's social concern can be seen in many of its products. One of its products is the Peace Pop, an ice cream bar on a stick, from which one percent of the profits go to build awareness for peace worldwide. To help preserve endangered rainforests, the company buys rainforest nuts for its Rainforest Crunch ice cream. It also buys brownies made by homeless people for its Chocolate Fudge Brownie ice cream and Brownie Bars.

Cohen and Greenfield's social awareness extends to their own employees as well. For instance, a seven-to-one salary ratio limits the pay of top executives to seven times that earned by the lowest-paid workers. This helps give all employees a sense of working together as a team. And, when the company expanded nationally, perhaps too quickly—it grew from 150 people to 300 virtually overnight—Cohen and Greenfield decided to slow its growth, so as to ensure the company's family atmosphere and its core values. Employees also get three pints of ice cream a day, free health club memberships, and a partially subsidized child care center.

Today, Ben & Jerry's continues to promote causes and events of value to the community rather than purchase advertising on television, radio, or in newspapers. The company sponsors peace, music, and art festivals around the country and tries to draw attention to the many social causes it embraces. One such cause is opposition to bovine growth hormone—a substance injected into cows to boost milk production—because Greenfield and Cohen fear that its use will drive small dairy farmers out of business.

Each year, Ben & Jerry's conducts a social audit to measure whether the company is fulfilling its self-imposed obligations. Nonetheless, the company will continue to struggle in its efforts to balance growth and profits with social responsibility. And Ben & Jerry's customers—mostly those 25 to 45 years old—will continue to buy its ice cream so that they may feel they are doing something good for society.

Questions

1. How did Ben & Jerry's develop a social responsibility philosophy?
2. How has Ben & Jerry's used its social responsibility philosophy to deal with issues like employee relations and consumer relations?
3. What kind of social responsibility strategy does Ben & Jerry's use?

Source: Pride, William M. and O. C. Ferrell, *Marketing: Concepts and Strategies,* Eighth Edition. Copyright © 1993 by Houghton Mifflin Company. Used with permission.

New Ventures and the Business Plan

The unprepared mind cannot see the outstretched hand of opportunity.

—Alexander Fleming

As the saying goes, "a thousand-mile journey begins with but a single step." So, too, must a new business venture. The decision to become an entrepreneur is the first step, followed by the choice of a product or service. Then the would-be entrepreneur must decide whether to:

▶ Create a new venture *or*
▶ Buy an existing business *or*
▶ Buy a franchise.

This chapter focuses on new ventures, while Chapters 5 and 6 focus on buy-outs and franchises. Also discussed are home-based businesses.

In starting a new venture, the pivotal step is to prepare a business plan, which calls for entrepreneurs to *anticipate*:

▶ The potential market for products or services.
▶ The potential costs of satisfying that market.
▶ The potential pitfalls in organizing operations.
▶ The early signals of progress or setbacks.

It is the rigor and thoroughness of the business plan that inform the work of successful entrepreneurs, not only at birth but throughout a venture's life.

The Need for Planning

Planning is really nothing more than decision making—that is, deciding what to do, how to do it, and when to do it. It is vital for business success. As one businessperson put it:

> Planning is so important today that it occupies a major part of the time of some of the most respected men in business. . . . Planning allows us to master change. It forces us to organize our expectations and develop programs to bring them about.
>
> Planning is a most effective way to draw out the best in all of us—our best thinking, our best interests and aims—and to enable us to develop the most efficient way of achieving our maximum growth.[1]

The very act of preparing a business plan forces entrepreneurs to think through the steps they must take—from the moment they decide to go into business for themselves, to the moment they open for business, to the years they are actively engaged in business. Indeed, the business plan, updated yearly, can serve the entrepreneur throughout a venture's life. This holds true whether entrepreneurs intend to be full-time or part-time, traditional or home-based.

▶ **Road Map**

In many ways the business plan resembles a road map, telling entrepreneurs how best to get from A to Z. Entrepreneurs may think, "Why should I spend my time drawing up a business plan?" The answer is that they cannot afford not to. A complex economy such as ours demands a business plan:

> Time was when an individual could start a venture and prosper provided he was strong enough to work long hours and had the knack for selling at prices above what materials or product had cost him. Small stores, grist mills, livery stables, and blacksmith shops sprang up in many crossroad communities as Americans applied their energy and native intelligence to settling the continent.
>
> Today, this native intelligence is still important. But, by itself, the common sense for which Americans are famous will not ensure success in a small business. Technology, the marketplace, and even people themselves have become more complicated than they were 100, or even 25, years ago.
>
> Today, common sense must be combined with new techniques in order to succeed in the space age. Just as one would not think of launching a manned space capsule without a flight plan, so one should not think of launching a new business without a business plan.[2]

▶ **Outside Pressures**

The idea of a business plan is hardly new. Big businesses have long been turning out business plans yearly by the thousands, especially for marketing new products, buying existing businesses, or expanding globally. What is new is the growing use of such plans by entrepreneurs.

In fact, outside pressures now force entrepreneurs to develop their businesses on paper before investing time and money in ventures that may have little chance of success. These pressures flow mainly from creditors and investors, the people the entrepreneur must approach for money. Most of them ask for a business plan before entertaining a request for money. These outside pressures are healthy:

▶ Entrepreneurs benefit because a business plan makes them better appreciate what it will take to succeed.

▶ Investors and such creditors as banks and suppliers also benefit because a business plan gives them better information with which to decide whether to help finance the entrepreneur.

As suggested in Exhibit 4.1, not only outsiders but also insiders have an interest in the business plan. The entrepreneur's employees in particular may use the business plan as a blueprint for harnessing their energies for years to come.

▶ **Scarcity of Formal Planning**

How many entrepreneurs actually prepare formal business plans? Probably fewer than 5 percent. The remaining 95 percent plan in less rigorous ways. Some, for example, do it entirely in their heads; still others simply write notes on the backs of old envelopes. This lack of formal planning may help explain why some entrepreneurs fail. In this same vein, Herman Holtz, author and consultant, offers these pointed comments:

> As Mark Twain observed about the weather, everyone talks about it—the need for a business plan, that is, but most people starting and running small businesses . . . do nothing about it. At least, not until later, after they

EXHIBIT 4.1
Parties potentially in need of a new venture's business plan.

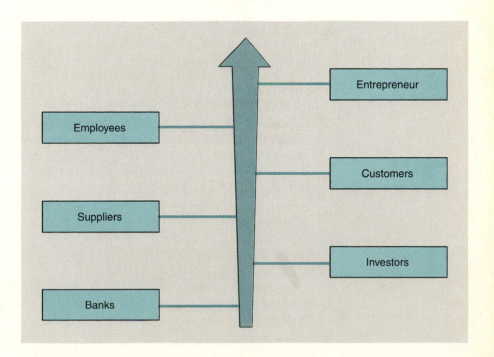

discover that it might have been helpful to have a plan, prepare for the unexpected, and have measures ready to cope with it.

The excuses given, according to David Bangs, a widely quoted expert on the subject, are numerous—for example:

▶ My business is unique.
▶ I haven't any competition.
▶ I'm bad with numbers.

. . . are among those most frequently heard. A complicating factor is that not everyone means the same thing by the term *business plan*; it has more than one meaning. . . . The phrase *business plan* is often a euphemism, actually referring to a loan application, a funding proposal, or a prospectus for prospective investors.[3]

Preparation of the Parts of a Business Plan

What should a business plan cover? For one thing, it should offer a thought-through analysis of not only personal skills but also the need for a particular product or service. Also, it should lay out the strategies for such vital areas as production and marketing, organization and legal aspects, accounting and finance. In short, a business plan should answer such questions as these:

▶ What do I want and what am I capable of doing?
▶ What are the most workable ways of achieving my goals?
▶ What can I expect in the future?

There is no single best way to begin the preparation of a business plan. The guidelines here are simply suggestions that entrepreneurs can modify to suit their individual needs. Exhibit 4.2 suggests the steps that entrepreneurs may take to prepare a business plan, as well as the time it generally takes to complete each step.

Exhibit 4.3 on pages 98 and 99 shows how all 16 steps in Exhibit 4.2 interconnect. It is apparent from the exhibit that certain key steps cannot be taken until earlier steps are completed. For example, entrepreneurs cannot research their market (step 4) until they choose a product or service (step 3); and they cannot prepare a marketing plan (step 8) until they research their market (step 4), forecast their sales revenues (step 5), and choose a site (step 6).

Exhibit 4.3 seems to suggest that there is no backtracking. In point of fact, however, every step is open to refinement *throughout* the planning process. For example, entrepreneurs may keep refining their marketing plans in response to new information about their markets.

Business plans are versatile tools. Although the guidelines in Exhibits 4.2 and 4.3 are tailored to new ventures, they are also applicable to the following situations:

▶ Buying out an existing business
▶ Buying a franchise

EXHIBIT 4.2
Suggested steps in developing a business plan.

Step	Description	Completion Date
1	Make the commitment to go into business for yourself.	
2	Analyze your strengths and weaknesses, paying special attention to your business experience, business education, and desires. Then answer this question:	Week 1
	Why should I be in business for myself?	
3	Choose the product or service that best fits your strengths and desires. Then answer these questions:	Week 3
	What need will my product or service fill?	
	What is unique about my product or service? How do I know it is unique?	
	What will my product or service do for customers? What will it not do?	
	What should it do later but does not now do?	
4	Research the market for your product or service, to find answers to such questions as these:	Week 6
	Who are my customers? Where are they? What is their average income? How do they buy? At what price? In what quantities? When do they buy? When will they use my product or service? Where will they use it? Why will they buy it?	
	Who are my competitors? Where are they? How strong are they?	
	What is the total market potential? Is it growing?	
5	Forecast your share of the market, if possible. Then forecast your sales revenues over a three-year period, broken down as follows:	Week 7
	First year—monthly	
	Second year—quarterly	
	Third year—yearly	
	Next, answer this question:	
	Why do I believe my sales forecast is realistic?	
6	Choose a site for your business. Then answer this question:	Week 7
	Why do I prefer this site to other possible sites?	
7*	Develop your production plan, answering these questions:	Week 9
	How big should my plant be?	
	How should my production process be laid out?	
	What equipment will I need? In what size?	
	How will I control the waste, quality, and inventory of my product?	

*This step applies only to entrepreneurs who plan to go into manufacturing.

EXHIBIT 4.2

Continued

Step	Description	Completion Date
8	Develop your marketing plan, answering such questions as these:	Week 9
	How am I going to create customers? At what price? By what kinds of advertising and sales promotion? Through personal selling? How?	
9	Develop your organizational plan, answering this question:	Week 13
	What kinds of skills and talents will I need to make my business grow?	
	Draw up an organizational chart that spells out who does what, who has what authority, and who reports to whom.	
10	Develop your legal plan, focusing on whether to form a sole proprietorship, a partnership, or a corporation, and then explain your choice.	Week 13
11	Develop your accounting plan, explaining the kinds of records and reports you need and how you will use them.	Week 13
12	Develop your insurance plan, answering this question:	Week 13
	What kinds of insurance will I need to protect my venture against possible loss from unforeseen events?	
13	Develop a computer plan, spelling out the ways that computer services can help you plan and control your business.	Week 13
14	Develop a program of total quality management (TQM), underscoring your venture's dedication to product excellence and to ethical behavior. The purpose of TQM is to help ensure customer satisfaction.	Week 13
15	Develop your financial plan by preparing these statements:	Week 15

A three-year cash budget. Show how much cash you will need before opening for business and how much cash you expect will flow in and out of your business, broken down as follows:

First year—monthly
Second year—quarterly
Third year—yearly

Balance sheets for the beginning and end of the first year

An income statement for the first year only

A profitgraph (breakeven chart), showing when you will begin to make a profit

Then determine how you will finance your business and where you expect to raise money.

16	Write a cover letter summarizing your business plan, stressing its purpose and its promise.	Week 16

- Expanding an existing business
- Floating additional shares of common stock
- Borrowing money from a bank

As they follow the guidelines in Exhibits 4.2 and 4.3, entrepreneurs should keep complete notes that *document* all facts, *back up* all assumptions, and *give the authority* for all opinions. Otherwise, they may lack credibility with investors and creditors.

Getting the Facts

By answering the guideline questions in Exhibit 4.2, entrepreneurs can prepare thoughtful and productive business plans. To use the guidelines well, however, they need to gather facts, opinions, and judgments from many sources. Though brief, the following suggestions for each step may be helpful.

▶ **Step 1: Making the Commitment**

The commitment to go into business for oneself requires little fact-finding. One must be sure, however, that the desire to become an entrepreneur dwarfs the desire to work for somebody else.

▶ **Step 2: Analyzing Oneself**

Analysis of personal strengths and weaknesses also requires little fact-finding. Entrepreneurs need only sit down and list their strengths, paying special attention to experience and education. Weaknesses may then be listed on another sheet of paper. Next, entrepreneurs should analyze their readiness to start a business.

Here, it is vital for entrepreneurs to understand that they can only build on strengths, that strengths offer the only true opportunities.

Precise planning lies at the heart of every venture's future success.

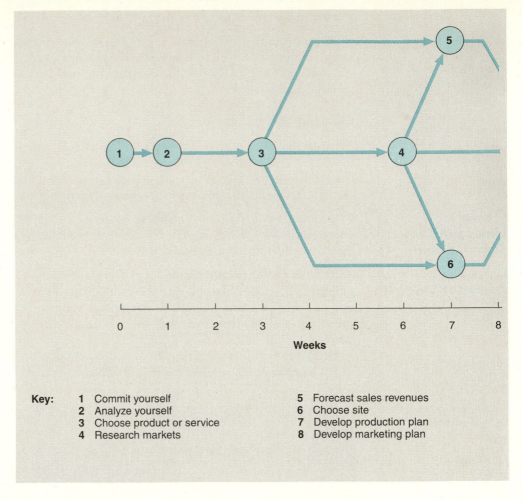

Key:

1 Commit yourself	5 Forecast sales revenues
2 Analyze yourself	6 Choose site
3 Choose product or service	7 Develop production plan
4 Research markets	8 Develop marketing plan

▶ **Step 3: Choosing a Product or Service**

Early on, entrepreneurs must ask, What business should I be in? This may seem absurd. "If there's one thing I know," said one entrepreneur, "it's what business I'm going into." However, entrepreneurs often *think* they know what business they have chosen without closely analyzing their choice. Take this example:

EXAMPLE ▶

Anthony DiBiasio started a business selling and renting boats. He thought he was going into the marina business. But when he got into trouble and asked for outside help, he learned that he was not really in the marina business.

Instead, DiBiasio was in several businesses. He was in the restaurant business with a dock-side cafe—serving meals to boating parties. He was also in the real estate business—buying and selling lots up and down the coast. And he was in the boat-repair business—buying parts and calling in a mechanic to help him. The fact was that DiBiasio was trying to be all things to all people. With this approach, he was spreading himself thin.

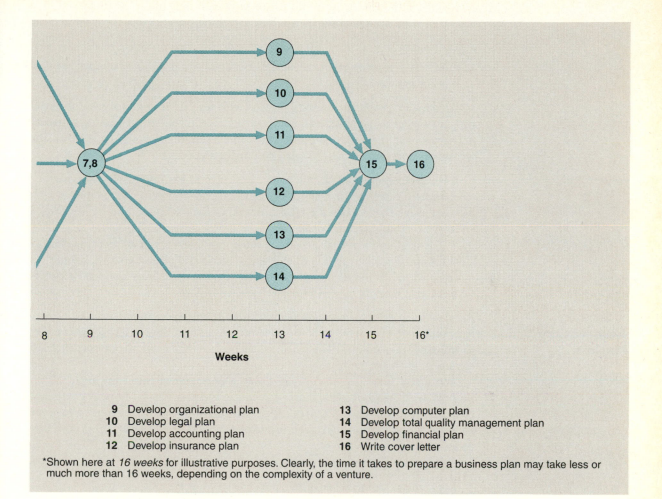

9 Develop organizational plan	**13** Develop computer plan
10 Develop legal plan	**14** Develop total quality management plan
11 Develop accounting plan	**15** Develop financial plan
12 Develop insurance plan	**16** Write cover letter

*Shown here at *16 weeks* for illustrative purposes. Clearly, the time it takes to prepare a business plan may take less or much more than 16 weeks, depending on the complexity of a venture.

Before he could make a profit, DiBiasio had to decide *what* business he really was in and concentrate on it. After much study, he saw that his business was really a recreation shopping center. From that point on, profits began to flow.[4] ▲▼▲

Thus, a vital first step for entrepreneurs is to define their business, preferably with precision and brevity. In this regard, Robert Townsend, a former board chairman of Avis Rent-A-Car Corporation, had this to say:

We defined our business as "renting and leasing vehicles without drivers." This let us put the blinders on ourselves and stop considering the acquisition of related businesses like motels and travel agencies. It also showed us that we had to get rid of some limousine and sightseeing companies that we already owned.[5]

Choosing a product or service forces entrepreneurs to look closely at their own skills and at industry trends to see how well they mesh. At this point, it is vital that entrepreneurs ask themselves searching questions such as these:

▸ Do I really have what it takes to succeed with that product or service?

▸ Do I really want to run that kind of business, do that kind of work, be that kind of person?

Because a new business usually opens with few, if any, employees, the entrepreneur serves as its heart and soul. As such, he or she must master a host of activities that may spell the difference between success and failure. In the words of Professor Arnold Cooper of Purdue University:

> If it is a clothing store, the manager must be good at buying the right merchandise, as well as displaying, advertising, and pricing it. The manager must also be able to do the selling, or train others to do it; and handle the recordkeeping, paying of suppliers, and a host of other day-to-day activities.
>
> An alert employee of a clothing store can learn many of these needed skills and become capable of starting a successful clothing store. People often start businesses in fields they already know to draw upon their previous backgrounds.[6]

▸ **Step 4: Researching Markets**

Because marketing research is so crucial to the proper preparation of a business plan, entrepreneurs should spare no expense in their quest for facts. The more they know about their markets, the greater their chance of creating customers at a profit.

Too often, however, entrepreneurs do a poor job in this vital area, relying on hearsay instead of facts, lacking even the foggiest idea of how best to reach customers. Many new ventures fade into oblivion because entrepreneurs fail to get the information they need to move products out of their hands and into those of customers.

The typical marketing research process has four steps:

1. Defining the need for facts
2. Finding the facts
3. Analyzing the facts
4. Taking action

In the quest for facts, it is logical to begin by asking, Who are my customers? The retailer entrepreneur who sweeps the market with a glance and decides, "Every one of the city's million people will want my product" is taking a casual approach that can only hamper later efforts to define a marketing strategy. Instead, the entrepreneur should obtain facts on where customers live and shop, their average income, how they buy, at what price, why they buy, and so on. Although this is a tall order, the information is both important and obtainable.

To research their markets, entrepreneurs should begin with their local chamber of commerce, which has information about what facts are available, either at hand or buried in government statistics. Trade associations are equally fruitful sources; they offer mountains of information, often at no cost. Virtually every industry has such an association. After collecting facts already unearthed by others, entrepreneurs should then leave their desks and do some firsthand fact-finding, as in this example:

An entrepreneur who is a certified public accountant plans to open an accounting service for small businesses only. As part of her business plan, the entrepreneur needs to estimate the total market potential for such a service. *Market potential* is the total dollar value of accounting services now purchased by small businesses in the marketing area.

To estimate market potential, the entrepreneur should begin by talking to prospects. She may choose about 25 small businesspersons at random and visit each one to get answers to such questions as the following:

▶ Will you buy my accounting service at competitive hourly rates if I promise my service will be quicker and better suited to your needs? If not, why?

▶ How much does your present accounting service charge you?

Armed with this information, the entrepreneur can now estimate her total market potential in this way:

a. Average hourly charge	= $50
b. Average number of hours per month of service time used by small businesses	= 4
c. Number of small businesses in sample	= 25
d. Number of small businesses in marketing area	= 5,000
e. Number of months in year	= 12
f. Yearly market potential (a × b × d × e)	= $12,000,000

Besides estimating market potential, the entrepreneur also should look at her competition, obtaining answers to questions like these:

▶ Who are my competitors?
▶ Where are they?
▶ How strong are they?
▶ What kinds of accounting services do they offer?

To answer the first two questions, the entrepreneur should thumb through the Yellow Pages and visit each accounting service to get a feeling for the scope of its operation. Then, on an area map, she should pinpoint each location.

Answers to questions about competitors' strengths and services should come from the entrepreneur's banker, who has access to a copy of each competitor's Dun & Bradstreet report, if available. These reports offer insights into a competitor's financial strength, credit rating, and line of accounting services. ▲▲

This fact-finding process is usually called *marketing research*. We discuss this vital tool more fully in Chapters 8 and 14.

▶ **Step 5: Forecasting Sales Revenues**

After estimating market potential, entrepreneurs should estimate the percentage share of that market they can reasonably expect to gain. This involves making realistic assumptions, taking into account the number and size of competitors and the amount of time it will take to reach their goals. The expected market share should then be expressed in terms of sales revenues. A good rule of thumb is to estimate sales revenues over a three-year period, broken down as follows:

▶ First year—monthly
▶ Second year—quarterly
▶ Third year—yearly

Because they are the basis for almost all other figure estimates, sales forecasts are crucial. It is vital, therefore, that sales revenues be forecast realistically, not picked out of the air. For example:

For her accounting service, the entrepreneur might now estimate her share of market as follows:

a. Total market potential = $12,000,000
b. Number of competitors = 59
c. Number of competitors *plus* entrepreneur = 60
d. Share of market (a ÷ c) = $200,000

Next, she should estimate how long it would take to reach that sales level. A realistic estimate might be three years. ▲▼▲

It bears repeating that sales forecasts must qualify as intelligent guesswork. Unless armed with careful forecasts, entrepreneurs cannot plan intelligently for such expenditures as buying or leasing long-lived assets, including buildings, equipment, or land; buying inventories and supplies; hiring employees; and financing customers who may take two or more months to pay their bills.

Sales forecasts are based unavoidably on assumptions as well as facts. Thus, the accuracy of sales forecasts hinges largely on the accuracy of supporting assumptions. Turning to Exhibit 4.4, note the decisive influence of sales forecasts on other key estimates.

▶ **Step 6: Choosing a Site**

Entrepreneurs usually have some idea from the very start of where to locate a business regionally. California, for example, may be preferred because of its

EXHIBIT 4.4

Example showing the decisive influence of sales forecasts on other key estimates (assumes entrepreneur is a grocer).

Might Require This—	A Grocer's First-Year Sales Forecast of—	
	$300,000	$600,000
▶ Number of employees	6	12
▶ Square footage of space	3,000	6,000
▶ Amount of inventory	$ 20,000	$ 40,000
▶ Amount of equipment	$ 75,000	$150,000

climate. Or a hometown location may be preferred because lifelong friend-ships are one source of raising money and customers. Wise entrepreneurs, however, balance personal preference with business logic. Because the two rarely match perfectly, entrepreneurs often must compromise.

For example, an entrepreneur going into chemical manufacture may have to locate his plant hundreds of miles from where he prefers to live regionally. The process he plans to use may require 10 pounds of raw materials to make just a pound of chemical product, forcing him to locate close to suppliers in order to cut transportation costs.

Equally important, at least to retailers and services, is location within a city or neighborhood. Too often, entrepreneurs jump at the first vacancy that comes along rather than base their choice on the results of their marketing research. Location is a critical decision that can mean the difference between success or failure. Chapter 8 discusses location in greater detail.

▶ Step 7: Developing a Production Plan

The need for a production plan applies only to entrepreneurs who intend to manufacture a product. In preparing such a plan, perhaps the most critical question an entrepreneur should answer is how big the plant should be. The estimate should be in volume of product per year and should flow logically from the sales forecast. General practice is to use the third-year forecast, or even the fifth-year forecast, to size a plant. However, the entrepreneur may find that a five-year forecast stretches too far into the future to be realistic.

After estimating size, the entrepreneur should lay out the production process. Efficient layout requires that equipment be arranged in ways that minimize manual handling of materials, make the best use of workers' time, and offer flexibility for expansion.

An especially helpful tool in the planning process is a flow diagram that shows how raw materials would enter the plant, how these materials would change into product, and how product would leave the plant.

The entrepreneur also must determine the type and size of the equipment needed for the production process. Each piece of equipment should be sized in a way that keeps the process free of bottlenecks. Equipment suppliers can generally offer expert advice on how to go about selecting and sizing equipment.

Finally, the entrepreneur should lay out plans to control waste as well as product quality and inventory.

▶ Step 8: Developing a Marketing Plan

This step forces entrepreneurs to detail how they plan to create customers prof-itably. If, in step 4, entrepreneurs have painstakingly researched their markets, then the marketing plan is likely to be creative and productive. It describes how the entrepreneur plans to use these marketing tools, among others:

▶ Marketing channels
▶ Price
▶ Advertising
▶ Personal selling
▶ Sales promotion

EXHIBIT 4.5
Selected marketing tools.
Proper coordination
of marketing tools
creates sales.

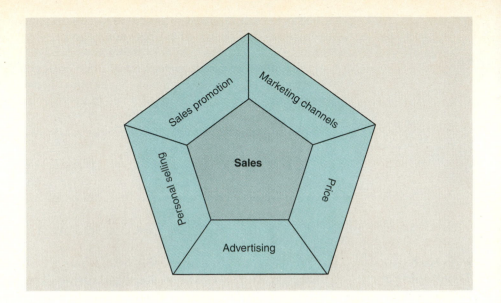

Properly combined and coordinated, these marketing tools help generate sales, as depicted in Exhibit 4.5. To clarify the role of marketing plans, let us go back to our earlier example:

EXAMPLE ▶

The entrepreneur estimates that her accounting service will generate first-year sales revenues of $100,000, which is half her third-year goal of $200,000. She then asks herself, How should I go about getting customers for my accounting service? In other words, what marketing mix should I use?

The entrepreneur knows that, on the average, her industry spends 10 percent of sales revenues on getting clients. This statistic tells her she should budget $10,000 for that purpose. So the next question she asks is, On what marketing tools, and in what combination, should I spend the $10,000?

Because of the importance of personal contact in providing accounting services to small businesses, the entrepreneur might decide that three-fourths of her marketing effort should be personal selling and just one-fourth should be advertising. In dollar terms, she would spend $7,500 for personal selling and $2,500 for advertising. ▲▼▲

For other kinds of businesses, the ideal mix would be quite different. We examine the marketing plan in some detail in Chapters 14 and 15.

▶ **Step 9: Developing an Organizational Plan**

Entrepreneurs must define precisely what skills and talents their ventures need to survive and grow. Then, they must decide how best to enlist the help of men and women who have those skills and talents.

Usually entrepreneurs cannot afford to hire full-time professionals such as marketing researchers or accountants. Even so, entrepreneurs should plan as if such professionals are affordable. Only through such a procedure can entrepreneurs ensure that any needed skills have not been overlooked.

Next, entrepreneurs should prepare an organizational chart, defining who does what and who reports to whom. This kind of chart is necessary even if the entrepreneur is the venture's sole employee.

Organizational planning and human relations are covered in Chapters 10 and 17.

▶ Step 10: Developing a Legal Plan

This step takes us into the legal arena. The entrepreneur must decide whether to go it alone as a sole proprietor, share the venture with one or more partners, or incorporate. Each choice has its advantages and disadvantages. Which one is best hinges on a host of issues, among them personal preference, taxes, and personal wealth.

At the first opportunity, the entrepreneur should see a lawyer for advice. The lawyer should be an expert in new ventures, preferably with experience in the entrepreneur's industry. These and other legal questions are addressed in some detail in Chapter 7.

▶ Step 11: Developing an Accounting Plan

Entrepreneurs often overlook the accounting side of their ventures. They reason that records can be put off until tomorrow, except that tomorrow never seems to come. They mistakenly prefer to work on more pressing matters, such as marketing and production plans.

Yet, from the start, entrepreneurs must keep records in order to know how well their venture is doing and, more importantly, in what direction it is moving. That is why they should have an accountant design a recordkeeping system before, not after, the venture starts.

The system need not be complex or consist of journals and ledgers and worksheets. It can be quite simple. If the system only requires that notes and figures be kept on the backs of old envelopes, so be it—as long as the notes and figures enable the entrepreneur to keep track of the business. As a rule, the best recordkeeping system is one that:

▶ Ensures a high degree of accuracy.

▶ Handles information at low cost.

▶ Turns out reports quickly.

▶ Minimizes theft and fraud.

The subject of accounting is discussed in some detail in Chapter 11; the related subject of control, in Chapter 12.

▶ Step 12: Developing an Insurance Plan

Like financial recordkeeping, planning for insurance is a step that entrepreneurs often ignore, sometimes until well after their ventures have been launched. This shortsightedness is hazardous. Entrepreneurs must protect themselves and their ventures from any unforeseen events that may threaten them, such as fire and theft.

To provide for protection, entrepreneurs should develop a program of risk management before the venture is launched. This program should specify:

▶ Where dollar losses may occur.

▶ How severe the losses might be.

▶ How to treat these risks.

To make sure their risk management program is tailored to their venture's needs, entrepreneurs should seek the help of an insurance agent and perhaps a lawyer as well. The subject of insurance is explored in much greater detail in Chapter 20.

▶ Step 13: Developing a Computer Plan

Few entrepreneurs can afford not to consider using a computer in their ventures. To plan and control their venture more efficiently, entrepreneurs should develop a computer plan that:

▶ Spells out the venture's need for information.

▶ Describes the benefits that would flow from a computer system.

▶ Evaluates possible computer systems.

▶ Recommends a computer system.

Because the entrepreneurs' knowledge of computers often is limited, it would be wise to seek expert advice, preferably from a consultant who focuses on small-business computer applications.

▶ Step 14: Developing a Total Quality Management (TQM) Program

To develop a TQM program, entrepreneurs must commit themselves totally, both to the pursuit of product excellence and to ethical behavior. The three principles of TQM are:

▶ The pursuit of total customer satisfaction.

▶ The constant improvement of products and services.

▶ The full involvement of every employee.

TQM is covered further in Chapter 10, which is devoted to organizational planning.

▶ Step 15: Developing a Financial Plan

A financial plan binds all the preceding steps by translating operating plans—production, marketing, organizational, and all the other plans related to the operations of the venture—into dollars. In other words, the financial plan is a dollar expression of the entrepreneur's operating plans.

Dollars are the common denominator by means of which dissimilar parts of a venture can be added or subtracted, multiplied or divided. For example, how could an entrepreneur possibly add together trucks and hammers or land and light bulbs unless the assets are expressed in dollars? This is one reason to prepare a financial plan.

Dollars also enable entrepreneurs to communicate more effectively. Investors and creditors understand needs expressed in dollars far better than needs expressed in physical terms. Only when reduced to dollars does an entrepreneur's need for, say, 15,000 square feet of floor space or a 55-foot distillation column make sense.

Dollars cannot paint a complete picture of a new venture, however, because some vital parts simply cannot be expressed that way. How can entrepreneurs put a dollar value on managerial skills, for example? Yet it is these skills that often spell the difference between success and failure. Nor can entrepreneurs put a dollar value on such intangible things as teamwork and morale, knowledge and idea-generating ability.

EXHIBIT 4.6

Cash Budget	Income Statement	Balance Sheet	Profitgraph

As depicted in Exhibit 4.6, a financial plan comprises four items:

▶ A cash budget

▶ An income statement

▶ Balance sheets

▶ A profitgraph (breakeven chart)

The Cash Budget   Of these statements, the most important is the cash budget, because it tells entrepreneurs how much money they need before and after they open for business.

The cash budget helps entrepreneurs make sure the money will be there when bills fall due. It also acts as a signaling device, enabling entrepreneurs to pinpoint future cash shortages and surpluses. A shortage, for example, signals a need to raise more money. Otherwise, marketing and production may have to be cut back to make ends meet.

As a financial tool, the cash budget is indispensable. It not only helps entrepreneurs spot possible cash-flow problems but also gives investors and creditors precise answers to questions like these:

▶ How much money does the entrepreneur need to carry out the business plan?

▶ When is it needed?

▶ How will it be spent?

▶ How soon can it be repaid?

The Balance Sheet and Income Statement   Besides the cash budget, entrepreneurs also should prepare two balance sheets and one income statement. Although less important than the cash budget, these statements are vital parts of every business plan. Banks, in particular, appreciate balance sheets because they show the dollar amounts that entrepreneurs expect to spend on such assets as inventories, machines, and land; and how they expect to finance these assets.

Entrepreneurs should prepare not one but two balance sheets—one projecting the beginning and the other projecting the end of the first year of business.

An income statement is also necessary. This statement summarizes both expected sales revenues and expected operating expenses. The difference between revenues and expenses equals profit or loss.

The Profitgraph   The last statement to be prepared is the *profitgraph,* commonly called a *breakeven chart.* We use the term *profitgraph* because *breakeven* suggests that entrepreneurs expect only to break even. Entrepreneurs naturally expect to do better than that.

The profitgraph shows how sales volume, selling price, and operating expenses affect profits. It also tells entrepreneurs how much product they must sell before they begin to make a profit. The profitgraph is covered in Chapter 12.

Preparation of a financial plan is anything but easy, and often frustrating to the entrepreneur who lacks financial knowledge. For help, entrepreneurs should turn to an accountant or a banker. These and other financial aspects are covered in greater detail in Chapters 9 and 13.

▶ **Step 16: Writing a Cover Letter**

Although not really part of the business plan, the cover letter nonetheless plays a vital role. It is a selling tool, addressed mostly to investors and creditors. In the letter, the entrepreneur summarizes the plan, giving special attention to its purpose and promise.

Home Businesses

Touted by some observers of the business scene as a phenomenon sweeping the nation, people more than ever before are launching businesses at home, either full time or part time. This phenomenon is taking place largely because, in the words of William Bridges, an author and a job skills expert:

> Something dramatic is going on in America. We are witnessing the disappearance of jobs. It is not just particular jobs in certain industries that are disappearing but the very thing itself, *the job,* that is vanishing today.[7]

So, among other reasons, as larger companies have been shedding employees in droves, many of these people—women more so than men (66% compared to 33%)—have opted to become self-employed at home. Even newly minted college graduates have joined with refugees from the corporate world to create jobs of their very own rather than look for a job with somebody else.

Thus, it appears that shrinking job security is spurring entrepreneurship—at any age. And so, many people are choosing to put their talent to work for themselves at home—in the belief that talent, not a job, is the *only* true security.

▶ **Newfound Respectability**

Reliable statistics on the number of home businesses are incomplete or unavailable, at least at this writing. We do know, however, that the landscape of entrepreneurial opportunities spreads far and wide. Turning to Exhibit 4.7, note the

EXHIBIT 4.7
Home-business
categories.

Source: *Home Office
Computing,* reported by
Steve Osborne, "Is a Home
Business for You?" *Home
Business News* (September
1995), p. 2.

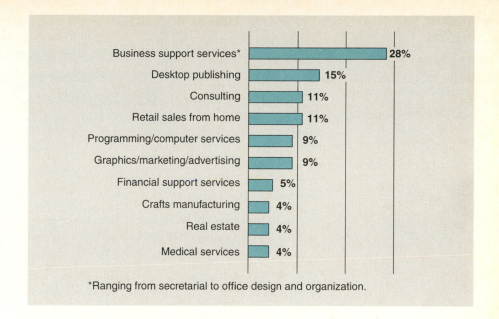

Business support services* — **28%**
Desktop publishing — **15%**
Consulting — **11%**
Retail sales from home — **11%**
Programming/computer services — **9%**
Graphics/marketing/advertising — **9%**
Financial support services — **5%**
Crafts manufacturing — **4%**
Real estate — **4%**
Medical services — **4%**

*Ranging from secretarial to office design and organization.

diversity of services offered by home-based entrepreneurs. Virtually every service industry has found a home, running the gamut from piano tuning to dentistry, from chimney sweeping to computer software.

As a result, home businesses are no longer second-class citizens of the business world. They have come of age, earning the respect of even the major media, including such prestigious newspapers as *The New York Times* and *The Wall Street Journal.* In the past, and in the mind's eye of the public, being self-employed and working at home often meant you were between jobs. At best, home businesses were called a fad. No more. Take this comment by *Entrepreneur* magazine in its cover story on home businesses, in 1995:

> The explosive growth of the home-based phenomenon shows that, far from just a trend, home-based business has become a way of life. Old stereotypes of bon-bon-eating . . . goof-offs are falling by the wayside as home-based entrepreneurs in every industry imaginable prove they're equal to, and often better than, their corporate counterparts.[8]

▸ **The Influence of Computers**

Indeed, so new is the home-business phenomenon that only recently has it caught the eye of academic researchers like Kathleen Christenson, a professor of environmental psychology at the City University of New York. When she pioneered the study of home-based businesses in the mid-eighties, Christenson could not find the words *home-based* or *telecommuting* in any reference source.[9]

That has changed dramatically, especially with the dawning of the Information Age. As computers have come affordably within virtually everyone's reach, so

EXHIBIT 4.8

How long home businesses using computers have been in business.

Source: "How Long Have You Worked Out of Your Home?" from *The New York Times,* October 15, 1995, section 3, p. 8.

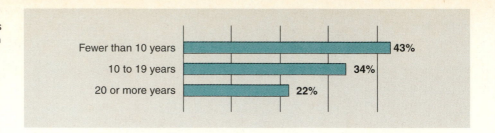

have home-based entrepreneurs gained credibility in the marketplace. One such entrepreneur put it this way:

> You may not be able to manufacture car parts in your den, but you can run a service or information business like a *Fortune 500* company in a spare room.[10]

According to a survey by the Gallup Organization, entrepreneurs who use computers in their home businesses do so overwhelmingly on a full-time basis; 85 percent use them full time, while 15 percent use them only part time. This finding underscores the vitality of home businesses in the marketplace. In particular, computers have been a boon to the disabled, offering a lifeline to those who are blind, quadriplegic, or have chronic illnesses that often make it all but impossible for them to work for anyone but themselves.

Gallup's survey also looked at the staying power of such businesses and found, as shown in Exhibit 4.8, that 56 percent have lasted more than 10 years—further proof that home businesses are neither whim nor passing fad. Even so, some entrepreneurs go to extraordinary lengths to look larger than they really are, as in this example reported by *The New York Times:*

EXAMPLE ▶

When Deborah Watring started a business in her bedroom [in 1986,] she wanted the giant telecommunications companies to whom she offered marketing advice to think she was running a much larger enterprise. Although pinched for money, she spent several thousand dollars on a "high-end image package" that included three-color professionally designed stationery and business cards printed on expensive paper.

[In 1994,] her company, Watring & Associates, [rang] up $1.5 million in … sales doing business for the likes of Nynex, MCI, and AT&T. Ms. Watring credits her success in part to the big-company attributes that her business had adopted—despite its structure as a small "virtual" corporation. Ms. Watring's "associates," it turns out, are 40 sole proprietors and small companies, most operating from home offices, spread over eight states.[11] ▲▼▲

▶ **The Need for a Business Plan**

A popular misconception is that starting a business calls for little planning. True, success for a home-grown business is not earned the same way as for other businesses, especially for full-time retailers or manufacturers.

Yet there are more similarities than dissimilarities. For one thing, regardless of its size and industry, every business needs a business plan. In the words of consultant Marv Gisser, who has worked full time from his home in Cleveland, Ohio, for more than 20 years:

As vital as a business plan is for any company, for the home-based business it is imperative. But, if you're planning on starting a business, don't look at your new world through rose-colored glasses. Wishful thinking can lead only to wistful thinking down the road, when you may be forced to close your doors because you were too optimistic.

Regardless of what the picture may hold for a newly formed home-based business, there won't be a future without legitimate tools like the business plan . . . that are needed to open and maintain a business.[12]

Would-be home entrepreneurs are also likely to find Exhibit 4.9 helpful. Suggested by the American Institute of Certified Public Accountants, it lists

---

EXHIBIT 4.9

Home-office checklist suggested for accountants by the American Institute of CPAs.

Advantages

Savings. You don't have extensive overhead such as rent, phone, utilities and furnishings.

Practice planning. Because you don't have to earn a monthly minimum just to meet overhead costs, you can afford to spend time developing the practice and client list you want, without taking on any client just to pay the rent.

Change of heart. If you find the sole practitioner life isn't for you, you haven't wasted rental money and you're not stuck with a useless commercial lease.

Travel savings. You don't waste time and money commuting. Ease of access means you can put in a few hours at night or on weekends.

Shared family commitments. Although you do need a well-defined work schedule, you can make time during the day for childcare and other household responsibilities. That is, you create your own "flextime" schedule.

Disadvantages

Client perception. Some clients may feel you are not as professional or as permanent as an accountant who works from a separate office. They may expect low fees because you have little overhead, leading to problems when you do move to a rental office and need to raise your fees.

Zoning. Some areas are zoned for residences only. Neighbors noting a stream of clients in and out of your home may report you. Check your local laws before making any decisions.

Accessibility. Clients will find it inconvenient if your home is located far from the other services they use, such as banks and restaurants. Some residential neighborhoods restrict parking for nonresidents.

Visiting clients. If you decide to save your clients time and avoid image problems by going to their offices whenever possible, you'll waste a lot of time traveling.

Insurance. Most homeowner's policies do not cover business losses, although some companies offer a rider.

Professional contacts. If you aren't near other businesspeople—those you can have lunch with—you could find yourself professionally and emotionally isolated.

Time distinctions. There isn't a rigid line between home and office time. Friends who are also clients may drop by just to chat because they think you're "at home."

Motivation. If you have trouble motivating yourself, you will find a lot of distractions at home.

Source: "Home-Office Checklist Suggested for Accountants by the AICPA" as adapted from Albert S. Williams, "CPA, On Your Own! How to Start Your Own CPA Firm" reported in "Home Office Pros and Cons Checklist," *Journal of Accountancy* (September 1995), p. 10.

in brief the advantages and disadvantages to weigh before opening a home business.

Although aimed at accountants, this list is equally helpful to entrepreneurs in other service industries. It does not, of course, take the place of a thought-through business plan.

SUMMARY

An essential step in getting a new venture off the ground is the preparation of a business plan. The process forces the entrepreneur to anticipate the potential market, the potential of satisfying that market, the potential pitfalls of organizing a new venture, and the early signals of progress or failure. The plan itself is the basis on which the entrepreneur runs the business, and in which investors and creditors make their decision to help the entrepreneur.

The text suggests 16 steps in preparing a business plan:

1. Make a commitment to go into business for yourself.
2. Analyze your strengths and weaknesses.
3. Choose the product or service that best fits your strengths and desires.
4. Research the market for your product or service.
5. Forecast your share of sales revenues.
6. Choose a site for your business.
7. Develop a production plan.
8. Develop a marketing plan.
9. Develop an organizational plan.
10. Develop a legal plan.
11. Develop an accounting plan.
12. Develop an insurance plan.
13. Develop a computer plan.
14. Develop a program of total quality management.
15. Develop a financial plan.
16. Write a cover letter that summarizes the business plan, stressing its purpose and promise.

These steps interconnect and overlap. This means that certain key steps cannot be taken until earlier steps are completed. In almost every stage of the development of a business plan, the entrepreneur must gather facts, opinions, and judgments from many sources. The plan will stand or fall on the completeness of the entrepreneur's fact-finding. In particular, the entrepreneur must dig out the facts that bear on the preparation of operating plans for production and marketing, organization and legal aspects.

Market research is perhaps the most critical step in the preparation of a business plan. The more the entrepreneur knows about the market, the greater the chance of attracting customers and earning a profit.

The operating plans form the basis for preparation of the financial plan. The financial plan is the dollar expression of the operating plans. This plan binds all the preceding steps in the preparation of a business plan by translating operating plans into dollars.

People more than ever before are starting businesses at home. Caused largely by shrinking job security and advances in computer technology, the widespread formation of home businesses is likely to continue unabated for many years to come.

One measure of the movement's vitality is that, of the home businesses *with* computers, 85 percent are full time and 56 percent have lasted more than 10 years, according to a survey by the Gallup Organization. Another measure is that virtually every service industry boasts successful entrepreneurs who work out of their home. As a result, home businesses now enjoy a respectability long denied them.

Discussion and Review Questions

1. Why should every would-be entrepreneur prepare a business plan?
2. Why do so few entrepreneurs prepare a business plan?
3. Why is the business plan as important to creditors and investors as it is to the entrepreneur?
4. To what situations, other than new ventures, is the business plan applicable? Explain your answer.
5. Explain how the steps taken in the preparation of the business plan interconnect.
6. Why, in preparing the business plan, must the entrepreneur document all facts, back up all assumptions, and give the authority for all opinions?
7. What questions does marketing research help answer?
8. Why is the entrepreneur's forecast of sales revenues the single most important dollar estimate?
9. What pitfall must entrepreneurs avoid when they choose a site for their venture? Explain your answer.
10. Why should a computer plan be part of the business plan?
11. In a business plan, how does the financial plan relate to operating plans?
12. Why is the cash budget more meaningful than either the income statement or the balance sheet?
13. What accounts for the growth of home-based businesses in our economy?
14. Why are business plans as necessary for home-based businesses as for traditional businesses? Explain fully.
15. Define these terms: *planning, business plan, market potential, marketing mix, organizational chart, TQM, cash budget.*

New Ventures and the Business Plan

Once an individual decides to open a business, the next step is to choose a product or service. Then, it is time to begin preparing a business plan.

Why a Business Plan?

In many ways a business plan resembles a road map, telling entrepreneurs how best to get from A to Z. It should answer questions like:

▶ What am I capable of doing?

▶ What are the most workable ways of achieving my goals?

▶ What can I expect in the future?

As pointed out in Chapter 4, planning involves decision making—that is, deciding what to do, how to do it, and when to do it.

Instructions for Worksheet 4

The purpose of Worksheet 4 is to describe how the traditional steps included in most business plans apply to your specific business. In part 1 of this worksheet, you should review and refine the type of business that you would like to start. Then in part 2, describe how each of the steps included in this chapter affect the business that you would like to start.

Part 1—What Business Would I Like to Start?

As part of the business plan exercise for Chapter 1, you were asked to define the business that you would like to start. Before answering the questions below, go back and review your definition.

1. After examining the material in the first four chapters of this text, do you still want to start the same type of business?

_____ yes _____ no

2. Is the definition that you developed for the business plan at the end of Chapter 1 still appropriate?

_____ yes _____ no

3. What, if any, changes should be made to the definition that you developed as part of the business plan in Chapter 1?

4. With these changes in mind, revise the definition for the business that you would like to start.

Part 2—The Steps in a Business Plan

Although there is no best way to begin the preparation of a business plan, there are a number of steps that should be included for any business.

5. For each of the following steps, give a brief explanation of how the step applies to your business. Do not be overly concerned with detail at this point; each step will be examined more thoroughly in later chapters and business plan exercises.

Step 1: Making the commitment
Step 2: Analyzing oneself
Step 3: Choosing a product or service
Step 4: Researching markets
Step 5: Forecasting sales revenues
Step 6: Choosing a site
Step 7: Developing a production plan
Step 8: Developing a marketing plan
Step 9: Developing an organizational plan
Step 10: Developing a legal plan
Step 11: Developing an accounting plan
Step 12: Developing an insurance plan
Step 13: Developing a computer plan
Step 14: Developing a total quality management (TQM) program
Step 15: Developing a financial plan
Step 16: Writing a cover letter

When Brenda Wade completed her studies in entrepreneurship at Cuyahoga Community College, her goal was to launch a home-based service firm. Its mission would be to satisfy the physicians' need to be paid promptly and accurately for their medical services. To help meet this mission, Wade is seeking a $5,000 line of credit from a local bank.

To prepare herself, and to give the bank the information it needs, Wade wrote the following business plan. It begins with a cover letter to the bank's loan officer.

Cover Letter to Bank

Ms. Diane Kowalski, Loan Officer
Lincoln Community Bank
One Euclid Avenue
East Cleveland, Ohio 44112

Dear Ms. Kowalski:

Attached is my business plan for a new venture, Physician Service Bureau. After reviewing my plan, you will, I am sure, agree that the potential for such a home-based business is good. Its mission would be:

> To satisfy the physicians' need to be paid promptly and accurately for their medical services by third-party payers such as Medicare.

To resolve any unforeseen cash-flow problems before they occur, and to give me peace of mind, I am seeking a $5,000 line of credit. Thank you for your help, and I look forward to hearing from you soon.

Sincerely,

Brenda Wade

Business Plan for Physician Service Bureau

Today, so vital is coding for physician services that it can mean the difference between a thriving practice and one whose future is in doubt. At issue are the mounds of paperwork spawned by the need to bill third-party payers such as Medicare. For relief, physicians have little recourse but to rely on expert coding if they are to:

▶ Maintain accurate, up-to-date information on their patients

▶ Receive quick, accurate payment of bills by third-party payers

How Coding Works

What is coding? It is nothing more than the process of translating medical information into shorthand by substituting numeric* or alphanumeric** codes for the actual services performed for the patient. This shorthand tells a third-party payer like Blue Cross what was done to the patient and why it was done.

Thus, coding controls the on-off switch for the payment of claims. This means that coding controls not only whether to pay a claim but also how to pay. So to make sure that claims are settled both quickly and effortlessly, physician services must be coded properly. To do so, we must first divide the practice of medicine into four parts:

▶ Procedures that are surgical, diagnostic, or therapeutic

▶ Services that cover office visits, consultations, or hospital visits

---

*Comprised of numbers only.
**Comprised of both numbers and letters.

EXHIBIT 4A.1
Brenda Wade at work.

- Supplies such as sterile surgical trays, bed pans, and splints
- Diagnoses that cover diseases, symptoms, and complaints

Each of these parts of a physician's practice must then carry a unique code, preferably one based on a system developed by the American Medical Association. This system, by the way, is used by most major third-party payers, including Medicare and Medicaid.

A Brief History of Medical Coding

Coding has been around for a long time. For nearly fifty years, health insurers have used coding systems to pay health-care claims. At one time, more than a hundred different coding systems were in use throughout the country, thus enormously complicating the lives of physicians who sought timely payment for their services.

But with the creation and huge growth of government health-care programs, such as Medicare and Medicaid, came a drive to limit health-care expenditures. It was at this time, in 1983, that the U.S. Congress created and mandated the use of a single coding system to track Medicare spending and to require all Medicare carriers to use it.

Why a Business of My Own?

Proper billing for physician services calls for a clear grasp of coding basics coupled with the ability to distinguish between the needs of third-party payers and those of physicians. In a word, that is why I am creating an insurance-claim coding venture. My expertise will help physicians to:

- Streamline their office routine
- Simplify the process of payment for their services
- Meet the challenges of health-care payment reform and of new health-payment mechanisms

At present, many physicians defer their billing matters to an inexperienced billing staff. As a result, their practice may face two serious problems:

- Loss of revenue
- Increased audit liability

Moreover, if improper billing practices occur over and over again, the physician may be singled out for an exhaustive audit by the U.S. Internal

Revenue Service. So it behooves physicians to have their billing performed by coders—like myself—with the knowledge, understanding, and skill in applying the rules of each coding system to obtain payment quickly and painlessly.

Marketing Research

My marketing efforts will be directed at both the single and the group practice that specializes in family services. This market segment consists of patients aged 18 and older, male and female alike, with most being professionals or retired persons. As the potential of this market segment grows, so will my share of market. Satisfying this segment will entail:

▸ Personal service, such as state-of-the-art software and coding manuals
▸ FAX capabilities to ensure fast turnaround of coding for quick payment of medical bills
▸ Timely mailing of claim forms

To attract clients, I will arrange appointments with physicians to inform them of my services *and* to underscore how they may benefit from them. To gain their confidence, I will not only follow through with letters but also with detailed descriptions of how my services would both save them money and speed up the payment of claims.

Sales Forecast

My estimate of total market potential for physician services in Greater Cleveland is $15.3 million a year, shared by 25 competitors. Assuming that I open my doors for business on January 2, 1996, my forecast of sales revenues for the first 3 years is as follows:

▸ *First-year forecast (monthly)*

January	$ 1,500
February	1,500
March	2,250
April	2,250
May	3,000
June	3,000
July	3,750
August	3,750
September	4,500
October	4,500
November	5,250
December	5,250
	$40,500

▸ *Second-year forecast (quarterly)*

First quarter	$15,750
Second quarter	18,000
Third quarter	20,250
Fourth quarter	22,500
	$76,500

▸ *Third-year forecast* — $90,000

My nearest competitors are two well-established firms: JMJ Medical Claims Service and Automated Medical Systems, Inc. To compete, I plan to charge much less than do these firms. They charge as much as $24 per patient per claim form, while I will charge no more than $15 per patient. I will also offer physicians such conveniences as maintaining a 24-hour communication network between myself and the physician's office and mailing all claim forms to the various insurance companies.

Location

My business will be located at home. The rent is $370 monthly, plus utilities. Starting my business in my home will reduce operating expenses, thus increasing profits.

Neighborhood businesses include several medical and dental clinics within five miles of my home. There are also supermarkets, service stations, restaurants, and a host of other kinds of businesses in the area.

Marketing Plan

In recognition of the cardinal importance of personal contact with physicians, I will devote three-fourths of my marketing effort to personal sales visits. With my computer knowledge, I will design an introductory letter graphically describing my services and requesting an appointment to discuss, among other benefits, how their income would increase. The question of pricing for my services would be deferred until the scheduled appointment.

Organization Plan

To my venture, I bring a 28-year range of managerial, secretarial, and computer experiences. I have worked at Cleveland State University as an administrative secretary, where I coordinated office functions for the Department of Health Care Administration. And I have been the liaison between the Healthy Family/Healthy Start Program, the City of Cleveland, Kaiser Permanente, and St. Vincent Charity Hospital.

My work experience also includes a position at Case Western Reserve University in its Medical Biology Department. As the office manager, I set up a record tracking system for five medical protocols. Maintaining these records involved a working knowledge of medical terminology and coding. Another position that gave me managerial experience was as treasurer of the Gethsemane Baptist Church Credit Union, where I was responsible for $100,000 of depositors' savings.

I am going to succeed with Physician Service Bureau because I have always dreamed of someday starting my very own business. After working for so many years for someone else, I know I have both the stamina and the willpower to create and run my own business.

Legal Plan

My venture will be a sole proprietorship. To help me with legal matters, I have engaged the services of Frederick White, Esquire, as my venture's lawyer.

Accounting Plan

My accountant is Nancy Jordan-Willoughby, who is a CPA. She has recommended that I purchase an accounting software package called #106 DOME Plus Small Business Accounting. This software is designed to get accounting records set up quickly. Moreover, with its advanced features,

it can satisfy my current and future needs splendidly. This versatile software can readily handle:

Sales records, cash receipts, accounts receivable, accounts payable, bank reconciliations, mailing lists as well as such vital financial reports as income statements, balance sheets, and cash budgets.

Thanks to the software's flexibility, I can change any of these features to best fit my needs during startup and through the stages of growth.

Computer Plan

Computers for use in physician offices will become a major growth segment in the medical computer market—mainly because of the sharp rise in the volume and complexity of patient information, thus forcing insurance carriers to demand more documentation before payment of claims. But thanks to advances in inexpensive computers and easy-to-use software, some of this information overload can now be transferred to machines. Even so, as a professional health-care coder, I must manage for my clients these four kinds of information:

▶ The history of illness, clinical findings, diagnoses, and treatments for patients

▶ The scientific information applied by physicians while caring for patients

▶ Administrative and accounting information involved in managing the accounts of patients

▶ Financial-management and practice-planning information that physicians need to evaluate the status of their practices—for example, such information as the level of income and expenses, the number and types of medical procedures they perform, and the demographic make-up of the patient populations they serve

Insurance Plan

Because my venture will be homebased, I will need to purchase a fire/theft insurance policy—to guard against the financial loss of computer

EXHIBIT 4A.2

Physician Service Bureau: Projected income statement for first-year operations.

Sales revenues		$40,500
Operating expenses		
Salary	$23,500	
Rent	4,440	
Advertising	3,600	
Computer lease	3,000	
Supplies	2,400	
Utilities	1,800	
Travel	1,200	
Telephone	600	
Insurance	360	40,900
Operating loss		($ 400)

equipment, furniture, supplies, and the like. An insurance representative, Henderson Deal of State Farm Insurance, will be working with me to secure the needed insurance coverage.

And most importantly, to guard against destruction of patient information, a back-up file of all completed claim forms will be transmitted to the physician's office by way of the computer linkage between our offices.

Financial Plan

As shown in Exhibit 4A.2, I am projecting a slight loss of $400 on sales of $40,500 the first year. Note that my salary of $23,500 is nearly 60 percent of sales. This means that I personally will be drawing nearly 60 cents for every dollar that I bill my clients, the physicians.

My projected beginning balance sheet appears in Exhibit 4A.3. Here, please note that, as a sole proprietor, I intend to finance the acquisition of

EXHIBIT 4A.3

Physician Service Bureau: Projected balance sheet at startup.

Assets			Equities	
Current assets			Liabilities	$ 0
Cash	$6,320		Owner's equity	10,000
Pre-startup expenses*	2,730	$ 9,050		
Fixed assets				
Computer office center	$ 350			
File cabinets	240			
Printer workstation	150			
Bookcase	60			
Chair	50			
Miscellaneous	100	950		
Total assets		$10,000	Total equities	$10,000

*Including supplies, advertising, utilities, insurance, accounting, and legal.

EXHIBIT 4A.4
Physician Service Bureau: Monthly Cash-flow Projection.

NAME OF BUSINESS Physician service Bureau		ADDRESS East Cleveland					OWNER Brenda Wade							
	Pre-Start-up Position		1		2		3		4		5		6		
YEAR 1996 MONTH			January		February		March		April		May		June		
	Estimate	Actual	Estimate	Actual	Estimate	Actual	Estimate	Actual	Estimate	Actual	Estimate	Actual	Estimate	Actual
1. CASH ON HAND (Beginning of month)	10,000		6,320		4,070		3,320		2,570		2,570		2,570	
2. CASH RECEIPTS (a) Cash Sales														
(b) Collections from Credit Accounts					1,500		1,500		2,250		2,250		3,000	
(c) Loan or Other Cash injection (Specify)														
3. TOTAL CASH RECEIPTS (2a + 2b + 2c = 3)														
4. TOTAL CASH AVAILABLE (Before cash out) (1 + 3)	10,000		6,320		5,570		4,820		4,820		4,820		5,570	
5. CASH PAID OUT (a) Purchases (Merchandise)														
(b) Gross Wages (Excludes withdrawals)			1,000		1,000		1,000		1,000		1,000		1,500	
(c) Payroll Expenses (Taxes, etc.)														
(d) Outside Services														
(e) Supplies (Office and operating)	750		200		200		200		200		200		200	
(f) Repairs and Maintenance														
(g) Advertising	400		100		100		100		100		100		100	
(h) Car, Delivery, and Travel	100		100		100		100		100		100		100	
(i) Accounting and Legal	500													
(j) Rent			370		370		370		370		370		370	
(k) Telephone	50		50		50		50		50		50		50	
(l) Utilities	150		150		150		150		150		150		150	
(m) Insurance	360		30		30		30		30		30		30	
(n) Taxes (Real estate, etc.)														
(o) Interest														
(p) Other Expenses (Specify each) Lease Computer/FAX	250		250		250		250		250		250		250	
(q) Miscellaneous (Unspecified)	270													
(r) Subtotal	2,730		2,250		2,250		2,250		2,250		2,250		2,750	
(s) Loan Principal Payment														
(t) Capital Purchases (Specify)	950*													
(u) Other Start-up Costs														
(v) Reserve and/or Escrow (Specify)														
(w) Owner's Withdrawal														
6. TOTAL CASH PAID OUT (Total 5a thru 5w)	3,680		2,250		2,250		2,250		2,250		2,250		2,750	
7. CASH POSITION (End of month) (4 minus 6)	6,320		4,070		3,320		2,570		2,570		2,570		2,820	
ESSENTIAL OPERATING DATA (Non-cash flow information) A. Sales Volume (Dollars)			1,500		1,500		2,250		2,250		3,000		3,000	
B. Accounts Receivable (End of month)			1,500		1,500		2,250		2,250		3,000		3,000	
C. Bad Debt (End of month)														
D. Inventory on Hand (End of month)														
E. Accounts Payable (End of month)														
F. Depreciation														

SBA FORM 1100 (1-83) REF: SOP 60 10 Previous Editions Are Obsolete

*Capital Purchases:

Computer office center	$350
3 two-drawer file cabinets	240
Printer workstation	150
Five-shelf bookcase	60
Chair	50
Miscellaneous	100
	$950

TYPE OF BUSINESS	PREPARED BY	DATE
Health Insurance Claim Service	Brenda Wade	

	7 July		8 August		9 September		10 October		11 November		12 December		TOTAL Columns 1—12		
	Estimate	Actual	Estimate	Actual	Estimate	Actual	Estimate	Actual	Estimate	Actual	Estimate	Actual	Estimate	Actual	
1.	2,820		2,170		1,270		370		220		70				
2. (a)															
(b)	3,000		3,750		3,750		4,500		4,500		5,250				
(c)															
3.															
4.	5,820		5,920		5,020		4,870		4,720		5,320				
5. (a)															
(b)	2,000		3,000		3,000		3,000		3,000		3,000		23,500		
(c)															
(d)	200		200		200		200		200		200		2,400		
(e)															
(f)	500		500		500		500		500		500		3,600		
(g)	100		100		100		100		100		100		1,200		
(h)															
(i)	370		370		370		370		370		370		4,440		
(j)	50		50		50		50		50		50		600		
(k)	150		150		150		150		150		150		1,800		
(l)	30		30		30		30		30		30		360		
(m)															
(n)															
(o)															
(p)	250		250		250		250		250		250		3,000		
(q)															
(r)	3,650		4,650		4,650		4,650		4,650		4,650		40,900		
(s)															
(t)															
(u)															
(v)															
(w)															
6.	3,650		4,650		4,650		4,650		4,650		4,650				
7.	2,170		1,270		370		220		70		670				
A.	3,750		3,750		4,500		4,500		5,250		5,250		40,500		
B.	3,750		3,750		4,500		4,500		5,250		5,250				
C.															
D.															
E.															
F.															

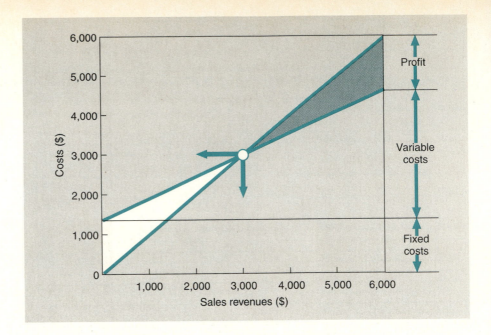

$10,000 worth of assets wholly out of personal savings. Thus, at startup, I will owe no one.

Turning to my monthly cash-flow projections in Exhibit 4A.4, note that my cash position drops perilously close to zero after August. That's why I need a $5,000 line of credit from your bank, as a cushion in the event my projections fall short.

The last piece of my financial plan is the profitgraph shown in Exhibit 4A.5. To prepare the profitgraph, I assumed that:

▸ My variable costs, which go up or down with sales, would be 60 cents for every dollar of sales (really, my salary plus supplies)

▸ My fixed costs, which stay the same regardless of sales, would be $1,250 per month

Questions

1. Would you advise Brenda Wade to get additional information before launching her venture? If so, what information?
2. Is Wade likely to succeed as an entrepreneur? Why or why not?
3. Evaluate Wade's business plan as a tool to get a line of credit from the bank. What other uses might her plan have? What suggestions, if any, would you make to improve it?
4. What are the key factors for success in the kind of business that Wade plans to pursue?
5. If you were the bank's loan officer, would you recommend granting Wade the $5,000 line of credit she seeks? Why or why not?

A Second Act in Business Life

"The great American dream is to be able to rise from nothing to something, on merit alone," believes Maria Wozniak. Born of immigrant parents from Poland, Wozniak was an over-achiever throughout her school years, graduating from the University of Texas in less than three years. Soon after graduation, she landed a job with a major electronics company in computer sales.

Wozniak soon became the classic corporate success, rising rapidly through the ranks. In 1990, just 15 years after she joined the company, she moved up to manager of a $370-million sales division. She was earning $127,000 a year.

Then tragedy struck. Wozniak lost her job. The company called her dismissal in 1995 the result of "corporate retrenchment." After the inner pain subsided, she floundered for a time, as one job interview after another never worked out.

Wozniak seemed to be drifting until an entrepreneur friend of hers suggested that she consider launching her very own business. In her mind's eye, her friend's suggestion raised such questions as:

▶ Can I bridge the gap in cultures, passing from the cocoon of a big business to the adventure of a small business?

▶ What new skills would I have to learn? Would I be able to do so, after having worked so many years in one narrow discipline: Computer sales?

One industry that Wozniak would avoid is management consulting. "Too many corporate refugees have turned to consulting as their second act in life," she says. Indeed, the U.S. Small Business Administration found that in 1995 there were 1.6 million people who said they were consultants, up from 1.0 million in 1988. Wozniak recalls reading about a Harvard professor who gave this advice to an aspiring entrepreneur:

▶ First, money is no obstacle.

▶ Second, decide what business you want to be in—if necessary, look through the Yellow Pages of the telephone book for an idea.

▶ Third, just go out and buy whatever business that you have chosen.

Questions

1. Is the Harvard professor's advice sound? Explain.
2. What would you recommend that Maria Wozniak do now? Explain.
3. How would you suggest that Wozniak put your recommendations into effect?

Raymond Wu came to the United States from Taiwan in 1973. Seventeen years later he struck out on his own to pursue the American dream of being his own boss. Captured by the entrepreneurial spirit that drives small-business owners to the nation's economy, he founded his general contracting business, Wu & Associates, Inc.

Like many small-business owners, Wu and his company had all the technical skills needed for success, but selling these capabilities to skeptical federal government buyers was a problem. Wu has two engineering degrees and is a licensed professional engineer. He served as project engineer on highway construction projects in the Far East, and since arriving in this country has managed multimillion-dollar contracts with public and private agencies.

Following the startup of his venture in 1990, Wu was low bidder on a succession of contracts for the U.S. Navy but was rejected. When a small business is the low bidder on a government contract and is rejected because its responsibility or eligibility is questioned, the bidder may appeal to the SBA for a Certificate of Competency (COC), which requires the contracting officer to award the contract to the lowest bidder. The U.S. Congress has given the SBA the final word in such cases.

The SBA's procurement assistance staff performed an independent study of Wu & Associates' credentials, found the fledgling company fully capable of performing the contracts, and issued the COC. Since then, Wu has received six additional contracts from the navy without SBA help.

In 1991, Wu & Associates' sales amounted to about $450,000, and Wu estimated $1.5 million to $2 million in total sales in 1992. "Now that I've got a track record, I am no longer a 'nonresponsible' bidder. I'm very thankful for the SBA's help. Without the SBA, I wouldn't be here."

Questions

1. To what do you attribute Wu's success?
2. What role did education play in Wu's success?
3. Why did the navy reject Wu's bids? How might a business plan have helped Wu?

Sources: "Wu and Associates, Inc." adapted from Pride, William M., Robert J. Hughes, and Jack R. Kapoor, *Business*, Fifth Edition. Copyright © 1996 by Houghton Mifflin Company. (Based on information from the U.S. Small Business Administration Annual Report, 1992, p. 52). Reprinted by permission.

CHAPTER 5

Buying Out Existing Businesses and Protecting Intellectual Property

I am never afraid of what I know.

—*Anna Sewell*

R ather than starting from scratch, would-be entrepreneurs may choose to buy out an existing business. This chapter focuses on how to make that choice wisely. It also covers intellectual property—in other words, the need to protect inventions, products, and ideas by means of patents, copyrights, or trademarks.

The Need for Planning

In the words of Price Waterhouse, the large certified public accounting firm, business plans "should sit and sing!"[1] This piece of advice applies equally to entrepreneurs who want to buy out an existing business and to those who want to start from scratch.

Magazine and newspaper articles often leave the reader with the feeling that business plans are for startups only. Nothing could be further from the truth. In fact, business plans are a remarkably versatile tool. As suggested in Chapter 4, if updated yearly, they can be used as a blueprint for action throughout a venture's life. Equally important, they can be used to help entrepreneurs buy out an existing business.

EXHIBIT 5.1
Performance of businesses
after buyout. Only a third
of all buyouts turn out to
be good, or satisfying, for
the entrepreneur.

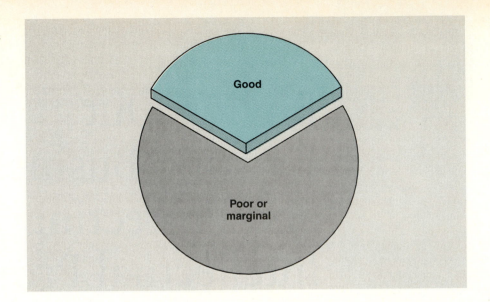

Good

Poor or
marginal

Planning Guidelines

In a study, Price Waterhouse found that only one-third of all buyouts succeed, as depicted in Exhibit 5.1. To boost their chances of success, entrepreneurs must prepare a business plan, following the guidelines laid down for new ventures in Chapter 4, *modified* to fit the special circumstances of the buyout. Among the benefits of preparing a business plan, before and after the buyout, are the following:

▶ A business plan serves to reassure entrepreneurs in a business world of quickening change. In fact, the very act of preparing the plan alerts the entrepreneur to potential pitfalls, perhaps early enough to escape them.

▶ The plan offers entrepreneurs, investors, employees, and others a clear sense of mission—of where the business stands, where it is going, and how to get it there.

Choosing a Product or Service

Having decided to buy out an existing business rather than start from scratch, entrepreneurs must now search for a business to buy out. Before they do so, however, they need to define, with precision and brevity, the kinds of products or services that best match their skills. Again, they must ask themselves questions like those we posed for new ventures in Chapter 4:

▶ Do I really have what it takes to market those products or services?

▶ Do I really want to run this kind of business, do this kind of work, be this kind of person?

The next step is for entrepreneurs, as potential buyers, to describe the criteria that a buyout prospect should meet, among them:

- **Specific products or services** For example, the buyer who is expert in the manufacture of precision measurement instruments might specify such products as gauges, meters, or thermometers.

- **Available financing** It makes little, if any, sense to look at a $1 million buyout prospect if just $100,000 is available—either from lenders or from investors (the buyer included).

- **Ideal sales range** The range should realistically fit both the buyer's expertise and the financing available. For example, with limited financing, a retail jeweler may be limited to seeking stores with sales revenues of, say, under $250,000 a year.

- **Location** Personal preference often narrows the buyer's range of buyout choices. For instance, some may prefer one geographical region to another because of climate, while others may prefer a rural site to either an urban or a suburban site because of space needs.

- **Seller's presence** The buyer may want the seller to stay on for, say, at least three months after the buyout, to help the buyer over the rough edges of transition.

> **Conducting the Search**

Armed with these criteria, entrepreneurs as buyers are now poised to carry out their search. To do so, they can pursue either of two avenues:

- Hire a finder or a business broker, someone who excels at matching buyers with sellers. *Finders* simply introduce buyers to potential sellers. *Brokers,* on the other hand, offer added services, among them access to databases on markets and expert help with negotiations.

- Randomly seek leads through bankers, lawyers, certified public accountants, management consultants, insurance agents, and venture capitalists.

Of these sources, and as shown in Exhibit 5.2, the conventional wisdom is that bankers offer the best leads, followed by lawyers and certified public accountants. The reason for this is that these sources generally have a long, trusting, professional relationship with their clients and thus are likely to know which are buyout prospects.

Surprisingly, venture capitalists are the least helpful.* Although they can offer buyers good advice on how to evaluate an existing business, the buyout prospects they suggest are almost always ones that they themselves have rejected.

Evaluating an Existing Business

Lawyers and bankers often advise entrepreneurs to buy out a business rather than start from scratch. The reason for this is that existing businesses, if

---

*Generally, venture capitalists make money available for investment in innovative smaller businesses, especially in high technology, in which both the risk of loss and the potential for profit may be high.

EXHIBIT 5.2

Ranking the best sources of leads to businesses available for sale (on a scale of 1 to 10). Generally, bankers are the best sources of candidates for purchase by entrepreneurs.

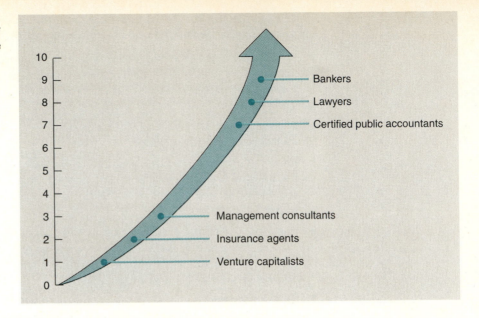

profitable, are less risky. The odds are better because a successful business already has proven its ability to draw customers and has likely established healthy relationships with bankers and suppliers, employees and the community.

Indeed, the track record of an existing business surpasses the guesswork required to evaluate the prospects of a new venture. Past records, however, do not eliminate risk. To lessen risk, entrepreneurs should ask questions like those posed in Exhibit 5.3. Note that this exhibit also describes a decision procedure, beginning with the choice of a product or service.

▶ Understanding the Seller's Motives

Among the valid reasons why owners are willing to sell are the following:

▶ **Personal and career reasons**   Owners may want to convert their holdings in a family-held business to cash.

▶ **Management succession**   Owners may doubt the ability of younger men and women in the business to carry on profitably in the future.

▶ **One-person management**   Owners may realize that their business is getting too big for them and that because of their own managerial shortcomings, they cannot continue to strengthen the business themselves.[2]

However, sellers commonly hide their true motives for selling. Some owners, seeing that today's technological advances will soon make their product or service outdated, may say they want to retire to California or teach small-business management at a local college. In most cases, though, the following reasons underlie their wanting to sell:

▶ Fear about the financial future of their business and family

▶ Fear that because they are company-rich but cash-poor, wealth built up over a lifetime would be lost

EXHIBIT 5.3
Deciding whether to buy
out an existing business.

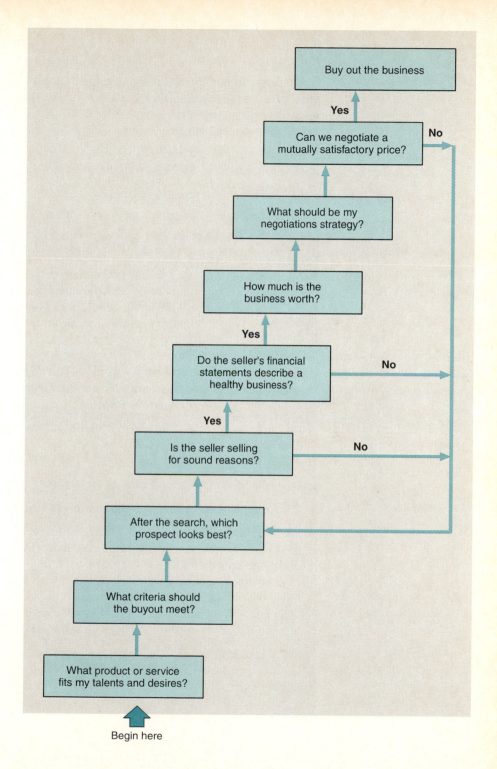

- ▶ Fear that technology, once simple, is now too complex to cope with
- ▶ Fear that the product or service is outdated[3]

Owners rarely express their fears; instead, they hide them and stress the good reasons for selling. This means that buyers must search out the real reasons. Otherwise, they may lack any basis for deciding whether they can solve the problems of the business to be acquired.

▶ **Evaluating Financial Aspects**

Let us now turn to the equally important problem of evaluating the financial aspects of a business. Financial evaluation raises the following questions:

- ▶ How healthy is the seller's business?
- ▶ How profitable has it been?
- ▶ How much is it worth?

The Role of Financial Statements   To help answer these questions, a buyer should begin with the seller's financial statements. Many buyers blindly accept any financial statements bearing an accountant's signature. Remember, however, that accountants work chiefly as advisers. They can make suggestions, but they cannot stop sellers from using any accounting method that best serves their purposes.

The idea that businesspersons can more or less select the profit level of their business may seem odd. But owners have this right. Few owners habitually juggle their books, but there are many ways in which they may legally overstate or understate profits. For example:

- ▶ Inventories can be accounted for in a half-dozen ways. Each method affects profits differently.
- ▶ Assets such as machines and buildings can be written up or down in value.
- ▶ Depreciation can be speeded up or slowed down.

One buyer, speaking from bitter experience, said:

We have studied companies for months before making an acquisition. We have made audits, sent in our controller, paid attention to every financial detail—or so we thought. In each case we found out something after we took over that we did not know before the deal was closed. Some of the differences between what we thought we were buying and what we did buy were major. We have learned. But this we believe sincerely. Financial statements don't really answer any questions, they just allow you to ask them.[4]

These problems are especially severe in small family-owned businesses. Here, accounting practices tend to vary widely. For example, owners may take every possible deduction to cut taxes, or they may use the fastest depreciation allowances permitted by the U.S. Internal Revenue Service, or they may expense rather than capitalize their costs.

Auditing   The buyer's first step in evaluating the financial aspects of a business should be to find out what adjustments need to be made to the seller's financial statements—in order to estimate what the business is really worth. To do that, the buyer should get the seller's income statements and balance sheets for, say, the past five years. These statements show, at least on paper, the business's financial health, as well as profitability. Armed with these statements, the buyer may now examine and question such information as the following:

▸ Bills owed by customers—to make sure they are collectible

▸ Inventories—to make sure of their existence and their quality

▸ Equipment—to make sure every piece of equipment works and is not held together by baling wire

▸ Bank loans, bills owed to suppliers, and other debts—to make sure payment can be made

▸ Leases, licenses, franchises, and contracts—to make sure they can be transferred

▸ Public records—to make sure the seller is the titleholder of record, has no tax liens against the property, has no outstanding product warranties, has no payments due under purchase contracts, and so on

To carry out this audit, the buyer normally needs the help of two professionals: a lawyer and an accountant. Their services are indispensable. Although the fees of these professionals are high, and their judgment is by no means flawless, they can reduce the odds of making the wrong choice.

As shown in Exhibit 5.4, investigation of the seller's business should be a team effort. It is the buyer's responsibility, however, to make sure that his or

EXHIBIT 5.4
Suggested procedure for investigating a potential buyout. Investigation of a potential buyout should be a team effort, involving the buyer, a lawyer, and an accountant.

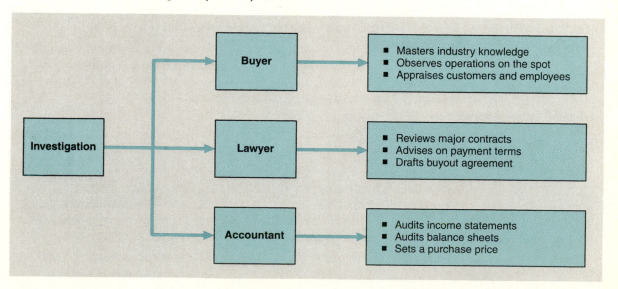

her efforts mesh with those of the lawyer and the accountant. The buyer must never lose sight of the need to exchange and correlate all information. For example:

> Suppose the accountant, reviewing the financial information, uncovers possible federal income tax deficiencies for past years by the seller. The buyer and lawyer should be told immediately. The lawyer then would proceed to protect the buyer—by contract—against the assumption of any legal obligations to pay back taxes. In turn, the buyer would evaluate the effect of the tax deficiencies on the seller's business. Is the business still viable and desirable?

▶ **Setting a Price**

Having thoroughly examined and questioned the financial records of the seller's business, the buyer now must tackle the problem of pricing it. Again, evaluating a seller's business is much more art than science. Questions about the worth and possible purchase price of a business cannot be answered with precision. Many factors, often immeasurable, influence the price that both buyer and seller place on a business. Thus, there is no best way to price a business. As a negotiating tactic, the buyer should look at a business not only from his or her own viewpoint but also from the seller's viewpoint.

In pricing a seller's business, the buyer may use either of two traditional approaches: earnings or assets. Earnings are synonymous with after-tax profits. As shown in Exhibit 5.5, the earnings approach requires the buyer to focus only on earnings, either past or future. The asset approach, on the other hand, requires the buyer to focus on assets only, without regard to their earning power.

The Earnings Approach   A buyer who chooses the earnings approach may use either of two methods: capitalizing profits or personal return. The *capitalizing profits* method assumes that the buyer is really buying a series of yearly profits. It requires the buyer to ask, What am I willing to pay for the chance to earn a certain profit each year for, say, the next 10 years? To clarify the meaning of this question, let us look at an example:

EXHIBIT 5.5
Traditional approaches for pricing a potential buyout. The buyer should price a potential buyout from both the buyer's and the seller's viewpoint.

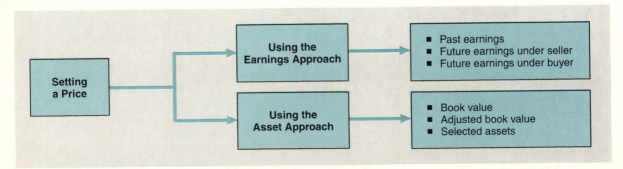

Suppose a buyer estimates that a bookstore will earn $20,000 a year after taxes for the next 10 years. What should the buyer pay the seller for this opportunity? To answer this question, the buyer should first estimate what return to expect on the investment. Let us assume that she expects a 15 percent return on investment after income taxes. Why 15 percent? Perhaps because she has other opportunities that will return at least that much. Or perhaps because she simply wants that much return, even though the next-best opportunity may be a bank that returns 5 percent on savings. Or perhaps because 15 percent is the seller's current return on owners' equity. Now we can arrive at the purchase price by capitalizing the buyer's estimate of average yearly future profits:

$$\$20,000 = 15\% \times \text{purchase price}$$
$$\text{Purchase price} = \$20,000 \div 0.15$$
$$= \$133,000 \text{ (rounded)} \quad \blacktriangle\blacktriangledown\blacktriangle$$

Capitalizing profits is a popular earnings method, although it often produces misleading results. For one thing, buyers can estimate after-tax profits in any one of several ways, among them:

▶ Last year's profits only

▶ Average yearly profits for the past five years

▶ Average yearly projected profits for the next five years, estimated on the basis of past profits

▶ Average yearly projected profits for the next five years, based on the buyer's belief that his or her superior managerial skills will boost profits

The first two ways have little to recommend them because they ignore any changes stemming from the transfer of ownership. Although the third way does suggest that the future will be different, only the fourth way recognizes the fact that, generally, entrepreneurs buy a business only if convinced their managerial skills will improve performance.

The *capitalizing profits* method is flawed, however. It looks at return, not from the entrepreneur's perspective, but from the business's, relating profits to total investment. A more commonsensible method, however, would be *personal return*, which looks at return only from the entrepreneur's perspective and which assumes that the entrepreneur stands separate and apart from the business. This means:

▶ Relating what he personally expects to take out of the business (salary, dividends, interest, perquisites), to what he personally invested, which may be a lot less than that invested by others—as explained in this example:

A seller offers her toy-making business to a buyer for $100,000. After some study, the buyer estimates that his yearly personal return would be $42,000:

$36,000	salary
4,000	perquisites (automobile, club memberships, etc.)
2,000	interest on long-term loan
$42,000	total personal return (cash flow or its equivalent)

Now let us assume that $100,000 is the seller's firm price for the business and that the buyer plans to finance the purchase price in the following way:

▶ $20,000 cash sale of stock to himself, keeping 60 percent of the business for himself

▶ $60,000 cash sale of stock to others at a premium, giving them just 40 percent of the business

▶ $20,000 long-term loan from the buyer to the business

Now what is the buyer's personal return on his investment? It can be estimated as follows:

$$\text{Personal return} = \$42,000$$
$$\text{Personal investment} = \$40,000 \text{ (including loan)}$$
$$\text{Personal return on investment} = 105\% \text{ a year} \left(\frac{\$42,000}{\$40,000} \times 100 \right) \quad \blacktriangle\blacktriangledown\blacktriangle$$

To summarize the two earnings approaches: The *capitalizing profits* method stresses after-tax profits expressed as a percentage of total business investment; the *personal return* method stresses the buyer's personal return expressed as a percentage of personal investment.

The Asset Approach   The asset approach ignores future earnings, focusing instead on just the seller's assets, such as buildings and equipment, inventories and accounts receivable. Although often not recommended, the asset approach is popular because it is easier to use than the earnings approach, which requires that the buyer perform the complex task of forecasting earnings to price a business. The three traditional asset methods are book value, adjusted book value, and selected assets.

Book value is the difference between what a business owns (assets) and what it owes (liabilities). It is a good starting point for pricing a business, because the buyer need only look at the seller's latest balance sheet. This method is full of pitfalls, however. It tells the buyer nothing about the true worth of a business. For example, a business may have a book value of $100,000 and still be worthless—because its assets are incapable of creating customers at a profit.

The *adjusted book value* method adjusts for any significant differences between the book and market value of assets. Market value measures what the assets could now be sold for, regardless of book value. For example, a buyer may adjust the price of land recorded in the seller's book at its original cost because its market value has since appreciated greatly.

With the *selected assets* method, buyers select only the seller's assets that they believe are needed. Unwanted equipment and inventories remain with the seller. In this way, buyers evaluate only parts of the seller's business, not all of it.

▶ **Negotiating a Price**

Estimating what to pay for a business is just the beginning of the pricing process. The buyer must now get down to the nitty-gritty of negotiating a price with the seller. Unless buyer and seller are of like mind, there may well be a wide gap between what the buyer believes the business is worth and what the seller believes it is worth. For reasons of sentiment if not greed, sellers are likely to inflate the asking price. For the buyer, no matter how well prepared, it is hard to see through such a practice.

Although negotiations depend in large part on numbers, the buyer also must look closely at the seller's human side. The seller, for example, may want iron-clad assurances that the business name, often the seller's name, will continue after the sale; that certain employees, especially relatives, will enjoy continued job security; or that product or service quality will continue to be improved.

Unless convinced the buyer will meet such *non*financial wants and needs, the seller may break off the negotiations. So it behooves the buyer to strike a delicate balance between the human side of the seller's business and its financial side.

Human aspects often carry a price, however. If the buyer, for example, agrees to keep unproductive relatives on the payroll, two salaries must be paid for one position. In that event, the buyer should negotiate a lower purchase price to offset the added cost.

Even after all this give and take, buyer and seller may still be miles apart on price. Their ability to agree hinges on their skills at the negotiating table and on how they see each other's strengths and weaknesses.

Before buying out an existing business, an entrepreneur must painstakingly evaluate both its past and its potential. These two entrepreneurs did just that.

New Ventures Versus Buyouts

For the pure entrepreneur, founding and molding a venture pose a greater challenge than taking over an existing business. They seek ventures that are truly their own creations, craving the creative satisfaction that stems from planting an idea and then nurturing it into a strong and sturdy business.

To be sure, the risks are also greater. With a buyout, records give the buyer some idea of how healthy and profitable the business is. But with a new venture, the best an entrepreneur can do is guess at what the profits will be. It may be intelligent guesswork, but it is guesswork nonetheless. There are some practical reasons why entrepreneurs prefer to begin from scratch:

▶ To avoid the effects of a prior owner's errors

▶ To choose their own banker, equipment, inventories, location, suppliers, and workers—without being bound by commitments and policies made by the previous owner

▶ To create their own loyal customers

How do entrepreneurs evaluate the prospects of a new venture? To begin with, they must study the market to estimate such things as total market, share of market, and sales revenues. This is difficult even for businesses the size of General Motors and Du Pont, let alone the small entrepreneur. Still, it must be done.

With a buyout, however, an entrepreneur has records that tell, for example, what its sales revenues were during the past five years and, more important, whether revenues are going up, standing still, or going down. From this information, the entrepreneur can then predict yearly sales revenues by assuming they will either follow past trends or outdo them.

Intellectual Property and the Entrepreneur

In this section, we discuss the need to protect intellectual property—a term used to describe the rights of entrepreneurs or others in intangible property created through ingenuity and mental effort. David Rosenbaum, author and patent attorney, offers this explanation:

> Fundamentally, rights in intangible property are virtually identical to rights in tangible property. The difference is that you can see and touch tangible property, while intangible property must be described or depicted in some tangible form.
>
> Tangible property includes land, motor vehicles, houses, bicycles, jewelry—all of which can be held and physically possessed. On the other hand, you cannot see and physically possess intellectual property rights, but they can still exist if you take the time to understand what they are and how they can be protected.[6]

To protect their intellectual property, entrepreneurs may use any one of three legal safeguards—patents, copyrights, or trademarks—depending on the nature of their ideas.

▶ Patents

Many entrepreneurs are also inventors. Often, these entrepreneurs must decide whether to apply for a *patent,* which grants exclusive rights to an invention. Patents can help entrepreneurs attract investors, earn licensing fees, and stop unfair competition. Patenting a product, however, takes time and money. Before launching a new venture, entrepreneurs should weigh both the benefits and the costs of patenting an invention by answering the questions listed here and depicted in Exhibit 5.6:

▶ Is my product patentable?

▶ Do I need or want patent protection?

▶ How do I go about getting that protection?

▶ If I do get a patent, can I keep competitors from circumventing it?

For legal protection, entrepreneurs should hire a patent attorney. Although entrepreneurs can get patents themselves, the process is so complex that they would be wise to leave it to an attorney.

Below are some guidelines, supported by an example, that every inventor-entrepreneur should follow, according to the Patent and Trademark Office of the U.S. Department of Commerce.[7]

▶ The Patenting Process

Suppose an entrepreneur has invented a new hydraulic bumper device that absorbs automobile collisions up to 30 miles an hour. The law says that, to be patentable, the device must be new, useful, and not obvious. If the device appears to meet these standards, the entrepreneur should take the following steps:

1. **Make a record** The entrepreneur should fix the time the device was invented, in case of a need to prove this later. The entrepreneur also

EXHIBIT 5.6
Some practical questions about patents. Entrepreneurs should weigh both the benefits and the costs of patenting an invention.

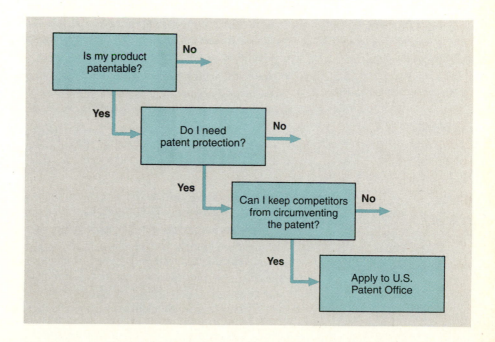

should write out a description of the hydraulic bumper device and illustrate it with sketches. In addition, he or she should sign and date the description and illustrations in the presence of knowledgeable witnesses.

2. **Make sure the invention is practical** The entrepreneur should learn enough about the automobile market to be sure there is some chance that the device will be used. Can it be made more cheaply than others on the market? Does it involve engineering problems for the manufacturer? Entrepreneurs should avoid patenting products that will not create customers at a profit.

3. **Hire a patent attorney** The entrepreneur should seek out an attorney from the *Directory of Registered Patent Attorneys and Agents*, which lists patent attorneys by state and city.[8]

4. **Have a search made** The entrepreneur should ask the patent attorney to get copies of existing patents on hydraulic bumper devices that might stop the entrepreneur from getting a patent.

5. **Prepare an application** If the search suggests that this hydraulic bumper device is the first of its kind, the entrepreneur should ask the patent attorney to prepare a formal application for a patent. The application must include:

   ▶ A petition—a request for a patent, addressed to the Commissioner of Patents of the U.S. Department of Commerce.

   ▶ The specification, which describes the entrepreneur's hydraulic bumper device, explains how it works, and describes how it is constructed.

   ▶ The claims of patentability, which define the entrepreneur's invention. The claims are intended to explain how the hydraulic bumper device differs from all other such devices not only on the market but disclosed in patents, magazines, and other publications.

   ▶ An oath, which the entrepreneur signs before a notary public. The oath requires one to swear that one believes oneself to be the first and sole inventor of this hydraulic bumper device.

The patenting process is complex, costly, and time consuming. In fact, it takes an average of two years, from the filing of the application to the receipt of the patent. Should the entrepreneur's patent application conflict with another patent, it can take much longer.

Once the patent is granted, the entrepreneur has the "right to exclude others from making, using, or selling the invention throughout the United States."[9] Such patent rights last 17 years. After the patent expires, anyone can make, use, or sell the invention without the entrepreneur's permission. The 17-year term cannot be extended except by special act of the U.S. Congress.

Meanwhile, competitors may try to "design around" the invention. To succeed, and thus avoid infringing on the entrepreneur's patent, a competitor need only eliminate a single element of the entrepreneur's patent claims.

▶ Copyrights

What do musical scores, computer software, and textbooks like this one have in common? Each of their authors is protected by the U.S. Copyright Act, which seeks to stop others from the unauthorized copying, duplication, or publication of their works. Not only are authors covered but also advertisers, artists, designers, photographers, and the like. Copyrights are invaluable because they endow entrepreneurs and others with:

> the exclusive right to use, reproduce, and charge a fee for reproducing their copyrighted works.

In contrast to patents, copyrights are easy to obtain. All that an entrepreneur or others need do is place a copyright notice on their work or the symbol ©, as well as the date and the entrepreneur's name. Though not required by law, the entrepreneur may then register the copyright with the U.S. Copyright Office in Washington, D.C.

Copyright protection covers the entrepreneur's life plus 50 years. But if the work is created by an employee but copyrighted by, say, the entrepreneur's business, then the copyright would be good for 75 years from the year the work was created.

▶ Trademarks

The golden arches of McDonald's, along with brand names like Xerox and Blockbuster Video, are vivid examples of trademarks. "A businessman's dream is to have his product readily identified by its trademark," according to David Rosenbaum.[10] Indeed, businesses often go to extraordinary lengths to create trademarks that consumers find both distinctive and memorable. A versatile marketing tool, trademarks come in many forms:

▶ They may be words, logos, or other symbols indicating that a product comes from a particular company. They may even be sounds, three-dimensional symbols—such as the well-known McDonald's golden arches—or colors. There are also service marks, which indicate the source of services. Service marks are often called brand names, like *Pepsi*; or slogans, like Apple's *The power to be your best.*[11]

Like copyrights, entrepreneurs or other trademark owners may protect themselves merely by using a trademark to help sell their products. To receive added legal protection, entrepreneurs may then register their trademark with the U.S. Patent and Trademark Office in Washington, D.C., preferably with the help of a patent attorney. Unlike copyrights, however, trademark protection may last indefinitely—in fact, for as long as the entrepreneur chooses to use the trademark to help sell products.

SUMMARY

Rather than start from scratch, some entrepreneurs choose to buy out an existing business. Whichever approach entrepreneurs take, an essential step is developing a good business plan. Remember that a business plan can be used as a blueprint for action throughout a venture's life. And, in a buyout situation, the process of developing the plan alerts entrepreneurs to potential pitfalls and gives them a clear sense of purpose.

In deciding whether to purchase an existing business, an individual should ask certain key questions: What product or service fits my talents and desires? What criteria should the buyout meet? Which prospect looks best? Is the seller selling for sound reasons? Do the seller's financial statements describe a healthy business? How much is the business worth? What strategy should I use in negotiations with the seller? Can we negotiate a mutually satisfactory price?

Before a price can be set, an evaluation of the financial aspects of the business is necessary. This evaluation is based on an audit of the business's financial statements. To place a value on an existing business, entrepreneurs may use either the earnings approach or the asset approach. The earnings approach— the *capitalizing profits* method or the *personal return* method—focuses only on earnings. The asset approach focuses only on assets, without regard to their earning power.

Why would entrepreneurs choose to buy out an existing business, rather than start a new one? The primary reason is that existing businesses are less risky because they already have proved their ability to draw customers at a profit and have established healthy relationships with bankers and suppliers, employees and the community. Of course, there are no guarantees that the business will continue to be successful. And a buyout, although challenging, does not offer the creative possibilities so crucial to the motivation of pure entrepreneurs.

Intellectual property is a term that describes the rights of entrepreneurs or others in intangible property created through ingenuity and mental effort. To protect such rights, entrepreneurs may use any one of three legal safeguards— patents, copyrights, or trademarks—depending on the nature of their ideas.

Patents protect inventors by seeking to stop others from making, using, or selling an invention for a period of 17 years. Entrepreneurs who are also inventors must decide whether to seek patent protection. Before doing so, however, they must first establish, with the help of a patent attorney, whether their invention is patentable—to make sure of its uniqueness and usefulness.

Copyrights protect advertisers, artists, authors, designers, photographers, and the like from the unauthorized copying, duplication, or publication of their works. Copyright protection covers the copyright owner's life plus 50 years.

Trademarks protect the distinctive name, term, or symbol registered with the U.S. Patent and Trademark Office. In contrast to patents and copyrights, trademarks have an indefinite life.

Discussion and Review Questions

1. Why should entrepreneurs prepare a business plan before buying out an existing business?
2. What are the advantages and disadvantages of buying out an existing business?
3. Outline a procedure that entrepreneurs can follow to decide whether to buy out an existing business.

4. Why do bankers and lawyers often advise entrepreneurs to buy an existing business rather than start from scratch?

5. Why does the seller of a business often give good rather than real reasons for wanting to sell?

6. Before buying a business, why is it vital to audit the seller's books? Which items in the seller's business deserve a close look? Why?

7. Would you consult with an attorney and an accountant before buying out a business? Why or why not?

8. Briefly describe the various ways of arriving at a purchase price for an existing business.

9. How does the *personal return* method differ from the *capitalizing profits* method?

10. Which is a better approach to pricing a business: earnings or assets? Why?

11. How important are nonfinancial considerations in negotiating the purchase price of an existing business? Explain your answer.

12. Compare the potential appeal to entrepreneurs of buying out a business versus starting from scratch.

13. Define these terms: *business broker, audit, capitalizing profits, personal return on investment, perquisites, book value.*

14. Is it necessarily a good idea to patent an invention? Why or why not?

15. How do copyrights differ from trademarks?

Building a Business Plan

Buying Out Existing Businesses and Protecting Intellectual Property

If you decided to buy out an existing business rather than start from scratch, you must find a business that is worthy of purchase. To do so, you can pursue one of the following two options:

▶ Hire a finder or a business broker. (*Finders* simply introduce buyers to potential sellers. *Brokers* offer added services that include access to databases on markets and expert help with negotiations.)

▶ Seek possible leads through bankers, lawyers, certified public accountants, management consultants, insurance agents, and venture capitalists.

Instructions for Worksheet 5

The track record of an existing business provides entrepreneurs with a great deal of information that can be used to evaluate a business, but it is your responsibility to evaluate the business before investing any money. In part 1 of this worksheet, you must determine why the current business owner wants to sell an existing business. In part 2, evaluate the financial aspects of an existing business. Then in part 3, set a price that you are willing to pay for the existing business.

Part 1—Understanding the Seller's Motives

There are many valid reasons why a business owner may want to sell an existing business. As discussed in this chapter, owners may sell for personal and career reasons as well as concerns about management succession, and even because they feel the business is now too big for them to manage. However, sellers commonly hide their true motives for selling an existing business.

1. What do you consider to be valid reasons why a business owner would sell an existing business?

2. What questions can you use to determine a seller's true motives?

Part 2—Evaluating the Financial Aspects of a Business

To determine the financial health of an existing business, an entrepreneur should begin with the firm's financial statements.

3. What type of information can be obtained by auditing the seller's financial statements?

4. When auditing the financial statements of an existing business, whom can you turn to for help?

5. In addition to the information contained on a firm's financial statements, what other types of information should a prospective business owner examine?

Part 3—Setting a Price

There are two widely accepted approaches for pricing an existing business: the earnings approach and the asset approach.

6. Describe how you would use the earnings approach to price out an existing business.

7. Describe how you would use the assets approach to establish a price for an existing business.

8. Which method do you feel is the best method for establishing the purchase price for an existing business? Why?

Western Reserve Business Review

In 1990, Bruce David took over a monthly business newspaper, the *Western Reserve Business Review,* as its owner, president, and publisher. Exhibit 5A.1 shows several headlines from the October 1990 issue. In its four-year history, the *Review* had never had a profitable month. But David was confident that he could reverse its fortunes on the strength of his experiences as a publisher of newsletters, manuals, and a weekly newspaper.

EXHIBIT 5A.1

Sample of headlines from the *Western Reserve Business Review.*

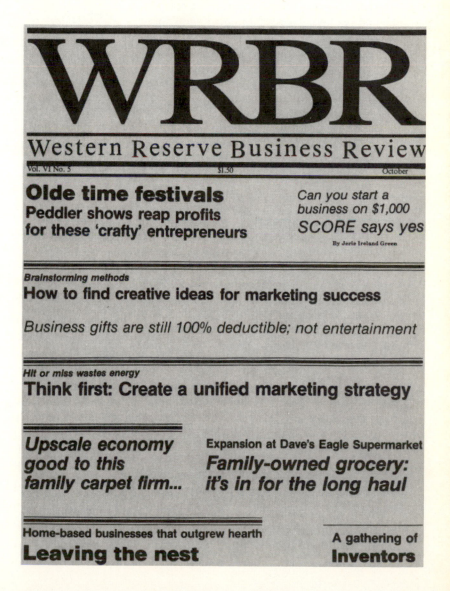

Background

David's entrepreneurial career began when he was just 11 years old. While working as a caddy at a private country club, he begged or bought used golf balls, clubs, and bags from members, then sold them to friends of his father at a profit.

Seventeen years would pass before he would launch a second venture. In the meantime, he indulged his love of study and reading. "I was, and still am, an information junkie," says David. "I've always been obsessed with the three Rs: reading, reading, and reading. There is nothing I enjoy more than researching ideas."

It was this obsession that carried David through high school and college. He attended Kent State University for two years and Arizona State University for one year, majoring in mass communications. But to the dismay of his parents, David dropped out after his junior year, despite a grade point average of 3.7. "I needed the excitement of new challenges," he explains. "I felt that I had already learned what I needed to know, to make it in the workaday world of business."

Reborn as an Entrepreneur

After leaving college, David worked at a progression of jobs, all of them having to do with advertising. Each new job brought with it added responsibility and authority as well as variety. For example, by the time he was 29 years old, David had already worked at:

▸ Designing publications and creating page layouts for *Beverage Industry, Video Retail,* and other trade magazines

▸ Writing feature stories about business executives

▸ Serving as the Midwest advertising manager of Harcourt Brace Jovanovich, a *Fortune 500* publisher.

It was all but inevitable that David would reenter the world of entrepreneurship. "I was ready, both mentally and professionally, to do so," he says. "I had developed the necessary talents and skills to succeed. At the same time, I began to tire of the corporate world and its rigidity. Working under somebody else's thumb was hard for me. I'm more productive and creative, and surely happier, acting as my own boss."

Publishing Ventures

While still with Harcourt Brace Jovanovich, David began a sideline venture called Worthprinting Limited. His investment came to just $300. As president and sole employee, David launched his first two publications, both of which were aimed at the advertising needs of small businesses:

▸ *The Shoestring Marketer,* whose purpose was "to show small-budget advertisers how they might promote their business without spending a fortune." Issued every two months and priced at $25 a year, the newsletter drew a total of 1,550 subscribers. In 1990, David sold the newsletter for $11,000.

▸ *Profitable Advertising, a Handbook for Small Business,* whose purpose was to offer entrepreneurs a ready reference of "proven techniques that they themselves might apply, without the financial pain of having to hire an advertising agency to do it for them."

As a result of these two publications, David soon found himself in demand as a speaker before chambers of commerce, Kiwanis Clubs, and other business groups. "One reason they wanted me was that I came for free," says David. His reputation as an advertising expert led to his creating a profitable set of seminars at local colleges.

These successes convinced David to leave the corporate world and become self-employed. His business cards identified him as an expert in three disciplines:

▸ Marketing consultant

▸ Mail-order publisher

▸ Seminar leader

David's decision to leave the corporate cocoon of regular paychecks and generous fringe benefits was made without his family's approval. In fact, his parents and wife tried to discourage him from going it alone.

Purchase of the Western Reserve Business Review

Five years later, a success financially and professionally, David again was ready for new challenges. "I was too many things to too many people. If I was really going to get anywhere, I realized that I had to focus my energies more sharply than I had."

And he did just that. The new focus of his energies was the *Western Reserve Business Review,* which was for sale. Founded in 1983, the *Review* never earned a profit for its founder, who treated it as a sideline business. "The founder made no effort to obtain national advertisers," says David. "The Review never grew at the rate it could have in terms of readership, graphics, and advertising."

Despite the *Review's* performance and image, David bought it for $25,000. The founder had wanted $45,000. David raised the money by selling all his other ventures, including *The Shoestring Marketer* and *Profitable Advertising.*

Financial Magic

A month after he bought the *Review,* David teamed with Ernest Brass and Ramesh Shah to form a new corporation, the Alpha Multi-Media Group. He sold the *Review* to the corporation in exchange for 45 percent of its ownership. The corporation's beginning balance sheet appears in Exhibit 5A.2.

Notice that the newly formed corporation owed David $20,000. When the loan is repaid, David will have launched what he believes will be a publishing empire with just $5,000 of his own money.

Notice also from Exhibit 5A.2 that Shah put in only $5,000 of his own money. Yet he holds 45 percent of the corporation's common stock, as does David. Both men rewarded themselves for founding the corporation by giving themselves enough common stock for 45 percent of its ownership.

EXHIBIT 5A.2
Alpha Multi-Media Group, Inc.: Beginning balance sheet (September 1, 1990).

Assets			Equities		
Cash			Long-term loan		
Brass	$ 5,000		David		$20,000
Shah	5,000				
		$10,000			
			Owners' equity		
Organizational cost			Brass	$ 5,000	
David	$42,500		David	22,500	
Shah	17,500	60,000	Shah	22,500	50,000
Total		$70,000	Total		$70,000

David's Partners

David was "pleased as Punch to have Ernie Brass and Ram Shah working with me, as members of my management team. I'm the product person, the one who gets out the work, who oversees the writing as well as the marketing. I'm not the manager that Ernie is; nor am I the financier that Ram is. Their skills and talents complement mine." Here are brief profiles of Brass and Shah:

▶ **Ernest Brass**   Brass works in two worlds: education and business. His educational world centers on Capital University, where he wears two hats. He teaches courses in accounting and in entrepreneurship; and he directs the university's Small Business Institute, which is financed by the U.S. Small Business Administration.

  In the business world, Brass is a management consultant. He markets his knowledge of accounting and management among entrepreneurs, helping them to survive and grow. He also works with nonprofit organizations and city and county governments, helping them boost the development of new and existing businesses.

  Brass earned his bachelor of arts degree from Bowling Green State University. He later completed his master of science degree in business administration at Case Western Reserve University. He is now pursuing a doctor of philosophy degree at Bradford University in England.

▶ **Ramesh Shah**   Born in India, Shah earned a bachelor of science degree from the University of Bombay. Soon after, he came to the United States on a student visa to pursue graduate study at the University of Illinois, where he earned a master of science degree in electrical engineering.

  Shah worked at a succession of jobs, ranging from the design of electronic instrumentation with Allis Chalmers to the management of computer systems with Bailey Controls. His last job working for somebody else was with the local chamber of commerce, as a management consultant helping minority businesses survive and grow.

  When he left the chamber of commerce, Shah founded his own venture. Called the Alpha Development Corporation, it served as a springboard for buying and managing apartment buildings and neighborhood shopping centers. In 1990, the market value of the corporation's assets topped $8.5 million.

Organization

Both Brass and Shah are unpaid members of David's management team, although both men play an active role—Brass as management advisor and Shah as financial officer. "I receive a lot of psychic income from being part of a publishing venture like Bruce's," says Shah. "It's a totally new world for me, and I'm fascinated by it all."

Other members of David's management team, all of them paid, include:

▶ Paul Bestgen, the production manager
▶ Thomas Hannan, the marketing manager
▶ Jerie Ireland Green, the *Review's* editor
▶ Betty Piotrowski, the circulation and office manager

"I'm satisfied that I now have the management team I need to turn the *Review* into a profitable publication," says David. Exhibit 5A.3 shows his organizational chart.

Preparation of a Plan

In 1990, the *Review's* losses were running at the rate of $2,000 a month. To help stabilize operations, David was looking for a $25,000 line of credit. In his words at the time: "The line of credit will help smooth out the up-and-down cycles of this traditionally slow cash-flow business. It will help pay the bills when they fall due."

To convince local bankers that Alpha Multi-Media Group, as the *Review's* publisher, was a

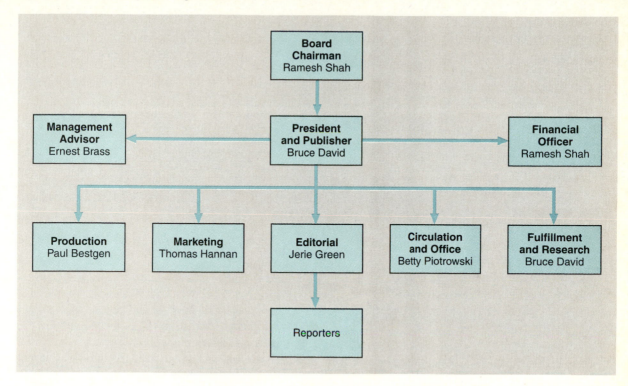

good credit risk, he prepared a plan. Here are excerpts from the plan's summary:

Alpha Multi-Media Group is a many-sided corporation whose mission is to fulfill the informational needs of entrepreneurs. Our marketing niche focuses on entrepreneurs with fewer than 50 employees, whom the larger but traditional media often overlook or ignore. To satisfy this niche, we will offer such special services and products as:

▶ Magazines such as the *Western Reserve Business Review,* which already serves the informational needs of entrepreneurs in our four-county area. Published monthly, each issue has news stories about local entrepreneurs as well as columns offering advice on a host of topics, ranging from estate planning to tax reform. Regular features cover awards, communications, economics, guest commentaries, upcoming conferences and meetings, and more.

In September 1990, we passed out 13,000 copies, of which only 400 were paid for. Sold at newsstands at $1.50 a copy, the *Review* reaches as many as 36,000 readers, of whom 80 percent are either entrepreneurs or managers.

▶ The *Western Review Business Show,* which will enable as many as 250 small businesses to exhibit their services and products to prospective customers.

▶ The *State Convention Directory,* which will feature listings and descriptions of special events scheduled in each of the state's 88 counties. Published yearly, this directory will help

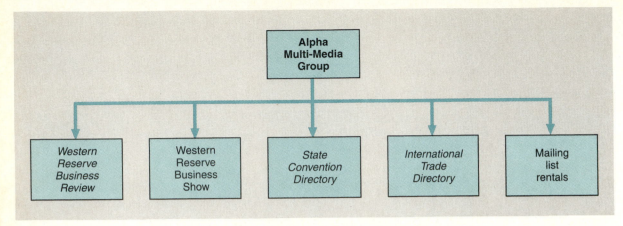

small businesses to market their services and products anywhere in the state.

- The *International Trade Directory,* which will tell entrepreneurs where best to find information that will help them to begin or expand their export-import activities. This directory will be updated yearly.

- Mailing lists, which will be rented to entrepreneurs who wish to expand by reaching more customers in their markets.

We expect to have all the foregoing activities in place by the end of 1991.

Exhibit 5A.4 depicts the corporation's services and products.

Financial Forecast

David expected sales revenues of $286,400 his first full year. His forecasted income statement for the year appears in Exhibit 5A.5. A breakdown of sales revenues by product appears in Exhibit 5A.6. His goal was "to reach sales revenues of $3 million within four years." With a team of seasoned managers in place, coupled with the need

by entrepreneurs for more and more good information, David believed that goal was attainable.

David expected most of the corporation's sales growth to come, not from the *Review,* but from the purchase of other publishing ventures and the founding of new publications. "We won't be sitting on our hands these next few years," he said shortly after taking over the *Review.* "We constantly will be looking for new opportunities. We will expand only into related marketing niches where we are strong competitively." By 1995, David expected two breakthroughs to take place:

- The corporation will have grown "so large that we will be able to go public and offer common stock to investors. We will then use the cash received from such an offering to expand even further."

- The corporation will diversify "dramatically into electronic broadcasting."

Nonmanagerial Employees

Pleased as David was with his team of managers, he had yet to grapple with the problem of how

EXHIBIT 5A.5

Alpha Multi-Media Group, Inc.: Forecasted income statement (1991).

Sales Revenues		
Western Reserve Business Review	$180,400	
Western Reserve Business Show	50,000	
State Convention Directory	38,000	
International Trade Directory	12,000	
Mailing list rentals	6,000	$286,400
Cost of Sales		
Printing	$ 29,600	
Typesetting	24,400	
Postage	18,400	
Outside services	14,800	87,200
Gross Profit		$199,200
Operating Expenses		
Commissions	$ 35,600	
Show	28,000	
Wages	25,200	
Salaries	21,600	
Automobile	7,200	
Rent	3,600	
Telephone	3,300	
Advertising	3,000	
Interest	2,250	
Travel and entertainment	1,440	
Insurance	1,200	
Supplies	780	
Legal and accounting	600	
Dues	600	134,370
Operating Profit		$ 64,830

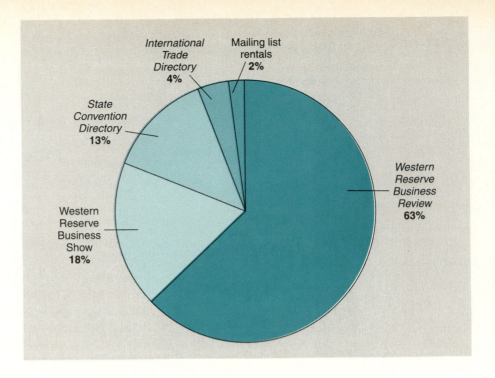

EXHIBIT 5A.6
Alpha Multi-Media Group, Inc.: Breakdown of sales revenues by product.

International Trade Directory 4%

Mailing list rentals 2%

State Convention Directory 13%

Western Reserve Business Review 63%

Western Reserve Business Show 18%

best to recruit and motivate the many nonmanagerial employees that would be needed if sales revenues soared to $3 million. He addressed this problem in his plan:

"If a business is to remain profitable and to serve its markets well, it must attract and keep *exceptional* men and women. We strongly believe that people are our most valuable asset, and that a climate must be created that will encourage people to give their best efforts. We can only be strong if we have motivated people who, by their work, display a sense of urgency about our business and about our customers.

Questions

1. Do you believe that Bruce David can make a success of the Alpha Multi-Media Group

venture? Why or why not? What is the venture's potential?

2. Comment on David's entrepreneurial experiences, especially as they bear on his management of the venture. On what should he concentrate his efforts? Why?

3. Is David's marketing strategy sound? Why or why not?

4. Comment on the team that David has assembled to help him manage the venture. How well do their talents mesh?

5. What does David stand to gain if the venture is successful? What will he lose if it fails?

Virginia Baerga

A graduate of Cuyahoga Community College with a major in entrepreneurship, Virginia Baerga believes she is now ready to go into business for herself. One opportunity that intrigues her is a women's apparel shop for sale in her community. She worked there on Saturdays when she was in high school and in college.

Now 33 years old and an assistant buyer with a major department store chain, Baerga knows the women's apparel business "inside out." Totally dedicated, she recalls a professor's advice:

▶ The secret to success is finding something worth doing that you enjoy doing so much that you would do it for free—and then learning to do it so well, that people will pay you well to do it.

Buying a business is, of course, a complex matter. Unavoidably, there are many analytical problems— among them, setting the purchase price, evaluating the business's future, and closing the "deal in a safe, legal, and equitable way." There are pitfalls all along the way.

The shop's owner told Baerga that she could review his latest financial statements. The latest income statement, in condensed form, appears in Exhibit 5B.1; the latest balance sheet, in Exhibit 5B.2.

The owner seeks $150,000 for his shop. "The business has provided a good living for me and

EXHIBIT 5B.1
Income Statement (1995).

Sales revenues	$357,000
Cost of goods sold	211,000
Gross profit	$ 46,000
Operating expenses	135,000*
Operating profit	$ 11,000
Income taxes	3,000
Net profit	$ 8,000

*Includes owner's salary of $54,000

EXHIBIT 5B.2
Balance Sheet (December 31, 1995).

Assets		Equities	
Inventories	$71,000	Accounts payable	$53,000
Other assets	22,000	Other liabilities	21,000
		Owners' equity	19,000
Total assets	$93,000		$93,000

my family," the owner told Baerga. "I'm sure that you, too, will benefit."

Questions

1. What steps would you recommend that Virginia Baerga take before deciding whether to buy the women's apparel shop?
2. Applying the methods of pricing a business described in the chapter, what do you recommend that Baerga pay for the shop if she decides to make an offer? Explain.
3. Imagine that you are an experienced women's apparel retailer and an old friend of Baerga's. Assuming that you know as much about the shop for sale as Baerga, what questions would you raise?

CASE 5C ▶ *Wilson Stove Company*

After 15 years as a loyal employee, Thomas Wilson bought what was to become the Wilson Stove Company. The company sells high-quality coal-burning stoves that are superior in design to most of its competitors' products.

To help manage the business, Wilson brought in his brother, Alvin. The brothers worked together profitably for many years, until Thomas retired. Soon after Alvin took over all operations, he expanded the product line to include fiberglass boats. This expansion proved to be a major mistake, and the firm suffered serious losses. Realizing that the company he helped build might be lost, Thomas came back to work and eventually sold the ill-fated boat division.

A Seemingly Endless Search

Thomas Wilson still wanted to retire, and he began to look for buyers. He finally sold the company to a group of business people in a neighboring state, but the business began to experience problems. Thomas, still keenly interested in the business, was aware of these problems. Eventually he decided to buy back the company.

Five more times in a period of less than five years, Thomas sold the business only to buy it back again because the new owners were either incompetent or were not running the business the way he felt it should be run. Today, Wilson is still looking for a buyer.

Questions

1. What is Thomas Wilson's real problem? What is really behind his efforts to sell?
2. If Wilson came to you for advice, what would you suggest that he do now? Why?

Source: Adapted from W. Gibb Dyer, Jr., *Cultural Change in Family Firms.* Copyright © 1986 by Jossey-Bass, Inc., Publishers. Used with permission.

CHAPTER 6

Franchises

To be what we are, and to become what we are capable of becoming, is the only end of life.

—*Benedict Spinoza*

In Chapters 4 and 5, we discussed two ways of going into business for one-self: Starting from scratch or buying out an existing business. A third way is to buy a franchise.

Today, few business topics spark more controversy than franchising. Opinions about its place in the economy differ sharply. Some see franchising as the last frontier of the would-be entrepreneur; others see it as a fraud. Neither extreme is correct—the truth lies somewhere in between. This chapter tries to put franchising in proper perspective.

A History and Definition of Franchising

Contrary to popular opinion, franchising did not begin with the boom of fast-food franchises like McDonald's in the 1950s. Rather, its beginnings date back to the early 1800s. But modern franchising got its first real push in 1898, when General Motors began franchising dealerships. Still alive and well today, that franchise system boasts 10,500 dealers scattered throughout the country. This is how the system works:

The franchised automobile dealer signs a contract with the manufacturer to serve as its representative in an area. The dealer then sells only that line of automobiles—for example, Saturns. In some areas, the dealer may even have a double franchise and sell, say, Thunderbirds made by Ford Motor Company as well as Saturns made by General Motors. ▲▼▲

Since the 1950s, franchising has grown so rapidly that it has made inroads into virtually every industry, ranging from bagels to on-call physicians, from nanny services to law enforcement. Moreover, franchising now accounts for more than one-third of all retail sales.[1] And between 1982 and 1991, sales

EXHIBIT 6.1

Franchise growth measured in sales revenues and by number. Between 1982 and 1991, the number of franchise units increased 22 percent, and franchise sales revenues increased 45 percent (sales in billions of 1991 dollars).

Source: As reported by Dan Fost and Susan Mitchell, "Small Stores with Big Names," *American Demographics*, November 1992, from the International Franchise Association. Used with permission of the International Franchise Association.

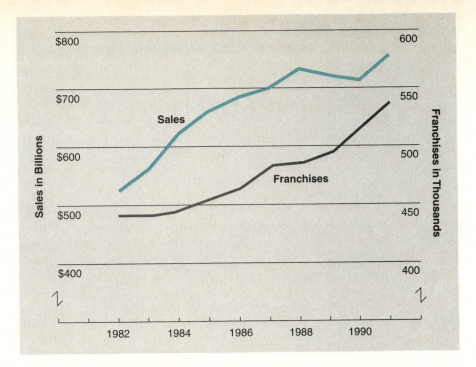

from all types of franchising—in manufacturing, retailing, services, or wholesaling—climbed 45 percent, to $758 billion, as shown in Exhibit 6.1.

The word *franchising* comes from the French word *franchir,* which means "to free"; originally it meant "to free from slavery." Today, it has several other meanings, depending on the industry. Some people even call franchising itself an industry, as if it were a product or service. But a typical franchise is simply an agreement between seller and buyer—an agreement that permits the buyer (*franchisee*) to sell the product or service of the seller (*franchisor*). The International Franchise Association defines it this way:

> A franchise is a continuing relationship between the franchisor and the franchisee in which the sum total of the franchisor's knowledge, image, success, manufacturing, and marketing techniques are supplied to the franchisee for a consideration.

The Appeal of Franchising

In essence, franchisees buy a ready-made business. And therein lies the appeal of franchising, since franchisees avoid having to build a business step by step, as must entrepreneurs who start from scratch. Rather, the franchisee's business materializes full blown, virtually overnight. And it often is a carbon copy of all the others in the franchise chain.

Franchises thrive in virtually every setting; here in the form of a candy vendor's kiosk in the lobby of an airport.

In return for their investment, franchisees expect to receive professional help that might otherwise be well beyond their reach. Such help might cover one or more of or—as in the case of large, familiar franchisors like McDonald's—even all of the following needs:

▶ Marketing strategy, with emphasis on advertising

▶ Store or office design and equipment purchasing

▶ Initial employee and management training

▶ Standardized policies and procedures

▶ Centralized purchasing with savings

▶ Continued management counseling

▶ Site selection and advice

▶ Negotiation of leases

▶ Computer applications

▶ Legal services

▶ Financing

As detailed in Exhibit 6.2, this is just the kind of help from the franchisor that fosters franchisee satisfaction—according to a study by Nerilee Hing of Southern Cross University in Lismore, Australia.[2] Besides professional help, franchisees might also derive other advantages, though mostly intangible, as

EXHIBIT 6.2

Initial franchisee support services contributing to franchisee satisfaction.

Initial Support Services	Highest Quality of Its Type as Rated by Franchisees
Initial training	One-on-one instruction at another outlet for 36 to 60 days, in addition to formalized training at a central location.
Help with site selection	Franchisor researched, negotiated, and selected sites on behalf of franchisees.
Help with purchasing equipment	Franchisor selected and negotiated prices, recommended suppliers, and so on.
Help with financing	Franchisor worked directly with financial institution on franchisees' behalf and supplied financial projections for the outlet.
Company supervisor of startup	Franchisor provided supervisory assistance for 30 days.
Help with facility design	Franchisor provided full turnkey* operations for franchises

*This term means that a franchisee would occupy an outlet only after the franchisor has finished readying *and* debugging the outlet.

Source: Adapted from Nerilee Hing, "Franchisee Satisfaction: Contributors and Consequences," *Journal of Small Business Management* (April 1995), p. 21.

shown in Exhibit 6.3; also shown are some likely disadvantages, chief among them a lack of independence, which will be discussed later.

Thus, franchising thrives largely because it combines the promise of personal ownership with the managerial skills of big business—as exemplified by familiar franchisors like McDonald's and Domino's. And, of course, personal ownership is one of the best incentives yet invented to spur commitment and hard work.

Franchising benefits not only the franchisee but also the franchisor. Specifically, it enables the franchisor to grow rapidly by using other people's (franchisee's) money. This is largely how familiar franchisors like McDonald's and Baskin-Robbins have mushroomed into billion-dollar businesses in so short a time. Besides enabling the franchisor to expand rapidly, franchising also allows the franchisor to expand into geographic areas that otherwise might not be likely locations for expansion. Because the franchisor needs fewer managers, payroll costs are lower and the potential for staff problems is decreased. In addition, franchisees are likely to be more highly motivated than company-employed managers.[3]

EXHIBIT 6.3
Selected advantages and
disadvantages of familiar
franchises

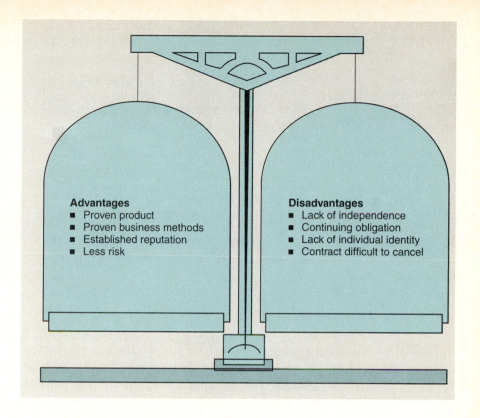

Advantages
- Proven product
- Proven business methods
- Established reputation
- Less risk

Disadvantages
- Lack of independence
- Continuing obligation
- Lack of individual identity
- Contract difficult to cancel

▶ The Reach of Franchising

Although it has grown vigorously since the 1970s, franchising appears to be slowing down. According to Mark Siebert, a franchise consultant in Olympia Fields, Illinois:

> The franchise boom isn't as aggressive as it was in the 1970s, but it's still a very dynamic market. We may be entering a new period of growth in franchising, with a significant increase in the number of large companies interested in franchising.[4]

Supporting Siebert's view is David Kaufman, a franchise lawyer in New York City, who says:

> One trend is the entry into franchising of some of the nation's largest corporations, which hitherto were not involved in franchising and indeed may have viewed it as somewhat suspect. Now these large companies are very much attracted to franchising and the benefits it affords, including the ability to rapidly penetrate a marketplace with minimum capital expenditure.[5]

Indeed, it appears that, as franchising matures and comes of age, bigness will follow. "Bigger is better" already seems to be the rule among franchisees who build multi-million-dollar empires by buying many more than a single

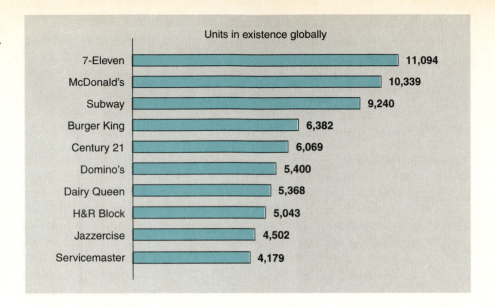

EXHIBIT 6.4
The ten largest franchisors by number of units globally (as of January 1995).

Source: Adapted from *Entrepreneur* Magazine and International Franchise Association; reported by Earl C. Gottschalk Jr., "Tax Shop? Gym? Finding a Franchise Without Losing Your Shirt," *The New York Times* (March 26, 1995), Section 3, p. 12.

franchise, thus tending to undermine the popular image of franchisees as "little guys."

"Bigger is better" is a creed that also drives major franchisors like McDonald's and Subway, so much so that they are now too costly for most people. In 1995, for example, the cost of a McDonald's franchise approached a half million dollars. The implications of the trend to bigness are plain. With familiar franchises like McDonald's or Jiffy Lube beyond their reach, most people may have no choice but to consider buying only less familiar franchises that "are not the safe and secure, absolute certainties that franchisors tout."[6]

Further evidence of franchising's trend to bigness appears in Exhibit 6.4, which lists the top ten franchisors by number of units. In 1995, most of these franchisors posted sales revenues in excess of a billion dollars.

Kinds of Franchising Systems

As shown in Exhibit 6.5, franchise systems may take many forms. These systems are by no means limited to chains like McDonald's and Jazzercise. For example, franchise systems may connect:

▶ Manufacturer and manufacturer
▶ Manufacturer and wholesaler
▶ Manufacturer and retailer
▶ Wholesaler and wholesaler
▶ Wholesaler and retailer
▶ Retailer and retailer
▶ Service provider and service provider

EXHIBIT 6.5
Variety of franchising.

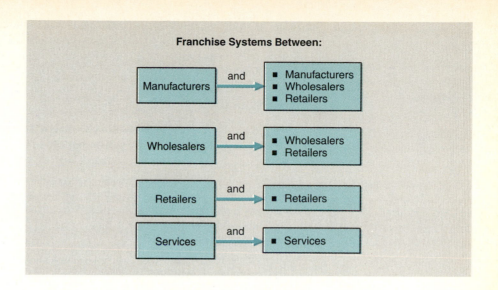

Let us look first at franchise systems between manufacturer and manufacturer. Suppose a chemical manufacturer patents a new way to make sulfuric acid. Because this process cuts the cost of making sulfuric acid by, say, 20 percent, other chemical manufacturers want to use it. The chemical manufacturer who invented the process then licenses the others, giving them the right to use the new process in return for a fee, called a *royalty*. In this case, the licensor is really a franchisor, and the licensee is a franchisee.

With a manufacturer-to-manufacturer franchising system, franchisees are relatively autonomous, all but free to do as they please. For example, policies and procedures can be of their own making; even the shop and equipment can be of their own design.

Another franchise system connects manufacturer and retailer. An example of such a system is that between automobile manufacturers and retail automobile dealerships. Still another example is service stations, which lease space and sell gasoline and oil bought under contract from oil refiners like Texaco. Franchise systems between manufacturer and wholesaler, wholesaler and wholesaler, and wholesaler and retailer run in similar ways.

Retail and service franchise systems like Domino's and Quality Inn differ markedly from manufacturer and wholesaler systems, because the franchisee is really an extension of the franchisor. Here, each franchise resembles a company outlet, the main difference being that the franchisor invested the franchisee's money instead of its own money to create the outlet.

Myths about Franchising

▶ **The Myth of Instant Success**

The fast growth of franchising has spawned a number of myths. Perhaps the most popular one is the promise of instant success. Get-rich-quick schemes abound. Many prey on lower-income men and women looking for a way to become rich without having to work for someone else.

Also perceived as easy prey are early retirees who seek a second act in life. Unethical franchisors take in the innocent, such as retirees, with overblown promises of instant success, or even overnight riches. Take this example, as reported by *The New York Times*:

> After a long career as a broadcasting executive, Gene Swanzy decided to take early retirement [in 1990] to run his own business.
>
> Impressed by Mail Boxes Etc., a San Diego-based chain of postal and shipping stores, Mr. Swanzy and his wife, Mary Anna Severson, a public television executive, took action. They bought two of the postal shipping service franchises in the Washington suburb of Arlington, Virginia.
>
> Today, Mr. Swanzy is sorry he ever heard of franchising. So far, he and his wife have invested $300,000 in the two stores, and still are $250,000 in debt without taking out a dime in salary. "It's been a horrendous experience," said Mr. Swanzy, now 63 [in 1995]. "I blew my retirement money, and now I'm trapped."
>
> The couple has joined 29 other franchise operators in a fraud and misrepresentation suit against Mail Boxes Etc. The company, which vigorously denies the charges, has filed a cross complaint against the Swanzys.[7]

▶ Failure Rates: Franchisees Versus Independents

Still another myth, so deeply embedded as to become the conventional wisdom, hails franchising as unquestionably the least risky road to success for would-be entrepreneurs. In 1994, for example, an advertisement in *Business Week* claimed that:

> A franchisee has a four times greater chance to succeed than an entrepreneur who launches a new independent business.[8]

But in stark contrast, and according to an exhaustive study by Timothy Bates of Wayne State University, franchising is anything but a safe, risk-free haven for would-be entrepreneurs. His study covered a sampling of 20,000 young small retailers, relying on nationwide data gathered by the U.S. Bureau of the Census. In analyzing these data, Professor Bates found that, of those retailers who were in business in 1987:

▶ 45 percent of the young *franchised* retailers had failed by 1991; but just—

▶ 23 percent of the young *independent* retailers had failed by 1991.[9]

Why so dramatic a difference between the conventional wisdom and Bates's findings? The most plausible explanation is that franchise associations and other interested parties have relied on survivor information supplied by the franchisors themselves—that is, by the companies selling franchises—rather than on information by the actual franchisees whose survival is at issue. In contrast, Bates's study took the opposite tack in its focus on franchisees rather than on the word of franchisors, many of whom are likely to have an interest in seeming more successful than they really are.

Another myth is that franchisees are independent businesspersons. In many cases, this simply is not so. Franchisees generally are not free to run their businesses as they see fit. They often are hamstrung by the franchisor's policies, standards, and procedures. Nor do franchisors encourage their franchisees to improve the way they do business. In fact, they often look for persons who are able to understand their systems but who have no wish to improve them.[10]

According to one franchisor, "The ideal franchisee [is] the sergeant type—midway between the general who gives the orders and the private who merely follows them. People who want their own business to escape taking orders from others frequently see franchising as the answer. They are subsequently frustrated by their lack of autonomy."[11] For example, the franchisee may not be able to change items such as advertising, inventory, and decor.

Selecting a Franchise

In a real sense, franchisees do not start from scratch. When they buy a franchise, they generally receive a ready-made business. Then all they need to do is follow the franchisor's instructions on how best to do business. Instructions cover a host of details, among them:

▶ What product or service to sell

▶ How to sell it

▶ How to control costs

▶ What reports to prepare

▶ How long to stay open each day

First Steps

Before buying a franchise, entrepreneurs first should make sure that the decision to become a franchisee is sound. Outlined in Exhibit 6.6 is a step-by-step procedure that they should follow.

Doing a self-analysis is the first step. This calls for entrepreneurs to identify and define their skills and desires. The next two steps—choosing a product or service and searching out likely franchises—should proceed at the same time because they focus on these pivotal questions:

▶ Do I really believe in, and would I be happy with, this product or service?

▶ Do I really want to be this kind of person, do this kind of work, and run this kind of franchise?

Reviewing a Checklist of Questions

These questions are just a beginning. To do a thorough job of analyzing a franchise opportunity, entrepreneurs should next go through a checklist like the one in Exhibit 6.7. This checklist of 25 questions may spare entrepreneurs the pain of making a wrong decision or being hurt by unkept promises.

Entrepreneurs interested in a franchise should make sure that the training program is thorough, that royalties and fees (such as advertising) are within

EXHIBIT 6.6

Procedure for evaluating franchise opportunities.

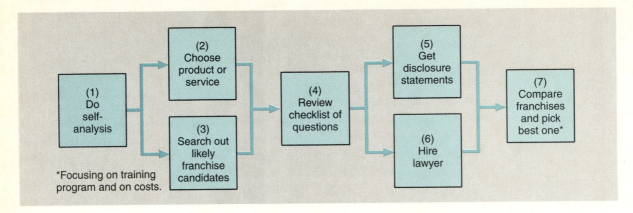

*Focusing on training program and on costs.

EXHIBIT 6.7

Checklist for evaluating a franchise.

On the Franchise Opportunity Itself

1. Did your lawyer approve the franchise contract after he studied it paragraph by paragraph?

2. Does the franchise call upon you to take any steps which are, according to your lawyer, unwise or illegal in your state, county, or city?

3. Does the franchise give you an exclusive territory for the length of the franchise or can the franchisor sell a second or third franchise in your territory?

4. Is the franchisor connected in any way with any other franchise companies handling similar merchandise or services?

5. If the answer to the last question is yes, what is your protection against this second franchisor organization?

6. Under what circumstances and at what cost can you pull out of the franchise contract?

7. If you sell your franchise, will you be paid for your goodwill, or will the goodwill you have built into the business be lost to you?

On the Franchisor

1. For how many years has the franchisor been in business?

2. Does the franchisor have a reputation for honesty and fair dealing among the local entrepreneurs holding its franchise?

3. Has the franchisor shown you any certified figures indicating exact net profits of one or more going franchises, which you *yourself* checked with the franchisee?

4. Will the franchisor help you with:

   a. A management training program?

   b. An employee training program?

   c. A public relations program?

   d. Merchandising ideas?

   e. Financing?

5. Will the franchisor help you find a good location for your franchise?

6. Is the franchisor adequately financed so that it can carry out its stated plan of financial help and expansion?

7. Is the franchisor a one-man company or a larger company with a trained and experienced management team—so that there would always be an experienced person as its head?

8. Exactly what can the franchisor do for you which you cannot do for yourself?

9. Has the franchisor investigated you carefully enough to assure itself that you can successfully operate one of their franchises at a profit both to them and to you?

On You—the Franchisee

1. How much equity capital will you need to buy the franchise and operate it until your sales revenues equal your expenses?

2. Where are you going to get the equity capital you need?

3. Are you prepared to give up some independence of action to get the advantages offered by the franchise?

4. Do *you* really believe you have the ability, training, and experience to work smoothly and profitably with the franchisor, your employees, and your customers?

5. Are you ready to spend much or all of the rest of your business life with this franchisor, offering its product or service to your public?

On Your Market

1. Have you made any study to find out whether the product or service which you propose to sell under franchise has a market in your territory at the prices you will have to charge?

2. Will the population in your territory increase, remain static, or decrease over the next five years?

3. Will the demand for the product or service you are considering be greater, about the same, or less in five years?

4. What competition exists in your territory for the product or service from nonfranchise firms and franchise firms?

Source: U.S. Department of Commerce, *Franchise Opportunities Handbook* (Washington, D.C.: U.S. Government Printing Office, June 1991), p. xi.

the industry norm, that any extra costs are affordable, and that suppliers offer competitive prices. Unless franchisees use a checklist to thoroughly analyze a franchise opportunity, they may make costly mistakes in judgment. An entrepreneur's best defense against such mistakes is the checklist.

▶ Getting Disclosure Statements (UFOCs)

To evaluate a franchise opportunity, an entrepreneur should ask the franchisor for its Uniform Franchise Offering Circular (UFOC), which is a disclosure statement. A priceless tool, this statement should enable entrepreneurs to answer many of the questions posed in the checklist. It also should enable them to compare one franchise with another, understand what to expect from the franchisor, and estimate the risks and costs involved.

All franchisors are now required by federal law to provide UFOCs. The law requires that these statements give detailed information on a number of subjects, a sampling of which follows:

▶ The franchisor's financial statements for the past three years

▶ A description of the lawsuits in which the franchisor and its officers, directors, and managers have been involved

▶ Information about the initial franchise fee and other initial payments that are required to obtain the franchise

▶ A description of the involvement of any celebrities or public figures in the franchise

▶ A list of the names and addresses of other franchisees

▶ A sample copy of the franchise agreement and any other legally binding documents the entrepreneur may have to sign

▶ An estimate of the entrepreneur's initial expenses, broken down into such categories as opening inventory and working capital, real estate expenses and leasehold improvements[12]

▶ Hiring a Lawyer

Entrepreneurs should rely on a lawyer to grasp the fine print of a franchisor's UFOC. It is a mistake to assume that the statement tells everything there is to know about the franchisor. Nor does it necessarily tell all about the consequences of signing a franchise contract. Moreover, arrangements between franchisor and franchisee vary widely, as Exhibit 6.8 suggests.

Thus, it is vital for entrepreneurs to seek the help of a lawyer familiar with the legal workings of franchising. This kind of lawyer can also inform entrepreneurs fully about their legal rights before they sign the franchise contract. Equally important, the lawyer can advise entrepreneurs about their legal obligations to the franchisor. But perhaps the lawyer's most creative role is to suggest changes in the contract that would better serve and protect the entrepreneur's interest. According to the U.S. Department of Commerce:

> At the very least, you should be certain that every promise you consider important made by the franchisor and its representative is stated clearly in writing in the franchise contract. If such promises do not clearly appear in the contracts you sign, you may have no legal remedy if they are not kept;

EXHIBIT 6.8
Franchising arrangements.

Business format franchises	Based on a specific operating system; consist mainly of retail and service businesses. Franchisor provides franchisee with formal training and continued support.
Piggyback franchises	Two or more franchised businesses that share space to offer a more comprehensive product or service to customers.
Conversion franchises	Independent businesses that become franchised units of existing franchises.
Distributorships	Franchisees that distribute products manufactured by franchisor or some other source.
Area franchises	Franchisees that have the right to run franchise on territorial basis; this allows franchisee to develop entire city, state, or region.
Single-unit franchises	Franchisees that have the right to run franchise at only one site.
Multi-unit franchises	Franchisees that have rights to open several franchise units at once.
Trade-name franchises	Franchises that develop from supplier relationships in ways similar to distributorship agreement. Franchisors supply product that franchisee sells under franchised trademark or logo.
Subfranchises	Franchised outlets sold by area franchisees to other businesspeople in their areas.

Source: Amy L. Weiss, "Franchising Arrangements." This article originally appeared in *Business Age*, the magazine for small business owners and managers, a publication of Business Trends Communication Corp., 135 W. Wells Street, 7th Floor, Milwaukee, WI 53203. For more information about *Business Age* call 1-800-635-8817. Reprinted with permission.

and you may be legally obligated to comply with your own continuing obligations under the franchise contract.[13]

Good Faith and Fair Dealing

Implicit in any contractual arrangement is the exercise of good faith and fair dealing by both parties. A franchisee who underreports sales revenues in estimating royalty payments betrays a lack of good faith, just as surely as a franchisor who imposes unreasonable fee demands to discourage the renewal of a successful franchise.

The U.S. Congress dealt with the principles of good faith and fair dealing in passing the Automobile Franchise Act of 1956. The act defines *good faith* this way:

> The duty of each party to any franchise is to act in a fair and equitable manner toward each other, so as to guarantee each party's freedom from coercion, intimidation, or threats of coercion.[14]

Here is an example of a franchisor who exercised good faith and fair play:

> Debra Olson, who opened the first USA Baby Inc. franchise in 1986 in Marietta, Georgia, says the franchisor made sure she did not fail. When construction problems delayed the opening of the infant furniture and accessories shop, the company agreed to guarantee her payments to major suppliers.
>
> In fact, the franchisor even dispatched a staffer to help Olson call worried suppliers and assure them about payment—a month late. "We had no credit and no track record in business," she says. "Corporate headquarters stood behind us."[15]

▶ Negotiating the Franchise Contract

The contract is the backbone of any franchisor-franchisee relationship. Selected franchisor guarantees and selected franchisee contractual obligations appear in Exhibit 6.9. Failure to understand the contract's fine print may cause the entrepreneur trouble later. For example, it is crucial to ask, "Under what conditions can I pull out of the franchise contract and what would it cost to pull out?"

Entrepreneurs should make sure they understand what they may lose or gain if they should decide to pull out, or if the franchisor decides to cancel the franchise contract. Typically, franchisors reserve the right to cancel a franchise contract if the franchisee:

▶ Fails to reach sales goals

▶ Tarnishes the image of other outlets by giving poor service to customers

▶ Fails to provide required weekly or monthly progress reports to the franchisor

Other, less precise reasons for canceling a franchisee's contract include:

▶ Failure to work hard and for long hours

▶ Failure to work smoothly with the franchisor

▶ Misuse of the franchisor's name and equipment

Typically, franchise rights run one to five years, with options to renew. An exception is McDonald's, which sells for $485,000 the right to operate a franchise at a specific site for 20 years. When the contract expires, the franchisee must put up another $485,000, adjusted for inflation, to continue operating at the same site. Unlike McDonald's, some franchise rights run indefinitely—but

EXHIBIT 6.9
Selected franchisor
guarantees and franchisee
contractual obligations.

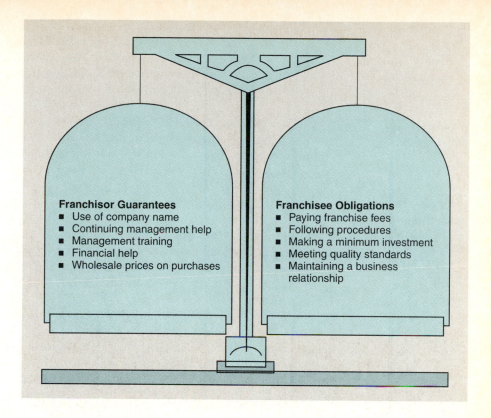

Franchisor Guarantees
- Use of company name
- Continuing management help
- Management training
- Financial help
- Wholesale prices on purchases

Franchisee Obligations
- Paying franchise fees
- Following procedures
- Making a minimum investment
- Meeting quality standards
- Maintaining a business relationship

generally the contract has a clause that gives either the franchisor or the franchisee the right to cancel with 30 to 60 days' notice.

Selling the Franchise

A problem may arise if the franchisee decides to sell out before the contract runs out. Such sales generally cannot be carried out without the franchisor's approval. This seems like a distinct drawback of franchising, as explained here:

> The right to sell or transfer the franchise determines whether or not a franchisee is truly an independent owner of a business, or merely an affiliate within a chain. Contract provisions should reflect your rights to build a profitable business and then sell it on the open market. The reputable company will do everything to protect its trademarks, patents, and uniquely developed services, but it should not—and must not—deprive you of the right to sell or transfer *your* business.[16]

Another sore point is the price at which a franchisee may sell the franchise, either to another entrepreneur or back to the franchisor. The franchisor often forces the franchisee to sell at a price lower than its value to a prospective buyer. For example, a franchise may be worth $50,000 more than its book value to a prospective buyer. If the franchise is sold, who deserves the gain of $50,000, the franchisor or the franchisee?

Franchisors may claim that it was their image that generated the $50,000 gain. Franchisees may counter that it was really their hard work that created the gain. To avoid the problem, entrepreneurs should make sure they have the right to sell the franchise at the highest possible price and that they can pocket the entire selling price. McDonald's has an enlightened attitude in this regard:

In 1991, a franchisee sold his McDonald's restaurant for $660,000. Its value on the books was about $220,000. The franchisee got to keep the entire capital gain of $440,000. McDonald's had an interesting though imprecise way of arriving at the purchase price of the franchise. It took the most recent year's sales revenues and multiplied by half. ▲▼▲

▶ Evaluating a Franchisor's Training Program

Perhaps the most crucial question to consider in evaluating a franchisor relates to the franchisor's training program. Reputable franchisors like Wendy's and Baskin-Robbins provide intensive training programs, including on-the-job training at an existing outlet. Some franchisors even provide refresher training after the franchisee has been operating for some time. Exhibit 6.10 traces the sequence of steps that, ideally, franchisors should follow in training their franchisees.

The main goal of these training programs is to supply entrepreneurs with the managerial skills they need to run a franchise profitably. Without this training, the inexperienced franchisee is likely to founder and fail. Entrepreneurs should make sure their franchise contract tells precisely how and where training will take place. McDonald's, for example, provides a three-step training program:

1. **Instruction at a training school** McDonald's has a school near Chicago called Hamburger University. After a three-week cram course on how to run a franchise profitably, franchisees receive a degree in "Hamburgerology." Courses cover everything from how to mop the floor to how to post a ledger.
2. **Instruction at an existing franchisee's site** McDonald's has every new franchisee spend at least one week with an established franchisee. While there, the new franchisee works at every job, from sweeping the parking lot to waiting on customers.
3. **Instruction at own site** McDonald's provides franchisees with an experienced instructor to help them over the rough edges of startup.

EXHIBIT 6.10
Franchisee training.

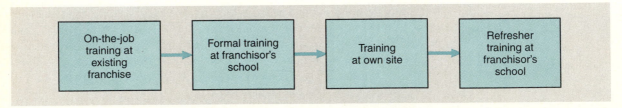

The instructor works side by side with the franchisee for at least a week—until the instructor is sure the franchisee can go it alone.

▶ Estimating the Costs to the Franchisee

Entrepreneurs should take pains to estimate what a franchise will cost, because franchisors often fail to tell entrepreneurs the full story. A franchisor may say, for example, that "all you need is $20,000 to buy a wall-cleaning franchise." But the $20,000 may cover just the right to use the franchisor's trade name and way of doing business. Hidden may be the costs of equipment, lease deposits, or even the signs needed to open the franchise—not to mention the money to finance inventory or to finance customers who buy on credit.

Entrepreneurs can avoid these problems by preparing a business plan, as discussed in Chapter 4. The cash budget, a key part of the business plan, identifies all cash costs, including the franchise fee, working capital, building and equipment costs, and royalties:

▶ **The franchise fee**   This gives the franchisee the right to do business at a specific address or in a specific territory. Depending on the franchise, this fee may range from nothing to millions of dollars. As mentioned earlier, McDonald's charges a fee of $485,000 for a 20-year contract.

▶ **Working capital**   This covers the money needed to buy inventory, pay salespersons, make lease payments, and so on—until customers buy and pay up.

▶ **Building and equipment costs**   The entrepreneur may pay for these in full or in part. Some franchisors lease both building and equipment to the franchisee, thus sparing the entrepreneur the need to make a large initial cash outlay. McDonald's charges a leasing fee of 8.5 percent of sales revenues.

▶ **Royalties**   These generally range from 0 to 15 percent of sales revenues. In return for the royalty payment, the franchisee may get such services as advertising, financial statements, and managerial advice. McDonald's, for example, charges a royalty of 3 percent on sales. Thus a franchisee with yearly sales of $1.2 million pays McDonald's $36,000 a year in royalties.

As with any other type of venture, financing a franchise can pose problems if entrepreneurs have little savings, although potential franchise buyers generally have higher than average incomes, as shown in Exhibit 6.11. Typically, the reputable franchisor wants the entrepreneur to put up at least half the money needed to get started, as equity capital. Often, the entrepreneur raises the money by selling stock to relatives and friends or borrowing from them to buy stock in his or her own name. The remaining half may be borrowed from a commercial bank, often with the franchisor as a cosigner of the note.

❋   ❋   ❋

The foregoing describes in some detail a procedure for evaluating and comparing franchise opportunities. In the process, one franchise opportunity is likely to stand out as being best suited to the entrepreneur's needs in terms of lifestyle, budget, location, and so on. Thus, this procedure enables an entrepreneur who, for example, may want to be a fast-food franchisee to compare

EXHIBIT 6.11

Percent of potential franchise buyers and of all U.S. households, by income. Potential franchise buyers generally have higher than average incomes.

Sources: Franchise Marketing & Sales Survey, 1990–91, and U.S. Bureau of the Census, reported by Dan Fost and Susan Mitchell, "Small Stores with Big Names," *American Demographics;* November 1992, p. 52.

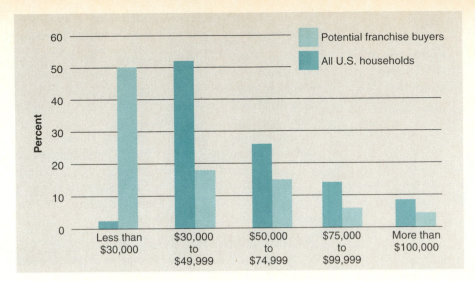

such franchisors as Burger Chef, Burger King, and Wendy's and be confident of making an intelligent choice.

Franchise Opportunities for Minorities

Until the mid-1960s, there were few minority franchisees. For example, in 1967, not a single McDonald's franchise was owned by a black entrepreneur. This picture has changed dramatically. By 1994, there were 658 black-owned units, or 7.2 percent of the total number of McDonald's U.S. units.[17]

Similar gains have been made in other industries, thanks to a more enlightened attitude toward minorities. In fact, more than 1,300 franchisors have declared that their franchises are open to all would-be entrepreneurs, regardless of race.[18]

It is vital, however, not to mistake progress for arrival. Minorities have a long way to go before they own their proportionate share of franchises. To quicken the pace, the federal government has been pushing franchising as a good way to improve the economic lot of minorities. Indeed, franchising offers special promise to minorities with little experience, enabling them to own businesses with the backing of big-business practices. Take this example:

EXAMPLE ▶

"One glance at the brightly colored African-print patterns on the walls and the faces of entertainers on the Apollo 'Wall of Fame' tells you there is something different about Carole Riley's McDonald's in Harlem. Then the mouth-watering scent of french fries and cheeseburgers and the smell of grease quickly remind you that this is a 'Mickey D' in Afro-centric clothing."

So began a 1992 feature story in *The New York Times* about two black partners—Carole Riley and Kelli Givens—who own two McDonald's franchises. Rarely do McDonald's franchisees put their personal stamp on their shops. But, contrary to form, these two women did. In fact, they designed their two McDonald's shops to reflect the "grace and style of Harlem U.S.A.," as they put it.

Among the unique touches are the African kente cloth uniforms worn by workers. There are also statues by George Mingo, a Harlem artist known the world over. Gracing the walls are paintings by prominent black artists. And their Apollo "Wall of Fame" features the faces of such entertainers as Duke Ellington and Michael Jackson.

Sound business logic underlies the shops' unique design. In the words of Givens, "People often don't realize that each McDonald's is a separately owned community business. We didn't want people in this area to feel this was just another large corporation taking their money. We think what we've done will make people more likely to patronize the stores."[19] ▲▼▲

Women in Franchising

Until the 1980s, few franchisees were women, especially in fast-food services, automobile dealerships, and other traditionally male-dominated industries. The number of franchises owned by women has grown, but male owners still far outnumber female owners.

As mentioned in Chapter 2, the SBA found that women are starting small businesses at a faster rate than men. Yet just the opposite is true with franchises. Why? Susan Kezios, founder of the Chicago-based association Women In Franchising, Inc., offers this explanation:

> Though there's been a lot of hype about recruiting women franchisees, there have been no numbers to back it up. Statistically, women in franchising are either treading water or sinking. They're starting businesses at twice the rate of men, but they aren't getting into franchising.[20]

Kezios believes that the number one reason for the absence of women in franchising is the white, "old boys' network." She claims many male franchisors "don't have a clue" about how to attract and deal with women franchisees. "There's outright sexism in the industry."

Indeed, it appears that franchising has failed to bridge the gap between good intentions and good results. Although franchisors often tout their commitment to equal opportunities, their lack of action belies their word.

Global Franchising

The decade of the 1980s brought with it a global boom in franchising. From Europe to Asia to Africa, U.S. franchisors have found receptive markets and vast opportunities to export their way of doing business. For example, on the opening day of McDonald's first restaurant in Kuwait in 1994, the drive-through line was *seven* miles long. In fact, so popular is McDonald's that half its profits came from overseas in 1994.[21] Small wonder, then, that familiar franchisors like McDonald's find global markets, which offer these advantages, among others:

▸ Franchisors can grow more quickly, by relying on a country's franchisees to finance their ventures.

▸ Franchisors can more readily penetrate markets by relying on the franchisees' knowledge of their country's unique culture.

Moreover, franchises are thriving globally because, unlike businesses seeking only to market U.S. products or to build U.S.-owned plants, they offer opportunities for local entrepreneurs within a foreign market. Especially appealing to those entrepreneurs is the opportunity to master U.S. business methods and technology.

Global franchising is, of course, a two-way process. Today, more and more foreign franchisors are looking for opportunities in the United States. Canadian franchisors enjoy the largest U.S. presence, followed by British and Japanese franchisors.

SUMMARY

Franchising plays a vital role in the U.S. economy, thriving especially in retailing and, to a lesser degree, in manufacturing. Since 1982, sales revenues from all types of franchises have increased by 45 percent, to $758 billion.

Franchising thrives because it combines the incentive of personal ownership with the managerial and technical skills of big business. To entrepreneurs, franchising offers a shortcut to growth: They receive a ready-made business. To the franchisor, franchising offers quick expansion by letting entrepreneurs finance its growth through the sale of franchises.

There are several advantages to owning a franchise. First, entrepreneurs work for themselves. They also have access to proven business methods, training, and an established reputation—all of which may help minimize the financial risk. The disadvantages are that unethical operators may take in an innocent with overblown promises of instant success, that franchisees often are not free to run their businesses as they see fit, and that they are hamstrung by the franchisor's policies, standards, and procedures.

Before buying a franchise, entrepreneurs must do a thorough job of evaluating the opportunity. The selection process involves (1) doing a self-analysis; (2) choosing a product or service; (3) searching out likely franchise candidates; (4) reviewing a checklist of questions; (5) getting disclosure statements; (6) hiring a lawyer; and (7) comparing franchises and choosing the best one, primarily on the bases of training and costs.

The franchise contract is the backbone of any franchisor-franchisee relationship. The contract stipulates the obligations and guarantees on the parts of both parties.

Discussion and Review Questions

1. Is the franchisee an entrepreneur? Explain your answer fully.
2. What accounts for the importance of franchising in today's economy?
3. Why would someone choose to buy a franchise rather than start a venture from scratch or buy out an existing business?
4. Name the different kinds of franchising systems and describe how they differ.
5. Explain the myths about franchising.

6. Identify some franchising abuses and suggest ways to correct them.
7. How would you evaluate a franchise opportunity?
8. Why should would-be franchisees work closely with a lawyer before committing themselves to a franchise?
9. Describe the various franchising arrangements between franchisor and franchisee.
10. Why is the franchise contract the backbone of any franchisor-franchisee relationship?
11. What are some of the reasons for a franchisor to cancel a franchise contract?
12. Assume you are the franchisee of a pet shop. Somebody offers to buy the shop at twice its book value. In your opinion, should you or the franchisor reap the benefit of the difference between what the franchise is worth to the buyer and its worth on the books? Explain your answer.
13. What should a franchisor's managerial training program consist of to be of most benefit to the franchisees?
14. Why does franchising offer a good way for minorities to go into business for themselves?
15. Define these terms: *franchise, franchisor, franchisee, UFOC, franchise fee, working capital, royalties.*

Building a Business Plan

Franchises

Franchising, as a method of business, is designed to provide a tested formula for success, along with ongoing advice and training. And the success rate for franchised businesses may be higher than the success rate for independently owned businesses. But be warned: opinions about franchising differ sharply. As pointed out in the text, some see franchising as the last frontier of the would-be entrepreneur; others see it as a fraud. It is up to you to evaluate any potential franchise opportunity.

Instructions for Worksheet 6

While failure rates may be lower, a would-be franchise owner must still evaluate a franchise opportunity before investing any money. In part 1 of this worksheet, you should answer questions designed to narrow franchise opportunities to those that "mesh" with your own skills and with your own practical experience. Then in part 2, conduct a more in-depth evaluation of one particular franchise opportunity.

Part 1—Selecting a Franchise

Choose one particular franchise opportunity and answer the following questions. Note: You may want to answer these same questions for several franchise opportunities and then compare the results.

1. What are the advantages of this particular franchise opportunity?

2. What are the disadvantages of this particular franchise opportunity?

3. Do you really believe in, and would you be happy with, the product or service offered by this potential franchise?

4. Do you really want to do this kind of work and run this kind of franchise?

Part 2—A More In-Depth Look at One Franchise

Based on your answers to the questions in part 1, choose one specific franchise opportunity that deserves more thorough evaluation. Then, answer the 25 questions that are listed in Exhibit 6.7 on page 162 in your text.

5. Based on the answers to the questions asked in Exhibit 6.7, would this franchise be a good type of business for you to start? Justify your answer.

CASE 6A ▶ *Arthur Treacher's, Inc.*

James Cataland saw an opportunity in a problem. The problem was Arthur Treacher's, a seafood restaurant chain that was on the edge of failure. Awash in red ink, the chain had fallen from a peak of 777 stores in 1979 to 210 stores in 1984.

That year, Cataland became the chain's fourth owner. He has since made many changes to revive the chain. Although the chain has yet to turn a profit, Cataland and his management team are sure it will. One of their goals is to grow to 500 stores by the mid-1990s.

Background

"For almost as long as I can remember, I have wanted to be on my own, in a business of my own," says Cataland. "It's been a lifelong goal." Raised in a family that revered education, Cataland soon acquired the habit of learning. He graduated from high school with an A+ average; then continued to excel at Ohio State University, where he majored in marketing and earned a bachelor's degree in business administration, and at the University of Texas, where he earned a law degree and ranked in the top 10 percent of his class.

It was in law school that Cataland first "seriously entertained" the idea of striking out on his own. He went home to Youngstown, Ohio, where he first practiced law with an established firm for four years. Then, at age 28, he started his own law practice—with help from his wife, Martha, who worked as his secretary.

Cataland's practice prospered, in large part because of the Cataland name. Both his grandfather and father had earned reputations as sound citizens and businesspeople in the community.

Young Cataland received many referrals, so many that he soon had four lawyers working for him. The firm's specialty was trial law, which later led to his involvement with Arthur Treacher's.

First Encounter

Cataland prospered, with a yearly salary of more than $100,000. But the practice of law began to bore him. He wanted new challenges.

In 1982, a chance lawyer-client relationship changed his life forever. Two men had hired Cataland as their attorney to form a limited partnership called Lumara Foods. The partnership wanted to buy out a franchisee who owned six Arthur Treacher's stores in Youngstown. Eager to make a career change, Cataland agreed to do their legal work for no fee in return for a 10 percent share of the newly formed partnership.

Cataland began devoting most of his time to Lumara Foods. The more deeply immersed he became, the more fascinated he was with the tangled workings of the Arthur Treacher's chain. The chain had fallen on bad times:

▶ In just three years, the number of stores in the chain had dropped from 777 to 298. The total number of stores between 1975 and 1985 is shown in Exhibit 6A.1.

▶ Franchisees were fighting "horrendous legal battles" with the franchisor, claiming that the franchisor had failed to deliver back-up services, among them advertising materials and manuals containing policies, standards, and procedures.

A Proud Past

The failing chain of seafood restaurants had a proud history. It was founded in 1969 with a 32-seat restaurant and a large take-out menu. Its main offering was fish and chips, popular in Great Britain among Americans tourists and World War II veterans.

In ten years, the chain grew to 777 restaurants, each a near carbon copy of the original restaurant. To grow that quickly, the founders had capitalized on the name of the well-known British

EXHIBIT 6A.1
Arthur Treacher's, Inc.: Total number of company and franchise stores (1975–1985).

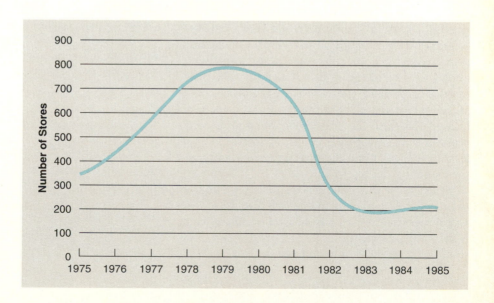

actor, Arthur Treacher, who starred for many years in the movies. His best-known role was that of the proper British butler, always played with a touch of weary dignity. Treacher also appeared regularly on the Merv Griffin television show.

As is often the case when celebrities lend their name to a product or franchise, Treacher never took part in the chain's management. Nor did he invest any of his own money. In return for the use of his name, the chain paid Treacher $80,000 a year.

Of course, Treacher's name alone did not trigger the chain's quick growth in the 1970s. Also contributing was the quality of the chain's main product, fish and chips. During the 1970s, the public was becoming aware of the need to cut back on salt and foods high in cholesterol. Riding the crest of this new concern, the chain focused its advertising on its "healthy" food:

▶ Unlike the hamburgers and hot dogs offered by other chains, fish and chips are low in salt.

▶ To cook its fish and chips, the chain uses peanut oil, which has no cholesterol.

▶ When heated, the liquid batter seals the fish and steams it, instead of frying it.

Decline and Fall

Through most of the 1970s, the chain enjoyed strong customer loyalty. In its heyday, the chain even produced humorous television commercials about the joys of eating fish and chips. One commercial described the chain's fish batter as "a secret recipe for a meal that you can't make at home." Then, in the late 1970s, the parent company and its franchisees began to squabble over the leadership of and the direction being taken by the chain.

In 1979, the founders, sensing that they had lost their influence and control over the franchisee network, sold the chain to a frozen seafood processor: Mrs. Paul's Kitchens, Inc., of Philadelphia. The founders realized $5 million from the sale.

When it took over the chain, Mrs. Paul's found nothing but problems. For one thing, the menu had not changed in ten years. Even the design of the equipment had stayed the same. It soon became clear to the new owners that if the chain was going to survive, changes had to be made—and quickly.

Lack of Leadership

The question was how best to solve the problems. The new owners found themselves facing an increasingly unhappy group of franchisees. They soon fell out over changes in the type of fish used, equipment design, and the menu.

The chaos led to a franchisee revolt and a long and costly lawsuit. Additionally, the franchisees stopped paying the new owners royalties, a move that put the chain's existence in jeopardy.

Cataland's Emergence as Sole Owner

Unable to cope with the crisis, Mrs. Paul's sold the chain in 1982 to Lumara Foods, the partnership Cataland had joined. At the time, Cataland knew very little about his partners, one of whom was later convicted of fraud and jailed. Four months after Lumara Foods bought Arthur Treacher's, the chain was forced into bankruptcy. Shortly, acting through the court, Cataland bought all of Lumara Foods.*

The Deal

Cataland bought the chain's operating assets for $700,000 without putting up a single penny of his own money—a fact that drew wide attention. Here is how it happened.

---

*Rona Ginden, "Cover Story: Can Cataland's Confidence Turn Around Arthur Treacher's?" *Restaurant News*, January 1, 1986, p. 115.

- El Charro, Inc., an inactive publicly held corporation in Denver, had raised $350,000 in 1983 (through sale of stock) to open a Mexican restaurant. When the plans fell through, the cash was left in a bank. Cataland heard of this after months of searching for such a company.

- He sold his new company, Arthur Treacher's Inc., to El Charro. When Arthur Treacher's emerged as the surviving corporation, the acquisition became a reverse takeover.

- To pay for his $700,000 purchase, Cataland used $350,000 from El Charro. He raised the remaining $350,000 by buying an Arthur Treacher's from Lumara Foods. In other words he was able to acquire Lumara Foods for $700,000.

- Still without the cash he needed to operate his new company, Cataland arranged for El Charro to sell $650,000 of stock.

During the entire course of these transactions, Cataland did not use any of his own money. Avoiding all risk, he was able to assign himself an $85,000 annual salary.

New Management Team

As shown in Exhibit 6A.2, Cataland ended up with 60 percent ownership of Arthur Treacher's. In Cataland's eyes, this strong control of the chain was vital. It gave him the freedom and flexibility to move quickly, without the advice and consent of others. One of his first acts was to put together a management team capable of turning the chain around:

- Arthur Baldwin serves as executive vice president. A graduate of Yale University with a bachelor's degree in economics, Baldwin came to the chain with a wealth of entrepreneurial experience. He is the founder of several successful businesses. A civic leader as well, he now serves as the part-time mayor of a small town.

- James Cataland, Sr., serves as a director. Before joining the chain, he worked for several furniture retailers as a salesperson, buyer, merchandising manager, and general manager. He is Cataland's father.

- Henry Schmidt is the treasurer. A certified public accountant for 36 years, Schmidt works

EXHIBIT 6A.2
Arthur Treacher's, Inc.: Shareholders' ownership.

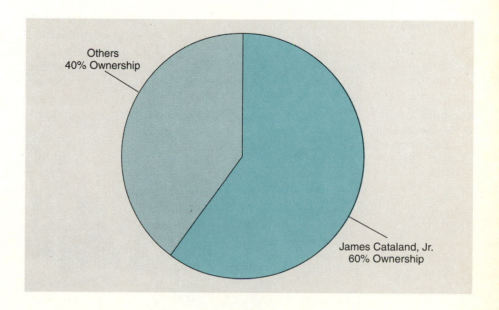

Others
40% Ownership

James Cataland, Jr.
60% Ownership

part time. His last full-time position was with Arby's, Inc., as their treasurer and controller.

- William Saculla is controller and secretary, in charge of office operations, including the computer. His work history includes a position as a controller with a Volkswagen automobile dealership. He is a graduate of Youngstown State University, with a bachelor's degree in accounting.

- Lloyd Allen is the director of company store operations. A prominent athlete, Allen played major league baseball with the California Angels, the Chicago White Sox, and the Texas Rangers. His work experience also includes a position as an area supervisor with Pizza Hut of America, Inc. He attended Fresno State University.

- Biagio Vittoria is the director of franchise operations. He first joined Arthur Treacher's in 1977, when the chain was in its heyday. Vittoria graduated magna cum laude from Southern Connecticut University.

- Linda Benton is the director of personnel and training. Her work experience includes positions as a high school teacher, an interior designer, and an account representative. She is a graduate of Youngstown State University.

Exhibit 6A.3 is a photograph of Cataland and his management team, with whom he meets daily except when he is out of town visiting one of the chain's stores. Exhibit 6A.4 shows the chain's organizational chart.

Cataland's Philosophy of Leadership

Cataland believes that integrity is the biggest lesson he has learned from his takeover experience. "It's my first priority," he says. "Integrity is vital to the success of any business, especially so of a fast-food chain like ours. I'm not interested in fooling anyone, let alone my customers. And, I expect integrity in return—from my employees, from my suppliers, from my stockholders, from my bankers."

Indeed, Cataland does not hire anyone unless he or she shares that philosophy. "It takes a special breed of cat to be part of a turnaround situation," says Cataland. "Ever since I took over in 1984, I've worked hard to surround myself with people who can help me reach my goals. One goal is for Arthur Treacher's to become a major player once again in the fast-food game. To succeed, I need team players who can stand up to the pressures of growth and not buckle."

Although confident that he will turn the chain around, Cataland is a realistic optimist. "Hey, we—my employees and I—could fail and still have done high-quality work. If the chain should fail, what will we have lost? It will have been a great

EXHIBIT 6A.3
Arthur Treacher's, Inc. management team. James Cataland is the person standing.

Arthur Treacher's, Inc.: Organizational chart during the mid-1980s.

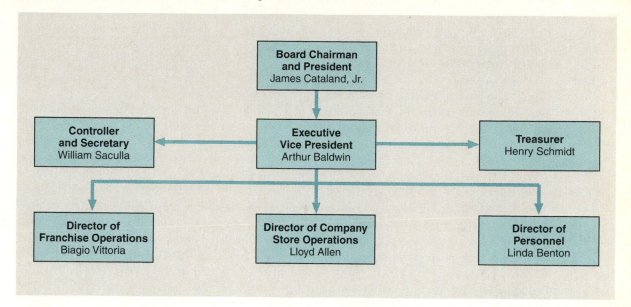

Morale and Performance

Cataland believes that his philosophy of leadership is working. As evidence, he jokingly cites the eating habits of the 22 employees at headquarters. "Nobody goes out for lunch," says Cataland. "They all eat at Arthur Treacher's."

Further evidence can be found in the chain's low employee turnover. Cataland's management team has stayed intact, without a single resignation. And at the company-owned stores, Cataland is "especially proud" of the fact that:

▶ The turnover of store managers is just 25 percent a year, as compared to an average of 100 percent in the fast-food chain industry as a whole.

▶ The turnover of store employees is 100 percent, as compared to the industry average of 300 percent.

Among his employees, executives included, Cataland stresses that loyal customers are the building blocks of the chain's foundation. "The longer that customers keep coming back," says Cataland, "the fewer new ones we'll need. The marketing cost of getting new customers far exceeds the cost of keeping those we already have."

"In all of this," continues Cataland, "our workers' morale plays a strong role. If worker morale is low, customers will sense it and not come back. But, if worker morale is high, customers will find their eating experience a pleasant one and keep coming back. It's the worker's pride in performance that stimulates customer satisfaction and creates customer loyalty."

Cataland also believes that lines of communication must be open within the chain. "Communication is a morale builder," he says. "Where employees have a voice to communicate with me and the other bosses, there is higher productivity, greater workforce stability, and deeper company loyalty—as compared to other company settings where employees sometimes have to strike to get their boss's attention."

The Struggle Back

In the spring of 1989, five years after Cataland took over the chain, he was pleased and proud of what he and his management team had achieved.

The chain's menu had been upgraded and expanded, although fish and chips still was its feature attraction. A broiled fish dinner had been added to increase dinner sales. In Cataland's words: "Along with the other nonfried items such as clam chowder, salad, and dessert—the broiled fish is responsible for the broadening of our customer base."

"Whereas we were attracting a very loyal base of people 45 to 65 years old, we're now developing new business from a younger group of people 25 to 45 years old. The new products appeal to their desire for low-calorie, high-protein, no-cholesterol foods."

Cataland's focus on food quality has won him and the chain national recognition. Recently *USA Today* reported that the Center for Science in the Public Interest (CSPI) chose Arthur Treacher's broiled fish as one of the five best fast foods in the country. (See Exhibit 6A.5.)

"That kind of recognition by so reputable a consumer group as CSPI does wonders for our image," notes Cataland. "It speaks volumes not only for the quality of our food but also for our management team. It was they who planned and produced so nutritious and delicious a food as our broiled fish."

EXHIBIT 6A.5

Arthur Treacher's, Inc.: Five best fast foods, rated by the Center for Science in the Public Interest.

1. Wendy's salad bar
2. Roy Rogers roast beef
3. D'Lites Jr. hamburger
4. **Arthur Treacher's broiled fish**
5. Wendy's chicken sandwich

Food Court Stores

As mentioned earlier, Cataland's overriding goal is to build the chain to 500 stores by the mid-1990s. He believes this goal is reasonable, although at present the chain has a total of just 109 stores, of which 34 are company-owned and 75 are franchisee-owned.

Cataland's optimism springs from his recent successes with restaurants in shopping malls and office buildings. In the past nine months, he and his franchisees have opened 20 food court restaurants. A photograph of one of the stores appears in Exhibit 6A.6. In Cataland's words: "It is important to the developer to provide a variety of noncompeting food types in a given food court. The Arthur Treacher system, with our unique seafood menu, is based on fast service from a relatively small space, which makes us a prized addition to any food court. We intend to use every effort to exploit this opportunity."

Dissident Franchisees

There are still some stores owned by dissident franchisees, although most have begun to pay royalties. Dealing with these franchisees has been Cataland's most pressing and frustrating problem. Although many franchisees agreed to come back into the system, their unhappiness with the previous franchisors has made it hard for them to trust a new franchisor with their royalty payments.*

Search for Financial Help

To build the chain of 500 stores by the mid-1990s, Cataland needs financial help. He plans to see a prestigious investment house called Financial America Securities, Inc. Its special talent is helping businesses in a turnaround position—companies

---

*Rona Ginden, "Cover Story: Can Cataland's Confidence Turn Around Arthur Treacher's?" *Restaurant News,* January 1, 1986, p.115.

like Arthur Treacher's—to raise money. According to its brochure:

▶ Financial America believes that the rebirth of America's entrepreneurial spirit is creating dynamic opportunities for investing in small but developing businesses. We are convinced that this area of investment offers the highest potential for gain by investors.

▶ We place strong emphasis on the experience and resourcefulness of top management in each business and on the soundness of the business plan. And, we have developed a resource of talented consultants to evaluate technologies and markets.

▶ We pride ourselves in giving existing clients as well as potential clients a fast and realistic opinion as to whether we can help them financially.

The chain's latest income statements and balance sheet appear in Exhibits 6A.7 and 6A.8.

Questions
1. Comment on James Cataland's managerial and entrepreneurial assets.
2. Does Cataland have what it takes to turn Arthur Treacher's around? Explain your answer.
3. What is Arthur Treacher's potential? Does Cataland's strategy of selling franchises in food courts make sense? Explain your answer.
4. Comment on Arthur Treacher's performance to date under Cataland's direction.
5. If you had the chance to invest in Arthur Treacher's, would you? Why or why not?

The management for Arthur Treacher's Fish & Chips has changed extensively since this case study was compiled during the mid-1980s. The food chain is currently under new ownership, so the management structure today and the direction for the future of the company are different from what this case study may imply.

EXHIBIT 6A.7

Arthur Treacher's, Inc.: Five-year income statements (year ending June 30, in thousands of dollars).

	1984	1985	1986	1987	1988
Sales revenues					
Company-owned stores	$2,376	$6,401	$7,913	$8,190	$7,339
Royalties	247	456	448	476	696
Total sales revenues	$2,623	$6,857	$8,361	$8,666	$8,035
Cost of sales	1,285	3,687	4,788	4,465	3,927
Gross profit	$1,338	$3,170	$3,573	$4,201	$4,108
Operating costs					
Company-owned stores	$ 816	$2,555	$3,127	$3,503	$3,308
Administration	213	572	587	454	520
Interest	64	215	240	247	225
Total operating costs	$1,093	$3,342	$3,954	$4,204	$4,053
Profit before depr.	$ 245	$ (172)	$ (381)	$ (3)	$ 55
Less: Depreciation	$ 109	$ 280	$ 335	$ 306	$ 317
Profit before taxes	$ 136	$ (452)	$ (716)	$ (309)	$ (262)
Income taxes	47	(36)	0	0	0
Profit after taxes	$ 89	$ (416)	$ (716)	$ (309)	$ (262)

EXHIBIT 6A.8

Arthur Treacher's, Inc.: Latest balance sheet (May 2, 1987).

Assets			Equities		
Current assets			Current liabilities		
Cash	$ 45,600		Notes payable	$ 473,400	
Accounts receivable	145,700		Accounts payable	340,800	
Notes receivable	22,800		Accrued expenses	1,207,100*	$2,021,300
Inventories	76,500				
Prepaid expenses	29,000	$ 319,600	Deferred royalties		34,300
Fixed assets		2,360,300	Lease obligations		1,099,300†
Other assets		146,000	Owners' equity		
			Stock	$ 967,600	
			Deficit	(1,296,600)	(329,000)
Total assets		$2,825,900	Total equities		$2,825,900

*$1,068,100 of which is taxes owed.

†$89,000 of which is current liabilities.

Sir Speedy, Inc.

Sir Speedy, Inc., is a leading franchisor of printing centers. Sir Speedy provides full-service printing, and its franchisees enjoy the highest average sales per store in the fast-printing and copying industry. In fact, Sir Speedy's top 25 centers average more than $1 million in yearly sales even though, remarkably, 97 percent of its franchisees have no prior experience in the printing industry.

In the past 10 years, the quick-printing industry in the United States has grown an impressive 170 percent in sales. By contrast, the Sir Speedy network has mushroomed more than 700 percent. As of December 31, 1994, a total of 838 franchised Sir Speedy Printing Centers dotted 46 states and 12 foreign countries.

All Sir Speedy Printing Centers are owned by franchisees. To ensure their franchisees' success, Sir Speedy provides comprehensive training, guidance, and support.

Training begins with an intensive two-week course at Sir Speedy–Copies Now University at corporate offices in California, where franchisees learn the four-part operating system. The first part covers how to develop a business plan and how to maintain daily financial control. For example, franchisees learn about pricing, estimating, forecasting, budgeting, and accounting procedures.

Next franchisees study how to prepare local marketing, advertising, and public relations plans. Then franchisees receive training in prepress, printing, and finishing methods as well as how to deal with suppliers. The operating system concludes with sessions on how to hire, pay, train, and develop staff.

The training continues with on-site instruction and counseling during the first two weeks at the franchisee's printing center. When the center opens for business, franchisees have on hand all the equipment and supplies they need to start generating sales.

The franchisor provides continuous support to help each center run smoothly and prosper. For example, the franchisees receive regular visits from Sir Speedy's management consultants. In addition, Sir Speedy offers various communications programs, such as newsletters, seminars, regional franchise meetings, franchisees' advisory councils, local advertising associations, and a yearly international convention.

The franchise package cost of a Sir Speedy Printing Center is $160,000, plus working capital. This sum breaks down as follows:

▶ $17,500—*Franchise Fee*. This amount covers the use of the trade names, logos, trademarks, and methods of doing business.

▶ $32,500—*Startup Costs*. This amount covers training, travel and lodging in connection with training, first year's accounting service, market survey, lease negotiation assistance, grand opening promotion, small equipment items, supplies, and initial inventory.

▶ $110,000—*Equipment*. This amount covers an impressive list of equipment, cabinets, counters, shelving, and furniture—all color-coordinated to attract customers and provide pleasant working conditions.

▶ $65,000—*Working Capital*. Here, a franchisee is recommended to have a minimum amount set aside to cover operating expenses before and after startup. This amount may vary depending on location.

Questions

1. Give some examples of the types of services provided by Sir Speedy Printing Centers.
2. Why would entrepreneurs buy a Sir Speedy franchise when they have the resources to open a center on their own?

3. Must a prospective Sir Speedy franchisee know about the quick-printing and copying business? Explain.

4. Can Sir Speedy, Inc., guarantee that a Sir Speedy Printing Center will be successful? Explain.

Source: Case "Sir Speedy, Inc." adapted from Pride, William M., Robert J. Hughes, and Jack R. Kapoor, *Business,* Fifth Edition. Copyright © 1996 by Houghton Mifflin Company. Reprinted by permission.

CASE 6C ▶ *Mary Poldruhi*

A pioneer in the effort to lure fast-food customers away from such traditional fare as hamburgers and pizza, Mary Poldruhi founded and built a successful restaurant in Parma. Her restaurant offers customers a nontraditional but stout and tasty meal of pierogies.

What are pierogies? They might best be described as "half-moons of soft dough filled with a potato-and-cheese mixture, or sauerkraut, and topped with butter and onions." Pierogies rarely, if ever, appear on the menus of fancy restaurants where bottles of champagne may cost more than a month's pay.

"People love pierogies," says Poldruhi. "It's a tradition among ethnics from Eastern Europe." So great is the tradition in Parma that a chamber of commerce executive was inspired to compose and record a song called "Pierogi Song." It laments the grief of a couple visiting a restaurant only to find it sold out of pierogies:

> It didn't take us long
> To find another spot
> We went right into Stash's place
> And through the crowd we fought
> We were going to have pierogi
> We were going to have our wish
> To our table came our waitress
> She said—try another dish.

Poldruhi's Ethnic Ingenuity

Poldruhi worked at a succession of nine-to-five jobs before she decided to launch her very own restaurant. At a telephone company she worked first as a secretary, then as a customer service representative, and last as an advertising consultant for the Yellow Pages Directory.

Disenchanted with office politics, Poldruhi left to strike off on her own. "Everybody has that American dream to start their own business," she says. "You start from nothing with a lot of energy. I feel if you're committed to it and do a lot of hard work, you can succeed."

And work she did—indeed, with ethnic ingenuity. To breathe life into her idea, she needed money, of course. Friends and relatives came forward to invest what they could. Then she came up with the idea of thumbing through the Yellow Pages Directory to call ethnic professionals who might have spare money to invest. Specifically, she looked for names of dentists, lawyers, and physicians that ended in the syllable "ski" or "sky."

This strategy worked brilliantly. Poldruhi soon found a total of 80 ethnic investors who put in $3,000 to $4,000 each. In short order, she was in business for herself, serving heaping platters of pierogies. This achievement earned her a mention in *Time* magazine. And, in the summer of 1992, candidates Bill Clinton and Al Gore dropped by for pierogies during their campaign. Clinton later invited Poldruhi to his inaugural.

Basking in the glow of such intense attention, Poldruhi is "thinking global." She is now laying plans to franchise her Parma restaurant and its logo, a pink flamingo in white socks. "The world will get to know Parma," she says. "The sky's the limit. Every city has ethnics. I think we will be the next hottest fast-food chain in the country."

At present, Poldruhi does not know how much to charge for a franchise. "We're in the planning stage," she says. "Our timetable will depend on the path we choose and when we feel we're ready. But we're going to do it."

Questions

1. What steps would you recommend that Mary Poldruhi take before franchising her restaurant? Explain.
2. How would you suggest that Poldruhi put your recommendations into effect?
3. If she franchises her restaurant, what qualifications should Poldruhi look for in the selection of franchisees? Explain.

Sources: Marcus Gleisser, "Parma Restaurant Owner Thinking Global," *The* [Cleveland] *Plain Dealer* (February 4, 1993), p. 1-D; Gloria Brown, "Looking for Mr. Pierogi," *The* [Cleveland] *Plain Dealer Magazine* (January 19, 1992), p. 14; author's interview with Mary Poldruhi on January 15, 1992, and on March 14, 1992.

CHAPTER 7

Legal Aspects

Laws should be like clothes. They should be made to fit the people they are meant to serve.

—*Clarence Darrow*

We pride ourselves on being a nation governed by laws—so much so that today it is all but impossible to move in many walks of life without first consulting a lawyer. Starting a business venture is no exception.

This chapter deals with the would-be entrepreneur's need for legal help, focusing on choosing a lawyer, selecting a legal form of organization, and coping with government regulations. Also covered are contract law and tort law.

The Need for Legal Advice

One of the entrepreneur's first acts should be to get a lawyer. To avoid breaking laws and to spot opportunities permitted by law, entrepreneurs need expert legal help. Only a lawyer can help resolve a maze of legal questions that range from questions on incorporation to questions on the rights of consumers. Exhibit 7.1 lists some of the legal questions faced by entrepreneurs.

A venture's complexity determines which questions must be addressed. For example, an entrepreneur launching a 20-employee, million-dollar plant to make hazardous chemicals would most likely be concerned with all the questions listed in the exhibit. On the other hand, an entrepreneur launching a part-time consulting practice, working out of her home, with herself as the sole employee, would likely be concerned with only a few of them.

Some entrepreneurs believe they need a lawyer only if they are sued or are suing others. This attitude is short-sighted. Lawyers are by no means merely actors in tense courtroom dramas; in fact, many lawyers never set foot in courtrooms. Their more creative role is to advise clients so that they need never go to court. Indeed, the best remedy for legal mistakes is to keep from

EXHIBIT 7.1
Selected legal questions
faced by entrepreneurs.
To avoid legal mistakes,
entrepreneurs should have
a yearly legal checkup.

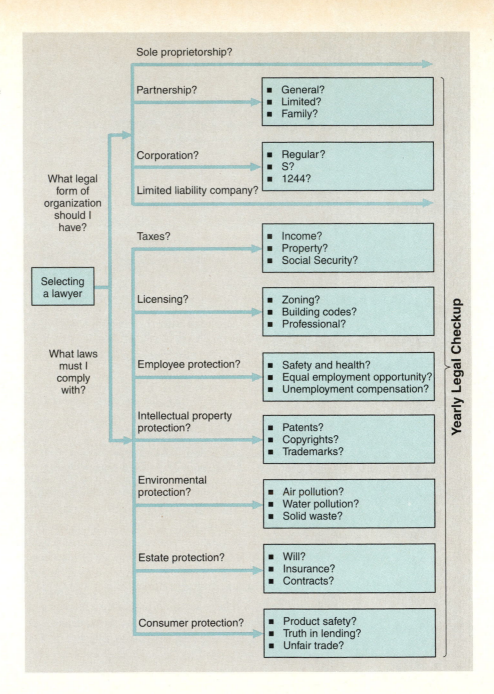

making them. So, perhaps the most apt way to describe the lawyer's role is as a kind of preventive medicine. This is why entrepreneurs should undergo a yearly legal checkup, as suggested in Exhibit 7.1.

▶ Choosing the Right Lawyer

Entrepreneurs should select a lawyer months before they launch their venture, and with the same care they would use to choose a neurosurgeon. A common mistake is to hire someone recommended by friends, neighbors, or relatives whose needs for legal help may differ sharply from the entrepreneur's. Precious few lawyers are general practitioners, expert in all aspects of the law:

EXAMPLE ▶

A criminal lawyer probably could not draft an entrepreneur's will, and one who writes wills probably could not find the way to tax court. And those who try child-custody cases may not be handy at incorporating an entrepreneur's franchise. ▲▼▲

In short, small business should be the very heart of the lawyer's practice with a well-earned reputation for expertise. To find such a lawyer, entrepreneurs might follow the guidelines described as follows and as depicted in Exhibit 7.2:

▶ Seek out a lawyer held in high esteem by the small-business community. The best sources of names are entrepreneurs who are both seasoned and successful. As such, they are likely to offer honest opinions about the skills of the lawyers who helped them get started. Other good sources are the loan officers of banks.

▶ Use the *Martindale-Hubbell Law Directory* to check the backgrounds of lawyers who are recommended to you. The American Bar Association updates this directory yearly.

▶ Narrow the list of names to those whose law firms are small. These firms are likely to be more accessible, more personal, and less expensive than large firms.

▶ Choose the right lawyer. Be sure that the lawyer's expertise is joined by a reasonable match in personal chemistry.[1]

Even with the right lawyer, it is a mistake to leave all decisions to the lawyer. The lawyer should only advise and inform the entrepreneur, while the entrepreneur should make the actual decisions based on the information the lawyer provides. To do so wisely, entrepreneurs should become familiar with the pertinent law. As Dr. Patrick R. Liles, who taught at the Harvard Business School, suggests:

A major difficulty for the inexperienced entrepreneur is the host of strange terms and phrases which are scattered throughout most legal documents. The novice in this kind of reading should have some understanding not only of *what* is contained in such documents, but also *why* these provisions have been included.

EXHIBIT 7.2
Suggested procedure for
selecting the right lawyer.

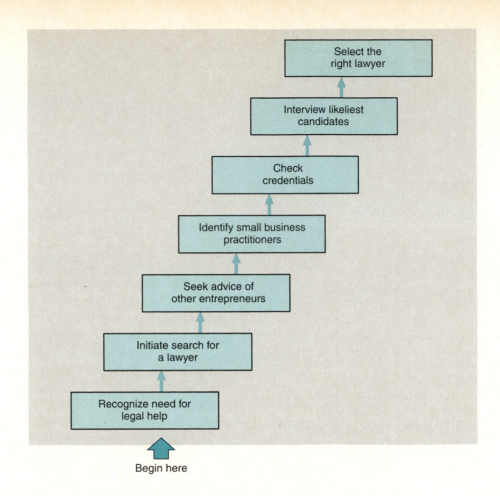

If an entrepreneur cannot find the time or take the interest to read and understand the major contracts into which his company will enter, he should be very cautious about being an entrepreneur at all.[2]

▶ What Entrepreneurs Want from Their Lawyers

To round out our discussion of lawyers and the need for legal advice, let us now look at what entrepreneurs may want from their lawyers:

▶ **Good chemistry**   Entrepreneurs should feel that they, and others in the venture, can trust their lawyers to do what is best for them and for their venture. Relations should be marked by mutual respect, decency, and trust.

▶ **Ideas**   Entrepreneurs often look for fresh ideas on how to run their ventures more efficiently, and thus more profitably. These ideas are likely to come from their lawyers' observations as to how other entrepreneurs do business.

▶ **Availability**   A lawyer should be available for advice when needed, responding virtually the very moment the entrepreneur calls—especially so in a crisis.

► **Timeliness**   The lawyer should observe deadlines religiously. If the lawyer promises to review a contract by a certain date, for example, she should make sure to meet that deadline. Moreover, if the lawyer says, "I'll get back to you on that," she should do so promptly.

► **Personal counsel**   Although entrepreneurs hire lawyers for their legal expertise in business matters, invariably there comes a time when they also need legal advice about such personal problems as buying a house or drafting a simple will.

Of course, this list of wants and their order of importance varies with each entrepreneur, but good chemistry should always be a top priority.

► **Understanding the Legalities of Franchises and Buyouts**

The need to find the right lawyer is just as pressing for entrepreneurs who buy a franchise or buy out an existing venture as for those who start from scratch. In fact, the need is often more pressing, because many of the legal aspects already have been reduced to writing.

Franchise agreements, for example, often cover dozens of pages. Because franchisees have little choice but to observe the franchisor's fine print, they need a lawyer to translate the "strange terms and phrases" that Liles mentions.

Similarly, though in greater depth, buying out an existing business calls for an audit of the seller's legal documents, including deeds, sales contracts, employment contracts, purchase contracts, and the like.

The need to find the right lawyer, one who will resolve the entrepreneur's legal problems by not allowing them to arise in the first place, is raised in Exhibit 7.3. Note the high expectation that entrepreneurs have of being sued. Such entrepreneurs, more likely than not, need the right lawyer to pinpoint their exposure to legal liability *and* to suggest safeguards—to restore their peace of mind.

Legal Forms of Organization

Choosing a legal form of organization—a sole proprietorship, partnership, or corporation—ranks among the entrepreneur's most vital decisions. This choice

EXHIBIT 7.3
The larger the small business, the more its entrepreneurs expect to be sued.

Source: Survey by the National Federation of Independent Business; reported in "Legal Briefs," *You and the Law* (July 1995), p. 12.

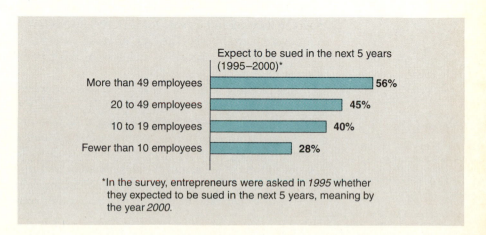

Expect to be sued in the next 5 years (1995–2000)*

More than 49 employees	56%
20 to 49 employees	45%
10 to 19 employees	40%
Fewer than 10 employees	28%

*In the survey, entrepreneurs were asked in *1995* whether they expected to be sued in the next 5 years, meaning by the year *2000*.

affects a number of managerial and financial issues, including which taxes the entrepreneur would pay, as well as their amount; whether the entrepreneur could be personally sued for unpaid business bills; and whether the venture would end automatically when the entrepreneur dies.

Entrepreneurs often ask if there is one best form of organization. The answer is no. The best form of organization depends on the entrepreneur's preferences and tax bracket, and on the venture's complexity and needs. According to the SBA:

> No one legal form of organization, or for that matter no combination of two or more of them, is suited to each and every small business. To try to say what is the best form for all enterprises would be like trying to select an all-purpose suit for a man.
>
> In choosing a legal form of organization, consideration to the parties concerned must be made—their likes, dislikes and dispositions, their immediate and long-range needs, and their tax situations. Seldom, if ever, does any one factor completely determine which is best.[3]

Let us now look at each of the major legal forms of organization from the entrepreneur's viewpoint, paying attention to both advantages and disadvantages.

▶ **Sole Proprietorships**

Sole proprietorships are the most popular legal form of organization, accounting for 75 percent of all businesses. Because most of them are small, often employing only the entrepreneur, laypeople tend to equate small businesses with sole proprietorships. However, sole proprietorships may be as large as a million-dollar foundry or as small as a corner newsstand. The advantages and disadvantages of sole proprietorships are discussed below and summarized in Exhibit 7.4.

Advantages   Freedom is the most striking feature of sole proprietorships. Because they own all of the venture, sole proprietors answer to no one but themselves. They alone reap the rewards of a successful venture or the bitter fruit of failure.

Another feature of sole proprietorships is their simplicity. They are easy to form. Often, entrepreneurs need only nail a shingle on the door telling the world they are in business for themselves. No law forces them to register with a governmental body. The lack of complex procedures is why this legal form of organization appeals so strongly to do-it-yourself, independent-minded entrepreneurs.

Still another attractive feature of sole proprietorships is their low startup cost. Legal fees are likely to be modest, mostly because entrepreneurs are spared the high cost of incorporating, which we discuss later.

In addition, sole proprietorships offer tax benefits for those new ventures likely to suffer losses before profits begin to flow. Tax laws permit sole proprietors to treat their venture's sales revenues and operating expenses as part of their personal finances. Thus, they can cut taxes by deducting any operating losses from personal income earned from other sources.

EXHIBIT 7.4
Sole proprietorships:
Selected advantages and
disadvantages.

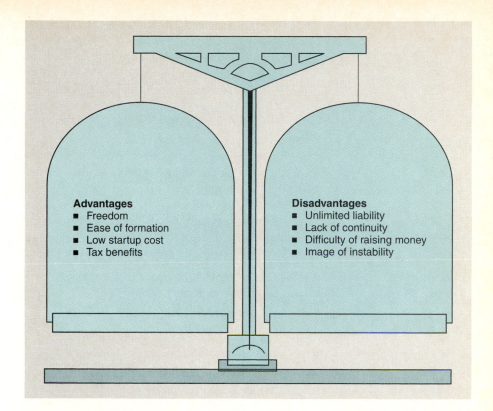

Advantages
- Freedom
- Ease of formation
- Low startup cost
- Tax benefits

Disadvantages
- Unlimited liability
- Lack of continuity
- Difficulty of raising money
- Image of instability

*Men and women often form
equal partnerships with each
other, as did these two
Russian immigrants shown in
their gourmet goods market.*

Disadvantages   The chief disadvantage is unlimited liability. In other words, entrepreneurs are personally liable for all debts incurred by their venture. Thus, they must pay bills out of pocket if their venture fails to generate enough cash flow. Within limits, creditors may step in and claim the entrepreneur's savings, house, or other possessions.

Lack of continuity is another drawback. Legally, a venture dies when the sole proprietor dies. It may, of course, be reorganized after the proprietor's death if a successor has been trained to take over. But executors or heirs often must liquidate because no one is capable of running the venture.

Yet another disadvantage is the difficulty of raising money. Sole proprietors generally find it hard to raise money, not only to start up but also to expand. Bankers, for example, tend to reject proprietors who are the sole strength of their ventures, fearing they may be unable to recover their loan if a proprietor becomes disabled. Moreover, bankers tend to equate sole proprietors with instability because many are part-time entrepreneurs.

▶ **General Partnerships**

As defined by the U.S. Uniform Partnership Act, a partnership is a "voluntary association of two or more persons to carry on as co-owners a business for profit." The act was approved in 1914 by the National Conference of Commissioners on Uniform State Laws. It has now been adopted in virtually all states.

A general partnership is really a sole proprietorship multiplied by the number of partners. The most striking feature of the general partnership is its ability to grow by adding talent and money. In this way, the partnership avoids one of the most serious drawbacks of a sole proprietorship—the dependence of success on the resources of a single individual.

All partnerships begin with an agreement of some kind. It may be written, oral, or even unspoken, although the wise entrepreneur insists on a written agreement to avoid trouble later. This agreement should spell out:

▶ Who invested what sums of money in the partnership.

▶ Who gets what share of the profits.

▶ Who does what and who reports to whom.

▶ How the partnership may be dissolved and how assets left over would be distributed among the partners.

▶ How surviving partners would be protected from the decedent's estate.

The advantages and disadvantages of general partnerships are discussed here and summarized in Exhibit 7.5.

Advantages   General partnerships may draw on a larger pool of talent than sole proprietorships. There is no legal limit to the number of partners: there may be as many as 100 or more, or as few as 2. As a result, a partnership has multiple sources of money. Moreover, partners may invest equal or unequal sums of money, and the profits they earn may bear no relation to their investment. For example, in a two-person partnership, a partner with no investment could reap 50 percent or more of the profits.

EXHIBIT 7.5
General partnerships: Selected advantages and disadvantages.

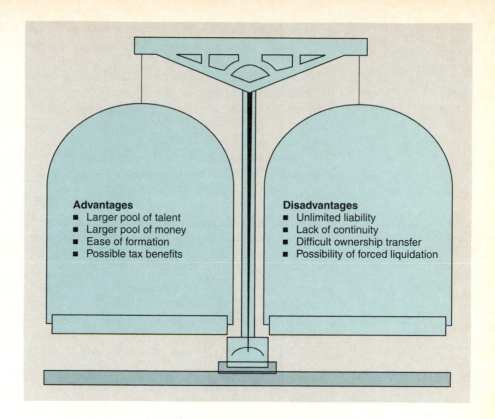

Advantages
- Larger pool of talent
- Larger pool of money
- Ease of formation
- Possible tax benefits

Disadvantages
- Unlimited liability
- Lack of continuity
- Difficult ownership transfer
- Possibility of forced liquidation

Like sole proprietorships, partnerships generally are easy to organize, with few legal requirements. For example, partners need not apply for approval with any governmental body. Nor, as suggested earlier, need there be a written agreement between partners. Of course, if there is no written agreement, the problem of proving the partnership's existence is ever present.

Tax benefits are another advantage. In the eyes of the law, a partnership is simply two or more individuals working together. This lack of legal standing means that the U.S. Internal Revenue Service taxes partners as individuals. Thus, if partners find themselves losing money, they may claim their losses on their personal tax returns—a benefit unavailable to corporate shareholders.

Disadvantages As with sole proprietorships, unlimited liability is the worst drawback of partnerships. By law, each partner is liable for debts incurred in the name of the partnership. And, if any partner incurs a debt unbeknownst to the other partners, they are all liable if the offending partner cannot pay the debt. This legal wrinkle holds even if the partnership agreement calls for all notes and bills to be endorsed by the other partners. Unlimited liability is the main reason why general partnerships are the least popular legal form of organization, accounting for only 7 percent of all businesses. Take this example:

Sidney Jordan and Robert Barron established a housepainting partnership called Bright Spot. Unwisely, they used a sprayer on a windy day and spattered dark red paint on 10 automobiles parked in a lot next to the building they were painting. Jordan and Barron had to pay for the automobiles to be repainted. Several were expensive automobiles needing fancy paint jobs, so the bill totaled nearly $5,000.

After this disaster, Barron left town and Bright Spot went broke. Jordan was liable to pay the whole $5,000 from his personal funds.[4] ▲▼▲

Another disadvantage is lack of continuity. When one partner dies or withdraws, the partnership legally dies as well, even if the other partners agree to stay on. A related drawback is the difficulty of transferring ownership. Because the law regards the partnership as a close, intimate, and personal relationship, no partner can sell out without the consent of the other partners. Thus, a partner who wants to retire or to transfer his interest to a son or daughter must first get the consent of the other partners.

Moreover, the life of a partnership often depends on the ability of retiring partners to find someone compatible with the other partners to buy them out. Failure to do so may force liquidation of the partnership.

Surviving partners also may be faced with liquidation when a partner dies. Liquidation of a partnership, however, need not cause a loss of sales. If they want, the surviving partners can quickly form a new partnership to retain the business of the old partnership.

▶ Other Partnership Forms

The problem of unlimited liability may be avoided by forming a *limited partnership*. Limited partners simply invest money; they cannot take an active role and they cannot be held liable for debts undertaken by the active partners. If the business goes under, limited partners are liable only to the extent of their investment.

More complex than general partnerships, limited partnerships require legal help to organize. All partners, for example, must register in each state in which the partnership plans to do business. Limited partners must take care never to become active in the day-to-day routine of the business. Otherwise, they risk losing their preferred status as limited partners.

Two other forms of organization have evolved to offset the defects of the general partnership. One is the *family partnership,* which enables partners to divide income among members of their families to avoid high taxes. The other is the *real estate investment trust (REIT)*. Managed by a trustee, the REIT enjoys both continuity of life and ease of ownership transfer.

▶ Kinds of Partners

The roles that partners play in the different forms of partnerships vary. For example:

▶ An *ostensible partner* is both actively involved in the venture and known as a partner.

▶ A *secret partner* is actively involved in the venture's day-to-day operations but is not known.

▶ A *dormant partner* is neither active nor known.

▶ A *silent partner* is inactive but is known to be a partner.

▶ A *nominal partner* is not an active partner in any sense but may pass himself off as one, or permit others to say that he is an active partner. Nominal partners may be held liable for their actions, just as if they were active partners.

▶ A *limited partner* risks only her investment in the venture, as long as she does not take an active part in the venture's management or operations.[5]

▶ Regular Corporations

Corporations dominate the business world, as shown in Exhibit 7.6. Although they make up only 18 percent of the total number of U.S. businesses, they account for 90 percent of all sales revenues. And, turning to Exhibit 7.7, note the strong relationship between the legal form of organization and the size of a business's yearly sales revenues.

Most people equate corporations with big business. The very word *corporation* inspires awe and respect, bespeaking bigness and power. But the tiny corner newsstand has as much right to incorporate as a giant steel mill. And it matters not whether a venture has thousands of shareholders or just one. In short, the corporation is a versatile legal tool capable of serving the entire spectrum of a venture's size and complexity.

In the words of John Marshall, former chief justice of the U.S. Supreme Court, a corporation is "an artificial being, invisible, intangible, and existing

EXHIBIT 7.6

Relative importance of legal forms of organization. Most businesses form sole proprietorships, but corporations account for most sales revenues.

Source: U.S. Bureau of the Census, U.S. Department of Commerce, *Statistical Abstract of the United States* 1995 (Washington, D.C.: U.S. Government Printing Office, 1995), p. 543.

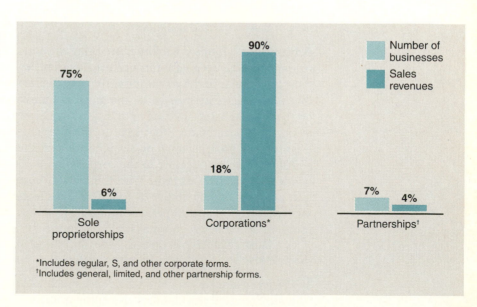

Legend: Number of businesses; Sales revenues

Sole proprietorships: 75%, 6%
Corporations*: 18%, 90%
Partnerships†: 7%, 4%

*Includes regular, S, and other corporate forms.
†Includes general, limited, and other partnership forms.

EXHIBIT 7.7

Size of yearly sales revenues versus choice of legal form of organization.
At one extreme, 85 percent of all businesses with sales under $25,000 a year are organized as sole proprietorships; at the other extreme, 85 percent with yearly sales more than $1,000,000 are organized as corporations.

| | **Number of Businesses with:** | | | |
	Yearly Sales Under $25,000	**%**	**Yearly Sales More Than $1,000,000**	**%**
Sole proprietorships	10,558,000	84.9	60,000	7.9
Partnerships	956,000	7.7	55,000	7.2
Corporations	924,000	7.4	647,000	84.9
		100.0		100.0

Source: U.S. Bureau of the Census, U.S. Department of Commerce, *Statistical Abstract of the United States 1995* (Washington, D.C.: U.S. Government Printing Office, 1995), p. 543.

only in contemplation of the law."[6] By these words, the Supreme Court defined the corporation as a legal person. A corporation, therefore, can:

▶ Sue and be sued
▶ Buy, hold, and sell property
▶ Make and sell products to consumers
▶ Commit crimes and be tried and punished for them

The advantages and disadvantages of the regular corporation are discussed here and summarized in Exhibit 7.8.

Advantages   Limited liability is probably the major reason why lawyers often recommend the corporate form of organization; it limits investors' liability to their investment in the corporation. Entrepreneurs should remember, however, that limited liability may be meaningless in some cases. For example, if all of one's personal assets are tied up in a venture, limited liability offers little protection. Also, no matter what legal form of organization entrepreneurs use, at least some of their personal possessions are protected by law.

Another striking feature of the corporation is its continuity. Its life is independent of the lives of those who founded it. In other words, if the corporation prospers, it may outlive its founders. This feature stems from the fact that a corporation is a legal person. As such, it is independent of the lives of its founders and may go on forever, at least in theory.

A related advantage is ease of ownership transfer, which takes place through the sale of stock. Stock may be either *preferred* or *common*:

▶ *Preferred stock* pays a fixed dividend, much like the interest payment on a loan. Preferred stockholders also enjoy priority or preference over common

EXHIBIT 7.8

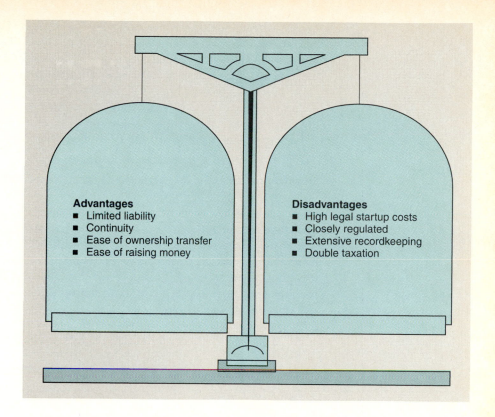

Advantages
- Limited liability
- Continuity
- Ease of ownership transfer
- Ease of raising money

Disadvantages
- High legal startup costs
- Closely regulated
- Extensive recordkeeping
- Double taxation

stockholders in terms of dividends and assets if a venture liquidates. Few small corporations issue preferred stock.

▶ *Common stock,* on the other hand, is issued by every corporation. Shareholders enjoy an ownership interest in profits and assets, though below that of all creditors and preferred stockholders.

Each common shareholder owns part of the corporation, as evidenced by stock certificates. These certificates give common shareholders the right:

▶ To elect the directors of the corporation.

▶ To cast one vote per share at shareholders' meetings.

▶ To receive dividends in proportion to the number of common shares they hold.

▶ To sell their shares to anyone who wants to buy them—unless the shareholders must offer to sell them to the corporation first. Moreover, before new common stock is offered for sale, shareholders usually have the right to buy the new shares in proportion to the amount of stock they already own.

Ownership interest, however, does not give common shareholders the right to act for the corporation or to share in its management. General Motors, to cite an extreme example, has more than a million shareholders; yet only a handful have a voice in the way the company is run. The only way that shareholders can influence the running of the corporation is by casting their votes for directors once a year; in most cases, though, voting is meaningless, because corporate managers tend to offer just one slate of directors for election.

Ease of raising money is still another advantage, which stems largely from the corporation's ability to sell shares of stock to investors. Moreover, should the entrepreneurs wish to sell their business, they may do so without dissolving the corporation.

Disadvantages One disadvantage of the corporation is that it is closely regulated. In fact, the corporation often is referred to as "a creature of statute," which means that a corporation can be formed only by complying with requirements spelled out in the statutes of the state where it is located. One requirement is that incorporation papers be prepared and filed with the state, giving such information as the corporation's name, its intended business activities, and how it is going to be financed. This document is called the *corporate charter*. Legal requirements for receiving a corporate charter differ from state to state in many vital matters, among them:

▶ Taxes

▶ Business fees

▶ Liabilities for debts

▶ Rules for issuing stock

▶ Minimum number of directors

▶ Minimum sum contributed by the founders

Because of their legal complexity, corporations cost more to form than either sole proprietorships or partnerships. Therefore, legal help is needed to ensure that the founders observe every legal requirement. Also, legal advice may be needed regarding directors' and shareholders' meetings, dividends, rights of shareholders, and the like.

Another disadvantage is extensive recordkeeping. Virtually all states require that corporate recordkeeping include the minutes of board meetings, financial records, and the documentation of business activities. Another requirement is that corporations make reports to the state agency that regulates corporations.

The greatest potential drawback of the corporate form, however, is double taxation. Corporations must pay income taxes on their profits; and shareholders, in turn, must pay income taxes on dividends. Because dividends are not tax-deductible, they come out of after-tax profits. This means that dividends are taxed twice.

Exhibit 7.9 compares the regular corporation with the sole proprietorship and the general partnership forms of organization. Note that the regular corporation is the most attractive in most ways.

▶ **S Corporations**   The S corporation, an alternative to the regular corporation, first appeared in 1958 with the enactment of Subchapter S of the U.S. Internal Revenue Code.

EXHIBIT 7.9

Comparison of selected features of main legal forms of organization.

	Sole Proprietorships	General Partnerships	Regular Corporations
Ownership transfer	Difficult	Difficult	Easy
Raising money	Difficult	Difficult	Easy
Preserving continuity	Difficult	Difficult	Easy
Protecting against liability for debts	Difficult	Difficult	Easy
Government regulations	Few	Few	Many
Formation	Easy	Easy	Difficult
Income taxation	Once	Once	Twice

It soon became a popular legal form of organization because it avoids double taxation: Shareholders are taxed as partners and so do not have to pay taxes on dividends twice. The S corporation keeps all other corporate advantages, such as limited liability, but with some strings attached. For instance, to qualify as an S corporation, a venture must meet some stiff legal requirements:

▶ It must be a domestic corporation that is not part of another corporation. In other words, it must be independently owned and managed.

▶ It must have no more than 35 shareholders.

▶ Only individuals and estates are permitted as shareholders. This requirement keeps other corporations from buying shares of its stock.

▶ Nonresident aliens are excluded as shareholders.

Moreover, once the venture gets under way, the entrepreneur must make sure that no more than 25 percent of sales revenues come from dividends, rents, interest, royalties, annuities, or stock sales; and that no more than 80 percent of sales revenues come from foreign nations.

Many lawyers question whether the S corporation really differs from the regular corporation. They argue that it is simply a corporation with limited size and capital structure. Even so, its ability to avoid double taxation qualifies it as a separate legal form of organization, blending the regular corporation and partnership forms.

The S corporation's popularity is due largely to limited liability and, of course, to its avoidance of double taxation. Nearly half of all corporations are S corporations (48% S corporations, compared to 52% regular corporations).

▶ **1244 Corporations**

To encourage people to invest in small businesses, the U.S. Congress enacted Section 1244 of the U.S. Internal Revenue Code. Under this legislation, persons whose investments in a small business become worthless may treat the loss as an ordinary rather than a capital loss. This means that investment losses of up to $50,000 a year can be deducted from ordinary income. In contrast, investment losses in regular corporations can be no more than $3,000 a year.

To qualify as a Section 1244 corporation, a small business must meet the following tests, among others:

▸ No more than $1 million can be raised for a new venture from the sale of common stock.

▸ For an existing venture with common stock already outstanding, the combined value of that stock and any additional stock issued under Section 1244 cannot top $1 million.

▸ The stock must be issued for cash or property, not in exchange for services.

▸ The tax break applies only to individuals—not to corporations, estates, or trusts.

Like S corporations, 1244 corporations appeal strongly to the entrepreneur seeking money to launch a risky venture. Potential investors are more likely to invest in the entrepreneur's venture if they know that losses, if any, would be deductible as ordinary losses.

▸ **Limited Liability Companies**

Thus far, we have discussed the traditional legal forms of organization, focusing on sole proprietorships, partnerships, and corporations. A new and promising alternative to these traditional forms is the limited liability company (LLC).

Not unlike S corporations, LLCs are hybrid organizations that combine the best features of partnerships and corporations. As such, an LLC enjoys these advantages:

▸ Like a partnership, it pays no tax of its own.

▸ Like a corporation, it offers liability protection.

Although the LLC is really no more than a variation on the S corporation theme, it has many more advantages, chief among them:

▸ An LLC may have an unlimited number of shareholders; in contrast, the S corporation may have no more than 35 shareholders.

▸ An LLC, as its shareholders, may have foreigners, regular corporations, and co-owners of partnerships; in contrast, the S corporation may not.

These advantages make the LLC attractive to any type of business, according to Grant Thornton, the large accounting firm.[7] Still another advantage is its flexibility, as underscored by this LLC expert:

William Bagley, a Cheyenne, Wyoming, lawyer, says that although the limits on liability and the partnership taxation are the major reasons entrepreneurs are choosing the LLC, there is a third motivation: flexibility.

"That is often the best reason," says Bagley, co-author of *The Limited Liability Company* and publisher of a newsletter on LLCs. "It's easy for owners to do what they want with the business without restriction. They are not hamstrung by lots of rules from the IRS or from statutes" governing corporations.[8]

Further evidence of the LLC's flexibility is that a few states already allow sole proprietors to organize themselves as sole-member LLCs, thus giving liability protection to individuals who never had it before. This innovative feature may soon spread to every state, thanks to a law being drafted by the National Conference of Commissioners on Uniform State Laws that would provide for sole-proprietor LLCs.

Government Regulations and Paperwork

Few subjects spark more complaints among entrepreneurs than government regulations and the resulting paperwork. In the federal government alone, there are now more than 90 regulatory agencies issuing hundreds of new rules each year. The force of these rules is felt by every person and every business, large or small. Moreover, regulatory agencies exist, not only at the federal level, but also at local and state levels.

Only with a lawyer's help may entrepreneurs learn about, and cope with, the maze of regulations and paperwork that affects their venture. The complex details with which they must comply are exemplified here:

EXAMPLE ▶

In Houston, a small real estate developer wants to build a number of housing units in a local subdivision. To do so, the developer first must get clearance from a local zoning board and also must file for a local construction permit. At the state level, the developer must comply with environmental protection laws and housing codes. At the federal level, the developer must comply with various U.S. Housing and Urban Development regulations and U.S. Environmental Protection Agency requirements. Federal regulations differ, depending on the size and location of the subdivision and whether the homes are planned for low-, middle-, or upper-income buyers.[9] ▲▼▲

Small wonder, then, that so many entrepreneurs complain about federal regulations. In point of fact, the burden of regulation has surged since the late 1980s, as depicted in Exhibit 7.10. This surge has struck entrepreneurs especially hard because, as mentioned in Chapters 1 and 2, they are the economy's engine of jobs.

There is little, if any, question that the high cost of regulation leads to job losses, higher prices, and heavier taxes—so much so that consumer groups and other interested parties have joined with entrepreneurs to resolve the problem. In testimony before the U.S. Congress, the SBA said:

Small business owners spend at least one billion hours each year filling out government forms at a cost of $100 billion a year.[10] Indeed, just to open a dry cleaning store, an entrepreneur has to fill out roughly a one-foot-high stack of paperwork, according to the National Federation of Independent Business, which is the nation's largest small business organization.[11]

EXHIBIT 7.10

How small-business profits vary with the tax and regulatory burden.

Source: Joint Economic Committee of the U.S. Congress; adapted from "Crippling Regulations," *Small Business Reports* (April 1993), p. 5.

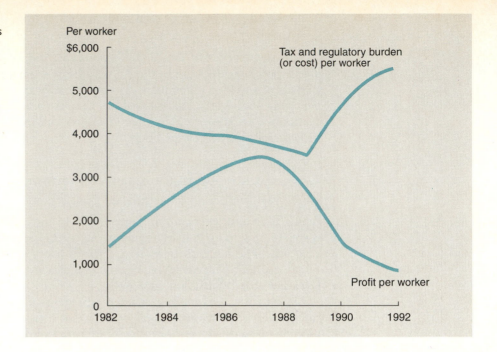

In its 1994 study, *A Citizen's Guide to Regulation,* The Heritage Foundation cited a number of what it calls "regulatory horror stories." Following are but two such stories:

▶ John McCurdy, owner of a very small herring smokehouse, recently had a run-in with the U.S. Food and Drug Administration (FDA). Despite producing over 54 million fillets over 20 years without a single reported case of food poisoning, the FDA told McCurdy he would have to change his methods.

  Unfortunately, that would require $75,000 in new equipment. Facing the hopeless choice between installing equipment he could not afford or fighting a legal battle with the FDA, McCurdy chose the only other alternative—he closed his business and laid off his 22 employees.[12]

▶ E. O. Schonstedt is president of the Schonstedt Instrument Company in Reston, Virginia. Schonstedt's company holds about 70 patents on various engineering inventions and has the capability of holding many more if the company were to employ more than the 50 people it now does.

  But, even though he wants to hire additional engineers to create more inventions, Schonstedt fears the burdens of Form EEO-1. This form requires that organizations with more than 50 employees and with government contracts totaling more than $50,000 must submit hiring information to the government.

After a fellow businessman ended up in the hospital with stress-induced problems due to the burdens of his 8-pound Form EEO-1, Schonstedt decided not to expand his workforce. Schonstedt calls this rule "the robber regulation . . . because it robs people of jobs, robs the nation of much-needed inventions, and robs the nation of competitiveness." He adds, "Just think how fortunate we are that Thomas Edison did not have to contend with today's regulations."[13]

A Balanced View

To give a balanced view, we should emphasize that many regulations benefit both society and the entrepreneur. Few entrepreneurs would disagree, for example, with the need to:

▶ Ban monopolies that undercut competition.

▶ Regulate banking practices to protect savings.

▶ Protect the environment from pollutants.

▶ Give women and minorities equal employment opportunities.

▶ Help the old, the poor, and the disabled lead meaningful lives.

▶ Protect natural resources from exhaustion.

Without government regulations, these needs and others most likely would not be met. We tend to forget that eight-year-old newsboys worked 16-hour days at the turn of the century for just a dollar a day. At the time, the courts only grudgingly accepted laws designed to make working conditions more humane.

▶ **The Need for the Entrepreneur's Political Involvement**

These days, with the business world becoming increasingly fast paced and complex, entrepreneurs must involve themselves politically, especially in issues that affect the way, and sometimes where, they can do business. Turning to Exhibit 7.11, note the results of a poll by *Inc.* magazine of entrepreneurs who, in 1994, led the 500 fastest-growing, publicly-held small businesses. Surprisingly, health-care reform was well down on their priority list of political concerns. Take these comments by an involved entrepreneur:

If you don't get involved and know what laws are being passed or changed and how they affect you, you could wake up one morning and find yourself out of business. Maybe that sounds strong but think about this:

▶ If a law is passed that you have to provide employees with health care regardless of the size of your business, could you do it?

▶ Or, if someone files an action against you on discrimination, can you support your position with proper documentation?

▶ Or, do you even know if you are in the right under the law that covers discriminatory practices?[14]

EXHIBIT 7.11

Issues that *Inc. 500* entrepreneurs believe the federal government should address (1995).

Source: Poll conducted by *Inc.* magazine, "The 500 Survey," *Inc.* (August 1995), p. 8.

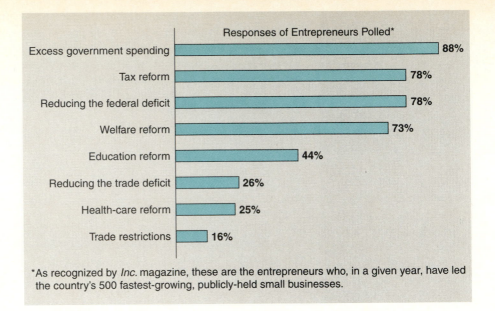

Responses of Entrepreneurs Polled*

Issue	Percentage
Excess government spending	88%
Tax reform	78%
Reducing the federal deficit	78%
Welfare reform	73%
Education reform	44%
Reducing the trade deficit	26%
Health-care reform	25%
Trade restrictions	16%

*As recognized by *Inc.* magazine, these are the entrepreneurs who, in a given year, have led the country's 500 fastest-growing, publicly-held small businesses.

Another entrepreneur had this to say about the virtues of becoming involved politically:

> My involvement is important because the environment today is so hostile to business . . . Politicians have realized they can continue to dole out benefits without increasing government spending by putting mandates on business.
>
> The pace of legislative attacks on business has quickened. Business is supposed to clean up the environment, preserve the family, protect employees from drugs, discrimination, and their own lack of responsibility. In the meantime, the media portray business people as heartless, greedy rogues.[15]

Contract Law and Tort Law

Today's sophisticated society depends on an intricate web of promises for its quality of life—that is, on the act of making promises and then keeping them. It would be all but impossible for society to work, at least as we know it today, without our honoring the promises we make.

It was society's commitment to ensuring that promises are kept that gave birth to contract law; a *contract* is any agreement between two or more parties that is enforceable in the courts. Contract law reflects society's values and expectations. For example, the law reflects:

▶ The degree to which society allows businesspersons, as well as laypersons, to make promises that are legally binding.

▶ The reasons that are acceptable to society for breaking such promises.

▶ The promises that society disallows because they violate its best interests.

- The degree to which society can hold accountable, say, a five-year-old or an adult who is mentally retarded for promises unkept.
- Society's sense of fair play that businesspersons, as well as laypersons, should be held accountable if they unwittingly make promises based on false information.

Dealing with these questions forms the very core of contract law. In a word, the law's purpose is to make sure that promises are legally enforceable.

Let us digress for a moment to distinguish between the moral and legal obligations created by a promise. Promising to visit an employee in the hospital and then failing to do so, for example, does not create a legal liability; however, it does create a moral obligation.

Of course, some promises carry both a legal and a moral obligation—for example, promising to hire a person who is blind and then failing to do so.

▶ The Requirements of Contract Law

Although contract law underpins our economy, entrepreneurs and others often rely on a sense of duty and good faith to do business. Even so, in a time of crisis, they may abandon principle and fail to live up to their promises. This is where contract law would be brought into play:

- To make sure that promises are kept, *or*—
- To offer the innocent victim some form of relief.

Contract law, then, is a system of procedures for enforcing promises. The six requirements of an enforceable contract are discussed below.

- **Agreement**   For a contract to be legal, there must be two parties, one of whom makes an offer that the other accepts.
- **Consideration**   This means that something of value must be promised by one party to convince the other party to accept.
- **Competence**   Both parties must have the competence to act intelligently and responsibly as they enter into the contract.
- **Legality**   This means that the contract's purpose must be beyond reproach, that it cannot violate the public's rights. For example, contracts in restraint of trade would violate federal law and thus harm the consumer, who may have to pay higher prices as a result.
- **Genuineness**   The agreement by both parties must be genuine in the sense that there is truly a meeting of the minds. A contract cannot be entered into under, say, some form of duress or fraudulent behavior.
- **Form**   Both parties must put the contract into the form required by law. To be enforceable, certain contracts—for example, for the sale of land or for the sale of products priced at $500 or more—must be written, not oral.

▶ Breach of Contract

If a contract meets all six of these requirements, the contract is legally enforceable. But what can the entrepreneur do if the other party breaches the contract by failing to live up to its terms?

Contract law offers a number of remedies to protect both parties. As the injured party to a breach of contract, the entrepreneur might simply cancel the contract because the other party failed to act in good faith. Or the entrepreneur might sue the other party for damages in the amount lost because of the breach. Take these examples:

▸ An entrepreneur might cancel a contract for paving a parking lot if the contractor fails to show up.

▸ An entrepreneur might sue for damages if a wholesaler fails to deliver merchandise in time for the holiday season.

▸ Tort Law

A *tort* is a noncriminal act that harms a person or property. Tort law, then, applies to civil or business relationships that are not governed by contract law. Fraud and misrepresentation are among the most common torts. An example of misrepresentation is when a used-car salesman lies to a customer and says, "Yes, that's a brand-new engine, not a rebuilt one."

One of the most controversial areas of tort law is product liability. Other controversial areas include negligence and intentional torts:

▸ **Strict product liability**   Here an entrepreneur may be held liable for injuries caused by a defective product, even if the entrepreneur used all reasonable care in making and selling its product. Recent cases have focused on illnesses traced to toxic waste that had been disposed of legally.

▸ **Negligence**   Charges of negligence are involved in most tort suits. These suits range widely, covering employees' actions as well as those of entrepreneurs—for example, the delivery truck driver who strikes a pedestrian. An example of employee negligence would be the entrepreneur who fails to remove snow in front of his store—a failure that causes a passerby to slip and break her arm.

▸ **Intentional torts**   These torts issue from the deliberate actions of businesses and their employees. For example, an intentional tort may result if an entrepreneur fails to add an inexpensive safety device to a toy or if an entrepreneur allows an employee to sexually harass a customer without taking action against the harasser.

SUMMARY

All new ventures require a lawyer's services. It is critical that would-be entrepreneurs not make the mistake of neglecting the legal aspects of their ventures. The legal questions faced by entrepreneurs fall into two major categories: What legal form of organization should I have—sole proprietorship, partnership, corporation? And what laws do I need to comply with—taxes, licensing, employee protection, intellectual property protection, environmental protection, estate protection, and consumer protection?

A good business lawyer is a kind of preventive medicine. The real value of lawyers is their ability to solve problems by not letting them arise in the first place. The process of selecting the right lawyer should include recognizing the need for legal help, initiating a search for a lawyer, seeking the advice of other entrepreneurs, identifying small-business practitioners, checking credentials, interviewing the likeliest candidates, and, finally, selecting the best candidate.

Again, a key concern is the form the organization will take. The three main legal forms of organization are sole proprietorships, general partnerships, and regular corporations. The advantages of sole proprietorships are the owner's freedom, ease of formation, low startup cost, and tax benefits; the disadvantages include unlimited liability, lack of continuity, difficulty raising money, and an image of instability.

The advantages of general partnerships include a larger pool of talent and money, the ease of business formation, and possible tax benefits; the disadvantages include unlimited liability, lack of continuity, the difficulty of transferring ownership, and the possibility of forced liquidation.

The advantages of regular corporations include limited liability, continuity, and the ease of transferring ownership and raising money; the disadvantages include government regulation, high legal startup costs, extensive record keeping, and double taxation.

A new and promising alternative to the traditional legal forms of organization is the limited liability company. Among its advantages are liability protection, avoidance of double taxation, and operating flexibility.

Few subjects spark more complaints among entrepreneurs than government regulations and the resulting paperwork. The burden of regulation has surged since the late 1980s, causing job losses, higher prices, and heavier taxes. To reverse this trend, entrepreneurs must involve themselves politically, especially in issues that affect the way, and sometimes where, they can do business.

Entrepreneurs also should know the workings of contract law and tort law, both of which reflect society's values and expectations. Contract law deals with any agreement between two or more parties that is enforceable in the courts. In contrast, tort law focuses on civil or business relationships that are not governed by contract law. Common torts include fraud and misrepresentation; the most controversial area of tort law involves product liability.

Discussion and Review Questions

1. Why might you, as a would-be entrepreneur, need legal help early in planning your venture?
2. What sort of legal questions must entrepreneurs answer?
3. How would you go about finding the right lawyer for your venture?
4. Why do bankers prefer not to lend money to sole proprietors?
5. How do general partnerships differ from limited partnerships?
6. Why should partners draw up a written partnership agreement?
7. Why does the public often equate big business with the corporate form of organization?
8. What is the basic difference between a corporation and the other legal forms of organization?
9. Interest on loans is a tax-deductible expense. Should dividends on corporate profits be treated the same way? Why or why not?

10. How do regular corporations differ from S corporations? From 1244 corporations?
11. Define these terms: *sole proprietorship, partnership, corporation, limited liability, corporate charter, contract.*
12. Is there one best legal form of organization, applicable to all entrepreneurs? Explain your answer.
13. How do limited liability companies differ from S corporations?
14. What current political issues affect small-business entrepreneurs? Why are these issues so important to entrepreneurs?
15. How does contract law differ from tort law?

Building a Business Plan

Legal Aspects

The future of a small business is affected by legal decisions that must be made early in the startup process. The most important of these choices is the legal form of business organization that the owner chooses.

Forms of Ownership

There are three forms of ownership generally available to an owner: sole proprietorship, partnership, and corporation. Each has advantages and disadvantages that must be analyzed before making a decision. Before completing Worksheet 7, you may want to review the material on each form of ownership in text—see pages 191 to 203.

Instructions for Worksheet 7

The purpose of this worksheet is to review the type of business that you want to start and then match your type of business with a form of ownership. Worksheet 7 is divided into three parts. To complete this worksheet, in part 1 you must review the definition of your business that was last revised at the conclusion of Chapter 4, and then choose a form of ownership that is appropriate for that type of business. In part 2, list the advantages and disadvantages of the form of ownership you chose in part 1. Then in part 3, provide a rationale for your ownership decision based on the information that you provided in parts 1 and 2.

Part 1—Choosing a Form of Ownership

Review the definition for your business that was last revised at the conclusion of Chapter 4.

1. After reviewing the definition for your business, choose a form of ownership that is appropriate for a business like yours.
2. In your own words, define the form of ownership you chose.

Part 2—The Advantages and Disadvantages for the Form of Ownership Chosen in Part 1

As discussed in this chapter, no one legal form of ownership is suited to each and every small business. In fact, each form of ownership has advantages and disadvantages.

3. List the major advantages for the form of ownership chosen in part 1.
4. List the major disadvantages for the form of ownership chosen in part 1.

Part 3—The Rationale for Your Ownership Decision

5. Based on the information above, is the form of ownership chosen in part 1 a reasonable choice?
6. Describe the primary reasons why you chose this form of ownership.

CASE 7A ▶ *ColeJon Mechanical Corporation*

ColeJon was founded as a remodeling firm. After seven years as a maintenance service firm, ColeJon's sales revenues reached $4,753,000. This record of fast growth earned its two founders, Lonzo Coleman and James Jones, national recognition as Minority Contractors of the Year.

Coleman and Jones believe that ColeJon is positioned to become one of the nation's largest contractors. In the next several years, they expect sales revenues to increase sixfold, to $28 million a year. About 75 percent of their sales, however, come from government contracts; just 25 percent, from the private sector. "I wish we could reverse that ratio," says Coleman. "The question is how?"

Background

Coleman first thought about starting his own business when he realized that his opportunities as

a tradesman were limited. An apprentice for five years and later a master pipefitter, Coleman could aspire only to be foreman for contractors specializing in maintenance service.

"I realized there was no way I could become an executive if I remained a pipefitter," says Coleman. "No way I could reach the boardroom. I knew, too, that the main reason employers hired me was to satisfy EEO requirements on a particular project.* The total lack of opportunity kept preying on my mind. More than ever, I was convinced that I could succeed at what I wanted to be, but only if I started my own business."

Coleman met Jones while they were working together, installing a heating system at a local college. Jones had apprenticed for four years as a sheet metal worker and was now a master tradesman.

---

*EEO is equal employment opportunity.

He soon shared with Coleman his frustration with his lot as a tradesman.

Jones agreed with Coleman that "there were many talented people working in subservient roles who would never be able to use their talents and receive the proper recognition." The chemistry between the two men was such that, on the day they met, they made up their minds to become partners and start their own business.

At the time, both men had secure jobs with reliable incomes. Coleman, for example, earned $25,000 a year as a pipefitter. Now his wages, as well as Jones's, would drop to zero.

The Early Years

Coleman and Jones scraped together $5,000 each to start their own remodeling firm. They named their firm *ColeJon*, which is a contraction of their surnames, *Cole*man and *Jon*es. "It truly gave us and our families a sense of pride to form a company named after us," says Coleman.

The two men harbored no illusions about the sacrifices they would be called on to make. Coleman mortgaged his house and Jones borrowed money from relatives. "We couldn't go to the movies anymore," says Coleman. "My wife learned to cook hamburgers in a hundred different ways. Without our wives, I doubt that we would have survived the first year. They truly were supportive and never complained about the change in our lifestyles, severe as it was."

Two months passed before the men landed their first job, installing air conditioning systems in 13 stores in a shopping center. "We made just $500 profit from that job," says Jones. Their firm's first-year income statement and end-of-year balance sheet appear in Exhibits 7A.1 and 7A.2.

"Even though things often looked bleak our first year in business," says Coleman, "not once did Jim and I consider giving up and folding our firm. To us, that would have been a fate worse than death. We would persevere." Jones adds, "Perseverance is what made ColeJon survive and succeed, and it has paid off handsomely."

EXHIBIT 7A.1
ColeJon Mechanical Corporation: 1984 income statement.

Sales revenues from contracts	$56,100
Cost of contracts	43,500
Gross profit	$12,600
Operating expenses	5,100
Profit before taxes	$ 7,500
Federal income taxes	0
Profit after taxes	$ 7,500

Education

Both Coleman and Jones believe that "lack of preparation" was the main reason for their poor performance that first year. They were not prepared to run a business of their own. Neither man had ever supervised anyone and certainly had never managed a business.

"I did learn about the ways of business by observing the contractors I had worked for," says Jones. "But it was a negative learning experience. The contractors were such poor managers that I learned what *not* to do, especially in the treatment of tradesmen like myself. They rarely trusted me and other tradesmen to put in a full day's work."

Ironically, it was the contractors whom Jones had worked for who helped him decide to launch his own venture. "I just knew I could do better," he says. "I just knew that I was a motivator, that I could help others to excel. What better way to use that talent than in a business of your own?"

Coleman and Jones have similar educational backgrounds. Both are graduates of large urban high schools who did well in their studies. Although encouraged by their teachers to go on to college, both men instead decided to learn trades and earn money. They both married and raised families soon after graduation.

They have not ignored education since. Coleman now believes that education should be a

EXHIBIT 7A.2

ColeJon Mechanical Corporation: Balance sheet (December 31, 1984).

Assets			Equities		
Current assets			**Current liabilities**		
Cash	$17,700		Accounts payable	$12,700	
Accounts receivable	16,100		Payroll taxes payable	1,600	
Other	200	$34,000	Accrued expenses	1,600	
			Other	4,000	$19,900
			Shareholders' loans		8,000
Fixed assets					
Equipment	$ 2,700		**Owners' equity**		
Less: Accumulated depreciation	300	2,400	Common stock	$ 2,000	
			Retained earnings	7,300	9,300
Other assets					
Deposits, organization		800			
Total assets		$37,200	Total equities		$37,200

"continuous thing," and he takes courses as he needs them at a local college. He has studied small business management, marketing, construction management, and engineering design. Jones also has taken courses to improve his technical skills.

Both men also attend seminars regularly all over the country. "What I like most about these seminars is the networking," says Coleman. "Jim and I get to meet with other contractors to share information and solutions to problems. We often come away feeling excited about what we've learned. In essence, Jim and I have learned to learn and learned to think for the rest of our lives."

Bonding Problem

Bonding companies, which protect customers and suppliers by selling bonds for a certain percentage of the contract price, have traditionally influenced business for contractors. There are three main kinds of bonds:

- Bid bonds, which assure customers that contractors are prepared to work according to the terms of their contracts if their bids are successful
- Payment bonds, which assure suppliers that they will be paid by the bonded contractors
- Performance bonds, which assure customers that jobs will be completed by the bonded contractors according to plans and specifications

These same bonds, however, create problems for new contractors looking for business. The U.S. Small Business Administration (SBA) describes these problems this way:

The effect that bonding companies have had on contractors is evident in the area of competition. The customer, by requiring that the contractor be bonded, is more or less assured of adequate completion of the job. Therefore, contractors are compared on the basis of price. Also, commercial banks are often more lenient to bonded contractors.

Bonding companies usually require the contractor to have proven experience and the organizational financial capacity to complete the project. This can be a real stumbling block to the new contractor.

With the widespread use of bonding requirements, the competition that is generated often leads the inexperienced contractor to submit bids that are unrealistically low. One or two such mistakes often can spell bankruptcy.

The SBA . . . has a surety bond program designed to help small and emerging contractors who might have previously been unable to get bonding. The SBA is authorized to guarantee up to 90 percent of losses incurred under bid, payment, or performance bonds on contracts up to $500,000.*

In the early days, ColeJon was faced with the problem of bonding in securing contracts: "As much as anything else, the bonding restraints imposed on us kept us from growing," says Jones. "The odd thing was, we could do the work, but we couldn't get the bonding that would let us do the work." Coleman adds, "The bonding restraint was like a millstone round our necks. The most we could get was a $25,000 bond, based on our personal assets, mine and Jim's. That meant we could only bid on $10,000 jobs."

Catch 22

Coleman and Jones tried to take advantage of the standard bond market, but they were turned down because of their inexperience as contractors. "It was a classic Catch-22 situation," says Jones. "We couldn't get work because we couldn't get bonding; and we couldn't get bonding because we couldn't get work. Amazing!" Later, the SBA helped Coleman and Jones through its surety bond program, enabling the two men to succeed.

*U.S. Small Business Administration, *Business Plan for Small Construction Firms* (Washington, D.C.: U.S. Government Printing Office, 1984), p. 7.

"Credibility is something you can't put dollars and cents on," says Coleman. "Jim and I spent, and still spend, most of our waking hours building up our credibility. We got our first job bidding low, just so we could gain some credentials, some credibility. It was a $3,000 job and we made no money. That first year was so rough, I did not draw a single penny of salary. Nor did Jim."

In their third year of business, the two men created an informal advisory council to give them the managerial help they needed. "We had too many managerial shortcomings, Lonnie and I," says Jones, "so we vowed to do something about it. For instance, our financial statements were such a mess that bankers laughed at them." In particular, they had little knowledge of project management or cost estimation for projects. These skills are crucial for contractors, as the SBA confirms:

Whether an entrepreneur succeeds as a contractor—makes a profit or not—depends to a great extent on his or her bidding practices. Therefore, the contractor must make careful and complete estimates.

Many of the more successful contractors attribute their success to their estimating procedures. They build the job on paper before they submit a bid. In doing this, they break the job down into work units and pieces of material. Then, they assign a cost to each item. The total of these costs will be the direct project cost.

Contractors must also figure on the indirect costs of a job. For instance, they will have overhead expenses such as the cost of maintaining an office, trucks, license fees, and so on. The estimate should also consider any interest charges that contractors will pay on money they borrow to get the job underway.

There are also insurance fees to pay, surety bond premiums, travel expenses, advertising costs, office salaries, lawyer's fees, and so on. These must also be paid out of the contractor's sales revenues.

The decision whether to bid on a particular job should be determined by several factors.

First, does the contractor have the capacity to complete the job on schedule and according to specifications? The contractor should beware of overextending himself or herself out of business. He must operate within his known capabilities. On any job, he must follow all the details of the work himself, or find competent supervision.*

Professional Help

The first and only professional that Coleman and Jones added to their advisory board was their attorney, Bernard Mandel, who is also an expert in cost accounting. In the first two years with ColeJon, Mandel did not charge for his services.

"What a super guy Bernie is," says Coleman. "He never even realized we could afford to pay him. He just went on doing legal work for us—writing subcontractors' agreements, filing legal papers, resolving disputes—as if we still could not afford his services. Of course, all this has changed, and Bernie now charges us his normal fee."

"We've always had pressing legal problems," says Coleman. "It's the nature of the industry. It's comforting to know that all I have to do is pick up the phone and ask Bernie for help. He can handle anything, even negligence suits against disreputable suppliers."

Federal Markets

After three years of lackluster performance, ColeJon's fortunes took a decided turn for the better. With Mandel's help, Coleman and Jones decided to devote almost all their marketing efforts to federal contracts. The federal government is the world's largest buyer of products and services. In fact, one of the SBA's major responsibilities is to see that small businesses like ColeJon obtain a fair share of this vast federal market.

To obtain their fair share, Coleman and Jones drafted a marketing strategy:

- Learning about federal markets. They wrote to Washington and ordered the *Small Business Subcontracting Directory,* the *Small and Disadvantaged Business Utilization,* the *Commerce Business Daily,* and other documents.

- Talking with specialists at the SBA and attending every workshop and seminar on federal markets that they could.

- Watching awards of major contracts to large companies in their area, companies that deal directly with subcontractors like ColeJon.

- Preparing descriptive literature and brochures about ColeJon's capabilities in the federal market. In order to do so, they learned how best to land federal contracts.

- Making frequent visits to small business specialists at the various federal agencies in their trading area.

- Carefully studying the terms of contracts, to make sure ColeJon can satisfy them to the letter.

The SBA's 8(a) Program

The federal program that appealed most to Coleman and Jones was the SBA's 8(a) program, which directs federal contracts to minority-owned businesses. This program has been highly controversial. Its critics claim that it has "made millionaires of a handful of minority entrepreneurs," in the process pouring "millions of dollars . . . into businesses that didn't work." Its supporters argue that the program has enabled minority entrepreneurs to succeed. "Without such help," says Jones, "we never would have made it."*

Mandel volunteered his services to guide Coleman and Jones through the maze of paperwork

---

*U.S. Small Business Administration, *Business Plan for Small Construction Firms* (Washington, D.C.: U.S. Government Printing Office, 1984), p. 6–7.

*Sanford L. Jacobs, "Company Sees Beneficial Side of Much-Maligned SBA Plan," *The Wall Street Journal,* (June 18, 1984), p. 21.

required by the SBA. To apply for certification as an 8(a) contractor, they had to give detailed information about their firm and themselves. The SBA's regional office then determined that ColeJon was eligible—a decision that later was reviewed and approved in Washington.

Coleman and Jones soon began landing government jobs, both local and federal. They overdid every job to build their credibility in the marketplace. At the same time, they expanded their business to include service maintenance, as described in their brochure:

> ColeJon designs and installs state-of-the-art plumbing, heating, air conditioning and fire protection systems, as well as power and process piping. ColeJon provides contract maintenance to industry and governmental units, protecting their mechanical "lifelines" against failure through constant vigilance.

Financial Performance

Sales began to soar as word spread in government circles that ColeJon performed well. Because ColeJon had won certification by the SBA as an 8(a) contractor, bonding was no longer a problem. ColeJon's yearly financial performance is summarized below and graphed in Exhibit 7A.3:

Year	Sales Revenues	After-tax Profits
1984	$ 56,100	$ 7,500
1985	82,300	(3,300)
1986	252,700	(8,600)
1987	601,500	(9,100)
1989	1,248,400	(10,800)
1989	3,756,800	71,500
1990	4,753,000	71,600

"We're proud of this record, Jim and I," says Coleman. "Never in our wildest dreams did we expect to be the founders of a multimillion-dollar corporation in so short a time. Our perseverance really paid off. When we started, all we could get was a bonding line of $25,000; would you believe that we now have a bonding line of $1.5 million? When we started, we could bid on nothing larger than a $10,000 job; now it's up to $1 million."

Today, ColeJon's largest service maintenance contract is with NASA's Lewis Research Center, which requires 80 employees. In addition, the company

EXHIBIT 7A.3
ColeJon Mechanical Corporation: Financial performance.

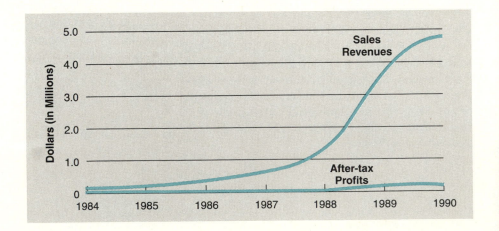

provides maintenance at the Environmental Protection Agency in Narragansett, Rhode Island. Its other clients include LTV, Union Carbide, and other giant corporations.

Coleman and Jones are especially proud of the fact that they have never lost a client. "Once we land a job," says Jones, "the client sticks with us and keeps renewing our contract. What better proof of our acceptance in the marketplace?"

Motivating Employees

Both Coleman and Jones credit much of their success to their methods of organization. "I'm a fiend for organization," says Coleman, "and I'm a good motivator." His philosophy on employee motivation is as follows:

▸ Avoid deception or rationalization among employees by relying on solid reasons and arguments.

▸ Give employees options, not orders, while at the same time retaining authority.

▸ Respect confidences, always making the effort to create trust by keeping the flow of information open.

▸ Build mutually satisfying relationships with employees and respect their individual purposes and needs.

The two men recognize that each employee has unique gifts and that their firm must allow employees to use these gifts. As a result, the words *trust* and *mutual respect* often are heard at ColeJon.

"The moral of this working philosophy is clear," says Jones. "If we treat our employees the way they themselves would like to be treated, our employees will then return the compliment in the form of productive and high-quality work. A work atmosphere that is not based on this kind of sensitivity is like a marriage without mutual respect. It's bound to collapse like a house of cards."

And they hire only foremen and managers whose working philosophy coincides with theirs.

"We go to great lengths, Lonnie and I, to hire the right person for the right job," says Jones. "We tell every job candidate that we look for managers who will fondle a job the same way we would if we were doing the job ourselves, away from the office."

It was this idea that led them to hire a seasoned mechanical engineer as a consultant in every facet of project management. "His formal knowledge of bidding and of project management was just what we needed to perform efficiently," says Coleman.

The engineer had once owned a small business himself and had been a chief engineer with a major contractor. Coleman and Jones filled the slots shown in the organizational chart in Exhibit 7A.4 with men and women of this caliber.

Control

To control ColeJon's performance, both men recognize the need for feedback at various stages of project management. As sole owners of ColeJon, they must plan, direct, and control each project efficiently. Throughout this process, ColeJon also needs constant financing, so their controls must supply them with the information they need to keep ColeJon's operations "on the money."

To manage each job efficiently, they analyze job costs to make sure it will turn a profit. "That is why good records are so important," says Coleman. "How can we possibly bid intelligently on a job unless we know what the costs are?"

As ColeJon has grown, their information and recordkeeping needs have become larger and more complex. Although all of ColeJon's accounting is done in house, most of it is done by a minicomputer programmed to generate:

▸ Quarterly income statements and balance sheets for the entire company

▸ Profit and cost comparisons of all projects

▸ Quarterly operating budgets

▸ Daily cash position

▸ Cash forecasts

▸ Payroll

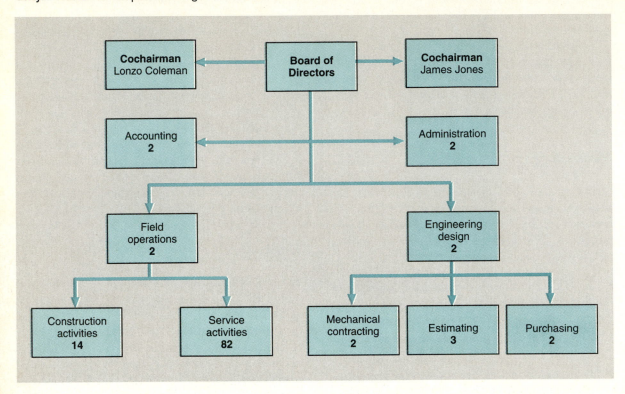

"The computer is our firm's memory," says Jones. "Most of our historical data is locked into the computer's memory. All we have to do is press a few keys to recall the data we need, especially for bid estimation."

The Future

"We want to be one of the country's major contractors," says Coleman. "We started out as remodelers, changed to service maintenance, and now may move into development programs for the federal government." Over the next few years, Coleman and Jones expect sales revenues to reach $28 million a year, up from $4,753,000 in 1990. ColeJon's income statements appear in Exhibit 7A.5.

Although work for local and federal government clients has been largely responsible for ColeJon's

success, Jones worries about that relationship. As shown in Exhibit 7A.6, roughly 75 percent of ColeJon's sales revenues come from government contracts; only 25 percent come from the private sector. "I would like to see that ratio reversed," says Jones. "Right now, ColeJon is highly vulnerable. The SBA's 8(a) program, for example, runs for just five years. When this program dries up, we've got to make up for the loss of business by landing more private-sector clients. That means we'll have to become even more competitive than we are now. Set-aside programs like 8(a) can't last forever."

Jones worries, too, that ColeJon is not as fully accepted in contract maintenance as it should be. "Just the other day, we had four auditors looking at our books, at our operations," he says. "We're always being investigated to see if we're capable." A photograph of Coleman and Jones and a client's building appear in Exhibit 7A.7 on page 220.

EXHIBIT 7A.5

ColeJon Mechanical Corporation: Three-year income statements.

	1988	1989	1990
Sales revenues from contracts	$1,248,400	$3,756,800	$4,753,000
Cost of contracts	1,077,700	3,157,700	3,585,500
Gross profit	$ 170,700	$ 599,100	$1,167,500
Operating expenses	183,700	483,200	979,100
Operating profit	$ (13,000)	$ 115,900	$ 188,400
Interest expense	7,400	17,700	18,700
Profit before taxes	$ (20,400)	$ 98,200	$ 169,700
Federal income taxes	(9,600)	26,700	98,100
Profit after taxes	$ (10,800)	$ 71,500	$ 71,600

EXHIBIT 7A.6

ColeJon Mechanical Corporation: Dependence on government markets.

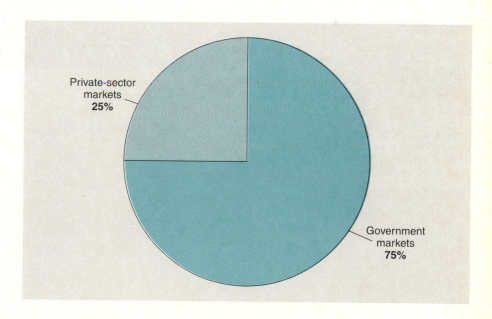

Private-sector markets 25%

Government markets 75%

Questions

1. Comment on the need for federal programs like the 8(a) program.
2. What are ColeJon's prospects?
3. Analyze ColeJon's financial performance.
4. What accounts for ColeJon's success?
5. What advice would you give Lonzo Coleman and James Jones about their plans for growth?

Roberta Zahniser

Roberta Zahniser, a CPA, had been a partner of a 33-strong accounting firm in Cincinnati for 11 years when she chose to quit and go into business for herself. Several of the firm's top small-business clients, as well as a junior partner, chose to follow Zahniser.

Zahniser's expertise was in helping small businesses weave their way through the Internet maze. One business she worked with had doubled its sales in a year by exclusively marketing its premium wines and gourmet foods over the Internet. This was one of the small businesses that chose to follow Zahniser.

Tempers soon flared over the buy-out price of Zahniser's partnership interest, deemed to be worth $105,000. Of that sum, $35,000 reflected the cash she had initially invested in the firm; and the rest was her share of the firm's growth in value during her years there.

Under the terms of the partnership agreement in effect when Zahniser left, the firm was obligated to pay her $105,000, but only on the condition that she had "committed no act harmful to the value of the remaining partners' interest in the partnership." After she left, the firm paid Zahniser $35,000 but refused to pay her a penny more—on the grounds that she had "irreparably harmed" the firm by:

▶ Launching her own accounting practice in competition with the firm

▶ Taking with her one of the firm's junior partners who had shown "considerable promise as a CPA"

▶ Taking with her several of the firm's top small-business clients, "thus causing the firm a financial loss"

Undaunted by her old firm's actions, Zahniser filed a lawsuit to recover the rest of her partnership interest, which came to $70,000. "It's mine; there's no question I earned it," says Zahniser.

Questions

1. How can an accounting firm protect itself against losses that may ensue when a partner, such as Roberta Zahniser in this case, leaves and takes with her a significant number of clients?

2. How would you argue in favor of the accounting firm in this case? In favor of Zahniser?

3. What ethical or social considerations, if any, are traded off to ensure freedom of choice on the part of clients?

Richard Melman, the founder of Chicago-based Lettuce Entertain You Enterprises, has a knack for knowing what the dining public wants just at the moment they start wanting it. Although Melman's expertise is restaurants, his eateries offer much more than just tasty food and a place to eat it. Melman creates total dining experiences. As a result, sales revenues at his thirty restaurants have grown to more than $100 million a year.

As a young boy, Melman worked in his father's delicatessens; and in 1967, he asked his father and his father's partner if he could become a third partner. They turned him down and, dejected, he quit, deciding to launch his own restaurant. In 1971, Melman opened R. J. Grunts—a restaurant that has become a Chicago landmark because of its good food and pleasant atmosphere.

With the Grunts' success behind him, Melman used his knowledge, instincts, and determination to build Lettuce Entertain You—today a lucrative nationwide chain of thirty restaurants. Although no two restaurants are alike, a common legal thread runs through them. Melman relies deeply on the partnership form of organization; in fact, twenty-one of his thirty restaurants are run as partnerships.

By going into business with partners in many parts of the country, Melman has achieved a comfortable and successful balance between strict control of his interests and freedom to pursue new ventures. The partnership for any given restaurant consists of Melman, his three most senior partners, silent partners who invest cash, and a managing partner who operates the restaurant.

In the belief that management should remain in close touch with the dining public, the managing partner is totally responsible for all day-to-day activities. If something goes wrong, Melman is called in to solve any problems.

Melman's partners include several celebrities. He opened "the Eccentric" with actress and talk-show host Oprah Winfrey, and he opened another one with quarterback Jim McMahon. Melman's success should continue to attract partners of all kinds, which in turn should free up Melman's time to "continue creating additional unique dining experiences."

Questions

1. When describing Lettuce Entertain You Enterprises, Richard Melman says, "We don't want to be the biggest, we just want to be the best." In what ways can a restaurant manager use this concept when managing day-to-day operations?
2. What are the advantages for Melman in using partnerships rather than other legal forms of business ownership? What are the disadvantages?

Source: Adapted from Pride, William M., Robert J. Hughes, and Jack R. Kapoor, *Business,* Fourth Edition. Copyright © 1993 by Houghton Mifflin Company. Used with permission.

Location

If you want a place in the sun, you've got to put up with a few blisters.

—Abigail Van Buren

Common in business circles is the saying that "the three most important factors in a retailer's success are location, location, and location." Though an exaggeration, this saying underscores the need for would-be retailers—such as grocers and clothiers—to research their markets thoroughly.

Similarly, location plays a vital role for would-be wholesalers, though much less so for service providers. But, for would-be manufacturers, the decision of where best to locate is especially crucial, mostly because of the heavy investment generally needed to make a product—as opposed, say, to a service like accounting, which requires little investment.

This chapter discusses how best to select the right site for a venture, focusing on marketing research as the indispensable factor in doing so.

The Varying Importance of Location

Location is more vital in some industries than in others, depending, for example, on whether customers must travel to the entrepreneur's place of business or the entrepreneur must travel to customers; on whether the business offers a unique product or service with little competition; or even on whether convenience is a key selling point.

In services such as accounting and management consulting, the question of location is often trivial. A management consultant's office, for example, may be within walking distance of prospective clients or an hour's drive away. Here, neither distance nor accessibility affects the consultant's ability to attract clients, because generally it is the consultant who must visit clients to solve their problems—and not the reverse.

At the other extreme are industries where location can make or break a venture. It matters a great deal, for example, where a grocer locates a supermarket. For one thing, it should be within walking distance for neighborhood residents, and no more than perhaps a five-minute drive for most residents in the trading area, with ample parking space available. It also should not be near another supermarket.

Marketing Research in Site Selection

As mentioned in Chapter 4, marketing research is one of the entrepreneur's most crucial tasks. Focusing as it does on the quest for information about the needs of customers, marketing research is indispensable. Only through such research, for example, may entrepreneurs carry off the site selection process depicted in Exhibit 8.1. This process—though applicable mostly to retailers and less so to manufacturers, service providers, and wholesalers—involves the choice of:

▶ A geographical region
▶ A city within that region
▶ An area within that city
▶ A specific site within that area

Few entrepreneurs go through so logical a process. Instead, they often allow personal preference to cloud their judgment on where best to locate. Entrepreneurs who enjoy warm weather the year round, for example, may choose to locate in the Deep South or the Southwest; on the other hand, those who enjoy

EXHIBIT 8.1
Process for selecting the right site.

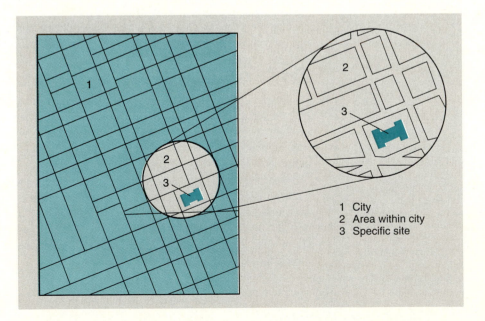

1 City
2 Area within city
3 Specific site

the four seasons may prefer New England or the Midwest. And still others may choose to stay in the neighborhood where they were born and raised. Even so, it would be a mistake to allow personal bias to take the place of pure marketing research.

How may entrepreneurs dig out the information they need to do a textbook job of marketing research? They might best begin by tapping such fertile sources of information as the federal government, trade associations, and chambers of commerce. The U.S. Bureau of the Census, for example, offers exhaustive demographic* information, by census tract, for all cities with 50,000 or more inhabitants. Each census tract resembles a large neighborhood, with an average population of 4,000 to 5,000. For example:

EXAMPLE ▶ An entrepreneur opening a women's clothing shop might use census information such as family income, family size, ethnicity, occupation, and the like to support a likely site for her shop. ▲▼▲

Thus, a good starting point for marketing research might well be someone else—such as the U.S. Bureau of the Census—who has *already* done research, often on the very same subject as the entrepreneur's. Finally, if the entrepreneur should find her problem unfathomable and all but impossible to define precisely, there often is no better recourse than a reference librarian.

Marketing research is discussed in greater detail in Chapter 14.

Selecting a Site

▶ **Locating a Retail, Service, or Wholesale Venture**

As suggested earlier, the process of site selection varies because each venture is unique. Suppose, for example, that an entrepreneur wants to open a drugstore. Before selecting a site, the entrepreneur first must ask questions such as those listed here, the answers to which would come from marketing research:

On the City

▶ Is the city growing? If so, how fast? What parts of the city are growing most?

▶ What is the city's population breakdown by age, income, and occupation?

▶ How many drugstores are there now in the city? Where are they? How well are they doing?

▶ What is the civic spirit like? Is the city progressive? Do residents work well together on civic projects?

▶ What is the quality of the city's schools, churches, parks, and culture?

On an Area Within the City

▶ What do area consumers buy when they go to a drugstore?

▶ What is the area's population? Is it growing? Are the people chiefly native-born or foreign?

Demographics is a marketing term covering such personal characteristics as age, ethnicity, income, occupation, race, sex, and the like.

- How do people make their living? Are they mostly white-collar workers, laborers, or retired persons?
- Are there people of all ages or are they mainly old, middle-aged, or young?
- What is the average family income? What is their total buying power?
- How many other drugstores are in the area? How successful are they?

On a Specific Site Within the Area

- Are neighboring businesses healthy?
- How close is the nearest competing drugstore?
- Is the site surrounded by well-kept homes?
- Is there plenty of parking space available next to or near the site?
- Is the site accessible by bus?
- What zoning requirements must be met?
- How far will customers have to travel to shop in the drugstore?
- Is there a steady flow of foot traffic by the site?
- What is the floor area? Is there any room to expand?
- Can deliveries be made from the rear?
- Will nearby stores draw customers to the site?
- Is the appearance of the site pleasing? Will customers want to shop there?
- Is there a divider on the road that may discourage some potential customers?

Thus, to choose the best site, entrepreneurs must pay painstaking attention to detail, narrowing their choices, and then ferreting out the facts about each one—as suggested in this brief example:

EXAMPLE ▶

An entrepreneur, Paula Lynne Berke, wants to open a children's apparel store in the Dallas, Texas, area. Berke prefers to locate in the Dallas area because it offers "just the continuity of life I'm looking for." She went to college there and later worked as a manager in a local department store; and she is an enthusiastic supporter of the Dallas Cowboys. As part of her business plan, Berke must justify which suburb offers her the best chance of success.

Berke's marketing professor had suggested that she look at *Sales and Marketing Management*'s "1995 Survey of Buying Power" to find data about the Dallas area. Grateful for the professor's advice, Berke visited the local library and examined its copy of the survey for various Dallas suburbs. She then narrowed her choices to the three described in Exhibit 8.2.

Of these three suburbs, Denton looks like the most favorable. It has a younger population than either Plano or Collin, and the median income is satisfactory. Having chosen Denton, Berke proceeds as suggested below.[1] ▲▼▲

▶ Shopping Areas Available to Retailers and Service Providers

In our example, the entrepreneur chose a particular suburb in which to locate her children's apparel store. The next step is to choose within that suburb a shopping area, of which there are two major types—planned and unplanned. These are described on the following page and depicted in Exhibit 8.3.

EXHIBIT 8.2

Data relevant to children's apparel store (Dallas area) (As of January 1, 1995).

Dallas Suburb	Percentage In Age Group		Population	Median Household Effective Buying Income
	18–24	25–34		
Denton	12.4	21.1	327,000	$46,100
Plano	7.1	17.9	164,200	69,720
Collin	8.0	18.8	335,300	60,180

Source: "1995 Survey of Buying Power," *Sales & Marketing Management* (1995), pp. c-140–c-146.

EXHIBIT 8.3

Major types of shopping areas available to retailers and service providers.

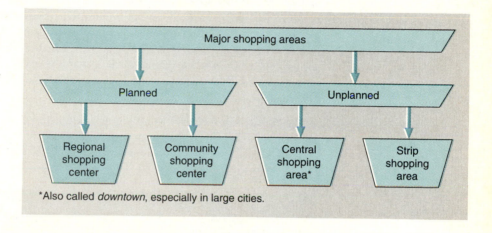

*Also called *downtown*, especially in large cities.

▶ Planned Shopping Areas

Regional Shopping Centers   Planned and built according to a master plan, these shopping centers generally have more than 100 shops each, with at least two department stores serving as anchor tenants. These shopping centers are designed to serve more than 100,000 people, who live up to a 30-minute drive away. And typically, they are enclosed, climate-controlled malls with free parking.

In their diversity and size, regional shopping centers have recreated the sweep of products and services traditionally offered by central shopping areas. Moreover, these shopping centers have become their community's social and cultural focal point. In fact, a survey by *U.S. News & World Report* found that "Americans spend more time in shopping centers than anywhere else outside their home and workplace."[2]

Community Shopping Centers   Also the result of much planning, community shopping centers may have just one department store, though smaller than those found at regional shopping centers. Community shopping centers are designed to serve 20,000 to 100,000 people, who live up to a 15-minute drive away. These shopping centers usually have no more than 25 shops.

Like regional shopping centers, community shopping centers apply the concept of balanced tenancy, properly balancing different kinds of businesses. For example, certain products or services attract similar customers. In other words, they draw mutually beneficial trade into the shopping center. This is why an entrepreneur might locate a dress shop next to a beauty shop.

▶ Unplanned Shopping Areas

Central Shopping Areas   Until World War II, the central shopping areas of cities and towns bustled with shoppers. Here were located the largest stores and the widest selection of products and services. Here, too, were located office buildings and major banks. And this is where major cultural events took place.

But since the war, the exodus of consumers to the suburbs and beyond has led to the economic decline of central shopping areas. Moreover, many have become eyesores, further discouraging consumers from shopping there and so hastening their decline.

Even so, spurred largely by their chambers of commerce, businesspeople are fighting back with the tools of imagination and innovation. Among the most highly publicized success stories is Boston's historic Faneuil Hall area. Until entrepreneurs banded together to revitalize the area, it had a dirty, down-at-the-heels look. Now fully restored, Faneuil Hall throbs with consumer activity the year round.

Strip Shopping Areas   Boasting shops clustered in a row, usually on one side of a street, these shopping strips generally sell convenience products—products that are low cost and that are purchased often and with little effort.

Planned shopping areas like Boston's Faneuil Hall Marketplace bustle with pedestrian traffic throughout the day.

A supermarket or a drugstore may be the largest store in a strip. Other businesses may range from barber shops to gasoline stations, from beauty shops to fast-food outlets. On-street parking is common.

Locating a Manufacturing Plant

Thus far, our discussion has centered on locating a retail store or a service firm. The process of deciding where best to locate a manufacturing plant is more complex and requires painstakingly thorough marketing research, as depicted in Exhibit 8.4.

To find the right site for their plants, entrepreneurs generally should try to balance three site factors:

▶ Potential sales revenues

▶ Manufacturing costs

▶ Transportation costs

These factors vary in importance, depending on the entrepreneur's marketing area. For example, if planning to sell their product to customers within a narrow geographic area, entrepreneurs should attempt to minimize transportation costs in relation to customers and ignore the location of rivals.

Questions of markets and costs are by no means the only ones that entrepreneurs should answer. The following factors also should be looked into:

▶ **Labor force**   Does the labor supply have the skills needed to run the plant productively?

EXHIBIT 8.4
Comparative difficulty of selecting the right site, by major industry group (on a scale of 1 to 10). Generally, manufacturers have the greatest difficulty finding the right site; service ventures have the least difficulty.

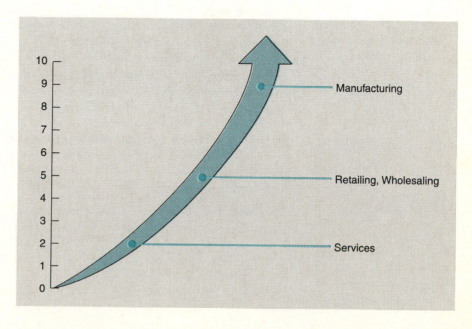

- ▶ **Community size**   Should the entrepreneur locate in a nonmetropolitan area? What is its standard of living? Its quality of life?
- ▶ **Transportation**   Will there be quick access to an interstate highway that allows overnight delivery to markets far from the site?
- ▶ **Water pollution**   What minimum levels of water pollution control must the entrepreneur adhere to?
- ▶ **Air pollution**   What kind of equipment must be installed to treat emissions of air pollutants?
- ▶ **Land**   How much land will be needed not only for making the product but also for parking and for air pollution-control equipment? Should the entrepreneur buy more land than needed at present to provide for future expansion and as a hedge against the upward trend in land prices?
- ▶ **Fuel and power**   Will there be ample sources of energy available now and later?
- ▶ **Taxes**   What effect will state and local taxes have on the cost of manufacture?
- ▶ **Financing opportunities**   Will the community or the state help finance the plant?[3]

This list of questions is by no means complete. But it does underline the complexity of picking the right site for a manufacturing plant. An example illustrates how the process of site selection might work:

EXAMPLE ▶

Glenn Myers, an entrepreneur, wants to build a small plant to make ammonia. There are no competing manufacturers in the state. A chemical engineer and former plant manager, Myers already has done some homework on basic problems:

- ▶ Because ammonia is the product of the reaction between natural gas and air, Myers wanted to make sure there would be an ample supply of natural gas in the future. The gas company assured him there would be.
- ▶ Because the manufacture of ammonia requires high pressures and temperatures, Myers wanted to make sure he could build such a plant. The state development department informed him that he could, as long as the plant was located at least a mile from the nearest residence. That way, if an explosion occurred—a remote possibility—the lives of residents would not be endangered.
- ▶ Because hot water and other pollutants would foul the environment if discharged by the plant, Myers must be sure that all pollutants will be neutralized. The designer of the plant has assured him that pollution control equipment placed throughout the plant would neutralize all pollutants.

Myers already has received promises from five fertilizer manufacturers that they will buy ammonia from him if his price is lower than that of competitors. He is sure he can underbid out-of-state competitors. Manufacturing costs will be the same regardless of location. Myers's main concern is to locate the plant in a place where the cost of transporting ammonia to the five fertilizer manufacturers is minimized.

To help him decide, Myers studied the map in Exhibit 8.5, which reveals that the five fertilizer manufacturers are located almost symmetrically about the state. The solution to the

EXHIBIT 8.5
Location of ammonia plant
in relation to customers.

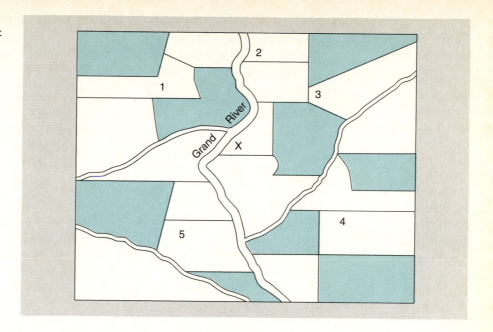

location problem now becomes apparent. Myers should locate the ammonia plant in an area roughly equidistant from the five customers, as shown in the exhibit. Because the manufacture of ammonia requires a lot of water, he also should place the plant near the river shown. ▲▼▲

In this example, Myers chose his plant site by inspection. In the real world, symmetrical markets and purchase areas are the exception; so choosing a site by inspection is usually difficult. Therefore, entrepreneurs should do an exhaustive analysis to measure the attractiveness of several likely sites, using return on investment as a financial yardstick. That is, how does each plant site affect potential sales revenues, manufacturing costs, and transportation costs? How do any changes affect potential profits?

Note the differences between locating a plant and selecting a store or office location. One major difference is that the choice of a region or community may be far more vital to manufacturers than the choice of a site within the community. Another difference is the lasting effect of a plant location. Once a plant is built, the entrepreneur is committed to the manufacture of a certain line of products for some time. If the entrepreneur has made a poor decision, relocation would probably mean financial collapse. Thus, thorough marketing research is a must before building a plant.

To carry out their marketing research, entrepreneurs may seek expert help, much of it free, from a number of ready sources. According to the SBA:

> You can get local help in choosing a site and securing data. For example, your electric, gas, or telephone utility may have a person who is designated to help companies with their location decisions.

Also, some banks and insurance companies provide such service. Other helpful services are found through local chambers of commerce and real estate agents who specialize in industrial sales, as well as through the industrial development departments of railway companies. Moreover, state governments usually provide agencies that specialize in providing facts for those entrepreneurs considering location.

Generally, there is no charge for the services of the groups listed here. But if you are unable to secure satisfactory data from any of these groups, you might consider hiring a professional consultant or a college professor who specialized in the field.[4]

▶ Site Criteria Used by High-Technology Companies

There is little question that high-technology companies will continue to fuel the nation's economy. What do these companies look for in selecting a plant site? The Joint Economic Committee of the U.S. Congress surveyed 691 high-technology companies to find out what criteria they use in choosing plant sites and how they evaluate the various regions of the country. The most important criterion is affordable labor. Other factors, in order of importance, are:

- ▶ Labor productivity
- ▶ A favorable tax climate
- ▶ Prestigious universities that can provide research support
- ▶ An affordable cost of living
- ▶ Accessible transportation
- ▶ Easy access to markets
- ▶ Limited regulatory controls
- ▶ A ready supply of affordable energy
- ▶ Cultural amenities
- ▶ A favorable climate
- ▶ Easy access to raw materials

▶ The Influential Role of Planned Shopping Areas and Industrial Parks

Even in those industries—such as apparel and shoes—where site selection matters a great deal, entrepreneurs lack the freedom to decide for themselves where best to locate; rather, that decision often is made for them by shopping center developers. The reason for this reversal of roles is the widespread dominance of *planned* shopping centers and industrial parks. In fact, more than 30,000 shopping centers and more than 4,500 industrial parks dotted the country in 1995, all but saturating the country—so much so, that only a handful of new shopping centers surfaced that year.[5]

One by-product of this phenomenon is that shopping center developers generally favor large chains as tenants, at the expense of the fledgling entrepreneur who may want to locate at the shopping center. Thus, the entrepreneur may have no recourse but to settle on another site, which may be inferior, and thus riskier.

Just as developers of shopping centers often determine the location of retail and service ventures, so do the developers of industrial parks often decide where the manufacturing entrepreneur may locate. The location of an industrial park frequently is dictated by ecological concerns, as well as access to transportation or markets. In fact, many communities have passed laws that force developers to meet the following requirements:

▶ No discharge of smoke into the air
▶ No despoiling of land around a plant
▶ No discharge of refuse, acid waste, or other pollutants into a stream
▶ Sufficient off-street parking, concealed by landscaped and grassy areas
▶ Recessed loading docks, so that trucks are not visible from the street

Developers of shopping centers and industrial parks must now go to great lengths to justify their proposals. Gone are the days when developers had only to make a marketing research study, buy up some vacant land, and build a complex of air-conditioned shops.

▶ **Best Cities for Small Business**

Our discussion of location would be incomplete without devoting some space to those cities—large, mid-sized, or small—that are especially open and hospitable to small business. Which cities go an extra mile in support of small business? Which are the best cities for small business?

To answer those questions, a statistical analysis was carried out by *Entrepreneur* magazine with Dun & Bradstreet, the large credit-reporting firm. In their analysis, they looked at six factors for each city:

▶ Business failures
▶ New incorporations
▶ Payment performance
▶ Personal income
▶ State small-business programs
▶ Cost of living

Results of their analysis appear in Exhibit 8.6. The cities listed there were hailed by *Entrepreneur* magazine as the "25 Best Cities for Small Business," meaning they offered the country's most favorable climate for entrepreneurs—at least for 1994. In commenting on the worthiness of these choices, which he helped make, Doug Handler of Dun & Bradstreet said:

Choosing these cities is more an art than a science. There is an element of arbitrariness in selection.[6]

EXHIBIT 8.6

25 best cities for small business (1994).

Size of Cities		
Large	**Mid-sized**	**Small**
1 Atlanta, GA	1 Amarillo, TX	1 Medford, OR
2 Minneapolis/St Paul, MN	2 Springfield, IL	2 Clarksville, TN/Hopkinsville, KY
3 Kansas City, MO	3 Canton, OH	3 Eau Claire, WI
4 Columbus, OH	4 Springfield, MO	4 Columbia, MO
5 Phoenix, AZ	5 Eugene/Springfield, OR	5 Biloxi/Gulfport, MS
6 Seattle/Everett, WA	6 Tulsa, OK	
7 Cleveland, OH	7 Salem, OR	
8 St. Louis, MO	8 Knoxville, TN	
9 Chicago, IL	9 Portland, OR	
10 Tampa Bay/St. Petersburg, FL	10 St. Cloud, MN	

Source: Cynthia Griffin et al., "25 Best Cities for Small Business," *Entrepreneur* (October 1994), p. 98.

SUMMARY

Selecting the right site for a venture is important to all businesses, but it is more vital for some than for others. Because the site chosen influences the venture's chances for success or failure, it is essential that the entrepreneur determine whether the sites under consideration meet the needs of the specific business. Must customers travel to the business? Or will the entrepreneur travel to the customers? Will the business offer a special product or service with little competition? Is convenience a key selling point in what the business will offer its customers?

To answer these questions and to select a site, entrepreneurs must rely on marketing research. Only through research can entrepreneurs best choose a geographical region, a city within that region, an area within that city, and, finally, a specific site within that area. Here, too, the nature of the business comes into play. That is, the process for selecting the right site depends on whether the business is a wholesale, retail, or service venture, or is a manufacturing plant.

In selecting a shopping area, for example, the entrepreneur must answer certain basic questions and then choose between a planned shopping area (a regional shopping center or a community shopping center) or an unplanned shopping area (a central shopping area or a strip shopping area).

The process of selecting a site for a manufacturing venture is more complex. Here, the entrepreneur must balance three site factors: potential sales revenues, manufacturing costs, and transportation costs. In addition, the entrepreneur must consider such factors as labor force, community size, transportation, water pollution, air pollution, land, fuel and power, taxes, and financing opportunities.

Discussion and Review Questions

1. Why is selection of the right site so important? Why is it more vital in some industries than in others? Give two examples.
2. What role does marketing research play in locating a venture?
3. What role should personal preference play in locating a venture? Explain your answer.
4. Describe some of the ways you might get outside help in locating a venture.
5. How would you go about selecting a site for your own venture?
6. What are some of the questions that a retailing entrepreneur should ask in selecting a city? In selecting an area within the city?
7. How do regional shopping centers differ from community shopping centers?
8. If you were thinking about opening a retail store, why might you choose to locate it near other retail stores that are healthy and prosperous?
9. In locating a manufacturing plant, what site factors should the entrepreneur try to balance?
10. In what ways is locating a manufacturing plant perhaps more critical than locating a retail store or service?
11. What are the site criteria used by high-technology ventures?
12. Since World War II, how has the rapid growth of shopping centers and industrial parks influenced the question of where best to locate a venture?
13. Do you believe that within a generation or two, most manufacturing will take place in industrial parks? Explain your answer.
14. In your judgment, how supportive of small business is your local community? Your city, county, or state? Give specific examples.
15. Define these terms: *marketing research, buying power, census tract, ecological concerns, industrial park.*

Location

As pointed out in the text, the three most important factors in retailing are location, location, and location. And it goes without saying that location is also important for other types of businesses as well.

Factors That Affect the Choice of a Location

The process of site selection varies because each business venture is unique. The characteristics of businesses that determine the importance of location include: (1) whether customers must travel to the business or whether the entrepreneur (or employees) must travel to customers, (2) whether the business offers a special product or service with little competition, and (3) whether convenience is a key selling point for the product or service that the business offers to customers.

Instructions for Worksheet 8

To complete this worksheet, in part 1 you must consider factors that affect the choice of location. In part 2, describe the ideal location for the business you would like to start. Finally in part 3, determine the cost for a specific location.

Part 1—Factors that Affect a Location Choice

Before completing this part, review the definition for your business that was last revised at the conclusion of Chapter 4.

1. Describe the typical customer who will buy your product or service.

2. Based on your answer to question 1, where does your typical customer shop for the product(s) or service(s) that your business sells?

Part 2—The Ideal Location

Entrepreneurs who are "stretched" for cash often settle for a cheap location. This philosophy can lead to disaster. As you answer the questions in this part, concentrate on identifying the ideal or "perfect" location for your business.

3. Based on the information in part 1, describe the ideal location for the type of business you would like to start.

4. How much space or square footage do you need for a business like yours?

5. When considering a location, are there any special needs or features that a business like yours may need?

Part 3—Balancing Cost and Location

To complete this part, make telephone calls, interview leasing agents, or talk with real estate agents to determine how much a location for your business—like the location you described in part 2—will cost.

6. To obtain the ideal location and the amount of space you need for your business, how much will it cost each month? How much will it cost each year?

7. Is the location you have chosen worth the cost? Justify your answer.

8. Can you afford this location? If the answer is no, what other locations are available at a lower cost?

Chocolate Emporium, Inc.

Paul Scott, a small business counselor, put down the receiver after speaking with Jon Lewis, a new client. Lewis was scheduled to come into the office in two hours to discuss his new business. Jon Lewis was referred to Scott by a mutual friend. Lewis's new business, Chocolate Emporium, Inc., was experiencing some difficulty.

The situation wasn't unusual; most new businesses experience some early difficulties. Paul Scott agreed to analyze Chocolate Emporium, Inc. and its market. As Paul reviewed the information he had gathered on Jon's business, he realized a two-prong attack was needed to make a go of the business—namely to increase revenues and to decrease costs. He also realized that abandonment was an alternative.

Background

Jon Lewis worked for 15½ years in insurance sales and agency management, before deciding to engage in his present venture, Chocolate Emporium, Inc. His insurance job, which required extensive traveling throughout the Midwest, restricted his family life. Jon chose a medium-sized Midwestern college town as the location of his business. This atmosphere closely resembled that of his youth. Jon liked the schools and the accessibility to a larger metropolitan area 35 miles away.

Of greater importance though, was the fact that the location Jon chose had no major chocolate specialty shop. Jon began researching the idea of a chocolate store two years before he actually opened the doors of Chocolate Emporium, Inc. His interests in such a store had been triggered by two successful examples in his hometown. One such chocolate store in particular appealed to Jon; it projected a "sit down," "family" image. It was this image that Jon hoped to reproduce in his own chocolate store. With this image in mind, Jon prepared to start his business.

Site Analysis

Jon was aware that pedestrian traffic would play a vital role in whether his venture succeeded. He visited the local chamber of commerce to get information on shopping areas and pedestrian traffic patterns. After observing several areas, Jon decided that downtown was best. From the start, however, he encountered problems of high rent, long leases, and rundown buildings. All available downtown sites were dropped for one or more of these reasons.

Jon then considered alternatives to downtown, among them several free-standing buildings that housed one or more stores. After six months of searching for a site, Jon identified a new shopping mall under construction along a major trafficway. The mall was the only one in the city and was located in its southern part. Jon viewed this location favorably because recently much of the city's growth had been in that direction. As shown in Exhibit 8A.1, Jon ultimately selected a corner location in the mall because of a favorable lease, year-round access, and new physical facilities. In addition, Jon anticipated that the other stores would draw customers, thus enhancing customer traffic around his store.

Competition

Jon wanted the Chocolate Emporium to be a retail store for high quality chocolates and candy. As Jon's marketing research progressed, he became convinced that chocolate and candy sales were seasonal and that he could expect sales peaks, mostly during the holiday seasons. He decided to expand

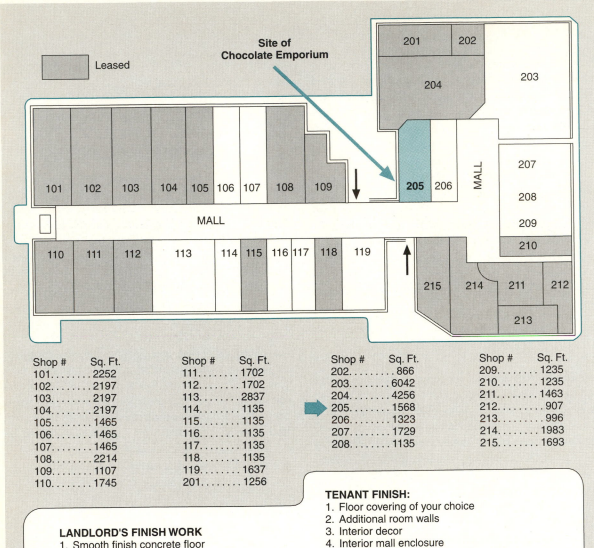

Shop #	Sq. Ft.
101	2252
102	2197
103	2197
104	2197
105	1465
106	1465
107	1465
108	2214
109	1107
110	1745

Shop #	Sq. Ft.
111	1702
112	1702
113	2837
114	1135
115	1135
116	1135
117	1135
118	1135
119	1637
201	1256

Shop #	Sq. Ft.
202	866
203	6042
204	4256
205	1568
206	1323
207	1729
208	1135

Shop #	Sq. Ft.
209	1235
210	1235
211	1463
212	907
213	996
214	1983
215	1693

LANDLORD'S FINISH WORK
1. Smooth finish concrete floor
2. Ceiling height – 10'
3. Drop ceiling (2' x4' acoustical panels)
4. Strip lighting
5. Side walls (Gypsum wallboard, taped and sanded)
6. Electrical outlets and minimum 100 amp panel
7. One (1) employee's bathroom – complete with hot/cold water supply. Bathroom enclosed with unpainted partitioning with door.
8. Individual space heating and air conditioning installed. Duct work to room.

TENANT FINISH:
1. Floor covering of your choice
2. Additional room walls
3. Interior decor
4. Interior mall enclosure
5. Signage

LEASE INFORMATION:
Term – Prefer minimum 3 years
Base Rent – $6.65 to $7.75 per square foot per year
Prorata share of common area maintenance and real estate taxes.
Utilities – Metered separately.
Hours of Operation – 10:00 A.M. to 8:30 P.M. Monday through Saturday and noon until 6:00 P.M. on Sundays. May vary for special events (i.e., Christmas).

his product line to include soda fountain items. This aspect of the business was not initiated, however, until after the shop opened. Thus, product lines eventually included chocolates, candy, and such fountain items as ice cream and carbonated beverages.

A factor underlying Jon's decision to choose the Midwestern college town was the lack of direct competition in the local chocolate market. However, there were several competitors in the candy and soda fountain markets. As noted in Exhibit 8A.2, Jon's chief competitors would be:

▸ *The Candy Store* (See CS in Exhibit 8A.2.)— The Candy Store carried few chocolates and sold mostly candies. Located downtown and privately owned, the Candy Store was probably the only direct competitor in candy sales.

▸ *Dairy Queen* (DQ)—Dairy Queen was long known for its fountain operations and had recently increased its efforts in the restaurant segment of its operation. The stores were located east and south of Chocolate Emporium and were franchises.

▸ *Baskin-Robbins* (BR)—Baskin-Robbins was solely a fountain operation. The name Baskin-Robbins was associated with 31 flavors of ice cream and was likely to have repeat customers. The store was located east of Chocolate Emporium on the same trafficway and was a franchise operation.

▸ *Zarda Dairy* (ZD)—Zarda Dairy had extended its market segment to include convenience stores with ice cream and fountain items provided by the dairy operation. Zarda Dairy was located nearby and was privately owned. The store was located west of Chocolate Emporium on the same trafficway.

▸ *Perkins* (P)—Although Perkins was mostly a restaurant, it did carry a limited selection of ice cream and fountain items. In addition, Perkins had recently run a market campaign highlighting the variety of deserts on their menu. Perkins was a franchise located across the parking lot from Chocolate Emporium.

There was also indirect competition from local grocery stores, all of which carried a variety of candies and chocolates, although the chocolate lines were not as widely varied as those at Chocolate Emporium. The major difference was that the grocery stores sold pre-packaged candies, while Chocolate Emporium weighed out what the customer wanted to buy. Jon preferred this personal touch.

Retail Preparation

Jon had no previous retail experience. Although he felt "very good about his ideas and their prospects," Jon realized that a positive attitude alone was insufficient. So, before deciding to start his own venture, he searched for franchise opportunities. After investigating several disappointing options, as summarized in Exhibit 8A.3, Jon decided to go it alone and explore the chocolate market on his own. He talked with suppliers of various chocolates and candies.

During this time, Jon became closely acquainted with the manager of a chocolate retail store in a nearby metropolitan area boasting a population of two million. This store was owned by a chocolate factory in the same area. Ultimately, this factory became Jon's major supplier of chocolates. He arranged to work at the retail store 2 to 3 days a week for six months, learning all he could about chocolate retailing.

The retail store that Jon worked with was in a large shopping mall that had opened in the heart of the metropolitan area five years before. Pedestrian traffic in the mall was brisk all year. Jon noticed that people often "browsed" among the different candy and chocolate counters. The store had many repeat customers. The manager told Jon that some customers had been regular patrons from the time she began running the store. It was Jon's hope that he could recreate such success in his very own retail store.

During this six-month period, Jon attended several chocolate and candy conventions. He enjoyed "discussing products with the suppliers and

EXHIBIT 8A.2
Chocolate Emporium, Inc.: Location of competitors.

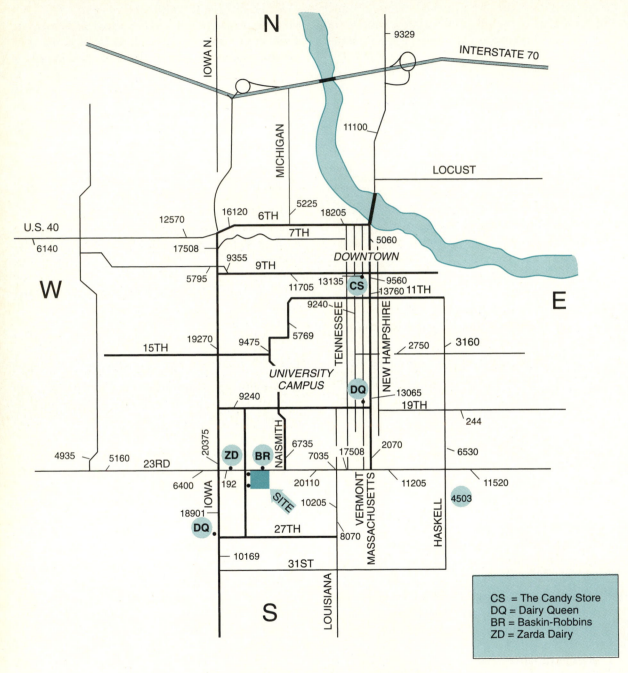

The numbers given by each major road are the traffic count for a 24-hour period. For example, 4503 vehicles were counted on Haskell just south of 23rd Street.

EXHIBIT 8A.3

Chocolate Emporium, Inc.: Potential franchises explored by Jon Lewis.

Name of Franchise	Results of Investigation
1. Godiva	▶ Very expensive chocolates, specializing in box chocolates.
	▶ Did not have a bona fide franchise arrangement.
	▶ Would have had minimum space and inventory requirements.
	▶ Cost prohibitive at $14 per pound
2. Russell Stover	▶ Were not ready to franchise at time of investigation.
	▶ Anticipating change in near future and willing to discuss franchise arrangements at that time.
3. Hershey's	▶ Did not provide franchises for retail operations.
	▶ Was willing to sell carload quantities for retail sales.
4. Swenson's	▶ Originally Jon wanted access to ice cream vs. bona fide franchise.
	▶ Price negotiations fell through.
	▶ Had to withdraw and see other sources.
5. Häagen Dazs	▶ Wanted to provide exclusive ice cream dealership; no chocolates or candies.
	▶ Withdrew because of above restrictions.

prospects for the future." Jon became knowledgeable about the chocolate industry. He arranged to receive specialty items not available through his major supplier. Eventually his sources of supply included chocolate and candy producers located across the country. Jon prided himself in his ability to locate suppliers and to expand the kinds of chocolates and candies he carried in stock. For the fountain and ice cream product line, Jon relied solely upon one supplier. His rationale was that these items are refrigerated and the closer his supplier the less problem with shortages and spoilage. Jon had had no problem with back orders from any supplier.

Jon could usually rely upon delivery of goods within a week of placing an order. Given the nearness of his major chocolate and dairy suppliers, he would receive goods sooner if he personally picked them up. The terms were cash on delivery. Since Jon was a newer small retailer, his suppliers were hesitant to extend credit. Jon hoped these suppliers' terms would change over time.

Financing of the Business

Jon was able to acquire a bank loan of $66,000 through a local bank, giving as collateral his personal portfolio of stocks and bonds. In addition, Jon invested $32,000 of his own money. A $19,000 loan from a relative provided the rest of the financing.

Current Situation

In talking with Jon Lewis, Paul Scott was impressed with Jon's knowledge of the chocolate industry.

The history and refinement of the cocoa bean often entered their discussions. Jon was truly fascinated with the industry and market he chose to enter. Both energetic and enthusiastic, Jon Lewis was the epitome of the entrepreneur. Indeed, he usually worked 60 or more hours a week.

Shopping Mall Status

The shopping mall that Jon chose had been vacant for two years prior to his lease arrangement. In discussing this fact with the developer, Paul Scott received no apparent explanation. The developer simply explained "the retail interest originally anticipated never surfaced." At the time of Paul's analysis, the mall was two-thirds occupied, as shown earlier in Exhibit 8A.1. Occupants included the following:

▶ Four specialty shops (sites 118, 115, 104, 105).
▶ An electronics store (109)
▶ A video game center (108)
▶ A large nightclub (210–215)
▶ A travel agent (201)
▶ A flower shop (202)
▶ A fitness center (204)
▶ Jon's chocolate/fountain shop (205)
▶ Clothing store (101–103, 110–112)

In addition, a cafeteria was under construction in the east end of the mall, shown as sites 203, 207, 208, and 209 in Exhibit 8A.1. The increase in occupancy was partly due to the efforts of the older occupants. In fact, Jon chaired a committee of current occupants that actively promoted the mall to stimulate new retail interest. When asked, Jon knew of no advertising campaign by the developers to promote the mall.

When Paul Scott spoke with a colleague about the mall's advertising strategy, his colleague mentioned a study performed by the developers. Paul's colleague made the following comments on the findings of the study:

▶ The study was geared toward the supply of labor rather than toward customers–that is, can you hire enough workers for your store?

▶ A study of customer potential was included but not customer flow.

▶ Projections from the study were unrealistically high.

▶ The mall opened with little information about customer needs and wants.

The shopping mall bordered one of the busiest traffic intersections in the city. To the west of the mall was a major department store and to the east a vacant lot. Behind the mall, to the south, were single- and multiple-family dwellings. The entire area south of the mall was zoned for residential use. Across from the mall, to the north, were several fast food restaurants. The area north of these businesses, though, was zoned for residential use. Essentially, the mall was part of a "strip development" along a major traffic-way.

Paul Scott had visited the shopping mall on a number of occasions. He observed that there were few people browsing in the mall itself. Jon agreed with Paul's observation. Jon expressed concern about the cafeteria being constructed next to him on the east side of the mall. He was fearful that people might enter the cafeteria from outside (on the north) and thus eliminate any location advantage he might have (see Exhibit 8A.1).

Facilities

A major advantage of the mall location was its new facilities. The mall had restrooms and access for the disabled. At the time of Paul's analysis, one end of the mall was vacant, as shown in Exhibit 8A.1. The other end of the mall was occupied by a clothing retailer. Because new occupants were still entering the mall, much construction was in progress.

Jon did not provide carryout service. He felt strongly about maintaining a "sit down" image. Since the fountain was a later addition to the business, Jon admitted that remodeling may be needed to ensure an efficient workflow. For example, he had more than 30 flavors of ice cream but could only display nine flavors at any one time. Jon planned to remedy this problem by the next peak fountain season.

Jon also wanted to ensure that he had adequate storage space. Consequently, he had a 10- by 12-foot walk-in freezer installed. Turn to Exhibit 8A.4 for the store layout. Paul noticed that the freezer was two-thirds empty and discussed the freezer capacity with Jon. Jon stated that he expected monthly sales revenues of $25,000 and felt that a 10- by 12-foot freezer would be large enough to accommodate that level of business. Paul discovered later that a nearby Baskin-Robbins store had a 10- by 6-foot freezer.

Jon purchased a van truck in order to provide special deliveries for chocolate orders. Jon charged

EXHIBIT 8A.4
Chocolate Emporium, Inc.: Store layout.*

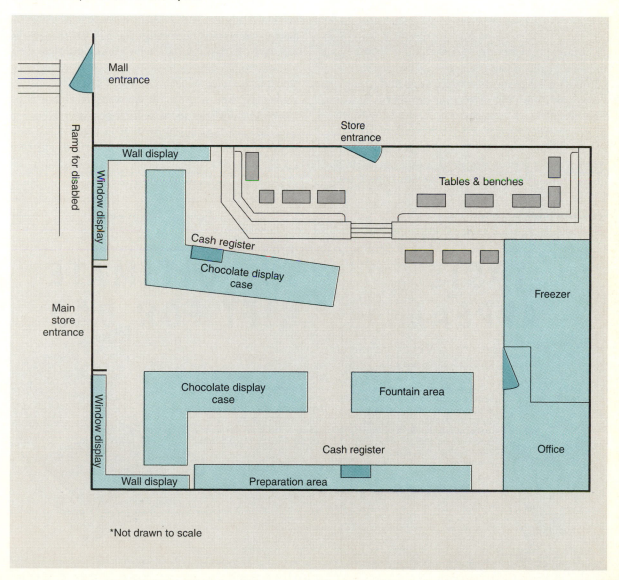

*Not drawn to scale

$1 for delivery. He recounted a delivery incident to Paul Scott:

> On Valentine's Day he had advertised giving candy instead of the traditional flowers. He received a request from a sorority house. When Jon arrived in the van to make the delivery, several of the sorority women questioned him about what he was doing and to whom it was to be delivered. Jon felt that incidents like these provided visibility for the business.

Marketing Factors

In analyzing Chocolate Emporium, Paul Scott focused upon the market area. The city in which Chocolate Emporium was located had a population of 53,000. There was no dominant industry. The chamber of commerce actively promoted the town as an attractive location for businesses. Several "Fortune 500" companies had located smaller branches in the area; however, none had more than 300 to 400 employees. There was a large rural population and many of them used the city for shopping on weekends. A twenty-year city plan called for improvement of the downtown shopping area to cope with retail traffic. In fact, the City Commission rejected a proposal for a new shopping mall in favor of promoting the downtown improvement plan.

The largest employer in the area was the university, which had 25,000 students.* During the fall, the football games created a high potential for business volume. In the summer, however, most of the students returned home. Thus, business was highly seasonal. The student population had grown steadily during the 1970s, but in the last two years there had been almost no increase.

Jon was aware of the importance of advertising and was actively experimenting to find "the answer to his market woes." He advertised in both the university and the local newspapers as well as on the radio. Examples appear in Exhibits 8A.5 and 8A.6. He wanted to design an advertisement that

---

*One-third of whom were considered residents of the town.

EXHIBIT 8A.5
Chocolate Emporium, Inc.: Newspaper advertisements.

Recapture the flavor of honest to goodness soda fountain treats. You'll find all your favorites, made with our delicious ice cream and luscious toppings. Savor the richness of a creamy Soda, Malt, Sundae, or New York Egg Creme...or try an old-fashioned Phosphate. Not to be missed are our delicious Banana Splits and our special Pink Panther.

Open weekdays till 10:00
Weekends and Holidays till 11:00

For the Dad who has everything . . . .a box made of milk chocolate. Fill it with Jelly Bellies, Almond Toffee, White Chocolate Pretzels, Raspberry Creams, Sour Balls, or a combination of your Dad's favorites. We're restocked and ready to surprise your dad with the Ultimate Gift.

Open Weekdays till 10:00 P.M.
Weekends & Holidays till 11:00 P.M.

EXHIBIT 8A.6

Chocolate Emporium, Inc.: Radio advertisements.

(1) Narrator:

Are you burning the midnight oil?

Do you have three exams tomorrow?

Did your roommate leave last week?

Are you lonely?

Well, wake up! Take a study break! Chocolate Emporium is pulling for you too, with an "all nighter" tonight only. The coffee pot's hot, the ice cream's cold, and they have lots of nibbles for you!

They'll be open all night! Tonight only! So, wake up at Chocolate Emporium in the Southern Hills Mall, 23rd and Ousdahl.

Chocolate Emporium! Chocolate Emporium! Chocolate Emporium!

(2) (S) Jonsey!

(J) What? Who said that?

(S) It's me, your sweet tooth!

(J) My what?

(S) Your sweet tooth. You're not going to get another box of that pre-packaged junk that passes for candy, are you?

(J) Well, what else is there?

(S) Fresh chocolate candy. Or wickedly rich fudge. An ice cream cone or a delicious soda from Chocolate Emporium in _____.

(J) Where?

(S) Chocolate Emporium in _____. They have everything to satisfy your sweet tooth, and a satisfied sweet tooth is a *quiet* sweet tooth, Jonsey.

That's Chocolate Emporium at _____.

promoted a "sit-down" and a "family" image. The shopping mall had one large central sign with space only for the shopping mall's name. Each business was permitted to hang a banner below the sign for the 30 days following its grand opening.

To partially overcome this situation, Jon parked the van every day so that the Chocolate Emporium logo faced the traffic. As mentioned earlier, Jon also used the van for occasional deliveries. This aspect of the business contributed little to sales, and the van usually "remained parked in its usual spot." Paul felt that this method of advertising was innovative but questioned its effectiveness. Jon was also experimenting with using classified advertisements in the local newspapers and in the coupon books sold by local service clubs.

Financial and Inventory Status

Paul Scott found that Jon kept accurate records but that no summaries, income statement, or balance sheet had been prepared. One of Paul's first tasks was to provide an income statement and a balance sheet, as shown in Exhibits 8A.7 and 8A.8. Paul also provided a detailed list of operating expenses, shown in Exhibit 8A.9; and charted sales revenues by product line, shown in Exhibit 8A.10. Paul discovered that Jon was four months behind in his rent. In discussing the mall with the developer, Paul learned that one-half of the occupants were behind in their rent. The developer did not view late rents as a severe problem because his major concern was to increase the mall's occupancy.

Paul was also curious about the sales revenues and the operating expenses traceable to the van's operation alone. He found that the van:

▸ Averaged sales of only $15 to $20 a month, peaking at $150 to $170 during the Easter holiday.

▸ Was purchased for $12,231 and to date had cost $972 to run. Depreciation on the van to date was $3,737.

The ice cream and chocolates were stored in the walk-in freezer. When reviewing inventory control procedures, Paul noted that orders were based on a stock tally sheet placed on the freezer. Whoever took a container of ice cream or a quantity of chocolate from the freezer made a notation on the sheet. Paul could not help noticing that Jon had a large volume of ice cream in stock. In fact, he discovered later than Jon had three weeks' stock on hand. When discussing ice cream inventory with a nearby competitor, Paul learned that the competitor never kept more than a one-week stock of ice cream. The competitor said the inventory level might vary slightly during the summer

EXHIBIT 8A.7

Chocolate Emporium, Inc.: Income statement (February 10, 198X to September 25, 198X).

Sales revenues		$42,689
Cost of goods sold		31,012
Gross profit		$11,677
Operating expenses:		
Variable expenses*	$33,073	
Fixed expenses**	27,927	61,000
Operating loss before		
depreciation and interest		($49,323)
Less:		
Depreciation	$ 7,087	
Interest	5,383	12,470
Net operating loss		($61,793)

*Variable expenses are items of expense that vary directly and proportionately with sales revenues. For example, if sales increase by 10 percent, variable expenses would also increase by 10 percent.

**Fixed expenses are items of expense that do not vary at all with sales.

EXHIBIT 8A.8

Chocolate Emporium, Inc.: Balance sheet (as of September 25, 198X)

Assets

Current assets:		
Petty cash	$ 195.00	
Savings	371.84	
Deposits	35.00	
Merchandise inventory	6,075.94	
Office supplies inventory	901.77	$ 7,579.55
Long-term assets:		
Moveable assets	$39,813.92	
Cash value of insurance	26,319.00	
Leasehold improvements	21,922.74	
Van	8,493.75	95,549.41
Total assets		$104,128.96

Equities

Current liabilities:		
Suppliers owed	$ 5,297.26	
Rent owed	4,661.07	
Sales tax owed	396.57	
Payroll taxes owed	400.00	$ 10,754.90
Short-term bank loan		66,451.50
Long-term liabilities:		
Family loan	$19,000.00	
Loans against insurance	5,198.70	
Contract labor owed	6,394.74	30,593.44
Owners' equity:		
Owner's investments	$58,122.50	
Retained earnings	(61,793.38)	(3,670.88)
Total equities		$104,128.96

EXHIBIT 8A.9

Chocolate Emporium, Inc.: Breakdown of operating expenses (February 10, 198X to September 25, 198X)

Wages	$15,285
Advertising	11,268
Contract labor	8,118
Officers' salaries	7,385
Rent	4,550
Utilities	2,202
Payroll taxes	2,074
Insurance	2,059
Taxes (mostly sales tax)	1,521
Freight	1,113
Car expense (van included)	972
Legal (cost of incorporation)	960
Licenses and permits	613
Machine rental	578
Telephone	521
Life insurance	475
Office supplies	371
Travel	237
Dues and publications	176
Employee benefits	102
Education and training	95
Postage	90
Miscellaneous items	74
Entertainment	65
Bank fees	58
Overdraft	38
Property tax	NA*
Total	$61,000

*Not available

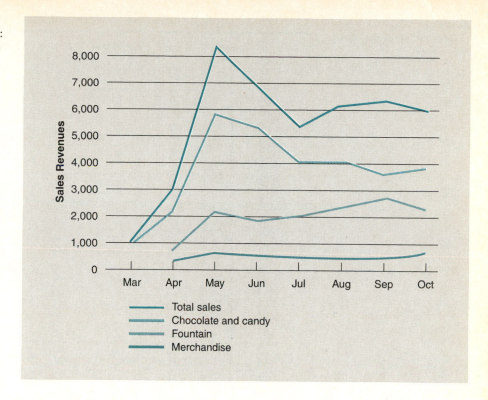

EXHIBIT 8A.10
Chocolate Emporium, Inc.: Sales revenues by product line (198X).

Legend:
- Total sales
- Chocolate and candy
- Fountain
- Merchandise

months. Paul then discussed inventory with Jon and discovered that Jon had 53 suppliers.

Personnel

Jon was the only full-time employee at Chocolate Emporium. His only hiring requirement was that each employee must work more than 10 hours a week. When working, the employees could help themselves to whatever they wanted in the store. Jon had no formal training program for new employees. His turnover was low; and, in fact, only one person had quit in 10 months of operation. All of Jon's help were students who received a minimum wage with the exception of his assistant manager. As Jon put it, "I don't like to underpay people, I found out that a nearby competitor pays as little as $2.00 an hour!" At least two people worked during most hours of operation, as shown in Exhibit 8A.11 on page 250. In addition, Jon helped out if customer traffic was heavy.

Questions

1. How serious is Jon Lewis's situation?
2. How did the current situation occur?
3. What are the alternatives available to Lewis? What are the consequences of each alternative?
4. As Paul Scott, lay out a detailed business plan for Jon Lewis. What should Lewis do? When? Why?

Source: Case "The Chocolate Emporium" by Dr. Marilyn Taylor and Dr. Alan Aidiff. Distributed by the Cases Research Association. Used with permission.

Time	Monday	Tuesday	Wednesday	Thursday	Friday	Saturday	Sunday
A.M. 9:30	—	1	1	1	1	1	
10:00	—	1	1	1	1	1	
11:00	1	2	1	1	1	2	
P.M. 12:00	1	2	1	1	1	2	1
1:00	2	2	1	1	1	2	2
2:00	2	2	2	2	2	2	2
3:00	2	2	2	2	2	2	2
4:00	2	2	2	2	2	2	2
5:00	2	2	2	2	2	2	2
6:00	2	2	2	2	2	2	2
7:00	2	2	2	2	3	3	2
8:00	2	2	2	2	3	3	2
9:00	2	2	2	2	3	3	2
10:00	2	2	2	2	3	3	2
	1	1		1			1

Note: Mall is open from 10:00 A.M. to 8:30 P.M. Figures include the assistant manager, but not Jon Lewis.

CASE 8B ▶ *Susan Johnson*

Susan Johnson recently purchased a 100-room motel in a small town in northern California. The area was once a popular resort community, but over the past 10 years, tourism has decreased significantly. Many businesses have closed, and currently only a few motels and restaurants are still operating.

This drop in tourism is primarily the result of an image problem the town has had. It is located on a river that is quite scenic but several years ago had a pollution problem. It has since been solved, and testing has indicated that the water is now clean. But during this time another problem also arose: The number of families visiting the area gradually decreased, and a rougher clientele began coming up from the nearby metropolitan area.

Johnson hopes to revitalize the area and win back the tourist trade it once had. The town has many advantages: It is located between two major cities, is surrounded by national parks, is on the outskirts of the California wine country, and is only about a half hour from the Pacific Ocean. The town itself also is interesting, having several historic buildings and an old covered bridge.

Johnson has convinced several local business owners to meet with her and formulate a plan to bring tourists back to the area.

Questions
1. What particular attractions might be developed to appeal to tourists? Explain.
2. How should the local businesses market their community? Explain.

Source: From: *Introduction to Hospitality Management* by Kathleen M. Iverson. Copyright © 1989 by Van Nostrand Reinhold. Used with permission.

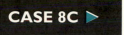 **CASE 8C ▶** *Donut Village*

Donut Village is a successful franchisor of doughnut shops throughout the United States. One of the most important services it offers franchisees is site selection research. The company recognizes that even the most successful operator can be hindered by a poor location. Because it typically negotiates for 20-year leases, Donut Village also knows the long-term consequences of site selection.

Site Selection Criteria

Donut Village applies these site selection criteria to its traditional main-road suburban stores:

▶ The correct side of the street is critical. The firm is aware that potential customers dislike crossing double-lined roads or making U-turns. When it does vehicular traffic counts for prospective sites, then, it heavily discounts vehicles traveling on the opposite side of the road.

▶ The busiest time for doughnut shops is typically before work, from 6:30 A.M. to 9:30 A.M. Traffic counts at this time of day are vital.

▶ Also vital is site visibility from the road. A site with poor visibility means that potential customers might pass the shop before they actually see it. This sharply reduces sales potential.

▶ Doughnut stores need to be close to a large population base to prosper. The most successful stores often are located near office buildings, factories, and colleges and universities.

▶ The company's required ratio of parking spots to store square footage is much less than that of McDonald's or Burger King. The reason is that customers spend much less time in a doughnut shop than in a hamburger-based franchise because of the doughnut shop's large take-out business and limited menu.

▶ Residents' income, age, and education are relatively unimportant factors.

Nontraditional Sites

Because good traditional sites are increasingly hard to obtain, Donut Village has begun looking at nontraditional sites for new shops. It must look at new kinds of locations if it is going to continue growing.

By studying the operations of McDonald's and Burger King, Donut Village discovered that each has been creative in its use of nontraditional locations. For example, McDonald's and Burger King have shops in naval installations, high schools, zoos, hospitals, office buildings, and parks, and on turnpikes. Burger King also has mobile units that can be moved to different sites.

Despite the popularity of these new sites, Donut Village understands that its business is very different from hamburger-based franchising. For example, the doughnut business is more snack oriented and has a higher percentage of take-out business; and doughnuts more often are purchased in multiple units.

This is how Donut Village views a number of nontraditional sites now under consideration:

Office buildings   Franchisees can sell products from coffee wagons in buildings that offer high concentrations of people. The office environment fits well with the breakfast and coffee-break orientation of Donut Village. Special arrangements would have to be worked out with each building owner.

Mobile units   These units can be sent to specific sites with high but temporary concentrations of people, to sporting events, parades, and dog shows, for example. This is a flexible approach. Separate arrangements would have to be made with each event manager for the right to sell Donut Village products.

Highway locations   Quick-stop units would offer an ideal place for car drivers and their passengers, bus passengers, and truck drivers to take a coffee break. Doughnuts and coffee could be consumed in the customer's car. This kind of operation could be open 24 hours a day.

College and university cafeterias   Self-contained operations located alongside schools' conventional cafeterias could be developed in a standard prototype format. These operations would offer quick service and portability, and the advantages of large concentrations of people and no need for additional parking facilities. Other advantages include evening and weekend business selling to dormitory students and catering small parties. Special arrangements would have to be made with each school. In many cases, cafeteria operators have exclusive rights to sell food on a campus.

Questions

1. What are the advantages and disadvantages of each of these options for doughnut shops: isolated store locations, unplanned business district sites, and planned shopping center sites?
2. Evaluate the criteria used by Donut Village in planning for its traditional sites.
3. Develop a site location checklist for use by Donut Village to evaluate nontraditional sites. How would you weigh each criterion?
4. Evaluate the four nontraditional sites proposed by Donut Village. Which kind of site is best? Explain your answer.

Source: From *Retail Management*, Fourth Edition by Berman/Evans, © 1989. Reprinted by permission of Prentice-Hall, Inc., Upper Saddle River, NJ.

Financing

The use of money is all the advantage there is in having money.

—*Benjamin Franklin*

Like many works of art, a business begins on a piece of paper. The would-be entrepreneur may sit down and design a small electronics plant to meet customers' needs and make a fine product, but without money the plan might never become a reality. This is why entrepreneurs should understand how to estimate the amount of money they need, and then how to go about raising that money.

This twin problem fascinates entrepreneurs, perhaps more so than any other part of launching a new venture. This fascination may stem from a romantic view of how some multimillion-dollar businesses began on a shoestring of just a few thousand dollars. Apple, for example, was started with just $600.

Despite its romantic aspects, financing a new venture frustrates many entrepreneurs. Often, they do not know where to begin; and if they do know, they go at it haphazardly. Relieving that frustration is one purpose of this chapter. It addresses two questions:

▶ What is the best way to estimate the money needed to launch a venture?

▶ What is the best way to raise that money?

Estimating Money Needs

Before estimating how much money they need, entrepreneurs must know what they plan to do. Unfortunately, many entrepreneurs do not, often because they have failed to work out a business plan. Yet the very act of preparing such a plan enables entrepreneurs to crystallize their thinking on how best to launch their ventures. It forces them to move logically and systematically from the stage of dreams and ideas to that of action and results.

The centerpiece of the business plan is its *cash budget,* which translates operating plans into dollars. Without a cash budget, entrepreneurs have no way of estimating their financial needs. So vital is this budget that few investors or creditors will entertain a request for money without one. More than any other piece of information, the cash budget enables them to make an intelligent decision about whether to finance the entrepreneur. The cash budget, for example, helps the banker obtain answers to core questions such as these:

▶ How much money do you need?

▶ How will you spend the money?

▶ How will the loan benefit you?

▶ How soon will you pay us back?

The Price of Failing to Budget

The process of budgeting has many guises. Some individuals divide the money from their weekly income into piles that they then place in envelopes earmarked for groceries, clothes, entertainment, and so on. Many giant corporations proceed in an orderly system that reflects both long- and short-range goals. And the federal government engages in a lengthy procedure of debate and compromise between the U.S. Congress and the President.

Whatever the approach, what we are describing is *budgeting,* or financial planning. Although such planning is widely practiced by big business, entrepreneurs do little of it. This is a mistake. To many entrepreneurs, financial skill

The existence of user-friendly software enables entrepreneurs to prepare, painlessly, a cash budget for their business.

is something best left to Wall Street. Yet financial skill is as vital to a venture's survival and growth as any other skill. One reason for their reluctance may be their discomfort with numbers. In the words of the Bank of America:

> The mere language of finance . . . sounds so official, important, and difficult that many businesspersons automatically assume it is beyond their understanding. They feel that anything so obviously "textbookish" is better left to the professionals.[1]

With this attitude, it is hardly surprising that so many entrepreneurs find themselves in trouble from the start. Yet they often blame investors and creditors for their plight rather than themselves. An entrepreneur might say, "If only I had $10,000, I could really make my idea work." Generally unprepared, these entrepreneurs fail to convince potential investors and creditors of their need for money. Clearly, the odds favor the prepared entrepreneur. As Branch Rickey, former owner of the old Brooklyn Dodgers, once said, "Luck is the residue of design."

▶ **Preparing a Budget**

Touched upon in Chapter 4, budget preparation will be explained here in some detail. Before beginning to work on their budget, entrepreneurs must first spell out their operating plans, covering such activities as marketing and production, organization and legal aspects—all key parts of their business plan.

Before we describe how to translate these operating plans into dollars, let us point out two limitations of budgeting:

▶ All budgets depend on estimates of what will happen in the future. No one can accurately predict what will happen, however, so budgets can be no better than the underlying estimates. Thus, entrepreneurs must be thorough in their efforts to prepare workable operating plans.

▶ A budget cannot account for the effects of intangible qualities or unpredictable events. It cannot reflect, for example, how skilled and able the entrepreneur may be, nor can it reflect teamwork and morale. A budget can deal only with future events that can be expressed in dollars.

Still, budgeting is a handy tool, offering as it does a tidy way of reducing the future to a single statement, *and* in language that investors and creditors understand well—as detailed in this example:

EXAMPLE ▶

An entrepreneur plans to open a store selling Scandinavian furniture. She has estimated her sales revenues for the first three years, as shown in Exhibit 9.1.

This sales forecast is a result of the marketing plan that she worked out as part of her business plan. Although rough, the sales forecast is her single most important estimate, because it is the basis for most other estimates. For example, a store with yearly sales of $2 million rather than $400,000 may call for five times as many salespersons, four times as much floor space, and three times as much inventory.

Having forecast her sales, the entrepreneur next estimates the cost of the fixed and current assets she will need to support those sales. ▲▼▲

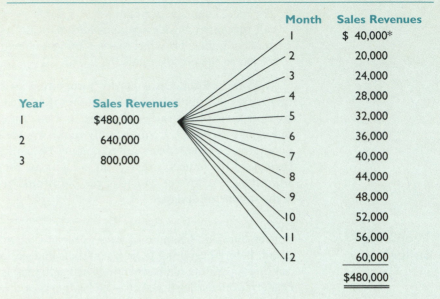

EXHIBIT 9.1
Scandinavian Furniture Store, Inc.: Forecast of sales revenues.

Year	Sales Revenues
1	$480,000
2	640,000
3	800,000

Month	Sales Revenues
1	$ 40,000*
2	20,000
3	24,000
4	28,000
5	32,000
6	36,000
7	40,000
8	44,000
9	48,000
10	52,000
11	56,000
12	60,000
	$480,000

*Assumes sales revenues would be relatively high the first month because of the store's grand opening.

Before proceeding with our example, let us see how fixed and current assets differ.

Fixed assets are resources whose use will benefit the entrepreneur for more than one year. An example is a building bought for $300,000. If the entrepreneur expects the building to last 25 years, she would receive $12,000 worth of shelter benefits a year. Other examples of fixed assets include machines, land, trucks, desks, and fax machines.

These examples are resources the entrepreneur can touch and see, but fixed assets also can be intangible. For instance, suppose an inventor sells an entrepreneur the patent rights for a new pollution control device for $160,000. The entrepreneur might expect to benefit from the patent rights for the next 10 years. These rights cannot be touched or seen; nevertheless, they are a long-lived asset that would benefit the entrepreneur for more than one year. Other examples of intangible assets are licenses and goodwill.

In contrast to fixed assets, *current assets* are resources whose benefits will last less than one year. Commonly, current assets are cash, accounts receivable, and inventories. *Accounts receivable*—the bills owed by customers who buy on credit—are a current asset because the entrepreneur expects to collect within a short time. Similarly, inventory is a current asset because the entrepreneur expects to recover the investment in inventory by selling it shortly after purchasing it from a supplier.

Returning to our example, let us assume that the entrepreneur, as part of her business plan, has prepared the cash budget in Exhibit 9.2 plus the balance sheets in Exhibit 9.3 and the income statement in Exhibit 9.4. How did she prepare them?

EXAMPLE ▶

(continued)

In estimating startup costs, the entrepreneur has decided to:

▶ Construct a one-story, free-standing building with 5,000 square feet of floor space to display and store furniture. Cost: $300,000 at year zero.

▶ Keep a base inventory of furniture large enough to generate twice the average monthly forecast of sales revenues; in addition, buy enough inventory monthly to cover the following month's sales forecast. She plans to pay for all inventory within a month of purchasing it. Cost: $72,000 at year zero.

▶ Lay an asphalt surface on a parking lot next to the building. Cost: $32,000 at year zero.

▶ Finance customers who buy on credit. The entrepreneur is assuming that all sales would be credit sales, with customers taking a month to pay, on the average. One month is the industry's average collection period.

▶ Buy fixtures, office equipment, and a half-ton delivery truck. Cost: $52,000 at year zero.

▶ Incorporate with a lawyer's help. Cost: $4,000.

▶ Design a record-keeping system with the help of an accountant. Cost: $2,000.

▶ Buy a three-year prepaid insurance policy. Cost: $12,000.

▶ Buy city, county, and state licenses. Cost: $2,000.

▶ Promote the store's grand opening. Cost $4,000.

She would now group these cost items into three categories—current assets, fixed assets, and other assets—to arrive at the total cost of assets before startup:

Current assets		
Accounts receivable	$ 0	
Inventory	72,000	$ 72,000
Fixed assets		
Building	$300,000	
Equipment, fixtures	52,000	
Parking lot	32,000	$384,000
Other assets		
Prepaid insurance	$ 12,000	
Professional fees	6,000	
Promotional costs	4,000	
Licenses	2,000	$ 24,000
Total assets		$480,000

Instead of constructing the building, the entrepreneur could lease a building and its parking lot, thus reducing the asset costs from $480,000 to $148,000. If she did lease, however, she probably would have to pay rent in advance, covering at least the first month or two.

EXHIBIT 9.2

Scandinavian Furniture Store, Inc.: Cash budget to estimate money needs ($).

	Before Startup	Month After Startup			
		1	2	3	4
Sales revenue forecast		40,000	20,000	24,000	28,000
Cash inflow	0				
Collections from credit customers		0	40,000	20,000	24,000
Cash outflow					
Purchasing inventory	72,000	12,000[a]	14,400	16,800	19,200
Paying operating expenses		12,800	12,800	12,800	12,800
Subtotal	72,000	24,800	27,200	29,600	32,000
Buying fixed assets	384,000				
Buying other assets	24,000				
Subtotal	408,000				
Total cash outflow	480,000	24,800	27,200	29,600	32,000
Cash flow summary					
Total cash inflow	0	0	40,000	20,000	24,000
Total cash outflow	480,000	24,800	27,200	29,600	32,000
Surplus or shortage	(480,000)	(24,800)	12,800	(9,600)	(8,000)
Cumulative shortage	(480,000)	(504,800)	(492,000)	(501,600)	(509,600)
Money needs					
Maximum shortage	525,600				
10% allowance for contingencies	52,560				
Total money needs	580,000[c]				
Cash balance at start of month	580,000	100,000	75,200	88,000	78,400
Surplus or shortage	480,000	(24,800)	12,800	(9,600)	(8,000)
Cash balance at end of month	100,000	75,200	88,000	78,400	70,400

[a]Obtained by multiplying the next month's sales forecast by 60 percent (0.60 × $20,000 sales in second month = $12,000 purchase cost in first month).

[b]Assumes a sales forecast of $60,000 in the thirteenth month after startup.

[c]Rounded upward.

5	6	7	8	9	10	11	12
32,000	36,000	40,000	44,000	48,000	52,000	56,000	60,000
28,000	32,000	36,000	40,000	44,000	48,000	52,000	56,000
21,600	24,000	26,400	28,800	31,200	33,600	36,000	36,000[b]
12,800	12,800	12,800	12,800	12,800	12,800	12,800	12,800
34,400	36,800	39,200	41,600	44,000	46,400	48,800	48,800
34,400	36,800	39,200	41,600	44,000	46,400	48,800	48,800
28,000	32,000	36,000	40,000	44,000	48,000	52,000	56,000
34,400	36,800	39,200	41,600	44,000	46,400	48,800	48,800
(6,400)	(4,800)	(3,200)	(1,600)	0	1,600	3,200	7,200
(516,000)	(520,800)	(524,000)	(525,600)	(525,600)	(524,000)	(520,800)	(513,600)
70,400	64,000	59,200	56,000	54,400	54,400	56,000	59,200
(6,400)	(4,800)	(3,200)	(1,600)	0	1,600	3,200	7,200
64,000	59,200	56,000	54,400	54,400	56,000	59,200	66,400

EXHIBIT 9.3

Scandinavian Furniture Store, Inc.: Beginning and ending balance sheets.

Assets	Beginning	Ending	Equities	Beginning	Ending
Current assets			Liabilities	$ 0	$ 0
Cash	$100,000	$66,400[a]			
Accounts receivable	0	60,000[b]	Owners' equity		
Inventory	72,000	84,000[c]	Common stock	$580,000	$580,000
Subtotal	$172,000	$210,400	Retained earnings		2,000[f]
			Subtotal	$580,000	$582,000
Fixed assets					
Building	$300,000	$288,000[d]			
Equipment	52,000	46,800[d]			
Parking lot	32,000	28,800[d]			
Subtotal	$384,000	$363,600			
Other assets	24,000	8,000[c]			
Total assets	$580,000	$582,000	Total equities	$580,000	$582,000

[a]Obtained directly from Exhibit 9.2 (cash balance at end of twelfth month).

[b]Obtained directly from Exhibit 9.2 (all revenues in twelfth month will be owed by customers at month's end).

[c]Assumes a base inventory ($48,000) plus enough inventory ($36,000) to support the thirteenth month's sales forecast of $60,000.

[d]Reflects depreciation of fixed assets during year (see Exhibit 9.4).

[e]Reflects write-off of prepaid expenses during year (see Exhibit 9.4).

[f]Obtained directly from Exhibit 9.4 (assumes profits will be plowed back into the venture).

So far, the entrepreneur has estimated what it would cost just to open for business. She must now go one step further and estimate what it would cost to stay open through the first year, by month:

Monthly cash expenses (excluding cost of goods sold):	
Entrepreneur's salary	$ 4,800
Part-time employee wages	2,400
Advertising	1,200
Electricity, heat, telephone	800
Delivery	800
Accounting, legal	800
Supplies	400
Other	1,600
Total	$12,800

Note that these monthly expenses are unlikely to change with sales revenues. That is, even if first-year sales are double the $480,000 forecast, monthly expenses would not be

EXHIBIT 9.4

Scandinavian Furniture Store, Inc.: Income statement (for first year of operations).

Sales revenues		$480,000[a]
Cost of goods sold		288,000[b]
Gross profit		$192,000
Operating expenses		
Administrative and selling	$153,600[c]	
Depreciation	20,400[d]	
Write-off of prepaid expenses	16,000[e]	190,000
Operating profit		$ 2,000

[a]Obtained from Exhibit 9.2 by adding monthly budgeted sales revenues.

[b]Obtained by multiplying total budgeted revenues of $480,000 by 60 percent because the gross margin is 40 percent.

[c]Obtained from Exhibit 9.2 by adding monthly operating expenses.

[d]Obtained as follows:

Building depreciation	=	$300,000 ÷ 25-year life	=	$12,000
Equipment depreciation	=	52,000 ÷ 10-year life	=	5,200
Parking lot depreciation	=	32,000 ÷ 10-year life	=	3,200
				$20,400

[e]Obtained as follows

Professional fees	=	$ 6,000
Insurance	=	4,000 (one-third of $12,000 prepaid policy expires during year)
Promotional costs	=	4,000
Licenses	=	2,000
		$16,000

significantly greater than $12,800. The only expense item likely to increase significantly would be part-time wages: As sales increase, the entrepreneur would probably need to add more part-time salespeople to wait on customers.

To these costs, the entrepreneur would add the purchase cost of furniture sold. These purchase costs, as mentioned earlier, would vary with sales revenues. Assuming a profit margin of 40 percent, the entrepreneur would realize a gross profit of $40 on every $100 sales of furniture:

$100	paid by entrepreneur's customers (sales revenues)
60	paid to entrepreneur's suppliers (cost of goods sold)
$ 40	contribution to all other expenses and to profit (gross profit)

Having collected the cost figures, the entrepreneur would now draft a cash budget for the first year. One method appears in Exhibit 9.2. Note that this budget shows:

▶ Expected inflows and outflows of cash.
▶ The money needed to finance the venture.
▶ The cash balance at the end of each month.

As shown in the exhibit, the entrepreneur needs $525,600, assuming that things go as planned. They rarely do—so the entrepreneur might add a cushion of 10 percent to the $525,600, to allow for an uneven flow of money in and out of her venture, and to absorb any unexpected bills. Rounding the figure, the entrepreneur arrives at $580,000 as the total amount she must raise to launch her venture.

Besides a cash budget, the entrepreneur would prepare beginning and ending balance sheets plus an income statement. These financial statements appear as Exhibits 9.3 and 9.4. Note that most of the figures come from the cash budget. The balance sheets assume that all the entrepreneur's assets would be financed through the sale of common stock, an unrealistic assumption. Below, we discuss more realistic ways of financing new ventures. Note also that the income statement shows that the venture would be profitable during its first full year of operation. ▲▼▲

Equity Capital Versus Debt Capital

Having estimated how much money they need, entrepreneurs must next decide what fraction of this money should come from investors as *equity capital* and from creditors as *debt capital*.

The ratio of debt capital to equity capital is a controversial topic. At one extreme, bankers generally recommend that entrepreneurs and their investors put in at least a dollar of their own money for every dollar they borrow. At the other extreme, some entrepreneurs prefer to put in as little of their own money as possible, while keeping 100 percent control of their ventures.

These differences arise because bankers generally are not risk takers. They are in the business of renting depositors' money, not risking it. So they tend to avoid ventures backed by small amounts of investors' money. Remember that it is the investors' money that protects bankers when adversity strikes. As losses occur, investors' money bears the first impact of loss. So the greater the amount of investors' money, the greater the likelihood that the bank will recover its loan.

Entrepreneurs, on the other hand, are risk takers. Many are willing to risk their life savings in their ventures if they have to. Some try to sell common stock in their ventures to investors. By doing so, they may raise all the money they need, lessen the risk to their personal savings, and still keep control of their ventures:

EXAMPLE ▶

(continued)

The entrepreneur needs $580,000 to finance her venture but has just $60,000 in savings. To help bridge the gap, let's say she decides to float 6,000 shares of common stock at a par value of $20 each.

Next, she manages to raise $300,000 by buying 3,000 shares herself at $20 each and by persuading friends to buy the remaining 3,000 shares, not at $20 each, but at $80 each. This assumes that her friends think enough of her venture's prospects to pay a $60 premium for the stock.

The rest—$280,000—the entrepreneur may now readily borrow from a bank. With $300,000 of investors' money behind her, most banks would welcome her as a borrower because her ratio of equity capital to total capital would top 50 percent ($300,000 ÷ $580,000 = 0.52). ▲▼▲

Our example shows how a venture may now be launched on a shoestring. With just $60,000 of her own money, the entrepreneur was able to raise another $520,000 and still keep control.

There are other ways as well. Take the following example:

EXAMPLE ▶

"You want to start what kind of business? A specialty chemicals manufacturing venture? From scratch? From point zero? Hmmm. Very, very interesting."

This was the typical response that Michael Rybka received from the more than 100 accountants, bankers, lawyers, and friends he had approached to finance his venture. Undaunted, Rybka continued to knock on doors, whether welcome or not.

Rybka's perseverance finally bore fruit. On the advice of another entrepreneur, he took a noncredit, four-month course on business plans taught by two professors of business administration. So thorough was his plan that it won first prize in a competition sponsored by the local chamber of commerce. The following day, the business section of the daily newspaper ran a lead story and a photograph applauding his achievement and his desire to finance his dream.

Rybka's business plan soon struck chords of recognition in the business community. Several private investors came forward with offers to help finance his venture. All told, he estimated that he needed $150,000 to carry his venture through its first year of operations. Lacking money of his own, Rybka decided:

▶ To give himself 50 percent of the common stock—to "reward myself for starting the venture and making a go of it."
▶ To sell investors the remaining 50 percent of the stock.

After raising $150,000, Rybka found that he needed $40,000 more, which he obtained by borrowing from a bank on the strength of investors' signatures. His beginning balance sheet appears in Exhibit 9.5.

Thus, without putting up a single penny of his own money, by investing just his ideas and energy, Rybka created a chemical manufacturing venture and owned 50 percent of it. ▲▼▲

However, it is generally safer for entrepreneurs to finance a new venture with more investors' money than creditors' money, for two reasons:

▶ Creditors' money involves a definite promise to repay the lender. Almost all loans require the borrower to meet a repayment schedule that demands not only repayment of the loan but also payment of interest—usually monthly. Failure to meet this twin obligation could force the entrepreneur's venture into bankruptcy.

EXHIBIT 9.5

Rybka Corporation: Beginning balance sheet.

Assets		Equities	
Cash	$ 15,000	Bank loan	$ 40,000
Raw materials inventory	15,000	Owners' equity	
Equipment	155,000	Rybka $150,000	
Organizational costs	150,000	Others 150,000	300,000
Other assets	5,000		
Total assets	$340,000	Total equities	$340,000

▶ Investors' money, on the other hand, does not involve a definite promise to repay. Investors buy shares of stock at their own risk. Later, if they want to sell their shares, they cannot force the entrepreneur to buy them back. Investors are on their own to find somebody willing to buy their shares. Neither are investors entitled to a dividend on their investment. In fact, only if the venture makes a profit may a dividend be declared.

Entrepreneurs who want 100 percent ownership of their ventures try to invest as little as they can and borrow as much as they can. Such entrepreneurs generally want to answer to nobody but themselves, but they may be deluding themselves. The entrepreneur's freedom to act may be as limited with creditors as with investors. For example, creditors with a large stake in the entrepreneur's venture might take over if the entrepreneur fails to pay bills or to repay loans.

Sources of Money: Equity Capital

One of the most puzzling questions for an entrepreneur is where best to raise money. As Exhibit 9.6 shows, a bewildering variety of sources awaits the entrepreneur. We will now look at these sources, beginning with equity capital, which is investors' money; and then debt capital, which is creditors' money.

▶ **Venture Capital Firms**

A venture capital firm typically receives more than 1,000 requests for money each year, the vast majority of which are rejected. Of every 100 requests, 80 are dropped after less than a day's study, 10 are dropped after a week's study, 8 are dropped after a month's study. Only 2 are finally accepted after one or more months of detailed study.

EXHIBIT 9.6
Selected sources of money.

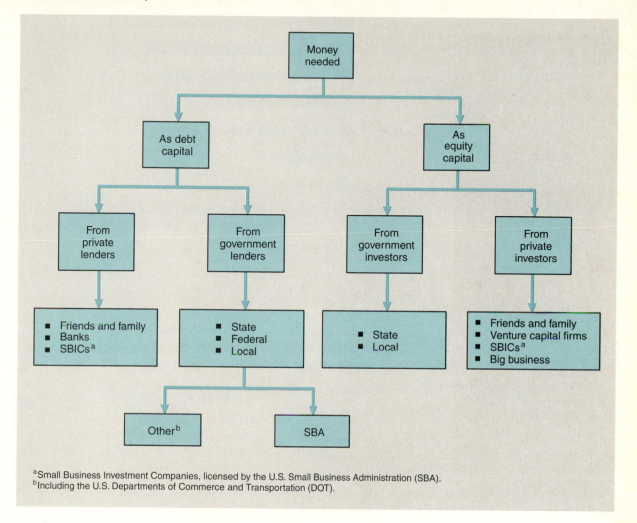

^aSmall Business Investment Companies, licensed by the U.S. Small Business Administration (SBA).
^bIncluding the U.S. Departments of Commerce and Transportation (DOT).

Most of the requests that are dropped within a day lack business plans. In fact, venture capital firms do not even look at a written request for money unless a business plan accompanies it.

Among the principal kinds of venture capital firms are the following:

▶ **Traditional partnerships,** which often are established by wealthy families to manage a portion of their money aggressively by investing in small businesses

▶ **Professionally managed pools,** which are formed by such institutions as pension funds and foundations

EXHIBIT 9.7
Where venture capital is invested.

Source: "Venture Capital Survey," Coopers & Lybrand, New York City (February 1995); reported in "Venture-Capital Trends," *Inc.* (June 1995), p. 92.

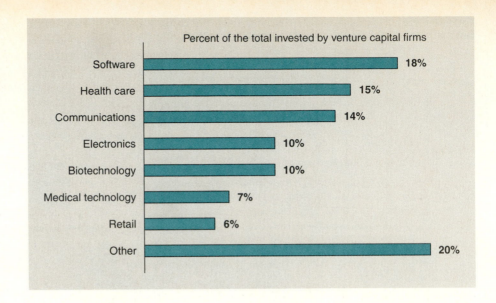

▶ **Investment banking firms,** which occasionally form investor syndicates* for venture proposals

▶ **Insurance companies,** which tend to be more conservative and often require a portion of equity capital as protection against inflation before they lend to small businesses[2]

A popular misconception about venture capital firms is that they also invest in so-called mom-and-pop shops—the corner drugstore or the neighborhood restaurant. They do not. Their interest lies in ventures that promise to grow rapidly in sales and in profits. As is dramatically illustrated in Exhibit 9.7, they find idea-rich, high-technology industries such as software and health care especially attractive.

▶ **Small Business Investment Companies**

Small business investment companies (SBICs) are another source of equity capital. SBICs began in 1958 after the U.S. Congress passed the Small Business Investment Act, whose purpose was to encourage private investors to finance entrepreneurs. This act gave investors an incentive to form SBICs, which run as private, profit-motivated businesses, but under these conditions:

▶ Investors would invest only in small businesses, especially in high-risk ventures boasting new products with promising market potential, favorable competitive positions, the possibility of growth through a favorable buy-out, and strong management.

▶ The SBA would oversee the SBICs, including their licensing and regulation.

---

*A syndicate is a group of individuals who get together to finance a particular project—for example, to build a shopping center.

In 1995, there were more than 310 SBICs scattered throughout the nation. Some are run by banks; some by engineers, scientists, or experts in technical fields; others by lawyers, accountants, and other specialists. All have one thing in common: a willingness to assume risks for a share of owners' equity, although in varying degrees. Some SBICs even act like banks, making loans rather than buying shares of stock. They are the exception rather than the rule.

SBICs often take a more balanced approach in their investment choices than do venture capital firms, as this example shows:

> Traditionally, SBICs have been the workhorses of venture capital, investing more in traditional businesses than in flashy new fields such as electronics. "Venture capitalists are realizing that everything is not high technology, and some of the older industries that aren't as sexy still have a lot of growth," explains Barbara Stack, vice president of Rand Capital Corporation, a Buffalo SBIC.
>
> [One year] besides investing $150,000 in an electronics company that invented an energy-control device, Rand also invested $300,000 in a manufacturer of wood furniture founded 50 years ago. Stack believes that both companies are affected favorably by the economy:
>
> ▶ The electronics company benefits from widespread concern about controlling the use of energy.
> ▶ The furniture company benefits from a growing trend among homeowners to buy high-quality furniture.[3]

SBICs expect precisely the same kinds of information as do venture capital firms, so entrepreneurs must have their business plans in hand when they go to an SBIC for financial help. Otherwise, they stand little chance of success.

▶ **Big Business**

Still another source of equity capital is big business. Many of the nation's major corporations have formed departments that seek out promising entrepreneurs to invest in. Their motives are mixed, ranging from a desire to boost profits to a desire to identify candidates for buyout.

Regardless of the motivation, investment by big business in small business is a healthy idea because corporations can offer not only equity capital but also managerial skills. It is not so much lack of money that plagues entrepreneurs as lack of managerial skills, of which major corporations have an abundance. A partial list of major corporations now aggressively seeking out promising entrepreneurs reads like a *Who's Who* of American business, among them Du Pont, General Motors, and Microsoft.

▶ **Other Sources**

There are many other fertile sources of equity capital. In fact, studies show that equity capital is more likely to be raised not from venture capital firms but from entrepreneurs themselves, from their family and friends—or even from so-called "business angels," as described in this example:

EXAMPLE ▶

"Business angels" are wealthy investors willing to back an invention or a novel marketing concept. Besides deep pockets, the best angels have managerial expertise and are willing to offer advice to new ventures.

An example of a business angel is Ronald Ritchie, a former executive of Texas Instruments, the large aerospace company. He is thinking seriously of investing in two innovative ventures. One planned to make semiconductor test equipment; the other to sell multimedia educational software.

If he invests in these two ventures, Richie believes he can make at least 35 percent a year on his money. "I am looking out five to ten years, by which time the companies should be sold to a larger enterprise or go public," he says.[4] ▲▼▲

In contrast to venture capital firms, business angels work alone, as solo investors. As such, they are beholden to, and accountable to, no one but themselves. Energized largely by the promise of generous monetary rewards, they are "a lot busier" than venture capital firms. For example, the Center for Venture Research at the University of New Hampshire estimated that in 1994:

▸ Business angels invested $15 billion in 60,000 new ventures, while—

▸ Venture capital firms invested but $2.6 billion in just 1,000 new ventures.[5]

Contrary to popular opinion, it often does not take a lot of money to start from scratch and still succeed. In fact, a study of successful entrepreneurs by the National Federation of Independent Business found that many began with little money—as shown in Exhibit 9.8. Note that 20 percent of all ventures began on an investment of less than $5,000. Indeed, one of the nation's best-known computer companies—Apple, whose visionary founders, Steven Jobs and Stephen Wosniak, launched the personal computer revolution—began in a garage on a shoestring of just $600.

EXHIBIT 9.8
Amount of money invested before the first sale.

Source: Data developed and provided by the NFIB Foundation and sponsored by the American Express Travel Services Company, Inc. Used with permission.

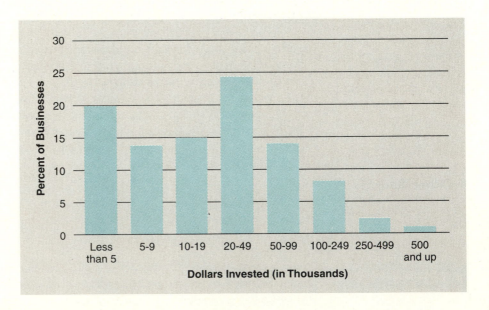

Sources of Money: Debt Capital

So far, we have focused on ways of raising equity capital. We now turn to ways of raising debt capital. Many entrepreneurs believe that banks and the SBA often lend money to ventures that have yet to earn their first dollar. They are wrong. Most bankers, for example, reject the loan applications of would-be entrepreneurs unless:

▶ A wealthy friend or relative guarantees repayment of the loan by cosigning the bank note.

▶ The entrepreneur offers personal holdings, such as a house or top-rated bonds, as security for the loan.

▶ The entrepreneur needs the loan to construct a building that could be repossessed without loss of dollar value if the venture fails.

Turning to Exhibit 9.9, note how sparingly fledgling entrepreneurs make use of banks, with only 6 percent getting startup money from a bank, according to a survey by Coopers & Lybrand, the large accounting firm. In stark contrast, entrepreneurs rely overwhelmingly—73 percent—on themselves, or family and friends, for startup money.

There are various ways that entrepreneurs may borrow money, however—before *and* after they launch their ventures. We begin by looking at private lenders, such as banks; and then at government lenders, such as the SBA.

EXHIBIT 9.9
Where the money comes from to start a business.

Source: Adapted with permission, Inc. magazine, (August 1994). Copyright 1994 by Goldhirsh Group, Inc., 38 Commercial Wharf, Boston, MA 02110.

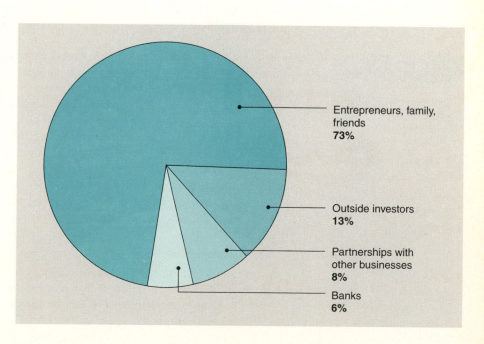

Entrepreneurs, family, friends
73%

Outside investors
13%

Partnerships with other businesses
8%

Banks
6%

▶ Private Lenders

Private lenders range from banks to storefront finance companies, from insurance companies to family. Of these, banks offer entrepreneurs the most help. Besides lending money, banks generally provide a host of other services, among them:

- ▶ Professional financial advice
- ▶ Financial references
- ▶ Credit information
- ▶ Trust administration
- ▶ Transfer of funds

Bankers are as indispensable to entrepreneurs as are lawyers. This is why entrepreneurs should strike a working relationship with a banker months before launching a venture. According to the SBA:

> Too many entrepreneurs go to their banker only when they need to borrow money. If the entrepreneur deals with her banker in day-to-day financial matters, the banker can get to know her and her business. Not only will the banker often give aid and advice on current financial operations, but when she really needs to borrow money, the banker will be familiar with her business and will be better able to evaluate her loan application.[7]

Banks generally make two major kinds of loans: short-term loans and long-term loans. They differ as follows:

Short-Term Loans   As a rule, banks like to see a fast turnover of loans, so they tend to prefer *short-term loans*—that is, loans that fall due within one year. These loans generally finance inventories or customers who buy on credit. The entrepreneur then repays when inventories are sold or when the customers pay their bills. Take this example:

EXAMPLE ▶

An entrepreneur opens a store to sell air conditioners. He must build up his inventory of air conditioners in the spring, just before the summer selling season. Because his need is only temporary, he may take out a short-term loan to buy the air conditioners. He would then repay the loan when his inventory of air conditioners is sold and paid for. ▲▼▲

This example points up the central feature of short-term loans: They satisfy the entrepreneur's temporary need for money. Short-term loans also are called *self-liquidating loans*.

Because short-term loans last a short time, they often are made on an *unsecured* basis. Collateral is not required because the bank relies on the entrepreneur's credit standing. Only if the borrower's credit is poor or not yet established may the lender require collateral as protection against possible default on a loan. Loans backed by collateral are called *secured loans*.

Long-Term Loans   Long-term loans help satisfy the entrepreneur's permanent need for money. *Long-term loans* run for more than one year and enable the entrepreneur to finance the purchase of long-lived assets, such as buildings and land, machinery and computers. These loans generally are repaid from profits.

EXHIBIT 9.10

Comparison of short-term and long-term financing needs.

Source: Adapted from William M. Pride, Robert J. Hughes, and Jack R. Kapoor, *Business,* Second Edition. Copyright © 1988 by Houghton Mifflin Company. Used with permission.

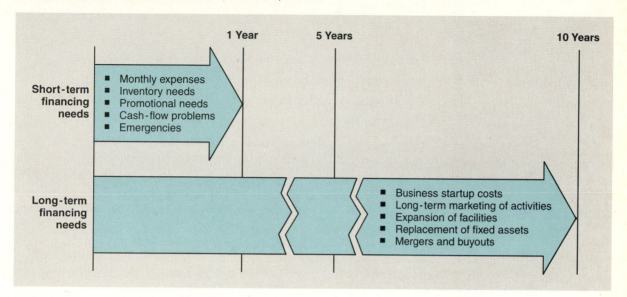

Long-term loans also enable an entrepreneur whose venture is growing rapidly to finance the permanent expansion of inventories, as well as customers who buy on credit. A comparison of long-term and short-term financing needs appears in Exhibit 9.10. The following example illustrates how long-term loans work:

EXAMPLE ▶

An entrepreneur who owns a small machine shop needs a $15,000 turret lathe. Lacking the cash, he takes out a $15,000 loan. If he continues to be successful, the entrepreneur will repay the loan out of profits plowed back into his venture.

The entrepreneur and the bank agree to a repayment schedule that calls for the $15,000 loan to be repaid in five yearly payments of $3,000 each plus interest. This kind of loan enables the entrepreneur to build up his equity over the life of the loan—in the same way that a homeowner builds up equity with each payment on a mortgage loan. ▲▼▲

▶ **Supplier Credit**

This source of debt capital works only for entrepreneurs who have a good credit rating. Others have to pay their suppliers in cash. By allowing suppliers to finance them, entrepreneurs benefit from the cash released for other purposes. An example shows how this kind of financing works:

EXAMPLE ▶

An entrepreneur who owns a tire supply store buys tires monthly. Her supplier offers credit terms of 30 days, which means that payment is expected 30 days after the entrepreneur receives a supply of tires. Thus, if she sells out her inventory roughly once a month, she needs virtually no money of her own to finance the purchase of tires. ▲▼▲

There are many government lenders, not only at the federal level but at the state and local levels as well. At the federal level, these lenders include the SBA and the U.S. Department of Commerce. At state and local levels, lenders generally include agencies that are designed to boost economic development. Of all these lenders, federal and otherwise, the SBA offers entrepreneurs the most help. To qualify for SBA help, businesses must:

▶ Be independently owned and run, and not dominant in their fields.

▶ Be unable to get private financing on reasonable terms.

▶ Qualify as small according to the SBA's industry standards, shown in Exhibit 1.2 on page 5.

Often called the entrepreneur's best friend, the SBA plays a life-giving financial role. Illustrative is this excerpt from the magazine, *Changing Times:*[7]

EXAMPLE ▶

Some things that really matter to small businesses—such as guaranteed loans for companies that bankers won't touch—the SBA does with remarkable efficiency. Enough so that some folks even go back again.

Take the case of Xavier and Dominique Noel and Patrick Chatel of Houston, owners of Paris Gourmet, a wholesaler of premium imported and domestic foods. Banks in economically troubled Texas were not too eager to lend to fledgling businesses in 1986, when the three men needed an infusion of outside money for their company to grow. With an SBA guarantee, a bank was willing to lend them $65,000, payable over four years.

The guarantee was critical for getting Paris Gourmet off the ground. "Without the SBA we never would have gotten where we are today," says Xavier Noel. Paris Gourmet now has 15 employees and more than $2.5 million in yearly sales revenues, up from $200,000 when they started in 1983.

Dealing with the SBA wasn't at all painful, either. It took Paris Gourmet about three months from filling out the papers to cash in hand. In fact, it went so smoothly that last year they got another $200,000 guaranteed loan to finance expansion, and next year they expect to go to the well a third time for money to build a warehouse.[8] ▲▼▲

Despite what many entrepreneurs believe, the SBA rarely lends money. Rather, it is the bank that lends money, and in turn the SBA merely guarantees repayment of the loan to the bank. In 1996, the SBA had 22 lending programs, among them:

▶ **Loan guarantees on conventional loans** Also called the 7(a) program, it enables entrepreneurs to borrow from a bank with the SBA guaranteeing to pay back part of any loss suffered by the bank. The SBA may guarantee up to 90 percent of the loan amount, not to exceed $500,000. These loans can be made for as long as 25 years. Through this program flows most of the SBA's lending activity.

This program, which sparks three-fourths of the SBA's loan activity, has earned high praise from many quarters, among them the National Institute of Business Management, publisher of a weakly newsletter, *Business Briefing:*

The SBA loan guarantee program is, arguably, one of the most successful government programs of this century. In fact, the SBA has guaranteed more than 400,000 loans totaling nearly $50 billion since its creation by the U.S. Congress in 1953.[9]

A variation on this program is the LowDoc loan program, introduced in 1994. Capped at $100,000, this program streamlines the application process for startup ventures. Its appeal is that entrepreneurs need only fill out a one-page loan application, and that the SBA replies all but instantly, within the week.

Still another variation is the GreenLine guarantee loan program. Also introduced in 1994, this program is the SBA's first revolving credit-line plan, which entrepreneurs momentarily strapped for cash find especially appealing.

▶ **International trade loan guarantees**   This program guarantees up to $1 million for the purchase, construction, renovation, modernization, improvement, or expansion of productive equipment to be used in the United States in the production of products and services for sale in other countries.

▶ **Small loan guarantees**   This program's purpose is to help entrepreneurs who need loans of $50,000 or less.

▶ **Displaced business loans**   These loans enable entrepreneurs to stay in business or to relocate if the SBA determines that an entrepreneur's business has suffered financially because of a government project. The loans may cover the purchase of, or construction on, other property, whether or not the entrepreneur owned the original property occupied by the business.

▶ **Regulatory compliance loans**   Entrepreneurs may borrow money to help comply with government laws that would otherwise cause them undue financial harm. Examples of such laws are the Occupational Safety and Health Act and the Clean Air Act.

▶ **Energy loan guarantees**   This program offers loans to help entrepreneurs save energy by producing energy from wood or grain, using windmills to generate electricity, burning garbage to produce energy, and other conservation strategies.

▶ **Local development companies (LDCs)**   The SBA works through a profit or nonprofit corporation founded by local citizens who want to boost their community's economy. The SBA can lend up to $500,000 for each small business helped by an LDC.

▶ **Pollution control loans**   The SBA helps entrepreneurs who need long-term loans for the planning, design, and installation of pollution control equipment—up to a maximum of $1 million per small business.

▶ **Handicapped assistance loans**   This program is designed to help entrepreneurs who are physically disabled.

Special Programs for Minority Entrepreneurs

Since the late 1960s, a number of special programs have surfaced to help minorities become entrepreneurs. Local agencies, such as chambers of commerce and

LDCs, as well as federal agencies like the SBA and the U.S. Department of Commerce, support these programs, among them:

▶ **Economic Opportunity Loan Program**   Under this program, the SBA can make or guarantee loans to minority entrepreneurs only. The most that can be borrowed under this program is $100,000 for up to 15 years.

▶ **MESBIC Program**   A MESBIC is a minority enterprise small business investment company, whose major purpose is to marshall the skills of big business, banks, and the federal government to help develop minority entrepreneurs. Individuals or companies can form a MESBIC by putting up at least $150,000 of their own money. After investing most of this sum in minority ventures, the MESBIC may then increase its original capital fifteenfold through a combination of federal and private financing. Like SBICs, MESBICs may either buy shares in minority ventures or lend them money.

EXAMPLE ▶

A MESBIC decides that a minority manufacturer who needs $200,000 to start production should be financed in this way:

▶ $40,000 in a 15-year loan from the MESBIC
▶ $160,000 in a 15-year loan from a commercial bank, 90 percent of which would be guaranteed by the SBA

Notice that the bank's exposure to loss would be only $16,000—or 8 percent of the total loan amount of $200,000. ▲▼▲

Many other federal programs do not lend money but do help entrepreneurs upgrade their managerial skills or get federal contracts. Similar programs often exist at both state and local levels as well. In the next chapter, we look at these programs in some detail, especially those offered by the SBA.

SUMMARY

To estimate the amount of money needed to launch a venture, entrepreneurs must prepare a cash budget. The cash budget is the centerpiece of their business plan that translates operating plans into dollars, and opens the door to potential investors or creditors. In addition to the cash budget, the entrepreneur must prepare beginning and ending balance sheets and an income statement.

After estimating how much money is needed, entrepreneurs must estimate what fraction of this money should come from investors (equity capital) and what fraction should come from creditors (debt capital). It is generally safer for entrepreneurs to finance a venture with more investors' money than creditors' money because creditors' money involves a definite promise to pay the debt, while investors' money does not.

There are many sources of money. Equity money comes from:

▶ Venture capital firms.
▶ SBICs.
▶ Big business.
▶ Personal sources.

Debt capital comes from private lenders, including banks and insurance companies, and government lenders. The most important government lender is the SBA, which currently has 22 programs that range from guaranteeing conventional loans to offering funds for the planning, design, and installation of pollution control equipment. Several programs are also in place to help finance minority entrepreneurs.

Discussion and Review Questions

1. Explain why a financial plan is so important in estimating money needs for a new venture.
2. Why do venture capital firms, banks, and the SBA generally ask for a business plan?
3. Why do entrepreneurs tend to ignore budgeting as a financial tool?
4. How would you, as an entrepreneur, go about estimating how much money is needed to launch your venture?
5. In preparing a cash budget, which figure is the single most important estimate? Why?
6. Explain the difference between equity capital and debt capital.
7. What are the hazards of financing a new venture with debt? Explain your answer.
8. Do banks generally help finance an entrepreneur who is just starting out? Explain your answer.
9. Why should an entrepreneur strike a working relationship with a bank early on?
10. What services do banks offer besides making loans?
11. How does repayment of a long-term loan increase the entrepreneur's equity in a venture?
12. How do "business angels" differ from venture capital firms?
13. Do SBA loan programs compete with private lenders like banks? Explain your answer.
14. Describe two programs designed to help minority entrepreneurs finance their ventures.
15. Define these terms: *cash budget, fixed assets, current assets, intangible assets, SBIC, secured loan, long-term loan, MESBIC.*

Financing

The very act of preparing a business plan forces entrepreneurs to formalize their planning on the type of business that they want to start. This type of detailed planning also allows entrepreneurs to budget their startup expenses and their ongoing operating expenses.

The centerpiece of a business plan is the cash budget, which translates operating plans into dollars. Without a cash budget, entrepreneurs have no way of estimating their financial needs for production, marketing, staffing, and other business needs.

Instructions for Worksheet 9

To answer the questions on Worksheet 9, it will be necessary for you to estimate the cost of specific items required to open your business and build a balance sheet for your business before startup in part 1. In part 2, estimate your monthly sales revenues, cost of goods sold, and operating expenses. Then in part 3, determine the most likely source of financing for your business.

Part 1—Startup Costs

Would-be entrepreneurs often try to start a business on a shoestring with too little available financing. To avoid this problem, entrepreneurs must be careful to estimate the "true" startup cost for their business.

1. List all of the startup costs that are necessary to open your business.

2. Based on your answer to question 1, construct a balance sheet that contains the one-time, startup costs for your business. (You may want to review the balance sheet presented in Exhibit 9.3 before completing this exercise.)

Part 2—Ongoing Monthly Expenses

While it is true that a budget can be no better than the estimates it contains, it is essential that you do the best job possible when estimating monthly expenses for your business. (Before answering the questions in this part, you may want to review Exhibit 9.2.)

3. Estimate what *monthly* sales revenues will be for the first twelve months your business is in operation.

4. Assuming that your business will sell merchandise to customers, what is the *monthly* cost of goods sold for the first twelve months?

5. List the *monthly* expenses for the first twelve months your business is in operation.

6. Using your answers to questions 3, 4, and 5, construct a cash budget like the one illustrated in Exhibit 9.2 for your business.

Part 3—Sources of Financing

When determining the total cash requirements for your business, many experts recommend that you include your total startup costs *plus* at least six month's monthly expenses.

7. With this recommendation in mind, what is the total investment required to start your business?

8. Considering your cash requirements and the different sources of financing discussed in your text, what are the two most likely sources of financing for your business?

CASE 9A ▶

Trolley Tours of Cleveland, Inc.

The year was 1988. Heady with success, Sherrill Paul was convinced that she could expand her young business to other cities. That business, Trolley Tours of Cleveland, had posted operating profits of $100,500 on sales revenues of $694,800 in 1987.

"My trolley tour service is unique, one of a kind," says Paul. "My dream was to duplicate, nationwide, my success in Cleveland. Of course, I needed money to do that, money I didn't have. Neither bankers nor venture capitalists look too kindly on services like mine. How was I going to convince them that my dream was worth backing?"

Background

Until April 1985, Cleveland was the butt of jokes, especially on national television. It seemed as though no one, not even its own citizens, believed in the city. Then, on April 15, a bright red and green trackless trolley, named "Lolly" showed up in Cleveland's Public Square to do tours.

Sherrill Paul, president of Trolley Tours of Cleveland, sees herself as a born entrepreneur. At the age of 12, she was baby-sitting for $0.35 an hour. And at Ohio Wesleyan University, she cut hair and drove students who were going home for the holidays to the airport. "It has been said that most entrepreneurs start at least 3.8 businesses before they are successful," says Paul. A photograph of Paul and one of her trolleys appears in Exhibit 9A.1; her résumé, in Exhibit 9A.2.

A Near Failure

Although Paul enjoyed working in retail sales management for others, her deepest satisfaction came from her work as a volunteer tour guide at the historic theaters in downtown Cleveland. It was this volunteer experience that led her, in 1982, to purchase a convention meeting and planning company called Bestconventions. The company specialized in walking tours of Cleveland and tour guide services for bus tours passing through the city. Unfortunately, Bestconventions turned out to be a breakeven business at best, hamstrung by several factors:

▶ The existing staff of tour guides quit the company to start a competing venture once the company had been sold to Paul.

▶ Paul did not have the money to promote its services.

EXHIBIT 9A.1
Trolley tours of Cleveland,
Inc.: View of Sherrill Paul
and Lolly the Trolley.

▶ The convention activity in Cleveland had begun its deepest decline ever.

Despite these problems, Paul survived. She hired and trained new tour guides, expanded her range of contacts, and did work for local companies by offering private city tours in buses, vans, and her own car.

A Need Waiting to be Filled

One request that Paul received repeatedly during the summer months was for tours of Cleveland by small groups of 2 to 10 people. The only service available was the cruise boat on the Cuyahoga River—a good tour, but limited in scope. Local bus companies ran sightseeing tours only sporadically, for groups of 20 or more. The need was there, but Paul was not sure how best to meet it.

Then, in October 1983, Paul and her husband, Peter, attended a friend's wedding in Boston. During some free time, they decided to tour the city and hopped on board Lolly the Trolley at historic Faneuil Hall. Enchanted with the trolley, they made plans to bring the concept to Cleveland. A brief description of the trolley appears in Exhibit 9A.3.

EXHIBIT 9A.2

Trolley Tours of Cleveland, Inc.: Sherrill Paul's résumé.

Work Experience

1982–present	Bestconvention, Inc.
	President and owner of a convention meeting and planning company
1981–1982	Ohio Bell Telephone Company
	Marketing representative
1977–1980	Executone of Cleveland, Inc.
	Began as director of customer service; was promoted to sales representative
1975–1977	Bass & Associates, Inc.
	Telecommunications consultant and client services coordinator
1973–1975	Task Force Temporary Help Services, Inc.
	Administrative supervisor and sales representative
1972–1973	Franklin Simon Stores, Inc.
	Assistant store manager
1968–1972	May Company Department Stores, Inc.
	Began as assistant buyer; was promoted to branch department manager

Education

1966–1970	Ohio Wesleyan University
	Received bachelor of arts degree in journalism

Personal

Health	Excellent
Interests	Cleveland history, aerobic dancing, cross-country skiing, golf, tennis

Voluntarism

Past president of Business & Professional Women's Club

Member of the chamber of commerce speaker's bureau

Member of the Junior Committee of the Cleveland Orchestra

Member of the Cleveland Waterfront Coalition

Guide for the Playhouse Square Foundation

Member of the Historic Warehouse District Development Corporation

EXHIBIT 9A.3

Trolley Tours of Cleveland, Inc.: Brief description of Lolly the Trolley.

Consider the romance and nostalgia of the trolley. The first tiny "sparklers" appeared more than 100 years ago and soon grew to become a major form of urban transportation. Not only was it the major form of transportation for the worker, but, come Sundays and holidays, it carried the whole family to the amusement parks that sprang up at the end of the line of most trolley systems. The trolley will forever be an important segment of our history.

Lolly the Trolley is no scaled-down version of this nostalgic mode of transportation. It is a handcrafted exquisite vehicle that has taken the talents of many fine Old World craftspeople to develop. Lolly seats 32 adults, in a half-open, half-closed body. The interior reflects careful attention to authentic detail. Seats are natural red oak, with ornate cast-iron ends finished in brilliant enamels. The natural red oak ceiling makes Lolly a sight to behold. It's a fun vehicle, a trip with the bell clanging and music playing. It's an experience for the whole family.

Lolly the Trolley is constructed to simulate as nearly as possible the trolley cars long familiar in San Francisco. This nostalgic vehicle makes transportation a new experience for residents, and it provides a natural promotional tool for an area. From postcards to television and newspaper coverage, the trolley brings with it a great deal of attention.

Lolly the Trolley can be operated in large or small areas, citywide or countrywide, for promotional purposes or for practical purposes. It is a solid, safe vehicle, backed by General Motors' guarantees.

Source: Adapted from a promotional brochure prepared by Trolley Tours of Cleveland, Inc.

"As naive entrepreneurs often do," says Paul, "we believed the project could be started in a hurry, by May 1984, a scant seven months away." She was firm in her belief that the skills and contacts she had assembled from Bestconventions would help her launch the new venture.

Business Plan

Once home, Paul began to collect and analyze the information she needed to create a business plan. While tracking down the trolley manufacturer, she talked with the owners of the Boston trolley company. They advised her to open with at least four trolleys if her business was going to make it the first year. She ignored their advice, projecting instead that she would need that number of trolleys later, in her third year. This decision would come back to haunt her.

Paul's business plan included balance sheets, income statements, and a cash budget. She learned how to prepare financial statements by studying and asking questions. "The financials were a great personal accomplishment," says Paul, "because accounting was an eight o'clock winter course in college, and I got a *D*." To get her venture off the ground, Paul estimated that she would need $180,000, as shown in Exhibit 9A.4.

"The odyssey during 1984 and early 1985 was intense," says Paul. "I talked with everyone I knew, and many others I didn't know, about investing in my dream—a trolley tour of Cleveland that both visitor and citizen would love."

EXHIBIT 9A.4

Trolley Tours of Cleveland, Inc.: Projected opening balance sheet.

Assets		Equities	
Cash	$ 46,620	Bank loan	$150,000
Cost of two trolleys	106,000	Owners' equity	30,000
Startup costs	27,380		
Total assets	$180,000	Total equities	$180,000

Many people told Paul her idea was foolish. After talking with more than 300 people, she finally found six investors who believed she had the drive and ability to make the trolley tour service a reality. They invested $24,000.

Help from Friends and Community Leaders

Paul soon found that bankers were even more difficult than investors to penetrate for the $150,000 she needed to purchase trolleys and other assets. According to Paul, the general response was "Honey, we don't finance startups."

An old college classmate came to her rescue. He introduced Paul to a friendly banker, who listened with "wonder to the wild-eyed plan for tours of Cleveland." After several false starts, Paul arranged for a genuine Lolly the Trolley to stop in Cleveland on a Sunday morning on its way to delivery in Boston, for the banker to see. The banker was "caught up by the trolley's magic spell and soon began to work on behalf of the project."

But another hurdle presented itself. The bank was willing to finance the project only if Paul got the U.S. Small Business Administration (SBA) to guarantee repayment of the loan. So she assembled and filed the proper papers. At first, the SBA did not see the project's potential. Once again, Paul's contacts carried the day. This time, several community leaders spoke to the SBA on her behalf. Several days later, the SBA agreed to guarantee repayment of the bank's $150,000 loan.

The Grand Opening

It was now March 1985. Although getting organized had been difficult, Paul's plans were moving ahead to a grand opening party, timed to coincide with delivery of the first trolley. Then came word from the manufacturer that delivery would be delayed.

Paul already had invited more than 400 people, and she was determined that they would enjoy themselves. So she insisted that the dealer in Florida somehow supply a trolley. On the afternoon of the big party, in the middle of a raging rainstorm, a trolley arrived in time for all the guests to take a ride. At the end of the party, the borrowed trolley returned to Florida.

Two weeks later, when the real Lolly the Trolley arrived just in time for the Cleveland Indians' opening day parade, the Florida dealer did the driving. Why? Because Paul had never driven a trolley before. She spent the weekend learning how to drive. The tours were to begin officially on Monday, April 15.

Monday dawned with Paul behind the wheel for the morning, noon, and afternoon tours. Although nobody showed up, the tours went on anyway. An employee taped Paul as she drove and talked, so that a script could be developed for new tour guides. "The first day was a terrible letdown," says Paul.

Fast Growth

The next day, two senior citizens showed up for the morning tour and were "treated royally."

EXHIBIT 9A.5

Trolley Tours of Cleveland, Inc.: Total number of potential customers in marketing area.

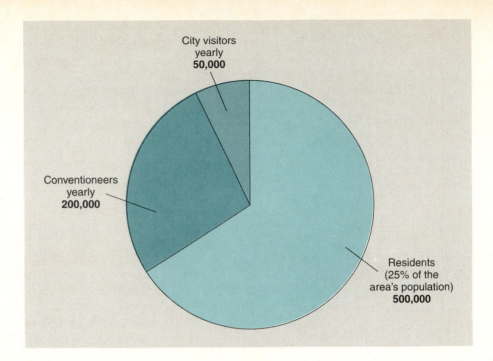

City visitors
yearly
50,000

Conventioneers
yearly
200,000

Residents
(25% of the
area's population)
500,000

They were thrilled that the tour went on with just two riders and vowed to tell others what a good time they had had. Paul refined the tour several times in the first month, as business grew.

The novelty of Paul's service soon attracted the media. Cleveland's daily newspaper devoted a full page to Lolly the Trolley. And the local *PM Magazine* devoted a whole show to the trolley. Paul relies on this kind of publicity and word-of-mouth advertising to attract riders. Her potential markets are depicted in Exhibit 9A.5.

By July, the media attention had the phones ringing off the hook, just as the second trolley arrived. During the day, Paul and her tour guides answered the telephones, typed orders, sold tickets, and did tours. In the evening, Paul and her husband washed the trolleys and ran charter tours.

Business grew faster than Paul had expected. She hired a secretary, and her husband left his job as a corporate executive a year earlier than planned. Mr. Paul was working for no salary; the business plan had called for just one salaried person, Sherrill Paul.

Everything the Pauls owned now depended solely on the business's success. By the end of the

first season, Trolley Tours had carried about 30,000 passengers. Ten people were on the payroll. And two used trolleys were added to the fleet in late fall. "These two battered red trolleys from the battlefields of Boston streets were not the prime specimens originally described by the seller," says Ms. Paul.

Liability Insurance Problems

In November 1985, a registered letter came informing Paul that Transit Casualty Insurance Company had gone bankrupt, and that within seven days Trolley Tours would no longer be covered by insurance. A mad scramble ensued. Paul found other coverage, but only with difficulty and at a greater cost.

"Insurance carriers unfairly rate businesses like Trolley Tours as though they are Greyhound or Trailways bus lines with over-the-highway coaches that travel thousands of miles at high speeds," says Paul. "The liability insurance problem has been a constant source of irritation because no credit seems to be given for a safe driving record. That's unfair."

"In fact, from the first day of operations, our company has had no claims," says Paul. "Yet we maintain standing orders with several insurance brokers to search out better prices for insurance coverage because the threat of doubled premiums is a yearly event."

Cash-Flow Crisis

Although sales revenues topped expectations, Trolley Tours' first season ended with an exhausted owner and staff. Moreover, there was not enough cash to carry the company through its off season. Both Pauls had seen the crisis coming during the fall, while they were juggling their insurance problems.

Ms. Paul turned for help to their trolley dealer in Florida, who owned a large trolley business in Miami. The dealer offered to find work for both Pauls and their four trolleys *if* they would come to Florida for four months.

Having drawn no salary since October, Ms. Paul borrowed money from her parents for personal expenses, then left for Florida on January 9 with her husband, a mechanic, and two trolleys. The other two trolleys were brought down two weeks later. Finding a modest apartment for the winter season, the Pauls worked as hired drivers. Trolley Tours received an hourly fee for rental of the trolleys to the Florida dealer.

Meanwhile, back in Cleveland, the bank reluctantly agreed to accept interest-only payments for three months. This reduction in monthly cash outflow, coupled with the money sent up from Florida, enabled Trolley Tours to stay alive. "The winter of 1985–86 was not a success, but we survived," says Ms. Paul.

Expansion Follows Adversity

In recognition of Ms. Paul's staying power, the original six investors, all of whom were fellow entrepreneurs, came through in the spring of 1986 with more money. This investment, coupled with a less-than-enthusiastic new loan from the bank, enabled her to buy two more trolleys, which expanded the company's capacity to take in more income without boosting overhead costs.

Sales revenues surged. The company's reputation for quality and service, molded in 1985, doubled ridership—to 60,000 people—with lots of repeat and referral business. This surge prompted:

▸ The hiring and training of new tour guides.

▸ A strict reservations-only policy for public tours.

▸ The launching of a successful low-cost school program to encourage use of the daily tour as an educational field trip during nonpeak months.

▸ The design by Mr. Paul of a new heating and storm window system, so that the trolleys could run during the winter months.

The success of their second season generated enough cash to see the Pauls and their company through the winter without migration to Florida.

Problems with the Bank

As the third season began, Ms. Paul ordered two more trolleys in anticipation of another banner year. Their purchase was financed by profits plowed back into the business and by still another bank loan. She found it very difficult to deal with the bank.

"The bank shifted the Trolley Tours account to a junior loan officer," she says. "The new person was less enthusiastic, understanding, and supportive than the original loan officer. Her conservative attitude was going to make it harder for me to obtain future loans to support our growth."

Taken aback by this attitude, the Pauls talked with other bankers and small businesspeople. Ms. Paul described the following scenario:

A company begins with one bank and is grateful for its help, although treated fairly to poorly during the early risk-laden years. As the company begins to grow, it still is treated like a green startup ready to fail, especially when growth calls for more borrowing to purchase revenue-producing assets.

Finally, the company succeeds and, because it was treated so coldly in the early years of its existence, abandons the bank for another one. Meanwhile, the abandoned bank warmly accepts a new but mature client, one that had itself been treated coldly by its original bank—thus coming full circle.

The Pauls had lunch with the bank's senior vice president to talk over the scenario. The vice president assured them that the bank supported them. But soon after, service on their account worsened.

Tour Guides a Critical Problem

"Finding good tour guides is the second most critical problem in the tour business, next to insurance," says Ms. Paul. "The two tie together very closely. In fact, transit insurance requires that all trolley drivers be over age 26 with a clean driving record. So college students cannot be tour guides."

Much is asked of tour guides. For example, they must drive and talk at the same time, often in heavy traffic. They also must memorize a 43-page script, as written, so that the tour flows easily.

"The work is seasonal and calls for a personable, mature, patient, disciplined, and extremely well-spoken person who loves people and Cleveland," says Ms. Paul. "Being a tour guide is a hard job to master; but once mastered, it is the most gratifying job in the world. Where else can you get told how wonderful you are up to three times a day?"

To help ensure high performance, Ms. Paul had designed a training program for both driving and tour guiding. So rigorous is the program that only two out of every ten people who apply complete the program and go on to become tour guides. Paul recruits likely candidates through advertisements that appeal to homemakers with grown children, theater arts and communications people, teachers, and retirees—with most success in the last two categories.

"Our training program is strict, intense, and ongoing," says Ms. Paul. "The turnover of tour guides who make it is low, although we constantly are looking for new guides as we grow." Paul plans to market her training program nationally some day.

The Third Season and Success

In the spring of 1988, with a third season behind her, Ms. Paul was proud of her achievements. "We had succeeded, Peter and I, despite the naysayers, despite the odds," she says. Indeed, Trolley Tours had grown dramatically, as shown in Exhibit 9A.6. A detailed income statement appears in Exhibit 9A.7; a balance sheet, in Exhibit 9A.8.

Ms. Paul credits much of her success to her organizational planning. An organizational chart

EXHIBIT 9A.6

Trolley Tours of Cleveland, Inc.: Summaries of recent income statements.

	1985	1986	1987
Sales revenues	$164,200	$403,600	$694,800
Cost of sales	95,200	223,900	391,200
Gross profit	$ 69,000	$179,700	$303,600
Operating expenses	130,200	160,300	203,100
Operating profit	$ (61,200)	$ 19,400	$100,500
Nonoperating income	1,700	(24,400)	(24,500)
Profit before taxes	$ (59,500)	$ (5,000)	$ 76,000

EXHIBIT 9A.7

Trolley Tours of Cleveland, Inc.: Detailed income statement (1987).

Sales revenues		
Daily tours	$284,800	
Charters	198,700	
Rentals	108,400	
Advertising	57,000	
School mini-tours	33,400	
Other	12,500	$694,800
Cost of sales		
Wages of tour guides and drivers	$132,100	
Depreciation of vehicles	91,000	
Vehicle insurance	45,200	
Gasoline and oil	25,100	
Payroll taxes	20,700	
Vehicle parts	17,900	
Wages of mechanics	15,500	
Advertising consultant	15,100	
Cleaning and maintenance wages	11,100	
Licenses and permits	6,700	
Vehicle tools and supplies	6,200	
Other	4,600	391,200
Gross profit		$303,600
Operating expenses		
Salaries of officers	$50,000	
Advertising	28,500	
Salaries of office staff	24,000	
Travel and entertainment	16,400	
Office and garage rental	14,400	
Professional fees	14,300	
Office supplies	10,500	
Telephone	10,200	
Office repairs and maintenance	7,700	
Bad debts	7,300	
Equipment rental	5,900	
Utilities	4,200	
Hospitalization insurance	2,200	
Commissions	1,700	
Dues and subscriptions	1,500	
Property insurance	1,400	
Depreciation of office equipment	1,400	
Other	1,500	203,100
Operating profit		$100,500

EXHIBIT 9A.8

Trolley Tours of Cleveland, Inc.: Latest balance sheet (September 30, 1987).

Assets			Equities		
Current assets			**Current liabilities**		
Cash	$140,200		Accounts payable	$ 6,100	
Accounts receivable	15,000		Notes payable	74,500	
Other	16,900	$172,100	Accrued wages	15,400	
			Withheld taxes	9,300	
			Other	3,600	$108,900
Fixed assets			**Long-term liability**		
Vehicles	$348,600		Notes payable		286,700
Equipment and furniture	20,200	368,800			
			Stockholders' equity		
			Common stock	$81,000	
			Retained earnings	64,300	145,300
Total assets		$540,900	Total equities		$540,900

appears in Exhibit 9A.9. As chairman and president, she manages all tour designs and scripting, public relations and marketing, and community relations. As vice president, Mr. Paul manages the day-to-day operations as well as all financial and accounting work.

Ms. Paul's success has not gone unnoticed. From all over the country, she has received calls from people who rode the trolley while visiting Cleveland and now want to launch "a little trolley business in their own town." Many ask Ms. Paul if she would mind telling them everything they need to know to start.

To Ms. Paul, these calls showed that a service like Trolley Tours was marketable in other parts of the country. She already had drafted criteria that cities must meet in order to duplicate a service like hers, "writing plans for the future that will take my service to other cities."

"We've worked hard and smart in this business and have learned a lot in a short time," said Ms. Paul in 1988. "Our dealer in Florida tells us that we have learned as much in three years as he learned in seven years. We make our service look so easy that lots of people think they can run a trolley tour service."

Ms. Paul credited her vision for many of her achievements. "What differentiates me from other small businesspeople is my vision, that I'm always looking to the future while dealing with day-to-day problems. Many small businesspeople get so bogged down with current concerns that they lose their sense of direction, which is the key to growth and success." Her goal was to achieve yearly sales revenues of $1 million by the fifth year of operation.

Questions

1. What accounts for the success of Trolley Tours of Cleveland?
2. Was Trolley Tours likely to grow in the future as fast as it had in its first few years

EXHIBIT 9A.9

Trolley Tours of Cleveland, Inc.: Organizational chart.

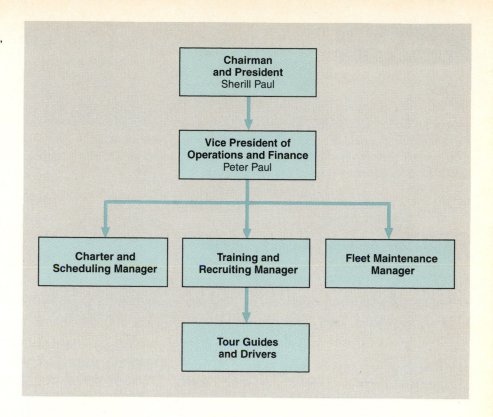

3. In your judgment, what would it have taken for Sherrill Paul to duplicate nationwide her success in Cleveland? Should she have franchised her operation? Explain your answer.
4. Comment on Ms. Paul's experience with and perception of insurance firms and banks. Why do they often seem unfair and unfeeling toward fledgling entrepreneurs, especially those in service industries?
5. If you had the chance to invest in Trolley Tours, would you? Why or why not?

of operation? What new markets could the business serve? Explain your answers.

Swisshelm Clothing Store, Inc.

John Carollo has just bought a small clothing store for $120,000. He paid the sellers $30,000 cash and gave them a five-year note on the remaining $90,000 at an interest rate of 15 percent a year.

Background

A graduate of Stanford University with honors, Carollo worked for 11 years with Sears, Roebuck Company. His experience there included:

▶ Selling men's suits and appliances on the floor.

▶ Managing a men's clothing department.

▶ Serving as assistant branch manager.

All along, his ambition was to have his own clothing store. Sears, he believed, would be a good place to learn every aspect of store operations. After all, Sears was one of the nation's biggest retailers.

Carollo worked for ten years to learn the business. Then he started to search for a clothing store in a small city. A year went by before he learned from a banker that a clothing store was for sale in New Philadelphia, a city of 16,000 people. Three months later, he and the sellers agreed on a purchase price of $120,000.

Cash Budget

One week after he took over, Carollo and his accountant are sitting down to prepare a cash budget. It is early August. Carollo knows that he will need a short-term loan to build up his inventory in anticipation of high consumer demand in September, when schools start, and again in December, when Christmas buying is in full swing.

A cash budget should help him decide how much to borrow and when to borrow. After analyzing past records, he came up with these estimates:

Sales Revenue Forecast	
June (actual)	$24,000
July (actual)	20,000
August	28,000
September	52,000
October	44,000
November	76,000
December	96,000
January	22,000
February	32,000

Monthly Expenses	
Rent	$3,000
Depreciation	500
Other expenses	900
Wages and salaries	
August	2,800
September	3,200
October	3,200
November	3,600
December	3,600
January	2,800

▶ Sales are 30 percent cash, 70 percent credit.

▶ Of the credit sales, 80 percent are paid within one month of purchase, 20 percent are paid within two months.

▶ Credit sales outstanding on August 1 consisted of $14,000 from July and $3,360 from June.

▶ Gross profit on sales is 25 percent.

▶ Enough inventory will be purchased monthly to cover the next month's budgeted sales.

▶ All inventory purchases will be paid for in the same month they are made.

▶ A minimum cash balance of $8,000 will be maintained.

▶ The cash balance was $19,000 on August 1.

▶ All borrowings will be in multiples of $1,000 and will be made or repaid on the first of the month.

▶ Interest at 1 percent a month will be paid when borrowings are repaid in full.

Questions

1. How much should John Carollo borrow to meet seasonal demand? When should he repay his loans? Prepare a cash budget on a

separate piece of paper using the worksheet in Exhibit 9B.1 as a guide.

2. How profitable does Carollo expect the store to be during the six months covered by his budget? Prepare an income statement.

3. Why is the cash budget useful to both Carollo and his banker?

EXHIBIT 9B.1

Swisshelm Clothing Store, Inc.: Cash budget worksheet.

	August	September	October	November	December	January
Cash inflow						
Sales revenues						
Credit sales						
Collections from:						
One month before						
Two months before						
Subtotal						
Cash sales						
Total cash inflow						
Cash outflow						
Inventory purchases						
Wages and salaries						
Rent						
Other expenses						
Interest						
Total cash outflow						
Cash gain or loss						
Borrowings						
Opening cash balance						
Balance before borrowing						
Borrowings						
Ending cash balance						
Cumulative borrowings						

Helen Sexton

Helen Sexton, a loan officer at the Byron National Bank, services loan applications made by small businesses. Two fledgling small businesses have each approached her for a one-year loan of $40,000. Highlighted below are some of the facts and figures Sexton drew from their business plans:

▶ A home-remodeling supplier for do-it-your-selfers, the Alpha-Beta Corporation has posted profits in each of the three years of its existence. This past year, it earned after-tax profits of $32,000 on sales of $608,000. Its most recent balance sheet appears in Exhibit 9C.1.

   So quickly has news of Alpha-Beta's expertise spread by word of mouth in its community, that Alpha-Beta expects sales to soar 40 percent this year. To support such an increase, Alpha-Beta wants to borrow $40,000 to stock more inventory and to carry more credit customers.

▶ Similarly, Susan's Gift Shoppe has been profitable throughout its brief three-year existence.

This past year Susan's earned after-tax profits of $29,000 on sales of $384,000. Its most recent balance sheet appears in Exhibit 9C.2.

   Susan's wants to borrow $40,000 to pay for stocking a new line of greeting cards and for redesigning the shop's interior. In Susan's judgment, backed by marketing research, these changes would boost sales by as much as 20 percent in the year ahead.

Questions

1. If you were Helen Sexton, to which company would you be more willing to lend $40,000? Why? Support your answer by identifying and analyzing the favorable and unfavorable factors that bear on each company's ability to pay back the loan in the next year.
2. What other information would you seek before making a final decision?

EXHIBIT 9C.1

Alpha-Beta Corporation: Balance sheet.

Assets			Equities		
Current assets			Current liabilities		
Cash	$ 24,000		Accounts payable	$160,000	
Accounts receivable	120,000		Loan payable	80,000	$240,000
Inventory	200,000	$344,000	Mortgage loan		160,000
Fixed assets			Owners' equity		
Land	$ 40,000		Common stock	$200,000	
Building	200,000		Retained earnings	40,000	240,000
Equipment	56,000	296,000			
Total assets		$640,000	Total equities		$640,000

EXHIBIT 9C.2

Susan's Gift Shoppe Inc.: Balance sheet.

Assets			Equities		
Current assets			Current liabilities		
Cash	$ 8,000		Accounts payable	$64,000	
Accounts receivable	40,000		Loan payable	10,000	$ 74,000
Inventory	108,000	$156,000	Long-term loan		28,000
Fixed assets			Owners' equity		
Equipment	$ 32,000		Common stock	$50,000	
Organizational costs	4,000	36,000	Retained earnings	40,000	90,000
Total assets		$192,000	Total equities		$192,000

CHAPTER 10

Organizational Planning and Total Quality Management

Never mistake knowledge for wisdom. One helps you make a living; the other helps you make a life.

—*Sandra Carey*

Major corporations employ hundreds, if not thousands, of *knowledge workers*—that is, those who master a body of knowledge, as do software providers and cost accountants, corporate lawyers and marketing researchers.[1] By contrast, would-be entrepreneurs generally cannot afford the services of such experts.

So if they have no recourse but to stand alone, how may entrepreneurs fill their need for knowledge workers? One way is to avail themselves of the expert help offered by the SBA and a host of others dedicated to giving entrepreneurs a helping hand, often for no fee. To make the most of such help, entrepreneurs must first ask themselves two questions:

▶ What skills do I need to launch my venture successfully?

▶ How can I get the help of individuals armed with those skills?

Also covered in this chapter is total quality management—a concept that affects every business, large or small, and that is closely related to the subject of organizational planning.

The Need for Organizational Planning

In today's age of microchip complexity, few entrepreneurs are equipped with the diversity of skills they need to survive and grow on their own. Until World War II, they worked in a business world of few regulations, few taxes, few

EXHIBIT 10.1
The circular nature of
organizational planning.

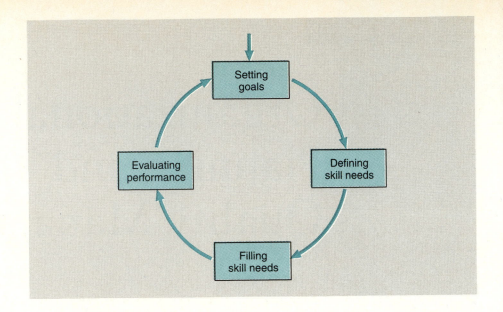

records, few giant competitors, and no personal computers. Simplicity has since given way to complexity. No longer may entrepreneurs be their own troubleshooters, lawyers, bookkeepers, financiers, and the like.

So to survive and grow in today's business world, entrepreneurs must identify and define precisely the kinds of help they need. Unless they do so, as part of their organizational plan, they are likely to flounder, if not fail.

Yet despite the need for organizational planning, many entrepreneurs ignore it, failing to see that it really is the organization itself that carries a venture—its goals and all its personnel and activities.

Turning to Exhibit 10.1, note the circular nature of organizational planning. This circular model suggests that, besides defining and filling skill needs, entrepreneurs need to know if their *actual* performance differs from *planned* performance. If it does, then entrepreneurs must find out why, which in turn may trigger a redefinition of skill needs to get back on track.

Defining Skill Needs

An *organization* is any team of people who work together to meet common goals. For example, a professional football franchise may hire 52 players, each with different skills, to fill its cavernous 80,000-seat stadium. Whether they fill it depends largely on how well they play as a team. Losses usually mean empty seats, which is why coaches spend so much time each year scouting college players. Take this example:

EXAMPLE ▶   A football franchise's all-pro defensive tackle is about to retire. The coach is looking hard for a replacement who earned at least all-conference honors as a defensive tackle, weighs at least 280 pounds, is at least 6 feet 4 inches tall, sprints 40 yards in less than 5.0 seconds, bench-presses at least 450 pounds, and plays with the "hurts." ▲▼▲

This is a tall order to fill, but note that the coach knows precisely what he needs to win. Equally important, he knows precisely what kind of player he is looking for to meet that need.

Entrepreneurs should define their skill needs in a similar way. There is a catch, though: Usually they cannot afford to hire a full-time marketing researcher or a full-time accountant, for example. Even so, entrepreneurs should plan *as if they can* afford them.

Thus, only by going through such a procedure may entrepreneurs assure themselves that they have neither overlooked nor ignored the skills they need to succeed. Take this example:

EXAMPLE ▶ Let us assume a chemical engineer is about to become a maker of plastic. Resourceful and imaginative, he has just invented a process to make fiberglass-reinforced plastic for sports cars like the Corvette. His novel process is not only faster and cheaper than competing processes but also pollution-free. Working evenings and weekends in a rented garage, it took him two years to design the process.

With business plan in hand, our chemical engineer now is ready to exploit his invention by launching a venture of his own. As part of his plan, he has set a first-year sales goal of $900,000; he has also defined what skills he needs to support that level of sales.

To do that, and guided by his business plan, he drew up a table like the one in Exhibit 10.2. Note that our engineer seems best qualified to perform, at least at startup, seven of the steps shown in the exhibit. For the rest, he must rely on:

▶ Outside experts, or professionals, who as knowledge workers have mastered a body of knowledge.
▶ A skilled staff of workers to carry out the day-to-day routine of making and marketing plastic profitably.

Following is a description of how entrepreneurs, including the engineer in our example, may go about finding the right professionals and the right workers for their ventures. ▲▼▲

Finding the Right Professionals

In his quest for help, the engineer in our example should look for professionals who work in his industry. For example, there are accountants who specialize in chemicals just as there are lawyers who specialize in musical recordings. By using specialists, the engineer may benefit from their experience with similar problems in other businesses in the same industry.

Before opening for business, entrepreneurs generally need the following kinds of professional help:

▶ An accountant, to set up the books
▶ A lawyer, to advise on legal matters
▶ A banker, to advise on financial matters
▶ An insurance agent, to ensure that the venture is protected from dangers that cannot be foreseen or controlled
▶ A computer consultant, to advise on computer uses

EXHIBIT 10.2

Identifying skill needs.

Step Number	Description of Step	Skill Needed	Expert Best Suited to Meet Need	
			Entrepreneur	**Other**
1	Decide to go into business	Knowledge of self	√	
2	Analyze yourself		√	
3	Choose product or service	↓	√	
4	Research markets	Knowledge of marketing research		Marketing researcher
5	Forecast sales revenues			Marketing researcher
6	Choose site	↓		Marketing researcher
7	Develop production plan	Knowledge of chemical engineering	√	
8	Develop marketing plan	Knowledge of marketing		Advertising account executive
9	Develop organizational plan	Knowledge of skill needs	√	
10	Develop legal plan	Knowledge of law		Lawyer
11	Develop accounting plan	Knowledge of accounting		Accountant
12	Develop insurance plan	Knowledge of insurance		Insurance agent
13	Develop computer plan	Knowledge of computers		Computer consultant
14	Develop total quality management plan	Knowledge of customers	√	
15	Develop financial plan	Knowledge of finance		Loan officer
16	Write cover letter	Knowledge of venture	√	

The work of these professionals does not stop, however, when the entrepreneur makes the first pound of product or closes the first sale. In point of fact, the need for their services continues throughout the life of the venture. For example, there is an ongoing need for:

▶ An accountant, to prepare monthly income statements and yearly balance sheets.

▶ A lawyer, to do legal checkups once a year and to keep the entrepreneur up to date on such matters as tax, labor, and worker-safety laws.

▶ A banker, to help finance either expansion or renewal.

▶ An insurance agent, to make sure the growing venture is safely covered against the unknown.

▶ A computer consultant, to make sure the venture keeps abreast of the latest technological advances.

Building a Staff

Accountants, lawyers, bankers, insurance agents, and computer consultants provide outside professional help, but entrepreneurs also need inside help. In some ventures, the entrepreneur may choose to be the only employee. For example, an entrepreneur who opens an employment agency may need only herself and a telephone answering service to start out. After business begins to pick up, she may then add a receptionist or an interviewer.

Many entrepreneurs do not choose to begin as one-person ventures, however. The chemical engineer mentioned earlier is one such entrepreneur. He expects sales revenues of $900,000 the first year in his fiberglass-reinforced plastic business. Based on his experience in the field, he knows that to support that level of sales, he would need, say, two chemical operators, one supervisor, and one secretary-bookkeeper besides himself.

▶ **Job Descriptions**

Because they spell out who does what, who has what authority, and who reports to whom, job descriptions spare entrepreneurs a disease that infects many ventures, especially as they grow and add employees. The disease is called *organizational muddle*. It generally is caused by the entrepreneur's failure to plan the organization. Typically, entrepreneurs allow their organizations to evolve naturally, with everybody reporting to one boss or with some employees reporting to two or more bosses. The resulting mixups often lead to anger and frustration, waste and duplication of work. As one management consultant put it: "Like a good golf swing, an organization should become so well grooved that people can go about their jobs without thinking twice about who does what."[2]

Job descriptions need not be fancy and elaborate. In point of fact, they may be as simple and straightforward as the one in Exhibit 10.3, prepared by a restaurateur for her short-order chef—a calling familiar to most.

Job descriptions are but one aspect of the organizational plan. Entrepreneurs also should define the personal qualifications needed for above-average performance in each position. To expect less could result in a merely average venture. Earlier, we defined an organization as a team of people working together to meet common goals. It follows, then, that the more qualified the team, the greater the likelihood of success.

▶ **Organizational Charts**

No organizational plan is complete without an *organizational chart,* which traces the lines of responsibility and authority between jobs. In a new venture, an entrepreneur may have to wear several hats, as would the chemical engineer in our example. His organizational chart might look like the one in Exhibit 10.4.

This kind of organization is called *line-staff.* Notice in the exhibit that each jobholder reports to a single boss, represented by a black line connecting their boxes. There is no overlap, but note also that those holding the staff jobs of

EXHIBIT 10.3
Sample job description.

Job Title:	Short-order chef
Duties:	Major:

- Cooks breakfasts, lunches, and dinners to customers' specifications.

Minor:

- Orders fresh food
- Prevents waste of food
- Maintains a clean kitchen
- Prevents spoilage and infestation
- Maintains clean kitchen equipment

Relationships: Supervises two cook's helpers who aid in the preparation of foods and kitchen cleanups
Reports directly to the manager

Experience Required: Two years' experience as a chef for a reputable restaurant or diner

Skills Required: Knows how to operate:

- Gas stove
- Gas grill
- Electric mixer
- Microwave oven
- Electric meat slicer and grinder

Knows how to:

- Cook popular dishes and to order

accounting and human resources have some control over those holding the line jobs of production and marketing, represented by the blue lines connecting their boxes. Although this may seem like an overlapping of authority, it is not. To see why, let us now define what we mean by line and staff:

- **Line authority**   Line positions give those in authority the right to lead others. They are the ones in a position to say, "Do it and do it now." The strength of their authority usually stems from their power to hire and fire.

- **Staff authority**   People in staff positions hold power that is subtler than that of line authority, as they exercise their expert knowledge to help those in line positions solve their problems. Line managers may say, "Do it and do it now," while staff managers may say, "You *ought* to do it in this way because it's the best way."

EXHIBIT 10.4
Sample organizational
chart.

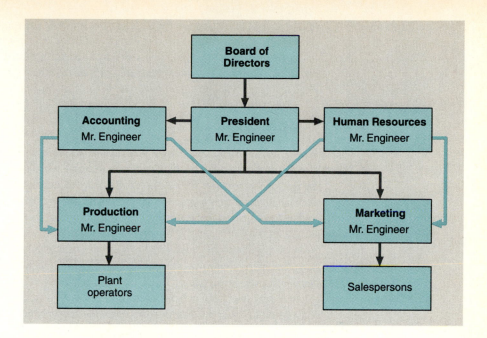

In other words, line authority is the power of *authority* that one person has over another, while staff authority is the power of *knowledge* that one person has over another.

Another way to distinguish between line and staff is to say that line is charged with making the product and closing the sale. Staff, on the other hand, is charged with generating ideas to keep the venture profitable and competitive. It is not enough for staff to simply generate ideas, however; they should also be adept at putting their ideas to work.

So far, we have focused on the line-staff form of organization. There are others, among them:

▶ **The line organization**   Every jobholder reports to a single boss; no one has a staff function. This form of organization is common among ventures with fewer than 10 employees.

▶ **The functional organization**   A jobholder may report to two or more bosses. In this kind of organization, a production supervisor may report directly to an accountant, a purchasing agent, and a researcher, as well as to a production manager.

The functional organization usually leads to chaos. With two or more bosses, a jobholder may never know where to turn when a problem comes up; and no single boss is responsible for the way jobholders perform.

Switching Organizational Forms   The line organization is a practical choice for ventures that start small. But once they begin to grow beyond 10 employees, entrepreneurs should consider switching to a line-staff form of organization. This switchover often causes problems, however, especially in ventures that have grown quickly. For when the entrepreneur gives up one of many hats to perhaps a newly hired accountant or a marketing researcher, veteran jobholders are likely to resent the change and to treat the new staff person as an intruder. This attitude is reflected in statements like these:

> We got along without them before, so why do we need them now? Besides, what do they know about the way we do things around here? They never even get their hands dirty. They're just overhead.

The best way to solve such attitudinal problems is to avoid them in the first place. This approach calls for entrepreneurs to plan their organization as if they could afford to fill each job, as did the engineer in our example. Recall that he drafted descriptions for each job, defined the qualifications of persons to fill those jobs, and prepared an organizational chart showing who reports to whom, with the engineer himself filling most of the job slots at the start.

With this kind of organizational plan, each jobholder knows from the start how the entrepreneur plans to run his venture. Each also knows that the entrepreneur is wearing many hats only temporarily. Later, as his venture grows, knowledge workers would be hired to wear those hats, thus releasing the entrepreneur to spend more time charting his venture's future.

Limitations of Organizational Charts   Entrepreneurs should also be aware of the limitations of organizational charts. Although they do indicate how entrepreneurs plan to get the work out, they often impress more than they express. Few ventures run precisely the way their organizational charts indicate. In a growing venture, organizational charts soon become dated, especially when unpredictable events change the course of an entrepreneur's plans. For this reason, wise entrepreneurs update their organizational charts at least once a year.

Organizational charts are also limited by their inability to show how all the jobs within a venture tie in. Trying to do so would result in solid and broken lines crisscrossing the page in undecipherable confusion. Good organizational charts are simple and highlight only key jobs and lines of authority.

▶ **Finding the Right Employees**

The founder of a small management-consulting firm thought she had hired the right person to counsel entrepreneurs poised for growth. His credentials seemed impeccable. After all, the employee had graduated with honors from a prestigious business school and had worked as a senior management consultant with a large, well-known firm.

Indeed, the new employee seemed an ideal fit, an aggressive self-starter who brought in the kinds of numbers the owner liked to see. But months after he joined the firm, a less than redeeming quality had surfaced: his creative flair with profanity and with offensive nonverbal behavior.

Other employees and several entrepreneur-clients were deeply offended. The owner puzzled over how best to resolve the issue. She feared that a "boys will be boys" attitude could turn into a crisis, one that would result in her getting slapped with a lawsuit.[3]

This problem was caused largely by the owner's failure to look beyond the printed word of her job description for the new employee. Granted, education

To help ensure total quality, successful businesses encourage their workers to share information face-to-face as well as by the written word.

and experience are vital, but so is chemistry. She might have spared herself the pain of hiring the wrong employee had she asked herself some deeper questions. For example, is the chemistry between:

▶ The prospective employee and herself as well as her current employees likely to be creative and productive, warm and fulfilling?

▶ The prospective employee and the firm's clients likely to enhance her firm's reputation in the small-business community as a caring problem solver that takes pains to satisfy?

As important as chemistry, and especially in the hiring of a venture's first employees, are such traits as flexibility and the willingness to work hard and for long hours. Is the prospective employee willing to work at a variety of jobs, no matter how menial they may be?

Often, fledgling entrepreneurs must look for people who are willing to work for less pay in order to grow with the venture. Moreover, they often cannot afford to offer paid holidays, hospitalization insurance, and other fringe benefits, that large corporations offer in abundance.

Finding such employees is by no means easy. There is no one best hiring method, as each method has its advantages and disadvantages. Some—like newspaper advertisements that require the screening of all who apply, or notices on college bulletin boards that may be slow in attracting applicants—are time consuming. Others—like employment agencies that expect entrepreneurs to pay the fee—can be costly. But, if entrepreneurs are prepared to pay an employment agency to save the time of screening applicants, it may be worth letting the agency handle the job alone.

On the other hand, advertisements in the local newspaper, notices on college bulletin boards, and letting friends in the business community know about the entrepreneur's needs—are all compatible with one another and are more likely to attract the right employees than any one of them alone.

This selection procedure is depicted in Exhibit 10.5.

▶ Delegating Authority

Once they have found the right employees, entrepreneurs should consider delegating authority. Few entrepreneurs enjoy doing so, mostly because it means letting others make decisions that call for spending the business's money. Yet, as their ventures grow from single- into many-person businesses, entrepreneurs have little recourse but to let go and delegate if their ventures are going to continue to grow *and* prosper. In the words of the SBA:

> Delegation is perhaps the hardest job that entrepreneurs have to learn. Some never do. They insist on handling many details and so work themselves into early graves. Others pay lip service to the idea but actually run a one-person shop. They give their employees many responsibilities but little or no authority.

EXHIBIT 10.5
Procedure for finding the right employees.

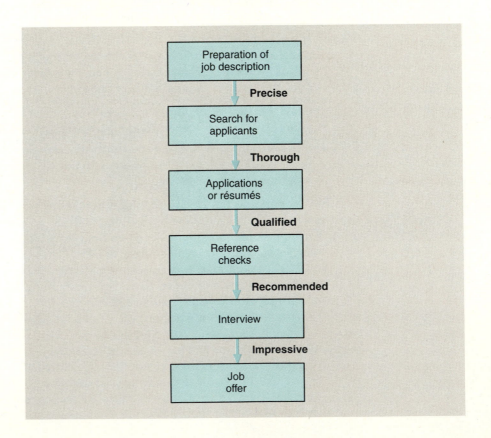

- Preparation of job description
  - **Precise**
- Search for applicants
  - **Thorough**
- Applications or résumés
  - **Qualified**
- Reference checks
  - **Recommended**
- Interview
  - **Impressive**
- Job offer

Yet, if entrepreneurs are to run a successful business, they must delegate authority properly. How much authority is proper depends on one's situation. At the very least, entrepreneurs should delegate enough authority:

▶ To get the work done.

▶ To allow key employees to take initiative.

▶ To keep things going in the entrepreneur's absence.[4]

Total Quality Management

In the 1990s, total quality management (TQM) is an idea whose time has come. Virtually every large business has embraced TQM in order to survive and grow in a global economy that demands quality. Entrepreneurs can do no less. In the words of one:

> "It is strictly a survival issue," says Tom Klobucher, owner of Elmhurst, Illinois-based Thomas Interior Systems Inc., an 80-employee firm with $35 million in sales. "Any company that is not involved in some sort of quality process is already outclassed. If they don't begin to learn the quality language and quality life, they will be out of business."[5]

TQM is really nothing more than the pursuit of excellence, by design. That is why entrepreneurs should make TQM a top priority, *before* not after, launching their ventures—as suggested in Chapter 4. Turning to Exhibit 10.6,

EXHIBIT 10.6
Results of a survey on what customers want most. Customers look for quality more than any other factor when rating suppliers.

Source: From *Purchasing*, as reported by Mark Hendricks, "Quality Makes a Difference," *Small Business Reports*, (December 1992), p. 29. Reprinted by permission of Purchasing Magazine, Copyright by Cahners Publishing Company.

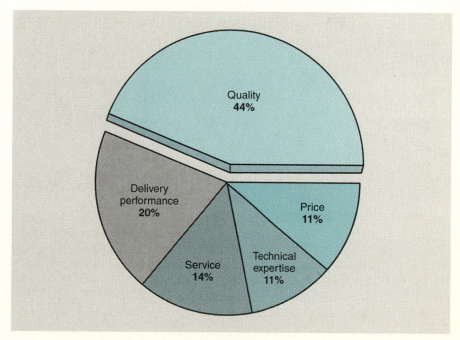

Quality
44%

Delivery
performance
20%

Price
11%

Service
14%

Technical
expertise
11%

note that a survey by *Purchasing* magazine of what customers want most found that 44 percent of all respondents valued quality most.

The overarching goal of TQM is total customer satisfaction. That would mean, in the case of a retailer, for example, accepting all returns without question and then making proper amends. One business that functions that way is the Saturn Corporation, a subsidiary of General Motors. If a customer is dissatisfied with her Saturn automobile, she can return it to the dealer, who then offers her two options if the automobile is beyond repair:

▶ Her money back, *or*—
▶ Another Saturn automobile.

▶ The Essence of TQM

This example goes to the heart of TQM, which is that only customers can define quality. More than just some obscure theory, TQM is a way of business life, a way of offering one's best to customers. To many would-be entrepreneurs, TQM also is a new style of working, perhaps even a new style of thinking, about their venture. Here is what the U.S. Office of Personnel Management says about TQM:

> Products and services that satisfy a customer don't happen by accident. Neither does TQM. It takes a lot of hard work, careful planning, listening to the customer, and involvement of *everyone* in the process, from the top of an organization to the bottom.
>
> It also takes systematically looking for ways to improve products and services, to measure performance frequently, and to maintain always an esprit de corps that comes from people in the organization feeling appreciated. All these factors need to build on each other, and be guided by a *shared* vision of what's important and what's needed to achieve it.[6]

▶ Definition of Quality

Although the meaning of quality varies widely, depending on its context, entrepreneurs must define quality from the customer's viewpoint:

> *Quality* means satisfying the customer's needs and expectations, the first time *and* every time thereafter.

Of course, doing something right the first time and every time thereafter means that everyone, entrepreneur and worker alike, must be partners in the pursuit of excellence, of TQM. For, how well entrepreneurs do depends largely on how well their workers do. Yet, as shown in Exhibit 10.7, most businesspeople fail to create an atmosphere in which their workers feel free to suggest and make changes themselves.

Now take this contrasting example cited by Tom Peters, the noted management consultant and best-selling author, who singled out this entrepreneur as "an unsung hero" for her efforts to satisfy a customer:

> Last year, during a freak October blizzard, Esther Gottberg, a cellular consultant with Kansas Cellular in Salina, Kansas, took a call from an irate customer. He was on the road, using his new phone to call Gottberg, but he couldn't receive incoming calls.

EXHIBIT 10.7

Results of Gallup survey on ways to improve job performance. In a Gallup survey of 1,200 workers, 33 percent said that the best way to improve job performance, and therefore quality, is to "give them a chance to take action."

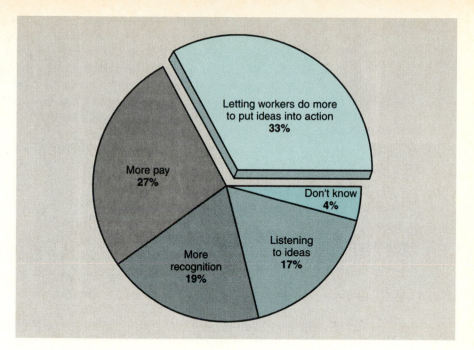

Come on in, she told him; we'll take care of it. By the time he arrived, about 5:20 P.M., the company's service representatives had gone for the day.

Though phone repair is outside her usual sales work, Gottberg and her colleague, Cara Walker, donned their overcoats and grabbed a tool kit. They pulled out the back seat of the customer's car, reprogrammed his phone and installed a new antenna.

"If it was going to happen, I had to figure it out," Gottberg explains. Forty minutes later, with the snow still falling, Walker's car door had frozen shut, so Gottberg drove her to pick up her young son.

Gottberg also knows how to sell. "Esther may be 50 years plus, but she outsells people half her age," says Mark Lacey, the Director of Marketing and Sales. Her secret? "She has an ability to focus on customers and make them feel like the most important people in the world," says Lacy. "It's not rocket science; but she's genuine, and it works."

"We started in July 1990 with *no* customers," she says. "We now (November 1992) have close to 20,000, and we're recognized throughout the state for our service."[7]

▶ **TQM Myths**

Despite its merits, TQM often is overlooked or ignored by entrepreneurs. A popular myth seems to be that TQM is a tool for big business alone. True, TQM first proved its worth with large manufacturers, among them Du Pont and IBM. Yet, the success stories of small businesses like those cited previously prove otherwise.

In fact, their very smallness may give them an edge in achieving customer satisfaction. How? For one thing, small businesses often have the speed, flexibility, and innovativeness to satisfy customers better than their larger competitors. For another, they tend to be closer to their customers.

A second myth about TQM is that it lends itself to use by manufacturers alone. Not so. In point of fact, retailers and service firms can adopt TQM as readily as manufacturers can. Take this example:

> Tom Peters offers the readers of *On Achieving Excellence* cash back if they do not find an issue useful. In his words, "If you don't get value from this or any upcoming issue, call us. We'll send you $10 for your trouble."[8]

▶ Competition and Cooperation

Often lost in the portrayal of TQM as "the race without a finish line" is its subtle effect on our understanding of competition. Implicit in our discussion of TQM so far has been the idea that TQM is everyone's job, not just the entrepreneur's. If that is so, then for TQM truly to work, entrepreneurs must imbue their ventures with:

▶ Not only the spirit of competition, which keeps employees on their toes and makes things happen, but also—

▶ The spirit of cooperation, which calls for an atmosphere of trust and sharing so that employees willingly help each other to excel—as touched on in Chapter 3.

Many businesspeople would likely question whether competition and cooperation can co-exist *and* thrive as equals, especially in a business world of swirling change. Yet it is already happening, with TQM providing much of the thrust, as suggested in Exhibit 10.8. In the words of Daniel Kielson of the Lake Forest Graduate School of Management in Illinois:

> In the business of the future, leaders will be seen as energy transformers, and the organization as a power station. The new paradigm of competition means that people will not seek to distance themselves from others, but rather from their former selves: Instead of becoming better than you, I want to become better than I was.
>
> In tomorrow's business world, the competitive spirit will press us constantly to move forward. Propelling and sustaining this movement will be the awakening that comes from learning and understanding, and the joy and enthusiasm that come from shared accomplishments.
>
> When we come to realize that there is a communal thread that weaves and connects the values and goals of people, businesses, and nations, then we will know that competition and teamwork are indeed compatible. The fact is, a sense of community is the requisite force that liberates and directs the competitive spirit to its true mission.[9]

EXHIBIT 10.8

The new paradigm of competition versus the old paradigm.

Source: Adapted from Daniel C. Kielson, "A New Paradigm for Competition," *The Futurist* (November/December 1994), p. 64.

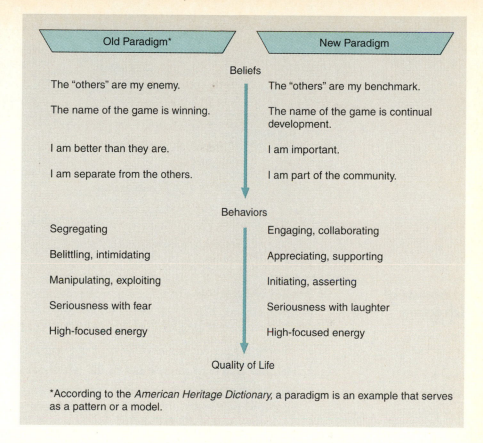

Old Paradigm*	New Paradigm
Beliefs	
The "others" are my enemy.	The "others" are my benchmark.
The name of the game is winning.	The name of the game is continual development.
I am better than they are.	I am important.
I am separate from the others.	I am part of the community.
Behaviors	
Segregating	Engaging, collaborating
Belittling, intimidating	Appreciating, supporting
Manipulating, exploiting	Initiating, asserting
Seriousness with fear	Seriousness with laughter
High-focused energy	High-focused energy
Quality of Life	

*According to the *American Heritage Dictionary*, a paradigm is an example that serves as a pattern or a model.

Fulfilling Management Needs

In chapter 9, we discussed the entrepreneurs' need for financial help. In the following sections, we discuss their need for management help, focusing on these sources:

▸ Boards of directors
▸ Management consultants
▸ The federal government, especially the SBA
▸ Trade associations
▸ Small-business networks
▸ Pooling resources

Turning to Exhibit 10.9, note how management help contrasts with professional help.

EXHIBIT 10.9
Management versus
professional help.

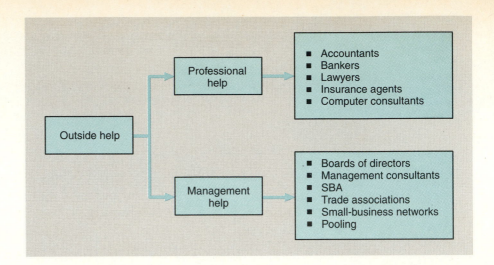

Boards of Directors

Potentially, boards of directors offer entrepreneurs a wealth of help, especially as problem solvers. Elected by shareholders, the directors are legally responsible for the venture and are given full authority. In theory, they do such things as:

▶ Choose the president and officers of the venture.

▶ Delegate power to run the day-to-day affairs of the venture.

▶ Make policy on paying dividends, financing major spending, and setting executive pay, including the entrepreneur's salary.

If the venture is a sole proprietorship or a partnership, the entrepreneur does not have to form a board. However, if the venture is a corporation, the entrepreneur, by state law, must have a board to protect shareholders. This requirement holds even if the entrepreneur is the sole shareholder.

Board Failings   Studies show that most boards of directors fail to perform, largely because entrepreneurs tend to ignore them. Yet studies also show that *outside* directors are one of the richest and least-used resources available to entrepreneurs. Even so, only about 5 percent of all small businesses have active boards with outside directors.[10] The rule is to have family and friends as board members.

As such, and lacking outside directors, the boards tend to be derelict in their duties, especially in their failure to set corporate goals and, most importantly, in their failure to ask wise, probing, penetrating questions. Like puppets, they dance on strings pulled by the entrepreneur.

Thus, because they are chosen arbitrarily by the entrepreneur, board members tend to act as his representatives, not as his challengers. Rarely do they ask sharp questions about falling profits, for example. Nor do entrepreneurs encourage them to ask such questions. Their attitude seems to be, "It's my money and my company, so I'll do as I please." Friendly board members share this attitude and, in turn, ask, "Why bother?" In contrast, consider these two examples:

One entrepreneur credits his outside board with helping his specialty baked goods concern develop an upscale image and a new line of brand names for its cookies. "You can see the influence of the board here," says the owner proudly, encompassing an array of attractive products with a sweep of his arm.[11]

The founder and president of a high-technology contractor says his outside directors helped him make crucial government contacts and lay long-range plans. He would advise other high-technology startups to name a board of "outside experts who understand the business," he says, "so you can avoid pitfalls by drawing on their experiences."[12] ▲▼▲

Finding the Right Board Members   Of course, some boards do perform well, especially as problem solvers. How might entrepreneurs select board members who will contribute to the success of their venture? Preferably, board members should be drawn from the community's ranks of successful entrepreneurs and professionals:

▸ Ideally, a successful entrepreneur should be familiar with the startup venture's industry. For example, an entrepreneur about to create a computer services venture might appoint to the board a retailer who sells personal computers.

▸ Generally, professionals would include accountants, lawyers, bankers, or computer consultants. For instance, the same entrepreneur might appoint to the board a professor of computer sciences who also consults.

Boards should remain small. A board with more than five members may become unmanageable and unproductive. It is better to spend some time selecting five problem-solving members than to hastily assemble ten members incapable of anything but idle talk.

In Exhibit 10.10, note where the board of directors fits into the organizational structure of a corporate venture.

▸ **Management Consultants**

The Value of Management Consultants   Giving advice to management about management has grown into a major industry. Yet, management consulting is a much-maligned profession: Opinions vary widely about the worth

EXHIBIT 10.10
Role of board of directors. One of the board's main duties is to elect officers capable of running the venture successfully.

Source: Adapted from William M. Pride, Robert J. Hughes, and Jack R. Kapoor, *Business,* 5th ed. (Boston: Houghton Mifflin, 1996), p. 120. Copyright © 1996. Houghton Mifflin Company. Used by permission.

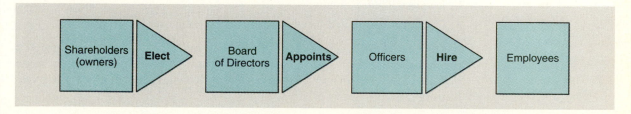

of outside consultants. Entrepreneurs, in particular, seem unhappy with consultants. Here is a typical criticism:

> In most cases, outside consultants simply don't solve the problem. They may be fully qualified and can give endless technical advice, but they can't tell us how to put their knowledge to practical use. Quite often I have had to take off my own coat and work with such fellows, doing more explaining of our problem to them than they do explaining their special knowledge to me.[13]

If clients complain about their consultants, consultants in turn complain about their clients—that they wait too long before seeking help and want hand-holding rather than an unbiased analysis of their problems.

What should entrepreneurs do to ensure that they get their money's worth from consultants? First, they should know what it is they want to know. The sharper the focus of their questions, the better the answers they will get. Instead of asking broad questions such as "What advertising method should I use to reach my prospective customers?" they should first ask well-focused questions, perhaps like the ones below, that a retailer might ask:

▶ Who are my customers? Where are they? In what census tracts?

▶ How do they buy? At what price? In what quantities?

▶ What motivates them to buy?

Finding the Right Consultants   How may entrepreneurs check a consultant's credentials? Testimonial letters are generally worthless. Only the large firms have well-established reputations, and their fees are beyond the reach of most entrepreneurs. Unlike medicine and law, management consulting is not considered a profession. In fact, anyone with printed business cards may claim to be a magician of the entrepreneurial world. There is no law requiring, say, a master's degree in business administration, five years of business experience, and passing grades on a comprehensive test given by the state before one can become a practicing consultant.

The large firms have formed a group called the Association of Consulting Management Engineers (ACME), whose purpose is to raise the standards of consultants to a professional level. ACME suggests, for example, that entrepreneurs should watch for such unprofessional practices as these:

▶ High-pressure salesmanship that promises quick, sure results

▶ Preliminary surveys offered cold at a fixed fee

▶ Requests for fees in advance

▶ Offers to consult at a low fee until results are shown

Despite ACME's efforts, consulting still has a long way to go before it reaches the status of a profession. Entrepreneurs, therefore, must do some investigating of their own before selecting a consultant. These are the questions they might ask:

- How long has the consulting firm been in business?
- What is the background of its consultants?
- What entrepreneurs has it served?
- What do these entrepreneurs say about the quality of its work?
- Has it had experience applicable to the entrepreneur's problem?

Sources of likely consultants include chambers of commerce, college professors, and entrepreneurs who have used consultants.

▶ The Federal Government

Let us now look at the sources of help offered by the federal government. Since the 1950s, the idea that entrepreneurs need management help to survive and grow has spread to virtually every corner of the country. Exhibit 10.11 shows the many sources of management help now offered at little or no fee to entrepreneurs, both before and after they go into business for themselves. Note that the services available to high-technology and to low-technology entrepreneurs differ, in recognition of the greater level of management sophistication required to launch a high-technology venture.

Note, too, that Exhibit 10.11 covers not only federal help but also help from other sources such as community colleges and universities, chambers of commerce, and organizations made up of small businesses. Exhausting this long list can only help entrepreneurs in their efforts to get the right advice.

Heading the list is the SBA. Since its birth in 1953, the SBA has helped hundreds of thousands of entrepreneurs—not only to borrow money but, even more importantly, to prepare themselves *managerially* for the job ahead. For, anybody can spend money; the question is, "Can they spend it wisely?" As one small-business expert put it:

> No small business ever failed because of a lack of funds. The supply of funds and the availability of cash to meet obligations is merely a thermometer that measures the wisdom and discipline with which the entrepreneur has committed his funds. When and if he runs clean out of working cash, his thermometer reading is zero. It indicates his inability to live within his means.[14]

SBA Management Counseling Programs Though obviously an exaggeration, the comments above underscore the central importance of management skills in any venture, large or small. What counts most is the entrepreneur's skill at managing resources, of which money is only one. The SBA offers entrepreneurs four major management-counseling programs to upgrade their management skills and to help them get federal contracts: SCORE (Service Corps of Retired Executives), ACE (Active Corps of Executives), SBI (Small Business Institute), and SBDC (Small Business Development Center).

- **SCORE program** If entrepreneurs need help in launching a venture, they can get it free through SCORE. All of its members are retired executives who enjoyed successful careers in either small or large business; all are volunteers.

EXHIBIT 10.11

Sources of management help for entrepreneurs.

Management Help Offered by	Where Available	Before They Go into a Business Whose Technology Is		After They Go into a Business Whose Technology Is	
		High	Low	High	Low
U.S. Small Business Administration					
Counseling by					
Staff	N		√		√
Service Corps of Retired Executives	N		√		√
Active Corps of Executives	N				√
Small Business Institutes	N			√	√
Small Business Development Centers	S	√	√	√	√
Prebusiness workshops	N		√		
Nonaccredited courses and seminars	N				√
Publications	N		√		√
U.S. Department of Commerce					
Seminars and workshops	N			√	√
Publications	N	√	√	√	√
Other federal agencies (example: U.S. Internal Revenue Service)					
Seminars and workshops	N				√
Publications	N				√
State, county, and local governments					
Counseling	S				√
Seminars and workshops					√
Publications	S				√
Local development corporations and similar companies					
Counseling	N				√
Seminars and workshops	N				√
Universities					
Accredited courses	S	√	√	√	√
Nonaccredited courses and seminars	S	√	√	√	√

Management Help Offered by	Where Available	Before They Go into a Business Whose Technology Is		After They Go into a Business Whose Technology Is	
		High	Low	High	Low
Universities—*continued*					
Publications	S	√	√	√	√
Counseling	S	√	√	√	√
Community colleges					
Accredited courses	S		√	√	√
Nonaccredited courses and seminars	N	√		√	√
Counseling	S		√	√	√
Small-business groups (example: National Federation of Independent Business)					
Seminars and workshops	S				√
Counseling	S				√
Publications	N		√		√
Large corporations (example: Bank of America)					
Publications	N		√		√
Counseling	S				√
Trade associations					
Publications	N			√	√
Seminars and workshops	N			√	√

N = Nationally; S = Some parts of nation

Under this program, the SBA tries to match the expert to the need. For example, if an entrepreneur needs a marketing plan and does not know how to put one together, the SBA pulls from its list of SCORE counselors a person with marketing experience. Take this example:

EXAMPLE ▶

Trained as a chemist, Diane Anderson admits "I had no idea how to run a business" when she started Agriculture & Priority Pollutants Laboratories (APPL) Inc. 10 years ago in Fresno, California. The company, an analytical laboratory that deals with environmentally sensitive issues, now has 50 employees.

Anderson turned to a SCORE counselor who "brought valuable papers and suggestions on such subjects as cash flow and long-term projections." The counselor returned every three months for the first few years to go over the books with her, until "one day he said I didn't need him anymore."

Anderson continued to call upon him periodically for advice, including once when she and her husband were considering expanding into another location. "He told us to go for it, and we've gone for it ever since."

Anderson has twice received loan assistance from the SBA and is currently taking part in its mentoring program. "I decided it was time for me to do something nice for someone else."[15] ▲▼▲

▶ **ACE program** Like SCORE, ACE is designed to help the entrepreneur who cannot afford expensive consultants. The SBA recruits ACE volunteers from virtually every industry. All ACE members currently enjoy successful careers, generally as entrepreneurs themselves.

Together, SCORE and ACE have more than 14,000 counselors working out of 400 chapters throughout the country. In 1995 alone, they counseled more than 150,000 entrepreneurs.

▶ **SBI program** The Small Business Institute draws on talents available at colleges and universities, including students working toward advanced degrees as well as professors of business administration. Under the professors' guidance, the students work with entrepreneurs to help solve their problems. Earning degree credit for their work, the students are graded on their solutions. In 1995, 510 colleges and universities took part in the program, counseling more than 20,000 entrepreneurs.

▶ **SBDC program** SBDCs offer in-depth training, counseling, research, and other specialized help at more than 700 locations nationwide. Participants include universities and chambers of commerce.

At some locations, the SBDC program roughly parallels the widely acclaimed Research and Extension Service of the U.S. Department of Agriculture, which mobilizes, through state universities, the latest technical and management advances in farming and makes sure this knowledge reaches all farmers. Here is an example of how an SBDC helped a minority entrepreneur to survive:

EXAMPLE ▶

A Maryland SBDC helped Lenny Ung when the company he owns with his wife, Lien Tran, had a run of bad luck at the time it opened in the summer of 1991.

The problems began when a plumber who was supposed to fix a grease trap at the noodle-making company failed to do so, and the system failed inspection. Then the plumber tried to elude Ung, so the business owner found a lawyer. But communication between Ung and his lawyer wasn't good either.

In addition to these nuisances, Ung and Tran had to worry about typical startup concerns, among them financing, paperwork, taxes, and marketing. "Everything makes you crazy," says Ung.

Then he learned about his local SBDC, run by a partnership of the state of Maryland, three local counties, area colleges, and the SBA. The counselors at the SBDC helped him get his business back on track by facilitating talks with his lawyer and by helping him solve his problem with his plumber. Now SBDC staff members are helping Ung find capital and are teaching him how to promote his business.

In short, the SBDC is helping Ung bridge a "very frustrating" cultural gap, says Adrian Gardner, minority-business commissioner for Prince George's County, Maryland.[16] ▲▼▲

Cooperation among SBA Programs   These four counseling programs often work jointly, if it is in the best interests of the entrepreneur. It is not uncommon, for example, for both SCORE and ACE counselors to work closely with an SBI professor to solve an entrepreneur's pressing problem. These programs also work together to offer prebusiness workshops, small-business management courses, and seminars on taxation and other special topics.

Among these special workshops is one that encourages women to consider small business as a career option. Another deals with war veterans and their problems as entrepreneurs. Special seminars also are given to encourage persons under 30 years of age to consider forming their own ventures.

Minorities benefit from special workshops and from the SBA's Minority Enterprise Program, whose main goal is to help close the gap between minority entrepreneurs and other American entrepreneurs. The SBA has joined with local communities, banks, and major corporations to match minority individuals with sound business opportunities. The SBA then works closely with the minority entrepreneur, often helping with financial statements and occasionally with preparing a business plan. SCORE, ACE, SBI, and SBDC counselors are deeply involved in this effort.

Of the many programs offered by the SBA, the foregoing are the most helpful to the entrepreneur about to launch a venture. These same programs are also helpful to those already in business for themselves. By the way, many of today's household names in the business world owe much of their early success as entrepreneurs to the SBA—among them Steven Jobs, Ross Perot, and Donald Trump.[17]

▶ **Trade Associations**

Trade associations are uniquely qualified to help their members survive and grow because their expertise and guidance relate directly to the entrepreneur's industry. There are more than 2,500 trade associations in the country, one for virtually every industry.

Many trade associations offer skilled help in a wide range of subjects, such as research, finance, labor relations, taxes, government regulations, and marketing. They also offer expert guidance, helping entrepreneurs:

▶ Pursue new opportunities in the marketplace.

▶ Take advantage of the latest technology.

▶ Adopt the latest operating methods.

▶ Solve operating problems.

▶ Increase sales revenues.

▶ Read market trends.

A composite picture of the many services offered by trade associations is outlined in Exhibit 10.12. Keep in mind, however, that not all associations offer all these services to their members. Even so, entrepreneurs should join the

EXHIBIT 10.12
Selected services offered by trade associations.

Source: U.S. Small Business Administration, *Association Services for Small Business* (Washington, D.C.: U.S. Government Printing Office, 1990).

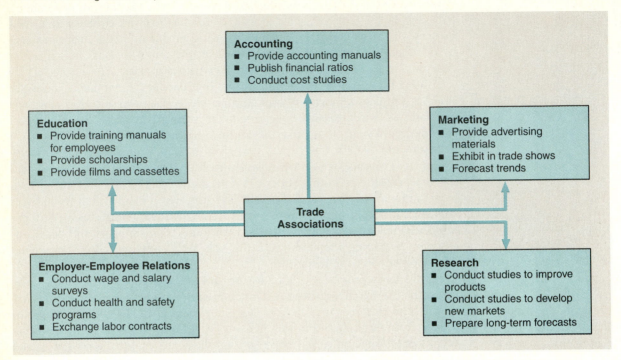

trade association in their industry, because the benefits usually far outweigh the costs. Membership dues are generally a fraction of 1 percent of the venture's yearly sales revenues. In the words of the SBA: "Considering the services available, the forward-looking entrepreneur will regard association dues not as an expense but as a form of investment toward improving the venture."[18]

▶ **Small-Business Networks**

Networking is an excellent source of help that now enjoys widespread popularity. Entrepreneurs network by meeting regularly and discussing mutual problems and opportunities. Small-business organizations have been founded all over the country for just this purpose. One such organization is the Council of Smaller Enterprises of Cleveland, which in 1995 had a total membership of 13,000 entrepreneurs, the largest number in the country. It offers educational programs and fringe benefits tailored to the needs and wants of its members.

Women and minority entrepreneurs, in particular, have found networking to be an effective problem-solving tool. Take this example, drawn from a column in *The Wall Street Journal:*

Ruth Lambert and her partner, Dianna Minnick, were hesitant to use a consultant to help them in their $2 million-a-year real estate forms business. Lambert says their reluctance was a matter of gender. "Men have no personal script against getting help. But women do; they get into I made the apple pie all by myself."

However, the partners aren't trying to run their New Haven company, Forms & Worms Inc., alone anymore. They joined a group of 10 women business owners who meet monthly to help one another with business problems. Known as the Chief Executive Roundtable, the group is sponsored by the New York-based American Woman's Economic Development Corporation and includes women who own and operate companies in the New York area with annual sales of $1 million to $10 million.

"You are alone at the top," says Doris Colgate, president of Offshore Sailing School Limited. "The roundtable gives me the opportunity to hear what someone else has to say. They are much more capable of analyzing a problem sometimes because I am too close to it."

The women have helped one another with an array of problems: important customers who chronically pay late, conflicts between partners, troublesome employees, financing expansion. "You get suggestions that are real and actionable," says JoAnn Friedman, president of Health Marketing Systems Inc. "There aren't many people who will tell you that you have a pimple on your nose."[19]

▶ Pooling Resources

To leverage their limited resources and save money during and just after startup, entrepreneurs may elect to share their space, their equipment, and even their workers. Says Jennifer Starr, a lecturer at Babson College's Center for Entrepreneurial Studies in Massachusetts: "Sharing resources is not only a way to economize; it's being innovative."[20]

It was in that entrepreneurial spirit that business incubators were first formed in the early 1980s. So popular have they become among fledgling entrepreneurs that there were more than 550 incubators in 1995, according to the National Business Incubator Association.

Typically, incubators are housed in an abandoned factory or warehouse. They generally are run by a university or a group of private investors, often in partnership with the local government. As tenants, entrepreneurs become the beneficiaries of low rent, shared computer and accounting services, and counseling.

▶ Just a Beginning

We have barely scratched the surface here. There is help available everywhere; entrepreneurs need only look for it. They may not be able to hire a $50,000-a-year marketing researcher or a $100-an-hour management consultant, but they can always use the many free services available from the SBA and other sources.

SUMMARY

Would-be entrepreneurs often cannot afford high-priced lawyers, accountants, and computer programmers. It is essential, then, that they engage in organizational planning to ensure that the support they need to run their business venture is available at a price they can afford.

In their search for help, entrepreneurs should look for professionals who also work in the same industry. Before opening a business, entrepreneurs generally need the following kinds of help:

▶ An accountant, to set up the books

▶ A lawyer, to advise on legal matters

▶ A banker, to advise on financial matters

▶ An insurance agent, to ensure the venture is protected from dangers that cannot be foreseen or controlled

▶ A computer consultant, to advise on computer uses

In defining staffing needs, entrepreneurs must think in terms of skills rather than individuals. To do this, they need to begin with the business plan, identifying all the skills needed to complete each step and then identifying people who have those skills. And they need an organizational chart, which traces the lines of responsibility and authority between positions. Finally, to find the right employees, entrepreneurs should look beyond job descriptions for flexibility, the right chemistry, and a willingness to work hard for long hours.

To survive and grow, entrepreneurs need to adopt total quality management (TQM) before, not after, launching their ventures. TQM is the pursuit of excellence by design in order to achieve total customer satisfaction. It is the careful planning of an operation by everyone involved to ensure quality. It is also the systematic searching for ways to improve products and services, the frequent measurement of performance, and the maintenance of an esprit de corps within an organization.

The organizational plan should have two parts: one that deals with internal help and another that deals with external help. In assessing their needs for outside help, entrepreneurs should take equally great pains to define the kinds of professional and management services they need. Two sources of management help are boards of directors and management consultants. In addition, many agencies and organizations are dedicated to giving entrepreneurs a helping hand. Among them are the SBA, which runs management consulting programs—for example, SCORE, ACE, SBI, and SBDC—trade associations, small-business networks, and resource pools.

Discussion and Review Questions

1. Explain the need for organizational planning.
2. Why is a business plan so vital in planning the organization?
3. What kinds of professional help are available to the entrepreneur?
4. How would you, as an entrepreneur, go about estimating the skills and staff needed to launch your venture successfully?
5. How helpful are organizational charts? Explain your answer.
6. What is *organizational muddle* and how can it be prevented?
7. Describe line-staff organization. When should you use this organizational structure?
8. Why do boards of directors tend to be ineffectual? Can they be made to work well? How?

9. Why is it that sole proprietorships and partnerships do not have boards of directors? Should they? Explain your answer.
10. What is total quality management and why is it so vital to a venture's survival and growth?
11. How would you go about getting the right consultant?
12. Describe how entrepreneurs can get help at little or no cost.
13. Which is more important, management skill or money? Explain your answer.
14. What kinds of help are available from private and government sources? How do they differ?
15. Define these terms: *organization, job description, organizational chart, line authority, staff authority, quality, board of directors.*

Building a Business Plan

Organizational Planning and Total Quality Management

An organization is any team of people who work together to meet common goals. Although entrepreneurs usually cannot afford to hire all the employees they need, they should plan as if they could afford them.

Creating the Organization

Organizing any small business requires two steps: (1) a division of jobs that must be performed and (2) assignment of those jobs to specific individuals. Only by going through this procedure can entrepreneurs be sure that they have not overlooked the skills or personnel essential for success.

Instructions for Worksheet 10

To answer the questions on Worksheet 10, in part 1 it will be necessary for you to determine different jobs that must be performed for your

business to be successful and identify who will perform each job. In part 2 you should choose a form of organization that is appropriate for your business. Then in part 3, construct an organizational chart for your business.

Part 1—Specific Tasks Necessary for Success

As discussed in this chapter, entrepreneurs must identify and define precisely the kinds of help they need if they are to survive and grow. Unless they do so, they are likely to flounder.

1. List all of the tasks that must be accomplished for your business to be successful.

2. Based on the above information, indicate whether the entrepreneur or a specific employee would most likely perform each task.

Part 2—Choosing a Form of Organization

Before answering the questions below, you may want to review the material on line, functional, and line-staff organizations that were discussed on text pages 297 to 302.

3. Based on the information in part 1, which type of organization is appropriate for your business?

4. What are the advantages for this type of organization?

5. What are the disadvantages for this type of organization?

6. In your own words, describe why this type of organization is appropriate for the business you would like to start.

Part 3—Constructing an Organizational Chart

No organization is complete without an organizational chart, which traces the lines of responsibility and authority between the entrepreneur and employees.

7. Construct an organizational chart that illustrates the lines of responsibility and authority for the people involved in your business.

CASE 10A ▶

Weaver Screen-Print

Two years after Mark and Helen Weaver began their silk-printing business, they are losing money, despite sales revenues approaching $150,000. "I'm not a smashing success yet," says Mr. Weaver, "but then again, I'm satisfied. In fact, I think I can double or triple sales in two years by expanding out of my plant into retailing."

To do that, though, Mr. Weaver may have to quit his job at Lubrizol Corporation. He has two years to go before he can "legally" retire and still get his pension benefits. Says Mr. Weaver, "I'm not sure what to do, how best to balance my desire for inner peace against my retirement benefits."

Background

There is little in the Weavers' background to indicate that they would someday become entrepre-

neurs. Both began their business careers at the same rayon manufacturing company, where Mr. Weaver worked as a chemist and Mrs. Weaver as a laboratory technician.

Shortly after they met there, they married and had two sons. One job change later found Mr. Weaver working as a project engineer for Lubrizol Corporation, a large chemical manufacturer. Mrs. Weaver also changed jobs to work for a large department store selling children's clothes.

At Lubrizol, Mr. Weaver rose from project engineer to warehouse manager. After 22 years with the company, he realized that he would rise no higher. He was 49 years old.

"I saw for the first time that I would never become a vice president," says Mr. Weaver. "Lubrizol is a great company to work for, but you've got to be a chemical engineer or a chemical researcher to get anywhere in the company. The top executives are mostly from one engineering school. So I began to look around."

In his search for a better job, Mr. Weaver soon found that his age worked against him. "Who wants to hire a 49-year-old?" Blocked off in one direction, he began to overflow with ideas in another. "Overnight, I made up my mind to go into business for myself. Just like that! Of course, I first talked it over with my wife and, without a moment's hesitation, she said yes. In fact, she even offered to quit her job at the department store where she enjoyed nine years of seniority. Working as a team, we just knew we couldn't fail."

Choice of Industry

For weeks, Mr. Weaver pondered what kind of industry to go into. When he was in his twenties, he had often thought about someday opening his own restaurant. He had moonlighted for five years at a drive-in restaurant, working at every job, including cook and dishwasher. But after watching many restaurants fail, he had concluded that a restaurant would be "too big a gamble. They're too faddish. They're popular for five years, then they go under."

Then opportunity beckoned. As president of Little League in his hometown, Mr. Weaver observed that the printing on the players' uniforms kept peeling off. So he approached the sporting goods retailer who had sold them the uniforms to find out why.

The retailer told Mr. Weaver that he was having a terrible time getting high-quality silk printing on T-shirts. "It came to me right there and then," says Mr. Weaver, "that if he was having trouble, then other sporting goods retailers had the same problem also. Wow, that very moment my thoughts jelled!"

In the next breath, Weaver asked the retailer a question: "Would you buy silk printing from me if I guarantee its quality?" "You better believe I would," replied the retailer. "I'll not only buy from you—if you guarantee the quality—but I'll also give you a guaranteed sales contract each year. If I buy less than the guarantee, I'll pay you the differ-

ence. And, if I buy more than the guarantee, I'll still pay you the difference. You can't lose."

"You just put me in business," laughed Mr. Weaver. "Would you put your offer in writing?" The retailer did, although he left out any mention of a guaranteed sales contract.

A Learning Experience

Of course, the Weavers now had a problem: How to launch their new silk-printing venture. They knew nothing about silk printing. In fact, they had never seen it done.

Undaunted, the Weavers spent "every spare second" for a month reading and studying every article and book they could find about the art of silk printing. Here the public library proved to be especially helpful.

After absorbing all they could, they leafed through the Thomas Register to get the names of local suppliers of silk-printing equipment. "We had to start somewhere," says Mr. Weaver. "I was sure that suppliers would help us get started if it meant we'd be customers."

And that is precisely what happened. Armed with the letter of intent from the sporting goods retailer, the Weavers landed a supplier who:

▸ Suggested how best to design a silk-printing plant

▸ Specified precisely what pieces of equipment the Weavers would need

▸ Suggested the name of their first employee, a "22-year-old who knows silk printing inside out"

"The supplier gave us quite an education," says Mr. Weaver. "So, just two weeks after talking to him, we took out a second mortgage on our house, borrowed $40,000 from the bank, and ordered the equipment from the supplier. We never even looked at another supplier." To justify the $40,000 loan, the Weavers gave the bank the statement that appears in Exhibit 10A.1.

EXHIBIT 10A.1

Weaver Screen-Print: Justification for $40,000 loan as presented to the bank.

We request a loan of $40,000.

Our minimum operating expenses per year will be:

$16,000	Operating expenses
14,400	Loan payments
12,000	Lease payments
6,000	Utilities
6,000	Miscellaneous expenses
1,000	Insurance premiums
$55,400	Total operating expenses

Necessary business volume to break even:

$$\text{Breakeven volume} = \frac{\$55,400 \text{ total expenses per year}}{\$3.00 \text{ sales price per unit}}$$

$$= 18,470 \text{ units per year}$$

$$= 1,540 \text{ units per month}$$

$$= 70 \text{ units per day (assuming 22 business days per month)}$$

The breakeven volume above can be achieved by the Weaver family, so no salary is necessary.

There is no apparent competition in Lake County.

The purchased equipment can produce 475,200 units per year, requiring 10 employees at $6.00 an hour.

Expected volume the first year is 90,000 units, or sales of $270,000. This sales figure is attainable because of a handshake agreement with Koenig Sporting Goods to sell them at least 60,000 units per year at $3.00.

In Business at Last

One month after being approved for the loan, the Weavers leased 1,000 square feet of space in an industrial park zoned for light manufacturing. "We first looked for an abandoned gas station, but we couldn't find one that was suitable, so we settled on an industrial park," says Mr. Weaver.

At the same time, they hired the "silk-printing expert" the supplier had recommended. Four months later, "everything was in place," and the Weavers opened for business. Their beginning balance sheet appears in Exhibit 10A.2.

When they started, the Weavers had just the retailer's letter of intent and *no* customers. Mr. Weaver continued to work days at his old job. Mrs. Weaver quit her job with the department store to become the new venture's manager. They named their business Weaver Screen-Print (see Exhibit 10A.3).

With overhead costs to cover, the Weavers' chief worry was how best to go about marketing

EXHIBIT 10A.2

Weaver Screen-Print: Beginning balance sheet.

Assets		Equities	
Cash	$13,800	Accounts payable	$ 1,000
Printing supplies	2,000	Bank loan	40,000
Office supplies	500	Owners' equity	1,500
Plant equipment	24,000		
Prepaid rent	1,200		
Other	1,000		
Total assets	$42,500	Total equities	$42,500

EXHIBIT 10A.3
Mark Weaver and his screen-print process.

their services. "We had to get customers in a hurry," says Mr. Weaver, "or else we'd run out of cash. So I thumbed through the Yellow Pages and worked up a list of every sporting goods store in the county—44 in all. Then I began paying a few of them a visit, cold."

The Weavers' first customer was a yacht club that wanted a message emblazoned across 48 T-shirts. With that order, and Mr. Weaver's after-hour visits to prospective customers, business began to pick up. By the end of their first year, the Weavers "managed to break even." Word had spread that they guaranteed their performance, a rarity in the industry.

This strategy did give the Weavers a competitive edge, so much so that the large sporting goods retailer followed through on his original promise to sign a guaranteed sales contract. By the fall of 1991, Mr. Weaver was landing half of all prospective customers he visited on his monthly round of sales calls. "If only I had more time," says Mr. Weaver, "I just know I could get many more customers." Financial statements for 1991 appear in Exhibits 10A.4 and 10A.5. The seasonality of sales is shown in Exhibit 10A.6.

Taking Stock

As their revenues approach $150,000 a year, the Weavers are taking stock of their business. Mr. Weaver says that they have grown so fast that they have to pause and see where they want to be two or three years down the road. Looking back, the Weavers believe that their years in business for themselves have been "highly rewarding."

To achieve revenues of nearly $150,000 a year, the Weavers had to expand their original idea of doing only direct printing on T-shirts. They also began to do transfers and promotional printing, and to sew decals and numbers—all on T-shirts, uniforms, and jackets.

To meet the demand for expanded services, the Weavers had to expand their shop space from 1,000 to 3,500 square feet. And it has cost them $34,000 to buy the latest silk-printing equipment.

EXHIBIT 10A.4
Weaver Screen-Print: 1991 Income statement.

Sales revenues		$146,600
Operating expenses		
Salaries and wages	$63,100	
Materials and supplies	30,200	
Utilities	12,600	
Rent	12,500	
Professional fees	8,500	
Depreciation	8,500	
Payroll taxes	5,600	
Interest	3,500	
Office supplies	1,300	
Property tax	1,100	
Freight	800	
Insurance	600	
Miscellaneous	300	148,600
Operating Loss		$ (2,000)

"I'm always looking for ways to invest in equipment of the latest technology," says Mr. Weaver. "Our competitors don't. Their equipment is so old it's held together by baling wire. Our equipment is one of the major reasons our quality is so good."

A Critical Time

The Weavers believe that the key to doubling or tripling their revenues is marketing their services. "I'm really in a puzzle," says Mr. Weaver. "With more time, I'm sure I could do a better job of selling. The only time I've got is after hours, when I'm done working at my other job at Lubrizol. I'm not sure whether to quit or not. I have just two years to go before I can retire legally and receive the pension benefits I'm entitled to."

The Weavers do not have a marketing plan. "We don't need one," says Mr. Weaver. "Ours is a

EXHIBIT 10A.5

Weaver Screen-Print: Balance sheet (December 31, 1991).

Assets			Equities		
Current assets			Liabilities		
Cash	$ 2,900		Note payable	$50,000	
Accounts receivable	8,080		Payroll taxes	830	$50,830
Supplies inventory	2,300	$13,280			
Fixed assets			Owners' equity		(1,650)
Printing equipment	$35,820				
Automobile	2,590				
Improvements	380				
Office equipment	130				
	38,920				
Less: Accumulated depreciation	3,100	35,820			
Deposit		80			
Total assets		$49,180	Total equities		$49,180

EXHIBIT 10A.6

Weaver Screen-Print: Seasonality of sales.

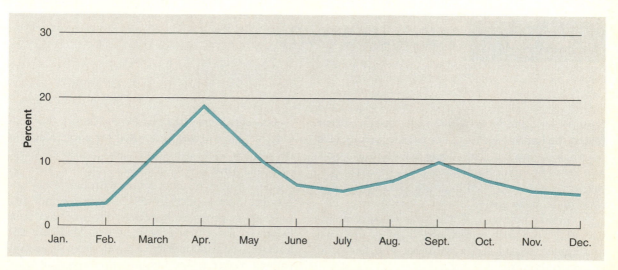

seat-of-the-pants operation. We just go from day to day; and so far, things have worked out well. I'm a do-it-yourselfer. I even put in all the equipment myself. My wife and I never needed legal help to get started. We just went ahead and did it. We're equal partners, she and I. Nothing's on paper, and we like it that way.

"Our business philosophy may be summed up in one word: trust. We trust our employees, and they trust us. We also trust our customers, and they trust us. That's the Japanese way." Mr. Weaver once spent two years in Tokyo with the U.S. Army.

Optimistic Outlook

To double or triple revenues, the Weavers are giving "serious thought" to expanding into retailing. "We might set up a dummy store in the city," says Mr. Weaver. "We could sell T-shirts with standard prints like the Superman logo and cartoon characters like Peanuts and Popeye. The exposure would be great."

To carry off such an expansion, the Weavers are counting heavily on their reputation as high-quality silk printers. Their quality has been so high that they rarely have lost a customer. "Even the few customers we lost have referred others to us," says Mrs. Weaver. She says the keys to their success are:

▸ Fast service—just one-week delivery for custom work

▸ The best equipment available

▸ Guaranteed performance

▸ Good, loyal employees

Questions

1. What are the strengths of Weaver Screen-Print? Its weaknesses?
2. Comment on the Weavers' justification for a $40,000 loan (see Exhibit 10A.1).
3. Should Mark Weaver quit his job with Lubrizol and devote full time to his venture? Why or why not?
4. How well has Weaver Screen-Print performed financially? What questions does your financial analysis raise?
5. Outline a step-by-step plan for the Weavers to follow before launching the expansion they are now considering, focusing on the questions they should answer before making a decision.

CASE 10B ▸ *All in the Family*

Susie never quite fit in. While older brother Brent joined the family business after college and appears on track to succeed Dad, Susie drifted. She barely got through high school, dropped out of college, married an unemployed high school dropout, and soon had a baby girl.

A divorce followed. While Susie received financial help from her family, she lived in her own apartment, worked as a waitress, and her child stayed in daycare.

One day, Susie stopped by the family business, entered Dad's office, and asked for a job. Dad saw the request as a positive step and put her to work.

While Susie's responsibilities did not promote regular on-the-job interaction with her father and brother, initial reports from her supervisor indicated satisfactory progress. However, circumstances soon began to deteriorate. First, it was tardiness and absenteeism. Productivity began to slide. When confronted by her co-workers and her boss, her retort was that she "would own them and this business someday."

She began to hang around the executive offices. Early one Friday afternoon, Susie demanded to know from her father why her brother got a plush office, high salary, and perks when she just got a worker's pay. "How can you deserve executive privileges when you can't even be here on time!" Dad said through clenched teeth.

"You never wanted me here anyway—so I'll quit, if that's what you want!" Susie shot back in a voice loud enough to be heard throughout the plant. She stalked out of the building.

She returned on Monday morning, and her father saw her punching in.

Questions
1. What would you recommend that Dad should do when he saw Susie punching in? Explain.
2. How might Dad have avoided the confrontation with Susie?

Source: Reprinted with permission, *The Family Business Advisor Newsletter,* Vol. 1, Issue 2. Copyright © 1992.

CASE 10C ▶ *Helen Bowers*

Helen Bowers was stumped. Sitting in her office at the plant, she pondered the same questions she had been facing for months: how to get her company's employees to work harder and produce more. No matter what she did, it didn't seem to help much.

Helen had inherited the business three years before when her father, Jake Bowers, died unexpectedly. Bowers Machine Parts, Inc., was founded four decades ago by Jake and had grown into a moderate-sized corporation. Bowers makes replacement parts for large-scale manufacturing machines such as lathes and mills.

Although Helen grew up in the family business, she never understood her father's approach. Jake had treated his employees like part of his family. In Helen's view, however, he paid them more than he had to, asked their advice far more often than he should have, and spent too much time listening to their ideas and complaints.

When Helen took over, she vowed to change how things were done and bring the firm into the twentieth century. In particular, she resolved to stop handling employees with kid gloves and to treat them like what they were—the hired help.

In addition to changing the way employees were treated, Helen had another goal for Bowers: she wanted to meet the challenge of global competition. Japanese firms had moved aggressively into the market for heavy industrial equipment. She saw this as both a threat and an opportunity. On the one hand, if she could get a toehold as a parts supplier to these firms, Bowers could grow rapidly. On the other, the lucrative parts market was also sure to attract more Japanese competitors. Helen had to make sure that Bowers could compete effectively with highly productive and profitable Japanese firms.

Contrasting Philosophies

From the day Helen took over, she practiced a philosophy altogether different from her father's to achieve her goals. For one thing, she increased production quotas by 20 percent. She instructed her first-line supervisors to crack down on employees and eliminate all idle time. She also decided to shut down the company softball field her father had built. She thought the employees really didn't use it much, and she wanted the space for future expansion.

Helen also announced that future contributions to the firm's profit-sharing plan would be phased out. Employees were paid enough, she believed, and all profits were the rightful property of the owner—her. She had private plans to cut future pay increases to bring average wages down to where she thought they belonged. Finally, Helen also changed a number of operational procedures. In particular, she stopped asking other people for their advice. She reasoned that she was the boss and knew what was best. If asked for advice and then didn't take it, it would only stir up resentment.

All in all, Helen thought, things should be going much better. Output should be up, and costs should be way down. The combination, therefore, should be resulting in much higher levels of productivity and profits.

Disappointing Results

But that was not what was happening. Whenever Helen walked through the plant, she sensed that people were not doing their best. Performance reports indicated that output was only marginally higher than before, but scrap rates had soared.

Payroll costs indeed were lower, but other personnel costs were up. It seemed that turnover had increased substantially, and training costs had gone up as a result.

In desperation, Helen finally had hired a consultant. After carefully researching the history of the organization and Helen's recent changes, the consultant made some remarkable suggestions. The bottom line, Helen felt, was that the consultant thought she should go back to that "humanistic nonsense" her father had used. No matter how she turned it, though, she just could not see the wisdom in this. People worked to make a buck and did not want all that participation stuff.

Suddenly, Helen knew just what to do. She would announce that all employees who failed to increase their productivity by 10 percent would suffer an equal pay cut. She sighed in relief, feeling confident that she had finally figured out the answer.

Questions
1. How successful do you think Helen Bowers's new plan will be?
2. What challenges does Helen face?
3. If you were Helen's consultant, what would you advise her to do?

Source: Case "Helen Bowers" adapted from Moorhead, Gregory and Ricky W. Griffin, *Organizational Behavior*, Fourth Edition. Copyright © 1995 by Houghton Mifflin Company. Reprinted by permission.

Accounting

It is not only what we do, but also what we do not do, for which we are accountable.

—Jean-Baptiste Moliere

How profitable is my venture? How wisely have I invested the money entrusted to my care by shareholders or creditors? What is my venture worth, at least on paper? Entrepreneurs are accountable for the performance and health of their ventures, and these are just a few of the questions that an accounting system should help answer.

We have already touched on accounting in earlier chapters. In this chapter, we focus on how entrepreneurs may use accounting to give them the information they need to make wise decisions.

The Uses of Accounting

Perhaps because accounting conjures up images of green eyeshades, yellow paper pads, and red ink, entrepreneurs often think that it is something better left to accountants. True, it is the accountant who designs the entrepreneur's accounting system, but it is the entrepreneur who must use the information supplied by the system to plan and control the venture.

As indicated in Exhibit 11.1, investors, lenders, and government agencies also need the entrepreneur's accounting information. Failure to recognize these needs may explain why some ventures make little profit or go under.

Entrepreneurs often blame their failures on low sales revenues, the wrong mix of inventory, high operating expenses, insufficient cash, or too much money tied up in fixed assets. Yet, with a well-designed accounting system, an entrepreneur can spot these problems early and head them off.

It is not enough for an accounting system to be well designed and carefully run, however. Unless the entrepreneur takes action based on information generated by the system, the system is useless. Three different entrepreneurs, for example, might use precisely the same accounting system—the same set of

EXHIBIT 11.1
Users and selected uses of
accounting information.

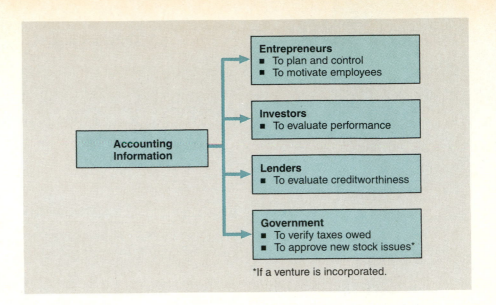

*If a venture is incorporated.

records and reports, the same means of collecting data—with wholly different
results:

▸ In one venture, the system may be useless because the entrepreneur never
acts on the information collected—and his employees know it.

▸ In the second venture, the system may be helpful because the entrepreneur
uses the information as a general guide for planning and control and has
educated her employees to use it in the same spirit.

▸ In the third venture, the system may be worse than useless because the
entrepreneur overemphasizes the importance of the figures and neglects
other and more important information—for example, that a competitor
has placed a better product on the market.

▸ Elements of a Good Accounting System

What should a good accounting system do? More than journals and ledgers
and worksheets, a good system:

▸ Allows the ready comparison of present financial performance with past
performance, industry performance, or budgeted goals

▸ Generates reports, tax returns, and financial statements quickly

▸ Ensures a high degree of accuracy and completeness

▸ Collects and processes information at low cost

▸ Minimizes the incidence of theft and fraud

However, there is no such thing as one best accounting system applicable to
all businesses, large or small. Any system works as long as it meets the goals
listed above. For example, the owner of a fruit stand may use nothing more

than the back of an envelope to keep records, if that is all he needs to stay on top of the job. Size unavoidably breeds complexity, however, as this entrepreneur would find if she joined a large retail chain:

EXAMPLE ▶

For the past seven years, an entrepreneur has profitably run a dress shop with the help of but one salesperson. Her accounting system is simplicity itself, consisting of daily cash register receipts, a checkbook, monthly bank statements, a file of unpaid bills, and a file of charge slips.

The information yielded by this simple system enables the entrepreneur's accountant to do her tax returns with ease. No other financial statements are needed, so fully in visual control is she of her shop's day-to-day performance.

Suppose, however, that the entrepreneur's shop were to join, say, a chain of 100 dress shops—the result of a buyout—there surely would be a host of changes imposed upon her. For one thing, the figures that she now keeps in her head, such as inventory and daily receipts, would be computerized so as to communicate them, perhaps daily, to the chain's headquarters.

In turn, headquarters would use these figures to make decisions about both the entrepreneur's shop and the chain as a whole. In addition, her performance would now be measured by these figures and then compared with that of the other shop managers in the chain.

Thus, the larger the venture, the more complex the accounting system. Managing alone, and with but one salesperson to look after, the entrepreneur has little need for records. She can see things on the spot—such as her inventory of dresses—that the chain's executives, far removed from her shop, can only find out about from reports produced formally, by computer. ▲▼▲

▶ The Need for an Accountant

Regardless of the simplicity of their ventures, entrepreneurs should call in accountants to help design their accounting systems. Designing a good system takes professional skill, especially as a venture begins to grow. Long gone are the days when entrepreneurs could do it all themselves, as did this entrepreneur:

A Greek restaurant owner in Montreal had his own bookkeeping system. He kept his accounts payable in a cigar box on the left side of his cash register, his daily cash returns in the cash register, and his receipts for paid bills in another cigar box on the right.

When his youngest son graduated as a chartered accountant, he was appalled by his father's primitive methods. "I don't know how you can run a business that way," he said. "How do you know what your profits are?"

"Well, son," the father replied, "when I got off the boat from Greece, I had nothing but the pants I was wearing. Today, your brother is a doctor. You are an accountant. Your sister is a speech therapist. Your mother and I have a nice car, a city house, a country home. We have a good business, and everything is paid for. So you add all that together, subtract the pants, and there's your profit."[1]

The Accountant's True Role   Today no entrepreneur should launch a venture without an accountant's expert help. Moreover, entrepreneurs should make full use of that help, ever mindful that the accountant's true role is creative, not passive. Accountants can do much more than passive tasks, such as the routine preparation of tax returns. For example, they can:

▶ Design accounting systems that best suit the needs of the entrepreneur

▶ Suggest changes in accounting systems as ventures grow

▶ Help analyze financial statements to spot problems and trends

▶ Help raise money by preparing special financial statements for prospective investors or creditors

▶ Help chart the future by translating operating plans into cash budgets

▶ Help save taxes at the federal, state, and local levels

The search for the right accountant is just as important as that for the right lawyer, and the search should begin months before a venture is launched. The best approach is to seek the names of reputable accountants from other entrepreneurs and then to narrow the list to those who work mostly with small businesses, preferably in the same industry.

It is also wise to choose a certified public accountant (CPA). The CPA designation means that the accountant is a college graduate who passed a qualifying state test. It helps assure the entrepreneur that the accountant is a professional. As such, only a CPA can certify—or *legally* guarantee—that an entrepreneur's financial statements have been prepared properly, in accordance with accepted accounting principles.

▶ Two Kinds of Accounting Systems

Entrepreneurs may choose between two kinds of accounting systems: the cash system or the accrual system. A tiny business, like a hot dog stand, is likely to use the cash basis for keeping records and for preparing financial statements. A larger, more complicated business—an automobile dealership, for example—would use the accrual system.

Under the cash system, sales revenues are reported only when cash payment is received. Similarly, operating expenses are deducted from sales revenues only when cash payment is made.

Under the accrual system, however, sales revenues are reported as earned, *regardless* of when the actual payment is received. For example, a dealer would recognize the sale of an automobile when delivery is made to the customer, *not* when cash is received. Operating expenses are treated similarly: They are recognized when they are earned, not when the entrepreneur pays the bill. For instance, the expense to the automobile dealer would be recognized when the automobile is sold, not when the dealer pays the manufacturer.

The accrual system is generally the better system to use because it offers a more accurate way of reporting financial performance, focusing as it does on the earning of sales revenues and operating expenses. This is good because no profit is shown until it has definitely been earned.

Financial Statements

▶ The Income Statement

A Summary of Operating Performance   The income statement tells entrepreneurs how well they are doing—that is, whether they have earned a profit or not. Because profit is largely a measure of customer satisfaction, entrepreneurs must prepare income statements frequently—at least every three months, if not monthly.

What does an income statement look like? In its simplest form, an income statement looks like the one in Exhibit 11.2. Note that profit is what remains after operating expenses have been deducted from sales revenues. Profit, then, is the net effect of two opposing flows of money:

▶ Money flowing into the venture from sales made to customers, either for cash or on credit (generally called *sales revenues*)

▶ Money flowing out of the venture from costs earned in connection with making those sales (generally called *operating expenses*)

The breakdown in Exhibit 11.2 is typical only for ventures in the service industries, which do not sell products that customers can touch and see. For the industry groups that do—retailing, wholesaling, and manufacturing—the income statement also should include an item called *cost of goods sold*, as shown in Exhibit 11.3.

For retailers, the cost of goods sold generally represents what they paid wholesalers for the products they resold to customers. For wholesalers, it represents what they paid manufacturers for the products they resold to retailers. And for manufacturers, it represents, for those products sold to customers, the cost of converting raw materials into finished products plus the cost of raw materials.

Exhibit 11.4 illustrates how financial flows differ depending on whether ventures deal with a product or with a service.

EXHIBIT 11.2

Computer Programmers, Inc.: Income Statement (for year ending December 31, 1995).

Sales revenues	$240,000
Operating expenses	210,000
Operating profit	$ 30,000

EXHIBIT 11.3

Hercules, Inc.: Income statement (for year ending December 31, 1995).

Sales revenues	$240,000
Cost of goods sold	140,000
Gross profit	$100,000
Operating expenses	70,000
Operating profit	$ 30,000

EXHIBIT 11.4
Basic financial flows.

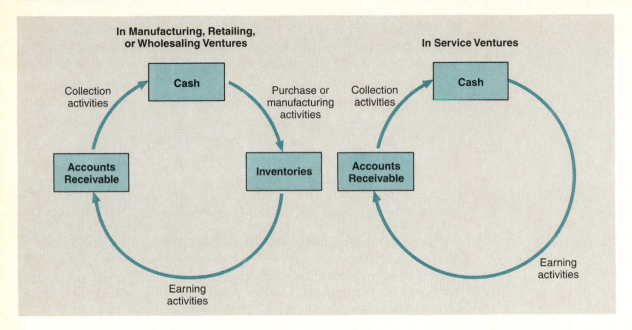

The Balance Sheet

A Summary of Financial Health   Just as the income statement summarizes how well a venture has done over time, the balance sheet summarizes its financial health as of a particular time. The balance sheet tells entrepreneurs:

▶ What their ventures are worth, at least on paper

▶ What they have invested in assets, such as inventories, land, and equipment

▶ How the assets were financed—that is, where the money came from to buy them

▶ Who has what claims against the assets

These are just a few of the questions that balance sheets help the entrepreneur answer. To clarify our understanding of the balance sheet, let us look at the following example:

EXAMPLE ▶

An entrepreneur, George Corrales, is about to lease space in a strip shopping area to sell men's shoes.

On February 1, he deposits $40,000 in a bank account opened in the name of his venture: Corrales Men's Shoes, Inc. His beginning balance sheet appears in Exhibit 11.5. This balance sheet says the venture has assets of $40,000 cash, with Corrales, the sole shareholder, having a 100 percent claim against that cash.

On February 2, he borrows $20,000 from a bank. His new balance sheet appears in Exhibit 11.6. It shows that the venture has assets of $60,000 cash. Now the bank has a one-third claim against total assets, and Corrales a two-thirds claim.

EXHIBIT 11.5

Corrales Men's Shoes, Inc.: Balance sheet (as of February 1, 1996).

Assets		Equities	
Cash	$40,000	Owners' equity	$40,000

EXHIBIT 11.6

Corrales Men's Shoes, Inc.: Balance sheet (as of February 2, 1996).

Assets		Equities	
Cash	$60,000	Bank loan	$20,000
		Owners' equity	40,000
Total assets	$60,000	Total equities	$60,000

EXHIBIT 11.7

Corrales Men's Shoes, Inc.: Balance sheet (as of February 3, 1996).

Assets		Equities	
Cash	$40,000	Bank loan	$20,000
Inventory	20,000	Owners' equity	40,000
Total assets	$60,000	Total equities	$60,000

On February 3, Corrales buys 400 pairs of shoes from a supplier for $20,000 cash. His new balance sheet appears in Exhibit 11.7. Note that the right-hand side of the balance sheet did not change between February 2 and 3. Only the left-hand side changed. Corrales simply exchanged one asset for another—cash for inventory—and received as much as he gave up. The key point here is that he really is no better off on February 3 than he was on February 2, because his equity of $40,000 remains unchanged.

On February 4, Corrales sells 20 pairs of shoes for $2,000 cash. His new balance sheet appears in Exhibit 11.8. Note that Corrales's equity has increased by $1,000 to $41,000, because he made some profitable sales. He sold shoes that had cost him $1,000 for $2,000—a 100 percent markup—giving him a profit of $1,000. His new income statement is shown in Exhibit 11.9.

Turning to Exhibit 11.10, note how the income statement in Exhibit 11.9 ties into the balance sheet in Exhibit 11.8. The income statement gives the details behind the changes that have taken place within the category of the balance sheet called retained earnings. Without

EXHIBIT 11.8

Corrales Men's Shoes, Inc.: Balance sheet (as of February 4, 1996).

Assets		Equities		
Cash	$42,000	Bank loan		$20,000
Inventory	19,000	Owners' equity		
		Common stock	$40,000	
		Retained earnings	1,000	41,000
Total assets	$61,000	Total equities		$61,000

EXHIBIT 11.9

Corrales Men's Shoes, Inc.: Income statement (for four days ending February 4, 1996).

Sales revenues	$2,000
Cost of goods sold	1,000
Gross profit	$1,000

EXHIBIT 11.10

Corrales Men's Shoes, Inc.: How the income statement ties into the balance sheet.

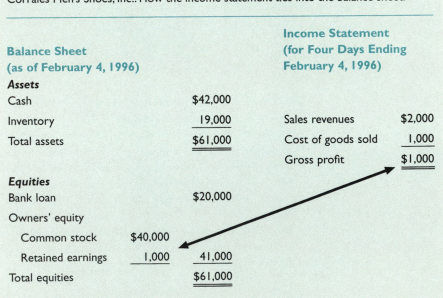

Balance Sheet (as of February 4, 1996)			Income Statement (for Four Days Ending February 4, 1996)	
Assets				
Cash		$42,000		
Inventory		19,000	Sales revenues	$2,000
Total assets		$61,000	Cost of goods sold	1,000
			Gross profit	$1,000
Equities				
Bank loan		$20,000		
Owners' equity				
Common stock	$40,000			
Retained earnings	1,000	41,000		
Total equities		$61,000		

EXHIBIT 11.11

Corrales Men's Shoes, Inc.: Balance sheet (as of February 5, 1996).

Assets		Equities		
Cash	$41,000	Bank loan		$20,000
Inventory	19,000	Owners' equity		
		Common stock	$40,000	
		Retained earnings	0	40,000
Total assets	$60,000	Total equities		$60,000

EXHIBIT 11.12

Corrales Men's Shoes, Inc.: Income statement (for five days ending February 5, 1996).

Sales revenues	$2,000
Cost of goods sold	1,000
Gross profit	$1,000
Dividends	1,000
Added to retained earnings	$ 0

the income statement, Corrales might never know what his sales revenues and operating expenses are. He also might never know what his profits are.

Suppose on February 5, Corrales pays himself a cash dividend of $1,000. His new balance sheet appears in Exhibit 11.11. At first glance, this balance sheet suggests that Corrales made no profit. As we know, his profits were really $1,000 on sales of $2,000. The net change in retained earning is recorded as zero because he paid himself a cash dividend, as shown by his new income statement, in Exhibit 11.12.

Although the balance sheet tells Corrales that his worth is $40,000, this is true only on paper. The true worth of his venture cannot be known until he tries to sell it. He could be worth more or less than $40,000, depending on what a prospective buyer is willing to pay.

This is an important point because entrepreneurs often believe that balance sheets report the real worth of their ventures. Not so. In fact, accountants do not even try to measure what a venture is worth unless the entrepreneur wants to sell it. ▲▼▲

Relationship between Assets and Equities Accountants generally define a balance sheet as a financial statement that lists assets on one side and liabilities and owners' equities on the other side. This definition is accurate but incomplete. It lacks the other messages that balance sheets try to give. For instance:

▶ The right-hand (equities) side of the balance sheet tells how entrepreneurs financed their venture.

▶ The left-hand (assets) side tells how entrepreneurs invested the money entrusted to their care.

Assets and equities always balance because all assets of a venture must be claimed by someone—either by investors or by creditors. And because the total dollar amount of these claims cannot exceed the total dollar amount of assets to be claimed, it always follows that:

$$Assets = Equities$$

The term *balance sheet* is an unfortunate one, however. It suggests there is something good about the balance between assets and equities. On the contrary, this balance tells nothing about the financial health of a venture. That is why accountants now recommend such terms as *position statement* or *statement of financial condition*. But the term *balance sheet* is so firmly rooted that few companies have adopted either of the two recommended terms.

▶ **The Cash Budget**

Measurement of Cash Flow　The income statement and the balance sheet, important as they are, fall short in one vital respect: They tell little about cash flow, the lifeblood of any venture. To be sure, the income statement measures operating results during a certain period, and the balance sheet measures the assets carried forward into the next period and the equities in those assets. But neither statement measures cash flow.

This fact escapes many entrepreneurs. They assume that if their ventures are earning profits, they must be financially sound. This is not necessarily so. In fact, even in the midst of soaring profits, entrepreneurs often have to scurry for loans to pay bills. What they soon learn seems paradoxical—that is, when it comes to paying bills, profits are not the same thing as cash in the bank. An example may help explain this paradox:

EXAMPLE ▶

A wholesaler begins a venture on January 1 with $30,000 in inventory and $48,000 in cash. She pays her bills promptly, and she bills customers 30 days net, meaning that payment is due within 30 days. She keeps an inventory equal to sales revenues expected during the next 30 days.

One month later, the wholesaler looks at her first income statement with pride. "A $10,000 profit isn't bad for a beginner," she says. Her January income statement appears in Exhibit 11.13, along with her projected income statement for February.

One day later, her banker calls to say she has run out of cash. "How come?" replies the wholesaler. "I made a profit of $10,000 in January. How can I possibly be out of cash?"

The answer is that the missing cash is tied up in inventory and in bills owed by customers. Customers owe her $40,000, and she used up her beginning cash of $48,000 to build up inventories in anticipation of February sales of $64,000. The $10,000 is but a paper profit. ▲▼▲

Accounting plays a creative role in analyzing a business's financial performance, especially so in seasonal businesses like ski resorts, which must keep an eye on cash flow the year round. This resort tries to smooth seasonal cash flow fluctuations by providing lift rides to mountain bikers in the summer.

EXHIBIT 11.13
Wholesaler's income statements.

	Actual January	Projected February
Sales revenues	$40,000	$64,000
Operating expenses	30,000	48,000
Operating profit	$10,000	$16,000

How might the wholesaler have avoided this cash flow problem? One way would have been to prepare a cash budget, which is a forecast of how much cash will flow in and out of a venture—as touched on in earlier chapters. The cash budget helps answer a vital question: Can we pay our bills on time?

The wholesaler's cash budget appears in Exhibit 11.14. Had she prepared such a budget earlier, she would have known that she would run out of cash by the end of January.

The lesson here is that the sales dollar does not necessarily return when inventory is sold, thus creating a drain on cash. In accounting terms, the lag is called *accounts receivable*. This lag can tie up cash for weeks or even months,

EXHIBIT 11.14

Wholesaler's cash budget.

	January	February	March
Sales revenues	$40,000	$64,000	$80,000
Cash inflows from sales	$ 0	$40,000	$64,000
Cash outflows for inventory	48,000	60,000	60,000
Cash gain or loss	($48,000)	($20,000)	$ 4,000
Beginning cash	48,000	0	(20,000)
Ending cash	$ 0	($20,000)	($16,000)

depending on credit terms. So, what really matters is not so much the volume of sales at any given time, but how soon the entrepreneur is paid for products sold. Also keep in mind that even when the dollars do come in, the entrepreneur may need to plow them right back into the venture to carry new inventory.

The Heart of the Cash Flow Problem　At the very heart of the cash flow problem are accounts receivable and inventory. Offsetting them are *accounts payable*—that is, what the entrepreneur owes suppliers but does not have to pay today. The balance and timing between these two sets of items determine how much cash the entrepreneur has available at any particular time.

Depreciation is another item that complicates cash flow. A noncash expense, depreciation recognizes the use of such long-lived assets as buildings and equipment by expensing their original cost over the years of their useful lives. Many entrepreneurs mistakenly believe that depreciation is a source of cash. It is not. Depreciation is merely a faucet that allows the entrepreneur to tap the flow of cash as it goes from sales down to net profit. It enables entrepreneurs to pay less taxes because it reduces net profit. But, unless there *is* a cash flow to tap, depreciation is just another accounting item on paper.

Many entrepreneurs run their ventures without cash budgets. In trying to survive and grow from week to week, they overlook the critical importance of budgeting as a managerial tool. But budgeting is indispensable. Not unlike a map, budgeting can help entrepreneurs keep on the right road. According to the SBA:

> In its simplest form, a cash budget is a detailed plan of future cash inflows and cash outflows. Combined with a projected income statement, the budget enables the entrepreneur to compare actual results with anticipated goals. For example, if operating expenses are higher than budgeted, the entrepreneur can start looking for ways to cut them; if credit customers fail to pay as expected, the entrepreneur can start looking for ways to tighten credit-and-collection activities.[2]

EXHIBIT 11.15
The entrepreneur's most
vital financial statements.

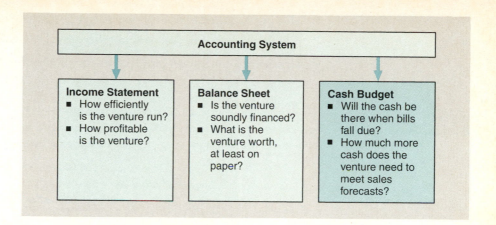

Exhibit 11.15 compares the cash budget with the income statement and the balance sheet in terms of the questions each can answer.

The Limitations of Accounting

As we saw earlier, accounting measures only a venture's paper value, not its true worth. It has other limitations as well that bear mention. One is the common belief that accounting figures are exact. They are not. Neither the income statement nor the balance sheet can give a precise picture of a venture. In fact, the figures in them are rough at best. Why? Because all ventures are highly complex, made up of highly dissimilar parts such as cash and policies, materials and incentives, buildings and morale, equipment and human beings. It is impossible to add all these dissimilar parts together to form a precise picture of a venture.

Another limitation is that assets are recorded at the price the entrepreneur paid for them, or at cost. The cost stays on the books even though the value of the asset may increase. Take this example:

EXAMPLE ▶   Suppose an entrepreneur buys a plot of land for $30,000. The asset would be recorded at $30,000. If, one year later, a buyer comes along and offers the entrepreneur $60,000 for the land, the entrepreneur would have strong evidence that it is really worth that much. Yet, recommended accounting practice prohibits changing the records to reflect the $30,000 gain in value. ▲▼▲

So the values at which assets appear in the balance sheet do not always reflect what they could be sold for. As a rule, the older an asset, the lower the probability that its book value matches its value to a prospective buyer.

Yet another limitation is that the balance sheet reflects dollars of differing purchasing power. For example, the balance sheet may show:

▶ Cash that reflects purchasing power today

▶ Inventory, stated in dollars that reflect purchasing power of a month ago

▶ Machinery, stated in dollars that reflect purchasing power of 5 years ago

▶ A building, stated in dollars that reflect purchasing power of 10 years ago

To reinforce our understanding of this limitation, let us look at another example:

An entrepreneur bought a 2 1/2-ton truck for $30,000 in 1990 and another 2 1/2-ton truck, just like the first one, for $36,000 in 1995. The entrepreneur's balance sheet would show both trucks at their *original* cost, unadjusted for price inflation:

$$\text{First } 2\tfrac{1}{2}\text{-ton truck} = \$30,000 \text{ (in 1990 dollars)}$$
$$\text{Second } 2\tfrac{1}{2}\text{-ton truck} = \underline{\$36,000} \text{ (in 1995 dollars)}$$
$$\underline{\$66,000} \ \blacktriangle\blacktriangledown\blacktriangle$$

Moreover, accounting is limited to recording only those facts that can be expressed in dollars, such as a $20,000 purchase of inventory or the receipt of a $2,000 bill from a lawyer. These are hard, objective, verifiable facts. But accounting cannot put a dollar value on teamwork, or a patent filing, for example. Nor can it report that a competitor has come out with a better product. It follows, then, that entrepreneurs should not expect to find in financial statements all the vital facts about their venture. Yet, nonfinancial information is often as vital as, if not more vital than, financial information—as depicted in Exhibit 11.16.

Despite its limitations, however, accounting does enable entrepreneurs to compress many complex events into just a handful of financial statements: notably the income statement, the balance sheet, and the cash budget. This is indeed a remarkable achievement.

EXHIBIT 11.16

Financial versus nonfinancial information. Accounting cannot accurately measure a venture's operating and financial health, because it cannot objectively measure nonfinancial information, which is at least as vital as financial information.

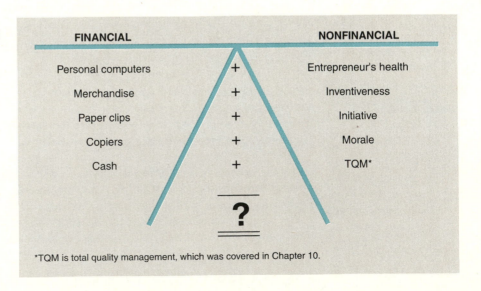

FINANCIAL		NONFINANCIAL
Personal computers	+	Entrepreneur's health
Merchandise	+	Inventiveness
Paper clips	+	Initiative
Copiers	+	Morale
Cash	+	TQM*
	?	

*TQM is total quality management, which was covered in Chapter 10.

SUMMARY

Accounting enables entrepreneurs to make better business decisions. It supplies entrepreneurs with the information they need to keep on top of their ventures, and enables them to see how profitable the business is and how wisely they have used the money entrusted to their care by investors and creditors.

Accounting information benefits a number of sources. Entrepreneurs use it to plan and control and to motivate their employees. Investors use accounting information to evaluate the performance of the venture. Lenders use it to evaluate the credit-worthiness of the business. And, finally, the government uses it to verify taxes owed and to approve new stock issues.

Generally, the end product of an accounting system is a set of financial statements that includes:

▸ The income statement, which reports how profitable a venture has been over a given period

▸ The balance sheet, which reports the financial health of a venture at a particular time

▸ The cash budget, which is a forecast of all cash inflows and outflows

Although all three statements are important, the cash budget is particularly important because it describes cash flow. Cash flow is the lifeblood of any business venture. The timing of cash inflows and outflows is far more critical than the amount of profit a venture makes.

Accounting does have its limitations. It cannot measure what a venture is really worth; it can report only its paper value. It also cannot measure such intangible assets as teamwork, morale, incentives, or the entrepreneur's health. In sum, accounting cannot give a precise and complete picture of the entrepreneur's venture.

Discussion and Review Questions

1. What is the need for accounting in a venture?
2. How would you, as an entrepreneur, use the information generated by your accounting system?
3. Why would you, as an entrepreneur, need an accountant?
4. What procedure would you follow to find the right accountant?
5. What are the main objectives of a good accounting system?
6. What is the accrual system of accounting?
7. Why is *balance sheet* a poor term?
8. How does the income statement tie into the balance sheet?
9. How often should income statements and balance sheets be prepared? Explain your answer.
10. What is the relationship between assets and equities?
11. Which financial statement is most important to the entrepreneur: the income statement, the balance sheet, or the cash budget? Explain your answer.
12. When it comes to paying the bills, is profit the same thing as cash in the bank? Explain your answer.

13. What is the importance of cash flow?
14. Describe some of the limitations of accounting. Can they be corrected? Explain your answer.
15. Define these terms: *accounting system, CPA, income statement, profit, cash budget, depreciation.*

Building a Business Plan

Accounting

As pointed out in the text, no entrepreneur should launch a venture without an accountant's expert help. And while there is no such thing as the "best" accounting system for all businesses, an effective accounting system should (1) help solve problems, (2) help pursue opportunities, (3) help express future plans, and (4) keep track of what is happening in the business. Above all, an accounting system should help the entrepreneur determine if the venture is earning a profit.

Instructions for Worksheet 11

To complete Worksheet 11, you must first prepare an income statement for your business at the end of the first year and analyze the results in part 1. Then in part 2, a balance sheet for your business at the end of the first year and analyze the results.

Part 1—Projected Income Statement at the End of the First Year

The income statement tells entrepreneurs how well they are doing—that is, whether or not they have earned a profit. For most small businesses, income statements are prepared at least every three months, if not monthly.*

1. Construct an income statement (based on your projections for sales revenues and operating expenses) for your business at the end of the first year.

2. Based on your projections, will your business be profitable at the end of the first year?

3. Based on the information contained in your projected income statement, what specific steps could you take to make your business more profitable?

Part 2—Projected Balance Sheet at the End of the First Year

The balance sheet summarizes the financial health of a business at a particular time. This statement tells entrepreneurs what their venture is worth, at least on paper. It also tells how assets were financed and who has what claims against the assets. Like the income statement, most entrepreneurs prepare a balance sheet at least every three months, if not monthly.

---

*Your answers for this part of the business plan are based on the estimates for sales revenues, operating expenses, assets, liabilities, and owner's equity that were included as part of the business plan for Chapter 9. You may also want to review the material on the income statement and balance sheet in the text on pages 332 to 338.

4. Construct a balance sheet (based on your projections for assets, liabilities, and owners' equity) for your business at the end of the first year.

5. Based on the information contained on your projected balance sheet, what specific steps could you take to improve the balance sheet for your business?

6. Many lenders examine the relationship between assets, liabilities, and owners' equity—all dollar amounts reported on a balance sheet—to determine if they will lend money to a business venture. Based on the information on your projected balance sheet, could you borrow more money to help finance your business?

CASE 11A ▶ ## *Majestic Molding Company, Inc.*

Margaret Ware Kahliff views with pride her achievement. She took over an ailing plastics company and improved its performance dramatically. Thanks to her, annual after-tax profits leaped from $7,000 to $115,000 in just three years. But sales revenues rose only slightly, from $1.4 million to $1.6 million a year.

Background

Kahliff caught the entrepreneurial fever from her father. He owned and managed a furniture store, a hardware store, and a funeral home in an Arkansas hamlet of 1,500 called Charleston.

Her father was a compulsive achiever. Besides managing three businesses at once, he served on the school board and ran the Methodist Sunday School. "He expected us to achieve, so we all did," says Kahliff. One brother, Carroll Bumpers, now heads two Greyhound subsidiaries in Phoenix, Arizona; another brother, Dale Bumpers, became a United States senator from Arkansas; and Kahliff heads a plastics company employing

102 persons. Speaking of her father's influence, Kahliff says, "If we kids made a 'B' in some subject and not an 'A,' father wanted to know how come. He never talked about money, but he talked about integrity and character."

Kahliff attended the College of the Ozarks. Years later, the college bestowed on her an honorary doctorate of humanities in recognition of her many achievements in business.

Creates Vending Machine Venture

Kahliff launched her first entrepreneurial venture at age 14, when she produced her own radio program. Later she helped finance her college education by singing at a public dance hall—until her father found out and stopped her.

Soon after college, she married a small businessperson who received a Dr Pepper franchise in a town 1,000 miles from Arkansas. The franchise failed. Out of need, Kahliff decided to go into business for herself with her husband's help. The business she chose was vending machines. She

EXHIBIT 11A.1

Ware Vending Company: Beginning balance sheet.

Assets		Equities	
Cash	$ 100	Bank loan	$1,000
Vending machine	1,000	Owner's equity	300
Other assets	200		
Total assets	$1,300	Total equities	$1,300

began with just $300 of her own savings and a $1,000 bank loan. Her beginning balance sheet appears in Exhibit 11A.1.

On this shoestring, Kahliff parlayed one vending machine into 500 vending machines ten years later. Her revenues soared from zero to $3.5 million a year. She credits this success to "knowledge, knowledge, and knowledge."

When Kahliff went into the vending-machine business, she knew nothing about it. A friend of hers had told her in passing that the "coming thing in vending machines was cups, not bottles." After sounding out vending machine suppliers and local bankers, she decided to plunge into the business.

To learn about the business, she talked to suppliers and attended sales seminars. She also took courses in accounting and marketing. "I was like a sponge, soaking up all the knowledge I could," says Kahliff.

Sells Venture

She did so well that she paid off all of her husband's debts. She eventually merged her business into a giant conglomerate—Servomation, Inc.— for 47,000 shares of common stock.

Meanwhile, she divorced her first husband and married William Kahliff, who had started his own plastics company during World War II.

Although she no longer headed her own business, Kahliff did not lose her habit of winning. She soon became group president at Servomation. By

her third year there, her division ranked second in profitability among the company's 200 divisions.

About that time, her second husband died. She inherited his business—Majestic Molding—with all shares of company stock now in her name. She was now head of one company and group president of another. She found herself working 80 or more hours a week.

This grueling work schedule all but overwhelmed her. She continued to do well at Servomation. But she soon found it physically impossible to oversee the affairs of Majestic Molding. As a result, the company began to flounder. In just one year, net profits plunged from $40,000 to $7,000. It looked as though the company would soon be awash in red ink. Worse yet, the company was now so cash-poor it could not pay its bills on time.

Accepts New Challenge

Drastic problems call for drastic solutions. So Kahliff quit her job at Servomation to devote herself full-time to Majestic Molding. She soon found that her husband had picked the wrong person to succeed him as company president. His successor was a chemical engineer who had been with the company for three years. Although competent as an engineer, he knew little about running a plastics business. "One of his first acts," says Kahliff, "was to abolish paid lunch hours. That, on top of his inability to get along with his workers, destroyed morale. Within three months, we had a union in the plant."

By mutual agreement, the engineer soon left. Kahliff then took over the day-to-day operations of the business. Overnight she began to put into practice the knowledge she gained running her own vending-machine business and managing a division for a conglomerate.

"How well you do depends largely on how well the people under you do," says Kahliff. Looking around her, she soon found that the engineer was not the only nonperformer. Such persons were everywhere, and they were gradually replaced. In fact, of the ten managerial employees she inherited, just one still works for her. She now has 102 employees, most of them hand-picked. "I test and interview almost every job applicant," she says. "I can't afford to be wrong."

Makes Sweeping Changes

Besides turning over the work force, what other changes did Kahliff make to earn such high marks for competency? For one thing, she put in several big-business practices:

▶ A cost-accounting system, including a chart of accounts, to keep daily tabs on costs and leaks. "How can you price a product unless you know, to the penny, what it would cost to make?" says Kahliff.

▶ Tuition-free education to all employees who take courses in high school or in college. "I've had as many as 16 employees in school at one time at my expense," says Kahliff. "I won't promote anyone unless they prepare themselves for a better job."

▶ A sharp separation between line and staff work. In fact, she carries this separation to extremes by placing her plant not under one manager but under two—each with equal but separate responsibilities and authorities. "I don't want the production manager to buy raw materials and still take a physical count," says

Kahliff. "That's wrong." Says Kahliff of her organizational chart, "I keep changing it at least once a year."

She took one look at her production process and decided to change that, too. Molding machines and raw materials were scattered helter-skelter throughout the plant. "It was messy and dirty," she says. Today, production is clean and orderly, flowing in a straight line from raw material storage through production and finally into finished-product inventory.

Kahliff also modernized her plant, replacing old molding machines with the latest models (see Exhibit 11A.2). She added a recycling process that all but eliminates waste. "We don't throw away anything," says Jack Kulasa, who is in charge of purchasing and inventory control.

With her employees' welfare in mind, Kahliff installed an exhaust system to cut air pollution, and she initiated a safety program to keep employees safety-conscious. Soon after, a government representative enforcing the Occupational Safety and Health Act inspected the plant and gave it a clean bill of health. The inspector told Kahliff, "This is one of the finest plastic-injection molding plants I have had the privilege of visiting."

In just three years, Kahliff worked a minor miracle, reversing the downward trend of profits dramatically, as shown in Exhibit 11A.3.

Her success became the talk of the town. She soon found herself in demand as a luncheon speaker, and she accommodated them by talking on "How to Get to the Top in a Man's World." Today, speaking requests flood in at such a high rate that she accepts only one in ten requests.

Of course, these sweeping changes took money, mostly hers. When she took over, the company's coffers were all but empty. She pumped $300,000 of her own money into the company. In addition, she borrowed $100,000 to enlarge the plant.

Motivated more by challenge than by money, Kahliff draws a salary of just $35,000 a year. "I'm interested more in building up my equity in the business than drawing a big salary," says Kahliff.

EXHIBIT 11A.2
Majestic Molding Company, Inc.

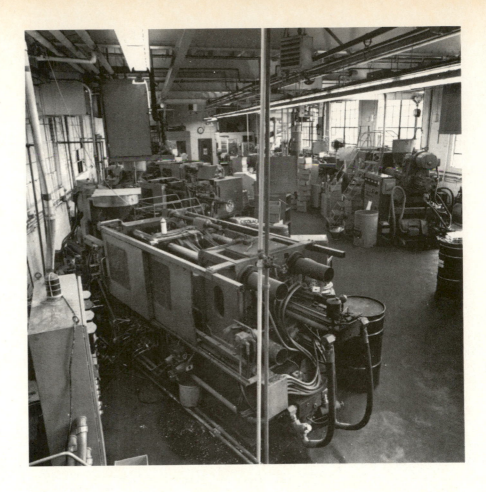

One of her personal goals at this time is to build up a million-dollar equity. She is just $50,000 shy of that goal.

Marketing

Has she set any long-range goals? No. "I've been too busy surviving to think about where we should be five years from now," says Kahliff. "But now that the company is on its feet, I'm going to think about the future, especially about ways to create more customers."

Today, her plant makes two kinds of products. One kind is called proprietary, or products made to the company's own design for sale directly to

EXHIBIT 11A.3
Majestic Molding Company, Inc.: Profits, 1987–1990.

Years	Sales Revenues	Net Profits
1987	$1,400,000	$ 7,000
1988	1,450,000	27,000
1989	1,510,000	91,000
1990	1,620,000	115,000

wholesalers or retailers. One such product is the Majestic Duck, a decorative piece for the home, office, or garden.

The other kind is called secondary, or products made to the design of other manufacturers. Into this category fall such diverse products as snowmobile wheels, shower knobs, tape cartridges, and football cleats—all made to order and all made to customer design.

Tape cartridges account for 38 percent of the company's revenues, up from 3 percent in 1987. This heavy dependence on one customer, which happens to be a giant corporation, worries Kahliff.

Today, products made for other manufacturers supply 75 percent of the company's revenues, and products made to Majestic's own designs account for only 25 percent of revenues.

For both types of products, Kahliff's market mix consists almost solely of word-of-mouth advertising. She employs no salespersons, nor does she advertise. But recently she hired an advertising agency to draw up flyers promoting the Majestic Duck. Nearly all her customers are repeat customers, landed by her late husband. "We've managed to keep them because we produce a quality product and deliver on time," says Kahliff.

Questions

1. What is Margaret Ware Kahliff's most pressing problem? Why? How would you suggest she solve it?
2. Comment on Kahliff's attitude toward goal setting.
3. Comment on Kahliff's marketing strategy.
4. Is Kahliff more an entrepreneur than a manager? Explain.
5. What should Kahliff do now?

CASE 11B ▶ *Lucy Henderson*

Instead of hunting for a summer job after finishing her junior year in college, Lucy Henderson started a lawn service business in her neighborhood. On June 1, she deposited $1,350 in a new account in the name of her corporation. The $1,350 consisted of a $500 loan from her father and $850 of her own money. In return for her investment, Lucy issued 850 shares of $1 par value common stock to herself.

Using the money in this checking account, Lucy rented lawn equipment, purchased supplies, and hired neighborhood high school students to mow and trim the lawns of neighbors who had agreed to pay her for the service. At the end of each month, she mailed bills to her customers.

On August 31, Lucy was ready to dissolve her business and go back to school for the fall term.

Because she had been so busy, she had not kept any records other than her checkbook and a list of amounts owed by customers.

Her checkbook had a balance of $1,760, and her customers owed her $435. She expected these customers to pay her during September.

Lucy planned to return unused supplies to Suburban Landscaping Company for a full credit of $25. When she brought back the rented lawn equipment, Suburban Landscaping also would return a deposit of $100 she had made in June. She owed Suburban Landscaping $260 for equipment rentals and supplies.

In addition, she owed the students who had worked for her $50, and she still owed her father $350. Although Lucy feels she did quite well, she is not sure just how successful she was.

Questions

1. Prepare one balance sheet dated June 1 and another dated August 31 for Henderson Lawn Care, Inc.

2. Compare the two balance sheets and comment on the performance of Henderson Lawn Care, Inc. Did the company have a profit or a loss?

3. If Lucy wants to continue her business next summer, what kind of information from her recordkeeping system would make it easier for her to tell whether or not she is earning a profit?

Source: Belverd E. Needles, Jr., *Financial Accounting*, Fifth Edition, p. 46. Copyright © 1995 by Houghton Mifflin Company. Used with permission.

CASE 11C ▶ *Karikas Fish Market*

James Karikas owns a fish market in Cape May, which is a popular summer resort area in southern New Jersey. A family business, the market was founded by his father, who immigrated to America from Greece in 1935.

Early each afternoon, Karikas purchases for cash as much as a thousand pounds of "whatever looks good" from incoming fishing boats. The day's catch consists mostly of tuna and bluefish, with an occasional sand shark. At day's end, Karikas sells any leftover fish to a cannery nearby that makes pet food.

His daughter, Athena, is appalled by her father's casual attitude toward accounting. "Dad, how do you know if you're making a profit?" asked Athena, who is now in her junior year at the University of Pennsylvania, majoring in entrepreneurship.

"All I need is the back of an envelope to record what I sell and what I buy," responded her father. "Everything's for cash, so what's the problem?" Athena retorted with these comments:

▶ Dad, in college we're taught that, to manage profitably any business, big or small, you need good records. Admittedly, your records need not be as sophisticated as those of giant corporations like IBM.

▶ What if you have to borrow from a bank? The bank will surely want to go over records you now don't have.

▶ Dad, let me help you set up an accounting system. Once you see what such a system can do for you, I'm sure you'll thank me.

Questions

1. Describe as completely as you can the kinds of information that you believe James Karikas needs to manage his business well.

2. Comment on his daughter's advice.

Planning and Control

Challenges make you discover things about yourself that you never really knew. They're what make the instrument stretch—what make you go beyond the norm.

—Cicely Tyson

In creating their ventures, entrepreneurs are both thinkers and doers. They are thinkers when they think through the steps of their business plans, and doers when they carry out those steps. These two processes are actually parts of one inseparable process. Thinking leads to doing; doing leads to rethinking; and rethinking leads again to doing—until finally the venture is created.

Called *planning and control,* this circular process is as vital to the health of a venture after its birth as it is before. In this chapter, we discuss the planning and control of the ongoing venture, focusing on coping with the problems of growth, setting goals, preparing budgets, and using the profitgraph, or break-even chart.

Problems of Growth

Most entrepreneurs want their ventures to grow. Often, though, growth takes place haphazardly, mostly because they ignore the lessons learned when they were launching their venture—namely, that planning and control help keep a venture on track. One reason for such behavior may be that planning and control are easily put off until a tomorrow that never seems to come.

Some entrepreneurs are like the climber who, after scaling the mountain, slips off the peak. In their eyes, planning takes place only before, not after, the birth of their venture. This failure to continue planning is one reason why so many ventures grow haphazardly, stand still, or go under.

▶ Four Stages of Growth

New ventures rarely take off like Olympic sprinters. Generally, they start slowly, sometimes inching along at a snail's pace. For example:

> An entrepreneur leased factory space to make pasta. Without any contracts in hand, he expected the first few months to be lean. It would take some time to debug the pasta-making equipment, to meet uniformly the quality standards of prospective customers, and to make pasta with negligible waste and at low cost. It would also take time to convince prospective customers, especially food chains, to buy the pasta, generally on a trial basis.
>
> Meanwhile, with sales limping along, and bills and wages piling up, the cash drain would become severe. Not until the marketplace begins to accept the entrepreneur's pasta would cash inflows begin to match and finally overtake cash outflows—perhaps months after startup.

Many ventures follow the pattern of growth shown in Exhibit 12.1. Generally, however, entrepreneurs fail to handle the later stages of growth as well as they do the earlier stages. They tend to do well during the *prebirth* and *acceptance stages*, even though progress in these stages often meets with obstacles. Prebirth involves taking all the steps necessary to reach startup. In the acceptance stage, entrepreneurs may struggle to break even as they introduce, say, a unique product. In this stage, they usually are so close to their ventures that they can spot obstacles and act quickly to remove them, though sometimes at great cost.

EXHIBIT 12.1
Stages in the growth of a venture.

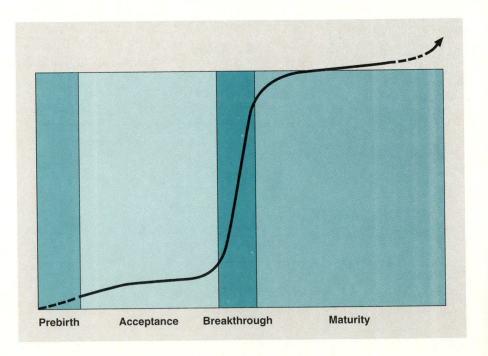

Prebirth   Acceptance   Breakthrough   Maturity

The *breakthrough stage* follows. Until then, growth may be slow—so slow that it often passes unnoticed—but in the breakthrough stage, the rate of growth may be so fast that the entrepreneur cannot keep up with it. Caught unprepared, many entrepreneurs falter. Sales may continue to spiral upward, as problems surface in areas such as these:

▶ **Cash flow**   Will we have enough cash when it comes time to pay bills?

▶ **Production**   Are we keeping costs down while producing a high-quality product?

▶ **Quality**   Are we handling customer complaints by practicing total quality management (TQM)—guaranteeing uniformly high quality?

▶ **Delivery**   Are we delivering promptly on all customers' orders?

Faced with such pressing problems, entrepreneurs often react rather than respond, applying Band-Aid solutions as sales level off or even drop. Later, upon sober reflection, they may stay the course and add such knowledge workers as a customer services representative or a TQM analyst.

No small thanks to such professionals, entrepreneurs may thus regain the agility they lost shortly after breakthrough. Finally, as their venture passes through the *maturity stage*, the cycle of growth may repeat itself as, for example, entrepreneurs introduce new products or enter new markets.

Take this example that describes the lessons learned by an entrepreneur during the early stages of a venture's growth:

EXAMPLE ▶

Michel Roth is the founder of a debt-structuring firm in Eugene, Oregon—his latest venture among others. One lesson he learned is that, in the beginning stages of a venture's growth, entrepreneurs must maintain a balanced perspective—especially when things are going well.

"Humans are so fickle, so forgetful when it comes to remembering bad times, that with a few months of success, we start thinking that we don't have to do the basics," says Roth. "That can get us off track easily."

To illustrate his point, Roth offers the story of one of his early ventures: a sporting goods company that got off to a rocky start. "All of a sudden, things started to click, and in three months we had $300,000 in sales," Roth recalls. "I thought I was God's gift to business. I just knew we had made money."

But, when the financial analysis was complete, the picture turned out to be very different. The actual cost of sporting goods was $305,000, and overhead expenses were far higher than originally projected. "We lost our shirt that first year," he says.

It was an expensive lesson, but Roth learned from it. In the excitement of having the business take off, of seeing the orders come in, he had gotten busy and careless. The nickels and dimes of product cost and overhead turned into dollars, and he had assumed incorrectly that he had ample profit margins to cover the expenses.

"Enthusiasm tends to mask a lot of potential problems. It makes you euphoric," says Roth. "But a monthly review of your financial circumstances will keep you grounded. It will keep you from thinking you have more than you do. Books are very neutral. They're the great equalizer. They have no enthusiasm; they're cut and dried; and they tell it like it is."[1] ▲▼

▶ Entrepreneurs as Managers

Some entrepreneurs who are good at creating and nursing a venture through infancy are less good at carrying its growth through to maturity. Other ventures never even survive infancy. Why do some ventures take off, while others fail? One answer may be that the qualities that equip entrepreneurs to succeed during a venture's infancy may not be helpful at the breakthrough stage. At that point, they must change hats and work at being managers as well as entrepreneurs by:

▶ Surrounding themselves with people who know more than they do about different aspects of the venture

▶ Orchestrating the skills of these people to make production efficient

▶ Keeping abreast of the latest management tools

Turning to Exhibit 12.2, note that, compared to large businesses, small businesses make little use of those management tools likely to give them a competitive edge. Especially shortsighted and neglectful is their failure to do long-range planning—just 7 percent do.

In becoming managers, however, entrepreneurs must not give up their entrepreneurial bent. On the contrary, they must continue to look for new opportunities, at the same time striking a balance between exploiting those opportunities and solving problems. Otherwise, their ventures may top out with little prospect for growth. What it means to shift from informal to formal planning is depicted in Exhibit 12.3.

EXHIBIT 12.2
Results of survey on degree to which selected management tools are used by small and large businesses.*

Source: Adapted from "Special Report: What Do Small Businesses Need from CPAs?" *Journal of Accountancy* (May 1995), p. 20.

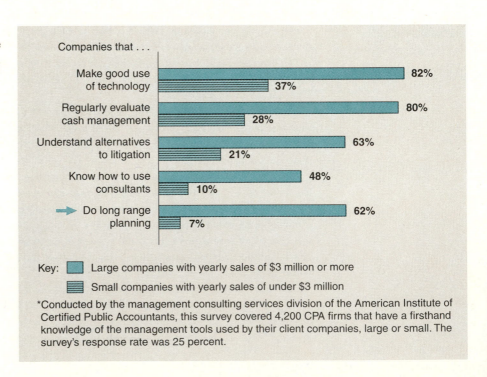

Companies that . . .

Make good use of technology — 82% / 37%
Regularly evaluate cash management — 80% / 28%
Understand alternatives to litigation — 63% / 21%
Know how to use consultants — 48% / 10%
Do long range planning — 62% / 7%

Key: ▮ Large companies with yearly sales of $3 million or more
      ▤ Small companies with yearly sales of under $3 million

*Conducted by the management consulting services division of the American Institute of Certified Public Accountants, this survey covered 4,200 CPA firms that have a firsthand knowledge of the management tools used by their client companies, large or small. The survey's response rate was 25 percent.

EXHIBIT 12.3
The shift from informal to
formal planning.

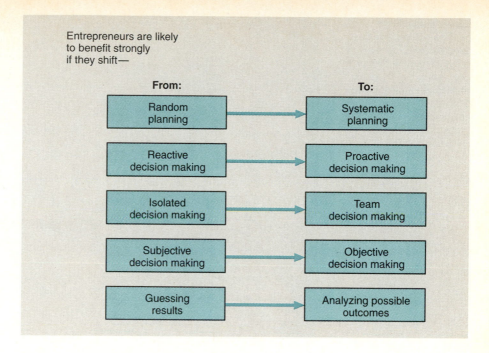

Entrepreneurs are likely
to benefit strongly
if they shift—

From:	To:
Random planning	Systematic planning
Reactive decision making	Proactive decision making
Isolated decision making	Team decision making
Subjective decision making	Objective decision making
Guessing results	Analyzing possible outcomes

▶ Keeping Profits in Perspective

As they shift to formal planning, if not before, entrepreneurs must always keep profits in perspective. Granted, no business can survive without profit. The entrepreneur's ability to satisfy customers, finance growth, reward employees, and contribute to their community—all hinge on the entrepreneur's ability to make a profit.

Yet, some entrepreneurs permit the pursuit of fast profits to blind them to what is healthy for their ventures, in the *long* run. For example, entrepreneurs can often boost profits in the short run by investing less in customer service or in product quality. But, in the long run, they are likely to pay a severe price for treating these areas cheaply, if not shabbily.

So it behooves entrepreneurs to keep profits in perspective and strike a proper balance between short-term profits and the need to invest for long-term strength and growth. They must never be so shortsighted as to jeopardize their survival by putting profit before product.

As discussed in Chapter 2, entrepreneurs must also understand the true meaning of profits: their just reward for a job well done in the sale of a product or a service that customers need or want. In other words, profits must be viewed as a yardstick that measures how well entrepreneurs are satisfying their customers. Generally, the higher the profits, the deeper their customers' satisfaction; conversely, the lower the profits, the poorer their customers' satisfaction.

▶ The Need for Lifelong Learning

In essence, then, a venture's true value resides in its customers, not in its products. Often defined as "consistently delighting your customers," customer

Customer satisfaction must be the be-all and end-all of every business, especially so in a pharmacy, dealing as it does with prescriptions. By keeping up with computer database innovations, pharmacists are able to keep better track of their customers' needs.

satisfaction must never be taken for granted. That is why entrepreneurs must continually ask themselves:

> What are we going to do, when we are no longer able to do, what we are doing now—in order to keep our customers satisfied.

This question has particular poignancy in these changing times, as virtually everything seems to be evolving faster and faster. So much so that, in the words of *Inc.* magazine, "Monday's hottest trend looks dented and dusty by Wednesday."[2] Though an exaggeration, this quotation underscores the need for entrepreneurs, in turn, to evolve faster and faster—to keep pace with the changing times *and* with their customers. Otherwise, they may become a victim of change rather than its master.

How might entrepreneurs master the challenge of change? By being not only competitive but by also becoming lifelong learners. In a 20-year study on what it takes to succeed in today's business world, Professor John Kotter of the Harvard Business School found that:

> The most salient characteristic is competitive drive—that is, a strong willingness to set ever higher standards and not walk away from competitive situations. [Successful entrepreneurs] try always to keep moving forward, knowing that sometimes they will fail.
>
> The second characteristic is a willingness to keep stretching themselves, to keep learning—even after they have achieved a certain level of success and could just take it easy. This capacity for lifelong learning has helped keep their skills relevant despite all the change.[3]

Unfortunately, few entrepreneurs view themselves as lifelong learners, much less their ventures as learning organizations. Yet, learning, and the knowledge it yields, are indispensable to entrepreneurs and their need to stay afloat in today's business world—a view shared by many expert observers of the business scene.[4,5]

Setting Goals

To keep their ventures alive and well, entrepreneurs must set goals in the same way they did before launching their venture. The act of setting goals is especially vital once a venture begins to grow rapidly and add more workers. This is when the entrepreneur, as manager, must lead others toward meeting the venture's goals. As Robert Townsend, former board chairman of the Avis Rent-A-Car Corporation, put it:

> One of the important functions of a *leader* is to make the organization concentrate on its goals. In the case of Avis, it took us six months to define goals, which turned out to be: We want to become the fastest-growing company with the highest profit margins in the business of renting and leasing vehicles without drivers.
>
> This goal was simple enough so that we didn't have to write it down. We could put it in every speech and talk about it wherever we went. And it had some social significance, because up to that time Hertz had a crushingly large share of the market and was thinking and acting like General Motors. . . .
>
> Once these goals are agreed on, the leader must be merciless on himself and on his people. If an idea that pops into his head or out of their mouths is outside the goals of the company, he kills it without a trial.[6]

As Townsend pointed out, the key to the pursuit of goals is concentration. Once goals are set, the entrepreneur must make sure that every employee understands and pursues them. In the words of Peter Drucker, noted author-lecturer-consultant:

> No other principle of effectiveness is violated as constantly today as the basic principle of concentration. . . . Our motto seems to be: "Let's do a little bit of everything. . . ." We scatter our efforts rather than concentrate them.[7]

▶ **Need for Precision**

In setting goals, entrepreneurs must decide what needs immediate attention and what needs long-range planning. With tongue in cheek, *The New Yorker* drew this distinction between immediate and long-range goals:

Long-Range Goals:
    Health—more leisure

    Money

    Write book (play)—fame///??

    Visit India

Immediate Goals:
    Pick up pattern at Hilda's

Change faucets—call plumber (who?)

Try yoghurt?[8]

If only it were this easy to set goals for an ongoing venture. If asked what their goals are, entrepreneurs are likely to say, "To make a profit, of course!" But they must learn to be as precise about their business goals as *The New Yorker* list is about personal goals. As one entrepreneur advises:

> Use your business plan to develop a program that will carry you through the challenge of startup to success and profitability. For example, if your business plan projects first-year sales of $100,000, what sales volume do you need to generate each month? And to do that, how many transactions do you need to complete each week?
>
> As you are setting the short-term goals that will take you to long-term success, make sure they are specific and recognizable, and assign each goal a timetable for completion. *Specific* and *recognizable* mean that you know exactly what you have to do and you will be able to tell when you have done it.
>
> The timetable imposes a deadline for action. For example, "build a successful business" is not a goal; "generate $5,000 per week in sales by the first of May" is.[9]

▶ Building on Strengths

To set meaningful goals, entrepreneurs must look first at their own strengths and skills. What can their venture do best? Self-examination is perhaps the most creative step in goal setting because it can lead to exciting challenges—for example, invading wholly new markets, dropping a product, or adding a product. The idea of setting goals based on one's strengths is built on these assumptions:

▶ In a highly competitive economy, success generally favors the venture that does its job with superior skill. Being an average performer may be almost as risky as being a poor one, especially in fast-moving markets like electronics and pharmaceuticals.

▶ A venture may create new customer demand for the job it does, if it does the job well.

▶ A venture's product or service may be outdated quickly, but its profile of special skills tends to continue for years to come.

One board chairman had this to say about the cardinal importance of building on strengths:

> Investors, financial people, and others from time to time ask about us. What's our productive capacity? How many tons will we ship? How do we figure depreciation? What profit will we make three years from next Michaelmas? And so on. All useful questions—no doubt.
>
> But rarely, if ever, do they ask the one, real, gutsy question—which is—what have you got for an organization? What sort of people are they? How do you recruit and train them? Who is going to run the business—

and do the thinking for it—5 years from now, 10 years, 20 years? This is the business. The rest is spinach.[10]

▶ **Management by Objectives**

One method of translating into concrete goals the insights gained from identifying a venture's strengths is *management by objectives* (MBO), as depicted in Exhibit 12.4. Practiced widely among giant corporations, MBO is a powerful tool. Its power lies in the simplicity of its premises:

▶ The clearer the entrepreneur's idea of what to do, the better the odds of success—if the intent is to make the most of the venture's skills and talents.

▶ True progress can be measured only against the entrepreneur's goals.

In essence, MBO is a system of cooperative goal setting that reaches from the top of a business to the bottom. Its purposes are to motivate employees and to make clear their role in the pursuit of goals.

To achieve these purposes, the entrepreneur meets with each employee individually to talk about goals. This meeting would normally take place yearly and focus on the coming year. The entrepreneur and the employee then agree on a set of goals for the employee to meet. These goals usually are expressed in numbers—for example, to boost sales revenues by 10 percent within six months. A year later, the entrepreneur would appraise the employee's performance, comparing actual results with goals.

EXHIBIT 12.4
The MBO cycle facilitates performance appraisal.

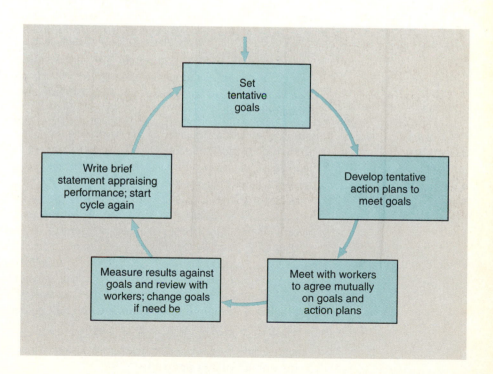

Set tentative goals

Develop tentative action plans to meet goals

Meet with workers to agree mutually on goals and action plans

Measure results against goals and review with workers; change goals if need be

Write brief statement appraising performance; start cycle again

Let us now look at an example of how MBO might actually work, focusing first on long-range goals and then on immediate goals:

As the owner of a Buick dealership, an entrepreneur sets two kinds of goals each year; one *long-term* and the other *immediate*. His latest hierarchy of long-term goals looks like this:

▶ To rank each year among the top 10 Buick dealerships in the nation, as measured by the number of new models sold yearly and the ratio of after-tax profits to sales revenues.

▶ To practice TQM by selling quality Buicks at reasonable prices, backed by excellent customer-oriented services. To meet strong competition from other dealerships, we must always give our customers superior service. Above all, we must be marketing-minded.

▶ To base our decisions on information collected and analyzed in light of the latest management tools. To compete profitably, we must be able to reach decisions and take action promptly and accurately. Our margin for error is wafer-thin. For example, only two cents of every dollar we took in last year was left for dividends and for financing future growth.

▶ To always be mindful of our responsibilities to our employees and to the community in which we work, in order to create a climate of warmth in which people will give their best to the dealership and to the community.

▶ To be known in the community as a dealership that offers equal employment opportunities for minority persons and people who are disabled.

The entrepreneur's *immediate* goals look like this:

▶ To increase new-car sales to 2,800, from 2,400 last year
▶ To increase the return on sales to 2.5 percent of sales, from 2.0 percent last year
▶ To increase the return on investment to 12.0 percent yearly, from 10.0 percent last year
▶ To establish a parental leave plan for all employees
▶ To beautify the grounds by planting elm trees ▲▼▲

Note how these two lists of goals are cast in descending order of importance, giving the entrepreneur a clear idea of how much attention to give each item. Separating the goals into short- and long-run lists also clarifies what needs to be done immediately.

▶ **Giving Employees a Voice**

Not only are the goals clear to the entrepreneur; they are also explicit enough to be shared directly with employees. To make sure of their support, the entrepreneur should set goals with the help of key employees—the new-car sales manager, the service manager, and the controller.

When employees have a voice in setting goals, commitment is more likely to filter through each layer of the organization, from the entrepreneur to the floor sweeper. The deeper the commitment, the greater the likelihood that goals will be met. As Dr. Douglas McGregor, the eminent behavioral scientist, put it, "The central principle . . . is that of integration: the creation of conditions such that the members of the organization can achieve their own goals *best* by directing their efforts toward the success of the enterprise."[11]

Finally, note that all these goals are actually guides to action:

▶ They facilitate decision making by helping the entrepreneur and the employees choose the best course of action in the solution of a problem or the pursuit of an opportunity.

- They clearly suggest specific courses of action. "To make profits" is a vague guide to action; "to rank each year among the top 10 Buick dealerships" is a precise guide.

- They specify ways of measuring the dealership's performance. The entrepreneur can tell how close he comes to the top 10 by comparing his new-car sales with those of other dealers throughout the nation. This measure is much more useful than an empty statement like "to compete in the new-car field."

- They challenge and excite the entrepreneur and the employees. Without such goals, the venture may lose its spirit and risk stagnation. Goals should not be too demanding, of course: Goals that are challenging but achievable spur performance best.

▶ Action Plans

Setting goals is just the beginning. Next, the entrepreneur must decide how best to meet those goals. This calls for the development of action plans that:

- Lay out precisely the steps necessary to achieve each goal.
- Fix the responsibility for each step on the entrepreneur or a key employee.
- Set deadlines for each step.

Action plans should be designed to make things happen. Without plans to breathe life into them, goals are meaningless. One example of an action plan is the *business plan*. Here is another:

EXAMPLE ▶

The entrepreneur in our earlier example worked out the following action plan for his new-car sales manager:

To help meet our goal of increasing new-car sales from 2,400 to 2,800 Buicks a year, you should:

- ▶ Send all salespersons to a marketing course at a local college to improve their ability to close a sale.
- ▶ Work with our advertising agency to create eye-catching television commercials with an appealing message.
- ▶ Invite all old customers to visit our showroom by letter and then by a follow-up telephone call.
- ▶ Meet with me and our controller each Monday at 10:00 A.M., to review our sales performance from the previous week. ▲▼▲

Action plans need not be fancy or elaborate; in fact, they can often be simple and straightforward. It is a good idea, however, to put them in writing, because a permanent record leaves little room for debate later.

Control and Budgeting

Setting goals and drafting action plans alone are not enough. The entrepreneur must also measure progress at frequent intervals. To do so calls for information that tells whether goals are being met.

Called *control,* this process of measurement helps assure entrepreneurs that their own actions, as well as those of employees, are on target. The heart of the control process is information that enables the entrepreneur to compare actual performance with planned performance. This information makes it possible to measure not only performance but also the suitability of goals and action plans—and, if need be, to adjust them.

In earlier chapters, we spoke of the cash budget as being the centerpiece of the business plan, especially in the entrepreneur's efforts to raise money before startup. The cash budget plays an equally vital role after startup, this time as a tool for planning and control. To see how budgeting might work, let us now look at this example:

The entrepreneur in our earlier example expressed his new-car sales in units, as Exhibit 12.5 shows. This unit budget would be used by the new-car sales manager to control the performance of her salespeople. Here, units have more meaning than dollars to salespersons and are an effective way of communicating goals to them.

But at the sales manager's level, dollars assume importance as a control. For example, to meet her unit goal of 2,800 new-car sales, the sales manager might overreact and tell her salespersons to sell at discounts or accept trade-ins that erode profit margins. To avoid that mistake, the entrepreneur would prepare another budget, this one translating units into dollars, as shown in Exhibit 12.6.

EXHIBIT 12.5
New-car sales budget—units.

| | Quarter | | | | |
Model	First	Second	Third	Fourth	Total
Small	200	400	400	200	1,200
Medium	100	200	200	100	600
Large	200	300	300	200	1,000
	500	900	900	500	2,800

EXHIBIT 12.6
New-car sales budget (net of trade-in).

| | Quarter | | | | |
Model	First	Second	Third	Fourth	Total
Small	$1,600,000	$ 3,200,000	$ 3,200,000	$1,600,000	$ 9,600,000
Medium	1,200,000	2,400,000	2,400,000	1,200,000	7,200,000
Large	3,000,000	4,500,000	4,500,000	3,000,000	15,000,000
	$5,800,000	$10,100,000	$10,100,000	$5,800,000	$31,800,000

EXHIBIT 12.7

New-car selling expense budget.

Item	Quarter First	Second	Third	Fourth	Total
Salaries	$ 800,000	$ 800,000	$ 800,000	$ 800,000	$3,200,000
Commissions	300,000	500,000	500,000	300,000	1,600,000
Advertising	80,000	150,000	150,000	120,000	500,000
Telephone	5,000	5,000	5,000	5,000	20,000
Total	$1,185,000	$1,455,000	$1,455,000	$1,225,000	$5,320,000

This control system is still incomplete, because the sales manager may overspend in her effort to meet her goal of 2,800 new-car sales. So the entrepreneur must prepare a third budget, dealing with selling expenses, as shown in Exhibit 12.7.

Armed with these three budgets, the entrepreneur can control the performance of the new-car sales department. By providing them with the information they need to make sound decisions, these budgets encourage the sales manager and the salespersons to do their best. These budgets also enable the entrepreneur to evaluate the performance of the sales manager and, in turn, the sales manager to evaluate the performance of her salespersons.

These evaluations of performance may result in promotions and in merit salary increases, or in remedial action and even dismissals. However, budget figures must never be the only measure of performance. For example, suppose an unexpected recession causes new-car sales to slump nationwide and results in the sales manager failing to meet the goal of 2,800 new-car sales. Should she be penalized? No. Her failure would be due to events beyond her control. In any case, it is the responsibility of the entrepreneur, not the sales manager, to foresee such a slump and adjust the budget accordingly. ▲▼▲

▶ Reporting Performance

To make the best use of budgets, an entrepreneur must establish a system that compares actual performance with budgeted performance. Such comparisons may be made on the back of an envelope for a one-person business; but for a larger business, like the automobile dealer's, only a comparative chart, like the one in Exhibit 12.8 is called for. The chart may then be shared with shareholders, managers, and even rank-and-file employees.

Note how this quarter-to-quarter comparison gives off immediate signals. For example, in the first quarter, actual performance topped budgeted performance for both small and medium models. This signals the entrepreneur that the new-car sales department performed well with those models. On the other hand, the sales department did poorly with large models, falling 20 cars short of the budgeted first-quarter goal. Because this figure is 10 percent off budgeted performance, the entrepreneur must find out why and then take remedial action.

EXHIBIT 12.8

Report on actual and budgeted sales—units.

	Small Model			Medium Model			Large Model		
Quarter	Budgeted	Actual	Difference	Budgeted	Actual	Difference	Budgeted	Actual	Difference
First	200	220	+20	100	100	+10	200	180	−20
Second	300	280	−20	150	150	−	250	220	−30
Third	300	310	+10	150	140	−10	250	230	−20
Fourth	200	180	−20	100	110	+10	200	190	−10
Total	1,000	990	−10	500	510	+10	900	820	−80

▶ **Return on Sales Versus Return on Investment**

So far, we have looked at ways the entrepreneur can control the performance of the salespersons and their manager. But what about the entrepreneur himself? Because the entrepreneur alone is accountable for the dealership's operating and financial performance, he must be evaluated against two of his budgeted goals:

▶ **A return on sales of 2.5 percent** A measure of *operating efficiency,* this return tells the entrepreneur how well he managed the dealership's day-to-day operations.

▶ **A return on investment of 12.0 percent** A measure of *financial efficiency,* this return tells him how wisely he invested the money entrusted to his care by investors.

At year's end, the entrepreneur would compare his actual performance with budgeted performance. For example, a return on investment of 13.0 percent would tell the entrepreneur that he had made good use of his investors' money.

Never confuse these two yardsticks of performance. Entrepreneurs often say, "My return is just 2 percent," creating the impression that their return on investment is 2 percent. They probably mean return on sales. Learn to distinguish between them. Exhibit 12.9 shows how they differ, as does this extreme example:

EXAMPLE ▶

An entrepreneur buys a product in the morning for 99 cents and sells it in the afternoon for a dollar. She does business this way 100 days a year. What are her return on sales and her return on investment?

Her return on sales is 1 percent, computed as shown in Exhibit 12.10; while her return on investment is 101 percent a year, computed as shown in Exhibit 12.11. From an investors' viewpoint, the better measure of performance is the return on investment of 101 percent, because it tells how efficiently the entrepreneur used her investment of 99 cents—how well she managed her resources to produce results. Although less important, the return on sales of 1 percent tells how efficiently she did business from day to day—how much she had left over as profit for each dollar of sales. ▲▼▲

EXHIBIT 12.9
Return on sales versus
return on investment.

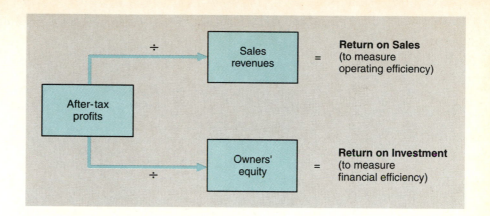

Return on Sales
(to measure
operating efficiency)

Return on Investment
(to measure
financial efficiency)

EXHIBIT 12.10

Example: Computing return on sales.

$$\text{Sales revenues} = \$100.00 \quad (\$1.00/\text{unit} \times 100 \text{ units/year})$$

$$\text{Operating expenses} = \underline{\;\;99.00\;\;} \quad (\$0.99/\text{unit} \times 100 \text{ units/year})$$

$$\text{Operating profit} = \$\;\;1.00$$

$$\text{Return on sales} = \frac{\text{Operating profit}}{\text{Sales revenues}} \times 100$$

$$= \frac{\$1.00}{\$100.00} \times 100$$

$$= \underline{\underline{1\%}}$$

EXHIBIT 12.11

Example: Computing return on investment.

$$\text{Operating profit} = \$1.00$$

$$\text{Owner's equity} = 0.99$$

$$\text{Return on investment} = \frac{\text{Yearly operating profit}}{\text{Owner's equity}} \times 100$$

$$= \frac{\$1.00}{\$0.99} \times 100$$

$$= \underline{\underline{101\% \text{ a year}}}$$

In Chapter 13, we discuss return on sales and return on investment in greater detail.

The Profitgraph

▶ **Uses of the Profitgraph**

Another helpful planning and control tool is the profitgraph, usually called a *breakeven chart*. The term *profitgraph* is better because the entrepreneur's goal is to make a profit, not just to break even. A remarkably versatile tool, profitgraphs give entrepreneurs visual answers to questions such as these:

▶ How many pounds of product must I produce and sell before I begin to make a profit?

▶ At what percentage of capacity must I run my plant before I begin to make a profit?

▶ How much must sales revenues increase to justify my hiring another salesperson?

The profitgraph can also give entrepreneurs visual answers to *what-if* questions. For example: What would happen to my profits if:

▶ Fixed expenses increase 10 percent but volume, prices, and variable expenses stay the same?

▶ Sales volume drops off 10 percent but prices, fixed expenses, and variable expenses stay the same?

▶ Sales volume goes up 10 percent but prices, fixed expenses, and variable expenses rise 5 percent?

These sample questions underscore how handy and versatile a tool the profitgraph can be.

The following example shows how to prepare a profitgraph:

EXAMPLE ▶

An entrepreneur has been profitably operating a restaurant in a shopping center for six years. Her success has encouraged her to think seriously about leasing space in another shopping center for a second restaurant.

Before she can make this decision, however, she needs to know how many customers she must average daily before she begins to make a profit. The entrepreneur and her accountant have estimated that variable expenses will be $0.40 on each $1 of sales, fixed expenses will be $36,000 a month, and the average customer will spend $10 for a meal.

Using this information, the entrepreneur can construct a profitgraph like the one in Exhibit 12.12. As shown, the new restaurant would begin to make a profit when its monthly sales top $60,000—or at least 6,000 customers a month.

In constructing the profitgraph, the entrepreneur drew a straight line parallel to the horizontal axis to signify fixed expenses of $36,000 a month—the same regardless of the number of customers patronizing the new restaurant. She drew a second line beginning at $36,000 on the vertical axis and increasing at the rate of $0.40 per $1 of sales, or $4 per average customer, to show total expenses. Finally, she drew a third line beginning at zero and increasing at the rate of $10 per average customer to signify total sales revenues.

EXHIBIT 12.12
Profitgraph.

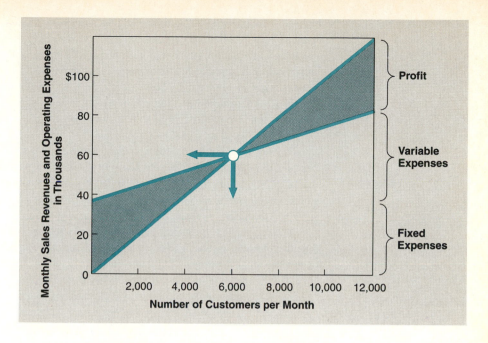

The point at which the sales and total expense lines intersect is the point at which sales revenues match total expenses. In other words, it is the point at which the entrepreneur would neither make a profit nor suffer a loss, but would break even. ▲▼▲

▶ Limitations of the Profitgraph

One word of caution about profitgraphs like the one described in the example: Volume-price-expense relationships are true only within relevant ranges of volume. For instance, if monthly volume in our example were to drop to 4,000 customers, the entrepreneur would undoubtedly slice her fixed expenses by perhaps doing away with the job of hostess, permitting customers to seat themselves; or by closing the restaurant on Sundays because volume is lowest that day.

Instead of constructing a profitgraph, the entrepreneur could have found the point at which she would begin to make a profit through the following calculation. First, she would estimate the contribution to fixed expenses made by each customer ($10 selling price – $4 variable expense = $6). This means that, out of each $10 sales, $6 is left over to cover fixed expenses. She would then divide this unit contribution into monthly fixed costs:

$$\frac{36{,}000/\text{month}}{\$6/\text{customer}} = \begin{array}{l}\text{6,000 customers a month} \\ \text{needed to cover fixed expenses} \\ \text{and begin to make a profit}\end{array}$$

This computation gives the entrepreneur her breakeven point, but it lacks the versatility of the profitgraph, which is also useful as a tool for visualizing the answers to a host of what-if questions. It enables the entrepreneur to anticipate a number of possible scenarios and their effect on profits.

SUMMARY

When entrepreneurs ignore the lessons they learned while launching their ventures—specifically, that planning and control help keep a venture on track—problems result. These problems coincide with the four stages of growth: prebirth, acceptance, breakthrough, and maturity. During the first two stages, entrepreneurs are usually so close to their ventures that they can spot obstacles and act quickly to remove them. In the later stages, however, entrepreneurs often are caught unprepared and experience problems with cash flow, production, quality, and delivery.

To keep a venture alive and well, entrepreneurs should continue to set goals the same way they did before launching their venture. These goals should be as precise as possible. In this way, both employer and employee understand what the venture's goals are as well as what the goals of each member of the enterprise are in working to meet the larger goals.

Setting goals is a critical first step in planning and control. The clearer the entrepreneur's idea of what should be done, the greater the chances it will be done. In addition, true progress can be measured only in relation to the entrepreneur's goals. The second step is to draft action plans to meet the goals. These plans should be similar to the business plan, which is a form of action plan. Finally, the third step is to measure progress at frequent intervals. This process, called *control,* helps assure entrepreneurs that their actions and those of their employees are progressing according to plan. The key to any system of control is information that enables entrepreneurs to compare actual with planned performance. This information indicates where the venture stands and, more important, in what direction it is moving.

Management by objectives (MBO), budgeting, and profitgraphs are three tools that help entrepreneurs plan and control more effectively. Management by objectives, which is practiced widely among corporate giants, is a method of translating concrete goals into insights gained from identifying a venture's strengths. It is a system of cooperative goal setting that reaches from the top of a business to the bottom, and whose purpose is to clarify the role of employees in the pursuit of goals and to motivate them. Budgets generally serve as a standard against which actual performance is compared. Profitgraphs illustrate the impact of sales volume, price, and expense on profit.

Discussion and Review Questions

1. What are the four stages of growth? Does an entrepreneur's venture essentially stop growing when it reaches the maturity stage? Explain your answer.
2. What are some of the problems of growth?
3. Why is lifelong learning so important?
4. What do profits measure? Explain fully.
5. Why is it vital to set precise goals? Give two examples of precise goal setting.
6. How would you, as an entrepreneur, go about setting goals for your venture?
7. What is the most important principle in the pursuit of goals? Why?

8. What is meant by the hierarchy of goals? Give an example.
9. What is MBO?
10. Explain the process of planning and control. Why is this process circular?
11. Why is budgeting a vital tool for both planning and control?
12. Which is the better measure of a venture's performance, return on investment or return on sales? Explain your answer.
13. Why is the profitgraph such a versatile tool in planning and control? Give two examples of how this tool may be used.
14. In your opinion, why do many entrepreneurs fail to plan and control their ventures in the ways suggested in the chapter?
15. Define these terms: *immediate goals, long-range goals, action plans, return on investment, return on sales, operating efficiency, financial efficiency.*

Building a Business Plan

Planning and Control

A goal is an end result that an entrepreneur wants to achieve over a certain period of time. A small business has at least two different types of goals, which include the firm's mission and specific objectives.

Types of Goals

The most fundamental type of goal is the firm's *mission,* the reason for the firm's existence. Texaco's mission is to earn a profit for its owners. Dallas County Community College District's mission is to provide an education for local citizens. The mission of the Secret Service is to protect the life of the president.

An *objective* is a specific statement detailing what the firm intends to accomplish as it goes about its mission. For McDonald's, one objective might be that all customers will be served within two minutes of their arrival.

Sears might adopt the objective that sales will be increased by 7 percent this year.

Instructions for Worksheet 12

To complete Worksheet 12, you must prepare a mission statement for your business in part 1. Then in part 2, list the objectives you want to accomplish during the first year of operation.

Part 1—What Is the Mission of Your Business?

Before completing this part of your business plan, you may want to review the definition for your business that you last revised in Chapter 4.

1. After examining the material in the first twelve chapters of this text, do you still want to start the same type of business?

_____ yes _____ no

2. Is the definition for your business that you last revised in Chapter 4 still appropriate?

     _____ yes   _____ no

3. What, if any, changes should be made to the definition that you developed for your business?

4. Given the current definition for your business, develop a mission statement for your business.

*Part 2—What Specific Objectives
Do You Want to Accomplish?*

Once an organization's mission has been described in a mission statement, the next step is to develop objectives. Objectives for a small business can deal with a variety of factors, such as sales, growth, expenses, customer satisfaction, and employee morale. For most firms, objectives represent specific activities that should be accomplished within a year.

5. Take a moment and visualize the type of business that you would like to own at the end of the first year. Now develop specific objectives that will help you build the business that you envision.

CASE 12A ▶

Chimo Enterprises, Inc.

Chimo Enterprises is seeking a $250,000 bank loan through the U.S. Small Business Administration (SBA). Its president, Stuart Ramsay, claims he needs that sum to expand sales revenues dramatically, from $530,700 to $820,400. The company markets lawn-care, landscaping, and tree services.

To justify his loan request, Ramsay has prepared a 112-page business plan. He prepared the plan when he was participating in a strategic planning course sponsored by the small business section of the local chamber of commerce. Taught by Dr. Jeffrey Susbauer and Dr. Robert Baker, this course is aimed solely at entrepreneurs whose ventures are poised for growth. Both men head their own consulting firms and are well known nationally for their knowledge of strategic planning.

Ramsay has just submitted his business plan to the SBA. The loan officer there promised to call him within ten days to inform him of the status of his loan request. Excerpts from the plan follow.

Company History

As suggested in our beginning balance sheet, shown in Exhibit 12A.1, we began humbly as a landscape maintenance and construction company in 1976. We also plowed snow during the winter. We directed our marketing efforts mostly at large accounts such as condominiums and apartment complexes, until we won several major

EXHIBIT 12A.1

Chimo Enterprises: Beginning balance sheet (June 30, 1976).

Assets		Equities	
Cash	$ 1,400	Liabilities	$ 0
Truck	5,000	Owners' equity	15,000
Landscape equipment	8,000		
Other	600		
Total assets	$15,000	Total equities	$15,000

construction contracts for new landscaping. Then we decided to focus on that market.

In our second year of operations, we purchased a lawn services franchise. We grew rapidly in the next two years and set sales records for the franchise.

In our third year of operations, we added a tree services division and developed new business by taking our existing customer base and selling additional but related services. This strategy has worked well, reducing both our marketing and transportation costs.

Since we are undercapitalized, fast growth has caused us to suffer financially. Thus, the $250,000 loan will enable us to:

▸ Relieve the financial strain

▸ Upgrade existing equipment

▸ Reduce maintenance costs sharply

▸ Market new products that match the needs of our existing customer base

Company Mission

We aim to market a total landscaping service to commercial and residential customers, offering them lawn fertilization, landscape maintenance, and tree services. We will earn a return of 15 percent on investment from this expansion. At first we will focus on selling additional services to existing, satisfied customers within a five-mile radius of our home office. Later, as penetration warrants, we will open branches in outlying areas, thus creating job opportunities for existing employees. We will do business in an ethical way, creating a work atmosphere that enables our employees to mature professionally.

Our five-year plan calls for the opening of three branches. We expect sales revenues to reach $600,000 a year at the home office and $200,000 at each branch. This expansion will be financed mostly through funneling profits back into the business and training current employees as potential managerial candidates.

Although winter operations have centered on commercial and industrial snowplowing, we will eliminate these services in favor of more profitable lines of work, such as hydraulic deep-root tree and shrub feeding and winter antidesiccant spraying.

Description of Business

We have three operating divisions:

▸ Chimo landscape services division, which does home designs, new construction, and lawn renovation work. This division specializes in high-quality, fully-guaranteed work, successfully marketed through a base of customers established by the other divisions.

▸ Chimo tree services division, which prunes and takes down trees. This division also specializes in preventive work such as tree spraying, hydraulic deep-root feeding, and tree surgery.

▶ A lawn services division, which fertilizes lawns. Using the only patented ground-metered equipment in the lawn-care industry, we provide the finest custom-applied lawn programs available.

Our market focuses on homeowner accounts in a small geographic area. A feature of such accounts is that we can sell them other services once they are satisfied with the work of one division. Computer records on all prospects and customers give us a database for marketing additional services unmatched in the industry. We expect to penetrate 10 percent of the homeowner market within a five-mile radius of our home office, expanding later to branches in outlying areas.

Our competitive position is strong, mostly because our equipment can tailor an application to a customer's specific lawn needs—a service not supplied by competitors at this time. Our salespeople evaluate lawn needs in person and make their sales presentations on the spot, resulting in a sales-to-closing ratio higher than that of our competitors.

One marketing goal is to employ salespeople throughout the year to penetrate the industrial, commercial, and institutional markets more effectively. Such a salesforce would help reduce the seasonal swings in our business as well as help create a stable workforce.

Our pricing strategy is to price to customer value, by guaranteeing high-quality work. This strategy helps retain our customer base at a level higher than that of competitors.

Major Changes in Marketing Direction

In 1983, we took a critical look at the markets we served and the services we offered. It quickly became apparent that some areas needed immediate changes. One such area was lawn mowing, which was highly unprofitable. Prices were so depressed that large buyers of lawn-mowing services were looking at price, not value, so we eliminated 95 percent of all lawn-mowing operations. Similarly, we found that snowplowing prices had dropped as much as 40 percent in the past three years, so we dropped those services, too.

In 1983, the upsurge in new-home construction suggested that the market for new landscape construction would rise sharply. We decided to go into that market heavily. To date, new landscape construction sales have leaped almost 400 percent.

We also identified hydraulic deep-root feeding as a highly profitable and much-needed service for both homeowner and industrial accounts. Although still in its infancy, this market will grow quickly if we provide high-quality service. In December 1982, this new service outsold our snowplowing.

Industry Structure and Our Position

As mentioned previously, we operate three divisions: Chimo landscape services, Chimo tree services, and lawn services. This line of services has positioned us as a complete landscape and exterior services company. No competitor offers as much. For example, we offer services such as:

▶ Dethatching
▶ Fertilizing
▶ Fungus control
▶ Lawn renovation
▶ New seed and sod work
▶ Plug core aerating
▶ Soil amendments

We also offer complete design and new landscape construction. Moreover, we have a service that provides a diagnosis of shrub and tree problems; and our tree services division does such work as tree removal, pruning, stump removal, tree spraying, and hydraulic deep-root feeding. Offering such a full line of services enables us to capture new business at reduced costs, since customers who are satisfied with one division's work will more readily buy services available from another division—as mentioned earlier. The statistics in Exhibit 12A.2 show that the markets we serve are the right ones.

In our industry, the most crucial aspect of cost control is geographic routing. Measured against an industry average of three miles per stop, our

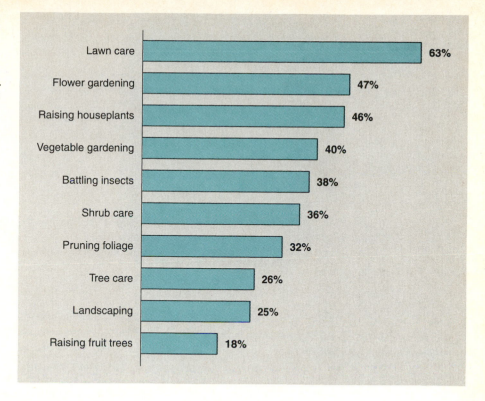

EXHIBIT 12A.2

Statistics on lawn and garden care. Seventy-one million U.S. households work on lawns or gardens, a $15 billion-a-year market. This graph shows the most common gardening activities.

Source: National Gardening Association

Lawn care	63%
Flower gardening	47%
Raising houseplants	46%
Vegetable gardening	40%
Battling insects	38%
Shrub care	36%
Pruning foliage	32%
Tree care	26%
Landscaping	25%
Raising fruit trees	18%

lawn services division does well indeed. We average less than two-tenths of a mile per stop.

We control our landscape services division similarly. When we market extra services such as plug-core aerating, dethatching, and lime applications, we route our service trucks in a geographic pattern that achieves the highest number of services for the miles driven.

The tree services division markets its services similarly. Our hydraulic deep-root feeding, tree spraying, and antidesiccant spraying services are all marketed intensively at different times of the year, and the trucks are routed to achieve the highest production for the fewest miles.

Competitive Position

The market for our lawn services division is highly competitive—at least seventeen major companies vie for the same customer base. Although our prices are among the highest in the industry, we offer the best services available. We have unique advantages over competitors in the following areas:

▶ Patented machines that "custom apply" both dry granular and liquid materials. As mentioned earlier, only our company is capable of customizing applications to individual lawn needs.

▶ Total landscape services. Some of our competitors offer additional services, but no one else offers a total service on a competitive basis.

▶ The industry's best written guarantee, as shown in Exhibit 12A.3. Note that we offer to redo any application free of charge if the customer is dissatisfied. Moreover, if the customer continues to be dissatisfied, we guarantee to refund the full cost of the last application.

Green Thumb Guarantee

As a Lawn Doctor dealer I guarantee satisfaction. If any application does not achieve satisfactory results —tell me. I will return and re-apply that application at no additional cost or refund the full cost of your last application. You don't have to sign a contract. I will continue to bring you this beneficial service from year to year until you tell me to stop!

▶ Both our name and green thumb logo, which project an image of professionalism that is seldom forgotten by customers.

Computerization

The computer boom has not escaped our eye. Because of the large number of customers, we found that it was simply too inefficient to process paper by hand. We were one of the first lawn services franchises in the country to install a computer.

We paid a programmer $25,000 to design programs tailored to our lawn-care business. Our computer system already carries four pages worth of data on each customer, and it has the potential to carry out many more functions. The computer also produces all of our truck routing, inventory control, financial statements, financial projections, account statuses, sales invoicing, and marketing letters. Our list of computer capabilities has grown to include updating and scheduling of customer services. Each customer's file includes what was done to the lawn and when and suggests additional services that may be needed. This system enables us to serve our customers more efficiently—on time with fewer errors—and to keep better track of the lawn's progress. If a problem develops, we can resolve it quickly.

Like many operations being introduced to a computer, we expected miracles when we first installed it. We expected our staff to be able to put out reports overnight. When we realized that it was not just that simple, we sent the whole staff to a ten-week orientation program to learn more about operating a computer system successfully. This decision for additional schooling paid off. We saved at least $10,000 in labor in the first year alone and recovered our investment in the computer system in two years. We foresee an unlimited potential for further computerization, as we install additional computer terminals, hire more employees to run them, and upgrade our operations in this way.

Like many other smaller businesses, we have discovered that computers are becoming more than just an economic advantage—they are almost mandatory.

Innovation

Lawn care is a $5 billion-a-year industry with a growth rate of 20 percent a year. It is our innovations that will always keep us ahead of our competitors. We will continue to introduce innovative ideas that save homeowners' money while optimizing their satisfaction with the services we perform. Some examples of innovative ideas are:

- Offering improved strains of shade grass seed that correct the problem of bare ground under trees

- Providing materials that ease the penetration of lawn roots, thus reducing the amount of water needed in summer

- Checking acidity, alkalinity, and thatch levels routinely

- Offering a range of corrective services to boost a lawn's endurance

Another new service that we plan to market is the Leaky Pipe, which is a low-cost alternative to sprinkler systems. This capillary-action, underground system may save customers up to 70 percent on water bills. Our conversations with distributors in other states have shown us that its market potential is huge. We can secure the exclusive distributorship covering our state. Our Green Thumb Newsletter describes the Leaky Pipe as follows:

Totally reliable, very inexpensive, and the most effective watering system on the market today, Leaky Pipe is installed three to eight inches beneath the surface of your lawn or garden. Leaking slowly and evenly through thousands of minute pores in a flexible rubber pipe, water gently seeps into the soil from the pipe and moves by means of capillary action to the plant roots. Leaky Pipe is ideally suited for use in any lawn or garden, regardless of size. Counted among its advantages over conventional sprinkler systems are that:

- Leaky Pipe saves time. It takes just a few hours to install and does its work without further effort.

- Leaky Pipe saves water. Because neither evaporation nor runoff takes place, water savings may run as high as 70 percent.

- Leaky Pipe saves on maintenance. Indestructibly strong and durable, it is installed wholly underground.

- Leaky Pipe saves money. It costs much less to install than conventional sprinkler systems. Its useful life exceeds 20 years. And, it lowers water bills.

These ideas will surely beautify our customers' lawns, causing our sales to rise significantly.

Management

Stuart Ramsay, who is the president and founder of Chimo Enterprises, was born in Montreal. While still in his teens, he left for the Canadian Arctic, where he worked as an apprentice carpenter. He received nine promotions in only three years while building the Canadian radar line.

On returning to Montreal, Ramsay became a district manager for the morning daily newspaper, where he worked for three years. Then, in rapid succession, he held a series of managerial jobs, each one more responsible than the preceding one:

- Manager, Branch Office, Sun Life Insurance Company, in a northern Canadian mining town.

- Industrial food sales representative, Procter & Gamble. With this company, he moved through the ranks to earn top honors in Canada as president of its National Sales Production Club.

- Sales manager, Commerce Label and Litho, a label and specialty printing manufacturer. He expanded the salesforce from one to nine salespersons and more than quadrupled sales.

- Commissioned salesperson with Premier Industrial Corporation. Within three months he was promoted to sales manager, a position that required him to move from Canada to a midwestern U.S. city.

In 1976, Ramsay left Premier Industrial to create Chimo Enterprises, initially as a landscaping and lawn maintenance business. His interest in lawn care was sparked by a horticultural project he headed while at Sun Life Insurance.

Shortly after forming Chimo Enterprises, Ramsay purchased a lawn services franchise. Mostly because of his energetic and competitive nature, it quickly became the fastest-growing new franchise in the franchisor's history.

[Ramsay's business plan continues:] Our company's success stems largely from our management team's dedication to excellence. An organizational chart appears in Exhibit 12A.4. Our managers often work as many as 60 to 70 hours a week, especially during spring and summer. Equally important, they are overachievers who perform to the best of their abilities. The team includes:

▸ Kathleen Ramsay, a founder of Chimo Enterprises and its vice president. A graduate of the University of Dayton, she held a number of managerial positions before marrying Ramsay and cofounding Chimo. As a buyer for a major department store chain, she was in charge of buying and planning for eight stores in the chain. At present, Ms. Ramsay oversees

EXHIBIT 12A.4
Chimo Enterprises, Inc.: Organizational chart.

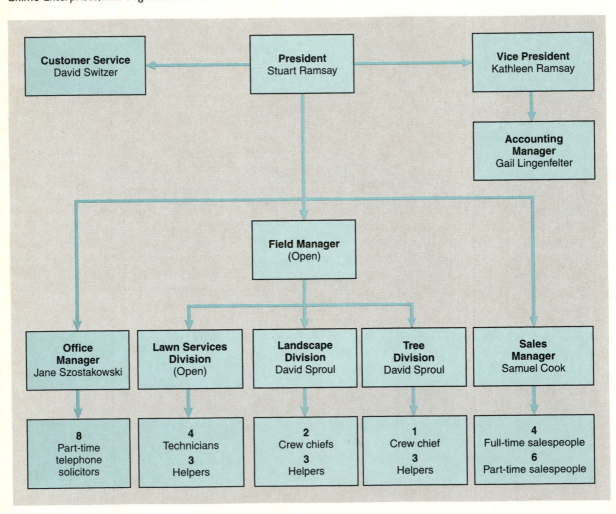

such vital functions as finance, credit and collection, purchasing, systems analysis, and organizational planning.

▶ David Sproul, manager of all tree and landscaping services. He is a graduate of Ohio State University with a degree in landscape design and construction. His responsibilities include all field operations, new design work, and landscape sales.

▶ Gail Lingenfelter, manager of our accounting activities and computer operations. She is a graduate of Cuyahoga Community College with a degree in accounting.

▶ Jane Szostakowski, home office manager. She is responsible for all secretarial duties, including order entry, printing, and general office management.

▶ David Switzer, customer service manager. His major responsibility is to resolve all customer complaints successfully. Before joining us, he was service manager for Orkin Pest Control, where he headed a team of twelve technicians and a fleet of ten trucks.

Financial Proposal

We seek a $250,000 loan, with a repayment schedule of monthly payments for seven years, through the guaranteed loan program of the SBA. We will use this money to:

▶ Purchase equipment and inventory
▶ Renovate our new office and storage building
▶ Update our truck fleet
▶ Liquidate a portion of our existing debt
▶ Maintain sufficient cash reserves for emergencies
▶ Provide adequate working capital

These uses of the loan will enable us to expand dramatically, to sales revenues of $820,400 in 1984, from $530,700 in 1983. Supporting financial statements are as follows:

EXHIBIT 12A.5
Chimo Enterprises, Inc.: Uses of $250,000 loan.

Repayment of loan to bank	$ 76,300
Operating equipment	
3 pick-up trucks	
2 turf tamers	
1 rear-tine rototiller	
1 sod cutter	
1 motorized tree chipper	
1 stump grinder	
1 tree sprayer	
1 dump truck	
1 utility vehicle	
1 one-ton van	75,700
Working capital	53,000
Three months' cash reserve	45,000
Total	$250,000

▶ Exhibit 12A.5 describes precisely how we will disburse the $250,000.

▶ Exhibit 12A.6 compares our 1984 and 1985 projected income statements with the 1983 statement.

▶ Exhibit 12A.7 contains our balance sheet as of June 30, 1983.

Questions
1. Comment on Chimo's financial performance.
2. What accounts for Chimo's recent success?
3. Do you believe Stuart Ramsay's business plan justifies his need for a $250,000 loan? Explain fully.
4. Comment on Ramsay's entrepreneurial qualities.
5. What are the company's prospects?

EXHIBIT 12A.6

Chimo Enterprises, Inc.: Actual and projected income statements.

	1983	Projected 1984	1985
Sales revenues			
Lawn Service Division	$304,900	$501,000	$ 680,600
Landscape and Tree Division	222,800	298,400	370,000
Special projects	3,000	21,000	36,000
Total sales revenues	$530,700	$820,400	$1,086,600
Cost of sales			
Cost of services sold	$190,100	$297,500	$ 357,400
Selling expenses	33,200	42,500	59,400
Advertising expenses	29,400	38,500	54,100
Total cost of sales	$252,700	$378,500	$ 470,900
Gross profit	$278,000	$441,900	$ 615,700
Operating expenses			
Royalties	$ 30,300	$ 49,900	$ 70,400
Officers' salaries	6,300	26,400	36,000
Clerical salaries	26,100	27,200	34,000
Depreciation	21,900	28,700	26,600
Office supplies	12,200	11,500	15,300
Payroll taxes	10,700	14,600	13,900
Rent	10,400	12,000	12,600
Insurance	6,200	7,600	10,000
Telephone	9,200	8,000	8,900
Professional services	3,700	7,200	6,000
Printing	4,300	3,600	5,500
Utilities	3,600	3,200	3,300
Hospitalization	2,000	2,800	3,100
Postage	2,000	2,200	3,100
Local taxes	1,800	2,100	2,800
Travel and entertainment	4,000	1,800	2,100
Dues and licenses	2,000	1,200	2,100
Total operating expenses	$156,700	$209,800	$ 255,700
Operating profit	$121,300	$232,100	$ 360,000
Non-operating adjustments			
Interest expense	$ 30,000	$ 38,300	$ 30,400
Gain on disposal	3,500	0	0
Total adjustments	$ 26,500	$ 38,300	$ 30,400
Profit before taxes	$ 94,800	$193,800	$ 329,600

EXHIBIT 12A.7

Chimo Enterprises, Inc.: Balance sheet (as of June 30, 1983).

Assets

Current assets

Cash	$ 1,800	
Accounts receivable	135,500	
Inventories	18,400	
Prepaid expenses	16,900	$172,600

Fixed assets

Assets under capital leases	$ 67,900	
Transportation equipment	40,000	
Machinery and equipment	26,200	
Furniture and fixtures	9,700	
Leasehold improvements	8,500	
	$152,300	
Less: Accumulated depreciation	96,500	55,800
Other assets		5,900
Total assets		$234,300

Equities

Current liabilities

Accounts payable	$ 62,700	
Accrued expenses	32,400	
Bank note payable	80,600	
Other notes payable	12,900	
Advertising fee payable	1,800	
Unearned revenues	118,600	
Royalty fee payable	2,800	$311,800

Long-term liabilities

Capital lease obligations	$ 9,600	
Shareholder loans payable	70,200	79,800

Owners' equity

Common stock	$ 16,000	
Retained earnings	(173,300)	(157,300)
		$234,300

Anthony Alomar

Seeking to launch a coin-operated drycleaning venture in Los Angeles, Anthony Alomar has all but completed his business plan. The only missing piece is a profitgraph.

The profitgraph would show Alomar as well as potential lenders how much business his venture must do to break even and turn a profit. Exhibit 12B.1 shows Alomar's estimates of monthly sales revenues and operating expenses. Note the heavy fixed expenses, which must be recovered if Alomar is to avoid sustaining a loss.

In any event, Alomar seems well-suited to run a coin-operated drycleaning store successfully. For instance, he passed an examination, but only after working for a year as an apprentice for a professional drycleaner and after taking courses in an

---

EXHIBIT 12B.1

Alomar Coin-Op Drycleaning: Estimates of monthly sales revenues & operating expenses.

Sales revenues			$17,400
Operating expenses			
▶ Variable			
Utilities	$1,200		
Cleaning supplies	900		
Laundry services	840		
Maintenance	300		
Advertising	90	$ 3,330	
▶ Fixed			
Depreciation	$4,200		
Wages	3,000		
Rent	1,800		
Interest	900		
Insurance	480		
Telephone	180		
Accounting	90		
Licenses	30		
Miscellaneous	90	10,770	14,100
Profit before taxes			$ 3,300

---

approved drycleaning school—as required by California law. Moreover, he had majored in small-business management at a community college, graduating with honors.

Questions

1. Given the information in Exhibit 12B.1, prepare a profitgraph. At what sales level would Anthony Alomar begin to make a profit?

2. How may Alomar use break-even analysis as a tool for profit planning and profit making? Explain by raising some of the so-called what-if questions that Alomar's profitgraph would help answer.

CASE 12C ▶ *Sidney Jordan*

Sidney Jordan owns a small manufacturing plant that makes hinges and small hardware used on kitchen cabinets. When he began three years ago, Jordan took a five-year, $110,000 loan from a commercial bank, using his private home as collateral.

During the first two years, Jordan was barely able to keep afloat. After meeting his bank obligations, he was able to take only a small salary for himself. In the third year, he decided to make several changes to boost sales and profits.

Jordan began to quote lower prices than he had before, in the hope that higher volume would lead to more profits. His reduced prices did improve volume, but this higher volume brought increased overtime as his employees worked to fill orders. When he realized how costly overtime had become, he decided to hire extra employees instead. This decision created crowded conditions that led to enormous inefficiency. Because of the crowded conditions, he could only purchase the materials that he needed and could not take advantage of quantity discounts from suppliers.

In addition, the larger volume of business meant higher accounts receivable and higher cash needs so, although he was needed to oversee pro-

duction, he spent more and more of his time on the telephone trying to get customers to pay more quickly.

When the February installment of his loan came due, Jordan found that he was unable to meet it. He could not even pay his own salary. He asked the bank for more money, but he was told that he had exhausted his credit. The bank agreed to let him postpone several payments until his cash flow improved.

When he looked at his books at year's end, Jordan found that he had earned even less than the year before. He had little recourse but to ask his family to help him keep the business afloat.

Questions

1. How did Sidney Jordan's managerial decisions affect the success of his business?

2. How important was "the people factor" in Jordan's business?

3. What specific money factors influenced the changes in this business?

4. How would you have tried to make this business more profitable?

CHAPTER 13

Analysis of Financial Statements, Investments, and Credit

The unexamined life is not worth living.

—Socrates

As their growing ventures strive toward maturity, some entrepreneurs fail to strike a balance between being entrepreneurial and being managerial. As we saw in Chapter 12, entrepreneurs who excel at launching new ventures often do poorly at managing their growth. This is not because they lose the spark of entrepreneurship, but because they fail to plan and control well.

Such entrepreneurs generally fail to use their financial statements to spot problems before they occur. They may also make unwise investment decisions, or refuse to consider computers to help them plan and control better. In this chapter, we focus on analyzing financial statements, evaluating investment opportunities, and appraising credit-and-collection activities.

Analysis of Financial Statements

To plan and control their ventures wisely, entrepreneurs must become skilled at analyzing the numbers in their financial statements. Many entrepreneurs believe that financial analysis is best left to the accountant. Not so. Although it is, indeed, the accountant's job to design accounting systems and prepare financial statements, it is not the accountant's job to analyze and interpret the numbers in the statements. This is the entrepreneur's responsibility.

Doing business is certainly not all numbers. In fact, few business problems can be solved solely by the collection and analysis of numbers. Equal thought must also be given to vital factors that cannot be reduced to numbers, such as teamwork and managerial skills. Entrepreneurs who put their trust in numbers alone, as well as those who trust intuition alone, would do well to keep in mind these words of wisdom:

> The real trouble with this world of ours is not that it is an unreasonable world, nor even that it is a reasonable one. The commonest kind of trouble is that it is nearly reasonable, but not quite. Life is not illogical; yet it is a trap for logicians. It looks just a little more mathematical and regular than it is; its exactitude is obvious, but its inexactitude is hidden; its wildness lies in wait.[1]

▶ The Essence of Financial Analysis

Comparison lies at the heart of all analyses of financial statements. For example, the statement "a venture earned a profit of $10,000" is, in itself, meaningless. The $10,000 becomes meaningful only when compared with some standard, such as last year's profit or this year's budgeted profit.

Comparisons like these are precise and concrete, but comparisons may also be imprecise and intuitive. For example, if a venture had sales of $10 million, we would know intuitively that a $10,000 profit is a poor return—just one-tenth of a penny for each dollar of sales. Turning to Exhibit 13.1, note the four bases that entrepreneurs may choose from to evaluate their financial performance.

The most meaningful comparisons are those that tell entrepreneurs how well they are meeting their goals. As suggested earlier, entrepreneurs have two kinds of goals:

▶ Financial goals, such as return-on-sales and return-on-investment targets

▶ Nonfinancial goals, such as psychic satisfaction and total quality management

EXHIBIT 13.1
Bases of comparison in financial analysis.

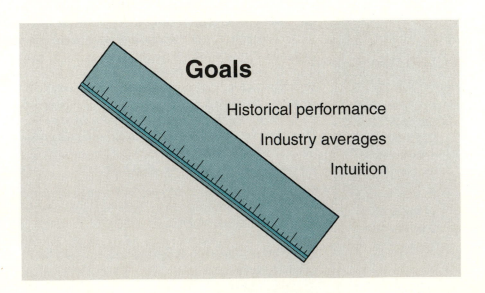

Goals

Historical performance

Industry averages

Intuition

Entrepreneurs must, of course, balance these goals in measuring their ventures' performance. Of the goals reducible to numbers, the most meaningful one is to earn a satisfactory return on the money invested, consistent with maintaining its financial health. Note the two-sided nature of this goal:

▶ To earn a satisfactory return
▶ To maintain financial health

Let us now discuss how entrepreneurs should analyze their financial statements, in their efforts to see how well they have done.

▶ Earning a Satisfactory Return

The best yardstick for estimating the return is called *return on investment* (*ROI*) and is computed by dividing net profit by investment. ROI tells entrepreneurs how many cents they earn in a year for each dollar of investment, in the same way that an interest rate tells savers how much they earn for each dollar of savings at a bank.

Because investment may be defined in three different ways—as either total assets, owners' equity, or permanent capital—entrepreneurs may compute their ROI in three different ways. Which is best? The answer hinges on what the entrepreneur wants to measure, as explained below:

▶ **Return on total assets** This yardstick measures how well entrepreneurs have invested all the money entrusted to their care, regardless of where it came from. In addition to shareholders, sources of money may include short-term creditors, such as suppliers; and long-term creditors, such as mortgage banks.

▶ **Return on owners' equity** This yardstick measures how wisely entrepreneurs have invested money from shareholders* *only*, thus purposely ignoring money from creditors. Highly popular because of its simplicity, this yardstick appeals strongly to shareholders, mostly because they chose to put their money in the entrepreneur's venture rather than elsewhere—in the belief they would earn a higher return. So naturally they would want to know if they had made the right choice.

▶ **Return on permanent capital** This yardstick measures how well entrepreneurs have invested *all* the long-term money entrusted to their care. It takes into account not only the investment made by shareholders but also any long-term loans made by banks, bondholders, and others, thus omitting money from short-term creditors.

The sum of owners' equity and long-term debt is called *permanent capital*. It reflects the total amount needed to finance fixed assets, such as machinery and buildings, and the fraction of current assets, such as cash and inventory, not otherwise financed by short-term creditors.

---

*Here, we assumed the entrepreneur's venture was a corporation, although we might just as logically have assumed it was either a sole proprietorship or a partnership.

▶ Maintaining Financial Health

Besides a satisfactory return on investment, shareholders also expect their investments to be protected against excessive risk. For example, suppose an entrepreneur finances an expansion solely by borrowing from a bank. This action might boost the shareholders' return—the return on owners' equity—but only by increasing the shareholders' risk of losing their investment. For, by financing the expansion with a loan, the entrepreneur must both repay the loan and pay interest. Failure to do both could throw the venture into bankruptcy.

To measure their degree of protection against risk, entrepreneurs may use any one of several yardsticks. One relates total debt to total assets; another omits current debt and relates just long-term debt to permanent capital. These yardsticks and others are described in the section of this chapter called "Tests of Financial Health."

▶ Ratio Analysis

To evaluate financial performance, the accepted way is a tool called *ratio analysis*. Putting the true value of ratios in perspective, Phil Nadel of the publication *Cash Flow Today* says:

> Some of the most important numbers you'll deal with are ratios. A ratio is a numerical value calculated by dividing one number by another, and it can be written as numbers, dollars, or percents. A single ratio has essentially no value, and a set of ratios has value only if they can be compared or benchmarked to other ratios.
>
> Think of a ratio like a thermometer reading. You take your temperature and get a reading of 100 degrees. Is that good or bad? You know the normal body temperature is 98.6 degrees, you also know that it's normal for your temperature to fluctuate depending on the time of day, what you are doing, your general health, and other factors. By knowing what the standard is and by taking into consideration various influences, you'll know whether your 100-degree temperature is something to worry about.
>
> Apply the same approach to your business ratios: they help you make comparisons, identify trends, and answer important questions:
>
> ▶ How different are you from other companies in your industry?
>
> ▶ How have you changed from the past year, or year before that?
>
> ▶ What caused those changes, and are they good or bad?
>
> ▶ What can you do to improve your ratios—and therefore your company?[2]

Dozens of ratios may be computed from just one set of financial statements, but usually only a handful are helpful to entrepreneurs. In the discussion that follows, and in Exhibit 13.2, we have grouped the ratios into two categories:

▶ Tests of profitability

▶ Tests of financial health

We shall now compute ratios for the various yardsticks of performance, based on the financial statements of a fictitious venture called Apollo Electronics. These statements appear in Exhibit 13.3.

EXHIBIT 13.2
Selected key ratios in
financial analysis.

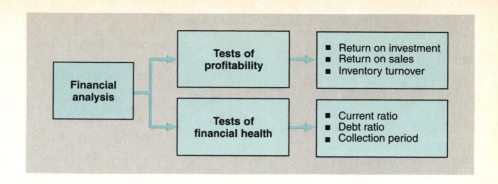

EXHIBIT 13.3
Financial statements for Apollo Electronics.

Balance Sheet (December 31, 1996)

Assets			Equities		
Current assets			Current liabilities		
Cash	$ 30,000		Accounts payable	$ 60,000	
Accounts receivable	75,000		Notes payable	30,000	
Inventories	120,000	$225,000	Accrued expenses	15,000	$105,000
Fixed assets					
Land	$ 30,000		Long-term liabilities		
Building	180,000		Loan payable		
Equipment	240,000	450,000	(12% interest)		225,000
			Owners' equity		
			Common stock	$150,000	
			Retained earnings	195,000	345,000
Total assets		$675,000	Total equities		$675,000

Income Statement (1996)

Sales revenues	$750,000
Cost of goods sold	525,000
Gross profit	$225,000
Operating expenses	123,000
Operating profit	$102,000
Less: Interest on loan	27,000
Profit before taxes	$ 75,000
Income taxes	22,500
Net profit	$ 52,500

Tests of Profitability

▶ **Return on Investment**

As we have just seen, entrepreneurs may estimate their return on investment using any of three ratios, depending on whether they define investment as total assets, owners' equity, or permanent capital. Computations follow:

$$\text{Return on total assets} = \frac{\text{net profit} + [\text{interest} + (1 - \text{tax rate})]}{\text{total assets}} \times 100$$

$$= \frac{\$52,500 + [\$27,000 \times (1 - 0.30)]}{\$675,000} \times 100$$

$$= 10.6\% \text{ a year}$$

$$\text{Return on owners' equity} = \frac{\text{net profit}}{\text{owners' equity}} \times 100$$

$$= \frac{\$52,500}{\$345,000} \times 100$$

$$= 15.2\% \text{ a year}$$

$$\text{Return on permanent capital} = \frac{\text{net profit} + [\text{interest} \times (1 - \text{tax rate})]}{\text{owners' equity} + \text{long-term liabilities}} \times 100$$

$$= \frac{\$52,000 + [\$27,000 \times (1 - 0.30)]}{\$345,000 + \$225,000} \times 100$$

$$= 12.5\% \text{ a year}$$

Note that to estimate the return on total assets and on permanent capital for Apollo Electronics, we added interest to net profit. It is common practice to do this because assets are financed by creditors as well as by investors, and the ratio should therefore reflect the return to both parties. Otherwise, the return would be understated.

Note, too, that the interest expense must be adjusted downward—to reflect the fact that it is tax-deductible. This means, for example, that if a venture's tax rate is 30 percent, then each dollar of interest really costs no more than 70 cents because each dollar of expense reduces taxes by 30 cents—as explained further in Exhibit 13.4.

▶ **Return on Sales**

In contrast to return on investment, return on sales measures how well entrepreneurs manage their venture's day-to-day operations. It tells them how many cents are left over as profit for each dollar of sales. To use this yardstick in analyzing Apollo Electronics, we would divide net profit by sales revenues, as follows:

$$\text{Return on sales} = \frac{\text{net profit}}{\text{sales revenues}} \times 100$$

$$= \frac{\$52,500}{\$750,000} \times 100$$

$$= 7.0\%$$

EXHIBIT 13.4

Example: Effect of income taxes on interest expense.

	Without Interest	With Interest
Sales revenues	$300,000	$300,000
Operating expenses	240,000	240,000
Operating profit	$ 60,000	$ 60,000
Interest expense	0	20,000(c)
Profit before taxes	$ 60,000	$ 40,000
Income taxes (30%)	18,000(a)	12,000(d)
Net profit	$ 42,000(b)	$ 28,000(e)

The interest expense of $20,000 (c) reduces net profit not by $20,000 but by only $14,000 (b − e). This venture pays $6,000 less in taxes (a − d) with interest expense than it does without interest. Thus, the effective cost of interest is only $14,000 (b − e) or simply [c × (1 − tax rate)] because of the effect of taxes.

This figure makes it possible to compare operating efficiency with that of other ventures in the same industry.* Averages are available for most industries, enabling entrepreneurs to rate themselves. If return on sales is low, it means the entrepreneur is inefficient, a sign that their venture needs attention.

▶ **Another Look at Return on Investment**

It is intuitively obvious that the more we make for each dollar of sales, and the more sales we make for each dollar of investment, the greater our return on investment. These relationships may be expressed as follows:

$$\frac{\text{Net profit}}{\text{Investment}} = \frac{\text{net profit}}{\text{sales revenues}} \times \frac{\text{sales revenues}}{\text{investment}}$$

This equation suggests that entrepreneurs may improve their return on investment in two ways:

▶ By improving the efficiency of their operations, resulting in more profit for each dollar of sales

▶ By making better use of their assets, resulting in more sales for each dollar of investment

▶ **Inventory Turnover**

Inventory turnover measures how well entrepreneurs are managing their inventories. Whether inventories are large or small depends mostly on the kind of industry and the time of year. For example, a fertilizer dealer with a large inventory in

---

*To see if they measure up, entrepreneurs may tap any number of sources that publish average ratios for companies in the same industry. Among the best-known sources are Dun & Bradstreet, which reports the ratios for 125 lines of business; and Robert Morris Associates, which reports the ratios for 300 lines of business. Also, most trade associations publish ratios for the industries they serve.

early spring is in a strong position to satisfy farmers. That same inventory in the late fall spells trouble. One way to tell whether inventories are high or low for Apollo Electronics is to relate inventory to the cost of goods sold, as follows:

$$\text{Inventory turnover} = \frac{\text{cost of goods sold}}{\text{inventory}}$$

$$= \frac{\$525,000}{\$120,000}$$

$$= \underline{\underline{4.4 \text{ times a year}}}$$

On the average, then, Apollo Electronics is selling out its inventory 4.4 times a year. To find out whether this turnover is high or low, Apollo Electronics may consult industry averages offered by its trade association or by Dun & Bradstreet, as suggested earlier.

To avoid a false reading, entrepreneurs in seasonal industries should be certain to relate *average* inventory to the cost of goods sold. This means they should average the beginning and ending inventories, or even average the monthly inventories, rather than simply accept the year-end inventory.

Tests of Financial Health

So far, we have discussed yardsticks that measure how well entrepreneurs manage their day-to-day operations and their assets. Let us now look at yardsticks that measure how well they manage the finances of their ventures.

▶ **Solvency**

A venture's *solvency* is its ability to repay long-term debts, including interest, when due. The more solvent a venture, the better protected its shareholders are from losing their investment. To measure this protection, entrepreneurs should use as yardsticks the *debt ratio* and *times interest earned*. Using Apollo Electronics as a model:

$$\text{Debt ratio} = \frac{\text{total liabilities}}{\text{total assets}} \times 100$$

$$= \frac{\$105,000 + \$225,000}{\$675,000} \times 100$$

$$= \underline{\underline{48.9\%}}$$

The debt ratio simply measures the degree to which a venture's assets are financed by creditors. Generally, a debt ratio of less than 50 percent is considered favorable by bankers. A variation on this yardstick is to omit current liabilities and to relate only long-term debt to permanent capital, as follows:

$$\text{Debt ratio} = \frac{\text{long-term liabilities}}{\text{owners' equity} + \text{long-term liabilities}} \times 100$$

$$= \frac{\$225,000}{\$345,000 + \$225,000} \times 100$$

$$= \underline{\underline{39.5\%}}$$

This ratio measures the degree to which Apollo Electronics used creditors rather than investors to supply permanent capital. The alternative would be to sell stock or to plow profits back into the venture.

Although widely used, these two yardsticks do not by themselves measure financial soundness. To complete the analysis, entrepreneurs should also apply a ratio called *times interest earned,* as follows:

$$\text{Times interest earned} = \frac{\text{operating profit before interest}}{\text{interest expense}}$$

$$= \frac{\$102,000}{\$27,000}$$

$$= \underline{3.8 \text{ times}}$$

Times interest earned measures how low profits can drop without straining a venture's ability to pay interest when due. Here, with operating profit topping interest 3.8 times, Apollo Electronics seems financially sound, its shareholders amply protected against financial ruin.

▶ **Liquidity**

Another yardstick that measures exposure to debt is the *current ratio.* By relating current assets to current liabilities, this yardstick measures a venture's ability to pay short-term bills when due. It is computed as follows:

$$\text{Current ratio} = \frac{\text{current assets}}{\text{current liabilities}}$$

$$= \frac{\$225,000}{\$105,000}$$

$$= \underline{2.1 \text{ to } 1}$$

The rule of thumb is that a current ratio of 2 to 1 is good, meaning that current assets could shrink 50 percent in value and still cover short-term bills.

An even tougher test of liquidity is the *quick ratio,* which omits inventories. It is computed as follows:

$$\text{Quick ratio} = \frac{\text{cash} + \text{accounts receivable}}{\text{current liabilities}}$$

$$= \frac{\$30,000 + \$75,000}{\$105,000}$$

$$= \underline{1 \text{ to } 1}$$

This yardstick measures a venture's ability to pay short-term bills if a real crisis strikes; it assumes that inventories would be worthless. Generally, a quick ratio of 1 to 1 or better is considered good.

▶ **Customer Credit**

The *collection period* is a measure of the degree to which a venture finances its customers who buy on credit. The entrepreneur should determine whether the actual amount of uncollected sales—accounts receivable—closely matches expectations, given the entrepreneur's credit terms. For example, if a venture gives its credit customers 30 days to pay up, it would normally expect to be owed only the most recent month's sales.

To apply this yardstick to Apollo Electronics, we would make two computations:

$$\text{Receivables turnover} = \frac{\text{credit sales}}{\text{accounts receivable}}$$

$$= \frac{\$750,000}{\$75,000}$$

$$= \underline{\underline{10 \text{ times}}}$$

$$\text{Collection period} = \frac{\text{days in the year}}{\text{receivables turnover}}$$

$$= \frac{360}{10}$$

$$= \underline{\underline{36 \text{ days' sales owed}}}$$

In this example, the "36 days' sales owed" means that Apollo Electronics carries its credit customers for 36 days, on the average. If its credit terms call for customers to pay up in 30 days, a collection period of 36 days is considered good. The rule of thumb is that the collection period should not exceed 1⅕ times the expected payment period.

Evaluation of Investment Opportunities

So far, we have discussed how to evaluate both operating and financial performance, focusing on how best to spot problems. Now, we focus on investment *opportunities,* to answer questions like these:

▶ Whether to lease or buy
▶ Whether to expand a plant
▶ Whether to add a new product
▶ Whether to make or buy a product
▶ Whether to add another retail outlet
▶ Whether to acquire another venture, in order to diversify
▶ Whether to replace a machine with one that reduces operating expenses

Each of these questions involves a choice that could make or break a venture. How? By locking the entrepreneur into a way of doing business for years to come, with but little room for change, as would be so if he were to build, say, a million-dollar plant to make a new product—as opposed to his putting up a lemonade stand.

▶ **Cash Payback**

The most popular yardstick of investment worth, *cash payback,* is simple to understand and easy to apply. It may be defined as the time required for the cash produced by an investment to equal the cash required by the investment. An example illustrates how this yardstick works:

EXAMPLE ▶

The owner of a machine shop makes many kinds of nuts and bolts. He carries a large inventory of steel stock as well as finished product. In an effort to cut costs, he is mulling over an opportunity to buy a forklift for $18,000 that could save him $6,000 cash a year in inventory handling costs.

Should the entrepreneur buy the forklift? He estimates it would take three years to recover his investment ($18,000 investment ÷ $6,000 savings per year). Whether this payback period is short enough depends on his own criteria. He may have decided intuitively to accept all investment opportunities with payback periods of less than four years, or to reject all those with payback periods of four years or more. In this example, the entrepreneur would buy the forklift. ▲▼▲

As a yardstick of investment worth, cash payback has a serious flaw: It fails to take into account savings earned *after* the payback period. In other words, it ignores what happens after the forklift has paid back the $18,000 investment. For, if the forklift's useful life is just three years, the return on the $18,000 investment would really be zero, and the investment would be worthless no matter how short the cash payback period. The entrepreneur, then, would have made the wrong decision.

To offset this drawback, it is important to measure the size and duration of cash return *beyond* the payback period. Another example shows how to do that:

EXAMPLE ▶

Let us now assume that the entrepreneur must choose between two kinds of forklifts, each of which has the same payback, as shown in Exhibit 13.5.

Which forklift should the entrepreneur buy? The two forklifts would be equally desirable as investments if he looks only at payback. But it is clear from Exhibit 13.5 that he should choose Model A. It not only recovers his cash investment of $18,000 but also promises to earn a return *beyond* the second year. ▲▼▲

Cash payback has another flaw: It fails to acknowledge that a dollar received today is worth more than a dollar received a year or more from now because

EXHIBIT 13.5
Example: Payback on forklifts.

		Cash Savings			
Forklift	Cash Outlay	First Year	Second Year	Third Year	Cash Payback Period
Model A	$18,000	$9,000	$9,000	$9,000	2 years
Model B	18,000	9,000	9,000	0	2

EXHIBIT 13.6

Example: Payback on forklifts.

Forklift	Cash Outlay	Cash Savings First Year	Second Year	Third Year	Cash Payback Period
Model A	$18,000	$ 9,000	$9,000	$9,000	2 years
Model B	18,000	13,000	5,000	9,000	2

other, more profitable investment opportunities may be available for today's dollar. Take this example:

EXAMPLE ▶

The entrepreneur must again choose between two kinds of forklifts, this time with the cash flows shown in Exhibit 13.6.

Which forklift should the entrepreneur buy? Each one pays back its initial investment in two years and earns the same total cash savings of $27,000. But Model B is better than Model A because it promises to earn more savings *earlier*. With Model B, the entrepreneur would have $4,000 more to reinvest at the end of the first year—a fact that the entrepreneur might neglect if he looks only at payback. ▲▼▲

▶ Return on Original Investment

Now let us look at another yardstick of investment worth. As we saw earlier, return on investment (ROI) tells entrepreneurs how much they earn yearly on each dollar invested. ROI also enables entrepreneurs to compare their estimates of return with their *cost of money*, as in this example:

EXAMPLE ▶

The owner of a small chain of seafood restaurants is thinking of adding another restaurant, this one in a strip shopping area. Her chain now earns an ROI of 10 percent a year—that is, each dollar of her investment earns 10 cents a year after taxes.

Here, the 10 percent also reflects the entrepreneur's cost of money. This means, for example, that every investment opportunity, such as her new seafood restaurant, must be promising enough to earn at least 10 percent a year. Otherwise, the opportunity would not be worth pursuing.

Suppose the entrepreneur is looking at two possible sites for the new seafood restaurant. Both sites would require the same investment of $200,000, but sales revenues, operating expenses, and profits would differ, as shown in Exhibit 13.7.

Which site should the entrepreneur choose? If her cost of money is 10 percent, she should choose Site A because its ROI would be 20 percent a year:

$$ROI_A = \frac{\$40,000 \text{ a year}}{\$200,000} \times 100 = 20\% \text{ a year}$$

Site B's ROI would be only 10 percent a year:

$$ROI_B = \frac{\$20,000 \text{ a year}}{\$200,000} \times 100 = 10\% \text{ a year}$$

EXHIBIT 13.7
Example: Choosing a site.

	Site A (yearly)	Site B (yearly)
Sales revenues	$660,000	$600,000
Operating expenses	600,000	570,000
Operating profit	$ 60,000	$ 30,000
Taxes	20,000	10,000
Net profit	$ 40,000	$ 20,000

The entrepreneur might also consider opening seafood restaurants at both sites, as long as Sites A and B are in areas that do not overlap. The reasoning here is that the entrepreneur should make as many investments as possible that promise to return at least 10 percent a year, which is her cost of money. ▲▼▲

▶ **Return on Average Investment**

In our example, the entrepreneur estimated her ROI by relating net profit to *original* investment. Another approach is to relate net profit to *average* investment: Here, the entrepreneur assumes that the seafood restaurant would lose value gradually over its estimated useful life, as in this example:

EXAMPLE ▶

If expected to last 10 years, the $200,000 seafood restaurant would decline in value at the rate of $20,000 a year. By the end of the tenth year, the investment would shrink to zero. Thus, the average investment outstanding would be $100,000, which is the midpoint between the restaurant's value of $200,000 at startup and its value of zero 10 years later ($\frac{1}{2} \times \$200,000 = \$100,000$). Notice that the ROI at both sites would be much higher:

$$\text{ROI}_A = \frac{\$40,000 \text{ a year}}{\$100,000} \times 100$$

$$= \underline{\underline{40\% \text{ a year}}} \text{ (versus 20\% using original investment)}$$

$$\text{ROI}_B = \frac{\$20,000 \text{ a year}}{\$100,000} \times 100$$

$$= \underline{\underline{20\% \text{ a year}}} \text{ (versus 10\%)} \text{ ▲▼▲}$$

▶ **Present Value**

So far, we have touched on three yardsticks for measuring investment worth:

▶ Cash payback
▶ Return on original investment
▶ Return on average investment

It is evident that these three yardsticks give very different results. In fact, one may produce figures twice those given by another. For example, an investment that shows a return of 10 percent a year on original investment may show a return of 20 percent a year on average investment.

To resolve this confusion, many large corporations have switched to a yardstick called *present value,* which falls beyond the scope of this textbook to explain in detail. It measures the true rate of return offered by an investment opportunity by taking into account the timing of cash returns and outlays over its useful life. The other yardsticks ignore these factors.

We have barely scratched the surface of how best to measure the worth of investment opportunities. It is a complex subject. Here, we are merely stressing the need to weigh the desirability of an investment opportunity carefully, using the yardsticks described above.

In earlier chapters, we looked at investment analysis from the viewpoint of entrepreneurs about to launch ventures. In this chapter, however, we have approached investment analysis from the viewpoint of entrepreneurs whose ventures are established and growing. These viewpoints differ sharply. In our discussion of the business plan, for example, we looked at the whole investment puzzle with all the pieces, as designed by the entrepreneur, already in place. In this chapter, we have looked at bits and pieces of an expanding and changing investment puzzle. Once a venture is under way, the investment picture is no longer static; it is constantly evolving and expanding.

Credit and Collection

In most industries, entrepreneurs must offer credit or lose customers. Although credit helps create customers, it also creates the risk that customers may not pay. So, it is vital that entrepreneurs understand how to extend credit without risking failure.

Consumers are bombarded with invitations to enjoy all manner of products and services right now and pay for them later. Most consumers accept freely, without guilt. No longer is it shameful to go into debt. In fact, the nation's prosperity depends on the widespread use of charge accounts, mortgage loans, bank loans, credit cards, and other means by which customers receive products and services before they can afford them fully. So deep is this dependence that any outbreak of resistance to credit would probably afflict the nation with joblessness, or even economic paralysis.

In short, credit is a way of life. To survive and grow, entrepreneurs must learn how best to give credit and, at the same time, how best to avoid nonpaying customers. If we look at each industry group, we find that credit supports:

▸ About 95 percent of all sales by manufacturers

▸ About 90 percent of all sales by wholesalers

▸ About 50 percent of all sales by retailers and by service providers

These high percentages mean that most entrepreneurs find themselves in the financing business as well. For, whenever customers buy on credit, the entrepreneur, in essence, is advancing them the money to buy. To do so means that large sums of money are tied up in accounts receivable. Clearly, entrepreneurs should manage their use of credit carefully, or they may find themselves in financial trouble, as in this example from the SBA:

Jack Woolson, owner of Woolson Filling Stations, developed a serious credit problem. Expanding from two to six stations in a three-month period, he personally hired all employees and trained them in the handling of credit.

Within another three months, he found that a very large number of accounts receivable were uncollectible. It took his accountant an additional two months to determine that two of the new station attendants, who worked evenings only, were granting credit to customers unauthorized to receive it. They had, in fact, given credit to customers on the firm's list of poor credit risks.

The firm's credit procedures called for having all credit sales checked at the home office every day. Because of the overload of work in the office, this important procedure had been bypassed.

Woolson could have avoided his losses had he enforced the procedures he originally established. His lack of planning and poor credit discipline proved to be costly. ▲▼▲

Entrepreneurs have the right to charge interest for financing their customers' purchases, and many entrepreneurs do just that. However, products should not be used as tools to sell credit. Remember, the main purpose of credit is to help sell products, not the other way around.

Giving credit can also be costly, unless entrepreneurs take pains to control their costs of credit and collection closely. Just how costly credit can be is underscored in Exhibit 13.8 and by this example:

An entrepreneur sells $1,000 worth of lumber on credit to the Nemo Corporation, which manufactures office furniture. She has done business with Nemo before. Although at times she had to send two or three invoices, Nemo eventually paid the bill. The entrepreneur's ratio of before-tax profits to sales revenues is 5 percent.

EXHIBIT 13.8
The cost of uncollected accounts.

If the Ratio of Before-tax Profits to Sales Is . . .	. . . Then, for Every $1,000 of Uncollected Accounts, Additional Sales in These Amounts Would Be Needed to Recover the Lost Profit
20%	$ 5,000
15	6,700
10	10,000
5	20,000
2	50,000

Three months go by, and the bill is still outstanding. When the entrepreneur pursues the collection, she finds that Nemo has gone out of business. Note in Exhibit 13.8 that, at a profit-to-sales ratio of 5 percent, the entrepreneur must sell $20,000 of additional lumber to offset the $1,000 that she cannot collect. ▲▼▲

▶ **Kinds of Credit**

There are two kinds of credit. *Business-to-business credit* is credit that an entrepreneur gives to other businesses; *consumer credit* is credit that an entrepreneur extends to individual customers.

Business-to-Business Credit   In retailing or services, entrepreneurs often may choose whether to sell for cash or credit. In wholesaling or manufacturing, they rarely have that choice, mostly because customers:

▶ Want to scan the delivered products before paying the seller

▶ Need to have the purchase financed by the seller

▶ Depend on the seller to deliver the product to locations far from the seller's site

Entrepreneurs cannot be too careful in their credit decisions. Selling to the more stable industries, such as chemical companies, rarely poses a credit problem. Corporations like Du Pont, for example, are almost as solid as the U.S. Treasury. But in many industries the reverse is true, especially in so-called fragmented industries marked by ease of entry, such as housing construction and dress manufacture.

To sell products and attract customers, many businesses must offer credit, as this electronics store does to youthful customers.

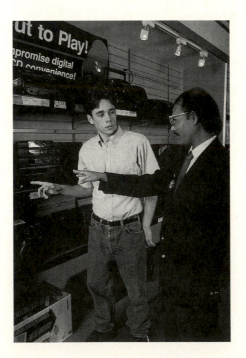

How may entrepreneurs protect themselves from bad credit risks? How can they tell whether customers will make good on their promises to pay? Naive entrepreneurs rely on blind trust; astute entrepreneurs put their trust in the customer's credit reputation. The key question is, "Will the customer pay promptly?"

To answer this question, entrepreneurs should turn to credit-rating firms like Dun & Bradstreet. This well-known firm reports on how promptly businesses pay their bills. Their files have up-to-date credit ratings on more than a million businesses. Dun & Bradstreet, for example, gives entrepreneurs who sell to other companies certain vital information:

▸ What kind of business the customer is in and how it is managed
▸ The customer's latest income statement and balance sheet
▸ An estimate of the customer's financial strength
▸ A record of the customer's promptness in paying bills

Besides ordering such credit reports, entrepreneurs must also ask for credit references. Usually, customers can list at least three creditors that they pay off regularly. Even so, it behooves the entrepreneur, when he calls those three creditors, to ask if they know of any *other* creditors for his customer. After calling them as well, what may now emerge is a more truthful reading of his customer's credit-worthiness.

▸ **Setting the Right Credit Policy**

It is apparent that entrepreneurs must design systems that enable them to extend credit with confidence of repayment, while helping customers do more business with the entrepreneur in the future. In this vein, Dun & Bradstreet offers the following advice:

> To conduct business more effectively, it is critical to closely manage your credit process. Setting terms and reviewing customers before you extend credit are the first steps in the process. The most important action you can take, however, is to develop a credit policy for your company—and stick to it. Decide whether an *open* credit policy or a *strict* one will best suit your needs:
>
> ▸ With an open policy, you would make every effort to extend credit to all reasonably qualified customers.
> ▸ With a strict policy, credit lines would be extended only to the most credit-worthy customers. New customers would have to earn the right to have credit with you by convincing you of their ability to comply with your terms.
>
> In deciding on the right policy for your company, consider market conditions, your sales revenues, your industry's credit-and-collection practices, your ratio of operating expenses to sales revenues, your current level of bad debt expense, and the availability of adequate staffing to monitor and collect from credit customers.[3]

Although this advice covers business-to-business credit, it applies also to consumer credit, which we discuss next.

Consumer Credit   Especially vulnerable to financial loss are entrepreneurs who sell directly to individual customers on credit. To screen these customers, entrepreneurs should first settle two vital questions:

▶ How much credit can the customer safely absorb?

▶ Does the customer have a history of paying bills promptly?

To answer these questions, the first step is to have credit applicants fill out a credit application. Then the entrepreneur should get a credit report on each applicant from the local credit bureau. This report makes it possible:

▶ To verify the information volunteered by the applicant

▶ To see whether the applicant pays promptly

After comparing the application and credit report, the entrepreneur can decide whether to extend credit. The promptness with which applicants pay their bills is the most important factor in this decision. Local credit bureaus have this information on virtually every person who has bought on credit at one time or another.

▶ **The Advantages and Disadvantages of Giving Credit**

We end our discussion of credit by listing some of the advantages and disadvantages of giving credit to customers. The advantages include the following:

▶ Credit customers are likely to become repeat customers.

▶ Credit enables customers to buy products or services they might otherwise have to do without.

▶ Credit customers tend to overspend.

▶ Credit customers pay less attention to prices.

▶ Credit sales require less selling effort.

▶ Credit customers tend to buy products of higher quality.

▶ Credit is a convenience to customers who dislike carrying cash.

The disadvantages include the following:

▶ Credit forces entrepreneurs to finance their customers, thus tying up money in accounts receivable.

▶ Credit refusal may cause ill will.

▶ Credit customers are more likely to abuse the privilege of returning products.

▶ Credit may obligate entrepreneurs to borrow and repay with interest.

▶ Credit adds to the cost of doing business because of investigations and the bookkeeping needed to keep records, bill customers, and collect payments.

▶ **Collection Systems**

Most entrepreneurs have trouble collecting from credit customers at one time or another. Slow-paying or nonpaying customers can severely strain the entrepreneur's financial resources. Take this example:

EXAMPLE ▶

The owner of a women's dress shop makes a $100 sale on credit. Unless the customer pays, the entrepreneur may lose at least $70 and possibly more. Why? Because it cost her $70 to buy the dress from a wholesaler, and the $30 markup is designed to cover other expenses, such as rent, utilities, and salaries, as well as profit. ▲▼▲

As the saying goes, a sale is not a sale until the customer pays in full. Otherwise, it is a bad debt. Often, all it takes is a little prodding to get a customer to pay; but sometimes entrepreneurs are saddled with bad debts that could have been avoided had they looked into their customers' credit history. Besides investigation, a good way to avoid bad debts is to design a collection system that:

▶ Accurately traces the history of each customer until the account is closed

▶ Alerts the entrepreneur the moment a customer is past due

▶ Separates credit customers into three categories: current; past due; and suspended, meaning the customer's account has been turned over to a collection agency or to a lawyer

▶ Updates customers' accounts daily, meaning that cash received from customers is posted daily

▶ Protects account files from theft, fire, or destruction

These principles underlie all sound collection systems. Details vary from venture to venture, especially regarding the use of forms and files, office machines and computers. But it behooves entrepreneurs to follow these principles to the letter. They can ill afford to be lax because, after all, uncollectible accounts erode profits and may even cause failure. Exhibit 13.9 graphically shows what might be called the law of diminishing returns, or what happens to slow or old accounts.

Aging of Accounts Receivable   Perhaps the backbone of any collection system is the analysis of accounts receivable—the amounts owed by customers. Entrepreneurs should prepare aging schedules, which keep track of how old

EXHIBIT 13.9
Diminishing returns on slow consumer accounts.

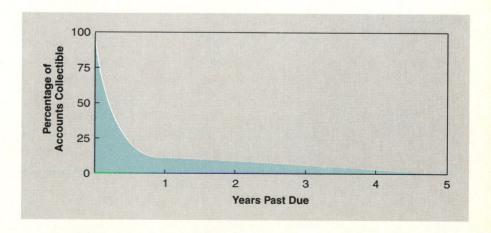

EXHIBIT 13.10

Aging schedule.

Age	Amounts Owed by Customers (Receivables)
Not past due	$13,600
1–30 days past due	5,400
31–60 days past due	1,200
61–90 days past due	800
More than 90 days past due	400
Total owed	$21,400

each debt is and thus measure the quality of the receivables. Such a schedule helps identify overdue accounts that demand extra attention. An example of an aging schedule appears in Exhibit 13.10.

The aging schedule works as a control device. Not only does it show the makeup of receivables, but it also directs attention to customers who are severely overdue. Aging schedules can be prepared for individual customers as well as business-to-business customers.

Collection Period   So far, we have focused on the collection of individual past-due accounts. Another question that merits discussion is, "How may entrepreneurs measure their credit and collection performance?" One yardstick is the collection period. Discussed earlier in the chapter, the collection period tells entrepreneurs how many days' sales revenues are tied up in accounts receivable. In other words, how long does it take, on the average, to collect from credit customers? Take this example:

EXAMPLE ▶   A women's fashion shop rang up revenues of $1,350,000 in 1996. Of this amount, $1,095,000 reflects charge-account sales. The shop's year-end balance sheet shows accounts receivable of $150,000. What is the average collection period? It is computed as follows:

$$\text{Receivables turnover} = \frac{\$1,095,000}{\$150,000} = 7.3 \text{ times}$$

$$\text{Collection period} = \frac{360 \text{ days}}{7.3} = 49 \text{ days}$$

How good a job of credit and collection is the shop doing? We cannot tell without also knowing its terms of sale. On net selling terms of 30 days, a collection period of 49 days might mean the shop is performing just below par; but, on net selling terms of 60 days, it would mean the shop is performing well. ▲▼▲

SUMMARY

The analysis of financial statements can help entrepreneurs make sound decisions in the areas of planning and control. By careful financial analysis, entrepreneurs can meet the two-sided goal of earning a satisfactory return on investment (ROI) and maintaining the venture's financial health. The technique used to analyze financial statements, and thus to discern financial health, is called *ratio analysis*— the analysis of ratios from a single set of financial statements.

The tests of profitability are formulas that indicate return on investment, return on sales, and inventory turnover:

Return on Investment

$$\text{Return on total assets} = \frac{\text{net profit} + [\text{interest} \times (1 - \text{tax rate})]}{\text{total assets}} \times 100$$

$$\text{Return on owners' equity} = \frac{\text{net profit}}{\text{owners' equity}} \times 100$$

$$\text{Return on permanent capital} = \frac{\text{net profit} + [\text{interest} \times (1 - \text{tax rate})]}{\text{owners' equity} + \text{long-term liabilities}} \times 100$$

$$\text{Return on sales} = \frac{\text{net profit}}{\text{sales revenues}} \times 100$$

$$\text{Inventory turnover} = \frac{\text{cost of goods sold}}{\text{inventory}}$$

The tests of financial health are formulas that compute solvency, liquidity, and customer credit. The debt ratio measures solvency:

$$\text{Debt ratio} = \frac{\text{total liabilities}}{\text{total assets}} \times 100$$

The current ratio and quick ratio are measures of liquidity:

$$\text{Current ratio} = \frac{\text{current assets}}{\text{current liabilities}}$$

$$\text{Quick ratio} = \frac{\text{cash} + \text{accounts receivable}}{\text{current liabilities}}$$

The collection period is a measure of the degree to which a venture finances its credit customers. It involves two computations:

$$\text{Receivables turnover} = \frac{\text{credit sales}}{\text{accounts receivable}}$$

$$\text{Collection period} = \frac{\text{days in the year}}{\text{receivables turnover}}$$

The formulas above are used to evaluate operating and financial performance. It is also important to evaluate investment opportunities. Investment decisions involve choices that can make or break a venture because they often commit the entrepreneur's resources for years to come. We use the following yardstick to measure the worth of investments:

▶ **Cash payback**   The time required for the cash produced by an investment to equal the cash required by the investment

▶ **Return on original investment**   How much entrepreneurs can earn yearly on each dollar invested

▶ **Return on average investment**   How much entrepreneurs can earn over the life of a venture

To survive and grow, entrepreneurs must learn how to extend credit and, at the same time, how to avoid the problem of customers who do not pay. When they grant credit, entrepreneurs essentially are advancing money to customers to buy products or services. Business-to-business credit is extended by one venture to other ventures; consumer credit is extended to individuals.

The advantages of giving credit are as follows:

▶ Credit customers are likely to become repeat customers.

▶ Credit enables customers to buy products or services they might otherwise have to do without.

▶ Credit customers tend to overspend.

▶ Credit customers pay less attention to prices.

▶ Credit customers require less selling effort.

▶ Credit customers tend to buy products of higher quality.

▶ Credit is a convenience to customers who dislike carrying cash.

Among the disadvantages of extending credit are the following:

▶ Credit forces entrepreneurs to finance their customers, thus tying up money in accounts receivable.

▶ Credit refusal may cause ill will.

▶ Credit customers are more likely to abuse the privilege of returning products.

▶ Credit may obligate entrepreneurs to borrow and repay with interest.

▶ Credit adds to the cost of doing business because of investigations and the bookkeeping needed to keep records, bill customers, and collect payments.

Discussion and Review Questions

1. How does the analysis of financial statements help entrepreneurs plan and control more wisely?
2. What is the main financial goal of a venture? Why?
3. Can problems be solved, or opportunities analyzed, solely by collecting and analyzing numbers? Explain, using examples.
4. Explain the three ways of estimating return on investment. Which way is best? Why?

5. If a venture makes a profit of $15,000, is its performance good or bad? Explain your answer.
6. Why is the *after-tax* cost of interest used in estimating the return on total assets or the return on permanent capital?
7. What are the best ways to measure the financial health of a venture? Explain fully.
8. How do solvency and liquidity differ? Which is more important to a venture's financial health? Why?
9. Explain the pitfalls of cash payback as a way to measure the worth of an investment opportunity. How might you avoid these pitfalls?
10. How is the saying "A bird in the hand is worth two in the bush" pertinent to investment decisions?
11. Why would investment decisions be critical to you as an entrepreneur? How would you evaluate investment opportunities?
12. Explain why credit is so vital in our economy. What are some of its advantages and disadvantages?
13. Explain the difference between business-to-business credit and consumer credit.
14. How does an aging schedule help minimize bad debts?
15. Define these terms: *ratio analysis, permanent capital, cash payback, cost of money, average investment, credit, aging schedule.*

Building a Business Plan

Analysis of Financial Statements, Investments, and Credit

To plan and control their ventures effectively, small business owners should become skilled at calculating financial ratios. A *financial ratio* is a number that shows the relationship between two dollar amounts on a firm's financial statements. The information required to calculate these ratios is found in the balance sheet and the income statement. Like the individual elements in a firm's financial statements, ratios can be compared with the firm's past ratios, with those of competitors, and with industry averages.

Instructions for Worksheet 13

Before answering the questions in this exercise, you may want to review the material on financial analysis on pages 384 to 392 in the text. The dollar amounts that you need for these calculations should be taken from the projected income statement and balance sheet at the end of year 1, which you constructed as part of the business plan for Chapter 11. To complete this worksheet, you must calculate specific ratios for profitability in part 1. In part 2, calculate specific ratios for tests of financial health. And in part 3, analyze the results of your ratio calculations.

Part 1—Tests of Profitability

A firm's net profit indicates whether the firm is profitable. It does not, however, indicate how effectively the firm's resources are being used. For this purpose, four ratios can be computed.

1. Calculate a return on total assets ratio.
2. Calculate a return on owners' equity ratio.
3. Calculate a return on sales ratio.
4. Calculate an inventory turnover ratio.

Part 2—Tests of Financial Health

As you might suspect, lenders are concerned about a business firm's ability to repay its debts. And business owners are concerned about their ability to obtain additional debt financing. Four ratios can be calculated to determine the ability of a firm to pay its debts.

5. Calculate a debt ratio that compares total liabilities to total assets.
6. Calculate a times interest earned ratio.
7. Calculate a current ratio.
8. Calculate a quick ratio.

Part 3—Analysis of Your Calculations

9. Based on your projected financial statements that were completed as part of the business plan for Chapter 11 and the ratio calculations above, how would you rate the financial health of your business at the end of the first year?
10. What steps could you take to improve the financial health of your business at the end of the first year?

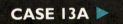

CASE 13A ▶ *Twining Lumber Company*

The time is the spring of 1996. As the scene opens, Ralph Twining, the owner of Twining Lumber Company, is in the outer office of the loan officer of the local bank. He is waiting to talk over the renewal of an overdue loan *and* an increase of $160,000 in his line of credit. At the moment, Ralph is quietly trying to marshal some telling arguments that would accomplish both goals.

Background

Ralph had opened the lumberyard in 1985. A graduate of the University of Oklahoma, Ralph had been sure of his readiness to strike off on his own. After all, he had worked in lumberyards as a delivery man, then as yard foreman, and finally as office manager. He knew lumber.

Lumber had been hard to get when he started out, but he had managed to get what he needed. Profits had been good, and as fast as lumber came in it was shipped out. There had been little need to worry about competition.

Meanwhile, the town had been growing. And as builders put up new houses and shops, Ralph's business had profited. In fact, owners' equity had grown from $30,000 in 1985 to more than $267,000 by December 31, 1995.

Arrival of Competition

But lately things had been getting tight. There had been strong competition in the past two years. Builders were asking concessions, and Ralph was hungry for new customers. While branching out into neighboring towns, Ralph had been cutting prices. Year by year, he was increasing his sales, but lately he was not making much of a profit.

The bank had been helpful. It opened up a line of unsecured credit on his own signature. Somehow, though, word was getting around that Ralph wasn't always meeting his bills to suppliers on time. In some cases, overdue bills were resulting in rather pointed reminders from his creditors.

Ralph's Progressive Loan Officer

A week ago, Ralph had mailed his latest financial statements to the bank. These, he knew, would be analyzed keenly, following which he would be called in to talk over the figures and make new loan arrangements. He owed the bank $28,000, which was overdue.

Ralph had written down on a sheet of paper the details of his balance sheet and his income statement, shown in Exhibits 13A.1 and 13A.2.

As Ralph gave these figures one last going over, George Linsenmann, the bank's loan officer, opened the door and called him in. He was known as a progressive bank executive. Priding himself on his knowledge of small business and credit risks, Linsenmann's special interest was borderline borrowers.

The U.S. Small Business Administration had referred many a harried entrepreneur to him with a financial problem, and many a borrower had he

---

EXHIBIT 13A.1

Twining Lumber Company Balance Sheet (December 31, 1995).

Assets			Equities		
Current assets			Current liabilities		
Cash	$ 948		Loans payable	$ 28,000	
Notes receivable	12,596		Notes receivable	9,684	
Accounts receivable	194,912		Accounts payable	304,480	
Inventory	313,644	$522,100	Taxes payable	10,880	$353,044
Fixed assets			Mortgage		20,000
Land and buildings	$ 92,516		Owners' equity		267,044
Equipment	25,472	117,988			
Total assets		$640,088	Total equities		$640,088

EXHIBIT 13A.2

Twining Lumber Company: Income statement (1995).

		Dollars	Percent
Sales revenues		$1,454,232	100.0
Cost of goods sold		1,233,376	84.8
Gross profit		$ 220,856	15.2
Operating expenses			
Wages	$117,655		8.1
Owner's salary	50,796		3.5
Delivery	18,792		1.3
Depreciation	14,400		1.0
Bad debts	7,228		0.5
Other expenses	7,101		0.5
Interest	1,400	217,372	0.1
Profit before taxes		$ 3,484	0.2

helped, including Ralph. Through sound advice, he had helped a number of small businesses to stay on their feet. They in turn had helped the town to grow. And as the town grew, so did the bank.

A Lack of Financial Knowledge

The loan officer motioned to his visitor. "Come in, Ralph; sit down." When Ralph was seated, the loan officer opened his desk drawer and pulled out a group of sheets containing columns of figures. Ralph guessed that they were his.

"Glad you came in," said the loan officer. "I've been wanting to talk with you for quite a while." Then followed a moment of silence as the loan officer stared out the window. Finally, he continued, "Ralph, you're a good salesperson, and you know lumber. But how well do you know your own figures?"

"I really don't know," replied Ralph. "My bookkeeper gives me monthly statements covering sales, cash, expenses. Most of the time, I'm too busy in the lumberyard to go into the books. I leave most of the details to her."

Working for Nothing

The loan officer then went on. "Let me ask you another question, Ralph. Why do you insist on doing business for nothing?" Ralph was startled, and he began to flush. He had been expecting to be taken to task for the overdue loan, but the conversation was now taking a turn for which he was unprepared.

"I'm *not* working for nothing," Ralph countered. "The last two years, it's been tough. I've been building up my business; you know that. Just look at my history. I'm worth more than . . ."

"Wait a minute, Ralph," interrupted the loan officer. "I know what you're going to say. But just look at your figures. Last year, your profit was just $3,484. The year before it was $750, and that was before income taxes. You could have done better working for someone else. You made virtually nothing on the money you invested."

"But how much *should* I have made?" Ralph asked.

An Academic Question

"You know, Ralph, the amount of profit a business should earn on its investment is something of an academic question. Some say that the ratio of after-tax profits to owners' equity should be about 10 percent a year. I look at it this way: If you had gone to work for someone else, and invested your $267,044 in blue-chip stock, you could have safely earned around 5 percent in dividends. That's about $13,400—almost four times your profits before taxes.

"Anyway, let's be practical. Your before-tax profit on sales for 1995 was only two-tenths of 1 percent. Your trade association of lumber dealers reports an average return for its members of 3½ percent on sales—17 times what you're getting!"

Ralph was quiet. The point had been driven home. "Maybe, Ralph, you've got all the money you're going to need," said the loan officer, as he spread out Ralph's figures over his desk. "You know, Ralph, I'm convinced you have been violating the three commandments of financial management."

"Now, wait a moment, Mr. Linsenmann!" Ralph countered. "You know as well as I do, I'll never borrow a dime I can't pay back, nor buy a two-by-four I won't pay for. I'm solvent. Look at my figures. I've got assets to pay."

The Three Commandments of Financial Management

As Ralph broke off, the loan officer picked up the figures and continued, "Don't get upset, Ralph. I know you're honest, and I know your intentions. If we weren't sure about that, I wouldn't be talking to you. The three commandments are: Don't overbuy; don't overtrade; and don't overexpand. Now don't you agree you've done all three?"

Ralph hedged, "Well, what makes you think so?"

"Look here," responded the loan officer. The two men drew up their chairs. "Let's start with your balance sheet. You show current assets of $522,100 and current debts of $353,044. Your current ratio is 1.5 to 1. That's dangerously close, according to your trade association. They've felt that the average lumberyard should show, at the very least, a ratio of 3 to 1.

What-If Questions

"What does all this ratio stuff mean?" Ralph interjected. "That fast figure work was a little over my head."

"It's simple enough if you figure it out in logical order, Ralph. Overtrading with finances is something like speeding in a car. At 20 miles an hour, a blowout is an inconvenience—but at 80 miles an hour?" The loan officer paused to let the point sink in.

"Look, Ralph, what if one of your big customers goes sour and you have to write some big receivables off as bad debts? What if prices take a quick tumble and your inventory drops in value? What if home building should suddenly stop because of a strike? Suppose creditors demand their money?

"Suppose . . ." and the loan officer smiled, "Suppose we called your loan?"

Ralph glanced up quickly. "Okay, Mr. Linsenmann, I see the point. How about the loan?"

"Let's think some things through first, Ralph," replied the loan officer. "We'll get to the loan; and we don't intend to see you forced out of business. But let's understand this: A soundly run business has the strength to survive blowouts. You haven't."

The Balance Sheet Revisited

"Now let's examine your balance sheet again, continued the loan officer. "Obviously, you need more cash. You have slightly less than a thousand dollars in your balance right now. Your overhead last year, eliminating depreciation and bad debts, was $195,744. That figures out to around $16,300 a month. You have less than enough cash to meet a week's overhead. I'm inclined to feel that a business should have enough cash to meet 2 weeks' overhead, at the very least.

"Next, think about your receivables. Your daily sales are about $3,980 on the average. Divide that into $194,912 in accounts receivable on the balance sheet, and you have an average collection period of about 49 days. Not so bad. That compares favorably with a 51-day average shown for other lumberyards by your trade association's studies. At least you're not in the banking business with your customers."

Inventory Deadwood

"Well, that brings us to inventory," said the loan officer. "Your company shows a relationship for cost of goods sold to inventory of—let's see, divide $1,233,376 in cost of goods sold by $313,644 in inventory—yes, that's right—3.9 times a year. Judging by a wide variety of other lumberyards in your line, it should be nearer to 6 times a year.

"How about that inventory, Ralph? Any deadwood in there?" The loan officer chuckled at the unintentional play on words.

"Well, it's like this," Ralph came back a little aggressively. "I took my inventory low. Why, I've got $40,000 worth of roofers alone that are up 20 percent since I bought them. Of course, it'll take me several months to move that much, but they'll go for a good profit."

A Questionable Practice

"I'm sure the roofers will sell, and if they do you'll be looking for more bargains," responded the loan officer. Tell me, Ralph, are you in business to make a profit as a marketer or as a speculator on price fluctuations? What will happen if you guess wrong?" Then said the loan officer rather emphatically, "You *will* guess wrong someday, you know?"

"But Mr. Linsenmann," remarked Ralph, rather plaintively, "does a guy have to shut his eyes to a good buy?"

"No, not if he can afford it. But you can't. You need that $160,000 right now to pay bills with—not to mention the loan that's overdue. Let's face it, Ralph. You're a perpetual overbuyer."

Rather vehemently, Ralph protested, "But business is a gamble!"

"So is driving an automobile, Ralph. If you were taking a trip to California, you'd want to make sure your car was in good shape. You'd have a mechanic go over your car carefully—checking brakes, tires, engine, and so on. You'd watch out for overloading, too, because you know that excessive strain might cause a breakdown. Right now you're driving your business under an overload of items that strain your financial resources."

Feelings of Self-Doubt

"Gosh, Mr. Linsenmann," Ralph mused, "this begins to look as though I don't belong in business. Is that what you want to tell me?"

"Not at all, Ralph," the loan officer replied. "What I've been doing is spotlighting a few disturbing facts to help clarify your thinking. You've been trying to take a quick and easy path around some roadblocks. In the process, you got lost.

"It isn't your balance sheet or your income statement that got you into trouble. Your statements are merely end products of some questionable managerial methods. The key to your problem, and to a possible solution, lies in the way you buy and sell lumber. Your income statement makes that fairly clear. Take a look at some comparative figures."

Some Revealing Comparisons

With that, the loan officer spread before Ralph two parallel columns of operating figures. One was Ralph's income statement expressed in percentages; the other represented a set of figures that Ralph had not seen before.

"Here are two sets of figures," continued the loan officer. "One you'll recognize. The other represents a sort of composite percentage statement based on some ratios prepared for last year by your trade association. They represent a picture of what lumberyards in our state have accomplished on the average. Here, study the figures for a minute and tell me what you see."

Ralph examined the statement, which appears in Exhibit 13A.3. After some pondering, Ralph began to shake his head. "Something's wrong," he

EXHIBIT 13A.3

Twining Lumber Company: Comparison of operating performance with lumber industry averages (1995). (All figures are percentages of sales revenues.)

	Twining Lumber Company	Lumber Industry Averages
Sales revenues	100.0	100.0
Cost of goods sold	84.8	75.0
Gross profit	15.2	25.0
Operating expenses		
Wages	8.1	9.8
Owner's salary	3.5	5.5
Delivery	1.3	1.0
Depreciation	1.0	0.9
Bad debts	0.5	0.4
Other expenses	0.5	3.2
Interest	0.1	0.7
Total expenses	15.0	21.5
Profit before taxes	0.2	3.5

mused. "I'm way ahead of the average on expenses, but way behind on profit."

The loan officer nodded. "What else, Ralph?"

A Pricing Problem

"Main thing I see is the difference in profit margin." responded Ralph. "How do these other fellows get the prices?"

The loan officer gave Ralph a keen glance. Then he spoke, "Doing much business with Brooks Builders over in Strongsville?"

"Sure," Ralph came back, "thousands of dollars a month."

"They're a new customer, aren't they? I hear they're pretty sharp buyers."

"Yeah, they're rough," Ralph admitted somewhat hesitantly. "But they're big-volume buyers."

"How much business do you do with home-builders, and how much with homeowners?" asked the loan officer.

"We don't bother much with that little stuff. It's a nuisance to cut and deliver a dozen pieces of two-by-four, six pieces of wallboard, and a pound of nails. We deal mostly in quantity with contractors."

Focus on Service

The loan officer gave no immediate reaction. Then he said, "They tell me you take business as much as 30 miles out of town. That would build up delivery costs, wouldn't it?"

Ralph nodded.

"I also hear that you're a bear on service, that you'll deliver a half load to any one at a moment's notice. I've seen your yardmen working overtime getting out deliveries. Sure, service keeps customers happy and brings in new ones. But there have to be offsetting compensations. Your trouble, as I see it, Ralph, is price.

"They tell me you'd rather miss a meal than lose a sale. Some people say you sold a carload of lumber to Brooks Builders just last week for $40 a thousand above cost. That's a pretty small mark-up on an item wholesaling for around $400 per thousand. Frankly, your competitors have been a little gleeful about it."

"But," Ralph responded, "isn't turnover an objective? Everybody is trying for volume nowadays. What about this business of 'Profits in pennies, volume in millions'?"

"It's a nice slogan, in its place," said the loan officer. "Many grocers work on a 15-percent margin, and their profit comes out at pennies per dollar. But their turnover is in goods. They move their goods daily and weekly. They aren't so likely to take inventory losses.

"And they sell for cash, mostly. Their volume is steady. But when a company like yours, Ralph, has to stock large inventories in advance of a season and has to carry receivables, cash flow can't help but slow down."

A Shift in Attitude

Anxiously, Ralph then asked, "All right, what do you think I should do—give up?"

The loan officer considered the question. Weighing his words, he replied. "No, that's the furthest thought from my mind. I don't think it's a question of quitting. You're too honest, likable, and hardworking. You know lumber. You're well-liked by your customers. Besides we, in the bank here, don't believe we can grow by driving people out of business.

"Actually, what you and I have been doing is diagnosing some symptoms of sickness. I've got a few suggestions that I believe will cure this patient—your company—if you care to listen."

Ralph's reply was quick, and relieved. "Sure, sure—I'll listen. What do you think we ought to do?"

Justifying the Loan

The loan officer continued thoughtfully. "Thinking over your situation carefully last week, I came to the conclusion that only part, but an important part, of your troubles are financial. Let's tackle them first. You could use $160,000 more cash, right?"

The answer was almost an echo, "Right!"

"Very well," said the loan officer. The immediate problem is the loan. I can't risk our depositors' money by granting you a larger loan. But I think we can do some refinancing. Your yard property appears to have appreciated in value enough so that we can consolidate the present mortgage and increase it $60,000. That will refinance your $28,000 note and leave $32,000 cash.

"Now let's look elsewhere. Suppose you were to cut back some of that inventory, say $100,000. Could you manage without causing sales to drop as a result? If you could, it would bring you down to an inventory turnover of about six times. You already have some appreciation on the $40,000 lot of roofers."

Ralph Concedes

This time Ralph was slow to answer. Reluctantly, he came to a decision. "Yes, I guess we could. Deliveries are coming in faster these days, and there's plenty of stuff on the market."

"Well, let's leave that one for a minute," continued the loan officer. "I have one more suggestion. I want you to give up that unprofitable Brooks Builders account. And I believe several others on your books have got to start paying you a better price. It's a cinch they'd have to if they did business elsewhere. If they're worth keeping, they'll go along. In other words, I would like to see you slice $200,000 worth of unprofitable sales volume off your books."

That was a shocker. Ralph had worked hard to land these accounts, even though the concessions forced upon him had been painful.

The loan officer continued, "It means no loss in profit. Also, it means buying thousands of dollars less each month. So you might say that, in a sense, it supplies that much more cash flow. Furthermore, it means carrying fewer receivables. Taken together, these items begin to get us closer to our objective."

Ralph's Future Brightens

Ralph brightened a little; the picture was beginning to look more attractive. Living with a daily burden of debt had been no fun.

"Next," said the loan officer, "let's look at some profit prospects. It looks as if this do-it-yourself market is here to stay. It's small, package stuff, but it can be profitable. All over the country, lumberyards are taking advantage of consumer business. They're putting in paint and hardware, renting power tools, and so on.

"Over in Strongsville, Ernie Manuel is grossing 40 percent on that type of business. He offsets delivery costs by adding service charges. His power-tool-rental income paid for his outlay the very first year. That's not so small, you know.

"These days, when homeowners buy, they want two things: service and quality. They'll spend money to get them. Some lumberyards are doing as much as 50 percent of their business with consumers. If you look at the facts carefully, you'll see that there's money to be made in it."

The Last Word

The loan officer continued. "We'd like to help you stay in business in spite of your present ratios. Well, what do you say?"

As he rose to leave, Ralph replied, "You know, Mr. Linsenmann, there's something about your

Adapted from a case prepared by the U.S. Small Business Administration.

approach that makes a lot of sense. Let me think the whole business through for a few days, as I get more figures together. Then I'd like to map it out with you. Meanwhile, could you get started on that mortgage? It would give me some breathing space."

The loan officer nodded approval, and the two walked to the door. In parting, Ralph remarked, "I think I can work it out. Heaven knows, I hope so." Then with a smile, he said, "Maybe, I'll turn out to be a good businessperson after all. Anyway, thanks for the education on those revealing ratios!"

Questions

1. Comment on the job that Ralph Twining had done managing his banking relationship. What were the important lessons to be learned from his loan officer?
2. Explain how Twining's future use of financial ratios could influence him in improving his lumberyard's profitability and financial health.
3. Why must Twining look beyond figures and ratios for the solution of his problems? Explain fully.
4. In your judgment, does Twining have what it takes to turn his business around? Is he likely to follow the loan officer's advice to the letter? Why or why not?
5. What other advice might you offer Twining? Why?

Ralls Men's Shoes, Inc.

In the early 1990s, one of the brightest spots in retailing was men's shoes. Professionals, especially those ranging in age from 21 to 34, have become more fashion-conscious than their older counterparts, shedding their drab guise and purchasing colorful footwear.

Riding this latest trend in shoeland is Robert Ralls. A former shoe clerk, buyer, and store manager, he is the sole owner of Ralls Shoes, Inc. He purchased the store three years ago, thus "avoiding the complexity of starting fresh." In essence, he bought title to a ready-made business, complete with inventory and a loyal following.

Mostly because of his ability to purchase and control fast-selling shoes, Ralls has doubled the store's sales revenues since he took over. This success has inspired him to consider expansion elsewhere, in a shopping mall within a mile of his existing store. "That would be exciting and challenging," says Ralls, "this time opening a second store from scratch, and molding it in my image."

However, expanding into a mall that already boasts several shoe store chains may pose problems for an independent entrepreneur as small as Ralls. For one thing, store chains may have a competitive edge when it comes to lower prices and a wider selection. "My secret weapon," says Ralls, "would be the little extras that turn customers into friends, such extras as offering to make repairs without charge on recently purchased shoes. I'll take anything back."

Ralls's accountant prepared the financial statements shown in Exhibits 13B.1 and 13B.2. "I'm going to sit down with my banker to see how much I can borrow to finance my second store," says Ralls. "I hope my financials impress him."

Questions

1. Compute the following ratios: Return on total assets, return on permanent capital, return on owners' equity, return on sales, inventory turnover, current ratio, quick ratio, and debt ratio.

2. What questions would you ask Robert Ralls, based on your analysis of these ratios?

EXHIBIT 13B.1
Ralls Men's Shoes, Inc.: Income statement (1995).

Sales revenues		$537,200
Cost of goods sold		333,100
Gross profit		$204,100
Operating expenses:		
Wages	$98,700	
Rent	42,900	
Advertising	13,400	
Utilities	7,500	
Depreciation	6,400	
Supplies	5,400	
Interest	5,100	
Insurance	4,300	
Licenses	3,800	
Professional services	3,200	
Travel	2,700	
Other	3,200	196,600
Profit before taxes		$ 7,500
Income taxes		1,700
Profit after taxes		$ 5,800

EXHIBIT 13B.2

Ralls Men's Shoes, Inc.: Balance sheet (as of December 31, 1995).

Assets			Equities		
Current assets			Current liabilities		$111,600
Cash	$ 8,100		Long-term loan (12%)		41,300
Accounts receivable	21,300		Owners' equity		
Inventory	141,200	$170,600	Common stock	$40,000	
Fixes assets			Retained earnings	12,700	52,700
Equipment	$ 47,300				
Accum. depreciation	16,100	31,200			
Other assets		3,800			
Total assets		$205,600	Total equities		$205,600

CASE 13C ▶ The Darvas Company

The Darvas Company, which makes high-precision machine tools, is wondering whether to replace two hand-operated lathes with but a single lathe—a newer model that features state-of-the-art computer technology. A marvel of engineering design, the newer model promises both to ensure product quality and to save the company money.

Boasting an estimated useful life of 10 years, the newer model would cost the company $90,000, delivered and installed. If it chooses, the company can finance the purchase with a bank loan at an interest rate of 12 percent.

The question is, "Would the yearly savings be large enough to justify spending $90,000 for the newer model?" The company came up with these estimates of savings:

▶ Labor costs would drop, as it would take just one skilled machinist to run the newer model—in contrast to the two older models, which now require the constant attention to detail of two machinists.

These machinists now earn $20 an hour, including social security taxes and such fringe benefits as medical insurance and a pension plan. Except for a two-week shutdown for vacations, the company operates one shift a day, five days a week, throughout the year.

▶ Other out-of-pocket savings, mostly from less scrap, would come to $5,000 a year.

▶ The newer model would also free up floor space, although the shop's layout was such that this freed space did not lend itself to use for some other purpose.

Furthermore, the company had financed the older models with a 10 percent bank loan, and still owed the bank $30,000. If replaced, the older models probably could be sold in their present condition for their book value of $20,000, after dismantling and removal costs.

Founded 11 years ago, the company has always prided itself on the fact that it has never lost a customer to a competitor. It expects to continue earning such loyalty well into the future. The company's latest financial statements appear in condensed form in Exhibit 13C.1.

Questions

1. What action, if any, would you recommend? Explain fully, using the tools described in the chapter, and answer the question: "Would the yearly savings be large enough to justify spending $90,000 for the newer model?"

2. Besides dollar savings, what other benefits might the Darvas Company reap by purchasing the newer model?

CHAPTER 14

Marketing Research and Marketing Channels

OBJECTIVES

▶ to explain the need for marketing research

▶ to outline the basic steps in carrying out marketing research

▶ to discuss how best to segment markets

▶ to distinguish between marketing research and intuition in solving marketing problems

▶ to explain the purpose of marketing channels and how they work

As long as one keeps searching, the answers come.

—Joan Baez

The entrepreneur's overriding goal must be to develop *totally* satisfied customers, at a profit. Marketing helps do this by moving products or services out of the hands of the entrepreneur and into those of customers. To carry off this effort, entrepreneurs may choose from a broad mix of marketing tools, each of which reinforces the others. Among these tools are:

▶ Marketing research
▶ Marketing channels
▶ Pricing
▶ Promotion
▶ Service

These tools, depicted in Exhibit 14.1, are covered in two chapters. In this chapter, we look first at marketing research and then at marketing channels. In Chapter 15, we cover pricing, promotion, and service.

EXHIBIT 14.1
Major tools of the
marketing mix. Marketing
research is the keystone of
the marketing mix.

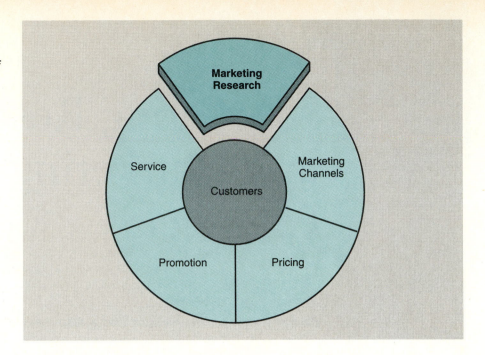

Marketing Research

The word *marketing* may be defined in several ways. The American Marketing Association (AMA) defines *marketing* as follows:

> Marketing is the process of planning and executing the conception, pricing, promotion, and distribution of ideas, goods, and services to create exchanges that satisfy individuals and organizational goals.[1]

Acceptable though the AMA's definition may be, especially by larger businesses, our definition is equally serviceable but simpler. We define *marketing* as "the effort to identify and satisfy customers' needs and wants." Even more simply, we may think of marketing as the effort to *get* and *keep* customers. In essence, then, it is the entrepreneur's job to build lasting bonds with their customers for life.

Before discussing marketing research and its pivotal role in that effort, let us first define what we mean by a market. A *market* is any group of customers who are willing and able to spend money, or its equivalent, to receive a product or a service that they need. A confusing term, the word *market* has many other usages—for example, to identify retail stores (the supermarket) and institutions (the stock market).

Marketing research is the collecting, recording, and interpreting of information about markets. Observers of the marketing scene often call it the most important marketing tool of all. Why? Because it helps satisfy the never-ending need for knowledge about markets:

- ▸ What products or services to sell
- ▸ Where to sell them, in what quantities, and at what prices
- ▸ What competitors are selling, where they are, and how strong they are

Thus, a venture's survival and growth depend strongly on the depth of its marketing research. As vital after startup as before, marketing research falls within the reach of every entrepreneur, no matter how small, as borne out by this example from the SBA:

EXAMPLE ▸

One of the simplest full-time ventures is the corner newsstand, a fixture in large cities like New York. An entrepreneur who is doing a successful job selling newspapers and magazines is doing marketing research. Before telling his supplier how many newspapers he wants each day, the entrepreneur has made some important marketing decisions.

He knows how many newspapers he usually sells each day of the week—a fact he has on tap from his own experience. Then he checks the weather each day and considers its effect on the number of people likely to stop and buy a newspaper. Our entrepreneur next checks to see if there are any special events, conventions, or meetings that might bring additional customers by his corner. He might even go so far as to check to see what stores are having special sales.

If our entrepreneur is really on his toes, he checks the early edition for special news events that might generate extra customer interest, or that he may be able to exploit for extra sales.

Our entrepreneur runs through this process every day before telling the supplier how many papers he wants. This process is called *marketing research.* In short, it means getting all the facts available on customers' interest, market potential, market mood, and environmental conditions. ▲▼▲

Chances are that entrepreneurs will do marketing research before start-up. Their decisions about where best to locate, what sales to expect, and how much money to raise are rooted in fact, *not* opinion. After startup, however, they often fail to dig out new facts, mistakenly assuming their markets will stay the same or change little.

This attitude is shortsighted, if not hazardous. Entrepreneurs who fail to remain in touch with their markets may find themselves without customers. Buying habits change so quickly that success favors the entrepreneurs who keep a close watch on their markets and, if necessary, quickly change their line of products or services to keep pace. For example, a change in fitness habits triggered a shift away from running shoes to tennis and aerobic shoes, today's fashionable leisure wear.

▸ **Uses of Marketing Research**

As suggested earlier, marketing research replaces opinion with fact, helping entrepreneurs offset the risks of doing business in today's fast-changing markets. It enables entrepreneurs to avoid taking such ill-conceived actions as:

- ▸ Adding a new product because their *nearest* competitor just did
- ▸ Drafting a new plan to build sales because they *think* it will work
- ▸ Adding a new service because they *hear* that customers like it

EXHIBIT 14.2
The marketing research process.

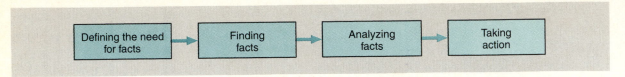

Small wonder, then, that some entrepreneurs fall by the wayside. They lose sight of the fact that their success begins and ends with the *customer;* that their one key to success is to know, better than their competitors do, what attracts customers.

Thus, it is the entrepreneur's unique calling to anticipate, adjust to, and capitalize on the sweeping changes that mark our times. Eminently fitting is this classic, if poignant, quotation from Theodore Levitt of Harvard University:

> An essential starting point is always to ask oneself: "What kind of society will we have in, say, five, ten, or twenty years? What does it mean for my company and its orientation?" Had the railroads asked themselves these germinal questions fifty years ago, they might now be making less frequent trips to Washington with tin cup in hand.[2]

Turning to Exhibit 14.2, and as detailed below, note how logical and straightforward marketing research can be.

▶ **Defining the Need for Facts**

The first step in marketing research is to raise the proper questions. Unless they know what questions are worth asking, entrepreneurs cannot research their markets wisely. In this regard, note below the kinds of precise questions a maker of personal computers might raise before, and after, startup:

▶ Who is buying or will buy
   What personal computer in
      What quantities of
         What specifications at
            What price in
               What kind of package against
                  What competitors?

▶ What competitors are supplying personal computers with
      What capabilities at
         What plant sites with
            What capacities?

▶ What opportunities are there for us with
      What personal computers of
         What quality at
            What price under

What marketing conditions in
What quantities in
What future periods?

This list by no means exhausts the number of questions the entrepreneur might raise. It does suggest, however, how entrepreneurs might define their need for facts. Note, too, that this list, though applicable to manufacturers such as a maker of personal computers, may easily be tailored to fit the needs of retailers, wholesalers, and service providers.

▶ Finding a Market Niche

The more facts entrepreneurs have, the better prepared they will be to carve out niches in the marketplace. To find their niches, or market segments, entrepreneurs must be futurists, always looking ahead. As such, they must dig out those facts that enable them to:

▶ Identify which market segments are the most profitable to pursue

▶ Identify soft spots in market coverage

▶ Choose new products or services that customers need

▶ Find out why existing products or services are selling well or poorly

▶ Set realistic sales goals

Let us now go through an example to see how an entrepreneur may find her niche in the marketplace. Assume she wants to open a travel agency, an industry she knows well, having worked three years for a local travel agency in various positions. A marketing major in college, she visits her library and unearths the data depicted in Exhibit 14.3.

Note that the exhibit covers the family's life cycle in nine stages, each stage differing according to age, marital status, and the presence or absence of children. Our entrepreneur knows that each stage of the life cycle uniquely influences the family's behavior as a potential customer of her travel agency. For example, she is likely to observe that childless married couples under age 45 are more affluent because both partners often work and do not have to spend money for child care. This observation can also be made for childless couples aged 45 to 64, who often are called *empty nesters*. Both of these niches are likely to be strong markets for travel.

Our entrepreneur would also note that the makeup of U.S. households is changing dramatically. For example, households with single-earner married couples with children had dropped to just 8 percent in 1990, from 21 percent in 1970.

▶ Finding Facts

Giant corporations can draw on many in-house resources for marketing research. These corporations have marketing research departments staffed with high-powered professionals, many with master's degrees in business administration. Du Pont, for example, has more than 700 professionals in its marketing research department.

EXHIBIT 14.3

Changes in the family life cycle between 1970 and 1990.

Source: U.S. Bureau of the Census, Current Population Survey, 1970 and 1990. (Washington, D.C.: U.S. Government Printing Office, 1992).

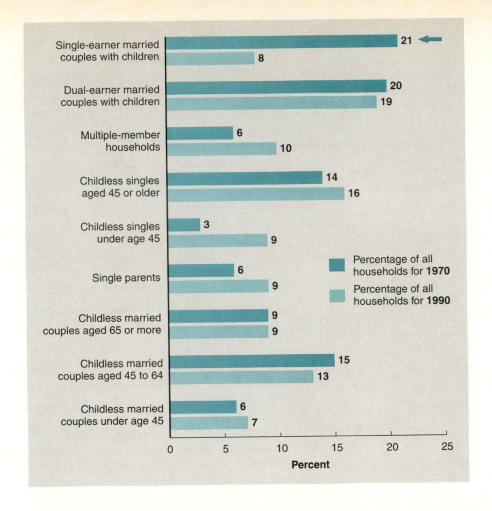

But few entrepreneurs can justify hiring a marketing researcher, let alone establishing a marketing research department. So how may entrepreneurs dig out the real facts about their markets? They can do so by:

▸ Tapping information already compiled by chambers of commerce, trade associations, the U.S. Department of Commerce, the marketing research departments of local daily newspapers, and libraries—as did the entrepreneur in the previous example

▸ Buying the services of a marketing research firm

▸ Organizing a part-time marketing research effort within their own venture

Using Statistical Information   Perhaps the best way to begin is by using statistical data already worked up by chambers of commerce, trade associations, and the U.S. Department of Commerce. Often available at no fee, this kind of information yields the greatest return on the entrepreneur's time and

Marketing research keeps businesses up to date on customer needs and preferences, as this entrepreneur does who is showing a customer a mat-and-frame sample against a print in her drapery shop.

effort. As we saw in Chapter 8, the U.S. Census Bureau can help draw profiles of markets. For example, using Census Bureau data an entrepreneur can learn:

▶ The percentage of the population in a marketing area under 10 years old, 10 to 19, 20 to 30, and so on

▶ The average yearly income per family

▶ The percentage of families who own their homes

▶ The percentage of families who own automobiles

From such statistical data, entrepreneurs may draw all kinds of useful conclusions about their markets. Take this example:

EXAMPLE ▶

A supermarket owner measured her market potential as follows:

16,500	Local population (from U.S. Census Bureau)
× $ 12,000	Local per capita income yearly (from U.S. Census Bureau)
$198,000,000	Gross local income per year
× 0.14	Percentage spent on groceries (from trade association)
$ 27,720,000	Total market potential

She then estimated her share of the market. Her yearly sales revenues are $5,544,000, so her market share is 20 percent:

$$(\$5,544,000 \div \$27,720,000) \times 100 = 20\%$$

The entrepreneur can now carry her analysis one step further, comparing her store's performance with that of other supermarkets in the area. There are three competing supermarkets, with average sales of $7,392,000 a year:

$$(\$27,720,000 - \$5,544,000) \div 3 = \$7,392,000$$

Clearly, our entrepreneur's work is cut out for her. Her competitors are doing 33 percent better than she is:

$$[(\$7,392,000 - \$5,544,000) \div \$5,544,000] \times 100 = 33\%$$

Of course, this analysis does not explain why her performance falls short. But it does raise several questions:

▶ Why are competing supermarkets attracting more customers?
▶ What are they doing to attract customers that she is not doing?
▶ What changes should she make in advertising, sales promotion, and personal selling to boost sales?
▶ Is she offering the right mix of food products?

Answering these questions may trigger further marketing research. Our entrepreneur may decide, for example, to do a consumer survey to find out what homemakers in her marketing area want in a supermarket, how they choose a supermarket, and their general feelings about supermarkets. ▲▼▲

Using a Marketing Research Firm   If initial marketing research leads to the decision to do a consumer survey, it would be wise to hire the services of a marketing researcher. Before doing so, however, it is crucial for entrepreneurs to be clear about what it is they want to learn from a survey. Consumer research is not for beginners. It takes the skills of a professional to work up a questionnaire that is free of bias—the basic requirement for a survey. Because the wording of a question may influence the reply, questions should be phrased so as to produce the most accurate answers and the greatest possible insight into motivation.

Besides drafting bias-free questions, a marketing researcher also designs the survey itself. Consumer surveys, for instance, cannot possibly interview all homemakers; instead, they use representative samples. Selecting a representative sample requires skill and ingenuity. For example:

EXAMPLE ▶

The Gallup poll uses a random sample of only 1,500 voters to learn the political preferences of a nation of more than 250 million people. The sample is called *random* because every voter in the nation has the same chance of being chosen for the sample.

Gallup selects 300 representative sections of the nation and randomly chooses 5 voters in each one. Then Gallup sends interviewers to poll them.

How accurate have Gallup's readings of voters' likes and dislikes been? Remarkably accurate. On average, its national election polls err by only 1.5 percent. ▲▼▲

Sampling is not a job for amateurs. Unless the sample is representative, the results will be misleading; which can be worse than no research at all.

EXHIBIT 14.4

Comparison of three ways to carry out surveys.

	Kind of Survey		
Points of Comparison	**One-on-One Interviews**	**Telephone**	**Mail**
Probability of cooperation	Medium	Low	Low
Cost	High	Medium	Low
Flexibility	High	Medium	Low
Potential bias	High	Medium	Low
Time to complete survey	Medium	Fast	Slow

Survey Methods   Turning to Exhibit 14.4, note that entrepreneurs may choose any one of three approaches to collecting information, each differing sharply from the others, depending on the point of comparison. Which approach to choose depends on two factors:

▶ The nature, complexity, and urgency of the entrepreneur's need for information

▶ The availability of resources—time, money, and trained staff—to carry out the survey

As summarized in the exhibit, each survey method has its good and bad points. For example:

▶ *One-on-one interviews* work best when entrepreneurs need a large amount of information, or when they must ask complex questions. Interviews, however, are the most expensive way to collect information.

▶ *Telephone surveys* work best when entrepreneurs need information quickly. A major drawback is that telephone surveys are limited to oral communication, which unavoidably excludes observation.

▶ *Mail surveys* recommend themselves to entrepreneurs looking for the least expensive way to collect information. Two major drawbacks are that responses from mail surveys tend to be low, often no more than 2 percent; and that the process takes much longer than the other two methods.

Organizing Part-Time Research   Although some aspects of marketing research, such as sampling, require professional advice, entrepreneurs should do much of it themselves. A good way to start is to keep a file of marketing data from trade publications and articles from magazines and newspapers. Taken singly, these facts may seem trivial. But when filed and studied over the years, they can be a fertile source for marketing research. For example:

▶ *The Wall Street Journal* carries information on marketing trends, thus alerting entrepreneurs to changes in customers' needs and tastes in their market.

EXHIBIT 14.5
Sources of marketing data.

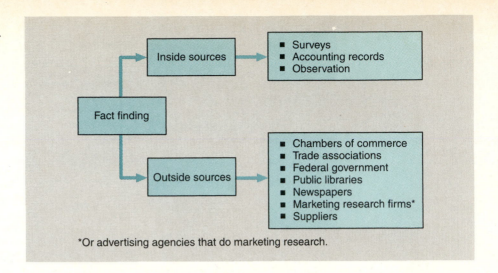

Inside sources
- Surveys
- Accounting records
- Observation

Fact finding

Outside sources
- Chambers of commerce
- Trade associations
- Federal government
- Public libraries
- Newspapers
- Marketing research firms*
- Suppliers

*Or advertising agencies that do marketing research.

▸ The local newspaper may publish data on population shifts, thus alerting entrepreneurs to opportunities emerging outside their immediate marketing area.

▸ Trade publications publish articles on highly successful ventures, thus alerting entrepreneurs to production, financial, and marketing methods they might try.

Exhibit 14.5 diagrams the approach to finding facts that we have just described. Note the inclusion of accounting records and observation as inside sources of data. Accounting records, for example, may indicate which products are selling well and which are not, while observation at the point of sale may indicate which displays attract retail customers. Note, too, the inclusion of suppliers as outside sources of data. Suppliers can provide insights into innovative changes made by noncompeting entrepreneurs in the same industry.

▸ Analyzing Facts

The third step in marketing research is analyzing facts. Its purpose is to distill meaning and direction from the data. What market segments should be targeted and pursued? Answering this question is a vital part of the entrepreneur's analysis.

Market Segmentation[3]   As suggested earlier, *market segmentation* is the division of markets into groups of customers with similar needs for either a product or a service. Thus, a *market segment* is any group of customers who share one or more traits and who therefore exhibit similar product needs. For example, say a clothier located in a large city decides to direct his marketing efforts at young professional men between the ages of 21 and 34. To satisfy this market segment, he would carry only apparel that his marketing research tells him would probably appeal to upwardly mobile young men.

As this example suggests, the market-segmentation approach requires entrepreneurs to focus on just one part or a few parts of the total market rather than

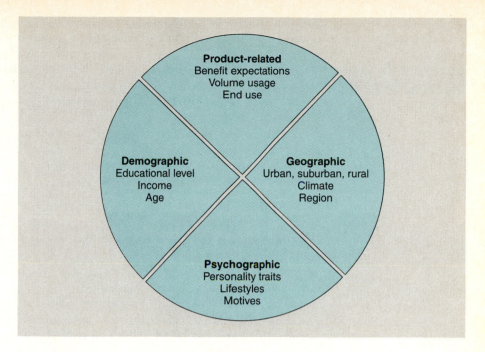

all of it. As Exhibit 14.6 shows, entrepreneurs may segment their markets by any one of four ways:

▶ Product-related

▶ Geographic

▶ Psychographic

▶ Demographic

Product-Related Factors   Some markets may best be divided according to the benefits that customers expect from a product. For example, one group of like-minded customers may be looking for a camera that takes reasonably good photographs, is easy to operate, and is inexpensive. Another group may want top quality photographs and may be willing to pay a higher price.

Other product-related ways to segment markets include volume usage and end use. *Volume segmentation* is based on the amount of product or service purchased. An entrepreneur may want to target marketing efforts toward the heavy user. Owners of professional baseball teams do this when they offer preferred seating as well as preferred parking to season ticketholders. *End-use segmentation,* on the other hand, is based on how customers use a product. For instance, to satisfy customers who use a product in a certain way, entrepreneurs may have to design some feature—say shape or size—that makes the product safer or easier to use.

Geographic Factors   Such geographic factors as terrain, climate, population density, and natural resources are also the basis for segmentation. Entrepreneurs may divide markets into regions because some geographic or cultural factor causes customers to differ from one region to another, as in this example:

Franchisors like Little Caesars and Domino's change their pizzas from one region to another because customers' preferences vary by region. Easterners want lots of cheese, Westerners prefer a greater variety of ingredients, and Midwesterners like both. ▲▼▲

Because of its influence on people's product needs, climate is a common geographic-segmentation factor. Air conditioning and heating equipment, building materials, yard equipment and furniture, and sporting goods are just a few examples of markets affected by climate.

Psychographic Factors The three most common psychographic factors used to segment markets are personality traits, motives, and lifestyles. Examples of personality traits are independence, ambitiousness, extroversion, introversion, and introspectiveness. This type of market segmentation works best when a product is similar to competing products and when other segmentation factors do not affect customers' needs significantly.

The easy thing about this kind of segmentation is that no measurement is necessary. All that entrepreneurs need do is select the personality trait valued by many, if not most, people in the target market. Take this example:

Dr Pepper, the soft drink company, found that 30 percent of youths tend to be introspective. Accordingly, the company developed an advertising campaign focusing on that inwardly directed market segment. ▲▼▲

Motives—that is, forces that move people toward goals—also can be used to segment markets. Examples of motives that influence what people purchase are convenience, status, economy, and product durability. When segmenting a market according to motives, entrepreneurs must examine customers' reasons for making a purchase. For example, convenience is one motive for buying power lawnmowers and snow blowers.

Demographic Factors Demographic factors are closely related to customers' product needs and purchasing patterns. Such factors can also be measured readily through observation or surveys. Clothing, diet foods, automobiles, and toys are examples of age-segmented product markets. Exhibit 14.7 shows a possible segmentation scheme for the toy market. Except for the age 12-to-adult segment, the segments reflect relatively short age spans. This is because of the rapidly changing nature of children's needs for, and interest in, certain toys. For example, three-year-olds are not likely to be interested in playing with a toy aimed at one-year-olds.

Income is another obvious way to segment markets, because it defines one's ability to buy and also influences one's lifestyle. Clothing, automobiles, furniture, and food are examples of such markets.

▶ **Taking Action** After identifying and researching their markets, entrepreneurs are poised for the final step in the marketing research process: taking action. They must now

EXHIBIT 14.7
Segmentation of the toy market.

Source: Adapted from William M. Pride and O.C. Ferrell, Marketing (Boston: Houghton Mifflin, 1989), p. 94. Copyright © 1989 Houghton Mifflin Company. Used by permission.

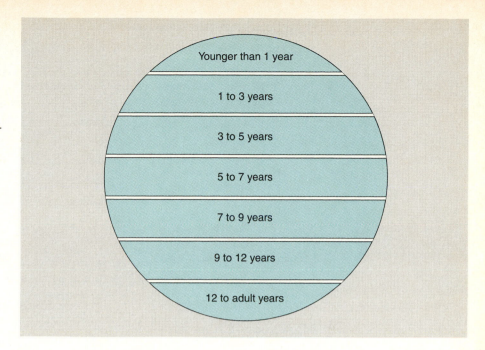

decide how best to create new customers and to keep existing customers. To do this, entrepreneurs must prepare their marketing mix, which, as depicted earlier in Exhibit 14.1, is made up of these tools:

▶ Marketing channels

▶ Pricing

▶ Promotion

▶ Service

The last three tools are covered in the next chapter; we describe marketing channels in the remainder of this chapter. Before doing so, however, let us first end our discussion of marketing research by contrasting it with intuition.

▶ **The Role of Intuition**

So far, our entire discussion of marketing research has ignored the role that intuition may play in making decisions. In fact, there are times when intuition may even be better than an analysis of marketing research data—for example, in applying common sense to solve small problems. But, when financial risks are high, perhaps to the point of threatening survival, entrepreneurs must do marketing research. Turning to Exhibit 14.8, note how sharply marketing research and intuition differ.

This is not to say that intuition lacks legitimacy. On the contrary, it makes good sense for entrepreneurs to blend marketing research with intuition in their decision making. Take this extreme example:

Xerox Corporation carried out a marketing research study that suggested the market for copiers was too small to enter. Xerox managers, however,

EXHIBIT 14.8

How marketing research and intuition differ as marketing decision aids.

Marketing Research Is:		Intuition Is:
Logic	versus	Feeling
Formal planning	versus	Instinct
Documented facts	versus	Memory
Statistics	versus	Experience
Use of computers	versus	Use of pencil and paper
Discipline	versus	Disorder

disbelieved the study and decided intuitively to market the copier anyway. That product was the Xerox 914 copier, which became one of the most successful products ever launched by a business.

Marketing Channels

What is a marketing channel? In essence, a marketing channel is the path that products and services may take as they pass from producers to consumers. Its purpose is to make products or services available to consumers at the right time, at the right place, and at the right quality—and to do so profitably.

As depicted in Exhibit 14.9, producers and consumers are always the beginning and ending points of each channel's path. However, there may be stops along the way that ease a product's passage—managed by wholesalers, retailers, and agents or brokers. What role does each play?

▶ **Wholesalers**   Wholesalers are intermediaries between producers and retailers. The popular view of wholesalers as those who sell at large discounts is untrue. Rather, wholesalers buy products from producers and then resell them to retailers.

As a product passes from producers to wholesalers and then to retailers, it does not change. The product's value, however, is enhanced by the wholesaler's services, among them offering credit and making the product available at convenient locations. An example is the wholesaler who stores a farmer's fruit and vegetables for resale to a wider market of grocers than the farmer alone could reach efficiently.

▶ **Retailers**   Like wholesalers, retailers are resellers. They buy a product from either wholesalers or producers and then resell it, unchanged, to ultimate consumers. For products like toothpaste and razors, for instance, ultimate consumers would be individuals who buy for either personal or household use.

Retailers, in turn, add value to products by offering services to customers, such as personal attention, a wide selection, and credit. An

EXHIBIT 14.9

Marketing channels available for products. Channels E, F, G, and H also apply to not-for-profit organizations.

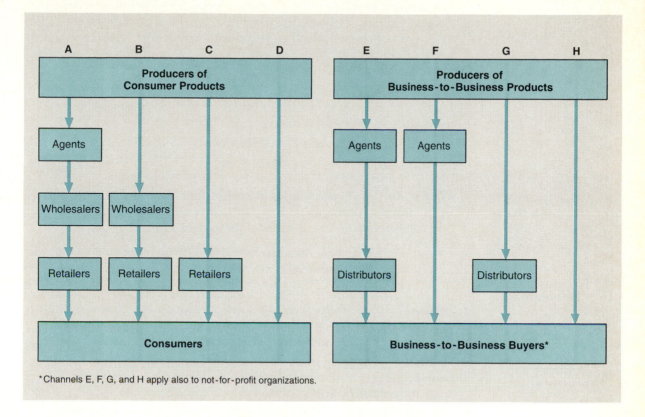

*Channels E, F, G, and H apply also to not-for-profit organizations.

example is a department store that sells a host of products, ranging from encyclopedias to sweaters to personal computers.

Note in Exhibit 14.9 that, for business-to-business products, distributors serve customers in the very same way that retailers serve theirs.

▶ **Agents or Brokers**   These intermediaries differ from wholesalers and retailers in that they do not take title to a product—that is, they never assume ownership. Rather, their overriding purpose is to bring buyers and sellers together.

Agents differ from brokers in that they work exclusively for the producer, in essence serving as the producer's sales force, although independently of the producer. One example is the agent who represents a small computer manufacturer in, say, a sprawling urban center.

In contrast, brokers do not work exclusively for one seller. Rather, they serve solely to bring buyers and sellers together. Real estate firms are one example of brokers.

Marketing Channels for Products: A Description

Let us now discuss briefly when entrepreneurs may best use a particular marketing channel, using Exhibit 14.9 as our guide:

▶ **Channel A**   This long channel—through which product flows from producers to agents to wholesalers to retailers and finally to consumers—lends itself to producers who want to introduce a new product or to enter a new market. Rather than hiring their own sales force, producers engage the services of an agent to call on wholesalers.

▶ **Channel B**   Here, producers are likely to use wholesalers if they are too small to sell directly to retailers. Retailers might also be too small to make direct sales an inexpensive option.

▶ **Channel C**   In this channel, producers bypass wholesalers and sell directly to retailers. In general, this channel works best if producers can field their own sales force and if retailers can buy in generous amounts.

▶ **Channel D**   Often called *direct marketing,* this channel enables producers to sell directly to consumers. To do this, producers use one of three methods: company-owned retail stores, door-to-door sales, or catalogs.

Channels A through D cover products that ultimately are sold to individuals, for either personal or household use. In contrast, Channels E through H, as depicted in Exhibit 14.9, cover products that ultimately are sold to businesses:

▶ **Channel E**   As with consumer products, producers are likely to use this channel to introduce a new product or to enter a new market. Producers may also use this channel if their customers buy in small amounts.

▶ **Channel F**   This channel appeals most to those producers who lack their own marketing effort but need marketing information, or who are too small to field their own sales force.

▶ **Channel G**   This channel is generally the choice of producers who aim their products at many customers. Examples include producers of building materials and office supplies.

▶ **Channel H**   This channel lends itself to producers of expensive equipment, such as aircraft and mainframe computers, which often require technical backup. Customers are more likely to receive the help they need in a direct channel like this one.

Marketing Channels for Services: A Description

So far, our discussion of marketing channels has dealt wholly with product flow. Looking next at services, we find that their marketing channels differ markedly from those for products.

The major point of difference is that most services are delivered directly to customers at precisely the time they are consumed. Turning to Exhibit 14.10, note that there are but three marketing channels, of which the most common is Channel K. Examples include professional and personal services as well as airlines and motels.

As suggested in the exhibit, services may also be sold through agents or brokers. Customers, for example, may buy airline and motel reservations through

EXHIBIT 14.10
Marketing channels available
for services. Channels I, J,
and K also apply to not-for-
profit organizations.

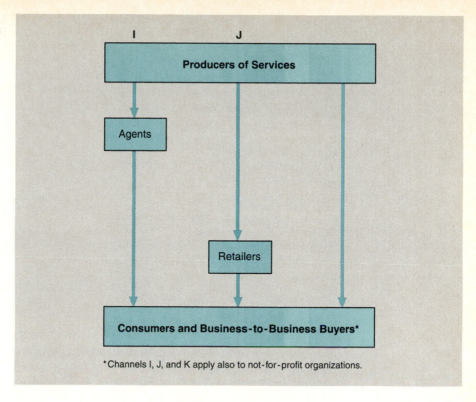

*Channels I, J, and K apply also to not-for-profit organizations.

travel agents, who may in turn double as enhancers of the value of the service by finding, say, the right tour abroad.

SUMMARY

The purpose of marketing is to move products and services out of the hands of entrepreneurs and into those of customers. To do this, entrepreneurs may choose from a wide spectrum of tools, each of which reinforces the others:

▶ Marketing research
▶ Marketing channels
▶ Pricing
▶ Promotion
▶ Service

Marketing research—the collecting, recording, and interpreting of information about a specific market—is, perhaps, the most important of these tools because it helps satisfy the never-ending need for knowledge about markets:

▶ What products or services to sell
▶ Where to sell them, in what quantities, and at what prices
▶ What competitors are selling, where they are, and how strong they are

The marketing research process is logical and straightforward. It has four basic steps:

1. Defining the need for facts
2. Finding facts
3. Analyzing facts
4. Taking action

The third step, analyzing facts, is used to determine which market segments should be targeted. *Market segmentation* is the division of markets into groups of customers with similar needs for either a product or a service. Entrepreneurs can segment their markets in any one of four ways:

▶ Product-related

▶ Geographic

▶ Psychographic

▶ Demographic

Although the information collected through marketing research is critical, intuition also plays a role in making marketing decisions. Of course, marketing research and intuition differ in many ways. Marketing research has to do with logic, formal planning, documented facts, statistics, use of computers, and discipline; intuition is more feeling, instinct, memory, experience, use of pencil and paper, and disorder.

Marketing research is just one marketing tool. Marketing channels are groups of organizations or individuals who direct the flow of products or services from producers to customers. The purpose of marketing channels is to make products or services available at the right time, at the right place, and at the right quality—and to do so efficiently. For products, the major intermediaries include the following:

▶ Wholesalers, who buy products from producers and then resell them to retailers

▶ Retailers, who buy products from either wholesalers or producers and then resell them to ultimate customers

▶ Agents or brokers, who bring buyers and sellers together

Most services are delivered directly from the producer to the consumer or business buyer, although one channel does make use of agents and another uses retailers.

Discussion and Review Questions

1. What is the purpose of marketing? Give an example of its use by a local entrepreneur.
2. Why is marketing research so vital a marketing tool?
3. What are some of the uses of marketing research?
4. Explain briefly the steps in the marketing research process.

5. What resources are available to entrepreneurs who need to find facts about their market but do not have the funds to hire a marketing research firm?

6. What are the advantages and disadvantages of these survey methods: one-on-one interviews, telephone surveys, and mail surveys?

7. Why is market segmentation so vital?

8. What are the most common psychographic factors used to segment markets? Give at least two examples.

9. How do entrepreneurs use demographic factors to segment their markets? Give at least two examples.

10. What are the differences between marketing research and intuition in solving marketing problems?

11. What is the purpose of marketing channels?

12. How do wholesalers differ from retailers and agents and brokers? Give an example.

13. How do the marketing channels for services differ from those for products? Give an example.

14. A small manufacturer of portable swimming pools has the problem of choosing her marketing channel. What are her alternatives? Which alternative would you recommend she pursue? Why?

15. Define these terms: *marketing*, *marketing research*, *random sample*, *market segmentation*, *product-related factors*, *intuition*, *agents*.

Building a Business Plan

Marketing Research and Marketing Channels

The old adage "build a better mousetrap and the world will beat a path to your door" simply does not apply to most entrepreneurs that own and operate small businesses. Today entrepreneurs know that the key to making their business a success is marketing.

What Is Marketing?

The text defines *marketing* as "the effort to identify and satisfy customer's needs and wants." Because the marketing concept is a business philosophy, anyone can say, "I believe in it." But to make it work, entrepreneurs must fully adopt and then implement it.

How Important Is Marketing Research?

Marketing research is the collecting, recording, and interpreting of information about a specific market. It answers questions that include:

▶ What products or services to sell

▶ Where to sell them, in what quantities, and at what prices

▶ What competitors are selling at what prices

Once marketing research is completed, it is the entrepreneur's job to anticipate, to adjust to, and to capitalize on the sweeping changes that mark our times.

Instructions for Worksheet 14

The purpose of this part of the business plan is to help you match the product and service that you sell with the customer you are trying to reach. To complete this part of the business plan, you must describe the type of products or services that you want to sell in part 1. Then in part 2, identify the potential customer and market for your product or service.

Part 1—What Products or Services Should I Sell?

Before answering the questions in this section, you may want to review the definition for your business that was last revised in Chapter 12.

1. In your own words, describe the type of products or services that you want to sell.

2. Is there anything unique about your product or service that stands out when compared to the competition?

Part 2—Who Is My Customer?

Once you have identified the products or services that you are going to sell, you must identify your target market. The target market for your business is a group of persons, businesses, or both that have the ability, willingness, and authority to purchase your product or service.

3. Describe the customer(s) for your product or service.

4. Based on your answer to question 3, how big is the total market for your product or service in your geographic area?

5. Briefly describe your competitors— other businesses that sell this same type of product or service.

6. How much of the total market do competitors already have?

7. How much of the total market can you expect to obtain within a reasonable period of time?

8. Are there any other factors that will affect the market for your product or service in the next five years?

Karabinus & Associates, Inc.

Last year, Karabinus & Associates, a photographic studio, had sales revenues of $88,100 and before-tax profits of $13,450. Its founder and president, Joseph Karabinus, was not happy with this performance. "I've been in business for myself now for six years, and I should be doing a lot better. What should bother me—and doesn't—is that I could be earning much more with less work and risk by working for somebody else—in fact, at least twice as much. I'm really good at what I do."

Background

Now 40 years old, Karabinus first became an entrepreneur when he was just 13. Entirely on his own initiative, he established a photographic studio in the basement of his parents' home. "I had a habit I couldn't afford," says Karabinus, "so I began selling my services to students. I charged them a nickel for each wallet-sized photograph. My dad, though, didn't like the idea of my becoming a photographer; he wanted me to be an electrical engineer.

"So I worked around him by appealing to my mom. She was so softhearted that she let me buy a $200 press camera. Believe me, 27 years ago, that was a lot of money to spend on a 13-year-old upstart like me. Somehow my dad never found out how much it cost. Good thing, too, because he was a strict disciplinarian, a patriarch from the old school, and he would have hit the ceiling."

Earning top grades in high school, Karabinus decided to further his education. He chose a university that had an undergraduate program in photography. "My mind was made up to become a professional photographer, in every sense of the word *professional*," he says. He graduated in the top third of his class, earning a bachelor of fine arts degree with a major in photography.

Momentarily Sidetracked

Soon after graduation, Karabinus married his high school sweetheart and began raising a family. Although he yearned to establish his own studio, Karabinus was convinced "it would be sheer madness to starve charmingly while I was struggling to make it as a professional photographer."

So he went to work for an aerospace company, Thompson-Ramo-Wooldridge, Inc. (TRW). "I never thought I'd ever work for a corporation that big," says Karabinus. Indeed, TRW is one of the top 100 corporations in the country, with sales of more than $7 billion a year. TRW had hired him to work in its industrial photography department.

Karabinus stayed there for 12 years. "It seemed like an eternity," he says. "The work was mundane. True, I was doing what I like best, taking photographs, but the psychic satisfaction just wasn't there. . . . It was annoying to work for bosses whose standards were so much lower than mine. The pay was good, but I just couldn't stand it."

Finally Breaking Away

Against the advice of his family, Karabinus quit his job with TRW. "When I told my boss that I was quitting, he told me how sorry he was to see me leave. I reminded him that I had done the same kind of photographic work for 12 years. Just think, I had one year's experience 12 times over. That's not growth. Then my boss reminded me that TRW had once laid off everybody else in my department but me. That's how much the company thought of me and my work.

"To go it alone, I knew my family had to support my decision completely, without compromise.

They did, eventually, although at first they tried hard to discourage me from striking out on my own. But after 12 years of leading a compromised life, there was no alternative for me. They saw that it was now or never for me."

In Business for Himself

When he opened his doors for business, Karabinus was so cash poor that he had to borrow all his startup costs—$6,000 at 13 percent interest. "It was a five-year signature loan," says Karabinus. "I didn't even have to mortgage my house. I'm sure the bank was impressed by my ability to earn money—if I really had to—to pay off the loan. They trusted me." His beginning balance sheet appears in Exhibit 14A.1.

He had two other problems besides financing: where best to locate and how best to organize legally. After talking with a friend of his who was also an entrepreneur, Karabinus decided to locate in the basement of his home until "my sales volume justified my moving away to larger quarters." He also decided to form a sole proprietorship because "it's a lot simpler than forming a corporation."

With $3,600 worth of camera equipment in his basement, Karabinus was fully equipped to satisfy customers in need of photographic services. "Of course, I never told prospective clients that my studio was next to the washer in my basement," he says. "If I had, they would have labeled me an amateur. Believe me, image is important."

Defining His Business

Indeed, for the first few months he spent almost all his time "beating the bushes," explaining his photographic services. He soon found that his experience at TRW worked against him. "There all I did was industrial photography," says Karabinus. "When prospective clients asked me what experience I had, they questioned my ability to do photographic art rather than straight industrial stuff." His goal was "to create photographic art for clients who do creative work"—advertising agencies, public relations firms, and architectural design firms.

Karabinus was bent on "creating photographic art rather than simply taking photographs. I wanted to do unusually creative things for clients, translating their words into visual images that evoke feelings. In a real sense, I saw myself as an interpreter, an artistic interpreter at that."

After six months of being on his own, Karabinus had landed just one client, an architect friend of his who needed photographs of several ice rinks that he had designed. His income from that one job was $753.10. "It's a good thing my wife was working," says Karabinus, "or I would have been on the bread line or out driving a taxi at night. A big part of my problem was that I knew nothing about business. I

EXHIBIT 14A.1

Karabinus & Associates, Inc.: Beginning balance sheet.

Assets		Equities	
Cash	$1,400	Accounts payable	$ 500
Photographic supplies	1,100	Long-term loan	6,000
Camera equipment	3,600	Owner's equity	0
Office equipment	300		
Other	100		
Total assets	$6,500	Total equities	$6,500

never took a single course in small business management when I was in college."

Turnaround

A professor friend of his recommended that he enroll in a small business program at a local college. He did so, taking all six courses devoted to small business management. "That helped a lot," says Karabinus. "The case studies really opened my eyes, gave me direction."

One of the things he learned was the value of having a "thought-through marketing strategy. I had my priorities all wrong. I never sat down and figured out how best to attract clients." When he finally did, he came up with this strategy:

▸ Spending one-third of his time finding new clients, mostly by visiting them sight unseen and armed with a sample portfolio of his best photographic art

▸ Updating his list of existing and prospective clients each quarter, focusing on architectural firms and advertising agencies, public relations firms, and downtown retail stores

▸ Offering clients a broader range of services by forming an informal partnership with someone knowledgeable in advertising

▸ Projecting an image of professionalism by incorporating the business and moving into spacious quarters downtown

▸ Guaranteeing his performance, offering to do a job over if he failed to satisfy a client's needs

The strategy seemed to work. Two years later, in 1986, revenues increased from almost zero to $28,760; and in 1987, revenues tripled to $86,960. "I thought I was on my way," says Karabinus. "But since 1985, my sales have been on a roller coaster ride.

▸ Revenues and profits since 1986 are graphed in Exhibit 14A.2.

▸ Condensed income statements appear in Exhibit 14A.3.

▸ A detailed income statement for 1990 appears in Exhibit 14A.4.

EXHIBIT 14A.2
Karabinus & Associates, Inc.: Sales revenues and profits by year (1986–1990).

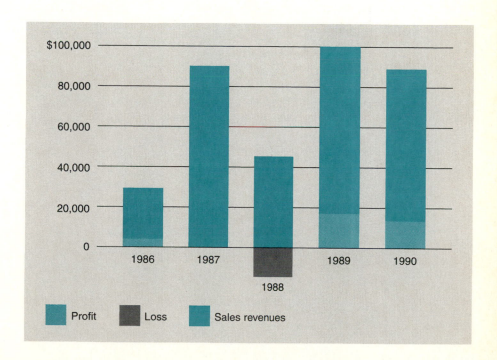

EXHIBIT 14A.3

Karabinus & Associates, Inc.: Condensed income statements (1986–1990).

	1986	1987	1988	1989	1990
Sales revenues	$28,760	$86,960	$ 45,360	$99,400	$88,100
Cost of sales	17,140	41,210	18,930	41,200	32,620
Gross profit	$11,620	$45,750	$ 26,430	$58,200	$55,480
Operating expenses	9,430	45,400	41,650	40,480	42,030
Operating profit	$ 2,190	$ 350	$(15,220)	$17,720	$13,450

EXHIBIT 14A.4

Karabinus & Associates, Inc.: Detailed income statement (1990).

Sales revenues		
Laboratory services	$30,260	
Advertising	28,820	
Commercial	15,130	
Industrial	5,510	
Materials	2,290	
Architectural	1,830	
Miscellaneous	4,260	$88,100
Cost of sales		32,620
Gross profit		$55,480
Operating expenses		
Salaries and benefits	$11,760	
Supplies	7,190	
Rent	6,610	
Maintenance	3,750	
Travel and entertainment	3,330	
Interest	3,190	
Professional services	2,260	
Utilities	1,790	
Insurance	1,120	
Dues and seminars	840	
Licenses	150	
Advertising	40	
Depreciation	0	42,030
Operating profit		$13,450

Problem Analysis

Karabinus is not sure why his "sales curve hasn't kept moving onward and upward. I'm doing all the things my professors told me to do. One thing I remember came from my small business professor. He kept stressing the importance of finding a niche in the marketplace, offering clients what your competitors aren't. That's why I guarantee performance on a no-questions-asked basis.

"In an industry like mine, competition is fierce. Everybody thinks he's an expert. Anybody with a $199 camera can set up shop and call himself a professional photographer. It's these amateurs who muddy the waters. Most people don't realize the years it takes to be a true professional." See Exhibit 14A.5 for samples of the quality of Karabinus's work.

One avenue that Karabinus pursued recently is an "informal partnership" with an advertising agency

EXHIBIT 14A.5
Karabinus & Associates, Inc.: Examples of Karabinus's work.

run by Jeffrey Wershing. The agency is now located in a corner of the same suite of rooms that Karabinus occupies.

"Working with Jeff is an ideal arrangement," says Karabinus. "I've expanded my market. I can now say to a prospective client that if you want an advertising brochure done, I can do the *whole* thing for you—the photographic art, the layout, the written word, everything. Believe me, the advertising industry can be lucrative; its potential is limitless. For example, a competing photographer working for an advertising agency recently shot two rolls of 35-mm film. He charged the agency $9,000 for just a half hour of shooting. After deducting the cost of the model and the set, his income was $4,000. Setup time, however, took a week.

"Other photographers I know in town get as much, if not more. But it takes time to get yourself established. Now that I'm in partnership with an advertising agency, I'm sure that I'll land more clients, especially those willing and able to pay $9,000 for just a half hour of shooting." See Exhibit 14A.6 for a description of a typical job.

EXHIBIT 14A.6

Karabinus & Associates, Inc.: Description of a typical photographic assignment.

A typical job begins with a client's seeking out a photographer, either with a layout in hand specifying the photographs to be taken or with an idea in mind. In essence, the client looks for a photographer who can contribute creatively to the client's concept. Karabinus describes one job below.

The job called for a fashion spread to be shot on location. My client's art director already had a location chosen but wanted to confer with me before going ahead.

The location was a small, private museum-to-be, not yet ready to be opened to the public. It had fire engines, old cars, farm buildings, a general store, and workshop stocked with antiques.

The next step was to select the live models and set the date. Because of conflicts in scheduling, my client and I chose to shoot the job on a weekend.

The amount of preparation is awesome on a shoot like this. Everything that might be needed must be packed and brought with you. Everything from coffeepots and lunch meat to clothespins and masking tape. For this particular job, we even brought an auxiliary power unit to run the strobes so we could shoot at night in the woods.

We started at 8:00 A.M. and got back about 11:00 P.M. About six hours were spent actually taking pictures. I then processed the film and made contact proof sheets.

Next came the long process of selecting the best photographs. Then I sized the photographs to fit the proportions of the layout that my client and I had worked on jointly, and the advertising copy was set in the selected typeface.

Last, on the client's approval, I sent the layout to the engraver for separations. Color keys were pulled for another approval, and the final run was made. All told, 100,000 copies of the layout were printed.

The Need for Improvement

In another recent change, Karabinus hired Chrissie Spuhler. She runs the receptionist's desk, keeps the books, and keeps after slow-paying customers. "I hired her because she's a self-starter," says Karabinus. "She doesn't have to be told what to do. I'm away so much, I need somebody to watch the shop."

Although his books are now up to date, Karabinus rarely looks at them. "I'm just too busy getting jobs, then getting them done," he says. He vows to "change my attitude and do some hard planning. I should have a budget but I keep putting it off. If my old professor ever saw how I run my little business, he would have cardiac arrest."

Questions

1. Comment on Joseph Karabinus's entrepreneurial and managerial qualities.
2. What questions would you raise after analyzing Karabinus's financial statements?
3. Comment on the quality of Karabinus's marketing research and his marketing plan.
4. Would you invest in Karabinus's venture? Why or why not?
5. If Karabinus came to you for advice on how best to boost sales, what would you suggest he do now? Why?

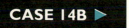

Shakey's Pizza

After the game, teams in Santa Monica's adult softball league head to the local Shakey's pizza parlor. A dozen watering holes near the playing fields offer food, drink, and a place to relive the game. But at their local Shakey's, the players can catch an instant replay of themselves on videotape, just like the big leagues.

It appears that the culture of narcissism has come to the pizza business. Videotaping local events like softball games, kids' soccer games, even community fashion shows is the newest wrinkle for pizza chains, which over the years have resorted to all kinds of gimmicks—big-screen TVs, videogame machines, large pipe organs, singing robots—to bring customers through the doors.

According to Dave Heiss, western marketing manager at Shakey's, 25 of the company's 180 western franchises have begun videotaping local events, with "more franchise holders jumping off the fence."

The Solution to a Problem

It all started when franchisee Mary Sunderlage invested in videocamera equipment to help overcome a poor location. Her Shakey's franchise is hidden in an industrial complex 3½ miles from the nearest residential area in San Diego. Here brisk business during the lunch hour was fading to a trickle at night.

The cost of the equipment was high, but Sunderlage kept her total costs in line by hiring six telecommunications students from the University of San Diego as her videotape crew. Eager for experience, they work for just $5.00 an hour. Has it worked? Videos gave residents in the community a reason to drive the 3½ miles, and Sunderlage's dinner business has doubled. Now Sunderlage wants to pay a subcontractor to do the videos so that she can concentrate again on making pizzas.

Harold Veum, a Shakey's franchise owner in fast-growing Sunnymead, attributes 30 percent of his business to videotaping everything from basketball games at a nearby army base to weddings. Veum calculates that an average videotape party brings in $200 in sales and costs less than $50 to produce after the initial equipment costs.

this form of entertainment developed a new market segment in fast-food service for Shakey's?
2. How else might Shakey's develop its new position in the fast-food market in terms of long-range investment in the community?

Questions

1. Assuming that pizza restaurant products are perceived as being much the same, how has

Source: Roger Neal, adapted from "You Oughta Be in Pictures," (May 6, 1985), p. 72. Reprinted by permission of *Forbes* magazine © Forbes, Inc., 1985.

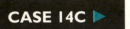 **CASE 14C** ▶ *Woolley Appliance Store*

The Woolley Appliance Store is a locally owned home appliance outlet that has been in business for eighteen years. It is located in Pelham, a town of 20,000 persons. For the last five years, the store's yearly sales revenues have topped $800,000.

Its owner, Sarah Woolley, has controlled the business since she founded it. Recently, she has considered expanding her business by opening a new

outlet in Emmett, a town not far from Pelham. Emmett has a population roughly equivalent to that of Pelham, but does not have an appliance store.

Woolley is eager to enter this new market before someone else does. During the past several months she has been compiling buying power information for the Emmett market. Using the data in Exhibits 14C.1, 14C.2, and 14C.3, she has

---

EXHIBIT 14C.1

Disposable income, savings, and discretionary purchasing power.

Items	Pelham Last Year	Pelham This Year	Emmett Last Year	Emmett This Year
Per capita	$8,180	$7,800	$4,540	$5,250
Personal savings (as percent of disposable income)	6	7	3	4
Discretionary purchasing power (as percent of aggregate consumer purchasing power)	40	45	20	25

EXHIBIT 14C.2

Percent of families in selected income classes (last year).

Income	Pelham	Emmett
Less than $10,000	10	25
$10,000–$15,000	25	35
$15,000–$25,000	30	20
$25,000–$35,000	20	15
More than $35,000	15	5

EXHIBIT 14C.3

Patterns of consumer spending for selected product (as percentage of total consumer expenditures).

Expenditure	Pelham	Emmett
Housing	14.5	13.7
Food for home consumption	16.1	18.2
Household appliances	1.4	0.9
Recreation	6.3	5.5
Clothing	10.3	8.6

compared the buying power of the two markets for last year and this year.

Questions

1. Indicate the relevance of each of the exhibits to Sarah Woolley's decision.
2. What recommendation would you make to Woolley concerning the opening of an appliance store in Emmett? Give specific reasons for your recommendation.
3. What factors other than buying power should Woolley evaluate before making her decision?

Source: Pride, William M. and O.C. Ferrell, *Marketing: Concepts and Strategies,* Second Edition, Copyright © 1980. Used with permission.

CHAPTER 15

Price, Promotion, Service, and Global Marketing

OBJECTIVES

▶ to explain how best to set prices

▶ to discuss the purpose of advertising, publicity, personal selling, and sales promotion

▶ to explain the marketing concept

▶ to discuss the marketing mix

▶ to summarize the opportunities available in, and approaches to, global marketing

There is only one boss—the customer. And he can fire everybody in the company from the chairman on down, simply by spending his money somewhere else.

—Sam Walton

❚ n Chapter 14, we focused on marketing research and its pivotal role as a marketing tool; we also looked at marketing channels. In this chapter, we discuss the other major marketing tools that entrepreneurs may choose from in their quest for ways to *get* and *keep* customers:

▶ Price

▶ Promotion

▶ Service

We begin by discussing how entrepreneurs might go about pricing their products or services, equating price with value. We then discuss in some detail such familiar promotional tools as:

▶ Advertising

▶ Publicity

▶ Personal selling

▶ Sales promotion

To live up to the marketing concept, which holds that marketing begins and ends with the customer, entrepreneurs must reach out to their employees as well as their customers. This service aspect of the entrepreneur's marketing effort is covered next.

This chapter also discusses the marketing mix, which calls for the blending of marketing research and marketing channels as well as pricing, promotion, and service in ways that are likely to create satisfied customers at a profit.

Global marketing is the last subject covered. Here, we focus on how entrepreneurs may look to global markets as new ground for expansion.

Price

In today's sophisticated society, what counts highly is perception of value. The question is, Am I getting the best value for my money? The answer hinges largely on price, especially its influence on how customers perceive product quality, and ultimately, its value. For example:

> For computer software, customers generally believe that a low price means low quality. But, for home appliances, customers generally equate a high price with high quality.

Thus, it behooves entrepreneurs to offer their customers value they cannot get elsewhere *and* to convince them that they would, indeed, be better off with this product. By doing so, entrepreneurs would also avoid falling into the trap of setting prices that are:

▸ Too high, because customers may then believe they have been misled, or even cheated

▸ Too low, because customers may then question the quality they got, since they generally equate a low price with low quality—a perception that may be false

▸ **Pricing Methods**   Entrepreneurs and other businesspersons are perhaps more mysterious about pricing than about any other aspect of their ventures. Few reveal how they go about setting prices. Often, setting a price poses no problem—especially if an entrepreneur's product is identical to that of competitors. For, no rational customer will pay a higher price than she knows is being charged elsewhere for a product that she regards as identical. Here, entrepreneurs have little choice but to follow their competitors—and work to keep costs below prices.

Pricing Formula   How are prices computed? Entrepreneurs generally need more than the simple arithmetic of costs and profits to set prices. The easiest formula to use is this one:

$$\text{Price} = \text{costs} + \text{profit}$$

But this simple formula is flawed. Why? Because costs and profit depend on sales volume, which in turn depends on price—among other factors. For example, a manufacturer with idle plant capacity and a growing market may temporarily cut prices to boost sales:

Saddled with excess capacity, a small manufacturer of nitrogen fertilizer reduced its price to $72 a ton, from $80, for a limited time only—in the hope of boosting profits. The manufacturer had reasoned that, at $72 a ton, the added sales would still be profitable because out-of-pocket costs to make fertilizer were just $50 a ton—though, of course, profits would be less on a per-ton basis. ▲▼▲

Let us now look at some questions that entrepreneurs ask before setting prices:

▶ How unique is my product or service? Is it different enough to command a premium price?

▶ How will my choice of a marketing channel influence price? What is the industry practice on prices, credit terms, and volume discounts?

▶ How will competitors react to my price? Will they cut prices? Improve old products? Increase service?

▶ What market conditions will influence my price? What role do inflation and federal taxes play? How does the rate of technological change affect the price?

▶ Are there any laws that may influence my price?

Pricing for Manufacturers   When manufacturers introduce a new product, setting a price is anything but simple. Entrepreneurs tend to charge as much as the market will bear—and so they should—because often it is the promise of high profits on their innovations that encourages them to risk money on research. This pricing practice is called *skimming*. It generally works well if:

▶ Customers are insensitive to price, because they believe the new product outperforms rival products by a wide margin.

▶ The cost of developing a new product is high, and the product may become obsolete in a short time.

▶ An entrepreneur's patent position on the product is strong.

Another pricing practice for new products is called *penetration pricing*. With this practice, entrepreneurs set a low initial price in an effort to capture customers quickly. It generally works well if:

▶ Customers are sensitive to the price of a new product. This means a lower price would boost sales to levels higher than they would be with a higher price.

▶ A low price is likely to discourage competitors from entering the market.

Price skimming was common, for example, among the first manufacturers of microwave ovens and personal computers. Penetration pricing, on the other hand, was common among the first manufacturers of digital watches and hand-held calculators. Both pricing practices, however, push toward the very same goal—namely, to optimize profits:

▶ With price skimming, by charging a *high* price for low sales volume

▶ With penetration pricing, by charging a *low* price for high sales volume

Clearly, setting a price for new products is complex. But for old, or mature, products, entrepreneurs generally have no pricing decision to make, charging the same price as competitors—unless they offer customers a special service, such as overnight delivery, that commands a higher price.

Pricing for Wholesalers and Retailers   Wholesalers and retailers commonly use a pricing method called *markup pricing*. *Markup* is simply the difference between the selling price and the purchase cost:

$$\text{Markup} = \text{selling price} - \text{purchase cost}$$

Markups vary widely, depending on the product. For instance, average markups may be as high as 100 percent or more for perfumes, or as low as 20 percent for books of fiction. Markups may be calculated either as a percentage of the selling price or as a percentage of the purchase cost. The formulas are:

$$\text{Markup percentage on selling price} = \frac{\$ \text{ markup}}{\$ \text{ retail price}} \times 100$$

$$\text{Markup percentage on purchase cost} = \frac{\$ \text{ markup}}{\$ \text{ purchase cost}} \times 100$$

Here is an example of how a retailer applies markup percentages in order to set prices:

EXAMPLE ▶

An entrepreneur runs a small shop selling office machines in a suburban shopping center. In anticipation of the spring selling season, she has just purchased a line of electronic typewriters for $91 each. She would like a 30 percent markup on the selling price, as suggested by the wholesaler. At what price should she sell the typewriters?

The entrepreneur sets her price using this formula:

$$\text{Selling price} = \frac{\text{purchase cost}}{100\% - \% \text{ markup on retail}} \times 100$$

$$= \frac{\$91}{100\% - 30\%} \times 100$$

$$= \underline{\underline{\$130}}$$

She would price her new line of electronic typewriters at $129.95 each (just below the $130 figure). ▲▼▲

Turning to Exhibit 15.1, note how markups may combine to set prices for a product as it passes through a familiar marketing channel:

▶ After markup, the manufacturer's price becomes the wholesaler's cost; and in turn—

▶ After markup, the wholesaler's price becomes the retailer's cost; and in turn—

▶ After markup, the retailer's price becomes the consumer's cost

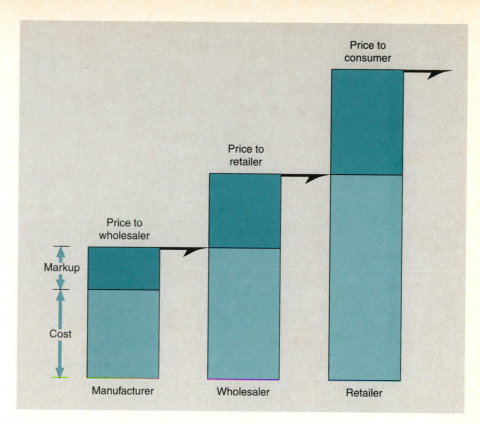

Note, too, the larger markups later in the marketing channel. These reflect the likelihood that, as a product passes closer to the ultimate consumer, entrepreneurs would sell smaller amounts of product and would also be more attentive to customer needs.

Pricing for Services   Unlike products, services are intangible, which makes it difficult to price them. An appliance repair shop, for instance, might price the repair of certain items—stove thermostats, refrigerator motors, and so on—based on the list prices of those items. Or the price might be based on labor plus parts. In addition, a price might be charged for analyzing the problem, another for actual repair work, and still another for travel time. Further, the chief repair person's work might be deemed to be worth more than that of assistants or apprentices.

How do lawyers, physicians, and other professionals price their services? Some charge a standard fee—for example, $500 for a physical examination or $1,000 for a divorce. Others, like certified public accountants and computer software consultants, charge by the hour.

Promotion

It is not enough simply to offer customers a product or a service. They must also be made well informed and, at the same time, be influenced to buy. This is

EXHIBIT 15.2
Major tools of the
promotion mix.

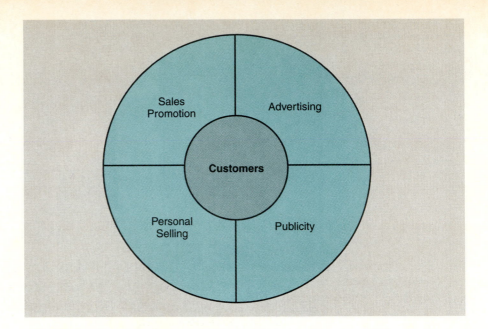

the purpose of promotion, which, as depicted in Exhibit 15.2, makes use of these four major marketing tools:

▶ Advertising
▶ Publicity
▶ Personal selling
▶ Sales promotion

▶ **Advertising**

Of the promotion mix's four tools, advertising generally forms the centerpiece of the entrepreneur's efforts to reach customers and to influence them to buy. It may be defined as the impersonal presentation of a sales-creating message aimed at customers targeted by the entrepreneur. As such, advertising has four purposes:

▶ To make customers aware of an entrepreneur's product or service
▶ To inform customers of the product's benefits or value
▶ To influence customers by underscoring the product's benefits through the use of imagery or testimonials
▶ To keep the product visible

The Advertising Message   To reach their customers, entrepreneurs may choose from a broad variety of messages, which for a retailer may take any one of several forms, among them:

▶ A two-column, 5-inch advertisement in a local newspaper, describing a particular product. The advertisement might also dramatize the ideas that surround the product—ideas designed to lead customers to think well of

All over the country, small businesses are using information technology once available only to large businesses to reach their markets.

Guerrilla Marketing On-Line

The Entrepreneur's Guide to Earning Profits on the Internet

Written by <u>Jay Conrad Levinson and Charles Rubin</u>

More than 30 million people use the Internet today, and that number is growing exponentially. The Internet is without question the greatest new marketplace. Jay Conrad Levinson's best-selling Guerrilla Marketing series has established him as the leading strategist for small-business marketing success. Charles Rubin is the author of many computer books, including The Little Book of Computer Wisdom. Now, in straightforward, step-by-step chapters, they show small and medium-size businesses how to profit from the Internet.

Guerrilla Marketing On-Line not only orients readers to the Internet by demonstrating how to apply Jay Levinson's proven marketing tactics to this frontier, it also unveils new weapons for launching attacks and promoting businesses electronically. In this definitive, A-to-Z guide, readers learn everything from the practical use of software to the unfamiliar culture of the Internet.

* <u>REVIEWS</u> * <u>LEARN MORE</u> * <u>TO BUY...</u> *

Title: Guerrilla Marketing On-Line: The Entrepreneur's Guide to Earning Profits on the Internet
Imprint: Houghton Mifflin
Available: Now
Category: Business & Economics, Computers
Pages: 320
Size: 6 x 9
ISBN: 0-395-72859-2 **Price:** $12.95 **Format:** Paper

[<u>Up</u> | <u>Nonfiction</u> | <u>Bookstore</u> | <u>HMCo</u> | <u>Feedback</u>]

the entrepreneur's venture, by making it clear that it is an honest venture to buy from and publicizing its role in bettering the community's quality of life. In this way, a venture can build a good reputation for itself among customers and suppliers, investors and the media.

▸ Multicolored posters splashed across storefronts heralding the specials of the day

▸ Thirty-second spots on television or radio telling customers why they should buy a certain product

▸ Neon signs flashing above a building, inviting customers to stop in for a look at the latest products

Few entrepreneurs can afford not to advertise. At the same time, few can afford to spend a million dollars for 60 seconds of prime time on national television. To make every dollar count, entrepreneurs must plan carefully, taking pains to:

▸ Offer the desired message

▸ Reach customers a sufficient number of times

▸ Earn a return on the advertising dollars spent

These goals are easy to set down on paper. Measuring progress, however, is extremely hard. Even giant corporations with multimillion-dollar advertising budgets find it hard to measure how well their advertising messages get across.

Still, entrepreneurs should keep these goals in mind when mapping their advertising campaigns, always striving to deliver the right message to the right audience at the right time.

But many entrepreneurs do not plan. For example, during a recession, some drop advertising in the mistaken belief that it is an unnecessary cost. Or, some advertise only when a media salesperson drops in with an attractive deal. Astute entrepreneurs, however, plan their advertising, consciously deciding on messages and media.

Planning Advertising Expenditures Advertising expenditures must be tied to goals. For example, suppose an entrepreneur introduces a new line of products for the youth market. Her sales goal may be $200,000 the first year. How much should she spend on advertising to reach that goal?

She should make this decision only after answering two other questions:

▶ What should my advertising message be?

▶ What media should I use?

Preparing the Advertising Message Before writing a message, the entrepreneur must study her market, estimating its size, income, age, and so on. Only by digging out such information can she prepare messages that appeal directly to the intended audience.

Note that getting the answers is really doing marketing research. Without the facts, the advertising message is likely to misfire. While writing it, the entrepreneur must put herself in the customer's shoes and ask several questions:

▶ What is unique about my product?

▶ What can it do for customers that competing products cannot? Will it save them money? Will it last longer? Is it of better quality?

▶ How can I convince customers that my product is better?

Selecting Media Because few entrepreneurs are advertising experts, it behooves them to work with advertising agencies. Agencies can be especially helpful in mapping out advertising campaigns. They are also adept at preparing messages of professional quality for newspaper or magazine advertisements and for radio or television commercials.

Advertising agencies also are qualified to recommend what media entrepreneurs should use to get their messages across. Media account for about 90 percent of advertising costs, so entrepreneurs can ill afford to pick the wrong medium. Advertising agencies can help decide among such media as the following:

▶ Radio or television

▶ Newspapers or magazines

▶ Handbills or direct mail

▶ Yellow Pages or outdoor signs

Turning to Exhibit 15.3, note the shares of the advertising dollar captured by selected media. Newspapers are the most popular medium, followed closely by television and direct mail.

EXHIBIT 15.3

Comparison of selected media in advertising expenditures.

Source: U.S. Department of Commerce, *Statistical Abstract of the United States* (Washington, D.C.: U.S. Government Printing Office, 1995), p. 584.

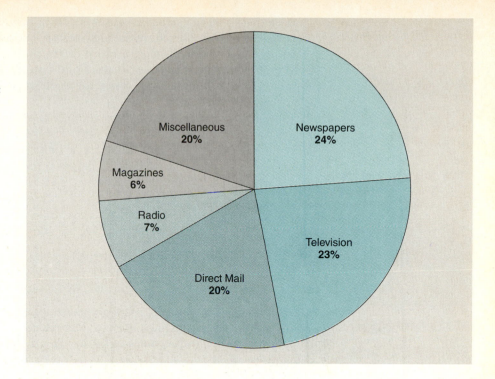

Miscellaneous 20%

Newspapers 24%

Magazines 6%

Radio 7%

Television 23%

Direct Mail 20%

▶ Publicity

Unlike advertising, *publicity* is an unpaid message about a venture or its products sent through a mass medium. Often overlooked by entrepreneurs, publicity can be a vital marketing tool. Its purpose is to attract attention to the venture and its products without paying media costs. For example, book publishers often place their authors on television and radio talk shows. Why? Because their very appearance is likely to spark interest—and book sales—without costing the publisher a single penny.

The news release is the most common form of publicity. It normally runs no longer than a single page of typewritten copy, or fewer than 400 words. Other forms of publicity include the captioned photograph, used to show a new or better product; and the press conference, used to announce a major news event.

▶ Personal Selling

Personal selling takes over where advertising leaves off. Advertising coaxes the customer to buy; it stimulates interest. Because advertising rarely closes the sale, entrepreneurs must also rely on personal selling—that is, meeting customers face to face to help them make up their minds.

Interaction Between Advertising and Personal Selling   Because one goal is to create loyal customers, entrepreneurs should strike the right balance between advertising and personal selling. To put it another way, they must decide how best to mesh their pull strategy with their push strategy. *Pull strategy* impels (pulls) customers to ask for the product; *push strategy* compels (pushes) them to buy it.

For example, say a customer is looking for a new, low-priced, two-door automobile. An advertisement in the local newspaper catches her eye. A dealer is offering a $400 rebate on the purchase of any automobile of a certain low-priced model. Her interest whetted, the customer decides to visit the dealer's showroom. This is pull strategy, since the dealer's advertisement stimulated the customer to take a look.

As the customer steps into the showroom, a salesperson offers to show her the new models and answer any questions. The salesperson reminds her that the $400 rebate is offered for a limited time only, so the customer should act quickly. Two days later, she decides to buy—in part because the salesperson was knowledgeable, helpful, and courteous. This is push strategy.

Note how these two strategies reinforce each other. Without advertising, the customer might not have set foot in the dealer's showroom; and without personal selling, the dealer might not have sold the customer an automobile.

The Personal Selling Process   Although no two selling situations are precisely alike, salespersons generally rely on the seven-step process shown in Exhibit 15.4. A brief explanation of each step follows:

▶ **Prospecting**   This first step relies on marketing research to suggest which potential customers are most likely to buy the product. Salespersons then home in on only prospects who appear to be willing and financially able to buy the product.

▶ **Approaching customers**   Because first impressions are vital, the salesperson makes every effort to discover the customer's needs and how the product can meet those needs.

▶ **Presenting the product**   In this step, the salesperson underlines the product's benefits to the customer as well as the ways in which it outperforms rival products.

▶ **Demonstrating the product**   This step reinforces the presentation and calls for the salesperson to demonstrate the product's superior qualities. In this step, the prospect may test the product personally.

▶ **Overcoming objections**   Here, the salesperson offers the prospect an opportunity to raise objections or to ask questions, thus giving the salesperson a chance to overcome objections that might block a sale.

▶ **Closing the sale**   This step is the most important as well as the most difficult, chiefly because it calls for the salesperson to sense when the prospect is clearly ready to buy. Thus, the salesperson must learn how best to recognize telltale signals from the prospect, including not only questions but also body language.

▶ **Following through**   This last step requires the salesperson to follow through on the order to make sure that the product is delivered on time, in the right quantity, and of the right quality. Equally vital, the salesperson must assure customers that she will respond instantly if and when problems arise after delivery of the product. Such single-minded attentiveness can only breed a lasting loyalty that all but ensures customer retention.

EXHIBIT 15.4
Personal selling process.

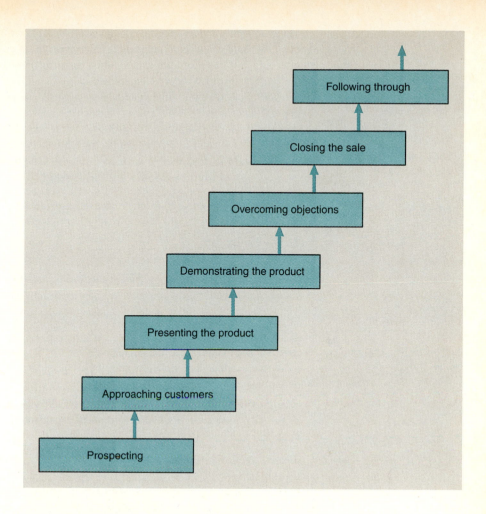

Finding the Right Salespersons   Personal selling varies in importance by industry. In retailing, for example, personal selling is indispensable. Salespersons give a store its personality; they help mold its image; and they help keep its customers from going elsewhere.

To build a nucleus of loyal customers, entrepreneurs must find the right salespersons. As suggested in Chapter 10, hiring methods include recruiting at schools, placing direct newspaper advertisements, and engaging an employment agency that specializes in placing salespersons. But before pursuing these methods, entrepreneurs must first decide:

▶ What the salespersons are expected to do
▶ What their salary and fringe benefits will be
▶ What their prospects for promotion are

In industries other than retailing, the requirements for salespersons vary widely. In manufacturing, for instance, a salesperson is usually a highly educated expert in the field. Sales engineers, for example, not only sell lathes to machine shops; as technical experts, they may also train their customers' machinists on how to run and care for the lathes. And, they may even help design lathes that better satisfy their customers' special needs.

Similarly, salespersons in wholesaling must be deeply knowledgeable about their products. Salespersons for a hardware supplier, for example, may sell to hardware retailers as many as 10,000 different items made by dozens of manufacturers. They must know all the items and their strengths and weaknesses, so they can help satisfy their customers' needs. On top of that, they must keep their customers posted on supply and price trends.

▶ Sales Promotion

Though not as visible as the other major marketing tools, sales promotion is no less important, especially in its role as handmaiden to advertising and personal selling. Both likely would fall short of their goals without the support of sales promotion and its variety of smaller tools, among them:

- ▶ Coupons to stimulate sales. Highly popular, this familiar promotion encourages retailer support as well as customer loyalty.

- ▶ Point-of-purchase displays that invite customers to try a product for the first time.

- ▶ Rebates that urge customers to buy now, not later. Here, the motive might be to stop a drop in sales—as might be the desire of a retail automobile dealer just after the holidays, in January.

- ▶ Contests to spur salespersons to sell more. For example, an automobile dealership may offer its top salesperson a two-week, all-expenses-paid vacation in Hawaii.

- ▶ Special price discounts to sell slow-moving inventory. For example, automobile dealers often offer discounts to sell slow-moving inventories just before the new models arrive from the manufacturer in early fall.

- ▶ Free samples to introduce a new product. For example, cosmetics manufacturers often give away tubes of a new face lotion at shopping centers.

- ▶ Piggyback premiums to introduce a new product. In this promotion, an unrelated item is attached to a product. For example, a manufacturer may attach plastic flowers to boxes of detergent.

- ▶ Exhibitions to build up a product's image. For example, a manufacturer may rent a booth at a trade show to demonstrate a product to potential customers.

Let us now see how one entrepreneur uses sales promotion to solve a summer problem:

EXAMPLE ▶ Each summer Richard Bennett, a Cleveland clothier, has offered customers $25 off on a new, tailor-made suit for each old suit they bring in. This promotion has worked so well that sales during the normally slack summer months of July and August almost match sales during May and June, the traditional peak months for the sale of suits. ▲▼▲

Service

In the marketplace, it often takes being different to be better than competitors. One way for entrepreneurs to give their competitiveness a finer edge is to pursue the ideal of total customer satisfaction by adopting the marketing concept.

The essence of the *marketing concept* may be captured in several ways. First, it is customer-oriented. This means all marketing thought begins and ends with the pursuit of total customer satisfaction, as practiced by these two entrepreneurs, both of whom were featured in 1996 by the magazine *Co-op America Quarterly:*

▶ **Jody Wright and Prakesh Laufer, Entrepreneurs**

When Jody Wright and Prakesh Laufer bought their home-based business in 1984, they thought it would be a "perfect little company," ideal for their young family. By 1993, their venture, named Motherware, was on *Inc.* magazine's list of the nation's 500 fastest growing small businesses. The company that designs, manufactures, and sells clothing for nursing mothers soon outgrew the family's basement and in 1996 employed a staff of 40 persons at business offices where more than 10,000 requests for mail order catalogs pour in each month.

Guided by their ideals, Wright and Laufer successfully wove principles and profits at Motherwear. Wright says that truly believing in what they were doing created the momentum that led to business fame and national acclaim. Matching their mission with a product, a social vision with a business plan, and an environmental agenda with their daily work—that was their formula.

Wright and Laufer take pride in developing Motherwear as a model business. Company innovations include allocating 6 percent of profits to nonprofit organizations, employing an environmental coordinator, and providing up to $60 a week for childcare expenses.

Now that Motherwear is growing up, Wright and Laufer aim to make their company more independent by encouraging workers to play a larger role. Weekly open-book financial sessions and training are broadening the scope; so will the Employee Stock Ownership Plan that Motherwear has planned.

Once Motherwear "leaves the nest," Wright plans to focus more on the values that brought Motherwear into the world in the first place. "I want to do more writing and speaking about breastfeeding," she says. Her aim—to increase the breastfeeding rate in America.[1]

▶ **Everyone's Responsibility**

As the previous example makes clear, it is the marketing concept that carries a venture. Only if entrepreneurs and employees alike embrace the marketing concept so wholeheartedly that it becomes routine may total customer satisfaction take shape—as depicted in Exhibit 15.5.

In short, it is everyone's responsibility to help make the marketing concept work. In all of this, of course, the entrepreneur's behavior is key. The entrepreneur must be willing to spend time and money to tailor the marketing concept to the precise needs of customers and employees.

This is not to say, however, that the marketing concept can be put into practice painlessly. It may look good on paper, but breathing life into it can be

EXHIBIT 15.5
The service connection to customer satisfaction.

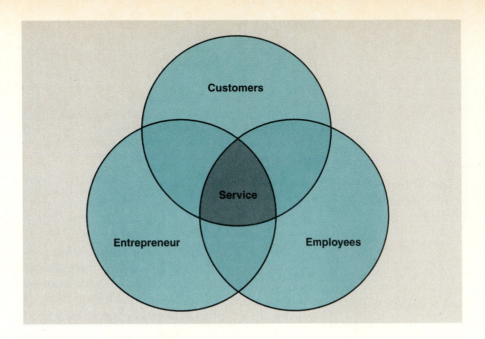

another matter. In fact, it behooves entrepreneurs to plan their venture's marketing concept from the very beginning, before they prepare a marketing mix, which we now discuss.

Preparing a Marketing Mix

After learning what it takes to create customers and to commit themselves to the marketing concept, entrepreneurs are ready to prepare the marketing mix. Its tools, or ingredients, are those we discussed before:

▶ Marketing research
▶ Marketing channels
▶ Price
▶ Promotion
▶ Service

Used either singly or in any combination, these ingredients must be blended in ways that enable entrepreneurs to get and keep customers at a profit. As a management consultant graphically put it:

> The entrepreneur, as the marketing man, is a kind of cook who is continually experimenting with new blends and new kinds of ingredients. He hopes ultimately to come out with the ideal combination that will produce the highest amount of sales at the lowest practical cost. In a sense, he is balancing a number of variables in which the contribution of each element to the total result is often extremely difficult to measure.[2]

The marketing mix varies widely from industry to industry. Even within an industry, it may vary among competitors. And it may also vary over the life of a venture. Take this example:

EXAMPLE ▶

Just before launching a sporting goods store, an entrepreneur places a three-column advertisement in the local newspaper heralding the store's opening. He also hires a model to pass out circulars in front of the store for three days before the opening. So his pre-opening marketing mix consists of advertising and sales promotion.

Once the entrepreneur opens the store, however, advertising is cut back and personal selling becomes the main ingredient in his marketing mix. Generally, customers are unsure about the sporting goods they want. A salesperson is needed to help customers make up their minds.

After peak selling seasons like early spring, the entrepreneur offers discounts to sell old inventory. At these times, his marketing mix consists of pricing and personal selling, as well as some advertising and sales promotion. ▲▼▲

Thus, the goal is to find a mix that creates satisfied customers at a profit; but entrepreneurs often avoid deciding which ingredients are likely to work best. Why? Because they believe that the marketing mix is the exclusive province of sophisticated giant corporations. Yet, the principle of a marketing mix is simple—and it may even be easier to apply in small ventures than in large ones.

Because marketing is also largely an *attitude* toward goals and their achievement, entrepreneurs must keep their venture market-oriented at all times. Some entrepreneurs tend to take their existing markets for granted. This is a mistake. Although products may seem to remain unchanged from year to year, markets are in fact changing, and it is a delusion to believe otherwise.

Entrepreneurs must also keep in mind that new products are the lifeblood of vigorous ventures. New products exploit changing markets, open new vistas, spark new investment, and charge a venture with excitement and vigor.

Global Marketing

Our discussion of marketing would be incomplete without touching on the vitality of global markets. Entrepreneurs often overlook or ignore these markets. Yet they offer a fertile source of sales opportunities—billions of dollars worth. The reasons that entrepreneurs tend to shun global markets are threefold:

▶ **Fear of the unknown**   Many entrepreneurs believe that their lack of knowledge about global markets is an insurmountable barrier. They reason that it is hard enough doing business locally, where information about markets is at their fingertips, let alone trying to do business abroad, where information may be much less handy.

▶ **Fear of long-distance relationships**   Many entrepreneurs believe that any relationship with a foreign country would be too hard to control. These entrepreneurs may be used to exercising on-the-spot control over local markets. In their view, global markets that are thousands of miles away would be all but impossible to control. They often perceive any such relationship as unstable, untidy, and more than likely to unravel—with unhappiness all around.

▶ **Fear of the complex** Many entrepreneurs believe that the very act of initiating a relationship abroad is too complex even to think about. These entrepreneurs believe that it is beyond them to grasp the complexities of language, legal systems, and money matters that often differ sharply from those at home.

▶ **Using Professional Help**

These fears are real, and no entrepreneur should ignore the risks involved in entering the global marketplace. But these fears may quickly dissolve once entrepreneurs avail themselves of the professional help, much of it free, available from the federal government and chambers of commerce.

For example, the first question an entrepreneur who is considering foreign markets must ask is, "How can I find out if there really is a market for my product or service abroad?" Answers to this question may take just minutes to get by tapping the information stored in a computerized file kept by the U.S. Bureau of International Commerce (BIC), a division of the U.S. Department of Commerce. BIC has information on more than 150,000 foreign importing organizations in all countries. Largely through its computerized file, BIC enables entrepreneurs:

▶ To find agents or distributors in virtually every country of the world.

▶ To get up-to-the-minute sales leads and representation opportunities from overseas. Some business in Hong Kong, for example, could be spotted instantly by an entrepreneur in, say, Miami.

▶ To obtain a detailed profile on an individual foreign company. A typical report would cover background information on the company, kind of organization, years in business, number of employees, size of the company, sales area, method of operation, products handled, names of officers, general reputation in financial circles, and names of the company's trading connections.

Besides these computerized services, BIC also offers the entrepreneur a host of personal services:

▶ **Free counseling** In Washington and other places, BIC offers guidance and in-depth counseling, and schedules appointments with knowledgeable officials in other federal agencies. This one-stop service is designed to give entrepreneurs the most amount of information in the least amount of time.

▶ **Publications** Thousands of government reports and booklets describe sales opportunities available abroad. One example is a survey of the sales opportunities for suppliers of machine tools in Australia, Germany, Mexico, and Sweden. For each country, this report lists the major users of machine tools, along with other vital marketing information, such as which machine tools are the most salable.

▶ **Workshops** The U.S. Department of Commerce also conducts workshops throughout the country on global marketing. And it holds seminars and organizes minicourses, generally in cooperation with local universities or community colleges.

The foregoing describes help available from the federal government. Equally helpful are local chambers of commerce. Many have special departments devoted to helping entrepreneurs sell their products abroad. Like the federal government, they organize trade missions, hold trade shows, and publish brochures on how best to expand into global markets.

Yet, despite governmental and private help, many entrepreneurs fail to consider the sales opportunities available to them abroad; and if they do, they often fail to seek professional help. For example, a U.S. company once launched a frozen food venture in a major country in the Far East before it realized that most homes in the market area did not have freezers. Had the company checked first with the U.S. Department of Commerce, it probably never would have made so costly a mistake.[3]

► Ways to Enter a Global Market

There are many ways for entrepreneurs to enter global markets. In Exhibit 15.6, some of these approaches are depicted, along with estimates of how they differ in degree of investment and control. Here is a brief description of each:

▶ **100 percent ownership**   Total investment in, say, a manufacturing plant abroad represents the strongest commitment that an entrepreneur can make. This kind of investment suggests that a country is politically stable and is open to investment by entrepreneurs from other countries.

▶ **Joint ventures**   This approach makes sense for entrepreneurs who lack the expertise and money to enter a global market. Normally, ownership is shared equally with a local company.

▶ **Licensing**   If entrepreneurs want to avoid the risks of producing and marketing products in another country, and still benefit, they might consider licensing. The danger here is that entrepreneurs risk losing control over product quality.

EXHIBIT 15.6
How various ways to market globally differ in degree of investment and control (on a scale of 1 to 10).

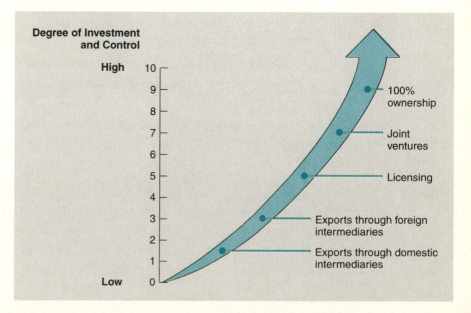

EXHIBIT 15.7
Marketing channels available
for exporting products or
services.

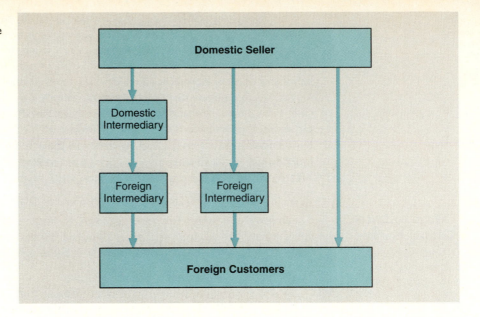

> **Exporting** This is the entrepreneur's most popular method for market entry abroad. It is both the least expensive and the least involved, mostly because responsibility for marketing is left to another company, either domestic or foreign—as depicted in Exhibit 15.7.

▶ **Preparing a Marketing Plan**

To best serve a global market, entrepreneurs must prepare a marketing plan. This plan would rely heavily on marketing research already done by others, mostly by the U.S. Department of Commerce, local chambers of commerce, and the foreign countries themselves.

Only after collecting and analyzing all available information should entrepreneurs prepare a marketing plan, following a procedure much like this one:

▶ Identify the most desirable market for the product or service.

▶ Identify potential buyers within that market.

▶ Prepare a proposal describing the product or service.

▶ Develop terms of sale that will satisfy the foreign buyer while protecting the entrepreneur's best interests.

To prepare the plan, entrepreneurs should seek the help of a lawyer versed in drafting international sales contracts, for example. An experienced lawyer can help describe what an entrepreneur has to offer in plain and concise language, so that the foreign buyer has a clear idea of what the entrepreneur is proposing. The lawyer can also help protect the entrepreneur's best interests when it comes time to negotiate a sales contract with the foreign buyer by determining what kind of contract will minimize risk.

SUMMARY

Because what counts is perception, equating price with value is of primary importance to entrepreneurs. If prices are set too high, customers may believe they are being misled or cheated. If prices are set too low, customers may question the quality of what they are buying. Consequently, it is vital for entrepreneurs to convince customers that they are getting more value for their money.

The purpose of promotion is to inform customers and, at the same time, to influence them to buy. Promotion makes use of four marketing tools:

▶ Advertising

▶ Publicity

▶ Personal selling

▶ Sales Promotion

Advertising serves four purposes:

▶ To make customers aware of the entrepreneur's product or service

▶ To inform customers of the product's benefits or value

▶ To influence customers by underscoring the product's benefits through the use of imagery or testimonials

▶ To keep the product visible

The purpose of publicity is to attract attention to the venture and its products without paying media costs. The purpose of personal selling is to close the sale in a face-to-face meeting with prospective customers. Finally, sales promotion is used to make advertising and personal selling more effective.

There are seven basic steps in the personal selling process:

▶ Prospecting

▶ Approaching customers

▶ Presenting the product

▶ Demonstrating the product

▶ Overcoming objections

▶ Closing the sale

▶ Following through

Marketing research gives entrepreneurs the information they need to make decisions. Marketing channels are the means they use to distribute their product or service. Pricing and advertising are tools entrepreneurs use to encourage customers to buy. But the ultimate success of the marketing effort rests on service, on total customer satisfaction. This is the marketing concept. Without total customer satisfaction, entrepreneurs have no strong customer base on which to build their business. And, although it is everyone's responsibility in the venture to make the marketing concept work, the entrepreneur's behavior is key. The entrepreneur must be willing to spend time and money to tailor the marketing concept to the needs of customers and employees.

The global marketplace offers multibillion-dollar sales opportunities to entrepreneurs who are willing to take the risk of entering that marketplace. Among the ways entrepreneurs enter global markets are:

▸ 100 percent ownership

▸ Joint ventures

▸ Licensing

▸ Exporting, through either foreign intermediaries or domestic intermediaries

Discussion and Review Questions

1. Why must prices match customers' perception of the quality they are getting? Give examples.
2. How do price skimming and penetration pricing differ? Under what conditions is one better than the other?
3. What is the purpose of promotion? Give examples.
4. What are the four objectives of advertising? Give examples.
5. Describe the steps in preparing an advertising message that will stimulate customers to buy.
6. How is publicity different from advertising? Give examples.
7. Why is personal selling so crucial to entrepreneurial success in most industries? Give examples.
8. How do personal selling and advertising interact? Give examples.
9. Describe the personal selling process.
10. How do sales promotion and advertising differ? Give examples.
11. What is the essence of the marketing concept? Explain your answer.
12. Why is the need for total customer satisfaction so important?
13. Compare a manufacturer's marketing mix for products sold to other manufacturers with the mix for products sold through retailers to consumers.
14. How would you, as an entrepreneur, go about exploring sales opportunities globally?
15. Define these terms: *markup, prospecting, push strategy, pull strategy, service, marketing mix, joint venture.*

Price, Promotion, Service, and Global Marketing

As part of the business plan for the last chapter, you were asked to describe the type of products or services that you want to sell in your business. You were also asked to describe the "typical" customer for your products or services. As part of the business plan for this chapter, we examine the issues of pricing, promotion, and service, and how they relate to the products or services that you will sell your customers. Each of these areas—pricing, promotion, and service—requires that you make decisions that are carefully thought out and based on solid marketing research.

Instructions for Worksheet 15

To complete this part of the business plan, you must determine an effective pricing policy for the products or services that you sell in part 1. In part 2, construct an effective promotion mix that can be used to "sell" your products or services. And in part 3, decide on a service policy that creates total customer satisfaction.

Part 1—Pricing Decisions

Before answering the questions in this part, you may want to review the information about the products or services that you included as part of the business plan for Chapter 14.

1. Describe the factors that will influence the prices you will charge customers for your products or services.
2. Will the price that you charge for your products or services cover your cost of goods sold, the cost of operating your business, and provide a reasonable profit?

3. Is your price policy consistent with the prices charged for similar products or services offered by competitors in your geographic area?

Part 2—Promotion Decisions

To tell customers about products or services, business owners must create a promotion mix that includes: (1) advertising, (2) publicity, (3) personal selling, and (4) sales promotion.

4. Based on the information in your text on pages 451 to 458, how can each of the above components be used to promote your products or services?
5. Based on your answer to question 4, which promotion component would do the best job of reaching potential customers?
6. What are the typical costs that small business owners pay for the type of promotion that you chose in question 5?
7. Can you afford to use this type of promotion to advertise your products or services?

Part 3—Service Decisions

As discussed in your text, it often takes being different to be better than competitors. One way that many successful business owners give their businesses a finer edge is to provide above-average service to their customers.

8. How can you use service (sometimes referred to as total customer satisfaction) to differentiate your business from competitors?

It was a Monday morning in September in San Francisco, and Julie Brighton was in her office analyzing recent data regarding consumer buying and behavioral trends in the barbecue industry. According to the Barbecue Industry Association, consumers had spent $4.35 billion in 1992 on all barbecue-related items.

This statistic greatly excited Brighton because Alma Products, Inc., the new venture that she had embarked upon with partner Jim Henly, intended to enter the barbecue market with its newly created charcoal starter. Once the company was realizing a profit, the plan was to gradually diversify, eventually building an entire line of barbecue-related items.

Critical Presentations to Markets

Brighton and Henly would carefully analyze the latest market information, shown in Exhibit 15A.1, before they made a final pricing decision for the company's first two models of a charcoal starter, which the partners had engineered two months previously. Although they had some idea what their competitors were charging for similar items, until now they did not have a clear picture of what the entire barbecue market looked like.

It was now one week before their presentations for next spring's programs to the buyers for both Williams-Sonoma, a mail-order marketer based in San Francisco, and Builders Emporium, a chain of home centers in the Los Angeles metropolitan area. With the new industry and census data in Exhibit 15A.1, the partners finally had as much information as they could get to make pricing decisions.

Brighton and Henly

With a master's degree from Stanford University and ten years' experience in retailing, Julie Brighton was a young businesswoman who had a restless urge for identifying and tackling new business opportunities. She had recently resigned her vice president's position with a leading retailer, where she had led the rapid growth of the retailer's newest division from 9 to 25 stores in just two years.

Jim Henley, who had been a close friend of Brighton since their time together in business school, worked full time as a real estate broker and investor. He thought the two of them together could have some fun and make some money building a business around their simple but ingenious new product.

Like many entrepreneurs, Brighton welcomed the challenges that came with new ventures but was easily bored and disliked the bureaucracy usually associated with running older, larger companies. Hence, she hoped to build Alma Products into a thriving enterprise and then sell it. Brighton knew other entrepreneurs who had been quite successful at this practice.

However, Brighton knew from experience that entering a market with the wrong introductory price could seriously undermine the success of any new product or business. For this reason, she planned on taking the next week to once again review all of the information related to costs, demand, target market, and the competition before coming up with a pricing structure for Alma's first products.

Product Descriptions

Initially, Alma Products planned to market only two products, namely, two models of the Easy Embers Charcoal Starter, identified as ED-12 and ER-12:

▶ The ED-12, with its brightly colored label, was intended for sale through hardware stores, home centers, and discount stores.

EXHIBIT 15A.1

Alma Products, Inc.: Marketing data for the barbecue industry.

Unit Sales: Barbecue Grills

Year	Charcoal	Gas	Electric	Total
1989	8,898,864	3,823,262	133,319	12,855,445
1990	8,661,621	4,002,279	190,809	12,854,709
1991	8,074,623	4,261,181	142,734	12,478,538
1992	7,946,738	4,283,387	155,895	12,386,020

Charcoal Briquette Sales—Tons

Year	Tons	% Change from Prior Year
1988	782,268	3.14
1989	745,317	(4.72)
1990	747,055	0.23
1991	752,699	0.75
1992	789,667	4.91

Selected Barbecue Industry Data

	1981	1991
% of households owning barbecue grills	79	83
% of households owning charcoal grills	73	62
% of households owning gas grills	15	54

Frequency of Barbecue Occasions

Barbecuing among Households Owning Grills, No. of Times/Year	% of Households*
More than 16	20
12–15	45
6–11	25
Less than 6	10

*According to the 1992 Statistical Abstract of the United States, the total number of households in the United States in 1990 was 94,312,000 and the total number of households in California was 10,381,000.

Source: Barbecue Industry Association and Alma Products, Inc.

▶ The ER-12, packed in a sturdy reshippable cardboard box, was intended for sale through mail-order retailers such as L.L. Bean, Williams-Sonoma, and Camper's World.

Shown in Exhibit 15A.2, the charcoal starters were simply metal cylinders, about a foot high and tapered toward the top, with an attached wooden handle and a heat shield. Inside, a metal grate to support the charcoal was located two inches from the bottom.

Instructions for use were quite simple. Two sheets of newspaper were crumpled and stuffed underneath the grate; then the charcoal starter was set inside the barbecue. Charcoal was poured into the top, and the newspaper then lighted from holes along the bottom rim of the device. Once the coals

were hot, they were ready to be dumped into the barbecue.

Brighton's tests showed that the charcoal starter was twice as fast as using lighter fluid, which was the most prevalent method of starting barbecue charcoal. The tapered design concentrated the rising heat around each briquette, allowing an even burn and a hotter fire.

Brighton and Henly had designed the product after observing some campers light charcoal using a crude device made of a three-pound coffee can with holes punched around the bottom.

Operating Costs

Brighton and Henly had negotiated an arrangement with a local metal fabricator, Santa Fe Engineering, to manufacture the Easy Embers in lots of 10,000 units at a cost of $3.00 each, which included all packaging, labor, and materials. Santa Fe was also charging a one-time tooling cost of $10,000 to make the dies with which the metal parts would be stamped.

Furthermore, since Alma did not own a warehouse facility, Santa Fe agreed to ship finished products directly to Alma's customers using shipping labels and packing lists provided by Alma. Brighton estimated that freight charges to ship the products to Alma's customers would average $6.00 per case for small orders, and about $3.00 per case when ten or more cases were shipped. Each case had 12 charcoal starters.

Another variable cost included sales commissions to be paid to a manufacturer's representative agency retained a month ago. Davis & Davis Associates, whose other clients included well-known manufacturers of barbecue grills, had agreed to a 10 percent commission on all sales made to retail stores, and exclusive coverage of retail accounts in California. (The partners planned to obtain commitments from mail-order marketers themselves.)

One of the main reasons for using an agency like Davis & Davis was cost; it would be much cheaper than hiring an internal sales force. Alma would simply pay the commission to the agency, which in turn was responsible for providing the salary, benefits,

EXHIBIT 15A.2
Alma Products, Inc.: Alma's first innovative product.

travel expenses, individual commission, and overhead expenses for each of its salespeople. In addition, Davis & Davis had well-established contacts with the retail buyers in the barbecue industry, contacts that could take years for Alma to form on its own.

Home-based at Startup

Fixed costs associated with running Alma were expected to be minor. Henly, working full-time in the real estate industry, and Brighton, living off consulting income and savings from her career as a retailing executive, had both agreed to forego salaries for the first year of business.

Using Brighton's home as an office for the company would save rent expense; and for now, only a part-time secretary would be needed to help handle orders. Total monthly office expenses, including the telephone and the secretary's salary, were expected to be about $500. Brighton thought that travel and other expenses that would be incurred in selling could be absorbed within this modest budget, at least in the first year.

Target Market

In its first year of business, Alma planned to target several national mail-order retailers, as well as retail stores located in California. Home centers, hardware stores, and mass merchandisers sold the most barbecue grills and would be the best marketing channels for the charcoal starters.

Brighton's knowledge of retailing told her that these chains would require a 40 percent gross margin on an item like Easy Embers. Mail-order margins would probably be higher, in the area of 60 percent.

Competition

In its home state of California, Alma found a few local retailers that sold a similar item, the Adamson QuickFire, for $9.95. However, this item was also new; and the manufacturer, Adamson, Inc., did not appear to have established itself with any large retail chains.

The only stores that carried the QuickFire seemed to be small, individually owned hardware stores. A clerk in one of the small stores told Brighton that the store bought the QuickFires from "some guy from Berkeley." Brighton was able to find no telephone listing for Adamson, Inc., in Berkeley or the surrounding area.

In the mail-order market, Brookstone featured a similar charcoal starter in its catalog for $16.00, and this product had been on the market for at least three years. Brookstone also carried this product, made by an apparently small company in St. Louis, in most of its nationwide retail stores.

Broader competition included manufacturers of electric charcoal starters, which sold for about $5.95 in most stores, and companies marketing charcoal lighter fluid. Lighter fluid sold for about $2.00 in most stores, and contained enough fluid to start 8 to 12 barbecue fires.

Brighton considered it a good sign that two other firms had found the charcoal starter idea a good one, and two direct competitors could hardly be regarded as market saturation. While she knew that others could also enter the market, Brighton felt that large companies, such as those that made charcoal grills, would not bother with a market niche of this size.

The Pricing Decision

Brighton knew that by Friday, she needed to have price lists prepared for both models, the ED-12 for retail stores and the ER-12 for mail-order marketers. She was not yet sure whether a skimming or a penetration pricing strategy made more sense, or even whether she should employ the same strategy for both markets. She did know, however, that her decisions must include her intended prices to the consumer—even though she could not really control the retailers' pricing, nor the prices she would charge the retailers and mail-order companies.

Brighton and Henly had no expectations of making much money their first year in business, but they did want to be certain to at least break even on a cash basis. Henly expected that Brighton would take the lead in the pricing decision, given her retail marketing experience and her understanding of retailer and consumer needs. It was time to get started.

Questions

1. Given the information in the case, how large is the market potential for charcoal starters in California?
2. What share of this potential is Alma Products likely to achieve during the first year?
3. What competitive factors must Alma consider?
4. What are the merits of skimming or penetration pricing strategies for Alma's products?
5. What price should Alma charge for each model, ED-12 and ER-12?

Source: This case was prepared by John W. Mullins and Christina L. Grippi of the University of Denver. Distributed by the Case Research Association. All rights reserved to the authors and the Case Research Association.

CASE 15B ▶ *Roy Olson*

Monaco Brothers is a small men's clothing store boasting a full line of coats and suits, shirts and accessories. Located in a mini-mall, the store caters mostly to young businessmen between the ages of 21 and 35.

One Saturday morning, a newly hired salesperson, Roy Olson, was reading the morning newspaper when a customer sauntered in. Dressed casually in a Harris tweed jacket, gray flannel trousers, and a modest maroon necktie, the customer began looking at the store's rich assortment of neckties. He looked to be "at least 55 years old," more than twice Olson's age.

With newspaper still in hand, Olson reacted quickly and, with eyes fixed on the customer, said, "We're having a great special on ties this week; we've marked all our ties down 25 percent." Bemused, the customer replied, "I see by the price tags that you have; thank you."

In the very next breath, Olson suggested, "That solid black tie would go nicely with your striped shirt." "You're right, I believe it would," replied the customer. When Olson then offered to slip the tie into a bag, the customer countered, "Not yet, please, I'm still looking."

At this time, a younger customer strolled in, wearing an old shirt with pants to match that appeared to have been reserved for painting the garage. Olson abruptly excused himself and left the older customer to wait on the younger prospect.

In Dogged Pursuit

When the younger customer appeared to be "nothing but a looker," Olson retreated to the older customer, who meanwhile had moved to a rack of sports jackets. "We only carry brand names you'll be proud to wear," said Olson. "What's your size— 44 long?"

Wordless, the customer then walked over to the shirt counter. Turning to Olson, who was in pursuit right behind him, the customer said, "I like plain broadcloth, button-down collars, and plain cuffs." Olson then took out a box of Style A shirts of the type the customer liked, as well as a box of Style B shirts, which were like the Style A shirts except for French cuffs and plain collars.

"They're all the same price," said Olson. "All my younger customers prefer the French cuffs." The customer then said, "I'll take one of the Style A, with plain cuffs." "How about one with the French cuffs to go along with it," Olson suggested. "Thank you, no," replied the customer.

Olson then wrapped the shirt, accepted the customer's credit card, and closed by saying, "Come back soon."

Question

1. Comment on Roy Olson's salesmanship. If you had been Olson, what would you have done differently? Why?

CASE 15C ▶ *Topnotch Performer*

For three years, Christine Martinez led the small manufacturer she worked for as a salesperson. She sold protective coatings to businesses in the food, beverage, and pharmaceutical industries. Her sales territory was one of seven targeted by the manufacturer.

Christine's reputation for working hard, imaginatively, and persistently spread throughout the business's sales force. On an average of every three months, her sales manager visited her territory to work with her for a day and then spent a genial hour or two with her over dinner.

But the last time he visited was different, and he was in for a shock. As they talked over coffee, Christine asked, as she had in the past: "Do you have any suggestions for improvement for me?" And her manager responded, as he had often done: "Hey, who am I to tell you how to work? You're succeeding, so why mess around with what works?"

After a short silence, Christine said: "I don't think you know how much you upset me when you say that." He was clearly taken aback. "What do you mean?"

"I know I'm good," she replied, "but I also know I can always do better. I depend on you to help me do better, and you don't help me."

Upon returning to his office, the sales manager shrugged as he told his colleagues: "Christine's a bit eccentric. What are you going to do?" The typical response was: "Put up with it. She's a topnotch performer."

Myths in Sales Management

Chances are that Christine's manager had too readily accepted some prevailing myths in sales management. One is that topnotch performers are loners—they have their own ways of working; and their drives are so strong that they do not need much attention and encouragement from outside. Another myth is that their self-confidence is so firmly rooted that they do not welcome help from their managers.

Aside from not being true, these myths can result in decreased productivity. Although there is often great urgency to help lesser performers become more profitable for the business, the reality that Christine's manager overlooks is that a small effort by him to help her can realize a much greater increase in productivity than a big investment of time and energy working with a lesser performer. For example, an improvement of 5 percent on $200,000 results in more sales than an improvement of 10 percent on a base of $80,000.

Questions

1. Should topnotch sales performers be treated differently from those less productive? Explain.
2. What benefits might the sales manager gain by working closely with Christine?
3. What recommendations would you make to the sales manager to generate even better results from topnotch performers like Christine? Explain.

Source: Adapted from Thomas L. Quick, "Help Your Star Performers Shine Even Brighter," *Sales & Marketing Management* (April 1991), p. 96.

Information Technology

The purpose of a computer is insight, not computation.

—Anonymous

Today's businesses, large and small alike, are witnessing an evolutionary force that is literally reshaping our world with dizzying speed, especially in the fusion of computer and information technology. In the words of the *Scientific American*:

The forces of innovation that are transforming our society, our economy, and our culture have swept beyond the laboratory and the specialized communities that the technologies originally served and are propelling us fast-forward into the future.[1]

This chapter focuses on the power and promise of information technology from the viewpoint of the entrepreneur, beginning with a discussion of the nature of information. We then take up some basics about computers and how entrepreneurs may benefit from their use. Next we look at how best to select a computer system. And finally, we discuss the new world of the Internet.

Information

Information reaches into virtually every nook and cranny of human endeavor. No one can escape its influence, let alone the need—more so with each passing day. Defined by the *American Heritage Dictionary* as "knowledge derived from study, experience, or instruction," information is not just facts and figures. Much more importantly, information is knowledge that endows us with insight and enlightenment.

As such, information comes in a rich variety of forms—among them, speech and music, tax returns and textbooks, balance sheets and income statements. To pass along such information, there emerged an equally rich variety of user-friendly avenues of access, ranging in complexity from the telegraph to the cellular phone, from the radio to interactive television, and from the pony express to overnight delivery. Note how these avenues of access—often called communication schemes—enable people receiving information to act in a timelier, or more productive, way.

Computers first came into being, both in government and in business, to further boost productivity. Thus, computers may best be viewed as both stretching and humanizing the roles played by communication schemes such as those mentioned above—for example:

▸ Computers can accept, store, and work logically with information, much as humans often do in their daily lives.

▸ Computers can also share information freely with one another, much as humans often do with each other.

▸ Taking Charge of Change

Without question, information technology is a priceless resource, one of which entrepreneurs must take advantage. Many fail to do so, mostly because its very dynamism invites discomfort, if not frustration. Turning to Exhibit 16.1, note the main frustrations experienced by entrepreneurs, according to a survey by *Inc.* magazine. Illustrative are these comments by frustrated entrepreneurs:

▸ I don't have a clue what to do about this thing called information technology. I don't know what's going on, and I'm too small to hire a techie. When I talk to techies about computers, I just nod my head and hope I don't show my ignorance.[2]

▸ You bet it scares me! I know I need the technology, but it's way over my head. How do I measure the value of information technology against what it would cost me?[3]

Clearly, such entrepreneurs see changes in information technology coming at them at a pace far faster than they believe they can absorb. As waves of change wash over one another, change sets its own pace, so much so that entrepreneurs who fail to take charge are likely to flounder. Yet, there is nothing about information technology that makes it any harder to grasp than, say, marketing or finance.

EXHIBIT 16.1
Results of survey on what frustrates entrepreneurs the most in making technology-investment decisions.

Source: "The Payoff Spots" and "The Inhibitors" from the *Inc. Technology Fax Poll Results,* 1995, No. 2, p. 78. Adapted with permission, Inc. Technology 1995. Copyright © 1995 by Goldhirsh Group, Inc., 38 Commercial Wharf, Boston, MA 02110.

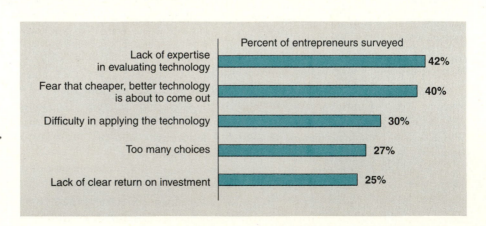

Percent of entrepreneurs surveyed

Lack of expertise in evaluating technology	42%
Fear that cheaper, better technology is about to come out	40%
Difficulty in applying the technology	30%
Too many choices	27%
Lack of clear return on investment	25%

Computer Basics

As recently as 1946, computers were invented. At the time, computers were so bulky—10 feet tall and 30 tons—that they filled entire rooms. But with the invention of the transistor and later the wafer-thin integrated circuit, computers have become progressively smaller and ingenious, yet more powerful and less expensive—so much so that virtually every business, regardless of size or complexity, lends itself to being computerized.

In essence, computers are machines capable of taking in information and then working that information into a form useful to the entrepreneur. Thanks to their ingenuity and power, today's computers boast a number of dramatic advantages over the entrepreneur. For instance, computers:

▸ Are lightning-fast, capable of clocking more than a billion operations per second

▸ Defy complexity, being capable of performing feats of logic denied the brain

▸ Have vast memories with total recall, capable of storing more than a billion pieces of information

▸ Are impartial, capable of making decisions without bias and without bending facts and figures to build a case

Thus, computers possess an all but infinite capacity to help entrepreneurs to think better in their efforts to make wise decisions. Even so, computers are really simpletons, serving at the beck and call of the entrepreneur. As such, they have no recourse but to follow orders to the letter, which the entrepreneur must take pains to put into simple language understood by the computer—as discussed later in the chapter.

▸ **Types of Computers**

There are three basic types of computers: mainframes, minicomputers, and microcomputers.

▸ **Mainframes**   Mainframe computers are not only the largest computers but also the fastest. They are multiuser computers, which means that they serve many users and perform many functions. Their large size—and high cost—limits their use to government agencies and giant corporations.

▸ **Minicomputers**   A smaller, desk-sized version of the mainframe computer, the minicomputer is used for operations that are too small for mainframes and too broad or specialized for microcomputers. Minicomputers are popular in mid-sized companies or within divisions of larger companies.

▸ **Microcomputers**   Commonly known as personal computers (PCs), microcomputers usually fit comfortably on a desktop; some may even be held on the entrepreneur's lap—hence the terms *desktop* and *laptop* PCs. Also available are *notebook* PCs, weighing but a few pounds and measuring an inch in thickness and covering the area of a letter-size sheet of paper

Though the least powerful of the three types of computers, PCs in 1996 still pack more power than did the largest mainframe computers in 1990—

a tribute to business's seemingly insatiable thirst for new and better computer products. Moreover, PCs now fall within the financial reach of virtually every entrepreneur, some costing less than $1,500.

In this chapter, when we talk about computers, we generally means PCs.

▶ Computer Hardware

Every computer consists of a basic set of physical components, known as *hardware*:

- ▶ The central processing unit (CPU), really the heart of the computer, which processes data
- ▶ An input unit, often a keyboard, on which the user enters data to be processed
- ▶ Primary (short-term) memory, which is built into the computer and which temporarily stores programs and data
- ▶ External storage (secondary or long-term memory), such as a floppy or hard disk for permanent storage of programs and data
- ▶ An output unit, such as a screen or a printer, for reporting results

▶ Computer Software

Software is the term used for computer programs, which give the computer its instructions. Using a computer language such as C++ or VisualBASIC, computer programmers write a set of instructions that tell the computer how to do certain tasks.

Although large corporations hire full-time computer programmers to write programs specific to their needs, many ready-made software packages geared to small businesses are available at reasonable cost. We discuss software applications later in this chapter.

Let us now look at how computers can help businesses, specifically small businesses.

Computers and Small Business

To make good use of computers, entrepreneurs must become computer literate. This may sound intimidating because people tend to equate computer literacy with knowledge of electronics. The two are only distantly related, however. In fact, knowledge of electronics is as unnecessary to using a computer productively as knowledge of fiction writing is to using the English language intelligibly.

▶ Benefits of Computer Use

As suggested earlier, the best reason to install a computer system is that it means good business. Among the benefits are improved productivity. In the words of the National Federation of Independent Business:

> Productivity means getting more output with less input. Some people like to call it "working smarter, not harder." Increasing productivity is absolutely necessary if a small business, or any business for that matter, is to remain competitive. . . .
>
> One way to increase productivity is to introduce new and more efficient equipment and machinery. Small-business owners do that all the time. A comparatively new type of equipment is the computer.

EXHIBIT 16.2

Results of survey on which areas entrepreneurs believe technology will benefit them the most.

Source: "The Payoff Spots" and "The Inhibitors" from the *Inc. Technology Fax Poll Results*, 1995, No. 2, p. 78. Adapted with permission, Inc. Technology 1995. Copyright © 1995 by Goldhirsh Group, Inc., 38 Commercial Wharf, Boston, MA 02110.

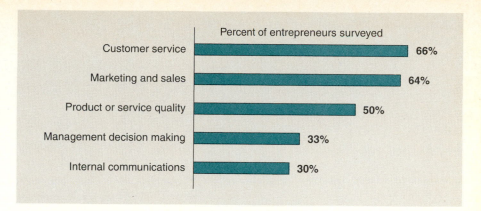

Small-business people who own computers generally consider them a valuable tool. While owners suggest many important benefits from computer use, almost all of these benefits relate either directly or indirectly to productivity increases.[4]

Because it improves productivity, the computer streamlines the flow of work and thus reduces labor costs. Hours upon hours of work may be eliminated if, say, order processing and invoicing are done by computer rather than by hand. If a customer calls to ask what happened to an order, someone can check the computer files rather than leafing through stacks of old invoices.

Turning to Exhibit 16.2, note the areas that entrepreneurs believe information technology will benefit them the most. Heading the list is customer service, followed closely by marketing and sales, according to the *Inc.* magazine survey cited earlier. Take this example:

EXAMPLE ▶

A small construction company called Buildco . . . competes against several other companies for building contracts. To prepare a bid for a contract, the owner must estimate the labor, materials, and time required to complete a project. The company with the lowest bid will win the contract, but if the bid is too low, the company that does the work will lose money.

Buildco installed a computer to do the calculations and print the reports needed to prepare a bid. A computer can act like a fast adding machine, but it can also function as a more general information machine. Buildco started using the computer to estimate what competitors would bid on new construction projects. The company collected data from past projects and past estimates by competitors and stored this data in the computer.

The computer's logical capability enabled it to find patterns in the other contractors' bids. For example, one company always bid very high on tall buildings, perhaps because it did not own a crane. Such information helped Buildco to win more contracts and earn greater profits. As the company grew, it found the computer more and more useful, especially in planning and managing projects. The complexity of construction work requires that supplies and subcontractors be scheduled well ahead of time but be available at just the right time. With its computer system, Buildco was able to schedule work much more precisely, increase its control over inventory, and reduce wasted time and resources.[5] ▲▼▲

EXHIBIT 16.3

Test to measure computer resistance.

Instructions: How well do the following statements describe you? Circle one number for each item, total your score, and check the key.

	Not at all						**Very much**

1. I have no desire to use a computer.

1–2–3–4–5–6–7

2. I don't trust computers.

1–2–3–4–5–6–7

3. I'm too old to learn how to use a computer.

1–2–3–4–5–6–7

4. I can't think of anything I would use a computer for.

1–2–3–4–5–6–7

5. Computers are too complicated for me.

1–2–3–4–5–6–7

6. The technical terms computer people use tend to intimidate me.

1–2–3–4–5–6–7

7. I'm not good enough with mathematics to be able to program a computer.

1–2–3–4–5–6–7

8. I don't know how to type, so I can't use a computer.

1–2–3–4–5–6–7

9. I'm afraid to buy a computer because new technology will soon make it obsolete.

1–2–3–4–5–6–7

10. Computers are too expensive.

1–2–3–4–5–6–7

Key

Total score = ___

10–29 = Low computer resistance
30–50 = Moderate computer resistance
51–70 = High computer resistance

Note: See interpretations on page 494.

Source: Adapted from Robert Kreitner, Barry L. Reece, and James P. O'Grady, *Business,* 2d ed. (Boston: Houghton Mifflin, 1990), p. 486. Used with permission.

Entrepreneurs have too much at stake to resist or ignore the computer's endless potential. To measure your computer resistance, take the test in Exhibit 16.3. Answer interpretations are provided on page 494.

▶ **Software Applications for Small Businesses**

Computers can help or hinder a small business depending on how they are utilized and on how adequately the entrepreneur and employees are trained. Planning a business's computerization is tantamount to success, and knowing which software to use is a critical part of that effort.

Advances in technology have made it easier and more productive for today's entrepreneurs to utilize information technology. The evolution of personal computers and the software that controls them has enabled more entrepreneurs to take advantage of technology through the use of a graphic user interface (GUI). A GUI is an interface that enables you to choose commands, start programs, and see lists of files and other options by selecting from windows, icons, and menus on the screen. GUIs are easier for most people to learn to use than command-driven interfaces, which require the user to learn commands and remember the correct command syntax for the software.[6] The GUI, and its more intuitive approach to problem solving, provides the entrepreneur the means to garner information from business events to make better decisions.

Most functions of a small business can be made more efficient and less costly through the appropriate use of technology. Some examples include accounting for business transactions, analyses of business trends, internal and external written communication, monitoring company records, and management of company projects. We now look in some detail at software applications from which small businesses could benefit.

Accounting Systems Every small business needs to capture and record its business events in an accounting system. Chapter 11 illustrated the need for and importance of keeping accurate accounting information. In this section, we explore the computerization of the accounting system.

Computerized accounting systems for small businesses are inexpensive and far more user-friendly than their predecessors. Most are based on the standard accounting model using debits and credits, journal entries, and ledgers, and require extensive accounting training and understanding. More recent accounting applications for small businesses have abandoned the traditional accounting model and based themselves on a business's source documents: the sales invoice, the purchase order, the purchase invoice, and the employee time card to name a few.

Intuit Corporation's QuickBooks software is one example of this advance in technology and business orientation to accounting. For less than $200, this accounting software will enable the entrepreneur to manage the accounting information generated by the business with much more ease and flexibility.

QuickBooks creates financial statements, like the one shown in Exhibit 16.4, with the click of a button. In this example, the Rock Castle Construction Company operations from July 1 through December 15 are available for analysis and review. A graph of income and expense is available for the same time period, which highlights the proportional cost of each job.

Entrepreneurs enter sales transactions into QuickBooks by generating invoices for services rendered or for products sold on-line. In other words, the sale is recorded one time: when the invoice is created. No additional journal or accounting entries are required.

Entrepreneurs may initiate inventory purchase transactions with purchase orders in an on-line fashion as well. Goods ordered are entered into a purchase order in QuickBooks, which is then printed and mailed to the vendor. When the goods are received, QuickBooks is updated via a receiving report, and the accounting records reflect a new balance in inventory and the corresponding liability to the vendor is recorded.

QuickBooks also tracks accounts receivable, inventory, and accounts payable on a transaction-by-transaction basis. In other words, entrepreneurs do not need to wait to the end of the month to keep an eye on the business. The entrepreneur is always aware of any large, unpaid, and potentially uncollectable customer balances; of inventory levels for reordering and sales commitments; and of vendor balances that are coming due.

Spreadsheets Spreadsheets are another indispensable tool for the entrepreneur. The standard spreadsheet design aligns data into columns and rows. Formulas are then written to establish relationships between the data provided.

EXHIBIT 16.4

Profit-and-loss report produced in QuickBooks.

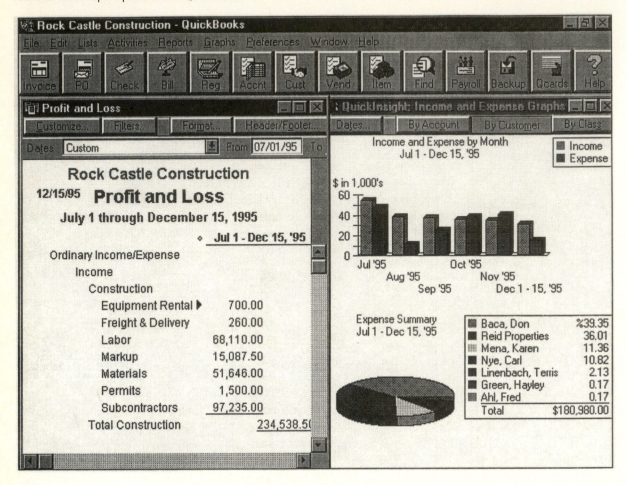

In a simple cash budget, for instance, the anticipated cash collections would include cash sales for the period as well as collection on the previous customer accounts receivable. If the entrepreneur expected 80 percent of the previous balance to be collected, a formula multiplying 80 percent by the previous receivable would be needed. Once created, entrepreneurs could use this spreadsheet for future periods where new data would be provided but the established relationships would continue.

The most recent versions of the spreadsheet design far exceed the basic matrix layouts of old. Powerful automated features such as Microsoft's wizards and built-in templates enable entrepreneurs to utilize the spreadsheet as an effective analytical tool without the advanced training required in the past.

One useful template, available in Microsoft's Excel for Windows 95 and shown in Exhibit 16.5, is the business planner. Advanced Windows features

EXHIBIT 16.5

The business planner template available in Microsoft's Excel for Windows 95™.
(Screen shots reprinted with permission from Microsoft Corporation.)

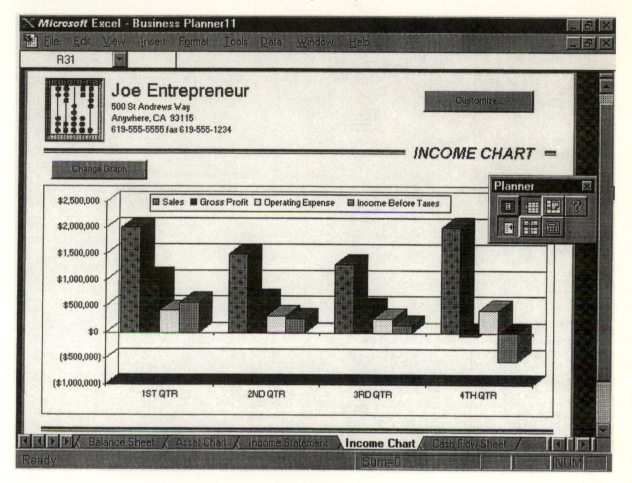

such movable toolbars, executable buttons, and multiple sheet tabs query entrepreneurs to provide answers to common business and financial questions. The resulting information is then provided in a variety of formats, including the graphic shown here.

Other new and useful tools available in today's spreadsheets include pivot tables, drag-and-drop editing, customizable templates, auto-correct, and auto-complete functionality. All of these and other functions provide rejuvenated power to spreadsheet users.

Word Processors   Word processors, long the work horse of business, have expanded their capabilities and have enhanced the entrepreneur's ability to compete with big business. In addition to the traditional typewriter capabilities, today's word processors utilize the what-you-see-is-what-you-get (WYSIWYG) approach, which makes creating a professional document downright easy.

A variety of professional and attractive documents can be created in today's word processors, including business plans, letters, memos, reports, and newsletters to name a few. In most word processors, these documents can be created manually or automatically, as in the case of Microsoft's Word for Windows 95.

The newsletter wizard, shown in Exhibit 16.6, walks entrepreneurs step-by-step through the creation of an eye-catching newsletter. Armed with this technology and an inexpensive laser printer, small businesspeople can create the types of documents previously done only by graphics production departments of large corporations.

Business letters, targeted mailings, and responses to product inquiries are all made easier with the latest word-processing technology. The mail-merge features of today's word processors enable the entrepreneur to customize

EXHIBIT 16.6
The newsletter wizard available in Microsoft's Word for Windows 95™.
(Screen shots reprinted with permission from Microsoft Corporation.)

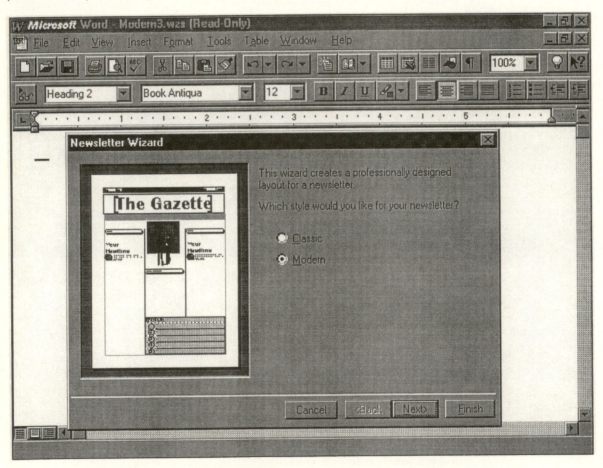

standard letters to each individual without the time and expense usually associated with such an effort.

Integrating these technologies has also had an influence on a small business's success. A word processing document can contain information created in a spreadsheet or a database (discussed below), which may be linked in such a way that as information in the spreadsheet or database is updated, the corresponding information in the word processing document is updated as well. Referred to as OLE (object linking and embedding) technology, this Windows-based feature extends the usefulness of the word processor to all areas of small business.

Databases Access to and utilization of the information available to a small business is becoming more and more important to today's entrepreneurs. For example, the advertising and promotion dollars spent by small businesspeople go wasted unless information from customers is analyzed and evaluated. Adequate inventory records must be maintained to help entrepreneurs plan for future purchases, promotions, and possible liquidation. In each of these examples, entrepreneurs would benefit from database management software.

A well-designed database can provide the entrepreneur efficient and convenient access to a business's information. The most popular type of information management software in use today is a relational database. One example of this type of database is Microsoft's Access, where information is stored in tables that are then associated with one another through common links or relations.

To design a useful database, entrepreneurs first determine the purpose of the database, which helps them decide which information must be gathered. For example, an entrepreneur may want to gather information on past sales to determine which products are selling best and what type of customer is buying those products.

Secondly, entrepreneurs must segregate information into separate subjects, such as orders, customers, and products. In Access, each of these subjects would be designed as a table. Each table then contains information about the subject, which is defined as a field. For example, the order table would include fields such as the order number, customer name, order date, product number, number ordered, and so on. The customer table would include fields such as the customer's name, address, shipping information, credit information, and key contact. Lastly, the product table would include information regarding product number, unit sales price, unit cost, and quantity on hand.

Each table is analyzed to determine how fields are related to one another, thereby linking tables together. For example, in the previously mentioned sales analysis, the order table's customer name field would be linked to the customer table's customer name field. Likewise the order table's product number field would be linked to the product table's product number field.

One final step in the database design process is creating forms to help organize and capture this information. Exhibit 16.7 illustrates an order form created in Microsoft's Access program, which uses information from all three tables referred to above.

EXHIBIT 16.7

An order form available in Microsoft's Access for Windows 95™.
(Screen shots reprinted with permission from Microsoft Corporation.)

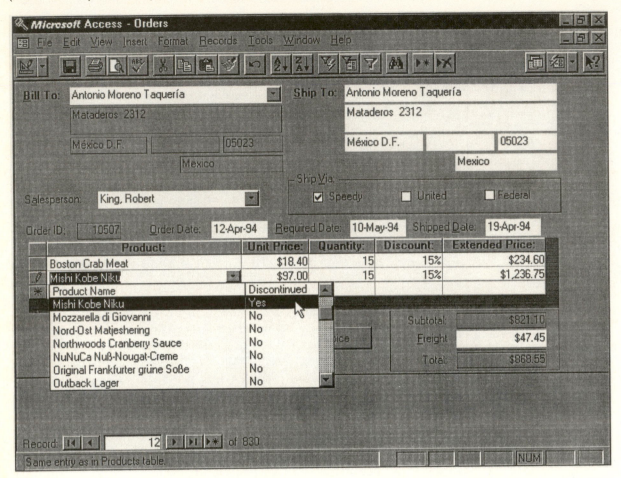

Installing a Computer System

Before installing a computer system, entrepreneurs must take the time to explore what the system can do for their business. It may take several weeks, or even several months, to learn enough to make an informed decision.

Entrepreneurs must take the utmost care to identify and define, in precise language, their need for computerization. As a rule, entrepreneurs lack the expertise to make the right decision themselves. Or they may be so busy with day-to-day operations that they cannot devote the time to do a feasibility study. Thus, many entrepreneurs find it advantageous to hire a computer consultant—as called for in this example:

Point-of-sale (POS) systems have become a mainstay in businesses, mostly in large companies that sell to consumers on a sales floor. To take advantage of these sophisticated systems, entrepreneurs need the help of a computer consultant.

POS systems usually include computerized cash registers and bar code scanners that record sales as they happen. Long common on groceries, bar codes are a series of vertical bars of varying widths printed on products and used especially for computer applications.

Nothing more than electronic tags, bar codes enable entrepreneurs to capture information when a sale takes place, carry it instantly to a database, and then feed it back in the form of sales summaries, inventory levels, and the like.

In a restaurant, for example, entrepreneurs can join a POS system to a database that lets them know how much of each basic ingredient the kitchen uses. If actual food use fails to track closely with expected use, they can look into the reasons why and take remedial action.[7]

▶ Hiring a Computer Consultant

In selecting a computer consultant, entrepreneurs must make sure the consultant understands their product. They might, for example, ask the consultant to write a statement summarizing how the product is produced and marketed and identifying areas that might benefit from computerization. From this statement, entrepreneurs can tell whether the consultant understands the business sufficiently. One clue is the consultant's working knowledge of the business's procedures and terminology.

The next step is to ask the consultant for a proposal for action plus a contract in draft form. The contract should specify what the computer system will be able to do for the business, and it should be written in language entrepreneurs can easily understand. Having a specific contract is one way to avoid the problem faced by so many businesses: buying hardware and software that do not meet the firm's specific needs.

The Wall Street Journal offers this advice:

> Seek a computer consultant who can communicate on your terms. Avoid those who begin by discussing solutions. Avoid those who are enamored of a particular hardware or software technology. Avoid consultants who can't explain what they are doing because it is "too technical."[8]

▶ Selecting Software

Although it might seem logical to choose a computer system and then choose the software to use on it, it is actually wiser to select the software first. In fact, identifying the right software is critical to the success of a computer system, because it is the software that tells the computer how to use data to perform business tasks and because a piece of software does not necessarily run on every computer model. Unfortunately, few entrepreneurs approach computerization this way. Small wonder, then, that so many computer systems fail to meet expectations. In the words of the Bank of America:

> A computer is only as good as its software. It isn't the equipment on the table that processes information, the software does. The software drives the machine. You buy a computer to perform a particular job. The software is the set of instructions that tell the computer what job to do and how to do it.

You can buy the finest state-of-the-art machine, but if its software fails to meet your needs, you're stuck with an expensive and useless piece of electronic equipment.

It can hardly be overstated: Do your software shopping *before* you shop for hardware.[9]

With so many software packages to choose from, it is often hard to select the one that suits a venture's needs best. Before deciding, entrepreneurs should talk with other entrepreneurs who already have chosen software, to find out their personal experiences. Talking with a noncompetitor in the same industry or profession can be especially helpful. For example, does a particular spreadsheet package handle sales forecasting for small independent grocers effectively? Or does a particular word processing package do a better job with form letters than does another package?

▶ Selecting Hardware

Having decided what software best fits their needs, entrepreneurs are now ready to select the hardware. Here is a brief checklist, in the form of questions, on how to do so:

▶ **Software needs**   Does the computer meet the entrepreneur's software needs? How well does the software run on this computer? Do the computer's graphics and memory support the software? How fast does the software run on the computer? Is the computer user-friendly?

▶ **Dependability**   Is the computer manufacturer well known in small-business markets? How many years has the manufacturer been in business? Does the manufacturer have a reputation for honest and fair dealings among local small businesses?

▶ **Expandability and adaptability**   Can the computer grow as the entrepreneur's venture grows for at least five years? If at the time, or even sooner, a more powerful computer is needed, are existing software and files readily adaptable to a new system?

▶ **Cost**   Will the hardware, software, and operating costs of the computer system be small compared to increased productivity? How much will it cost to train employees to use the system? What will it cost to debug the system? What help does the entrepreneur need to make a sound analysis of cost effectiveness?

▶ **Maintenance**   Will the computer manufacturer provide quick and competent technical support if the computer breaks down? Are spare parts readily available locally? Can the computer be repaired on site or must it be moved to another site? Is it preferable to have a third-party service company maintain the computer?

▶ **Compatibility**   What is the computer's compatibility with future versions of the software? Is the computer compatible with computer services offered by banks and database networks, so that the computers can "talk" with one another?

▶ Selecting a Vendor

Once a computer satisfies most, if not all, of the foregoing tests, entrepreneurs are in a good position to narrow the field of vendors, select the best one, negotiate terms, and purchase both software and hardware. The winning vendor should be a full-service shop, scoring well not only in its product but also in its people, service, and price.

Perhaps the best way to find a vendor is to ask other entrepreneurs—in short, to look for satisfied customers. Another way is to ask a computer consultant to recommend the best place in town to purchase software and hardware.

The Internet

Any discussion of information technology would be incomplete without devoting some space to the new world of the Internet, generally defined as a collection of computer networks. Functioning as a truly electronic global village, the Internet has aroused virtually everyone's curiosity, so much so that many entrepreneurs are looking to establish their very own presence on the Internet—and for good reason:

> With access to the Internet, entrepreneurs can put themselves in touch— freely and cheaply, instantly and interactively—with literally tens of millions of computer users the world over. Its possibilities as a major marketing tool thus seem endless.

Such high promise must be tempered, however, by the fact that the Internet is still in its infancy. Still to be proven is its value as a marketing tool on a par with advertising and sales promotion, at least as of this writing. Even so, the Internet is undeniably already changing the way we do business, in some cases dramatically. Illustrative of its promise and potential are these comments by users:

> "For small business, the Internet really is a great equalizer," says Carol Morgan, a market development executive at Apple Computer, who does seminars for Internet "newbies." "For the first time, you've got access to the same audience as big business."
>
> Agreeing with Morgan is Tim Mueller, co-owner of Vantage One Communications Group, which developed a World Wide Web* site on the Internet for the Rock and Roll Hall of Fame and Museum in Cleveland. "At one stroke, the playing field has been leveled," he says. "The smallest business can now compete on equal terms with the largest."[10]

All told, the Internet allows the smallest of businesses to research new markets, test ideas, and build close ties to customers—in much the same way that large businesses do. In the words of *Business Week*:

> All over America, small businesses are using information technology to become the Davids of marketing. The savviest are setting up databases to remember customers' favorite foods or [favorite] clothing designs and

---

*The World Wide Web (WWW) is a set of standards that enables computer users not only to see what is shared on a computer in another part of the world, but to see that information in full color, complete with pictures and sound—and for sophisticated users, even with moving pictures.[11]

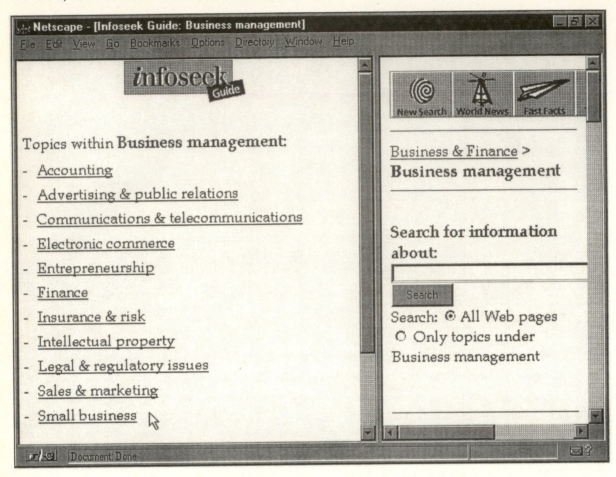

Utilization of the WWW by small business is growing daily from two very different approaches. In the first approach entrepreneurs are using the WWW to discover information on how to more efficiently operate businesses as well as to find new vendors. Using the WWW as a resource, entrepreneurs explore the Internet using one of many different search tools, such as the one shown in Exhibit 16.8. In this example, the entrepreneur is seeking information about business management techniques. After entering the search topic in Infoseek, the search tool provides a listing of topics found, which then points the entrepreneur to different sites on the Internet that provide information on that topic.

sharing tips online in an electronic version of the Rotary Club.* Making it all possible: the sweep of . . . networks into the core of everyday activities.[12]

---

*A major national and international service club.

The second approach to using the WWW provides entrepreneurs with access to new customers by promoting the business globally on the Internet. One example of this expanded customer base through the Internet is shown in Exhibit 16.9. Ingeborg's Chocolates has teamed up with a local Internet service provider to promote its products. This exhibit shows a portion of the order form, where customers can see a picture and description of the product, provide a credit card number, and have it shipped immediately.

Impressive as the Internet's potential may be, many questions remain unanswered. Among the real concerns are information overload and such sticky issues as pornography and privacy.[13] But whatever its future, the Internet has become a fixture in the life of the small-business community. Viewed within the context of a larger explosion of information access, the Internet is surely changing the way to get information and where to look for information.

EXHIBIT 16.9

The Netscape browser shown displaying a small business in Solvang, California, attempting to reach out globally for more customers.
(Used by permission of Ingeborg's Chocolates, Solvang, CA.)

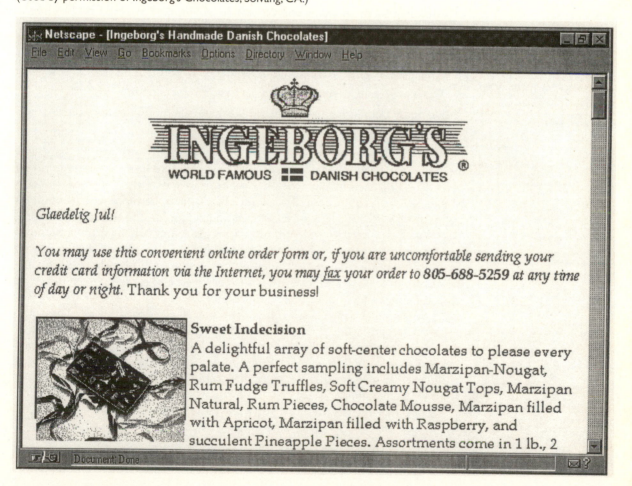

SUMMARY

Today's businesses large and small alike, find themselves in the midst of an evolutionary force that is reshaping our world with head-spinning speed. At its core is knowledge and its computer-aided communication in ways that provide entrepreneurs with the insight and enlightenment to manage wisely.

There are three types of computers to choose from:

▶ Mainframes are so large and complex that they are used only by the government and major corporations.

▶ Minicomputers are used by mid-sized companies, whose operations are too small for mainframes and too broad or specialized for microcomputers.

▶ Microcomputers—more commonly known as *personal computers* (PCs)—either fit on desktops or are small enough to use as portables.

All benefits from using a computer relate either directly or indirectly to increased productivity. So few, if any, entrepreneurs can afford to ignore the value of computerization. A remarkably versatile tool, the computer enables entrepreneurs to get more output with less input—in short, to "work smarter, not harder."

Although there are many ways in which a computer can increase productivity, the following applications are particularly important to small businesses:

▶ Accounting—for capturing and reporting business events

▶ Spreadsheets—for forecasting, modeling, accounting, and bookkeeping

▶ Word processing—for producing letters and documents

▶ Database management—for storing, organizing, manipulating, retrieving, and summarizing data

To locate the software that can perform these functions and the hardware on which the programs will run, entrepreneurs should hire a computer consultant. The first step in the process is making sure that the consultant understands the venture's product and needs. To this end, entrepreneurs should ask the consultant to write a statement summarizing how their product is produced and marketed and identifying areas that might benefit from computerization. Entrepreneurs then should commission a proposal for action, a proposal that specifies what the computer system will be able to do for the business. And, in all instances, they should be sure that the consultant is able to communicate in language they understand.

In the actual choice of a system, the first step is selecting software. These programs help define the type of hardware the business is going to need. Before making a software decision, entrepreneurs should speak with other entrepreneurs who already have chosen their software, to learn about their experiences with different packages. Talking with a noncompetitor in the same industry can be especially helpful.

Once they have selected their software, entrepreneurs are ready to select the hardware. There are six major criteria to consider in choosing a computer system:

- Software needs
- Dependability
- Expandability and adaptability
- Cost
- Maintenance
- Compatibility

The final decision is choosing a vendor. Here, again, the experience of other entrepreneurs can be a help, as can the recommendations of a computer consultant.

The Internet is a collection of computer networks that enables entrepreneurs to communicate freely and inexpensively, instantly and interactively, with literally tens of millions of computer users the world over. Although its value as a marketing tool has not yet been proven, the Internet is already changing the way entrepreneurs do business.

Discussion and Review Questions

1. What is information? Why is it important?
2. How do the three basic types of computers differ?
3. How do hardware and software differ?
4. What is computer literacy and why is it so important?
5. What are the most important benefits of computer use?
6. What are spreadsheets? Give one example of how they are used.
7. What is database management? Give one example of how it is used.
8. In what ways can project management software benefit the entrepreneur?
9. What is word processing? Give some examples of what it can do.
10. What is the best approach to securing the services of a computer consultant?
11. Why should the selection of software always precede the selection of hardware?
12. What are the criteria for selecting computer software? Hardware?
13. How should a computer vendor be selected?
14. What is the Internet? Why is it important?
15. Define these terms: *central processing unit, keyboard, floppy disk, printer, programmer.*

One close inspection, each of the ten items in Exhibit 16.3 turns out to be an excuse, not a *valid reason,* for not using a computer:

1. A stated desire to not want to use a computer often is an emotional response motivated by fear of failure.
2. Computers don't make mistakes; people do. Because billing mistakes and other administrative problems often are blamed on computers, people have come to mistrust them. Computers do what they are instructed to do. If they are given faulty instructions, they will produce faulty results. "Garbage in—garbage out!"
3. True, computers generally are associated with the young. But this is no reason for older people to shy away from them. Age is a state of mind, not a number.
4. A trip to the nearest computer store for some browsing can open up a whole new world of possibilities for using a computer for work or play.
5. Technically, computers are complicated. But user-friendly hardware and software are making them accessible to the average individual.
6. Computer users often do engage in terminology overkill. Again, as computer hardware and software become more user-friendly, the technical jargon will be pushed aside. Think of the modern telephone. It is a highly complex piece of telecommunications equipment. But it is so user-friendly that you do not need a technical vocabulary to make a phone call. All it takes is pushing a few buttons.

7. This item involves two mistaken notions. First, although computers often are used to solve complex mathematical problems, you do not need to be a math whiz to operate the typical business program. Second, you do not have to be a computer programmer to be able to work on a computer. All the programming has already been done for you when you buy an application program for word processing, spreadsheets, and so on. Analogously, you do not have to know how to build and repair an automobile in order to drive one.
8. Although it helps to be a fast touch-typist when entering data on a keyboard, many computer users do very nicely with their own version of hunt and peck. Moreover, other input devices, such as a point-and-push "mouse," eliminate the keyboard altogether.
9. True, computer technology changes rapidly. But the key to buying a computer is finding one that adequately performs the jobs you need to accomplish, for a reasonable price. Even when new computers come on the market, you will still have one that "gets the job done."
10. Personal computers have been around long enough to permit the growth of a used computer market. Used personal computers, still in good working order, can be purchased for surprisingly little today.

Source: Adapted from Robert Kreitner, Barry L. Reece, and James P. O'Grady, *Business,* 2d ed. (Boston: Houghton Mifflin, 1990), p. A–2. Used with permission

Building a Business Plan

Information Technology

Collecting, analyzing, and reporting information are vital activities for any small business. To help accomplish these tasks, many small business owners have turned to computers.

Benefits of Computer Use

The best reason for a small business owner to install a computer is that it means good business. Because using a computer improves productivity, the computer streamlines the flow of work and thus reduces labor costs. For example, hours upon hours of work can be eliminated if order processing and invoicing are done by computer rather than by hand.

Software Applications

Software is the term used for computer programs, which give the computer its instructions. Today, computers, with the help of the proper software package, can help entrepreneurs perform most business functions, including order processing and invoicing, purchasing, inventory control, payroll, bookkeeping, scheduling, and even typing.

Instructions for Worksheet 16

To complete this part of the business plan, in part 1 you must examine different business activities that need to be completed in order for your business to be successful. In part 2, you must explore different software programs that could be used to perform the business activities needed for success in your business.

Part 1—Potential Computer Applications

Before spending well over $2,000 to purchase and install a computer system, entrepreneurs must take the time to determine if a computer and software programs can really help them operate their business.

1. Develop a list of specific tasks that must be performed on a regular basis in your business.

2. Who is responsible for completing each task?

3. Which of these tasks could be performed with the aid of a computer?

Part 2—Software Applications

Before answering the questions in this part, you may want to review the software applications that were discussed on pages 480 to 485 in your text.

4. Describe how software programs could help you accomplish the business tasks that were listed in part 1 of this worksheet.

5. Will the use of new software programs require the purchase of new computer equipment?

6. What is the total cost required to purchase the software programs and the computer upgrade required to use the new software programs?

7. Can the new software programs be adapted or changed to meet the firm's needs?

8. What kind of training is available with the software programs?

9. Can you contact the vendor if you have questions or encounter problems when you attempt to use the new software programs?

10. Do the expected benefits of using the new software programs justify the cost?

Sulcus Computer Corporation

In 1984, Sulcus Computer Corporation was developing, making, and marketing microcomputer systems for the real estate industry, focusing on the land-title market. Sulcus had grown rapidly since its founding in 1979. Just five years later, it earned after-tax profits of $213,000 on sales revenues of $2.1 million.

In 1984, Sulcus purchased Lawtomation, a company based in Washington, D.C., that specialized in management systems for law firms. Sulcus hoped to win over the nation's law firms with the same methods it had used to cement the land-title market. One of Sulcus's founders, Jeffrey Ratner, wondered whether his small firm could compete against giant corporations like IBM in a market estimated at $10 billion a year. At the time, Ratner said, "We're playing hardball with the big boys, and we think we'll be among the major-league hitters. In three years, we'll either be a $100 million company or go bust."

Background

In 1984, Sulcus's microcomputer systems served these markets in the real estate industry:

▶ Title insurance firms and escrow companies

▶ Abstract companies and mortgage bankers*

▶ Financial institutions and law firms

Its most important product was a turnkey system consisting of hardware, software, supplies, training, and support. Sulcus furnished all the components and installed the microcomputer system *before* turning it over to the client, who then only had to "turn the key." The product was marketed nationwide through a network of distributors and dealers, regional representatives, and branch offices. Exhibit 16A.1 shows Ratner holding a Sulcus microcomputer.

Company Financing

Founded by Ratner and Richard Gross in 1979, the company started its corporate life under the name Ragtronics, Inc. Two years later, the firm bought all of Gross's stock, leaving Ratner the majority shareholder.

In 1983, the company borrowed a total of $275,000 from three Small Business Investment Companies (SBICs). Licensed by the U.S. Small Business Administration, SBICs are venture capital companies that invest in, or lend to, small businesses—especially high-risk ventures offering new products with promising market potential, unusually favorable competitive positions, and sound, aggressive management.

The three SBICs received stock options for 152,700 shares of common stock that can be exercised only after Sulcus repays the $275,000 loan. This loan bears 12 percent interest, matures in 1990, and is subordinated to the company's debt to trade creditors and financial institutions. (*Subordination* means that a creditor agrees that the claims of other specified creditors must be paid in full before he or she receives any payment. Here, the three SBICs are subordinate creditors.)

Later in 1983, Sulcus sold 17,450 shares of its 7 percent convertible preferred stock for $45 a share in a private placement. That preferred stock was convertible into 401,350 shares of common stock. Preferred stock has priority over common stock in receiving dividends, obtaining assets in the event of liquidation, and other matters specified before the sale.

---

*Abstract companies write concise histories, taken from public records, of the ownership of pieces of land. Each history includes a statement of all liens or liabilities that could affect a prospective purchaser.

Financial Performance

Since its founding, Sulcus had grown rapidly—so rapidly that it qualified as one of the most promising high-technology ventures in the country. In 1985, the company placed fiftieth among *Inc.* magazine's 100 fastest-growing, publicly owned small businesses.

Sulcus posted after-tax profits of $213,000 on sales revenues of $2.1 million in 1984, compared to profits of $128,000 on sales of $1.3 million in 1983. This performance far exceeded that of 1982, when Sulcus lost $49,700 on sales of $448,800. (See Exhibit 16A.2.)

Inc. described growth companies like Sulcus this way:

> Ten years ago, more than 80 percent of the companies on this year's *Inc.* list did not exist. Five years ago, most were still in the startup stage—small, struggling, and privately held.
>
> Today they are in the front ranks of America's resurgent economy. If . . . we are on the verge of a second American revolution, then the chief executive officers of the *Inc.* 100

are the Minutemen of the 1980s, the growth leaders of the entrepreneurial age.*

In August 1984, Sulcus became a publicly owned company, selling 19 percent of its common stock for more than $1.8 million. Exhibit 16A.3 shows Sulcus's three-year income statements; its two-year balance sheets appear in Exhibit 16A.4.

Controlled Growth

As chief executive officer and board chairman since the company's founding, Ratner was responsible for directing Sulcus's managerial and financial policies. He deliberately steered a course of controlled growth for the company. A newspaper article praised Ratner for his restraint:

> In an industry rife with firms willing to rush a product to market and hope for the best, Sulcus has taken a slow, calculating course. For the better part of six years, Sulcus

---

*Curtis Hartman, "The 1985 *Inc.* 100," *Inc.* (May 1985), p. 57.

EXHIBIT 16A.2
Sulcus Computer
Corporation: Sales and
profit growth (1979–1984).

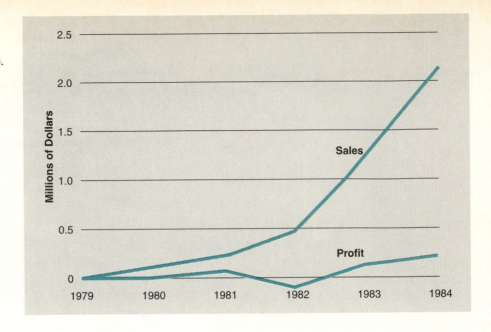

EXHIBIT 16A.3

Sulcus Computer Corporation: Three-year income statements.

	1982	1983	1984
Sales revenues	$447,800	$1,335,400	$2,148,400
Operating expenses			
Cost of sales	$208,500	$ 381,800	$ 531,300
Selling and administrative	193,300	550,700	977,600
Research and development	93,700	216,500	334,800
Interest	100	26,700	34,700
Depreciation	9,800	18,200	29,600
Total operating expenses	$505,400	$1,193,900	$1,908,000
Profit before taxes	$ (57,600)	$ 141,500	$ 240,400
Federal income taxes	(7,900)	13,500	27,000
Profit after taxes	$ (49,700)	$ 128,800	$ 213,400

EXHIBIT 16A.4

Sulcus Computer Corporation: Two-year balance sheets (December 31).

Assets	1983	1984	Equities	1983	1984
Current assets			**Current liabilities**		
Cash and cash equivalents	$1,017,800	$3,006,200	Notes payable	$ 0	$ 169,600
Accounts receivable	37,800	48,100	Accounts payable	50,400	72,600
Inventories	143,300	153,000	Bonus payable	40,000	
Other current assets	10,000	59,800	Other liabilities	34,700	41,300
Total current assets	$1,208,900	$3,267,100	Deferred revenue	29,900	64,400
			Taxes payable	13,500	27,200
			Total current liabilities	$ 168,500	$ 375,100
Fixed assets			Long-term debt	$ 275,000	$ 275,000
Equipment and fixtures	$ 104,200	$ 305,700	**Owners' equity**		
Less: Accumulated depreciation	30,600	59,600	Preferred stock	683,700	0
			Common stock	47,000	2,591,800
Total fixed assets	$ 73,600	$ 246,100	Retained earnings	108,300	281,900
Other assets	$ 0	$ 10,600	Total owners' equity	$ 839,000	$2,873,700
Total assets	$1,282,500	$3,523,800	Total equities	$1,282,500	$3,523,800

restricted its product to the land title industry, designing its computer software and hardware to automate real estate law, escrow, and title insurance firms.

"We never intended to be a broad-brush computer company," says Mr. Ratner. "We want to know every nook and cranny in our customer's business so we can add new products for them, make them more cost effective."*

Sulcus's strategy of focusing on a sector of the computer market and slowly nurturing its customers has worked well. By the time Sulcus began to mass-market its systems in 1983, they had been tested for nearly three years at several sites across the country, and a string of distribution centers was well established. In fact, Sulcus tailored its software to each state's real estate law and procedures. Support services were ready to respond to trouble, promising next-day replacement of any malfunctioning system.

In two years, Sulcus captured 75 percent of the 800 land-title companies estimated to have automated their offices. "We literally dominate that market," said Ratner, "and the customers keep coming back. Once we automate their business, our customers tend to look to us to do everything."

Marketing Network

The far-flung nature of Sulcus's marketing network is illustrated in Exhibit 16A.5. To market its turnkey

---

*Jeffrey Fraser, "Greensburg Firm Nurtures Software Niche," *Pittsburgh Press*, (May 10, 1985), p. B6.

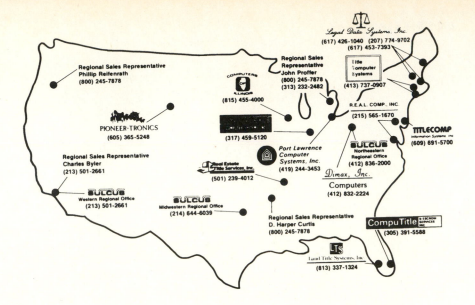

microcomputer systems efficiently, Sulcus designed a network made up of several parts:

Distributor-dealer network   Sulcus chooses its local distributors from among the entrepreneurial users of its products. They best combine product knowledge and familiarity with customers' needs. Distributors are required to:

▶ Develop their own territories and markets

▶ Inventory all Sulcus products

▶ Have full-time sales, training, and support personnel available

▶ Use the company's advertising and promotional programs

Branch offices   The branch office provides regional support to the distributor-dealer network as well as to the end users. In 1984, Sulcus had branch offices in Dallas and Los Angeles, and others were planned in the Northeast and Midwest. These branch offices allow prompt response to users' needs.

Regional representatives   The regional-representative program extends Sulcus's products into areas not currently served by distributors, dealers, or branches. Experienced salespeople also enable Sulcus to spread into new areas. In

1984, there were regional representatives in Oregon, California, Michigan, and Arkansas, and the company expected to add 20 to 25 more.

Advertising and Sales Promotion

In 1984, Sulcus's marketing efforts took a quantum leap. With a six-figure advertising budget, Sulcus expanded its reach in the marketplace, using a number of prestigious publications. Advertisements and articles about Sulcus appeared in *The Wall Street Journal, ABA Journal, National Law Journal, American Lawyer, Title News, Financial Computing, Legal Economics, MicroBanker, Mortgage Banking,* and *Computers in Banking.*

Sulcus also was active in trade shows, providing hands-on demonstrations to hundreds of its best prospects. The purchase of a 400-square-foot, 12-foot-high exhibit booth enabled Sulcus to maintain its leadership in the competitive national convention arena.

New Market

In 1984, Sulcus was poised to enter the market of law office automation. "We believe we have a

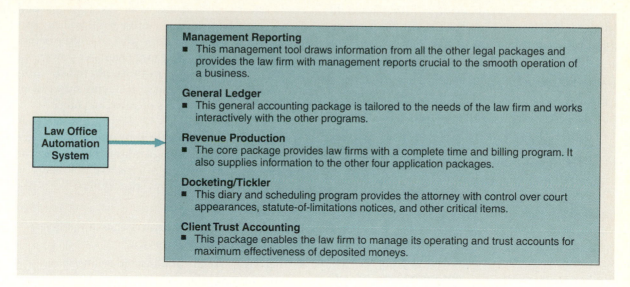

Management Reporting
- This management tool draws information from all the other legal packages and provides the law firm with management reports crucial to the smooth operation of a business.

General Ledger
- This general accounting package is tailored to the needs of the law firm and works interactively with the other programs.

Law Office Automation System

Revenue Production
- The core package provides law firms with a complete time and billing program. It also supplies information to the other four application packages.

Docketing/Tickler
- This diary and scheduling program provides the attorney with control over court appearances, statute-of-limitations notices, and other critical items.

Client Trust Accounting
- This package enables the law firm to manage its operating and trust accounts for maximum effectiveness of deposited moneys.

golden opportunity to be a major competitor in that market," said Ratner. "We know the needs of the small- and medium-sized law office."

Lawtomation software and manuals were rewritten to fit Sulcus systems. A new line of computers was readied. When Sulcus swooped down on the nation's 576,000 lawyers, it expected to compete successfully with IBM and other computer-industry giants. Exhibit 16A.6 shows the family of programs that Sulcus offered law firms.

Source: Adapted from a case prepared by Professor Richard W. Shapiro of Cuyahoga Community College. Used with permission.

Questions

1. Comment on the financing of this publicly held company.
2. Explain why Sulcus has succeeded in the crowded computer industry.
3. If you were Jeffrey Ratner, would you have expanded into the legal market in light of the stiff competition? Why or why not?
4. Would you buy shares of common stock in the company? Why or why not?
5. Comment on Ratner's marketing strategy.

CASE 16B ▶ *Dell Computer Corporation*

Always an entrepreneur in a hurry, Michael Dell was but 13 years old when he earned $2,000 selling stamps out of a rented post office box. In his next venture, at 16, he bought lists of the names of newlyweds from the county courthouse, and then telephoned them to offer subscriptions to the *Houston Post*. Dell broke the newspaper's sales records. A year later, he recruited several high school friends to help him, earning for himself $18,000—enough to buy a BMW.

Thus, even as a teenager, Dell had shown an uncanny knack for closing sales by telephone, working from a base of solid customer lists. He would later use this experience to good advantage in selling personal computers (PCs).

In the Beginning

Dell founded Dell Computers at the tender age of 19. At the time, he was a pre-medical student at the University of Texas, where he began building PC's in his dormitory room. He soon dropped out to launch his computer venture.

Dell's marketing strategy was the soul of simplicity. He would sell PCs by telephone, a strategy shunned by such major PC makers as IBM and the Apple Computer Corporation. Working out of a storefront in Austin, Texas, Dell offered custom-built computers to small businesses and to such professionals as accountants, lawyers, and physicians. Dell's strategy also called for his receiving half the money up front to buy off-the-shelf computer components, thus helping to keep his cash flow healthy. He worked 18-hour days and slept on an army cot in his office.

Dell's strategy worked. By plowing profits back into the business to finance his growth, Dell posted sales revenues of nearly $10 million his very first year, in 1984. By the beginning of 1985, he was already employing 39 people. This success spurred Dell to expand beyond state borders and launch a national advertising campaign, this time targeting both small- and medium-sized PC users.

Direct Marketing Strategy

Starkly simple, Dell's advertisements focused on offering buyers what his giant competitors would not—namely, customized PCs. All that buyers need do, explained the advertisements, was dial an 800 service number. In the same breath, buyers could select such features as drives, memory, and speed—with promises to deliver within 72 hours.

Dell's marketing strategy also covered pricing, offering buyers not only more computer power but at much lower prices than those offered by competitors—up to 25 percent less. Buying direct from Dell made such low prices possible, of course.

So brilliantly has this strategy succeeded that Dell himself has become one of the computer industry's icons, joining such household names as Apple's Steven Jobs and Microsoft's Bill Gates. It was Dell's vision that saw what others did not—for example, that:

▶ Selling PCs through dealers caused inefficiencies and led to poor service

▶ Bypassing dealers and instead selling direct would breed efficiency, boost service, and create happier buyers

Indeed, Dell's singleminded dedication to service has earned Dell blue-ribbon praise. In fact, Dell in 1992 ranked first in a customer-satisfaction survey by J. D. Power & Associates, a marketing research firm.

In 1995, Dell's sales revenues topped $5 billion, making Dell the fourth-largest PC maker in the country, behind IBM, Apple, and Compaq.

Moreover, Dell now bestrides the globe, selling PCs in 18 nations, including Japan.

Questions
1. Explain why Dell is a nonstore retailer and how Dell competes with computer stores.
2. How would you describe Dell's marketing strategy?
3. What are some of the issues that Dell must consider to ensure its future success?

Sources: Cover Story, "The Education of Michael Dell," *Business Week* (March 22, 1993), pp. 82–88; Cover Story, L. B. Gschwandtner, "Who is Michael Dell," *Personal Selling Power* (March 1993) pp. 14–24; Stephanie Anderson Forest, "PC Slump? What PC Slump?" *Business Week* (July 1, 1991), pp. 66–67; Kevin Kelly, "Dell Computer Hits the Drawing Board," *Business Week* (April 24, 1989), p. 138.

"I know it's taking me some time to learn these new gadgets, but I'm getting the job done," said Marvin Keller to Joe Richman. Marvin is a warehouse foreman in a manufacturing business employing 47 people. Joe is the founder's son and recently earned a master's degree in business administration.

"It's like this, Marvin," sighed Joe. "This has nothing to do with you and me being friends. The business we are in involves people like yourself becoming computer literate."

Marvin, looking every one of his 58 years, sighed as he replied. "Yeah, I know, everything you say is probably true, Joe. But I've spent 25 years with this business. You come on board with your fancy college degrees and want to turn us all into computer nerds. Well, there's a saying about teaching an old dog new tricks—and I'm an old dog."

Joe recognized that Marvin had an excellent record with the business, but Joe had made mastery of the computer system a major company-wide goal. And everyone, including Marvin, had to learn to become proficient at the computer system.

After a few weeks of little progress, Joe was now telling Marvin that the time had come for Marvin to cut the nonsense and get up to speed on the system with everybody else.

Excuses Don't Cut It

"Why don't you leave me alone?" asked Marvin. "It's hard enough trying to learn these machines. Not to mention my arthritis, which flares up when I type the warehouse reports, plus the headaches that screen gives me."

Joe was growing tired of having to wait up for Marvin: "It's about time you joined the 1990s, Marvin. Sorry about your personal afflictions, but you're getting paid to get a job done, so do it."

"Well, the way I see it, you just aren't giving me enough time to learn. Fact is, I don't see how you can expect anyone to learn it overnight."

"It's hardly an overnight assignment, Marvin. We've had this system in place for close to six weeks."

Marvin called in the next day with a flare-up of arthritis, which he claimed was aggravated by the computer keyboard. By the time he returned to work, Marvin was way behind the others in the computer orientation program.

Marvin realized that he was never going to catch up. And, he was so miffed at the whole workplace scene, that he wrote out his resignation and quit.

Different Views and Viewpoints

Marvin did not just quit. He decided to salve his irritation in court. And now, Joe faced a bigger irritant. Marvin's attorney claimed his client was unfairly discharged, because he just was not learning computers fast enough.

"It's an outrage!" claimed Joe. "I never threatened to fire Marvin. He just realized he was too set in his ways to learn computers and decided to quit. Nobody fired him!"

"Nobody says that you fired him, Mr. Richman," explained Marvin's lawyer. "What we are saying is that you made the working conditions so miserable for Marvin that he felt he had no choice but to quit. There's a major difference."

"That's not true," Joe sputtered. "I treated him the same as the other computer trainees."

"Let me remind you of a couple of incidents," purred the lawyer. "What about the tremendous pressure you put on him to get up and running on the computer, while at the same time you gave younger workers more time?

"And," he continued, "what about the suspension? When my client took a longer lunch break, which everyone did when they double-shifted, you suspended him."

"You're coloring the facts," defended Joe. "Everyone had to adapt to the computer quickly. The reason Marvin didn't get it was not because the younger guys had more time. He had his teachers so frustrated, a couple of them threw up their hands and walked away.

"And the suspensions were legit. He broke company policy, and he had to pay the price."

So, as it turned out, did the company. Despite the seemingly business-oriented reasons for the dismissal, a court decided that Joe Richman and his company were in the wrong and made a winner of the veteran Marvin.

Question

1. What steps should Joe Richman have taken from the beginning to avoid law suits like Marvin Keller's?

Source: Adapted with permission from *Manager's Legal Bulletin* by Alexander Hamilton Institute, Inc., 70 Hilltop Road, Ramsey, NJ 07446. To order please call (800) 879–2441.

CHAPTER 17

Human Relations

OBJECTIVES

▶ to explain the fundamental importance of human relations

▶ to identify the major forces influencing human behavior at work

▶ to detail the needs of employees and how best to meet them

▶ to identify what distinguishes the entrepreneur as a manager

▶ to summarize the most important aspects of wage, salary, and fringe benefit policies

Authority should go with knowledge and experience; that is where obedience is due, no matter whether it is up the line or down.

—Mary Parker Follett

Far from being a mysterious science, human relations is often nothing more than goodwill and applied common sense. Much of an entrepreneur's success in human relations depends on simple things, such as making a store a friendlier place to work or making a plant more comfortable and safe.

Entrepreneurs often ignore these simple things, especially when their businesses begin to grow. When they start their ventures, they typically have only themselves and perhaps a few employees to manage. A strong sense of purpose binds owner and employees together. But the addition of new employees tends to loosen that bond, unless the entrepreneur pays attention to so-called people problems. In this chapter, we discuss these problems by focusing on the entrepreneur's responsibility to recognize employees' needs and to manage them in ways that bring out their best.

The Importance of Human Relations

So massive are many businesses today that employees lose all sense of human contact with their employers. In many manufacturing industries, for example, the high degree of mechanization robs employees of their sense of personal pride and often their identification with the product they help make. In fact, employees often do not even know how customers use the product. The robotlike nature of much of their work thwarts their sense of self-respect. In the words of Fyodor Dostoyevsky, the famed Russian writer, "If it were desired to reduce a man to nothingness, it would be necessary only to give his work a character of uselessness."[1]

A "character of uselessness" is imposed on much of the work done in plants, stores, and offices. Many employees feel they have been swallowed by a big impersonal machine that robs them of their self-respect and identity. Out of this betrayal of the human spirit, the science of human relations was born to find ways to give employees a sense of usefulness, and thus improve their performance on the job—in the belief that life may be made more enjoyable by making work more meaningful.

Often, however, entrepreneurs lose sight of the importance of meaningful work in their rush to boost sales. They soon find themselves saddled with employees who do poorly. Why? Because they are unhappy. Entrepreneurs can buy an employee's time and physical presence at a given place, and a measured number of skilled muscular motions per hour. But entrepreneurs *cannot* buy an employee's enthusiasm, initiative, or loyalty.

Rather, the entrepreneur must *earn* these values by recognizing that employees need to feel that the work they do really matters, and that the entrepreneur is interested in them and appreciates what they do. Employees generally do better, for example, when they are singled out for individual attention. In return for their loyalty and enthusiasm, they expect the entrepreneur:

▸ To protect their right to work continuously, as long as they perform honestly and productively.

▸ To give them a chance to advance as the venture grows.

▸ To treat them with dignity and respect.

▸ **Putting Employees First**

Yet all too often, entrepreneurs as employers fail to recognize, let alone understand, such expectations. They tend to focus shortsightedly on the bottom line alone, ignoring the "productive power of putting people first."[2] As one disenchanted former employee of a small radio station put it:

> Though idealistic business folk envision employee and employer working hand-in-hand for a common goal, such a scenario cannot exist. No matter what the business, employer and employee live in different worlds and speak a different language. I'm firmly on the employee side of the workforce; or I was. I'm dislocated at the moment.
>
> I wonder whether employers truly appreciate how much their employees care about the quality and the purpose of the work, and their unique part in its creation. [Computers] and spread sheets are lifeless. They don't divulge the heart and soul of an organization. The books might balance, while the work, and mission, topple.[3]

By no means uncommon, this ex-employee's heartless work experience underscores why entrepreneurs should have a sense of moral obligation to their employees—and, in kind, why employees should have a sense of loyalty to the entrepreneur—not only because it is good business, but also because it is humane.

In stark contrast to the example above is this example set by an enlightened entrepreneur, whose humanity seemingly knows no bounds, much to the delight of the small world around her:

Love your customers, employees, shareholders, vendors, and community—in that order—and the profits will follow.

This philosophy has catapulted my company, Acucobol, from a six-person startup to an international software company with annual sales of over $4 million in just 40 months. And what about profit? It has been flowing since the 12th month of operation.

"But wait a minute," you may say. "Love and marriage go together, but love and *business?*"

You might ask how I get 60 employees to commit to showing "love" for customers. The answer is to "love" your employees. For example:

▶ Give them an environment where they can learn, make mistakes, grow, excel, and prosper; they in turn will put their energy and wisdom back into your company.

▶ Care about them as persons; care about their health, their families, and their career goals.

▶ Give them the tools to become more productive.

▶ And above all, make sure everyone is having fun. Chances are that, if they're having fun, your employees are committed to your goals.

I am committed to helping every Acucobol employee attain his or her dreams. I have given employees various opportunities for a fulfilling work environment. Many of my senior-level staff members work flexible hours, which lets them have their personal time when it's best for them and also encourages them to maximize their time at work.

We schedule events outside work and invite friends and families. This encourages camaraderie, openness, and greater productivity in the long run. To promote our employees' careers, I've encouraged them to join associations relevant to their work and to contribute articles to industry publications.

I've encouraged my employees to become involved with the community as well. Whether they help out at a shelter for the homeless, support blood drives and food collections, or work with local elementary schools, I want my employees to value the community and the contributions they can offer to make it better.[4] ▲▼▲

Truly, the entrepreneur in our example values people, their expectations *and* their motivations—a subject we discuss below, in the belief that an understanding of motivation may help entrepreneurs and their employees to fulfill themselves.

Human Needs and Employee Motivation

Some people define motivation as simply the reason we behave the way we do. Still others think of it as some mysterious force—such as ambition or the will to win—that is put into people to make them run, much as fuel is put into an automobile. Commenting on the mystery of motivation, D. R. Spitzer, author and consultant, had this to say:

What motivates people? No question about human behavior is more frequently asked or more perplexing to answer. Yet, knowing what motivates another person is basic to establishing and maintaining effective relations with others.[5]

▶ Maslow's Hierarchy of Needs

Several theories seek to de-mystify motivation. The best known, and most widely cited, is the theory called *hierarchy of needs,* as visualized by the noted psychologist, Abraham Maslow. Depicted in Exhibit 17.1, this theory classifies all human needs and aspirations according to their importance and presents them as a pyramid of five levels:

▶ Physiological needs

▶ Safety and security

▶ Belongingness and love

▶ Esteem

▶ Self-actualization[6]

According to Maslow, we, as human beings, strive to satisfy these needs in ascending order. Once a lower level is satisfied, we try to satisfy the next level of need. As shown in Exhibit 17.1, note that the first level is the satisfaction of *physiological needs*—air, water, and food. Once these needs have been satisfied, we need protection from hostile forces, such as criminals and cold weather. These needs form the second level, *safety and security.*

The third level, *belongingness and love,* refers to our need for affection and the acceptance of others. The fourth level, *esteem,* refers to the need for self-respect, self-esteem, and the esteem of others.

The fifth and highest level has to do with *self-actualization.* Activated only when all other needs have been satisfied, this level of needs reflects our desire to fulfill our highest potential as individuals. Self-actualization refers to our

EXHIBIT 17.1
Maslow's hierarchy of needs.

Source: *"Hierarchy of Needs"* from *Motivation and Personality* 2nd ed. By Abraham H. Maslow. Reprinted by permission of Addison-Wesley Educational Publishers Inc.

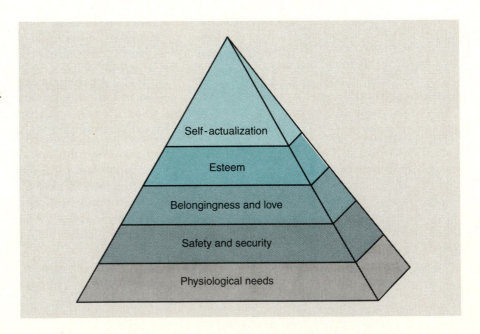

need to do what we are best suited to do, just as athletes must compete and entrepreneurs must create.

Turning to Exhibit 17.2, note how entrepreneurs may apply Maslow's theory to help motivate employees.

▶ Theory X and Theory Y

Building on Maslow's pioneer work, the equally noted psychologist, Douglas McGregor, came up with another theory, this one explaining the assumptions made by entrepreneurs and other business leaders about how best to treat their employees:

▶ **Theory X**   According to this theory, employees hate work and perform only if threatened with punishment. And consequently, entrepreneurs must bully their employees and undermine their security with threats to fire them. Thus, Theory X focuses on the first two levels of Maslow's hierarchy of needs: physiological needs and safety and security.

EXHIBIT 17.2

How Maslow's hierarchy of needs may be applied in a work setting.

Needs	Ways to Satisfy Needs
Physiological	Pay
	Company housing
	Breakfast or lunch programs
Safety and Security	Pay
	Pensions
	Seniority
	Company benefits plans
Belongingness and Love	Pay
	Work teams
	Sports teams
	Coffee breaks
	Company picnics and social events
Esteem	Independence
	Responsibility
	Pay as symbol of status
	Prestigious office location and furnishings
Self-actualization	Challenge
	Independence

Source: Gordon, Judith. *A Diagnostic Approach to Organizational Behavior,* Third Edition. Copyright © 1991 by Prentice-Hall Inc.

▶ **Theory Y**   Supporters of this theory believe that work is as natural as rest. Theory Y assumes that employees work hard to meet goals if they are committed to them, and that they seek responsibility and can use their creativity to solve problems. Thus, this theory relates to the higher levels of Maslow's hierarchy of needs: belongingness and love, esteem, and self-actualization.[7]

The overriding reason for embracing Theory Y rather than Theory X is that entrepreneurs are more likely to succeed by satisfying the needs of their employees than by ignoring them. Only by satisfying these needs would employees be strongly motivated to pursue excellence in their work. A comparison of Theory X and Theory Y appears in Exhibit 17.3.

▶ **The Hawthorne Experiment**

A classic example of what happens if employees are treated humanely was shown by the now-famous Hawthorne experiment.

In the 1920s, Elton Mayo of Harvard University asked 2,000 employees at the Hawthorne plant of the Western Electric Company how they felt about their jobs, their bosses, and the company they worked for. Mayo and his interviewers used checklists that carefully itemized every feature of the work situation. The lists included the lights, the materials used, the handling of equipment, rest periods, product knowledge, and so on. The employees, however, wanted to talk about other things, and to talk freely under the seal of professional confidence, which was never abused. Surprisingly, the interviews themselves seemed to improve productivity.

The results of the interviews were so inconclusive that the research teams decided to try some experiments. They increased and decreased lighting, temperature, and rest periods. They changed room colors. They isolated groups from one another. No matter what the change, however, production improved. The Harvard scholars were stumped. Finally, they asked the employees to explain. "Oh, don't you know?" one worker replied. "We're something special."

Although the employees did not know why, they knew they had been distinguished from all the other employees. They were now something more than

---

EXHIBIT 17.3
Comparison of Theory X and Theory Y.

Theory X	Theory Y
Employees have little ambition.	Employees crave responsibility.
Threats are necessary to motivate employees.	Employees dislike threats.
Employees avoid work because they hate it.	Work is as natural as rest.
Employees avoid all responsibility.	Employees want to satisfy their needs for belongingness and love, esteem, and self-actualization.

cogs in a machine. The special treatment had made them feel better about themselves and about their work. They recognized that their jobs were important, and so did their coworkers. They had achieved that something special—status, or the importance attributed to a work position by the employees themselves as well as by management.[8]

Expanding on Maslow's and McGregor's theories of motivation, we next discuss how managerial style may influence the performance of entrepreneurs as well as that of their employees.

The Entrepreneur as Manager

Although often viewed as the job of getting work done through others, managing really means much more. It also means making it possible for others to work easily and productively, and bringing out their best. How can entrepreneurs help employees do their best?

To begin with, entrepreneurs must want to help employees become achievers. Some do not, holding fast to the idea that employees do not crave satisfaction from their jobs. This attitude may cause problems like absenteeism and high turnover, shoddy workmanship, and a weakening of the will to work.

What many entrepreneurs lack is an understanding of just how deeply their managerial style may affect the survival and growth of their venture. How can they tell whether their managerial style is autocratic or participatory? One way is to use the chart in Exhibit 17.4, developed by Rensis Likert at the

For a business to thrive without conflict, the chemistry among fellow workers must be conducive to an easy give and take of differences in viewpoint.

EXHIBIT 17.4

Analysis of managerial style.

Record your answers at the proper point on the spectrum. For example, on the first question, if you answer "almost complete," put a checkmark between "substantial" and "complete," but closer to "complete." When you have answered each question, draw a line through the checkmarks from the top to the bottom of the chart. The result is a profile of your managerial style.

		System 1 Exploitive Authoritative[1]	System 2 Benevolent Authoritative[2]	System 3 Consultative[3]	System 4 Participatory[4]
Leadership	How much confidence do you demonstrate in your employees?	None	Little	Substantial	Complete ✓
	How free do they feel to talk to you about their jobs?	Not at all	Not very	Rather free	Fully free
	Do you seek your employees' ideas and use them, if worthy?	Seldom	Sometimes	Usually	Always
Communication	How much communication is aimed at achieving your venture's goals?	Very little	Little	Quite a bit	A great deal
	What is the direction of information flow?	Downward	Mostly downward	Down and up	Down, up, and sideways
	How is downward communication accepted?	With suspicion	Possibly with suspicion	With caution	With an open mind
	How accurate is upward communication?	Often wrong	Censored for the boss	Limited accuracy	Accurate
	How well do you know the problems your employees face?	Know little	Some knowledge	Quite well	Very well

		Style 1[1]	Style 2[2]	Style 3[3]	Style 4[4]
Motivation	Is predominant use made of 1 fear? 2 threats? 3 punishment? 4 rewards? 5 involvement?	1, 2, 3, occasionally 4	4, some 3	4, some 3 and 5	5, 4, based on group-set goals
	Where is responsibility felt for achieving your venture's goals?	Mostly at top	Top and middle	Fairly general	At all levels
Decisions	At what level are decisions formally made?	Mostly at top	Policy at top, some delegation	Broad policy at top, more delegation	Throughout but well integrated
	What is the origin of the technical and professional knowledge used in decision making?	Top management	Upper and middle management	To a certain extent, throughout	To a great extent, throughout
	Are your employees involved in decisions related to their work?	Not at all	Occasionally consulted	Generally consulted	Fully involved
	What does the decision-making process contribute to motivation?	Nothing, often weakens it	Relatively little	Some contribution	Substantial contribution

[1]This style describes those entrepreneurs who behave as absolute dictators. They believe that the proper employer-employee relationship exists only when employees do precisely as they are told—with no ifs, ands, or buts about the matter.

[2]Both job-oriented and employee-oriented, this paternalistic style describes those entrepreneurs who enhance their employees' quality of life as well as the content of their jobs, but who are just shy of seeking their advice and recommendations on how best to do their work.

[3]This style carries the prior style to a loftier level and invites employees to give advice and to suggest alternative courses of action on matters affecting them, but the entrepreneur alone makes the final choice.

[4]This style is the last word. It calls for entrepreneurs to let employees make their own choices and to open their books for all employees to see, thus instilling a strong sense of family and unity throughout a venture.

Source: Adapted from *The Human Organization* by Rensis Likert. Copyright © 1967 by McGraw-Hill, Inc. Reproduced by the permission of the McGraw-Hill Companies.

Institute of Social Relations of the University of Michigan. By answering the questions, entrepreneurs may learn a great deal about themselves and about the way they treat their employees.

Humorist Josh Billings once said: "It's not only one of the most difficult things to know yourself, but one of the most inconvenient ones, too." Although it may be an uncomfortable task, the more realistic one's view of oneself, the better one's performance as a manager. Flexible entrepreneurs change because they want to and because they must, in response to insights gained on the job.

▶ **Self-Image**

Entrepreneurs cannot begin to know their employees without first knowing themselves. Every human being, consciously or not, has a self-image. We may, for example, see ourselves as quick or slow, neat or sloppy, busy or lazy. Everything we feel, hear, or do is filtered through our self-image, with the result that we are what our self-image allows us to be. For entrepreneurs to grow as managers, they must recognize—and often change—their self image. To twist an old saying, it is not what entrepreneurs know that counts but rather who they are.

Thus, it is mainly through self-discovery and change of self-image that entrepreneurs may learn how employees work best. These processes go on continuously, yet many entrepreneurs ignore them. If entrepreneurs do not understand how their employees see themselves, and what motivates them, they cannot give their employees the tools they need to change. The result is often a poor product or a slipshod service that jeopardizes the firm's survival and halts growth. At a conference of business leaders, Robert Townsend, former head of Avis, Inc., offered these prescriptions:

> The boss should be constantly with the workers. So important is this that the paraphernalia of the boss should be entirely removed. He shouldn't have a mahogany office. He shouldn't have a limousine. He shouldn't have a space reserved outside for his car. He shouldn't be addressed by anything but his first name. And he shouldn't receive a salary more than five times that of the least of his employees. . . .
>
> What happens then? Well sir, morale is very high, workers have a sense of participation in the business, absenteeism all but disappears, and the problem is pretty well solved.[9]

This quotation suggests the need for entrepreneurs and employees alike to observe what a philosophy and ethics professor, Thomas Michaud, calls the *employee bill of rights,* which appears in Exhibit 17.5.

▶ **The Entrepreneur as Coach**

The art of bringing out the best in employees can be learned by observing the methods of successful athletic coaches. Just as coaches must be close to their players, so must entrepreneurs be close to their employees. Teams with top-flight coaches generally win consistently, mostly because they know their job and have a knack for communicating that knowledge to their players:

▶ Players understand how to carry out their assignments because their coach has meticulously laid out the game plan and the plays necessary to handle the competition.

You Have the Right to:	And You Have the Obligation to:
Refuse requests without feeling guilty	Help if you reasonably can
Change your mind	Have good reasons for your decisions
Be forgiven for honest mistakes	Forgive the honest mistakes of others
Accept gifts of nominal value	Refuse gifts that may be too valuable
Express views, positive or negative	State your views so they do not injure others
Criticize	Communicate criticisms constructively
Make requests in the workplace	Request help from one capable of helping
Start and build relationships	Stop attempts of friendship if the other party is unwilling
Stand up for your own interests	Remember that others may also have needs

Source: "Employee Bill of Rights" from Wheeling Jesuit College, as seen in "Workplace Etiquette" by Vikki Kratz, Business Ethics, October 1995.

▶ Players carry out their assignments with West Point precision because their coach has created an atmosphere of fairness, confidence, and camaraderie, which generates the will to win.

Creating this kind of work atmosphere is difficult. No two employees are precisely alike. What appeals to one employee may not appeal to another. So, to help employees achieve their best, entrepreneurs must understand each employee's unique needs.

▶ **Giving Recognition to Employees**

How may entrepreneurs help employees earn status and develop better opinions of themselves and their jobs? There are a variety of ways, among them:

▶ Sharing decision making with employees, as discussed earlier

▶ Giving employees greater responsibility when they are ready to assume it

▶ Taking employees' ideas and suggestions to heart

▶ Judging employees rigorously on merit and rewarding them accordingly

Entrepreneurs who follow these suggestions are likely to succeed. By building up their employees' self-image and improving their status, entrepreneurs are likely to keep growing in stature themselves—a process that feeds on itself.

Moreover, as a venture expands, talented men and women will be drawn to it. People generally prefer to work for a growing venture, mostly because growth creates opportunities for promotion. The possibility of promotion is, of course, a strong incentive for improved performance and for personal growth.

▶ **The McKinsey Study on Excellence**

Since the early 1980s, few business subjects have sparked more interest than excellence or, more accurately, the pursuit of excellence. One of the many books on this subject, *In Search of Excellence* by Thomas Peters and Robert Waterman, looked at the traits of such well-known giant corporations as IBM and 3M. It made *The New York Times* best-seller list for 59 straight weeks—a record for a book on business.

Authors generally focus on successful big businesses and what makes them tick, ignoring smaller businesses. An exception was a study by McKinsey and Company, the world's largest management consulting firm. This study found that successful small businesses do a number of things right to foster excellence—for example, they:

▶ **Innovate as a way of life**   Winners continue to generate a stream of new products, services, and ways of doing business that help them hone their competitive edge.

▶ **Create and develop smaller market niches**   It is important to expand into related niches only, where existing strengths such as distinctive technologies, good sites, and entrenched marketing channels already exist.

▶ **Compete on value, not price**   Winners deliver products and services that provide consistently superior value to all their customers. Often, these products and services cost the customers more rather than less.

▶ **Develop a strong sense of mission**   Winners have an unusually clear sense of their distinctive role—where they will and will not compete, what kinds of products they will and will not offer, what level of quality they expect to produce.

▶ **Attend to fundamentals**   Winners worry about return on investment. They employ strong financial disciplines to generate cash flow—designated for the innovation of new products and for increases in organizational strength.

▶ **Attack bureaucratization**   Winning companies consciously restrict overhead. They make use of temporary work groups and task forces to meet short-term goals.

▶ **Encourage experimentation**   Unlike companies that fire or demote risk takers who fail, winners bend over backward to avoid punishing failure, so that risk takers can learn from their failures and generate solid new ideas.

▶ **Think like customers**   Salespersons for some winners spend most of their time working in a customer's plant, looking for ways to save money or to boost performance for that customer. They have learned that the best way to make money for themselves is to make money for their customers.

▶ **Motivate with money**   Incentive pay tied to company performance tends to be much higher in winners than in competitive companies in the same industries.

▶ **Set examples at the top** The heads of winning companies show extraordinary perseverance, even obsession, about doing quality work. Despite their success, they continue to work hard and for long hours. They are deeply involved in details and can talk convincingly about their products or services, customer relationships, competitive positions, and the like.[11]

In the pursuit of excellence day in and day out, the entrepreneur must set the example. As the legendary football coach, Vince Lombardi, put it: "You don't try to win some of the time. You don't try to do things right some of the time. You do them right all of the time."[12]

Generally, excellence is a product of expectations. If entrepreneurs expect excellence from their employees, they often get it. If they do not, it rarely occurs. Only highly motivated employees are likely to offer superior products or services—the kind that cause customers to return again and again.

As suggested earlier, entrepreneurs crave the loyalty of their employees. Some entrepreneurs, however, believe that their employees should be blindly loyal to them. They expect employees to stick by them through thick and thin, regardless of how they are treated.

Such false loyalty weakens rather than strengthens a venture. For, true loyalty means working up to one's capabilities, doing the best one knows how. Thus, true loyalty is to the job, not to the entrepreneur.

▶ **Diversity**

We would be remiss if we failed to revisit the subject of diversity, given its importance to the practice of human relations. No longer an issue of race and gender alone, diversity touches every aspect of business, opening doors to new opportunities for entrepreneurs and other business leaders alike. In the words of Roosevelt Thomas Jr., founder of The Institute for Managing Diversity:

Managing diversity is much more than a concept, much more than a program, much more than an initiative. Businesses have come to know it as a process that goes far beyond the interests of a particular individual or group or individuals.

In the context of today's environment, they see managing diversity as providing a perspective that can enhance creativity and growth—not only with respect to the workforce, but also synergistic progress in other arenas such as diverse functions, acquisitions, and multiple lines of business.[13]

Indeed, and as suggested in Chapter 3, diversity is a competitive necessity in a global economy such as ours. Entrepreneurs and other business leaders must therefore be open, thoughtful, and accepting of other people's values, customs, and culture as our world and workplace grows smaller. Turning to Exhibit 17.6, note that diversity has already struck responsive chords, as businesses more and more embrace diversity in their appreciation of individual differences in the workplace—be they ethnic, religious, or cultural. As the distinguished historian Arthur Schlesinger Jr. reminds us:

The genius of America lies in its capacity to forge a single nation from peoples of remarkably diverse racial, religious, and ethnic origins. The American identity will never be fixed and final; it will always be in the making.[14]

EXHIBIT 17.6

Results of survey on diversity in the workplace.

Source: Society of Human Resources Management, reported by Donna Fenn, "Diversity More than Just Affirmative Action," *Inc.* (July 1995), p. 93.

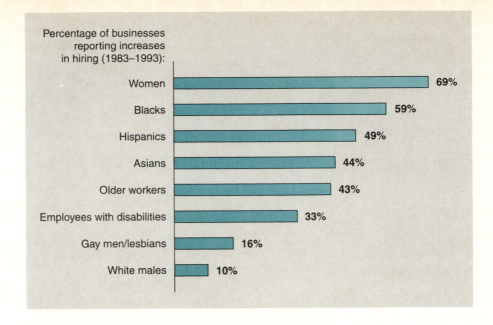

Percentage of businesses reporting increases in hiring (1983–1993):

Women	69%
Blacks	59%
Hispanics	49%
Asians	44%
Older workers	43%
Employees with disabilities	33%
Gay men/lesbians	16%
White males	10%

Wage, Salary, and Fringe Benefit Policies

To attract and keep good employees, entrepreneurs must make sure their pay scales compare favorably with those offered by competitors. It is also sound policy to pay employees on merit, gearing pay to performance. Employees, after all, expect their pay to reflect the skills and energies they put into their work.

▶ **Legal Obligations**   No matter how wages and salaries are set, however, entrepreneurs must meet certain legal obligations to employees. For example, for virtually every employee, entrepreneurs must pay social security taxes. So, they are required by law:

▶ To withhold a certain percentage of wages and salaries from each employee's paycheck

▶ To contribute a matching amount

▶ To deposit the withheld amounts in a bank, either monthly or quarterly, depending on the amounts

Entrepreneurs need legal and accounting help to make sure they honor all their legal obligations. New obligations keep appearing, and old ones keep changing. Besides paying social security taxes, all employers must meet certain legal obligations affecting employees, among them:

▶ **Federal income taxes**   Entrepreneurs who pay salaries and wages, or have employees who report tips, must withhold a certain amount from each employee's paycheck.

▶ **Workers' compensation insurance**   Entrepreneurs with fulltime employees must protect them from loss of income due to injury on the job.

- ▶ **State unemployment insurance** If they pay wages, entrepreneurs must also contribute to a state fund that is drawn on when any of their employees are laid off but are willing and able to work.

- ▶ **Federal unemployment taxes** If they have four or more employees who put in 20 or more weeks a year, entrepreneurs must pay federal unemployment taxes, which serve the same purpose as state unemployment insurance.

- ▶ **Federal wage and hour laws** Entrepreneurs who sell across state lines, hold federal government contracts, or have sales in excess of $500,000 must abide by federal laws that set a minimum hourly wage. These laws also regulate child labor and worker health and safety.

- ▶ **Civil Rights Act, Title VII** Entrepreneurs with employees covered under the federal wage and hour laws must also abide by the Civil Rights Act, which ensures that all job applicants and employees are treated fairly and equally, regardless of race, color, religion, gender, age, or ethnic origin.

- ▶ **Occupational Safety and Health Administration (OSHA)** Overseen by the U.S. Department of Labor, OSHA's rules and standards are intended to prevent workplace injuries and hazards. OSHA covers not only factories and construction sites but also offices and shops—in fact, anywhere employees may be found.

- ▶ **Americans with Disabilities Act (ADA)** Limited to businesses with 15 or more employees, ADA calls for disabled job applicants to be treated precisely the same as those without disabilities. This act also requires businesses to reach out to the disabled by, for example, widening doorways or modifying washrooms.

▶ Fringe Benefits

A form of pay, fringe benefits strongly influence the lives of employees. These benefits have given the nation's average employee a standard of living higher than ever before. The average employee now receives the following benefits:

- ▶ Paid vacations, holidays, and personal days
- ▶ Life, unemployment, and medical insurance
- ▶ A pension plan and social security
- ▶ Paid leave for illness or jury duty

Fringe benefits are a significant part of a business's payroll. As Exhibit 17.7 shows, these benefits in 1993 accounted for 41 percent of the average employer's yearly payroll. In contrast, fringe benefits in 1930 cost the average employer just 3 percent of the total amount paid for wages and salaries.

Generally, entrepreneurs must offer attractive fringe benefits for these reasons:

- ▶ To attract and hold good employees
- ▶ To help upgrade their employees' quality of life
- ▶ To keep pace with benefits offered by competitors
- ▶ To meet the legal obligations imposed by local, state, and federal governments

EXHIBIT 17.7
Fringe benefits as a
percentage of total payroll:
1993 versus 1930.

Source: U.S. Chamber of
Commerce Research Center,
Employee Benefits (Washington,
D.C.: U.S. Chamber of
Commerce, 1994), p. 5.

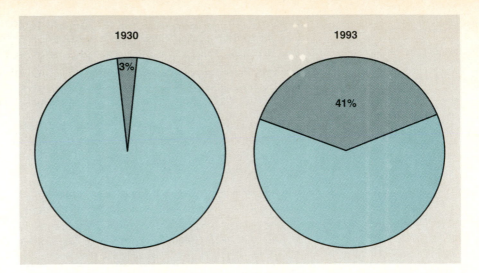

The most important of these reasons is the first—to attract and hold good employees. Other things being equal, they seek employers who offer a complete package of fringe benefits. This attitude often puts entrepreneurs at a disadvantage, as few small businesses can afford to offer the same package of benefits that giant corporations can. This means they often are forced to compete for talent on other terms, such as the appeal of contributing to a venture's growth.

Sooner or later, however, most employees come to expect the same fringe benefits, no matter whom they work for. Fringe benefits are so common today that employees look upon them as a right rather than a privilege.

SUMMARY

Good human relations are founded on goodwill and applied common sense. Entrepreneurs who practice good human relations treat their employees with dignity and respect, and recognize that they need to feel that the work they do really matters and that their employer is interested in them and appreciates their work. Above all, entrepreneurs must recognize that every employee is a complex individual with unique needs and wants.

In his hierarchy of needs, Abraham Maslow classifies all human needs in the order of their importance to the individual. He presents them as a pyramid of five levels:

▶ Physiological needs
▶ Safety and security
▶ Belongingness and love
▶ Esteem
▶ Self-actualization

Entrepreneurs lead by enabling employees to work easily and productively, as a way to bring out their best. They must want to help employees become achievers and, ultimately, must understand how their leadership style may affect the survival and growth of their venture.

An essential part of any venture is its wage, salary, and fringe benefit policies. With regard to wages and salaries, entrepreneurs as employers are legally obligated:

▶ To withhold a certain percentage of wages from each employee's paycheck
▶ To contribute a matching amount for social security
▶ To deposit the withheld amount in a bank

In addition, employers must meet other legal obligations, among them:

▶ Federal income taxes
▶ Workers' compensation insurance
▶ State unemployment insurance
▶ Federal unemployment taxes
▶ Federal wage and hour laws
▶ Civil Rights Act, Title VII
▶ Occupational Safety and Health Administration (OSHA)
▶ Americans with Disabilities Act (ADA)

Also, employees have come to expect fringe benefits that enhance their lives. These benefits include:

▶ Paid vacations, holidays, and personal days
▶ Life, unemployment, and medical insurance
▶ A pension plan and social security
▶ Paid leave for illness or jury duty

The availability of these benefits affects the entrepreneur's ability to attract and hold good employees.

Discussion and Review Questions

1. What does the term *human relations* mean to you? What is the importance of good human relations in the workplace?
2. Comment on the following statement by an entrepreneur: "We really need to take a hard look at behavior in our venture. Our employees are totally unmotivated. Nothing gets done when it should, or in the way that it should be done."
3. Are happy workers always productive workers? Explain your answer.
4. What kind of manager is likely to earn the respect and loyalty of employees?
5. Is there one best way to manage a venture that works for all entrepreneurs? Explain your answer.
6. What is the best way to measure the quality of human relations in a venture? Explain your answer.

7. Abraham Maslow classified human needs as a hierarchy with five distinct levels. Describe the characteristics of each level and discuss how each can be met.
8. What did the Hawthorne experiment show?
9. Describe one way in which entrepreneurs may create a work atmosphere that brings out the best in their employees.
10. How would you, as an entrepreneur, foster the pursuit of excellence among your employees?
11. Describe the entrepreneur's legal obligations in the area of human relations.
12. Why are attractive salary, wage, and fringe benefit policies so vital to the success of a venture?
13. Are fringe benefits a right or a privilege? Explain your answer.
14. How would you, as an entrepreneur, compete for topnotch talent if you could not afford to pay the same salaries that large corporations can pay?
15. Define these terms: *managing, Theory X, Theory Y, self-actualization, workers' compensation, fringe benefits.*

Building a Business Plan

Human Relations

As discussed in the text, much of an entrepreneur's success in human relations depends on simple things, such as making a store a friendlier place to work or making a plant more comfortable and safe. Unfortunately, many entrepreneurs often ignore these simple things.

The Importance of Human Relations

To be successful, entrepreneurs must earn employees' commitment by recognizing that they need to feel that the work they do really matters and that their employers are interested in them and appreciate what they do. In fact, there are a variety of methods entrepreneurs can use to help employees earn status and develop better opinions of themselves and their jobs.

Instructions for Worksheet 17

To complete part 1 of the business plan, you must describe the ideal employee(s) that you need for your business. In part 2, develop methods to increase employee ideas and suggestions. Then in part 3, determine if shared decision making is appropriate for your business.

Part 1—The Ideal Employee

Before answering the questions in this section, you may want to review the definition for your business that was last revised in Chapter 12.

1. How would you describe the ideal employee(s) in your firm?

2. What type of skills does your employee(s) need?

3. How much will it cost to obtain the type of employee(s) that you described in your answer to question 1?

4. Can you afford to hire this type of employee(s)?

Part 2—Employee Ideas and Suggestions

Although no two employees are precisely alike, successful business owners must understand each employee's needs if they are going to build trust and encourage the employee to generate ideas and make suggestions.

5. In what ways can you build a trusting relationship with employees?

6. Describe the methods you can use to encourage employees to share ideas and make suggestions.

Part 3—Shared Decision Making

In essence, shared decision making encourages entrepreneurs to seek out their employees' ideas and to organize work around jobs broad enough to have meaning.

7. Can shared decision making be used to improve productivity in your business? Justify your answer.

8. In what ways can you allow employees to share decision making in your firm?

9. In what ways can you recognize employees who perform above and beyond the call of duty?

CASE 17A ▶ *Newe Daisterre Glas*

Alfred Brickel founded Newe Daisterre Glas (*new dawn glass* in Old English) to create stained-glass windows and other works of glass art. His fledgling company has already designed and built the world's biggest kaleidoscope, mostly out of glass. But sales revenues have failed to match Brickel's reputation for artistic excellence. In fact, he has laid off half his workforce, cutting it from eight to four employees. He is wondering what to do to build up demand for his unique service.

Background

The son of a physician, Brickel qualifies as a dyed-in-the-wool entrepreneur. Just 25 years old, he has worked on and off for 11 years. At 14, he set up his own landscaping business in the summer. Then at 16, bored with school, he left home for Bloomington, Indiana. There he did odd jobs while earning his high school diploma.

Brickel's next stop was college, where he was promptly expelled for poor attendance and even poorer grades. After a brief stint clerking in a grocery store, he enrolled at another university to study art. This time he stayed four years, graduating with a bachelor of arts degree. In his junior year, he earned most of his living by painting houses on his own.

In his senior year, Brickel decided to go into the glass art business—by accident. He was sitting in his parents' living room one December day, when his eye caught a replica of a stained-glass window, used as a Christmas decoration. Its beauty fired his imagination. That was the unlikely beginning of a hobby that led him three months later to set up his own business turning out works of glass art.

Still in college, Brickel worked at his new venture part-time and also moonlighted in a bar 4 hours a night. All told, he was putting in 90 hours a week studying and working. After graduation, he gave up his job as a bartender to work full-time at researching his market and organizing his new venture. His beginning balance sheet appears in Exhibit 17A.1.

Takes Partner

Although he himself put up the entire $6,000 out of savings, Brickel took in Dale Mitchell as an equal partner. With the help of a lawyer, they drew up articles of copartnership specifying that:

▶ The two partners would share equally in the firm's profits

▶ Brickel would oversee all design, production, purchasing, financial, and employee relations activities

▶ Mitchell would oversee all marketing and public relations activities

On the advice of his lawyer, Brickel also hired a certified public accountant to design a simple bookkeeping system. "Every day I set aside time to make entries in my books," says Brickel. "Every three months the accountant picks them up to prepare an income statement and a balance sheet. He also does my tax returns for the city, county, state, and federal governments."

But Brickel does not find these financial statements helpful. "My business is so small, I can easily keep on top of things," he says. "There's little that goes on that I don't know about. I'm here day and night. Besides, my people and I are like a close-knit family. Each of us is interested in doing what's best for the others in the family."

From the start, Brickel's education has stood him in good stead, especially in design. And what he did not know, he quickly picked up through trial and error and from a 77-year-old glass cutter. "There are only 8 left in the whole country," says Brickel. "In the 1930s, there were more than 1,500. It's really a dying art."

EXHIBIT 17A.1
Newe Daisterre Glas: Beginning balance sheet.

Assets		Equities	
Cash	$1,000	Liabilities	$ 0
Supplies	800	Owners' equity	6,000
Equipment	2,400		
Organizational costs	1,100		
Prepaid expenses	700		
Total assets	$6,000	Total equities	$6,000

One of a Kind

Brickel's business is unique. His creations range from a stained-glass jack of diamonds to a turn-of-the-century ticket booth, from individualized Christmas ornaments to custom-made fiberglass kayaks. But his bread-and-butter trade comes from original stained-glass windows. Photographs of his creations appear in Exhibit 17A.2.

The work he is proudest of is a kaleidoscope that may be the world's largest. Ordered by a nightclub appropriately called The Kaleidoscope, it weighs 425 pounds and measures 12 feet in length and 3 feet in diameter. Brickel made it out of pulleys, rocks, glass, posters, and plywood. Today it sits in his studio waiting for a buyer with $3,000 to spare. He had to repossess it from the nightclub owner because "the guy couldn't pay."

Brickel's business is unique in other ways too. For example, he turns down repeat orders. "Everything I do is a one-of-a-kind, handmade thing," he says. "I don't like to repeat myself. I'm not a mass producer." Although in business to make a profit, he thinks of himself more as an artist than a businessman. He wants to bring back the esthetics of hand craftsmanship, an "ancient craft that some people think is dead."

All of his coworkers echo his business philosophy. For example, his vice president, Delbert Morrow, says: "The important thing is that we love

EXHIBIT 17A.2
Newe Daisterre Glas, Inc.: Examples of glass art.

what we do. We have ambitions only to the point of comfort, but we do get good money for what we do." Indeed, no item sells for less than $40, and most sell at prices in excess of $200.

Unit prices may be high, but revenues have failed to take off. In May 1989, revenues peaked at $12,800. By July 1990, monthly revenues had dropped off by half. This sharp drop forced Brickel to reduce his workforce from eight to four employees. "I hated to do it," says Brickel, "but I had no choice. There wasn't enough work for them."

All his coworkers are artistic. In fact, Brickel recruited them from classes he gives in glass art at his alma mater. None of them draws more than $200 a week in wages. And Brickel himself often draws less. "It's a labor of love," he says. "We could all be making much more."

Steps to Boost Sales

Brickel has looked for ways to boost revenues to levels that would enable him to rehire the artists he laid off. "I feel a responsibility toward them," says Brickel. "If I could drum up more sales, I could also increase their wages. Let's face it, $100 to $200 a week doesn't go very far these days."

To boost revenues, Brickel already has taken several steps:

▶ He replaced Mitchell with Morrow, whose main charge is to find new customers and, equally important, to come up with new product ideas. One idea Morrow has come up with is the manufacture of custom-built kayaks.

▶ He incorporated his business. It had been a two-way partnership. The new company was capitalized at $500, the minimum allowable in the state. Brickel put up the entire $500 himself, in return taking 80 percent of the stock. He gave Morrow and another coworker each 10 percent of the new company. He believes that "one way to make the company grow is to have employees with a vested interest."

▶ He installed a cost-accounting system to keep closer tabs on the cost of each job as it passes through production.

▶ He applied for a three-year $10,000 loan from a local bank, telling the loan officer he needed the money to increase wages, promote the company and its products in a wider market, purchase more materials, and expand into new product lines.

Brickel is sure these steps will lead to "much higher revenues." Recent financial statements appear in Exhibits 17A.3 and 17A.4. A photograph of his workshop appears in Exhibit 17A.5.

EXHIBIT 17A.3

Newe Daisterre Glas, Inc.: Income statement (for three months ending July 31, 1990).

Sales revenues		$19,140
Cost of sales		
Purchases	$5,960	
Less: Ending inventory	3,940	
Materials used	2,020	
Labor	6,460	
	8,480	
Less: Work in process	4,240	4,240
Gross profit		$14,900
Operating expenses		
Rent	$3,640	
Utilities	1,000	
Automobile	780	
Insurance	660	
Office supplies	460	
Maintenance	460	
Advertising	240	
Legal and audit	160	
Travel	120	
Telephone	100	
Rubbish	20	7,640
Operating profit		$ 7,260

EXHIBIT 17A.4

Newe Daisterre Glas, Inc.: Balance sheet (July 31, 1990).

Assets			Equities		
Current assets			Current liabilities		
Cash	$ 40		Accounts payable		$ 3,240
Accounts receivable	2,380		Other liabilities		
Inventory	3,960		Loan payable, officer		16,120
Work in process	4,240	$10,620			
Equipment and fixtures		17,000	Owners' equity		
			Common stock	$ 500	
			Retained earnings	7,760	8,260
Total assets		$27,620	Total equities		$27,620

EXHIBIT 17A.5

Newe Daisterre Glas, Inc.: View of workshop and Alfred Brickel.

Questions

1. If you were Alfred Brickel, what would you do to boost sales revenues?
2. Comment on Brickel as an entrepreneur.
3. How well has Brickel done so far?
4. Comment on the way Brickel organized and financed his venture.
5. If you had the chance, would you invest in Brickel's venture? Why or why not?

In just seven years, Dwight Hawkins, originally a carpenter, has seen his construction firm grow into the second largest home-building firm in Jacksonville, Florida. Last year alone, Hawkins Home, Inc., constructed more than 500 homes. Hawkins Home stands out among local land developers because it does an effective job of responding quickly to customers' needs and problems, while keeping construction costs well below average.

Hawkins credits the firm's effectiveness to what he calls "flexible organization." Each of his six field construction managers has broad decision-making authority. In his words: "I encourage each field manager to run his construction project as if it were his own business. I'm a jack of all trades, and I expect my managers to be, too. They don't come running to me to wipe their noses for every little problem. They know what needs to be done, and so I stay out of their way and let them get on with it." Hawkins often has told visitors and customers that they won't find any red tape at Hawkins Home.

During the past year, as commercial building has begun to catch up with the residential boom, Hawkins has been thinking seriously about diversifying into commercial construction. Unfortunately, Hawkins Home lacks the funds to buy or lease the heavy equipment needed to build schools, stores, and small office buildings.

A Possible Solution

At this point, the most promising alternative seems to be a merger with Interstate Builders, Inc., a large Chicago-based commercial builder. Interstate's legal staff has worked out a very tempting stock-trade arrangement.

From a financial viewpoint, the merger proposal looks good, but Hawkins is having second thoughts about how well he and his firm would fit into Interstate's huge operations. In the first place, he deplores the long time it takes to get something through the bureaucratic machinery at Interstate. For example, by the time a bid has passed through the engineering, planning, and legal departments at Interstate, ten months have gone by. At Hawkins Home, the bid cycle rarely takes more than three months.

Hawkins also doubts Interstate's ability to adapt to the wide variation in small-scale commercial jobs. Finally, Hawkins is not enthusiastic about the prospect of reporting to the president of Interstate indirectly, through three layers of management. During the recent merger talks, it took Hawkins three trips to Chicago and a half-dozen conferences before he even met Interstate's president.

Questions

1. Contrast the organizational styles of the two firms.
2. How do you suppose Dwight Hawkins's field managers would respond to working in an organization like Interstate?
3. If you were Hawkins, what organizational concessions would you demand from Interstate before agreeing to a merger?

Source: Adapted from Robert Kreitner, *Management*, 2nd Ed. (Boston: Houghton Mifflin, 1983) pp. 261–262 © Houghton Mifflin Company. Used by permission.

Empowerment in the Workplace

The Federal Commission on the Future of Worker-Management Relations was assigned the task of exploring ways that employee involvement could be increased in the workplace. The commission found that up to one-third of the workplaces now use employee participation in some form, and that another 50 million workers would like to have more say about their jobs. Companies that have included their employees in traditional management responsibilities show a clear pattern of high productivity and improved economic performance. Here are two examples:

▶ Several years ago, Chesapeake Packaging Corporation, a 145-employee corrugated-container manufacturer in Baltimore, was embroiled in a potential financial disaster. Management decided that one way to involve the employees in solving the problem was to open the books and ask for suggestions on how to improve profits.

One suggestion was to carefully monitor who was hired, retained, and fired. Now every job applicant goes through a series of job-related tests, is interviewed by a four-employee panel, and is subject to a peer review every 90 days for the first year. Fellow workers determine whether new employees are taking their jobs seriously and contributing intellectually or are merely showing up for work and their paychecks. The panel makes the final decision on which new employees become part of the regular work force.

▶ At Nucor, a mini-mill steel maker located in Charlotte, North Carolina, 80 percent of the employees are hourly wage earners organized into teams. Management encourages team members to pretend they own their own franchise. They are totally in charge of completing their tasks as efficiently and effectively as possible.

Nucor's bonus system allows employees to boost their pay to as much as three times the industry average, based on their team's productivity. Employees who are tardy lose their bonus for that day; those who are more than an hour late or who miss a day of work lose their bonus for the week. If one member of the team is not pulling his or her weight, the team works together to solve the problem quickly so that they can get back on track.

Questions

1. How would you feel about the power of the peer-review panel if you were a new employee at Chesapeake Packaging? How would your opinion change if you were a member of the panel?
2. Does Nucor's bonus system enhance or inhibit teamwork? How?
3. Do you find the concept of empowerment frightening or exciting? Explain.

Source: Reece, Barry L. and Rhonda Brandt Case "Empowerment in the Workplace," adapted from *Effective Human Relations in Organizations*, Sixth Edition. Copyright © 1996 by Houghton Mifflin Company. Used with permission.

Purchasing and Inventories

He who freely praises what he means to purchase, and he who enumerates the faults of what he means to sell, may set up a partnership with honesty.

—Lavater

How wisely entrepreneurs do their purchasing may well spell the difference between profit and loss. Thus, they must look sharply at the prices charged by suppliers for products and services—to make sure they get the most value for their money. Without question, if done wisely, purchasing offers entrepreneurs the opportunities to cut costs and boost profits.

In this chapter, we begin by discussing the central importance of purchasing. We then look at ways to manage purchasing efficiently. Next, we move to the related subject of inventories, and how best to control them.

The Importance of Purchasing

In a word, the goal of purchasing must be to improve a venture's profits. Keeping that goal uppermost in mind, entrepreneurs must make every effort to choose the products, services, and sources of supply that best meet their needs at the least possible cost—yet *without* sacrificing quality.

To some entrepreneurs, the idea that purchasing may make or break a venture seems far-fetched. But it is not, as evidenced by the fact that wholesalers, retailers, and manufacturers spend vast sums on purchases—for example, and as depicted in Exhibit 18.1:

▶ Wholesalers generally spend 80 to 85 cents of every sales dollar to purchase products for resale to retailers. This means, for example, that a wholesaler with sales of $1,000,000 a year may spend as much as $800,000 for the products it resells to retailers.

EXHIBIT 18.1
Relative importance of
what it costs to purchase
products,* by industry
group.

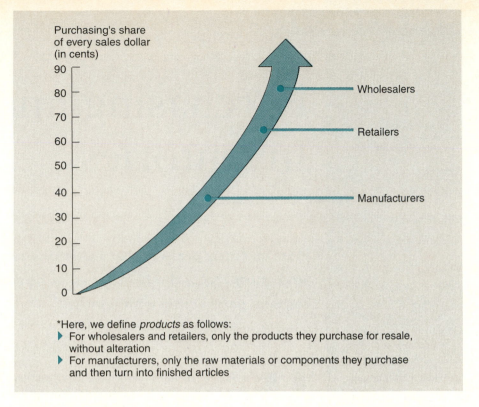

*Here, we define *products* as follows:
▶ For wholesalers and retailers, only the products they purchase for resale, without alteration
▶ For manufacturers, only the raw materials or components they purchase and then turn into finished articles

▶ Retailers generally spend 60 to 70 cents of every sales dollar to purchase products for resale to consumers.

▶ Manufacturers generally spend 20 to 50 cents of every sales dollar to purchase raw materials for conversion into finished product.

Clearly, with such vast sums at stake, entrepreneurs can ill afford to take lightly their purchasing decisions, especially on price. Further evidence of the central importance of purchasing appears in Exhibit 18.2, which shows dramatically the effect on profits of savings in purchase costs. Note the powerful incentive to save; for example:

If the entrepreneur's profit-to-sales ratio is only 2 percent, a purchase savings of just $1,000 would equal the profit earned on a sales increase of $50,000. Put another way, it would take a sales increase of $50,000 to have the *same* effect on profits as a savings of $1,000!

Purchasing Management

Purchasing covers much more than the mere act of buying. It also calls for such varied skills as the accurate forecasting of needs and the observance of ethical relations with suppliers. Computer knowledge is helpful as well, because many purchasing procedures can be refined by using a computer. Broadly speaking, purchasing involves:

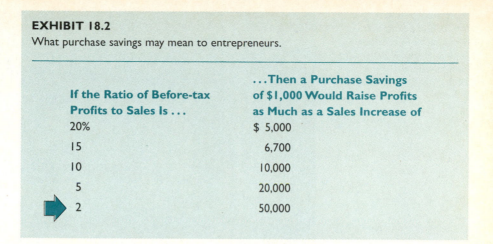

EXHIBIT 18.2

What purchase savings may mean to entrepreneurs.

If the Ratio of Before-tax Profits to Sales Is ...	...Then a Purchase Savings of $1,000 Would Raise Profits as Much as a Sales Increase of
20%	$ 5,000
15	6,700
10	10,000
5	20,000
2	50,000

EXHIBIT 18.3
Goals of purchasing management.

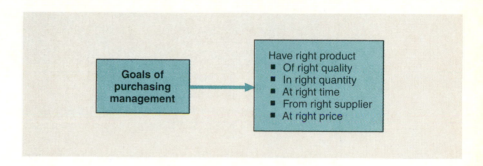

- Pinpointing the need for products and services
- Searching out and selecting suppliers
- Settling with suppliers such matters as price and payment terms
- Negotiating contracts or orders
- Making sure suppliers live up to their end of agreements

The classic rule of thumb for purchasing is to buy products and services of the right quality in the right quantity at the right time from the right supplier at the right price, as shown in Exhibit 18.3.

▶ Purchasing Guidelines

Let us now look more closely at each element in this rule of thumb.

Buying the Right Quality   Entrepreneurs must make sure that the products and services they purchase suit their needs. Manufacturers especially must see that raw materials meet their specifications to the letter. Otherwise, their product may turn out faulty. Take this example offered by the SBA:

EXAMPLE ▶

The owner of a small foundry one day complained bitterly about the amount of defective material he was receiving. "The raw material is guaranteed to meet quality specifications so as to contain less than 0.005 percent impurities. For the past three weeks, though, our

As in this toy factory warehouse, a business's decisions on what is best to keep in inventory depend on knowing precisely the demographic makeup of its market.

castings have been turning out rougher than they should. I'm sure that last shipment of raw materials wasn't as pure as it should have been. What do I do now?"[1] ▲▼▲

Buying the Right Quantity   Because they may have large sums of money tied up in inventory, entrepreneurs must make sure they buy the right quantity. In retailing, for example, too small a purchase may result in a loss of customers because of empty shelves. Too large a purchase, on the other hand, may mean excess inventory that threatens to become obsolete.

"Start out small" is the advice often offered by experienced suppliers, who have seen too many small businesses buried under oversized inventories. By starting with a small inventory, fledgling entrepreneurs are likely to be flexible enough to make changes quickly in response to customers' needs and wants.

Entrepreneurs must also be careful not to let personal biases stand in the way of sound marketing sense. In sporting goods, for example, new entrepreneurs tend to stock items with which they are familiar. But what suits them may not, for example, suit fishermen who want to choose from a selection of rods and tackle, or tennis players who want to choose from a selection of racket weights and types.

Buying at the Right Time   The timing of purchases is equally crucial. For manufacturers, buying at the right time means buying raw materials to meet production schedules without overloading warehouses with inventory. In times of inflation, it may also mean buying raw materials just before a price rise. Additionally, entrepreneurs should try to foresee what the economy will be like in the years to come. Will there be a recession or prosperity? Will there be shortages in raw materials? If so, they may have to look for substitute materials or stock up on materials early.

Timing is especially important in fast-moving industries like consumer electronics and apparel. In apparel, for example, fads and fashions come and go with dizzying speed. Yet, retailers often must order their stock months ahead of the selling season. Only with a keen sense of timing may they spot early shifts in customers' moods and tastes.

Buying from the Right Suppliers   Choosing the right supplier is one of the entrepreneur's most challenging decisions. A bad choice may cancel out meticulous plans for quality, quantity, price, and time of delivery. Some suppliers, for example, may be incapable of meeting precise specifications. Others may not be able to deliver on time. Still others may not sell at the right price. It is the entrepreneur's job to find the supplier who can offer the best mix on all these points, as in this example offered by the SBA:

EXAMPLE ▶   A manufacturer was wondering what to do about a new supplier of electronic components. "I got a good price on the first shipment, and so I signed an order for two more shipments. The bill I got for this last shipment is almost $600 over that of the first. I told the supplier to take it back or reduce the bill, and he said that his quotation gave him the right to increase prices as inflation and labor expenses rose for him. I know I could get the shipment for less elsewhere."[2] ▲▼▲

Entrepreneurs must continually review relationships with suppliers, looking especially for backup or better suppliers. For example, a wholesaler's reliance on a years-long relationship with a single supplier for a particular product may lead to trouble. The supplier's value to the wholesaler may vanish if, unbeknownst to the wholesaler, other suppliers have developed better products or fresh marketing ideas. In short, although relationships with reliable suppliers are vital, entrepreneurs must not ignore changes in the marketplace.

Entrepreneurs must also be cautious about purchasing a new product. It may look highly promising, but it is wise to make sure, perhaps beginning with a sample for testing and then small quantities for everyday use. Take this example:

EXAMPLE ▶   A small auto body repair shop could find itself seriously inconvenienced if it changed to a cheaper paint supplier too suddenly and ran into difficulties with color matching. One discontented customer can take away months of savings on a cheaper paint.[3] ▲▼▲

Buying at the Right Price   The right price is not always the lowest price. For one thing, a lower price may not supply entrepreneurs with the product quality that customers expect. A lower price may also mean poorer service from suppliers. So, in deciding on price, entrepreneurs must balance price with both quality and service.

Of these elements, quality must come first, followed by service. This means that suppliers must deliver products of the right quality in the right quantity at the right time. Last comes price, because little, if anything, would be gained by paying a lower price only to lose out on quality and service.

To compete against large corporations, resourceful entrepreneurs often form buying groups. For example, owners of small convenience stores often band together to couple the flexibility of their smallness with savings from high-volume purchasing, thus enabling member entrepreneurs to purchase most of their inventory at prices equal to those paid by large chains.

The Purchasing Cycle

Armed with these purchasing guidelines, entrepreneurs should now proceed by following the four steps of the purchasing cycle, as recommended by the SBA. Although the purchasing cycle is described below in retailing terms, all entrepreneurs who do purchasing—manufacturers, wholesalers, and service providers, as well as retailers—should find the concept helpful:

▶ **Estimating needs**   Before buying, entrepreneurs must estimate what they will need until their next review of the particular line of merchandise. For some items, estimating involves merely looking at inventory and past sales. For other lines, it entails risky decisions—which styles to select and how much of each to buy. Entrepreneurs do not want to be left with out-of-season or outmoded merchandise.

▶ **Selecting suppliers**   After estimating merchandise needs, entrepreneurs must find suppliers. If merchandise is available from only one vendor, the only decision is whether to carry the line. For most merchandise, however, there are several potential suppliers. In these instances, entrepreneurs must evaluate not only price but also quality and service, as well as reliable delivery, adjustment of problems, and help—with credit terms, with spacing deliveries, with inventory management, and in emergencies.

▶ **Negotiating purchases**   Negotiations involve the purchase price as well as quantities, delivery dates, single or multiple shipment deliveries, freight and packing expenses, guarantees on the quality of the merchandise, promotion and advertising allowances, special offers on slightly damaged materials or sellouts, and so on.

▶ **Following through**   Finally, to improve service, entrepreneurs must review their relationship with each supplier from time to time, to determine whether a change should be made. As necessary, they should search for backup or new suppliers.[4]

If a delivery date is crucial or a shipment is overdue, entrepreneurs must assume an even more active role. By every means available, they must negotiate with suppliers to speed up shipments. Doing so could prevent, for example, the shutdown of a plant due to shortages of vital raw materials.

▶ **Keeping Records**   At the very least, a good recordkeeping system must enable entrepreneurs to keep track of:

▶ All orders received and all shipments made to customers

▶ The rates at which purchased products are used

- Suppliers' quantities and delivery cycles
- Names of suppliers and their price lists
- Order cycles and quantities ordered
- Products returned by customers

These records enable the efficient handling of purchases, as suggested in this example:

An entrepreneur decides to replace worn-out tools with new ones. This decision sets a train of events in motion. First, his foreperson fills out a requisition stating the type and number of tools needed and gives it to the entrepreneur for approval. The entrepreneur then checks the requisition to make sure that the cost of the tools is correct, the description of the tools is complete, the quantity is sufficient, the delivery date is reasonable, and the routing is clear.

Next, the entrepreneur issues a purchase order, authorizing the purchase of the requisitioned tools. Two copies of this purchase order are sent to the supplier. One of these copies will later be returned, with the promised delivery date noted by the supplier. Other copies of the purchase order go to the entrepreneur's accountant and to the foreperson.

When the shipment comes in, the foreperson verifies its contents and sends her receiving copy of the purchase order to the accountant, thus completing the purchasing cycle. ▲▼▲

▶ Measuring Purchasing Performance

Entrepreneurs must measure their purchasing performance at least once a year, asking two key questions:

- How do my purchasing costs measure up to those of my competitors?
- What are my losses from shrinkage, spoilage, and theft?

The common way to measure purchasing performance is to compare a venture's cost of goods sold with the industry average. Published yearly by trade associations and professional organizations, industry averages are useful as standards of comparison, as discussed in Chapter 13. Take this example:

EXAMPLE ▶

The owner of a bookstore posted sales revenues of $360,000 and cost of goods sold of $240,000. To measure her purchasing performance, she would compare that performance with her industry's average for her size store, as follows:

	Entrepreneur's Bookstore		Industry Average
	Dollars	Ratios	Ratios
Sales revenues	$360,000	100.0%	100.0%
Cost of goods sold	240,000	66.7	64.0
Gross profit	$120,000	33.3%	36.0%

The entrepreneur spent too much on purchases—66.7 percent on sales compared to the industry average of 64.0 percent. Low performance is a signal to find out why and then to take remedial action. ▲▼▲

Losses from shrinkage, spoilage, and theft are discussed later in this chapter.

Inventory Management

Inventory has to do with the products that must be kept on hand, day in and day out, either:

▶ As products for wholesalers and retailers to resell, without alteration, or—

▶ As raw materials or components for manufacturers to turn into finished articles, or—

▶ As the finished articles themselves for manufacturers to sell

This definition excludes services like legal advice and shoe repair, because obviously such expertise can neither be stored nor stockpiled in the way that, say, laptop computers and rock salt can be.

Why have inventory at all? This rarely asked question is one that entrepreneurs must never overlook, as the answer bears strongly on how to best plan and control their inventories. Reasons for having inventory include:

▶ To avoid the loss of customers because a product is not in stock

▶ To enable customers to look over a product before buying it

▶ To capitalize on discounts in the price of raw materials

▶ To keep a plant from cutting back or shutting down

▶ To make a product in quantities that minimize costs

▶ To speculate against increases in price and cost

▶ To assure customers of prompt delivery

▶ To protect against strikes

Although this list applies to manufacturers, much of it also applies to wholesalers and retailers. Returning to our earlier example of the bookstore owner, let us now see how she might initially think through her need for inventory:

EXAMPLE ▶

From the vast crop of books in the marketplace, the bookstore owner must choose those titles suitable to her customers. It follows, then, that her inventory of titles must serve her customers' specific interests, and not her personal biases. This means she must be flexible and appeal to her customers' passions for, say, science fiction and mysteries, even if she has no personal interest in these subjects. ▲▼▲

▶ Forecasting and Control

To plan their inventory, entrepreneurs must always begin by forecasting sales revenues. At best, forecasts are intelligent guesswork. Only entrepreneurs with monopolies in unsaturated markets can estimate precisely what the future demand for their products will be, and thus exercise pinpoint control over their inventories. For most entrepreneurs, however, the two central questions—When should I order? How much should I order?—defy precise answers.

Who knows, for example, what the demand for Valentine cards will be? Whatever demand is forecast, however, demand surely will be zero after

EXHIBIT 18.4
Some pressures at work
that increase or decrease
inventory levels.

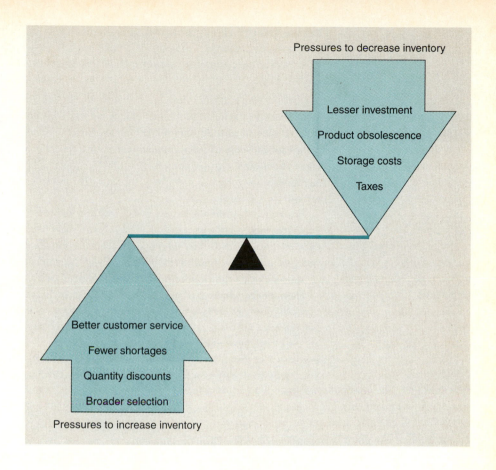

Pressures to decrease inventory

Lesser investment

Product obsolescence

Storage costs

Taxes

Better customer service

Fewer shortages

Quantity discounts

Broader selection

Pressures to increase inventory

February 14; thus, the entrepreneur can ill afford to be far wrong in her fore-cast. To decide on the right number of cards to order, the entrepreneur must rely on *inventory control*.

The goal of inventory control is to strike a balance among conflicting pressures—such as those listed below, and as depicted in Exhibit 18.4:

▸ Keeping ample inventory on hand at all times, in order to fill orders promptly. This way, customers would be satisfied and would keep coming back.

▸ Keeping inventories low, in order to reduce the sum of money tied up in them. This way, more cash would be available for, say, expansion. Return on investment also would be higher, because investment would be lower.

▸ In the case of manufacturers alone, keeping inventories high, in order to maintain steady production despite up-and-down demand. This way, the entrepreneur would avoid costly shutdowns and temporary layoffs.

▸ **Turnover
Analysis**

To strike a balance among these conflicting pressures, entrepreneurs must apply the concept of *turnover*. Together with a forecast, turnover analysis enables entrepreneurs to estimate roughly how many months' supply to keep on hand. As we saw in Chapter 13, turnover is generally the best measure of how well entrepreneurs manage their purchases. Take this example offered by the SBA:

EXAMPLE ▶

Stein Brothers Company [a food wholesaler in the East] buys most of its produce directly from farmers in various parts of the country. Buyers represent the firm in scattered, local communities. Some of these communities are on the West Coast, and delivery to the East takes about eight days—a considerable time for perishable products. Because of this long lag between purchase and delivery, the company is forced to speculate a great deal on prices.

Practice varies with the season of the year and with the current habits of customers, but purchases must usually be made long before sales. Stein Brothers sells to grocery supermarkets, institutions, and other wholesalers. Demand for any particular produce commodity varies continuously—depending on the quality of the product when it arrives in the East and on the amount of the same commodity available from other suppliers.

Daily closing inventories must be taken because each salesperson must know how much of specific lots and items is available for sale the next morning. The inventory is used to check out the sales for every case or bushel received in each railroad car or truck. Stein Brothers knows exactly how much profit is made on any given purchase. With an inventory turnover every two or three days (about two turnovers a week or 100 a year) the Stein Brothers office staff must always be on its toes to keep pace with changing market conditions.[5] ▲▼▲

A yearly turnover of 100 is the average for wholesale grocers. A lower turnover—say, 90—would signal that the grocer is carrying slow-moving or spoiled produce. On the other hand, a higher turnover—say, 110—would signal that the grocer is carrying fast-moving produce. If the level of sales revenues remains the same, the investment in inventory is lower with a turnover of 110 than with a turnover of 90. In general, the less money tied up in inventory, the better, as long as stockouts are held to an acceptable level. A *stockout* occurs when a store runs out of a product, leaving shelves temporarily empty.

The inventory turnover for wholesale grocers differs from that of most other wholesalers or retailers. Men's clothing stores, for example, have an average yearly turnover of 3; appliance stores, 4; and restaurants, 22. Manufacturers also have a broad range of turnovers. Some chemical manufacturers, for example, turn over their inventory 100 times a year. In contrast, some steel fabricators have turnovers as low as 3. The following example shows how entrepreneurs may use turnover as a tool to control inventory:

EXAMPLE ▶

A retailer of men's clothing forecasts sales revenues of $1,500,000 next year. In this industry, inventory turns over three times a year, on the average. How many months' supply should be on hand? How much investment should be in inventory? To answer these questions, the retailer would make the following computations:

$$\text{Months' supply} = \frac{12 \text{ months/year}}{3 \text{ turns/year}}$$

$$= 4 \text{ months' supply}$$

$$\text{Inventory investment} = \frac{\$1,500,000 \text{ revenues/year} \times 75\%^*}{3 \text{ turns/year}}$$

$$= \$375,000$$

These computations are only part of this entrepreneur's inventory-control system. Control also involves evaluating the turnover of each item of inventory, such as shirts, ties, and topcoats.

*The ratio of the purchase cost to the selling price. ▲▼▲

As a way to judge inventories, turnover is by no means flawless. Entrepreneurs often believe, erroneously, that the higher the turnover, the higher the profit. This is not always so. For example, turnover does not measure sales that are lost because a product is not available. Take this extreme example:

EXAMPLE ▶

A hardware store has an inventory consisting of just one hammer. No other product is on the shelves. The owner sells a hammer each day. After the sale, the owner goes to the nearby supply house and buys another hammer. At month's end, the inventory turnover is 30 times a month, or 360 times a year. But has the owner been efficient? Many productive sales were lost through lack of inventory. A proper inventory with a turnover of 5 times a year would have produced much better results.[6] ▲▼▲

Like so many other aspects of managing a venture, there is no one best way to control inventories. Various techniques have been proposed to answer the following questions:

▶ What is the best inventory level for a product?

▶ Where should inventories be kept?

▶ Should there be an inventory?

These techniques generally do little for entrepreneurs. Their simple formulas may be applicable to mass production or to chain store operations, but not to smaller, growing ventures. The technique itself is not as important as the method of reasoning that entrepreneurs may use to analyze their control of inventories.

▶ Physical Inventory

A *physical inventory* compares what is actually on hand to that shown in the records. If book inventory and physical inventory differ, the entrepreneur must find out why, in order to remedy the problem.

There are many possible reasons for an inventory shortage. For example, products may have been pilfered, lost, thrown away, or overlooked when the physical inventory was taken. Or receiving and billing procedures may be at fault. Of these reasons, pilferage is the most easily understood. The other reasons are more subtle but equally damaging. According to the SBA:

▶ If receiving procedures are faulty, a receiving clerk may not be counting actual amounts received and comparing them with those on the supplier's packing list or invoice. If the amount received is less than that invoiced, the entrepreneur is paying for the difference.

▶ A salesperson may be selling to customers without billing them, through oversight or carelessness. In such cases, the entrepreneur takes a loss equal to the cost of the product and also loses the profit that should have been earned on the sale.

▶ Clerks may be accepting returns of merchandise that is no longer salable because of damage, stains, or packing defects. Or, the entrepreneur may be ignoring opportunities to return merchandise to suppliers when it arrives unfit for resale.[7]

To minimize shortages and to keep employees alert, entrepreneurs must take a physical inventory regularly, even weekly if need be. According to the SBA, most entrepreneurs take careful steps to guard against theft, but few adopt serious procedures for protection from inventory shortages caused by factors such as poor receiving procedures, poor billing procedures, and damaged merchandise.

▶ **Inventory Costs**

To buy and hold inventories is costly. Yet, many entrepreneurs count only the purchase price of materials, ignoring so-called carrying costs incurred after their purchase. These costs include:

▶ Storage and handling
▶ Interest, insurance, and property taxes
▶ Obsolescence and spoilage
▶ Paperwork

How significant are these carrying costs? One estimate puts the average carrying cost at 21 percent of the purchase cost of inventory, as depicted in Exhibit 18.5.[8] However, carrying costs differ sharply from industry to industry.

The main reason entrepreneurs ignore carrying costs is their absence as such from accounting records. Interest charges and property taxes, for example, are easy to isolate and identify. But the other carrying costs are extremely hard to measure, particularly the cost of money and the cost of shortages:

▶ **Cost of money**   Often overlooked, the cost of money is perhaps the most crucial of all carrying costs. Why? Because money not invested in inventory could be invested elsewhere, in, say, plant expansion. The estimated return from this kind of foregone opportunity is the cost of money tied up in inventory.

▶ **Cost of shortages**   The costs connected with carrying too little inventory can be as severe as the costs of carrying too much inventory. Entrepreneurs often overlook this cost because shortages are less visible than excesses. The cost of shortages includes:

EXHIBIT 18.5
The true cost of inventory.

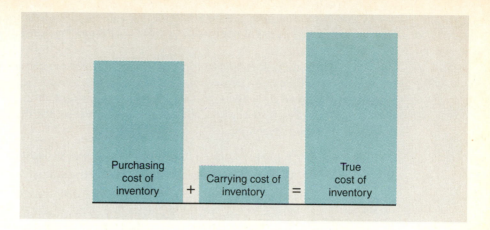

- ▶ Sales revenues lost because the entrepreneur could not fill a customer's order
- ▶ Excess costs incurred to speed up production or to break into the schedule of another product in order to avoid losing a customer's order
- ▶ Loss of goodwill and future orders

The costs of shortage defy computation. For example, if a $1,000 order is lost because of an inventory shortage, the cost of shortage for that order alone is precisely $1,000. But how many future orders from the same customer has the entrepreneur lost? This figure is impossible to estimate with any accuracy, but it still is a real cost.

SUMMARY

How well entrepreneurs do their purchasing and manage their inventories may well spell the difference between profit and loss. Like finance, marketing, and production, purchasing is a major entrepreneurial activity.

Entrepreneurs must plan and control their purchases with the same care they devote to other business activities. Guidelines for the purchase of products and services include buying:

- ▶ Of the right quality
- ▶ In the right quantity
- ▶ At the right time
- ▶ From the right supplier
- ▶ At the right price

At least once a year, entrepreneurs must measure their purchasing performance by asking two key questions:

- ▶ How do my purchasing costs measure up to those of my competitors?
- ▶ What are my losses from shrinkage, spoilage, and theft?

The answer to the first requires a comparison of the venture's cost of goods sold to the industry average. The answer to the second has to do with inventory control.

In most industries, inventory and purchasing are equally important. Without sufficient inventory, customers can be lost and services compromised. Inventory has to do with product that must be kept on hand, day in and day out—either to resell, without alteration; or to turn into another product. Entrepreneurs need inventory:

▶ To avoid the loss of customers because a product is not in stock
▶ To enable customers to look over a product before buying it
▶ To capitalize on discounts in the price of raw materials
▶ To keep a plant from cutting back or shutting down
▶ To make a product in quantities that minimize costs
▶ To speculate against increases in price and cost
▶ To assure customers of prompt delivery
▶ To protect against strikes

For most entrepreneurs, the two central questions in forecasting sales revenues are: When should I order? and How much should I order? Because these questions defy precise answers, entrepreneurs must rely on inventory control. The goal of inventory control is to strike a balance among conflicting pressures, such as:

▶ Keeping ample supplies on hand at all times, in order to fill orders promptly
▶ Keeping inventories low, in order to reduce the amount of money tied up in them
▶ In the case of manufacturers alone, keeping inventories high, in order to maintain steady production despite up-and-down demand

Turnover analysis is one tool entrepreneurs may use to balance such conflicting pressures. The objective of this and other methods of inventory control is to answer three questions:

▶ What is the best inventory level for a product?
▶ Where should inventories be kept?
▶ Should there be an inventory?

Discussion and Review Questions

1. Is purchasing as important an activity as finance and marketing? Explain your answer.
2. Why is the timing of purchases so crucial?
3. In the purchase of a product or service, which comes first: quality or price? Explain your answer.

4. Explain the five purchasing guidelines.
5. How do sound purchasing and inventory control practices help entrepreneurs boost profits?
6. How do inventories differ among the manufacturing, wholesaling, and retailing industries?
7. Explain why inventories are necessary.
8. How are inventories best controlled?
9. What tool might you, as an entrepreneur, use to judge your performance in managing your purchases and inventories? Why?
10. Would you, as an entrepreneur, try to maximize inventory turnover in order to maximize sales revenues? Explain your answer.
11. Why must entrepreneurs regularly take a physical inventory?
12. Explain why purchase costs are not the only cost of inventory. Give one example.
13. Why is it so hard to estimate the cost of money? The cost of shortages?
14. Are purchasing and inventory management equally important? Why or why not? How are purchasing and inventory-control performance measured?
15. Define these terms: *inventory, inventory control, turnover, carrying costs, cost of money, cost of shortages.*

Building a Business Plan

Purchasing and Inventories

Purchasing consists of all the activities involved in obtaining required materials, supplies, and parts from other firms. With this definition in mind, entrepreneurs should make every effort to choose suppliers that best meet their needs at the lowest possible price.

What Is Inventory Control?

Inventory control is the process of managing inventories in such a way as to minimize inventory costs, including both holding costs and potential stock-out costs. Simply put, holding costs are the costs associated with storage of raw materials, work-in-process, or finished products. Stock-out costs are the costs associated with running out of inventory. The goal of both purchasing and inventory control should be to improve a venture's profits.

Instructions for Worksheet 18

To complete this part of the business plan, you must examine the purchases that you must make to operate your business in part 1.

In part 2, describe how the factors of price, quality, and reliability affect your purchasing decisions. Then in part 3, estimate how much inventory you should maintain in your business.

Part 1—Purchasing Guidelines

Before answering the questions in this section, you may want to review the definition for your business that was last revised in Chapter 12.

1. List the type of raw materials that you need for your business.
2. List the type of component parts that you need for your business.
3. List the type of production and office supplies that you need for your business.

Part 2—Factors that Affect the Choice of Suppliers

The choice of suppliers should result from careful analysis of three factors: (1) price, (2) quality, and (3) reliability.

4. Considering the purchases described above, how does the factor of price affect your purchasing decisions?
5. How does the factor of quality affect your purchasing decisions?
6. How does the factor of reliability affect your purchasing decisions?

Part 3—Inventory Control

Experienced business owners realize the disasters that a shortage of needed materials can cause and will avoid this type of problem if at all possible. The simple fact is that shutdowns are expensive because fixed costs—such as rent, wages, and insurance—must still be paid.

7. How important is inventory to your type of business?
8. Based on your type of business, on the raw materials or merchandise you need for your business, and on your estimates for sales revenues, how much inventory should you have on hand? Justify your answer.

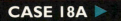

CASE 18A ▶ ## CWC Industries, Inc.

Located in an inner-city area, CWC Industries is "suffering from severe growing pains." It has reached its manufacturing capacity, with little room for expansion. Although it earned $75,000 on sales revenues of $1.6 million last year, CWC has found it hard to raise money to expand. "Every bank in town has turned us down," says Mary Jane Fabish, executive vice president. "It just doesn't make sense."

Background

The two entrepreneurs responsible for CWC's success are Fabish and Gerald Lancaster, founder and president. They have worked as a team since 1965, when Lancaster founded CWC. Before 1965, both had worked for Brooks Chemicals, Lancaster as executive vice president, Fabish as office manager. Lancaster had hired Fabish at Brooks.

"Our talents mesh beautifully," says Fabish. "I take care of finances and organizational planning. Jerry takes care of marketing, production, product development, and the overall direction of the com-pany. We share all of the decision making. If we dis-agree, we hammer out the pros and cons. And every time, we end up acknowledging the strong points in each other's argument to come up with what we both agree to be a good decision." Their résumés appear in Exhibits 18A.1 and 18A.2.

EXHIBIT 18A.1

CWC Industries, Inc.: Résumé of Gerald Lancaster.

Work Experience

1965–present	CWC Industries, Inc.
	Founder and president of an analytical testing laboratory that does work in the environmental sciences. This company is also the parent company of two wholly owned subsidiaries, Continental Chemical Company and Excelsior Varnish & Chemicals, Inc.
	These two companies make and sell chemical specialties. Continental Chemical sells directly to the end user, mostly industrial and institutional. Excelsior Varnish sells mostly to jobbers who use private labels; its product line includes cleaners, floor finishes, paints, and varnish.
1949–1965	Brooks Chemicals, Inc.
	Began as technical director developing products. Was promoted to vice president of technical operations. In 1954, was promoted to executive vice president of the entire company, including its marketing operations.

Professionalism

| 1949–present | Professional engineer, licensed to practice in Ohio, Pennsylvania, and Wisconsin |

Present Activities

	Air Pollution Control Association
	American Chemical Society
	National Association of Corrosion Engineers
	Water Pollution Control Federation

Education

1960–1965	Case Institute of Technology
	Received master of arts degree in environmental engineering
1945–1949	Hiram College
	Received bachelor of arts degree in chemistry

EXHIBIT 18A.2

CWC Industries, Inc.: Résumé of Mary Jane Fabish.

Work Experience

1965–present   CWC Industries, Inc.
Executive vice president. Oversees accounting, financial, marketing, and organizational aspects of the company.
This company is also the parent company of two wholly owned subsidiaries, Continental Chemical Company and Excelsior Varnish & Chemicals, Inc.

1956–1965   Brooks Chemicals, Inc.
Office manager. Handled purchasing of raw materials, did costing of products, wrote technical bulletins.

1952–1956   Murray Ohio Manufacturing Company
Secretary. Worked in production, personnel, and purchasing departments.

Activities Since

1970   Council of Smaller Enterprises—Chairperson
Chamber of commerce—Member of board and of executive committee
Ohio Motorist Association—Trustee
Regional Advisory Council of U.S. Small Business Administration—Board member
National Advisory Council of U.S. Department of the Treasury

Awards

1971 and 1977   Chosen Woman of the Year by American Business Women's Association

Education

1977   Dyke College
Studied accounting

1970   Case Western Reserve University
Studied marketing and creative writing

Rapid Growth

Since its founding in 1965, CWC's sales have grown from $40,000 to $1.6 million. "That's a dramatic growth rate," says Fabish, "even after adjusting for inflation." She credits CWC's success to Lancaster's "sheer guts, creativity, and willingness to take risks." With Fabish's help, Lancaster has built CWC in two ways:

▶ Through the acquisition of small chemical companies
▶ Through expansion into new markets

The acquisitions have fulfilled Lancaster's dream of someday running a "full-blown chemical manufacturing company." When he first went into business for himself in 1965, Lancaster bought a service company called Zero Air Filter Company. It cost him just $10,000. No manufacturing was involved, just the servicing of air filters. "It wasn't very exciting, picking up and cleaning grease filters from restaurants," says Lancaster.

Even so, it was a beginning, one that Lancaster shortly parlayed into a manufacturing company. After two years of doing nothing but cleaning filters, he learned that a "sick" company called Continental Chemical was for sale. Losing money at the rate of $1,200 a month, this company was in the same building as Lancaster's company. The owner was asking $75,000. Seeing the acquisition as an opportunity to become a chemical manufacturer at last, Lancaster decided to buy it.

The owner agreed to accept a $5,000 down payment and to finance Lancaster for five years at an interest rate of 7 percent a year. With the purchase of Continental Chemical in 1967, Lancaster became a manufacturer of specialty chemicals and coatings for maintenance work and water treatment.

Another Acquisition

Two years later, opportunity knocked again when Excelsior Varnish & Chemicals, Inc., came up for sale. This company manufactured paints, varnishes, and cleaning chemicals. Like Continental Chemical, it also was losing money.

"The asking price of $120,000 was very reasonable," says Lancaster, "but we had to buy it on the spot, or so said the lawyer representing the seller. In fact, the lawyer was so demanding that we had to have the bank call him to tell him that under the then-prevailing 'truth-in-lending' regulations, it was impossible to complete the transaction as quickly as he wanted to."

"Apparently he could understand that," says Lancaster, "and it was our bank that made the purchase possible. It loaned us the entire $120,000 we needed." For that purchase price, Lancaster received "inventory, receivables, cash, manufacturing equipment, and a customer list."

Period of Adjustment

Both Lancaster and Fabish dedicated themselves to "turning these acquisitions around and making them profitable." Neither was a stranger to hard work or sacrifice. When Fabish joined Lancaster in 1965, she agreed to a salary of just $200 a month. She took the rest of her salary in options to buy stock; later, when she exercised her options, she ended up owning 25 percent of CWC.

"We all reminisce about the early days of eating hot dogs and beans," she says. "There were many times that we never took home a paycheck, but our employees always did. There were days when you could only go in the corner and cry. But the next day, you knew you'd come back fighting because the competition was right around the corner."

Did their sacrifices and hard work pay off? The answer appears in their recent financial statements, shown in Exhibits 18A.3 and 18A.4. Notice that both sales and profits have gone up each year.

Of course, it took more than sacrifice and hard work to achieve these sales and profit levels. "Jerry and I never would have made it without our employees. They helped us a lot, although I sometimes had to whip and scream and holler. Our philosophy was, and is, to get all our employees to

EXHIBIT 18A.3

CWC Industries, Inc.: Comparative income statements (in thousands of dollars).

	1984	1985	1986	1987	1988
Sales revenues	$1,008	$1,105	$1,162	$1,396	$1,605
Cost of goods sold	469	511	540	681	712
Gross profit	$ 539	$ 594	$ 622	$ 715	$ 893
Operating expenses					
Factory and Warehouse			$ 179	$ 162	$ 190
Selling	$ 499	$ 534	187	268	282
Administrative			186	217	302
Depreciation	12	20	25	19	14
Total operating expenses	$ 511	$ 554	$ 557	$ 666	$ 788
Operating profit	28	40	45	49	105
Federal income taxes	3	6	9	10	30
Net profit	$ 25	$ 34	$ 36	$ 39	$ 75
Cash flow	$ 37	$ 54	$ 61	$ 58	$ 89

feel as if they're part of the team." CWC shares its profits with employees. Every employee, including Lancaster and Fabish, receives proportionately the same bonus at the end of the year.

Rewards of Success

CWC's success has brought with it community recognition. Word soon got around among businesswomen that Fabish was a successful entrepreneur. She was twice honored as Woman of the Year by the American Business Women's Association. This honor later led to her appointment to the board of the city's chamber of commerce. Only one of two women to be so recognized, Fabish now serves on the chamber's executive committee along with members from Fortune 500 corporations.

Moreover, in 1980, Fabish was elected by her peers as a delegate to the White House Conference on Small Business. She also has served as chairperson of the Council of Smaller Enterprises, which boasted a membership of 7,000 small businesses in 1988.

This council is the largest of its kind in the country, a product of her efforts to recruit small businesses.

Although she bemoans the fact that she never pursued a college degree, Fabish believes she already has earned an "MBA in the school of hard knocks. I've learned through doing." She often talks glowingly about her "crashing the good old boys' network in the city and becoming one of the guys."

Fabish believes it is a myth that women in business cannot get help when they need it. "Whenever I have a problem, I call on fellow businesspeople for help. They have never let me down. Often, just by discussing a problem with another person who's been there, I can work it out. Believe me, we can all learn from our competitors' experiences and mistakes—and I have."

Need for Expansion

Last year, CWC was faced with an acute shortage of space. Located along with other manufacturers in a rambling 99-year-old building complex, the

EXHIBIT 18A.4

CWC Industries, Inc.: Latest balance sheet (December 31, 1988).

Assets			Equities		
Current assets			Current liabilities		
Cash	$ 89,000		Long-term debt (current)	$ 28,600	
Accounts receivable	248,900		Accounts payable	115,000	
Inventories	168,200		Accrued taxes	26,800	
Prepaid expenses	21,600	$527,700	Accrued expenses	53,000	
Fixed assets			Income taxes payable	22,200	
Land and buildings	$ 52,800		Dividends payable	3,300	$248,900
Equipment	132,200		Long-term debt		
	$185,000		Notes payable	$ 32,400	
Less: Accumulated			Lease payable	10,100	
depreciation	130,100	54,900		$ 42,500	
Other assets			Less: Current portion	28,600	13,900
Goodwill	$ 8,000				
Deposits	2,000	10,000			
			Owners' equity		
			Common stock	$ 26,300	
			Preferred stock	33,000	
			Paid-in capital	1,600	
				$ 60,900	
			Less: Treasury stock	9,000	
				$ 51,900	
			Retained earnings	277,900	329,800
Total assets		$592,600	Total equities		$592,600

company needed room to meet the increased demands of its customers. "The only place to expand was into the street," says Fabish. Views of CWC's plant and chemical laboratory appear in Exhibit 18A.5.

A solution was fast in coming. At about the same time, a company called Penreco, located in 12 adjoining buildings, decided to move out. It seems that Penreco had just dropped its line of chemical products because of labor problems. "What luck,"

says Fabish. "Jerry and I both saw Penreco's imminent departure as the answer to all our problems. Penreco's plant was just what we needed."

They wasted little time initiating talks with Penreco's management. Its sprawling plant was four times the size of CWC's, and its equipment was more modern. Penreco's price was $900,000; but as shown in Exhibit 18A.6, CWC really needed an estimated total of $1.41 million to complete its expansion.

EXHIBIT 18A.5

CWC Industries, Inc.: Views of plant and of chemical laboratory.

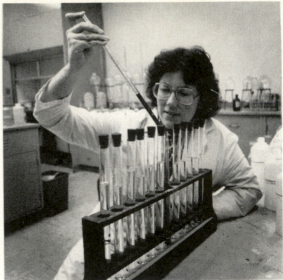

EXHIBIT 18A.6

CWC Industries, Inc.: Estimate of investment needs.

To complete the proposed plant relocation and expansion, CWC needs an estimated total of $1,410,000 itemized as follows:

$ 900,000	Purchase of Penreco plant (12 buildings with 3.10 acres of floor space, 3.04 acres of land, and equipment)
225,000	Working capital needed to expand
100,000	Boiler room equipment and installation
85,000	Dismantling and moving existing equipment
50,000	EPA and OSHA controls and equipment
50,000	Office computer
$1,410,000	Total investment

Two years ago, Penreco received from Cragin, Lang, Free & Smythe, Inc., an appraisal of $600,000 on the Penreco property. Several years ago, the Industrial Appraisal Company estimated the total value of Penreco's equipment at $1,221,400. On checking with the appraisers, CWC's principals were informed that these values are still reasonably true.

Thus the total fair market value of the Penreco plant is about $1,821,400. The principals of CWC have negotiated a firm offer of $900,000 for the plant with Penreco's management.

"That's a lot of money for a little company like ours to raise," says Fabish. "But with our reputation in the community, I was sure we could raise all of it through the banks."

With the help of their lawyers, CWC and Penreco soon negotiated a buy-and-sell agreement in principle. Penreco also gave CWC one year to buy the company out. "Our work was now cut out for us," says Fabish. "It's one thing to have a list of customers, and another to deliver. We had to move in a hurry to raise the entire $1.41 million."

Inner-City Location a Problem

Armed with résumés and financial statements, Fabish confidently approached the five largest banks in the city for a loan. Each turned her down. "They were nice about it," says Fabish. "Many of the bank executives I knew on a first-name basis. Even so, because we were located in a 99-year-old building in the inner city, they strongly felt it would be too risky to lend us all that money."

Being turned down by local banks only served to strengthen Fabish's resolve. "I knew we were a solid company because our income statements showed lots of profits (see Exhibit 18A.3) and our latest balance sheet showed lots of financial strength (see Exhibit 18A.4). So I wasn't about to take no for an answer. Somehow I was going to get the money Jerry and I needed to keep growing."

At this point, both Lancaster and Fabish knew they had to be creative in their financing. "You can't go to the banks with hat in hand," says Fabish. "You sometimes have to pound on the table and not give up. Not giving up—that's the hallmark of every successful small businessperson I know."

A Creative Solution

After numerous talks with other entrepreneurs, Fabish found that they had had similar problems in the inner city. What did they do to solve their financial problems? Based on the advice she received, Fabish "packaged a creative financial proposal" involving help from:

- The Union Commerce Bank, the city's fourth largest bank
- The U.S. Department of Housing and Urban Development
- The U.S. Small Business Administration (SBA)
- The planning commission of the city
- The chamber of commerce of the city
- The U.S. Department of Commerce

It took Fabish ten grueling months to prepare the proposal. "Being located in the inner city, there was just no other way but to involve the government, both federal and local," says Fabish. "The red tape was unbelievable. The running I had to do from one group to another almost got me down. If I had it all to do over again, I'd be too tired." To justify CWC's request for money, Fabish's financial proposal had to show that:

- CWC would create a significant increase in jobs in the community
- A major share of the new jobs would go to residents of the surrounding community

Especially worrisome to Fabish was the tenuous nature of her relationship to each of the organizations involved in the proposal. Each one had to satisfy itself that the others were equally committed. If just one pulled out, Fabish's proposal would collapse "like a house of cards."

Excerpts of her proposal appear in:

- Exhibit 18A.7, which shows how and from whom CWC planned to raise the $1.41 million it needed in order to buy out Penreco and complete its expansion
- Exhibit 18A.8, which shows the loan conditions set by the bank, from which CWC wanted a $750,000 loan
- Exhibit 18A.9, which shows how profitable CWC expected to be after it acquired Penreco's complex of 12 buildings
- Exhibit 18A.10, which shows how financially sound CWC expected to be
- Exhibit 18A.11, which shows how many new jobs CWC expected to create

EXHIBIT 18A.7

CWC Industries, Inc.: Tentative sources of money.

To finance the proposed plant relocation and expansion, CWC's principals have obtained tentative commitments to a commercial bank loan, a HUD action grant and loan, and a loan from Penreco itself:

$750,000   Seven-year term loan from the Union Commerce Bank. Approval of this loan has been granted subject to an SBA guarantee of two-thirds of the loan amount. In addition, CWC must obtain at least $300,000 from investors, shareholders, or a 2 percent HUD loan, all of which must be subordinated to the bank and to the SBA. Interest will be fixed at 12 percent.

$360,000   HUD action grant and loan. Of this sum, $230,000 will be a grant and $130,000 a loan payable in ten years at 2 percent interest. Approval of both the grant and the loan are subject to firm financial commitments by private parties for the rest of the money needed.

$300,000   Penreco loan. Penreco is willing to finance this portion of the purchase price of its plant. This loan will be payable in one year at 12 percent interest.

    The principals of CWC have approached other banks and private investors, and have been turned down outright or have been offered terms that would place excessive drain on the company's cash flow or would force the principals to yield control of CWC to others.

EXHIBIT 18A.8

CWC Industries, Inc.: Loan conditions set by bank.

The $750,000 seven-year term loan from the bank will be secured by a first lien on all buildings, property, machinery, and equipment, as well as on accounts receivable and inventories. It also is understood that all borrowings will be endorsed by Gerald Lancaster and Mary Jane Fabish. Reductions on the loan principal will be as follows:

Month	Monthly Reductions
1–12	$ 6,250*
13–48	$ 8,333*
49–84	$10,417*

    The loan is approved subject to maintenance of a sound financial condition. It is further understood that all borrowings will be subject to these conditions:

▸ Minimum shareholders' equity of $686,000

▸ Minimum working capital of $386,000

▸ Ratio of long-term debt to shareholders' equity not to exceed 1.75 to 1.00

▸ Quarterly financial statements and yearly audited financial statements

▸ No additional borrowing other than trade and subordinate loans

    Finally, it is understood that CWC will maintain its major deposit relationship in the years ahead.

*Plus accrued interest.

EXHIBIT 18A.9

CWC Industries, Inc.: Projected income statements (in thousands of dollars).

	1989	1990	1991	1992	1993
Sales revenues					
CWC Industries	$1,900	$2,270	$2,600	$3,070	$3,620
Penreco	1,020	1,500	2,000	2,500	3,000
Total sales	$2,920	$3,770	$4,600	$5,570	$6,620
Cost of sales					
CWC Industries	$ 840	$1,000	$1,200	$1,410	$1,670
Penreco	710	1,050	1,400	1,750	2,100
Total cost of sales	$1,550	$2,050	$2,600	$3,160	$3,770
Gross profit	$1,370	$1,720	$2,000	$2,410	$2,850
Operating expenses					
Administrative	$ 530	$ 570	$ 620	$ 760	$ 980
Selling	380	450	550	650	770
Factory and laboratory	290	370	430	510	610
Total Operating Expenses	$1,200	$1,390	$1,600	$1,920	$2,360
Operating profit	$ 170	$ 330	$ 400	$ 490	$ 490
Interest	120	110	100	90	80
Before-tax profit	$ 50	$ 220	$ 300	$ 400	$ 410
Income tax	—	80	120	160	170
Net profit	$ 50	$ 140	$ 180	$ 240	$ 240
Cash flow					
Net profit	$ 50	$ 140	$ 180	$ 240	$ 240
Depreciation	90	90	90	90	90
Total cash flow	$ 140	$ 230	$ 270	$ 330	$ 330
Debt service	$ 75	$ 100	$ 100	$ 100	$ 125

EXHIBIT 18A.10

CWC Industries, Inc.: Projected balance sheets (condensed, in thousands of dollars).

Assets	1989*	1900*	1991*	1992*	1993*
Current assets	$980	$1,350	$1,730	$2,090	$2,510
Fixed assets	920	830	730	640	550
Other assets	40	40	40	70	70
Total	$1,940	$2,220	$2,500	$2,800	$3,130
Equities					
Current liabilities	$510	$760	$950	$1,120	$1,350
Long-term debt	980	870	780	680	530
Owners' equity					
Capital stock	130	130	130	130	130
Retained earnings	320	460	640	870	1,120
Owners' equity	450	590	770	1,000	1,250
Total	$1,940	$2,220	$2,500	$2,800	$3,130

*Year end.

EXHIBIT 18A.11

CWC Industries, Inc.: Employment potential.

To carry out its projected rise in sales, CWC must add to its workforce. CWC's most conservative estimates of the new jobs to be created follow:

Year	New Jobs to Be Added in			Total New Jobs	Cumulative Increase in Jobs
	Plant	Laboratories	Office		
1989	4	1	2	7	7
1990	5	1	1	7	14
1991	5	1	1	7	21
1992	5	1	2	8	29
1993	5	0	1	6	35
Total	24	4	7	35	

Within weeks of the time CWC acquires the Penreco plant, the principals will have to hire at least six new people to enable CWC to meet its expanding backlog of orders and its forward commitments to customers.

Questions

1. Why is CWC having trouble raising money to expand?
2. Comment on CWC's written proposal to raise $1.41 million (see Exhibits 18A.6 through 18A.11).
3. Suggest financing alternatives other than the ones proposed by CWC. Would they be better? If so, how?
4. How have the managerial styles of Mary Jane Fabish and Gerald Lancaster contributed to CWC's growth?
5. If CWC's request for a $1.41 million loan is turned down, what should Fabish and Lancaster do next? Why?

CASE 18B ▶ *Linda Townsend*

Linda Townsend has just succeeded her father as the head of a small office-equipment company. Before working in the family business, and upon the advice of her father, Townsend worked elsewhere for four years.

"My dad wanted me to see how tough it can be outside," says Townsend. "I learned firsthand the realities of competition and business behavior—sometimes in ways that quietly shocked me. When the bottom line is at stake, it's truly amazing how deceitful some people can be."

Soon after she took over, Townsend found herself in a quandary. The reason? The buyer of a large public university had called her to place a $30,000 order for office equipment—but with a somewhat slippery twist.

At issue was the buyer's lack of authority to make any single purchase in excess of $10,000 without the approval of his superiors. So he had asked Townsend to divide the $30,000 price into three bills of $10,000 each. In that way, the buyer could approve payment on his signature alone.

"Nobody will get hurt," the buyer told Townsend, "and we'll both get what we want." In the same breath, he warned that if she would "not go along," he would place his $30,000 order with a competitor who would.

At first, Townsend was tempted to accept the buyer's proposal. It seemed reasonable enough. She soon began having second thoughts, however, as she recalled that her father had once told her that "no business can survive for long in a morality based upon what you can get away with."

Townsend was also keenly aware that, for a business as small as hers, a single $30,000 order was hard to ignore. Further complicating the issue was the promise of repeat orders, if she accepted the buyer's proposal. Moreover, this past year the business had stalled out as it barely broke even on sales of $720,000.

Question

1. If Linda Townsend came to you for advice, how would you identify and evaluate her options? Which one would you recommend that she pursue? Why?

Samantha Teen Shoppe, Inc.

Samantha Martynak owns a store that specializes in clothes for teenagers. Located in a suburban shopping mall, the store has been doing moderately well. Last year the store had:

▶ Sales revenues of $234,000

▶ A gross margin of 40 percent on sales

▶ An inventory turnover of 3

One day, Martynak learned from a supplier that her yearly turnover was below the average in her field, which was 4. This news prompted Martynak to take a long hard look at the clothes she carried.

She soon found that she had been carrying some slow-moving styles. So she replaced them with items that turn over more quickly—four times a year.

Questions

1. Assuming all other costs remained unchanged, by how many dollars did Samantha Martynak improve her cash position?

2. What related costs were affected by this increase in inventory turnover? How were they affected (up or down)?

Taxation

For every benefit you receive, a tax is levied.

—*Ralph Waldo Emerson*

F ew subjects spark more controversy than taxes. Most taxpayers grumble about them; entrepreneurs are no exception. Few entrepreneurs enjoy poring over their federal income tax returns. And, as Exhibit 19.1 shows, federal income taxes are just one of many taxes that entrepreneurs must pay. Entrepreneurs need to know precisely what taxes they must pay and, equally important, how taxes may affect the survival and growth of their ventures.

In this chapter, we look first at the need for taxes, and then at the ethical distinction between tax avoidance and tax evasion. Our focus then shifts to the effect on tax planning of the various legal forms of organization and of such other considerations as inventory values and estate taxes. We cover the need for complete tax records last.

The Need for Taxes

Referring to taxes, the English poet, Robert Herrick, once wrote, "Kings ought to shear their sheep, not skin them." His remark strikes a responsive chord in the minds of most entrepreneurs. Even so, few entrepreneurs would quarrel with the need for some taxes. As Oliver Wendell Holmes, former chief justice of the U.S. Supreme Court, put it, "Taxes are what we pay for a civilized society."[1]

In essence, taxes travel a circular route, as money paid out in taxes has a subtle way of coming back to entrepreneurs and other taxpayers in the form of benefits. In the imagery of *Time* magazine:

The complacent observer of high taxes points out that all the money somehow comes back to the people. A fresh-water clam in the well-balanced home aquarium pumps through his voracious lungs nine gallons of water a day, yet the fish around it do not starve. Rather, the tank is purified in the redistribution. So the Government pumps it in, and pumps it out for the greatest good of the greatest number. That's the idea.[2]

EXHIBIT 19.1
Entrepreneurs' tax
obligations.

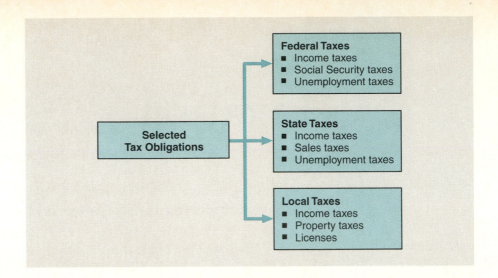

Entrepreneurs must pay their taxes promptly, with the help of an accountant if necessary to make sure that the tax code is observed to the letter.

EXHIBIT 19.2
Percentage of corporations
that do not pay U.S. income
taxes* (1991).**

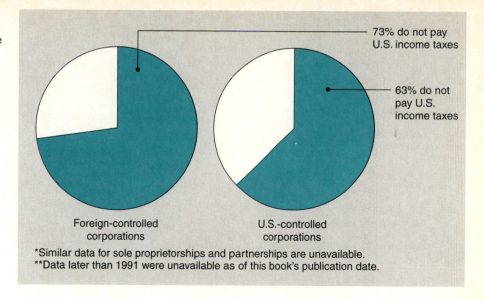

73% do not pay
U.S. income taxes

63% do not
pay U.S.
income taxes

Foreign-controlled
corporations

U.S.-controlled
corporations

*Similar data for sole proprietorships and partnerships are unavailable.
**Data later than 1991 were unavailable as of this book's publication date.

There is vast disagreement, however, about who should bear the burden of taxation. Business especially is the target of attack by politicians and journalists alike for seemingly paying too little in taxes. Admittedly, and as depicted in Exhibit 19.2, more than half of all corporations pay no income taxes at all—among them some giant corporations. This seemingly poor showing, suggestive as it is of unethical behavior, prompted one congressman to comment as follows:

> The annual reports published by giant corporations announce to stockholders that business is better and profits are improving. The tax statements of these same companies to Internal Revenue paint a picture that reduces their profit figure, which in effect reduces their total tax figure. Like the medieval European peasant, for their stockholders they wear wedding clothes; for the tax man they wear rags.[3]

Are these corporations breaking the law? Some may be, but most observe the tax law to the letter. In fact, no business, large or small, has a duty to pay more taxes than the law demands. But what the public often perceives is that businesses have their tax accountants cut corners in order to evade rather than avoid taxes.

This perception needs correction. For one thing, tax savings boost the economy by helping finance new products and new markets, in the process serving customers better and creating jobs. Also, when politicians criticize businesses for not paying enough taxes, they generally mean federal income taxes only. Yet businesses also pay social security taxes, property taxes, local taxes, and possibly even foreign taxes. These taxes merit the same attention as federal income taxes. Moreover, and as shown in Exhibit 19.3, all three levels of government—state and local as well as federal—play significant roles as tax collectors.

EXHIBIT 19.3

Share of total taxes collected by federal, state, and local governments (includes individual as well as business taxes).

Source: U.S. Department of Commerce, *Statistical Abstract of the United States* (Washington, D.C.: U.S. Government Printing Office, 1995), p. 299.

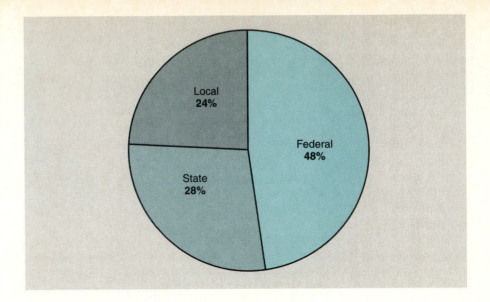

Tax Avoidance Versus Tax Evasion

Entrepreneurs must be clear about the ethical distinction between tax avoidance and tax evasion. Perhaps this is the best way to distinguish between them:

▸ *Tax evasion* is the willful failure to live up to the spirit and letter of the tax law.

▸ *Tax avoidance,* on the other hand, has the blessings of the U.S. Supreme Court, Congress, and state legislatures. In fact, the U.S. Internal Revenue Service (IRS) *expects* individuals and businesses to avoid all avoidable taxes—and gives them the information they need to do so.

Here is how the *Internal Revenue Manual* defines the conditions that must exist for fraud, a criminal offense, to be evident:

> Actual fraud is intentional fraud. Avoidance of tax is not a criminal offense. All taxpayers have the right to reduce, avoid, or minimize their taxes by legitimate means. The distinction between avoidance and evasion is fine, yet definite. One who avoids tax does not conceal or misrepresent, but shapes and preplans events to reduce or eliminate tax liability, then reports the transactions.
>
> Evasion, on the other hand, involves deceit, subterfuge, camouflage, concealment, some attempt to color or obscure events, or making things seem other than they are.[4]

Federal tax laws change yearly, often in ways that affect profits significantly. Some changes open the door to new tax savings, by hiking deductions or by reducing tax rates. Some boost taxes by wiping out tax shelters or by shaving deductions. To keep abreast of these changes, entrepreneurs should

EXHIBIT 19.4

What tax savings may mean to the entrepreneur.

If the Ratio of Before-tax Profits to Sales Is ...	...Then a $1,000 Tax Saving Would Boost Profits* as Much as a Sales Increase of
20%	$ 7,600
15	10,200
10	15,200
5	30,300
2	75,800

*Assumes a flat 34 percent corporate tax rate. A *word of caution:* This tax rate, as well as all other tax rates and depreciation tables in this chapter, are intended for illustrative purposes only. The U.S. Congress may change them at any time.

rely on their lawyer or accountant for the latest tax information. Moreover, these professionals can help entrepreneurs save taxes. How significant these savings can be to entrepreneurs is shown dramatically in Exhibit 19.4. Note the powerful incentive to save on taxes—for example:

> If an entrepreneur's profit-to-sales ratio is 2 percent—as it is among grocery stores, on average—a tax savings of just $1,000 would equal the profit earned on a sales increase of $75,800. Put another way, it would take a sales increase of $75,800 to have the *same* effect on after-tax profits as a tax savings of $1,000!

Entrepreneurs need tax help in other areas as well, since the laws governing state, county, and municipal taxes, social security taxes, and estate taxes are equally complex.

Let us now look at various ways in which entrepreneurs may save or postpone taxes, focusing mainly on the U.S. Internal Revenue Code.

Legal Forms of Organization and Tax Planning

How much a venture pays in federal income taxes depends deeply on the legal form of organization the entrepreneur chooses. The consequences of this choice may well spell the difference between profit and loss. As discussed in Chapter 7, there are several legal forms of organization, among them:

▸ Regular corporations
▸ S corporations
▸ Limited liability companies
▸ General partnerships
▸ Limited partnerships
▸ Sole proprietorships

Regular Corporations

Perhaps the first step in understanding federal corporate income taxes is to define what is meant by taxable income, which may differ from what corporations report as book profit, as explained below:

▶ *Book profit* is the profit that entrepreneurs report to their shareholders, in accordance with the ground rules laid down by the Federal Accounting Standards Board (FASB). These ground rules are called *generally accepted accounting principles* and are the bible of the accounting profession.

▶ *Taxable income,* on the other hand, is the profit that entrepreneurs report to the IRS, in accordance with the ground rules laid down by the U.S. Internal Revenue Code. These ground rules differ from those of the FASB.

The existence of two sets of ground rules—one for shareholders and the other for the IRS—naturally leads to some confusion. In any given year, for example, the entrepreneur may report taxable income that differs sharply from book profit. Does that make sense, reporting two profits for one and the same venture? It does if the entrepreneur understands that the goals of tax accounting differ unavoidably from those of financial accounting:

▶ The goal of *tax accounting* is to minimize taxes—by recognizing operating expenses as soon as is legally possible and by postponing the recognition of sales revenues as long as possible. This way, taxes are postponed to later years.

▶ The goal of *financial accounting,* on the other hand, is to report fairly the sales revenues, operating expenses, and profits earned in a given period.

The U.S. Internal Revenue Code recognizes the validity of both goals. For example, it permits entrepreneurs to use one depreciation method for tax purposes and another method for financial-reporting purposes. Let us now look at the depreciation methods that may be used for tax purposes.

As an incentive to invest in new fixed assets, the U.S. Tax Reform Act of 1986 permits entrepreneurs to depreciate the cost of most fixed assets over just a few years for tax purposes. This act also drops the use of the term *depreciation,* substituting instead the term *modified accelerated cost recovery system (MACRS).* Listed below are selected asset classes, together with examples of the items in each class:

▶ **Three-year asset class**   This class covers race horses, special tools, and some research and development equipment.

▶ **Five-year asset class**   This class covers automobiles and trucks; computers, copiers, and typewriters; and equipment for manufacturing chemicals, clothing, and electronic products.

▶ **Seven-year asset class**   This class covers office furniture plus any asset that is not designated by law as being in any other class.

▶ **Ten-year asset class**   This class covers barges and tugboats; some buildings; and equipment for manufacturing grain, sugar, and vegetable oil products.

EXHIBIT 19.5

Depreciation rates under MACRS.

	Depreciation Rates for Assets with Depreciable Lives of			
Year	3 Years	5 Years	7 Years	10 Years
1	33.33%	20.00%	14.29%	10.00%
2	44.45	32.00	24.49	18.00
3	14.81	19.20	17.49	14.40
4	7.41	11.52	12.49	11.52
5		11.52	8.93	9.22
6		5.76	8.92	7.37
7			8.93	6.55
8			4.46	6.55
9				6.56
10				6.55
11				3.28
Total	100.00%	100.00%	100.00%	100.00%

Source: U.S. Internal Revenue Service, *Depreciation: Publication 534* (Washington, D.C.: U.S. Government Printing Office, 1995.

Shown in Exhibit 19.5 are the yearly rates at which entrepreneurs may depreciate their cost of fixed assets for each of these four classes. To see how entrepreneurs may benefit from applying MACRS, let us now look at an example:

EXAMPLE ▶

To estimate depreciation expense, an entrepreneur plans to use two methods. To save taxes, he must use MACRS, but to report his financial performance to shareholders, he uses the straight-line method. This method assumes that depreciable assets provide equal benefits throughout each year of service. Thus, this method charges as an expense an *equal* fraction of an asset's cost each year.

Let us assume that, in the first year, the entrepreneur has sales revenues of $300,000 and operating expenses of $225,000 before depreciation. Depreciable assets cost $150,000; their average useful life is 10 years. The entrepreneur's book profit would differ from taxable income as shown in Exhibit 19.6. Note that taxable income is $15,000 less than book profit. This means, of course, that taxes would be lower. The entrepreneur, however, would end up paying the *same* total taxes over the life of his depreciable assets, regardless of the depreciation method.

In fact, the entrepreneur is merely taking advantage of the fact that cash received today—from postponing taxes—is worth more than cash received tomorrow, because it can be reinvested *sooner*. ▲▼▲

	First Year	
	Book Profit	**Taxable Income**
Sales revenues	$300,000	$300,000
Operating expenses before depreciation	225,000	225,000
Operating profit before depreciation	$ 75,000	$ 75,000
Depreciation	15,000*	30,000†
Operating profit	$ 60,000	$ 45,000

*Using the straight-line method: $150,000 asset cost × 10% depreciation rate = $15,000

†Using MACRS: $150,000 asset cost × 20% depreciation rate = $30,000

Remember that corporations are the only legal form of organization that the U.S. Internal Revenue Code recognizes as being a so-called legal person, separate and distinct from its owners. As a result, income tax rates for regular corporations differ from those applicable to either sole proprietorships or to partnerships. The only exception is the S corporation, which is taxed as if it were a partnership.

Notably, the tax law gives regular corporations a tax break if their taxable income is $75,000 or less:

Corporate Taxable Income	Tax Rate (1996)*
$0–$50,000	15%
$50,001–$75,000	25%
$75,001–$100,000	34%
$100,001–$335,000	39%
$335,001–$10,000,000	34%

This tax break recognizes the need to help small ventures survive and grow. To show its impact, let us now look at an example:

---

*Tax rates are subject to change by the U.S. Congress.

Assume that a small corporation has taxable income of $75,000. How much would it save with the tax break? Here are the computations:

With Tax Break

Taxable income	$75,000
Less: Federal income taxes	
on first $50,000 (× 15%) = $7,500	
on next $25,000 (× 25%) = 6,250	13,750
Net profit	$61,250

Without Tax Break

Taxable income	$75,000
Less: Federal income taxes ($75,000 × 34%)	25,500
Net profit	$49,500

The tax break saves this corporation $11,750 ($25,500 − $13,750), thus boosting the net profit to $61,250, from $49,500. ▲▼▲

▶ S Corporations and Limited Liability Companies

As we saw in Chapter 7, an S corporation is a hybrid form of organization, a cross between a regular corporation and a general partnership. Like a regular corporation, owners enjoy limited liability. But like a partnership, an S corporation is not subject to corporate federal income taxes. Instead, its profits pass through to the shareholders, to be taxed as if they were salary or wages. Thus, S corporations are free of the double taxation to which regular corporations and their shareholders are subject.

As discussed in Chapter 7, limited liability companies (LLCs) are a new legal form of organization. LLCs are similar to S corporations, including the way they are taxed. Thus, an LLC pays no tax of its own, since its profits flow through to the shareholders.

▶ General Partnerships and Sole Proprietorships

General partnerships and sole proprietorships are subject to almost precisely the same tax laws as the S corporation. In a general partnership, the partners themselves are taxed, not the partnership. The partnership merely serves as a pipeline through which profits or losses flow to the partners. To compute federal income taxes, the partners must report their share of the partnership's profit, even if plowed back into the business. In contrast, corporate shareholders must report only the cash dividends they receive.

Sole proprietors are taxed as individuals because the tax laws do not see the sole proprietorship as a separate and distinct legal entity. In contrast to corporations, sole proprietorships offer few opportunities for tax savings. Sole proprietors cannot take advantage of such corporate tax-sheltered benefits as life and health insurance, nor can they pay themselves tax-deductible salaries. Just two tax advantages are open to sole proprietors: If taxable income is low, individual tax rates may be lower than corporate tax rates; and if losses occur, sole proprietors can use those losses to offset their taxable income from other sources.

General partnerships offer more tax-saving opportunities than do sole proprietorships, although not as many as do corporations. Tax laws, for example, permit partners such intriguing options as these:

▸ A partnership agreement may call for profits to be shared, not by ownership percentages, but by the degree of effort or expertise required to run the partnership. This means a partner could earn, say, 20 percent of the profits even though she owns just 10 percent of the partnership—thanks to her expertise.

▸ A partnership agreement may permit the partnership to lease property or borrow money from its partners, benefiting *both* the partnership and the lender. This means, for example, that a partner could make a loan to the partnership and then benefit personally by earning interest income, while at the same time creating a tax-deductible interest expense for the partnership.

▸ **Limited Partnerships**

The traditional tax shelter vehicle is the limited partnership. Its partners are said to be *limited* because the tax law limits their personal liability to their investment as long as they do not take part in management. As with sole proprietorships and general partnerships, losses flow straight to the limited partners. They may then save taxes by deducting those losses from their taxable income from other sources.

Other Aspects of Tax Planning

▸ **Inventory Values and Taxes**

Inventory values may strongly affect entrepreneurs' tax bills, especially in times of fast-rising prices. The basic problem is how best to value ending inventory. The two most common approaches to this problem are called FIFO and LIFO:

▸ **FIFO (first in, first out)**   This method assumes that the oldest products are sold first. So, ending inventory consists of the products purchased most recently. FIFO generally corresponds to the natural flow of products through inventory. One exception is a coal pile, where coal from the top of the pile rather than the bottom is sold first.

▸ **LIFO (last in, first out)**   This method assumes that the youngest products are sold first. Ending inventory here consists of the oldest materials. LIFO generally corresponds to the economic flow of values through inventory.

Of the two methods, LIFO saves more in taxes. Particularly in a climate of rising prices, LIFO keeps book profits down by matching present selling prices with present costs: The spread is not so great. The following example shows how LIFO yields less taxable income than FIFO:

EXAMPLE ▸   The owner of a retail store is thinking of switching from FIFO to LIFO to save taxes, because prices are rising rapidly. She estimates that next year she will have:

- ▶ $200,000 in sales revenues
- ▶ $40,000 in operating expenses
- ▶ 2,000 units in beginning inventory
- ▶ 2,000 units in ending inventory
- ▶ 6,000 units of purchases
- ▶ An increase in the purchase cost of inventory, to $20 a unit from $10 a unit

With the help of her accountant, the entrepreneur prepares the table shown in Exhibit 19.7. The upper half of the exhibit shows her estimates of the cost of goods sold under FIFO and then under LIFO. Next, she prepares two income statements to compare the impact on both taxes and net profit.

Notice that federal income taxes would be $4,000 lower under LIFO than under FIFO. To simplify the arithmetic, we assumed that prices would double in one year, to $20 from $10 a unit. In real life, price increases would rarely be so steep. ▲▼▲

The U.S. Internal Revenue Code permits entrepreneurs to use LIFO for income tax purposes, but only if they also use LIFO in their published financial statements to shareholders and other interested parties. This is the only

---

EXHIBIT 19.7

How LIFO saves taxes: LIFO versus FIFO computations.

Items	Units	Unit Cost	Under FIFO	Under LIFO
Beginning inventory	2,000	$10	$ 20,000	$ 20,000
Purchases	6,000	$20	120,000	120,000
Available for sale	8,000		$140,000	$140,000
Ending inventory	2,000		40,000*	20,000†
Cost of goods sold	6,000		$100,000	$120,000

Income Statements		Under FIFO	Under LIFO
	Sales revenues	$200,000	$200,000
	Cost of goods sold	100,000	120,000
	Gross profit	$100,000	$ 80,000
	Operating expenses	40,000	40,000
	Taxable income	$ 60,000	$ 40,000
	Federal income tax‡	12,000	8,000
	Net profit	$ 48,000	$ 32,000

*Obtained by multiplying the ending unit cost of $20 by the 2,000 units in ending inventory.

†Obtained by multiplying the beginning unit cost of $10 by the 2,000 units in ending inventory.

‡Assumes a flat 20 percent corporate tax rate.

time entrepreneurs must use the same accounting method for both income tax and financial-reporting purposes.

▶ Targeted Jobs Credit

Entrepreneurs may avail themselves of the targeted jobs credit by employing certain disadvantaged people. This tax credit equals 40 percent of the first $6,000 of wages per eligible employee for the first year of employment only. Eligible employees include:

▶ Young men and women, ages 18 to 25, from low-income families

▶ Men and women with disabilities

▶ Vietnam veterans

▶ Ex-convicts

The employee must also come from an economically disadvantaged family, defined as having an income of less than 70 percent of the minimum living standard set annually by the U.S. Bureau of Labor Statistics. Take this example:

EXAMPLE ▶

An entrepreneur hires three disadvantaged youths, each certified as eligible for the targeted jobs credit. Each receives wages of $9,000 during the year. If the entrepreneur takes the tax credit, her tax bill would be reduced by $7,200, computed as follows:

$$\text{Targeted jobs credit} = (\$6,000 \times 40\%) \times 3 \text{ employees}$$
$$= \$7,200 \text{ ▲▼▲}$$

▶ Estate and Gift Taxes

In addition to federal income taxes, federal estate and gift taxes should be of major concern to every entrepreneur. Until passage of the U.S. Economic Recovery Tax Act of 1981, the tax laws encouraged entrepreneurs and their spouses to protect their estates by:

▶ Putting insurance policies in each other's names to avoid paying estate taxes after death

▶ Legally sharing the ownership of a home or other assets

The 1981 tax law eliminated the need for these actions. As a result, entrepreneurs may now leave everything to their spouses tax-free.

Changes in the estate tax law have had other effects, too. For example, the law now exempts all taxable estates of $600,000 or less entirely from federal taxes, no matter to whom they are bequeathed. If the estate is subject to tax, the maximum tax rate is 55 percent; the lowest rate is 37 percent.

Tax laws also permit an unlimited number of $10,000 gifts—$20,000 if the donor is married—tax-free each year of one's life. These tax-free amounts are in addition to the $600,000 tax credit mentioned above.

Today, with sound planning, an entrepreneur's estate can have a net worth of more than $1 million and still avoid paying any estate taxes as property passes from one generation to the next. To achieve this result, the entrepreneur needs the help of an accountant, a lawyer, or an insurance agent. Planning for minimizing estate taxes should:

- Take maximum advantage of the tax rules governing estates and gifts
- Make imaginative use of charities
- Use trust devices to prevent estate taxes from depleting wealth in each generation

Other Federal Taxes

The federal tax structure takes in a host of other taxes. The most important are employment taxes and excise taxes:

- **Employment taxes** Employment taxes cover social security and unemployment. Entrepreneurs must pay social security taxes for every worker who earns more than $50 in quarterly wages. (We discuss social security in more detail in the next chapter, which deals with insurance.) Furthermore, anyone who employs one or more people for 20 weeks each during the year must pay federal unemployment taxes.

- **Excise taxes** Excise taxes cover sales revenues, not profits. They apply to selected products and services, such as the use of highways by trucks and the manufacture of alcohol and tobacco products.

Keeping Tax Records

Compliance with federal, state, and local tax laws requires a staggering amount of paperwork. Recording and withholding taxes, as well as reporting and paying taxes, must be done accurately and promptly. In dealing with taxes, entrepreneurs play a double role. As debtors, they pay federal income taxes on profits. As agents, they withhold federal income taxes and social security taxes from their own salaries and those of employees, in order to pass them on to the proper government agency. For some entrepreneurs, these chores cause anxiety and confusion.

The best way to relieve this anxiety is to design an accounting system that also generates tax information. For example, an accounting system that turns out income statements should also generate data for preparing federal income tax returns.

Tax laws require entrepreneurs to keep permanent records on items such as the following:

- Sales revenues of products subject to excise taxes
- Tax-deductible operating expenses
- Inventories

How serious a problem is noncompliance? The federal government continually studies the problem in its efforts to reduce the gap between what taxpayers owe and what they fail to pay voluntarily. Turning to Exhibit 19.8, note that sole proprietors head the list of those found to be in noncompliance.

Filing Tax Returns

To make sure they meet their obligations, entrepreneurs must keep tax calendars reminding them of tax due dates. Failure to file returns or pay taxes on time can bring stiff penalties, such as high interest charges, fines, or even jail sentences.

EXHIBIT 19.8

Who fails to pay their share of federal income taxes?

Source: U.S. General Accounting Office; adapted from, and as reported in, "GAO Eyes Closing the Taxpayer Noncompliance Gap," *Journal of Accountancy* (September 1995), p. 27.

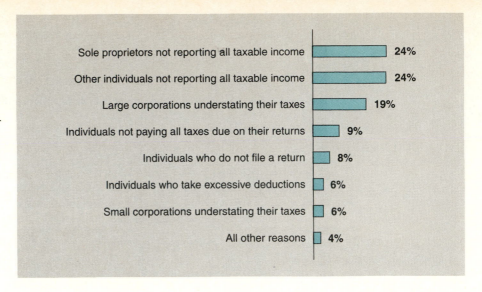

Sole proprietors not reporting all taxable income	24%
Other individuals not reporting all taxable income	24%
Large corporations understating their taxes	19%
Individuals not paying all taxes due on their returns	9%
Individuals who do not file a return	8%
Individuals who take excessive deductions	6%
Small corporations understating their taxes	6%
All other reasons	4%

The IRS can hold an entrepreneur personally responsible for taxes owed by the venture, even if it is incorporated. The IRS bears down especially hard on entrepreneurs who withhold income taxes and social security taxes from the wages of employees and then use these sums instead of passing them on to the government. Such illegal use of money often occurs with the best of intentions; the entrepreneur fully intends to pay up, eventually. If payment is delayed for long, however, the IRS can impose severe penalties.

▶ **Auditing**

Entrepreneurs can count on having their tax returns audited from time to time by the IRS. Government computers handle more than 150 million tax returns a year, helping speed refunds, spot violators, make sure taxpayers file the right returns, check the accuracy of arithmetic, and determine whether other taxes are owed before a refund is paid.

There are two main reasons why a tax return may be selected for audit. First, it may be selected at random. Second, and more serious, a return may be audited because it is inaccurate or incomplete. When the IRS selects a return for audit, it usually examines:

▶ The taxpayer's salary

▶ Sales revenues and operating expenses

▶ Inventories

▶ Large cash transactions

▶ Travel and entertainment expenses

Occasionally, the IRS does uncover fraud, but often there is honest disagreement between the IRS and the taxpayer on how certain items should be handled. For instance, they may disagree on when sales revenues and operating expenses should be recorded, how fixed assets such as buildings should be depreciated, or how intangible assets such as licenses and covenants not to compete should be amortized over their useful lives. The IRS requires the taxpayer to present proof of questionable deductions.

Clearly, it is vital to be painstakingly thorough in all tax matters. To support their tax returns, entrepreneurs must keep good records and *never* violate the tax law. Ignoring these precautions may trigger enormous problems.

SUMMARY

Although taxes spark controversy and grumbling from the individuals and businesses that pay them, they are necessary. Their purpose is to enhance the quality of life by paying for the nation's defense, schools, welfare programs, and other vital services.

Entrepreneurs must understand the difference between tax avoidance and tax evasion:

▸ Tax avoidance is legal. The IRS expects individuals and businesses to avoid all avoidable taxes and gives them the information they need to do so.

▸ Tax evasion is the willful failure to live up to the spirit and letter of the tax law.

A company's tax liability depends on its legal form of organization. The laws governing corporate income taxes make a distinction between tax accounting and financial accounting:

▸ The goal of tax accounting is to minimize taxes by recognizing operating expenses as soon as is legally possible and postponing the recognition of sales revenues for as long as possible.

▸ The goal of financial accounting is to fairly report the sales revenues, operating expenses, and profits earned in a given period.

There are many ways to postpone or reduce taxes. One—the modified accelerated cost recovery system (MACRS)—allows entrepreneurs to depreciate the cost of most fixed assets over just a few years, thus postponing tax liability. The LIFO (last in, first out) method of valuing ending inventory and the targeted job credit both reduce tax liability.

Computers enable the IRS to monitor closely the accuracy and completeness of income tax returns. Because there is a good chance of a return's being audited, entrepreneurs must be prepared to support every entry. Therefore, it is important to keep accurate, complete, and up-to-date records.

Discussion and Review Questions

1. How would you, as an entrepreneur, benefit from the payment of federal income taxes?
2. Distinguish between tax evasion and tax avoidance.
3. Why must entrepreneurs keep up with changes in the tax law?
4. Do you believe it is ethical for entrepreneurs to figure their income one way for federal income tax purposes and another way for financial accounting purposes? Why or why not?

5. Do you believe that the tax incentives for investing in new fixed assets are adequate? Explain your answer.
6. How significant may tax savings be to the entrepreneur? Give examples.
7. How does the legal postponement of tax payments benefit the entrepreneur?
8. Why and how does the U.S. Internal Revenue Code give small corporations a tax break?
9. Why are S corporations especially attractive to some entrepreneurs?
10. Describe some of the ways that entrepreneurs may minimize their federal income tax liability.
11. How do LIFO and FIFO differ? Why does LIFO save taxes?
12. Why is estate planning so vital? How would you, as an entrepreneur, go about it?
13. Explain how entrepreneurs act as both debtors and agents in managing the tax aspects of their ventures.
14. Why must entrepreneurs keep accurate and complete tax records?
15. Define these terms: *taxable income, MACRS, straight-line depreciation, targeted jobs credit, employment taxes.*

Building a Business Plan

Taxation

Few issues spark more controversy than taxes. And yet taxes cannot be ignored. As illustrated in Exhibit 19.1 in the text, small business owners must be concerned with many different types of taxes at the federal, state, and local levels.

Tax Records

Entrepreneurs have certain tax obligations they must meet. And compliance with tax laws requires a staggering amount of paperwork. The best way to relieve this anxiety is to design an accounting system that also generates tax information. Then it is possible to construct a tax calendar that will remind them of tax due dates.

Tax laws require entrepreneurs to keep permanent records on many items that include sales revenues of products and services, tax-deductible operating expenses, and employee wages and deductions.

Instructions for Worksheet 19

To complete this part of the business plan, in part 1 you must list the tax obligations at the federal, state, and local level that affect your business. Then in part 2, construct a tax calendar that lists tax due dates.

Building a Business Plan (continued)

Part 1—Tax Obligations

Before answering the questions that follow, you may want to review the material on pages 563 to 571 in your text.

1. List the specific federal tax obligations that you incur as a result of your business activities.

2. List the specific state tax obligations that you incur as a result of your business activities.

3. List the specific local tax obligations that you incur as a result of your business activities.

4. Are there other taxes that you must pay that were not described in your text? If so, describe these tax obligations.

Part 2—Tax Payment Dates

5. Based on the information in part 1, determine when payments must be paid to the federal government.

6. Based on the information in part 1, determine when payments must be paid to state governments.

7. Based on the information in part 1, determine when payments must be paid to local governments.

8. Now construct your own tax calendar, listing specific payment dates for all of the tax obligations that you incur.

CASE 19A ▶ *Kerscher Elevator Company*

Founded in 1912, Kerscher Elevator prospered for about 50 years. During the next 20 years, the company declined. When John Blatt bought the company, it was in "beat-up, rundown condition," says Blatt. "The company's building was a mess. The roof leaked, the washroom had no running water, and the windows had been shattered by vandals. Worse, the company had lost all respect in the community. Believe me, the company was all but dead." Undaunted, Blatt "plunged into deep water and bought the company anyway."

Blatt had worked for eleven years in the elevator division of Reliance Electric, a billion-dollar company, before striking off on his own to buy Kerscher Elevator. "I just hated working for a company that big," says Blatt. "I felt boxed in and couldn't stand the endless meetings. They were so boring. Besides, my job was a dead-end job, although I enjoyed going to Las Vegas and other resort cities on trouble-shooting jobs." Blatt had joined Reliance Electric soon after he was discharged from the U.S. Navy, where he had worked for four years as a nuclear engineer under the renowned Admiral Hyman Rickover. Before his stint in the Navy, Blatt attended Ohio State University, where he studied industrial management.

Blatt inherited his entrepreneurial spirit from his father, whom he deeply admired. A successful entrepreneur, his father owned a small retail automobile dealership selling Studebakers and Willys. "He did well enough to put me through college," says Blatt, "It was my dad who always encouraged me to be my own boss."

Financial Sacrifice

When he left Reliance Electric, Blatt was earning $60,000 a year as manager of elevator construction and technical service. His first two years with Kerscher Elevator, however, he paid himself only $15,000 a year. "It was worth the sacrifice, just to be my own boss," says Blatt. "I was reduced to scrambling for a living, and instead of working 40 hours a week, I found myself working 80 to 100 hours a week. Funny thing is, I really enjoyed it."

Blatt's wide travels as a trouble-shooter with Reliance Electric enabled him to observe firsthand the operations of virtually every other elevator company in the country. Long entertaining the thought of owning his own elevator company, he made mental notes of which companies "seemed ripe for purchase at a low price." He chose the Kerscher Elevator Company, which "was going under before my very eyes. I was sure I had the drive and imagination to turn the company around," says Blatt.

He bought Kerscher Elevator for $120,000, financing the purchase with just $10,000 of his own money and borrowing the rest from the seller. Interest was 8 percent, and the term of the loan was ten years. "Not a bad deal," says Blatt. "The banks never would have given me such generous terms." His beginning balance sheet appears in Exhibit 19A.1. Note that Blatt also loaned the company $15,000 to purchase inventories of elevator parts, and to finance customers until they pay their bills, as well as to repair and renovate the building, which had become an "eyesore."

When he bought the company, Blatt had decided to take in a partner whose experience with the elevator industry complemented his—someone who was an expert in sales and purchasing. Blatt, on the other hand, was an expert in installing and repairing elevators.

EXHIBIT 19A.1
Kerscher Elevator Company: Balance sheet at time of purchase (September 30, 1981).

Assets			Equities		
Current assets			Current liabilities		
Cash	$15,000		Note payable	$15,000	
Accounts receivable	42,000		Accounts payable	26,000	$ 41,000
Inventories	11,000	$ 68,000			
Fixed assets			Long-term liability		
Land	$ 5,000		Note payable		100,000
Building	47,100				
Equipment	2,000		Owners' equity		
Vehicles	18,000	72,100	Common stock		10,000
Goodwill		10,900			
Total assets		$151,000	Total equities		$151,000

Although he had incorporated his new company and made the total investment, Blatt had agreed, in writing, to share the company and all future dividends equally with his partner. In essence, then, Blatt had an equal partner who had invested not a single penny of his own money. "It was my way of letting him know that I needed and appreciated his skills," says Blatt. "In my eyes, he was my partner and I always spoke of him as such, even though the company was a regular corporation and not a general partnership."

Turning the Company Around

Kerscher Elevator had suffered a string of operating losses under the prior owner. "The challenge was awesome," says Blatt. "My partner and I agreed that our most pressing problem was to brighten the company's badly tarnished image. The question was, How?" After much thought, the two partners decided that Blatt would become the company's "Mr. Outside," making himself visible in the community as a volunteer to service groups and civic organizations like the Kiwanis and Rotary Clubs. A $1,000 job was done at the city zoo—and they charged $1. He would make himself available to serve the community at a moment's notice and, in this way, make every effort to boost the company's image.

At the same time, he would be "beating the bushes" to recapture clients lost by the prior owner. Here he would stress that Kerscher Elevator's new and aggressive management would focus on supplying better service than any competitor. For example, the company would be ready to respond "instantly—at any hour of the day and night—if a client's elevator broke down."

Blatt's partner, on the other hand, would be the company's "Mr. Inside," directing his energies at running the shop. He would be responsible for getting the work done right the first time and on time. He would also run the office and make sure that records were kept up to date and clients paid their bills on time.

The partners' strategy paid off immediately. As shown in Exhibit 19A.2, sales revenues moved

EXHIBIT 19A.2
Kerscher Elevator Company: Operating performance before and after purchase.

	1981*	1982	1983	1984	1985	1986	1987
Sales revenues	$312,000	$417,500	$667,500	$896,900	$1,396,500	$907,500	$969,000
Cost of sales	242,000	301,100	510,000	639,400	999,500	654,000	615,000
Gross profit	$ 70,000	$116,400	$157,500	$257,500	$ 397,000	$253,500	$354,000
Operating expenses	92,000	104,300	125,500	258,300	374,900	339,400	315,600
Operating profit	$ (22,000)	$ 12,100	$ 32,000	$ (800)	$ 22,100	$ (85,900)	$ 38,400
Interest		8,000	11,300	16,000			
Profit before taxes	$ (22,000)	$ 4,100	$ 20,700	$ (16,800)	$ 22,100	$ (85,900)	$ 38,400
Income taxes		200	1,100				
Net profit	$ (22,000)	$ 3,900	$ 19,600	$ (16,800)	$ 22,100	$ (85,900)	$ 38,400

*Under prior owner

steadily upward through 1985, although profits were erratic. "It surely was a heady feeling to know that it was our strategy that saved the company from certain bankruptcy," says Blatt.

To turn the company around, Blatt spent "part of almost every day" working to change its image. Soon after he and his partner took over the company, he was elected president of the small-business branch of the local chamber of commerce. In addition, his volunteer work soon drew the community's attention.

Workforce

When he and his partner took over the company, Blatt was aware that image and solid performance must go hand in hand. "It was vital," says Blatt, "to hire, train, motivate, and mold all employees in the image of excellence that we wanted to project."

Blatt has to hire his employees through the International Union of Elevator Constructors, which runs a closed shop, meaning that workers must first join the union before hiring on with elevator companies. The union supplies the labor for Blatt, although he retains the right to hire and fire specific employees. "If I need a worker," says Blatt, "I just pick up the phone and call the union. I don't have to advertise for help or call an employment agency."

The elevator industry rivals both the automotive and the steel industries in the generosity of its wage structure. In 1988, elevator mechanics earned an average base wage of more than $20 an hour plus fringe benefits of $5 an hour. "Not a bad wage," says Blatt. "In fact, my employees have often drawn more pay than me, and I'm the company president. My employees make more money than most college professors."

As well paid as his employees are, Blatt still goes to "extraordinary lengths" to make sure they meet his expectations of excellence. His promotional brochure claims:

The Kerscher team is kept constantly on the cutting edge of the state of the art in vertical transportation by attendance at Kerscher College. Our commitment is that our employees will be the best trained elevator persons in the area. Our supervisory personnel work directly with the field mechanics to reach this goal.

The Kerscher professional service team includes elevator mechanics and helpers with experience on hundreds of different makes and models of elevators. No other local company has as much breadth of talent as Kerscher's carefully selected team.

"I'm a poor motivator," says Blatt. "I'm not very good at it, and yet I need workers who are motivated to excel at providing service. It's not uncommon for elevators to break down in the dead of night or on a holiday. In such emergencies, our answering service gets on the phone immediately to persuade a mechanic to repair the elevator. But to get someone to come in at odd hours is often as easy as pulling teeth. Why, the other day I had to send a taxi to a mechanic's house to get a repair job done in a downtown office building."

At present, Blatt employs seventeen men and women, of whom fourteen work in the field and three in the office. "Our organization is a lot leaner than it was in our growth days," says Blatt. "We had too much overhead." Blatt's organizational chart appears in Exhibit 19A.3. Although he is its chairman, he has never called a meeting of the company's board of directors.

Note that the organizational chart omits mention of Blatt's partner. "We got tired of each other. We just couldn't get along and it took me four years to do something about our relationship. Had I known in the beginning what I know now, I never would have formed a 50-50 working partnership. We ran the company as equals, even though I had put up all the money to buy it."

Market Segments

Kerscher Elevator markets its services within a 75-mile radius of its offices. "Any building with an

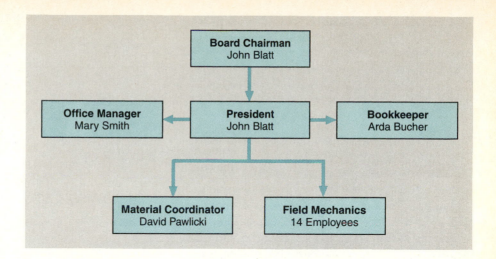

EXHIBIT 19A.3
Kerscher Elevator Company: Organizational chart.

Board Chairman
John Blatt

Office Manager
Mary Smith

President
John Blatt

Bookkeeper
Arda Bucher

Material Coordinator
David Pawlicki

Field Mechanics
14 Employees

elevator is a potential client," says Blatt. "In my marketing area alone, more than a thousand buildings have elevators of some kind."

Indeed, elevator service is in constant demand because buildings, tall or short, must now be accessible to the handicapped. Blatt says that two factors put building owners "at the mercy" of elevator service companies like his:

▶ The complexity of today's elevator systems. A single elevator system may have more than 10,000 separate parts, each one capable of causing a breakdown in elevator service.

▶ The technology of elevator systems. Manufacturers differ sharply in their designs as they try to outdo each other by using the latest advances in electronic technology.

These two factors complicate Kerscher Elevator's ability to service its clients properly. "That is why our training program, which I like to call the Kerscher College, is so necessary," says Blatt.

Kerscher Elevator recently diversified into the market for the handicapped with a complete line of porch lifts, residential elevators, stair climbers, dumbwaiters, and power-lift chairs. "We recognize this segment as a rapidly growing market into which we have moved with deliberation," says Blatt. In the next two years or so, Blatt plans to continue his diversification efforts by "invading the escalator market. This market is also growing rapidly," he says, "and we ought to exploit it, although not now."

Competition

Kerscher Elevator is the second largest elevator service company in its marketing area. The largest is Shindler of North America, which also manufactures elevator systems. "Competition in the industry for service work is severe and getting worse by the week," says Blatt. "To survive in this industry, you have to know your competition—their strengths and weaknesses."

Blatt responds to competitive pressures by exploiting his company's agility. "Response time is our niche in the marketplace," he says. "We respond quicker and faster than our competitors when clients need us. In bidding on a service job, for example, we're never more than fifteen minutes from a decision on a client's elevator problem; our competitors take a week or two. In fact, it usually takes me no more than a couple of minutes to price a service job."

Even so, Blatt is especially worried about the price-cutting war now under way. "I've always priced to value," says Blatt. "My clients have always been willing to pay a premium for the excellent service I give. They want fast, reliable, dependable service, and they know I have staked my reputation on giving such service."

Financial Crisis

About four years after buying Kerscher Elevator, Blatt and his partner negotiated their separation. This, as well as other problems, so distracted Blatt that he began to neglect the day-to-day operation of his business. As a result, sales revenues dropped to $907,500 from $1,396,500 the year before, and profits vanished as operating losses of $85,900 were incurred. "It was the worst period of my life," says Blatt, "but I never doubted my ability and courage to turn the company around, a second time."

The Second Turnaround

Taking stock of himself and his company, Blatt decided to stick to the philosophical course he had set originally. He would not panic and he would continue to focus on excellence to regain lost customers and gain new ones. He would not compromise his principles or engage in any price-cutting war. Although this strategy has not worked as well as he would have liked, Blatt has turned the company around once again. The year after the crisis, sales revenues rose to $969,000 and profits came to $38,400. "Coming on the heels of that whopping big loss the year before, I couldn't be more pleased," says Blatt. His 1987 income statement and balance sheets appear in Exhibits 19A.4 and 19A.5. Exhibit 19A.6 traces his sales and profit performance since 1981.

Optimistic, Blatt prepared both a financial plan, shown in Exhibit 19A.7, and a marketing strategy for 1988, described in Exhibit 19A.8. In addition, Blatt had drafted these objectives for 1988:

▶ To work with union workers to achieve a profit margin of 48 percent through improved job planning and scheduling

EXHIBIT 19A.4

Kerscher Elevator Company: 1987 income statement.

Sales revenues		$969,000
Cost of sales		615,000
Gross profit		$354,000
Operating expenses		
Office salaries	$130,500	
Interest	30,100	
Travel, entertainment	26,800	
Office supplies, postage	16,100	
Insurance	15,500	
Building rent	14,400	
Depreciation	13,100	
Professional fees	13,100	
Covenant not to compete	12,500	
Automobile and truck	8,200	
Employee benefits	6,600	
Utilities, security	4,100	
Dues and subscriptions	2,800	
Advertising	2,700	
Tooling	2,500	
Temporary help	2,100	
Personal property taxes	1,900	
Licenses	1,500	
Repairs and maintenance	900	
Penalties	700	
Freight	700	
Education	700	
Equipment rental	500	
Contributions	400	
Bad debts	200	
Miscellaneous	7,000	315,600
Operating profit		$ 38,400

EXHIBIT 19A.5

Kerscher Elevator Company: Balance sheet (December 31, 1987).

Assets			Equities		
Current assets			**Current liabilities**		
Accounts receivable	$144,900		Bank overdraft	$ 4,000	
Inventories	168,400		Accounts payable	75,100	
Other	8,700	$322,000	Long-term loan (current)	61,900	
			Payroll deductions	68,700	
			Miscellaneous	35,100	$244,800
Fixed assets			**Long-term liabilities**		
Equipment	$ 5,900		Installment notes	$ 17,600	
Furniture and fixtures	9,900		Long-term loan	162,500	
Vehicles	37,000		Owed to former partner	44,300	
	$ 52,800			$224,400	
Less: Accumulated			Less: Current portion	61,900	162,500
depreciation	37,200	15,600	**Other liabilities**		
Other assets			Covenant not to compete		31,200
Covenant not to compete	$ 31,200		**Owners' equity**		
Miscellaneous	2,100	33,300	Common stock	$ 10,000	
			Retained earnings	(77,600)	(67,600)
Total assets		$370,900	Total equities		$370,900

EXHIBIT 19A.6

Kerscher Elevator Company: Sales and profit performance.

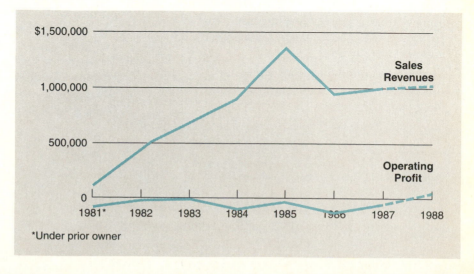

*Under prior owner

Sales revenues		
Maintenance	$600,000	
Repair	300,000	
Construction	75,000	
Handicap	5,000	$980,000
Cost of sales		
Maintenance	$300,000	
Repair	200,000	
Construction	66,000	
Handicap	14,000	580,000
Gross margin		$400,000
General and administrative		250,000
Operating profit		$150,000
Less: Profit-sharing		15,000
Profit before taxes		$135,000

▶ To develop an effective quality-control program, ensuring high-quality products and service at competitive prices and reducing callbacks* to three per day

▶ To design an inventory control system that reduces the investment in inventory by 10 percent

▶ To develop office procedures to ensure that all customers with contracts are routinely serviced and not overlooked

▶ To improve communications within the office to spark instant response to customer complaints

*A term that refers to "calling back" an employee to work overtime during odd hours to repair an elevator.

▶ To brighten the appearance of the company by keeping the shop and office both clean and orderly at all times and by improving lawn care and snow removal

He is so confident of his future that he is now seriously considering relocating to the nearby Control Data Business Technology Center. Founded by the giant Control Data Corporation, this center helps its tenants, small businesses like Blatt's, by providing:

▶ Layout and space design help

▶ Basic utilities such as heat and air conditioning

▶ A security system for controlling after-hours operations

▶ Word processing

▶ Clerical services

▶ Equipment leasing

▶ Shipping and receiving

▶ State-of-the-art computer services

It also provides the services of information specialists and a complete business and technical library that offers automated literature searches. "Of course, I cannot move into the Center until I resolve my financial problems," says Blatt. A view of the Center appears in Exhibit 19A.9.

Questions
1. What accounts for the company's recent problems?
2. Comment on John Blatt's entrepreneurial and managerial traits.
3. What are the key factors for success in a business like this one?
4. What are the company's prospects?
5. What should Blatt do now?

EXHIBIT 19A.8
Kerscher Elevator Company: Marketing strategy.

Product
We will maintain these product lines: Maintenance, repair, construction, and residential. We will expand our repair efforts through clearly stated specification sheets and simple price lists. We will sell Kerscher as "The Elevator Professional" and seek profitable opportunities to so demonstrate. We will seek to sell our product differentiation, including professionalism, personal attention, contractual freedom, insurance, company strength, 75-years' experience, local ownership.

Price
We will work from a standard price book and will later upgrade it to reflect actual competitive expenses. We will carefully price major contracts to reflect superlative service and will clearly demonstrate what we are selling so as to differentiate it from the competitor. We will always consider "Why should the customer buy from Kerscher?" If we have no good answers, we will not pursue that market segment.

Promotion
We will utilize appropriate trade shows and related opportunities to position Kerscher in the forefront. We will selectively advertise to promote the theme: "Professionals in vertical transportation." Personal selling will remain the backbone of our efforts with a profit-sharing bonus program geared to reward superior success. We will utilize a company brochure to help build company recognition. We will remain active in civic affairs to maintain our present positive reputation.

Distribution
We will continue with direct company salespersons in the present market. We will continue to serve an area 75 miles around. We will remain alert to governmental opportunities, or favored customers, to operate satellite branches. We will remain alert to the opportunity to consult or educate in remote areas where the profits remain attractive.

EXHIBIT 19A.9
Control Data Business Technology Center.

The Christopher Baseball Club

The Christopher Baseball Club was a flourishing limited partnership formed to carry on the business of a minor league baseball team in a small Midwestern city. The club's financial success, however, was not shared by its limited partners, at least not anything to the degree they had expected.

In fact, for all the years in which the club prospered, the general partner awarded the limited partners only 20 percent of their share of the club's profits. Yet, all of them were taxed *as if* they had received 100 percent of their share of the profits, not just 20 percent. The remaining profits had been reinvested, mostly to renovate a ball park that prior owners had neglected to keep in shape.

Although the limited partners complained bitterly, the general partner chose to ignore the issue. His cavalier attitude caused the limited partners to sue. In their suit, the limited partners claimed that their rights as investors had been violated and that they were entitled to 100 percent of their share of the club's profits. To confuse matters, the club's partnership agreement, which every limited partner signed, had failed to spell out how profits, if any, were to be distributed.

Much to their dismay, the limited partners lost the suit. The court ruled that, in the absence of a partnership agreement covering the distribution of profits, the decision to reinvest profits was strictly a managerial one—meaning the general partner could do with the profits as he saw fit. Thus, unless the limited partners could prove that the general partner's conduct had harmed the club financially, they had no recourse but to accept his decision *and* to continue paying taxes on money they never received.

Upon hearing the court's ruling, one of the limited partners said: "It just isn't fair; I never thought our case would play out the way it did."

Questions

1. In your judgment, is the legal rule that limited partners cannot take part in management fair? Why or why not?
2. Do you believe that, because limited partners cannot take part in management, the general partner has an ethical duty to the limited partners that goes beyond that permitted by law? If not, why not? If so, how would you define such a duty?

Ernest Allyson

Ernest Allyson began in construction as a carpenter, working for a builder who specialized in additions and new homes. He worked with the same firm for eight years. When he decided to launch his own business, he was in charge of six other carpenters.

Allyson established his own firm because large parcels of land were being developed nearby and he was certain that with his experience, he could earn more money. He rented a garage as his office, hired a work crew, and subcontracted for about a year, gradually building up his own reputation.

In three years, Allyson's business grew so much that he needed additional space. He bought a building to house the tools and equipment that were accumulating. With more space, he also was able to buy materials at wholesale and stock them in his building, both for use by his three work crews and for sale to other builders.

After operating for four years on his own, Allyson looked at his business:

▶ He had three work crews that were kept busy full time. Some employees had been with him from the start, and he wanted to keep them.

▶ He wanted to expand his building so that he could display more of his supply inventory and increase sales.

▶ He had purchased $22,000 in equipment in the past year alone and wondered if there was some way to recover those expenditures.

▶ He was beginning to think about saving some money for retirement.

▶ His taxes were rising sharply as the business grew. His accountant told him that his tax bill as a sole proprietor had been over $50,000 the previous year.

Questions
1. Should Ernest Allyson consider changing his legal form of organization? How might a different form benefit him?
2. If Allyson is checking his tax return for deductions or savings, what should he look for besides normal operating expenses?

Source: Adapted from a case prepared by the U.S. Small Business Administration.

Risk Management and Insurance

I am not afraid of storms, for I am learning how to sail my ship.

—Louisa May Alcott

O ur lives are fraught with risk and have been since the moment of birth. The saying that we can never know what tomorrow will bring is especially true in business. Entrepreneurs soon find that risk is their constant companion, and that their ability to manage it depends largely on their attitude. If entrepreneurs ignore risk, they are likely to blunder; but if they face up to it, they can enhance their chances of survival and growth.

In this chapter, we discuss how entrepreneurs may protect themselves and their venture from risk, focusing on risk management programs, insurance, and pension programs.

The Idea of Risk

Risk defies easy definition. To the layperson, risk generally means the possibility of losing one's health, reputation, or self-image. To the entrepreneur, however, risk means the chance of financial loss. When we discuss risk in this chapter, we mean *financial risk,* the kind that can result in dollar losses. These losses can show up in the balance sheet or in the income statement as:

▶ **Reduced sales revenues**   A fire may reduce a plant to rubble, and thus force the entrepreneur to lose sales until the plant is rebuilt.

▶ **Increased operating expenses**   A fire may force the entrepreneur to move into temporary but expensive quarters.

▶ **Reduced assets**   Inventory or equipment may be stolen, or a major customer who owes the entrepreneur money may declare bankruptcy.

EXHIBIT 20.1
Kinds of financial risks.

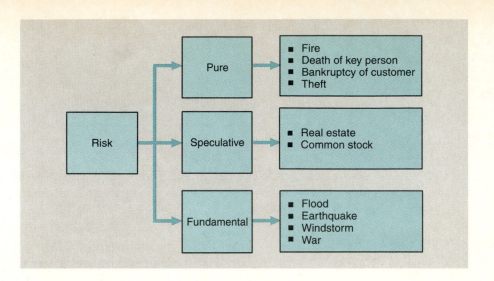

▶ **Increased liabilities**   The entrepreneur may fail to deliver on a contract or may lose a lawsuit.

Note that all of these potential losses have one thing in common: Their occurrence cannot be foreseen. When such losses do occur, the entrepreneur is caught completely by surprise.

As Exhibit 20.1 shows, there are three kinds of financial risk: pure, speculative, and fundamental.

▶ **Pure risk**   Risks qualify as *pure* if they may result in a loss or no loss, with no possibility of gain. Examples include fire, death of a key person, bankruptcy of a customer, and theft. The entrepreneur can do little to avoid pure risk. For example, any venture that owns a delivery truck faces the risk of accident, and any venture that owns a building faces the risk of fire.

▶ **Speculative risk**   With pure risk, the entrepreneur can only lose or break even. With *speculative risk,* however, the entrepreneur can either gain or lose. For example, an entrepreneur may decide to invest in land on the chance that it will go up in value. Unforeseen events, however, may lower its value. Any such investment qualifies as speculative because it is the entrepreneur, not fate, that exposes the venture to loss. Similarly, investment in common stocks can yield either a profit or a loss.

▶ **Fundamental risk**   *Fundamental risk* differs from both pure and speculative risk in its neutrality. In other words, fundamental risk plays no favorites. Fate does not single out just one venture and bypass all others. On the contrary, fundamental risk touches all ventures. It usually arises from the economic, political, social, or natural forces acting on society. Some specific sources of fundamental risk are floods and earthquakes, inflation and war.

Every business, regardless of size, must protect itself against a catastrophe, as did this manufacturer of women's clothes whose building was gutted by fire.

Risk Management Programs

It may seem self-evident that entrepreneurs are aware of all risks, especially those that could jeopardize the survival and growth of their venture. Yet, entrepreneurs often ignore risk, especially fundamental risk, which is not always apparent. Take this example:

Blizzards and heavy rains in the Northeast caused billions of dollars in losses during the winter of 1996. Especially hard hit were New York and Pennsylvania, where the rain and melting snow led to flooding that severely damaged thousands of small businesses and forced many to suspend operations.

    Tragically, only 1 percent of these businesses had flood insurance.[1] Moreover, those who bought coverage had insured only their buildings, not their inventory or equipment. ▲▼▲

In short, entrepreneurs must fully analyze their exposure to loss. Only through such analysis can they protect their venture against loss from pure or fundamental risk. Although easy to state, this goal—protecting a venture against possible loss—is difficult to achieve. The main reason is that risk management is more art than science, often defying precise analysis. Expert judgment plays the key role here. This is why entrepreneurs must rely on the expertise of an insurance agent to design a program of risk management that:

▸ Pinpoints risks that may cause dollar losses.

▸ Estimates how severe these losses may be.

▸ Selects the best way to treat each risk.

Pinpointing Risks

Because losses affect a venture financially, financial statements offer a good starting point for pinpointing where losses may occur. The balance sheet, for example, may show a building valued at $400,000. The entrepreneur must then ask, "What could happen to destroy its value of $400,000?" Among many other possibilities are the risks of a fire or windstorm. By continuing in this vein, the entrepreneur can identify all the points of exposure to loss, especially with the help of a checklist like the one in Exhibit 20.2.

For the entrepreneur, the job of pinpointing risks never ends. As a venture changes and grows, new risks arise. The manufacture of a new product, for example, may expose a venture to new risks. It is the entrepreneur's job to pinpoint these risks and gauge their possible effect on the venture.

Estimating the Effects of Losses

This step is perhaps the hardest, for there are no checklists to help estimate the effects of losses. So, it is a good idea to seek professional help. For example, a lawyer can help entrepreneurs estimate liabilities under the contracts they sign; or estimate liabilities for the potential hazards of a new product.

After estimating the dollar cost of each possible loss, entrepreneurs must estimate how often the loss may occur and how serious the loss may be.

These estimates are crucial, because they point to which risks offer the greatest loss and which the least. For example, the chances may be slim that a fire will break out; but if it does, it might ruin the venture. The entrepreneur cannot permit that to happen. One way to absorb the risk is to shift it to somebody else, by buying insurance protection.

Selecting Ways to Deal with Risk

With the help of an insurance agent, entrepreneurs must now select the best combination of ways to deal with a given risk. There are four choices:

▶ Avoid the risk entirely.

▶ Absorb the risk through self-insurance.

▶ Prevent the occurrence of loss, cut the chances of its occurrence, or reduce its severity.

▶ Transfer the risk to others, through insurance.

Entrepreneurs may *avoid risk* in dozens of ways. For example, by leasing rather than buying such assets as machines and trucks, they bypass the risks connected with owning them. By incorporating, they avoid many of the risks connected with the unlimited liability of general partnerships and sole proprietorships. And by depositing cash receipts at the end of each day, they avoid the risk of losing cash to burglars after hours.

Self-insurance is too costly a choice for most entrepreneurs. Few can absorb risk by setting aside excess cash for that purpose. Generally, self-insurance makes sense only if asset values are small compared to sales revenues. An example is an entrepreneur who runs a management consulting firm out of a rented office.

Prevention is also practiced by entrepreneurs, although not to the same extent as avoidance of risk. To minimize their exposure to risk, entrepreneurs should:

▶ Design their plants, shops, or offices to minimize the chance of fire and accidents to employees

EXHIBIT 20.2
Checklist for pinpointing exposure to loss.

Source: Reprinted by permission of SOUTH-WESTERN PUBLISHING CO.

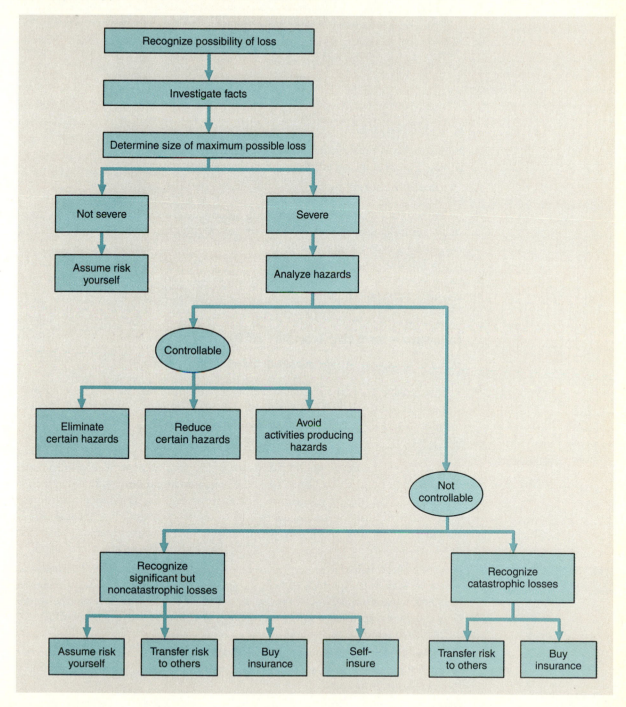

EXHIBIT 20.3
How entrepreneurs may
deal with risk.

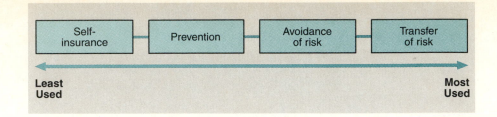

> Hold safety education programs for employees
> Inspect and repair safety devices regularly
> Protect assets by hiring guards, improving burglar alarms, and screening job applicants carefully

These practices prevent or lessen the impact of losses. For example, an automatic sprinkler system may not prevent fires, but it does keep fire from spreading and causing even greater loss.

As Exhibit 20.3 shows, *transfer of risk* is the method most widely used by small businesses. Because of its importance and complexity, this method merits more attention than the others.

Insurance and the Transfer of Risk

What is insurance? In the words of a group of experts:

> Insurance . . . is the business of transferring pure risk by means of a two-party contract. In order for a particular risk technique to qualify as insurance, all of the requirements of the above definition must be met.[2]

Thus, insurance is simply a means of letting an outside party absorb risk. For a fee, called a *premium,* the outside party agrees to pay a specified sum to cover losses suffered under conditions spelled out in a written contract called an *insurance policy.* By buying protection, the entrepreneur is in essence trading the uncertainty of a major loss—say, the loss of a $400,000 building through fire—for the certainty of a minor loss, the premium. Take this example:

EXAMPLE ▶

An entrepreneur decides to protect her venture against the likely loss of sales if her key salesperson were to die unexpectedly. To do so, she buys a $300,000 policy on the salesperson's life for $3,700 a year. This policy would provide her with $300,000 if the salesperson died—a sum large enough to enable her to survive the likely loss of sales from such a tragedy. ▲▼▲

How do insurers decide whether a particular exposure to risk—like the one in our example—is insurable? Basically, insurers say that a risk is insurable if it meets these four tests:

- ▶ The risk must exist in large numbers.
- ▶ The losses must be chance happenings that fall beyond the entrepreneur's control.
- ▶ The losses must be readily measurable.
- ▶ Possible losses must be so severe that the entrepreneur is incapable of absorbing them.

▶ **Risk in Large Numbers**

Risk must exist in large numbers for the law of averages to work for the insurer. Otherwise, the insurance industry could not possibly survive. Somewhat tongue-in-cheek, George Bernard Shaw described the workings of the law of averages as follows:

> An insurance company, sanely directed, and making scores of thousands of bets, is not gambling at all; it knows with sufficient accuracy at what age its clients will die, how many of their houses will be burnt every year, how often their houses will be broken into by burglars, to what extent their money will be embezzled by their cashiers, how much compensation they will have to pay to persons injured in their employment, how many accidents will occur to their motor cars and themselves, how much they will suffer from illness or unemployment, and what births and deaths will cost them: In short, what will happen to every thousand or ten thousand or a million people even when the company cannot tell what will happen to any individual among them.[3]

Because tens of thousands of ventures own trucks, for example, insurers are willing to insure against accidents. In essence, each entrepreneur bets with the insurer that his own truck will have an accident. And the insurer mathematically fixes the odds on the basis of historical facts showing the frequency of accidents by truck size, age of driver, and so on.

The odds are fixed so that the insurer runs only the slightest risk of losing financially. When thousands of cases are considered, the probability that an accident will take place somewhere is certain, but the probability in any single case is unknown. This combination of unpredictability in particular and predictability in general is what makes insurance a business.

▶ **Chance Happenings beyond Control**

An example of a chance happening beyond the entrepreneur's control is a fire caused by lightning that guts a building. This great financial loss could not have been predicted, so here the risk of fire is insurable.

Another example is key-person life insurance, mentioned earlier. Here, the risk is not whether the key person will die, but when. The key person cannot control the time of death except by committing suicide. Insurers do pay death claims from suicide, but only if the policy has been in force for a certain period, usually two years.

Losses from theft or shoplifting are often uninsurable, especially in the high-crime areas of the nation's large cities. So great are the chances of loss in these areas that insurers often can ill afford to insure the entrepreneur's exposure to risk. Burglary and fire insurance are also often denied in high-crime areas.

▶ Readily Measurable Losses

Losses must be measurable in dollars and hard to falsify. Without this test, insurers would have trouble verifying losses. Take this example:

EXAMPLE ▶

An entrepreneur insures a newly constructed building against fire. The building is appraised at $500,000. A year later, an explosive fire destroys the building, leaving in its wake only rubble and ashes. This kind of loss is readily verifiable. So, the insurer has no recourse but to pay the entrepreneur $500,000 to rebuild. ▲▼▲

Most financial losses, however, are not this cut and dried. The severity of losses from a burglary, for example, is often hard to verify. The insurer often has only the entrepreneur's word for the amount lost to burglars, especially for products that are portable and valuable, such as furs and jewels. Because these kinds of losses provide an opportunity for extensive fakery, insurers handle all such claims with extreme care.

Accidents on the job, especially injuries or ailments that defy precise diagnosis, are another gray area. One such ailment is the "bad back." Insurance files bulge with records of people who have collected huge sums for bad backs, because medical science cannot yet spot and measure such ailments with precision. Nor can physicians measure precisely how injuries disturb a patient's psychological well-being. The physician has only the patient's word. As a result, insurers are extremely wary of such claims.

▶ Severe Losses

Possible losses from exposure to risk must be so great that entrepreneurs cannot even begin to absorb them. For example, the possible loss of a factory from fire is insurable, because its loss may ruin the business. On the other hand, the possible loss of a 15-cent pencil from fire is not insurable, because its loss is trivial.

These four tests of insurability are by no means hard and fast. They vary from insurer to insurer and from situation to situation. Shown in Exhibit 20.4, and discussed below, are some common examples of insurable risks.

EXHIBIT 20.4
Selected insurable risks.

Source: From Samuel C. Certo, Stewart T. Husted & Max E. Douglas *Business* Second Edition. Copyright © 1984 by Allyn and Bacon. Reprinted by permission.

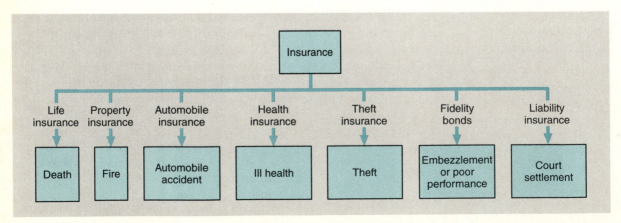

Kinds of Insurance Coverage

To protect against fire, windstorms, and other natural disasters, entrepreneurs must buy *property insurance*. This kind of insurance typically covers such assets as buildings, equipment, and inventories. To discourage their deliberate destruction, insurers traditionally keep the policy's face value below the assets' book value.

Another important kind of coverage is *liability insurance*. It protects against losses that may be caused by the entrepreneur's own negligence. For example, a customer may sue a manufacturer because he hurt himself using its product; or a customer may sue a retailer because she tripped on his premises and broke a leg. The liability judgments from such accidents often run into tens of thousands of dollars. With liability coverage, the insurer agrees to pay claims assessed by the courts, but only up to the limit set forth in the policy.

Key persons are vital to the success of any venture. This is especially true in the sole proprietorship. To protect heirs from being forced to sell the venture to pay estate taxes, sole proprietors can buy *key-person life insurance*. This kind of insurance can also benefit partnerships, to buy out the heirs of a deceased partner. Also insurable are the lives of such key persons as creative chemists or star salespersons.

If a small venture shuts down because of a major disaster, such as fire, but expects to re-open after restoration, it must keep paying operating expenses, such as salaries to key employees, taxes, interest, and so on—even though there are *no* sales. To protect against such losses, entrepreneurs can purchase *business-interruption insurance*.

To protect against theft and fraud committed by employees, entrepreneurs can buy *fidelity bonds* from bonding companies. The face value of this kind of policy is limited to the amount of cash, or the value of the products, accessible to employees. Here is an example:

EXAMPLE ▶

A father has a son who has fallen in with bad companions. The son is caught stealing and is sent to a reformatory. Upon his release, the son cannot get a job because of his record. A satisfactory employment record is necessary, however, if the son is to be rehabilitated, become self-supporting, and develop personal pride.

The father asks a friend to give the boy a job that will demonstrate the boy's honesty. The friend refuses, fearing that he too may suffer a loss. The father then agrees in writing to repay the friend for any loss suffered because of the dishonesty of the boy. On this basis, the friend hires the boy.

This agreement is a personal surety contract of the type known as a *fidelity bond*. The obligation guaranteed is the son's honesty. The parties to the contract are the father, the son, and the friend who employs the boy. The risk is the uncertainty of loss arising from the son's possible dishonesty.[4] ▲▼▲

Selecting an Insurance Agent

Perhaps no other industry is more carefully tailored to the needs of individual customers than the insurance industry. As a result, entrepreneurs can readily buy the insurance program that best suits their own needs as well as their venture's needs. To do so, however, they must rely on the expertise of a reputable insurance agent. Licensed by the state, agents are qualified by training and by experience to design an insurance program geared to the entrepreneur's unique needs. These two examples underscore the need to seek reputable advice:

EXAMPLE ▶

Ronald Gompertz, the owner of a small clothing store, was pondering the last bill he received from his insurance company. "These premiums are killing me. I must have insurance on everything under the sun, including my gold teeth. I have so many different policies that I wouldn't be surprised if some things were covered by two policies. There ought to be an easier way to get good insurance than this."[5] ▲▼▲

EXAMPLE ▶

Linda Johnson, the owner of a small India import shop, seemed to have just the opposite problem. "Six months ago this shop was broken into and burglarized, and I am still trying to collect from my insurance company. They say my policy only covers robbery, not burglary. Well, aren't they the same thing?"[6] ▲▼▲

How should an entrepreneur select a reputable insurance agent? One way is to ask bankers or lawyers, who are likely to know which agents are reputable and which offer one-stop service, selling all lines of insurance, including fire, health, liability, and life insurance.

The alternative to one-stop service is piecemeal service, in which the agent specializes in just one line, such as fire insurance or health insurance. This alternative is less attractive than a one-stop service. The reason is that agents who offer a one-stop service are more likely to do a painstaking job of analyzing all of the entrepreneur's insurance needs, mostly because they earn a commission on not just one but many lines of insurance. These agents, then, are more likely to favor the entrepreneur's best interests rather than the insurer's on any settlement claims made by the entrepreneur.

Moreover, it is generally best to select an *independent* agent, one who represents a number of insurers. Independence permits the agent to shop for the policies that best fit the entrepreneur's needs. For example, if one insurance company fails to offer what the agent believes to be proper coverage at a reasonable premium, the agent can select another insurer who does. Exhibit 20.5 lists the traits that entrepreneurs should look for in an insurance agent.

To make sure that an agent deals only with financially solid insurers, the entrepreneur must do some checking. One good source of information is *Best's Insurance Reports*, which rates each insurer's ability to pay claims promptly.

Fringe Benefits

We have already discussed several kinds of insurance that protect ventures from extraordinary financial loss. Other kinds protect not the venture but its employees. Often called *fringe benefits*, these kinds of employee insurance include life insurance, social security, and health and accident insurance.

EXHIBIT 20.5
Traits of a competent
insurance agent.

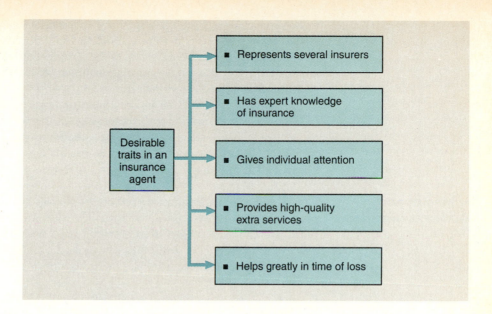

- Represents several insurers
- Has expert knowledge of insurance

Desirable traits in an insurance agent

- Gives individual attention
- Provides high-quality extra services
- Helps greatly in time of loss

▶ **Life Insurance**

Life insurance protects a family from loss of income on the untimely death of its breadwinner. The basic form of life insurance is *term insurance*. It provides pure protection, meaning that there is no savings plan connected with the insurance policy. The premium is just enough to cover the insured's death claim plus the insurer's expenses and profit. Term insurance gives protection only for an agreed-on number of years, after which the insurer can charge higher premiums, or even refuse to insure.

Another basic type of life insurance is *whole life insurance*, sometimes called *straight life* or *ordinary life*. It differs from term insurance in that premiums are paid throughout the employee's lifetime, with the whole amount of the policy payable on the insured's death. Here, the insurer cannot refuse to insure at any time during an employee's lifetime, as long as premiums are paid promptly.

Each of the hundreds of different life insurance plans is a variation on either term or whole life insurance. In one variation, employers of four or more people can buy *group life insurance*. This plan offers advantages denied to individuals. For instance, medical examinations are usually waived; thus, employees may qualify under a group policy even if their health disqualifies them for a personal policy. Another advantage is that group premiums are low compared to individual premiums, with savings running 50 percent or more. Most group life insurance plans are contributory—that is, employees pay part of the premium and employers pay the rest.

▶ **Social Security**

Run by the federal government, social security is a compulsory kind of insurance. It provides families with a minimum income to live on when a breadwinner dies, retires, or is unable to work. Today, social security covers about 90 percent of the nation's employees.

Because social security is compulsory, economists often refer to social security payments as taxes rather than premiums. In 1995, the law required entrepreneurs to withhold 7.65 percent of the first $61,200 earned by each employee in a calendar year. The law also requires entrepreneurs to pay a sum equal to that withheld from the earnings of each employee.

It was public demand for financial security that led the federal government to initiate *social insurance* with the passage of the Social Security Act in 1935. Since then, the federal government has steadily expanded its social insurance programs. In fact, the government now spends tens of billions of dollars each year for such programs.

▶ Health and Accident Insurance

Health and accident insurance protects employees against the high cost of hospitalization and physicians' services. The two most widely used insurance plans are Blue Cross and Blue Shield. Blue Cross pays hospital bills; Blue Shield pays physicians' bills. Besides paying such bills, health and accident insurance often offers benefits like the following:

▶ Up to 26 weeks of wages if an employee cannot work because of accident or sickness

▶ A percentage of wages if an employee suffers a permanent physical disability and can no longer work

▶ Lump-sum payments if an employee is dismembered

To reduce the cost of health care coverage, insurers have developed health maintenance organizations (HMOs). HMOs are insurance plans that contract with selected physicians and hospitals to provide health care for a fixed, prepaid premium.

Pension Plans

So far, our discussion has focused on how entrepreneurs can protect their ventures against the unknown. Now, let us look at how they can protect themselves against the risk of financial hardship when they retire. Such hardship is a real probability without a financially sound pension plan.

Pension plans first appeared in the 1940s, and they have since become a vital part of the nation's retirement system. Economists often refer to this system as a three-legged stool, supported by three sources of retirement income:

▶ **Social security** As discussed earlier, most Americans can count on social security benefits when they retire. For people who have nothing else to live on, however, these benefits offer no more than bare subsistence.

▶ **Personal savings** This source of retirement income is beyond the reach of many entrepreneurs and their employees. As one congressional task force concluded, "If past performance is a guide, private savings cannot be expected to contribute significantly to raising the level of income in old age."[7]

▶ **Pension plans**   This third source of retirement income offers the most reliable way to guarantee a financially comfortable retirement.

Unlike large corporations, however, few entrepreneurs can justify the cost of a private pension plan, either for themselves or for their employees. Given the fact that private pension plans operate best with large numbers of both dollars and employees, small businesses face some special problems:

▶ The cost of running a pension plan is disproportionately high.

▶ Pension moneys, set aside to earn a return, would be insignificant, because a small group means a small pension fund.

▶ Failure is common among new small businesses, thus making their pension plans, if they exist at all, more vulnerable to failure than those of major corporations.

▶ **Keogh Plans**

For sole proprietors and partners who own at least 10 percent of a venture, this bleak picture has become brighter. In 1974, the U.S. Congress passed into law the Employment Retirement Income Security Act (ERISA), which enables many entrepreneurs and their employees to shelter money from taxes while accumulating a nest egg on which to retire. Popularly called the *Keogh plan,* the act allows entrepreneurs and their employees to set aside, *tax-free,* as much as 20 percent of their taxable income—with a limit of $30,000 a year—in a retirement plan.

The plan works this way: Say an entrepreneur's taxable income is $29,000. If she puts $2,000 a year into a Keogh plan earning 10 percent a year, her nest egg at retirement would very likely be large enough to cover her financial needs. Exhibit 20.6 shows that, if she begins investing at age 35, by the time she reaches 65 she will have earned $301,900 in interest, giving her a grand total of $361,900.

EXHIBIT 20.6
How a Keogh plan builds savings.*

Start Plan at Age	Total Amount You Deposit*	Interest Earned**	Total Savings at Age 65
25	$80,000	$893,700	$973,700
30	70,000	526,300	596,300
35	60,000	301,900	361,900
40	50,000	166,400	216,400
50	30,000	39,900	69,900
60	10,000	3,400	13,400

*Also applicable to so-called IRA and 401(k) pension plans, discussed later in the chapter.

**Figures assume deposits of $2,000 a year at an interest rate of 10 percent.

The Keogh plan has several features, among them:

▶ All employees with three years or more of service must be included in the plan.

▶ All moneys contributed to the plan are fully tax-deductible.

▶ All moneys contributed are fully protected by law. In the event of a lawsuit, divorce, bankruptcy, or other financial problem, these funds cannot be claimed.

▶ *None* of the capital gains, interest, and dividends earned by the plan are taxed until the individual begins to withdraw retirement benefits. By then, most people are likely to be in a lower tax bracket.

To set up a Keogh plan, entrepreneurs should approach banks or insurance companies. Many of them have IRS-approved, tax-qualified master plans for investment of Keogh plan moneys.

▶ **Individual Retirement Accounts**

Another tax shelter available to entrepreneurs and their employees is an individual retirement account (IRA). The IRA gives *every* working person in the country the opportunity to set up a retirement plan and, at the same time, to shelter a part of their paychecks from federal income taxes. According to the Economic Recovery Tax Act of 1981, every employee can set aside up to $2,000 a year toward retirement. Additionally, employees can deduct that money from their taxable income.

Entrepreneurs can save for retirement using both a Keogh plan and an IRA. Thus, sole proprietors or partners can invest up to $30,000 a year or 25 percent of their income, whichever is less, in a Keogh plan. They also can invest up to $2,000 a year in an IRA—for a total potential deduction from taxable income of $32,000 a year.

The growth of savings at a 10% interest rate, as shown in Exhibit 20.6, applies to IRAs as well as to Keogh plans.

▶ **401(k) Plans**

So far, we have discussed pension plans that apply only to sole proprietorships, partnerships, and their employees. Another popular tax-deferral plan that entrepreneurs should consider is the 401(k) plan, which may be adopted by any business, regardless of its legal form of organization.

Named for the section of the U.S. Internal Revenue Code that makes them possible, 401(k) plans have been hailed by some pension experts as the cornerstone for retirement savings. Their major advantage is that entrepreneurs and employees alike can have pretax contributions deducted from their pay. For example:

An employee earning $30,000 a year and making a $3,000 contribution reduces her taxable salary to $27,000, which brings an immediate tax savings. This means that, if her federal, state, and city income taxes are at a combined rate of 30 percent, she would receive an immediate tax savings of up to $900.

Most 401(k) plans allow employees to set aside as much as 15 percent of their pay each year, up to a maximum amount set by law. That amount, adjusted yearly for inflation, was $9,240 in 1995.

Another advantage of 401(k) plans is that the entrepreneur's venture, if it so chooses, may match all or part of its employees' contributions. This means that if the venture puts up 50 cents for each dollar their employees contribute, employees would earn a 50 percent return on their money immediately.

And, as with IRA's and Keogh plans, taxes are deferred until withdrawals are made. How 401(k) plans can grow into a tidy nest egg at retirement if begun early enough is shown in Exhibit 20.6.

SUMMARY

To the entrepreneur, risk means the possibility of financial loss. This financial loss can be classified into three kinds of risk:

▶ **Pure risk**   Risk that cannot produce a gain. Examples include, fire, death of a key person, bankruptcy of a customer, and theft.

▶ **Speculative risk**   Risk whereby the entrepreneur can either gain or lose. Investing in land that may or may not increase in value is a speculative risk.

▶ **Fundamental risk**   Risk that touches all ventures—for example, floods, earthquakes, inflation, and war.

To develop an effective program of risk management, entrepreneurs must rely on the expertise of an insurance agent, who can design a program that:

▶ Pinpoints risks that may cause dollar losses.

▶ Estimates how severe these losses may be.

▶ Selects the best way to treat each risk.

There are four ways for entrepreneurs to deal with risk:

▶ Avoid the risk entirely.

▶ Absorb the risk through self-insurance.

▶ Prevent the occurrence of loss, cut the chances of its occurrence, or reduce its severity.

▶ Transfer the risk to others, through insurance.

There are a number of forms of insurance coverage. Among the most popular are the following:

▶ *Property insurance,* which covers assets such as buildings, equipment, and inventories.

▶ *Liability insurance,* which protects against losses caused by the entrepreneur's negligence.

▶ *Key-person life insurance,* which protects against the loss of persons who are vital to the survival of a business.

▶ *Business-interruption insurance,* which protects against losses caused by a shutdown due to a major disaster like a fire.

▶ *Fidelity bonds,* which protect against theft and fraud committed by employees.

A pension plan, which offers retirement income to all workers, should be a part of every entrepreneur's master retirement plan for employees. A pension plan supplements the other two main sources of retirement income: social security and personal savings. The most popular pension plans today are IRAs, Keogh plans, and 401(k) plans. Each one offers entrepreneurs and their employees an opportunity to shelter their income while accumulating a nest egg on which to retire.

Discussion and Review Questions

1. What does risk mean to an entrepreneur? Give one example.
2. Explain the difference between pure and speculative risk. Give one example of each kind of risk.
3. What is fundamental risk? Give one example.
4. What is risk management? How might you, as an entrepreneur, go about setting up a risk management program for your venture?
5. Explain the four ways of handling risk. Give an example of each.
6. Describe some of the ways that entrepreneurs can minimize their exposure to risk.
7. What is insurance? How does it work?
8. Describe the four tests that insurable risks must meet.
9. Describe some of the various kinds of insurance coverage.
10. Why is key-person life insurance so vital to the survival and growth of certain ventures?
11. Explain why entrepreneurs should select insurance agents with the same care they give to selecting accountants, bankers, or lawyers. How would you, as an entrepreneur, go about selecting an insurance agent?
12. Why is it generally best for entrepreneurs to select *independent* insurance agents?
13. Describe some of the ways that an entrepreneur can help employees protect themselves against financial loss. Why are they often called *fringe benefits*?
14. Why is a pension plan so important to the entrepreneur?
15. Define these terms: *avoidance of risk, self-insurance, transfer of risk, premium, liability insurance, term insurance, ERISA.*

Risk Management and Insurance

To the entrepreneur, risk means the chance of financial loss. If entrepreneurs ignore risk, they are likely to blunder, but if they face up to it, they can enhance their chances of survival and growth.

Risk Management

Risk management is the process of evaluating the risks faced by a firm and then minimizing the costs involved with those risks. A part of any effective risk management program is determining the most appropriate way to handle potential risks. While most people think of risk management as simply buying insurance, there are other ways to deal with risk, which include: (1) risk avoidance, (2) risk prevention, and (3) risk reduction.

Instructions for Worksheet 20

To complete this part of the business plan, in part 1 you must identify potential risks that could affect your small business. Then in part 2, examine methods that can be used to avoid risks, prevent risks, or reduce risks. Finally in part 3, determine the types of insurance coverage needed to protect your small business.

Part 1—Potential Risks

Before completing this part of the business plan, you may want to review the material on insurance coverage on pages 590 to 601 in the text.

1. Identify specific risks that could affect your small business.
2. Which of these risks are pure risks?
3. Which of these risks are speculative risks?

Part 2—Risk Avoidance, Risk Prevention, and Risk Reduction

As discussed in the text, it is impossible to escape some types of risk in today's world. In fact, for businesses, risk is a part of every decision. And yet there are situations where risk avoidance, risk prevention, and risk reduction can be well worth the time and money required to improve a potentially "risky" situation.

4. Based on the risks identified in part 1, what methods can you use to avoid potential risks?
5. Based on the risks identified in part 1, what methods can you use to prevent potential risks?
6. Based on the risks identified in part 1, what methods can you use to reduce risks in your business?

Part 3—Insurance Coverage

Perhaps the most commonly used method of dealing with risk is to shift, or transfer, the risk to an insurance company. A risk that insurance companies will assume is called an *insurable risk*. Insurable risks include the risk of loss by fire and theft, the risk of loss by automobile accident, and the risks of sickness and death. A risk that insurance companies will not assume is called an *uninsurable risk*. In general, pure risks are insurable, whereas speculative risks are uninsurable.

7. Based on the information in parts 1 and 2, what types of insurance coverage do you need for your business?

Preferred Gift Shop

Not content to rest on her laurels as an accomplished entrepreneur, Jeanette Van Pree is seeking new challenges. She has come to you for advice on how best to choose from among several challenges she has identified. In 1995, her company, Preferred Gift Shop, posted after-tax profits of $169,250 on sales of $3,000,000.

Background

Jeanette Van Pree bought out Reiff's Newsstand five years ago for $100,000. Reiff's had been in the business for ten years and had always made a fair profit of about 5 percent of sales, or $15,000 annually. At the time of the sale, Reiff's carried all the major newspapers, books, cigars, cigarettes, candy, magazines, and lottery tickets, and rented out a limited supply of video films.

Since acquiring the shop, Jeanette had expanded its physical space to 4,000 square feet. She redecorated the entire inside of the store, periodically changing the decor to reflect major holidays, such as Christmas, Hanukkah, Valentine's Day, Mother's Day, Halloween, and all the other important celebrations. She added a complete line of greeting cards for all events, imported unusual gifts from all parts of the world, and even stocked an inexpensive line of jewelry.

Jeanette also sold decorations for various types of parties. She still kept her national newspapers, magazines, and paperback books for the old clientele, but she moved them to a less conspicuous location. She did do away with the lottery tickets, however, since they seemed to cause more trouble than they were worth. When the weekly prize was big, people would crowd the shop, demanding the attention of all the clerks.

Moreover, so many people to watch added to the shoplifting problem.

Gradual Changeover

Six months after she purchased the shop, Jeanette gave it the new name, Preferred Gift Shop. She made her changes gradually and took her time in hiring new personnel, cautious not to make a mistake. After being hired, an employee had to work in every department to gain proficiency in all aspects of the shop's operation. Jeanette was proud of her employees; they were loyal, intelligent, and knowledgeable. Of course, she had to pay them more than they could earn elsewhere in the same line of business. But according to Jeanette's philosophy, if you want good people you have to pay for them.

For the year 1995 the income statement for Preferred Gift Shop was as follows:

Sales revenues	$3,000,000
Cost of sales	1,650,000
Gross profit	$1,350,000
Operating expenses	1,100,000
Profit before taxes	$ 250,000
Income taxes	80,750
Profit after taxes	$ 169,250

Jeanette is currently very satisfied with her business, but she feels she could expand it further. For one thing, the sale of her unusual gifts constantly prompts many phone calls from out-of-town recipients interested in placing orders. Jeanette estimates that she has made around $250,000 in sales outside her immediate area. She thinks perhaps a catalogue would help her distribute her gifts nationally, but she has no idea of how to produce one or how to manage a mail-order operation in general.

Besides the catalogue, Jeanette has also considered opening another store and expanding on a much slower basis. Some of her trained personnel are equipped to be managers.

Perhaps Jeanette should do both—produce the catalogue *and* open a second shop. In any case, she has come to you for assistance and guidance. She would like you to tell her which direction to take. She estimates that she could invest up to $250,000 in another venture or enterprise. In the meantime, she's off on another buying spree to Puerto Rico, the Dominican Republic, and Anguilla—her favorite places to buy exotic gifts.

Source: Reprinted with permission: *Cases in Small Business Management*, 3rd edition. Copyright © 1994 by John Edward de Young. Published by Upstart Publishing Company, Inc., a division of Dearborn Publishing Group/Chicago.

Questions

1. Why is Jeanette Van Pree's shop such a success?
2. What would you recommend to Jeanette regarding expansion? Should she go into the catalogue business or should she start another shop? Should she put her ideas for expansion on hold for a while? How should Jeanette approach this issue to arrive at the appropriate decision? Outline in detail.
3. What function would a business plan serve in this case? Outline the contents of your business plan.

CASE 20B ▷ # *Comer Bicycles*

In partnership with his wife, Michael Comer worked like a Trojan building up his full-service bicycle shop. He and his wife had invested their life savings of $44,000 in the shop. They were the co-owners, along with the bank that held the mortgage.

The bicycle shop had just begun to break into the black when Mr. Comer suffered a severe heart attack. His wife was overcome with shock, as Mr. Comer was but 33 years old and bursting with energy. He was a jogger to boot. She blamed his heart attack on overwork. In her words:

There's no doubt in my mind that Michael got sick because he tried to do almost everything himself. He'd work six and seven days a week, from dawn to dusk without any letup. He

hasn't taken a single vacation in the three years we've been in business for ourselves.

How many times have I begged him to let me do more in the shop? But he wouldn't listen. Although we're partners, Michael feels my place is in the home with our baby. Now look at what's happened. If he recovers, he's going to need a long rest at home. Meanwhile, who's going to run the shop?

Three days after he was stricken, Mr. Comer died. The shop now faced a serious problem. Harvey Brown, who was 66 years old and worked in the shop on repairs, kept things running; but Mrs. Comer knew it was too much to expect him to keep doing so. Soon after the funeral, the

EXHIBIT 20B.1

Comer Bicycles: Income statement and Balance sheet.

Comer Bicycles: Income statement (for year ending July 31, 1995)

Sales revenues		$276,000
Cost of goods sold		193,200
Gross profit		$ 82,800
Operating expenses:		
Mr. Comer's salary	$44,000	
Other	38,200	82,200
Profit before taxes		$ 600

* * * *

Comer Bicycles: Balance sheet (as of July 31, 1995)

Assets		Equities	
Current assets	$ 81,600	Current liabilities	$ 54,000
Fixed assets	69,000	Mortgage loan	60,000
		Owners' equity	36,600
Total assets	$150,600	Total equities	$150,600

shop's accountant worked up the financial statements shown in Exhibit 20B.1.

Mr. Comer had no will. Nor did he have much insurance. He had once told his wife that "wills and insurance policies are for older folk. I'm too young to think about stuff like that."

Questions
1. What should Mrs. Comer do now? Why?
2. Had you been Mr. Comer, what might you have done differently? Why?

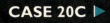

CASE 20C ▶ *Kevin Carney*

Kevin Carney and his wife Mary had jointly amassed an estate worth $750,000 in Lake County, Ohio. They had been equal partners in a thriving restaurant and catering service, which they had sold upon retirement. Married for 44 years, the Carneys had three children, six grandchildren, and six great-grandchildren. Mary died in January 1995.

In April, Kevin Carney, who was an avid golfer, moved to the neighboring county of Ashtabula, buying a house that bordered a picturesque 18-hole golf course. Soon after, in June, Carney told his three children that he was going to marry Laura McNea, a widow 22 years his junior, whom he had met in church only a month before. They married on July 1. A week later, using Laura's lawyer, Carney drew up a will in which he left all of his estate to her.

Within the month, Kevin Carney died unexpectedly. Suspecting foul play, his three children immediately contested the will in court, claiming that their father "was not of sound mind" at the time, and that his will reflected Laura's "improper and deceitful influence" over him.

In court, the children's witnesses from *Lake County* testified that, after Mary's death, Kevin Carney often drank heavily; had once tried to dig up her grave so that he could talk to her; and had often hallucinated that she visited him at night.

One witness claimed that Mary's death even caused Carney to "lose his concentration on the golf course."

On the other hand, the newly widowed Laura and her witnesses from *Ashtabula County* testified that they had never known Kevin Carney to drink, except socially, and then only in moderation. They also testified that, although Carney mourned Mary's death, he seemed determined to make a new life for himself with Laura's "loving help."

Questions

1. What two conflicting principles are at work here, and how would you resolve the issue?
2. In your judgment, what would be the fairest solution?
3. Is there any solution to the possible unfairness that may result from giving people the right to ignore natural heirs in their wills? Explain.

Sample Business Plan

NOTE: This is a sample business plan for a hypothetical company that illustrates the steps required for an effective business plan. Each step was described in Chapter 4 of the text. Additional information on constructing a business plan was included at the end of each chapter in your text. The preparation date for the business plan in this appendix is December 1, 1996. All-Pro Lawn Care will begin operations on January 1, 1997.

All-Pro Lawn Care, Inc.

Business Plan

**Step 1:
Making the
Commitment**

Back in 1991 I had a "dream" to own and manage a lawn-care service that would provide customers with landscape and fertilization services. Now, after five years of planning, saving for initial startup costs, and working in this type of business, I am prepared to transform the original dream into a reality. I am highly motivated to own and manage my own business because it will allow me to make decisions based on my ideas, experience, and research. Realizing the amount of hard work and money required, the potential risks involved, and the rewards of business ownership, I feel strongly that I am destined to be a small-business owner.

**Step 2:
Analyzing Oneself**

Even in 1991 I knew that it took more than just an idea for a business to be successful. Initially, I realized that I had to obtain three key ingredients to achieve success. First, I needed experience. To obtain practical experience, I took an entry-level job with a lawn-care service. Eventually, through employment at other lawn-care businesses, I became involved in all phases of the day-to-day management of this type of business. The second key ingredient that I needed to obtain was an educational background that would help me own and manage a small business. At the University of North Texas and Richland Community College, I successfully completed courses in entrepreneurship and small business management. Finally, the last key ingredient I needed was financing. To obtain the money necessary to open my business, I began a savings and investment program designed to provide the initial capital required to open the doors.

▶ Step 3: Choosing a Product or Service

The owner and employees of All-Pro Lawn Care will strive to provide quality landscaping and fertilization services on a dependable basis to the residents and businesses of the northern sector of Dallas County. Our services will include initial lawn preparation, seeding and distribution of sod, landscaping, renovation, and all aspects of regular lawn maintenance.

▶ Step 4: Researching Markets

All-Pro Lawn Care will operate in Dallas County in the state of Texas. Our service area will include the cities of Addison, Richardson, Plano, and the northern sector of the city of Dallas. There are over 100,000 upscale homes in the service area. And over 90 percent of the homes in this area of Dallas County have a market value in excess of $120,000. Many of the homeowners in this part of Dallas County are professional people between the ages of 30 and 50. And more importantly, a large percentage of the homeowners in the potential market area are very involved in their careers. As a result, they do not have the time needed to perform routine yard work. In addition to single-family homes, there are also over 11,000 apartment complexes and numerous office buildings and small strip shopping centers that need lawn-care services.

While it would be nice to assume that there are no other businesses offering lawn-care services in this area, there are competitors. At the present time, there are 36 lawn-care businesses listed in the Southwestern Bell telephone book. And yet, there are important differences between All-Pro Lawn Care and similar businesses. Perhaps the most important reason customers will choose All-Pro Lawn Care is dissatisfaction with their current lawn service. Customers whom I have talked with tell me that quality and dependability are the most important factors when choosing a lawn-care service. In fact, many customers have been forced to drop one company and choose another because they were dissatisfied with the service they received. An alarming number of customers indicated that their previous lawn-care services initially did quality work, but after a short time problems began to develop. Services like mowing and edging were not completed as scheduled. Other customers complained that many services—like fertilization and tree trimming—were never completed. And after five years of experience in the lawn-care industry, my own personal experience indicates that there is a definite need for a firm that will pay attention to the details.

▶ Step 5: Forecasting Sales Revenues

Based on a market survey of this section of Dallas County, slightly more than 40 percent of all homeowners use lawn-service companies during the spring and summer months. The average amount homeowners pay to have their lawn cut and edged is just more than $32 per week. Based on specific questions in our market study, many homeowners would also prefer to pay someone to perform landscaping, fertilization, and other lawn maintenance activities.

In addition to single-family homes, more than 85 percent of the apartments, offices, and strip shopping centers use a lawn-service company to maintain property. While it is difficult to obtain average prices that commercial customers pay, it is safe to assume that the average weekly charge is higher than it would be for single-family homes.

Based on the above assumptions, my forecast of sales revenues for the first three years of operations appears below.

ALL-PRO LAWN CARE
Three-Year Forecast of Sales Revenues

First-year forecast of sales revenues

January	$ 2,000
February	4,500
March	7,200
April	5,358
May	5,358
June	6,376
July	6,376
August	6,376
September	6,376
October	6,376
November	3,088
December	3,088
Total	$ 62,472

Second-year forecast of sales revenues

First quarter	$ 22,400
Second quarter	35,256
Third quarter	35,256
Fourth quarter	25,104
Total	$118,016

Third-year forecast of sales revenues
$149,850

Notice that sales revenues will increase in both the second and third years of operations. Revenue increases are primarily the result of increasing the number of lawns serviced during the second and third years. To support this sales increase it will be necessary to add additional team members in the second and third year during the peak mowing seasons. Also, notice that sales revenues for all three years have been adjusted downward for the slower winter months.

▶ **Step 6: Choosing a Site**

While All-Pro Lawn Care will provide on-site services at the customer's location, it will be necessary to rent office and storage space. Because the vast majority of our customers will be homeowners, apartments, and businesses in the northern sector of Dallas County, our office/storage location will be located in an industrial park or self-storage facility. A small portion of the facility will be used for an office, while the remainder will be used to store mowers, edgers, and other equipment.

▶ Step 7: Developing a Production Plan

Note: Since All-Pro Lawn Care is a service business, there is no production facility or production plan.

▶ Step 8: Developing a Marketing Plan

The lawn-care business is very competitive. In addition to the 36 professional businesses listed in the telephone book, there are a host of smaller firms that range from school kids cutting yards to earn money in the summer to unemployed individuals who are desperate to put food on the table. Thus, we must use marketing to let potential customers know why All-Pro Lawn Care is different.

Throughout this business plan, the characteristics of quality and dependability have been used to describe the services provided by All-Pro Lawn Care. It makes sense to develop a marketing program built on these two important elements. We must tell potential customers how and why All-Pro Lawn Care is different. The following components will be used to develop a marketing program that will establish a solid base of customers:

1. *Price.* Because the lawn-care business is competitive, price is a major concern. While our goal is not to be the most inexpensive lawn care business in Dallas, our prices will be competitive. We will meet the prices charged by our competitors for the same type of services. At the same time, we will provide the quality and dependability that customers in our market study said were important.

2. *Personal Selling.* During the months of January and February of the first year, personal selling will be used to establish an initial base of 40 to 50 customers. For this initial marketing effort, I will concentrate on three or four selected upscale neighborhoods. I will also contact the owners of apartment complexes, strip shopping centers, and small office complexes.

   As part of our sales presentation, I will explain how All-Pro Lawn Care will meet their lawn needs, including mowing, edging, fertilization, landscaping, and all other aspects of lawn maintenance. I will talk about my years of experience and point out how quality and dependability will make All-Pro Lawn Care different from our competitors. I will also tell potential customers that they are free to contact me at any time if they are dissatisfied with our services. Our goal is total customer satisfaction.

   I will use a similar approach to expand our customer base for the second and third year. Again, special effort will be made in January and February to obtain new customers before the mowing season begins. Because of our total customer satisfaction approach, a special effort will be made to encourage our existing customers to make referrals to friends and relatives.

3. *Advertising.*   We will use handouts and mailers to support our personal selling approach. Initially flyers describing our services and my experience in the lawn-care business will be placed on doors in selected neighborhoods to generate interest. Handouts describing when certain lawn-care activities (fertilization, planting, flower beds, and so on) should be performed will be distributed to both prospective and current customers. These handouts will emphasize our ability to provide these important services for the customer at a reasonable cost.

Ultimately, All-Pro Lawn Care must develop a customer base of between 150 and 200 regular customers by the end of the third year. While many of these customers will only want our mowing and edging services, we will attempt to convince them to allow All-Pro Lawn Care to provide *total* care for their lawns. In addition, we will begin to concentrate on increasing the number of commercial customers (apartment complexes, strip shopping centers, and office complexes) that will allow All-Pro Lawn Care to provide total care.

▶ **Step 9: Developing an Organizational Plan**

Although All-Pro Lawn Care will be organized as a corporation, it will be managed more like a sole proprietorship—especially the first year. Because of the seasonal nature of lawn care in the Dallas area, I will do the initial landscape work the first year during the months of January and February. I will also spend time talking with prospective customers during this time in preparation for the mowing season, which begins later in spring. Beginning in March, I will hire two employees who will work with me for the remainder of the first year.

During the first two months of the second year, the original three-member team will perform all landscape work for our customers. A special effort will be made during these months to talk with prospective new customers in preparation for the mowing season. When the mowing season begins, it will be necessary to expand and hire four additional employees and organize a second team; we will then have two team leaders—one for each team. Each team leader will report to me, and I will oversee the entire operation to ensure that quality and dependability are the cornerstones of All-Pro Lawn Care. I will also spend time marketing our service to new customers, especially apartment complexes, strip shopping centers, and small office complexes.

During the third year, we will need to expand again, forming a third team with a team leader and two additional employees. All three team leaders will report to me, and I will continue to oversee the entire operation and market our service to new clients to expand our base of satisfied customers. At this point, the organizational chart on the following page illustrates the relationships among the owner and employees for All-Pro Lawn Care.

Beginning with the first year, a special effort will be made to develop a team where each worker is responsible for all aspects of the lawn service that All-Pro Lawn Care provides its customers.

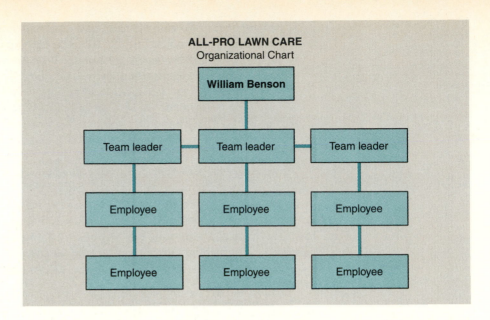

ALL-PRO LAWN CARE
Organizational Chart

William Benson

Team leader | Team leader | Team leader

Employee | Employee | Employee

Employee | Employee | Employee

▶ **Step 10:**
Developing a
Legal Plan

After consultation with Jackie Sutton, an attorney who specializes in new business ventures, we decided that All-Pro Lawn Care should incorporate to avoid potential legal problems. The principal reason we chose the corporate form of ownership was the limitation on personal liability. All necessary incorporation papers, along with fees, were filed with the Secretary of State in Austin, Texas, on 2 November 1996. On 30 November 1996, All-Pro Lawn Care received its corporate charter from the state of Texas.

At the initial meeting with Ms. Sutton, we discussed two other legal matters. First, we decided that she would develop a contract for customers who want to establish a long-term relationship with All-Pro Lawn Care; this contract is currently being developed. Second, Ms. Sutton suggested that All-Pro Lawn Care should obtain an employer identification number (EIN) from the Internal Revenue Service; an application was obtained, completed, and mailed to the IRS. A short time later, All-Pro Lawn Care was issued an EIN.

▶ **Step 11:**
Developing an
Accounting Plan

After consultation with Jackson Barrett, a certified public accountant, I decided to use a computerized accounting system that will be customized to meet the specific needs of All-Pro Lawn Care. For my business, I will need detailed records for cash receipts, accounts receivable, and cash disbursements to track the operations of All-Pro Lawn Care. In addition, the computerized accounting system will generate sales invoices that will be mailed to customers on a monthly basis.

We also decided that I will maintain the day-to-day accounting records. Mr. Barrett will examine my accounting records on a quarterly basis and prepare necessary financial statements and government reports.

▶ **Step 12:**
Developing an
Insurance Plan

After consultation with Samantha Sanders, an independent insurance agent, we determined that All-Pro Lawn Care does need insurance coverage in three areas. First, we need liability coverage to protect customers in the event that their property is damaged by employees. Second, we need insurance to meet requirements for operating a commercial truck in the state of Texas. Third, we need workers' compensation to protect employees while they are performing services for All-Pro Lawn Care.

Step 13: Developing a Computer Plan

Because of the large number of customers that we will serve and the fact that we provide each customer with customized lawn maintenance on a weekly basis, we will need a computer to help manage All-Pro Lawn Care. Specifically, the computer will be used to complete the following tasks:

1. Maintain all accounting records, including cash receipts, accounts receivable, and cash disbursements
2. Schedule jobs to be completed on a daily basis
3. Prepare all invoices for customers' lawn-care services
4. Maintain mailing lists for all current and prospective customers

After consultation with the accountant who is customizing the computerized accounting system, I decided to purchase a new IBM or IBM-compatible personal computer with a Pentium processor and at least 8 MB of memory. In addition to the computer and the computerized accounting system, I purchased several software packages to provide technological support for All-Pro Lawn Care.

Step 14: Developing a Total Quality Management (TQM) Program

Although there are many lawn-care services in this section of Dallas County, the two characteristics that will distinguish All-Pro Lawn Care from other businesses are dependability and quality. Both characteristics provide important building blocks for a successful total quality management (TQM) program. In fact, the concept of total quality management is so important to this business that I have developed the following statement to help ensure that total quality management is the driving force behind All-Pro Lawn Care:

The owner and all employees of All-Pro Lawn Care will make total customer satisfaction their number one priority. In addition, we will build a team of employees where every member of our organization constantly strives for methods that can be used to improve the services we provide our customers.

Step 15: Developing a Financial Plan

Realizing how important it is to accurately translate operating and marketing plans into dollars, I have paid particular attention to the financial details in the business plan for All-Pro Lawn Care. All projections are based on realistic expectations and are contained in Exhibits 1 through 4.

As shown in Exhibit 1 (projected beginning balance sheet), initial startup capital will come from two sources. I will invest $29,350; I will need to borrow $12,000 to help purchase a truck and trailer for use in the business. In addition to the truck and trailer, I will need to purchase lawn equipment valued at $4,800, office equipment valued at $3,100, and supplies valued at $250. Also notice that All-Pro Lawn Care will begin operations with a cash balance of $15,000. If needed, this amount can provide a reserve or cushion

EXHIBIT I

All-Pro Lawn Care, Inc.: Projected beginning balance sheet.

Assets		
Cash	$15,000	
Supplies	250	
Lawn equipment	4,800	
Office equipment	3,100	
Truck & trailer	18,200	
Total assets		$41,350
Equities		
Bank Loan	$12,000	
Owner's equity	29,350	
Total equities		$41,350

that can be used to pay operating expenses during the first year. Total assets on the projected beginning balance sheet are $41,350.

As shown in Exhibit 2 (cash budget), sales revenues exceed expenses in every month with the exception of January, November, and December. An operating loss should be expected in those months because of cold weather and diminished need for lawn-care services. In all other months, All-Pro Lawn Care will show a profit. While sales revenue and expense amounts are projections, they are based on conservative estimates. For example, revenue estimates for the months of June through October are based on obtaining 42 customers that want weekly lawn services. At the end of the first year, All-Pro Lawn Care will have a positive cash flow of $8,572 after paying all expenses.

As shown in Exhibit 3 (projected income statement for first year), All-Pro Lawn Care will earn an operating profit of $7,932 during the first 12 months of operation. It should be noted that all expenses will have been paid, including monthly loan payments on the truck and trailer.

Significant changes reported on the projected balance sheet at end of first year (Exhibit 4) include an increase in the cash account, a decrease in the amount owed to the bank, and an increase in the owner's equity account. While many small businesses show a loss at the end of the first year, our projections indicate that All-Pro Lawn Care should earn a profit that can be used to expand our customer base and operations during the second year.

EXHIBIT 2

All-Pro Lawn Care, Inc.: Cash budget.

	Jan	Feb	Mar	Apr	May	Jun	Jul	Aug	Sep	Oct	Nov	Dec	Totals
Sales revenue forecast	$ 2,000	$ 4,500	$ 7,200	$ 5,358	$ 5,358	$ 6,376	$ 6,376	$ 6,376	$ 6,376	$ 6,376	$ 3,088	$ 3,088	$62,472
Less expenses													
Salaries	$ 1,600	$ 1,600	$ 3,520	$ 3,520	$ 3,520	$ 3,520	$ 3,520	$ 3,520	$ 3,520	$ 3,520	$ 2,560	$ 2,560	$36,480
Gasoline/oil	120	120	240	240	240	240	240	240	240	240	180	180	2,520
Rent	210	210	210	210	210	210	210	210	210	210	210	210	2,520
Insurance	90	90	120	120	120	120	120	120	120	120	120	120	1,380
Utilities	210	210	210	210	210	210	210	210	210	210	210	210	2,520
Advertising	175	175	175	175	175	175	175	175	175	175	175	175	2,100
Telephone	110	110	110	110	110	110	110	110	110	110	110	110	1,320
Supplies	50	50	100	100	100	100	100	100	100	100	100	100	1,100
Loan repayment	330	330	330	330	330	330	330	330	330	330	330	330	3,960
Total expenses	$ 2,895	$ 2,895	$ 5,015	$ 5,015	$ 5,015	$ 5,015	$ 5,015	$ 5,015	$ 5,015	$ 5,015	$ 3,995	$ 3,995	$53,900
Cash surplus or shortage	($895)	$ 1,605	$ 2,185	$ 343	$ 343	$ 1,361	$ 1,361	$ 1,361	$ 1,361	$ 1,361	($907)	($907)	$ 8,572
Beginning cash balance	$15,000	$14,105	$15,710	$17,895	$18,238	$18,581	$19,942	$21,203	$22,664	$24,025	$25,386	$24,479	N/A
Ending cash Balance	$14,105	$15,710	$17,895	$18,238	$18,581	$19,942	$21,303	$22,664	$24,025	$25,386	$24,479	$23,572	N/A

EXHIBIT 3

All-Pro Lawn Care, Inc.: Projected income statement for first year of operation.

Sales Revenues		$62,472
Less expenses		
Salaries	$36,480	
Gasoline/oil	2,520	
Rent	2,520	
Insurance	1,380	
Utilities	2,520	
Advertising	2,100	
Telephone	1,320	
Supplies	1,100	
Depreciation	3,640	
Interest expense	960	
Total expenses		$54,540
Operating profit		$ 7,932

EXHIBIT 4

All-Pro Lawn Care, Inc.: Projected balance sheet at end of first year.

Assets		
Cash		$23,572
Supplies		250
Lawn equipment		4,800
Office equipment	$ 3,100	
Less: Accumulated depreciation	620	2,480
Truck & trailer	$18,200	
Less: Accumulated depreciation	3,020	15,180
Total assets		$46,282
Equities		
Bank loan		$ 9,000
Beginning owners' equity	$29,350	
Plus: Retained earnings	7,932	
Total owner's equity		$37,282
Total equities		$46,282

EXHIBIT 5

All-Pro Lawn Care, Inc.: Sample cover letter.

December 10, 1996

Ms. Betty Campbell
United Federal Bank
Main and Elm Street
Dallas, TX 75201

Dear Ms. Campbell:

Attached is my business plan for All-Pro Lawn Care, Inc. After reviewing the attached business plan, you will, I am sure, agree that the potential for success for this type of business is excellent. The key elements that will make this business a success include a quality service provided by an owner and employees who are dependable and not afraid of hard work.

Although estimates for sales revenues and profits for the first three years are impressive, I will need a bank loan of $12,000 to purchase a truck and trailer for use the first year. This loan, along with the initial capital ($29,350) that I will invest, should provide the startup financing needed to open the business and provide an adequate cash reserve. In fact, based on projections contained in the attached business plan, All-Pro Lawn Care should earn a profit of almost $8,000 the first year.

If you have any questions about the enclosed loan application or business plan, please do not hesitate to call me. Thank you for your consideration. I look forward to hearing from you shortly.

Sincerely,

William Benson
All-Pro Lawn Care, Inc.

Enclosures: Loan application
              Business plan

▶ **Step 16: Writing a Cover Letter**

NOTE: Since All-Pro Lawn Care, Inc., will need a small bank loan ($12,000) to purchase a truck and trailer, it is necessary to provide prospective lenders with a cover letter and a copy of the firm's business plan. Exhibit 5 shows a copy of the cover letter requesting a bank loan for All-Pro Lawn Care.

NOTES

Chapter 1

1. Edward C. Bursk, *The World of Business* (New York: Macmillan, 1963), I, 2.
2. G. R. Driver and John C. Miles, *The Babylonian Laws* (Oxford: Clarendon Press, 1955), II, 83.
3. John Case, "The Wonderland Economy," *Inc.* (1995), p. 29.
4. U.S. Small Business Administration, *The State of Small Business: A Report of the President* (Washington, D.C.: U.S. Government Printing Office, 1995), p. 3.
5. Adapted from the Office of Advocacy of the U.S. Small Business Administration, *The State of Small Business: A Report of the President* (Washington, D.C.: U.S. Government Printing Office, 1995), p. 111.
6. Adapted from a column by Maria Shao of the *Boston Globe* and reported by *The* [Cleveland] *Plain Dealer* (July 2, 1995), p. 1-H.
7. Adapted by the Office of Advocacy of the U.S. Small Business Administration from statistics prepared by the Dun & Bradstreet Corporations, *New Business Corporations* (various issues) (1994).
8. John Case, "The Wonderland Economy," *Inc.* (1995), p. 24.
9. Albert Shapero, "Numbers That Lie," *Inc.* (May 1981), p. 16.
10. Adapted from Robert N. Lussier and Joel Corman, "There are Few Differences between Successful and Failed Businesses," *Journal of Small Business Strategy* (May 1995), p. 21.
11. Joseph F. Coates and Jennifer Jarrett, *What Futurists Believe* (Bethesda, Maryland: World Future Society, 1990), p. 169.
12. Peter F. Drucker, *Managing in a Time of Great Change* (New York: Truman Talley Books/Dutton, 1995), p. 153.
13. Cecily Patterson, "Going Global," *Forbes* (October 19, 1992), p. 1.
14. Caren Goldman, "Popular Culture Studies Focus on American Lifestyles," *The* [Cleveland] *Plain Dealer* (October 6, 1992), Special Supplement on Education, p. 3.
15. Ibid.
16. "Global Changes, Urgent Choices," *The* [Cleveland] *Plain Dealer* (August 11, 1992), p. 2-C.

17. Michael White, "Cultural Diversity One of City's Greatest Assets," *Insights* (Spring 1992), p. 1.

18. "Diversity Training Goes to Court," *Training & Development* (November 1991), p. 11.

19. Martin Levin, "Phoenix Nest," *Saturday Review* (June 22, 1968), p. 4.

20. Ralph L. Stanley, *The White House Conference on Small Business: A Report to the President of the United States* (Washington, D.C.: U.S. Government Printing Office, November 1986), p. 13.

21. Peter F. Drucker, "Europe's High-Tech Delusion," *The Wall Street Journal* (September 14, 1984), p. 24.

22. John S. DeMott, "The High-Tech Challenge," *Time* (December 24, 1984), p. 38.

Chapter 2

1. Sandra L. Kurtzig, *CEO: Building a $400 Million Company from the Ground Up* (Boston: Harvard University Press, 1994), pp. 2–10.

2. James Gleick, "Making Microsoft Safe for Capitalism," *The New York Times Magazine* (November 5, 1995), p. 50; Philip Elmer-DeWitt, "Mine All Mine," *Time* (June 5, 1995), p. 50; Steven Levy, "TechnoMania," *Newsweek* (February 27, 1995), p. 25; Brent Schlender, "What Bill Gates Really Wants," *Fortune* (January 16, 1995), p. 35.

3. Joseph A. Schumpeter, *The Theory of Economic Development,* trans. Redvers Opie (Cambridge, Mass.: Harvard University Press, 1934).

4. Quoted by Office of Economic Research, the New York Stock Exchange, *Economic Choices for the 1980s* (January 1980), p. 9.

5. Irving Kristol, "Business vs. the Economy," *The Wall Street Journal* (June 26, 1979), p. 18.

6. Peter F. Drucker, *The Effective Executive* (New York: Harper & Row, 1966), p. 22.

7. Orvie F. Collins and David G. Moore, quoted by Patrick R. Liles, *New Business Ventures and the Entrepreneur* (Homewood, Ill.: Richard D. Irwin, 1974), p. 2.

8. Adapted from Lynn Beresford et al., "Young Millionaires," *Entrepreneur* (November 1995), p. 120.

9. David C. McClelland, *The Achieving Society* (Princeton, N.J.: Van Nostrand, 1961).

10. "The Updated Book of Jobs," *Time* (January 3, 1983), p. 25.

11. Adapted from Christina F. Watts et al., "Emerging Entrepreneurs," *Black Enterprise* (November 1995), p. 106.

12. Adapted from Ron Stodghill II, ed., "The People Who Make a Difference," *Business Week Special Issue* (1993), p. 112.

13. Adapted from Stephen Gleydura, "Risky Business," *COSE Update* (November 1995), p. 13.

14. Adapted from U.S. Small Business Administration, reported by Wendy Zellner et al., "Women Entrepreneurs," *Business Week* (April 18, 1994), p. 110.

15. Cited in Janet Gardner, "A Workaholic—and Happy That Way," *The* [Cleveland] *Plain Dealer* (March 14, 1980), p. 1-D.

16. Adapted from Christina F. Watts et al., "Emerging Entrepreneurs," *Black Enterprise* (November 1995), p. 110.

17. Marvin Bower, *The Will to Manage* (New York: McGraw-Hill, 1966), pp. 62–63.

18. U.S. Small Business Administration, *Small Business in the American Economy* (Washington, D.C.: U.S. Government Printing Office, 1988), p. 165.

19. Bryan Walpert, "Betting on Home Shoppers," *Small Business News* (June 1995), p. 49; Elizabeth Lesley, "Inside the Black Business Network," *Business Week* (November 29, 1993), p. 71.

20. U.S. Small Business Administration, *The State of Small Business: A Report of the President* (Washington, D.C.: U.S. Government Printing Office, 1995), p. 17.

21. Ibid.

22. Wendy Zellner et al., "Women Entrepreneurs," *Business Week* (April 18, 1994), p. 104.

23. SBA, *Small Business in the American Economy,* p. 118.

24. James M. Stuck and Jack A. Ruhe, "A Comparison of Women Managers in International Business Cases and Selected U.S. Corporations: A Preliminary Study," *Journal of Teaching in International Business* (Vol. 6, No. 4, 1995), p. 36.

25. U.S. Small Business Administration, *The State of Small Business: A Report of the President* (Washington, D.C.: U.S. Government Printing Office, 1991), p. viii.

26. Greg M. Thibadoux et al., "Plugging into Minority Markets," *Journal of Accountancy* (September 1994), p. 50.

Chapter 3

1. William J. Bennett, "Redeeming our Time," *Imprimis* (November 1995), p. 2.

2. Rushworth M. Kidder, *How Good People Make Tough Choices* (New York: William Morrow and Company, Inc., 1995), p. 38.

3. "Reich Cracks Down on Slave Labor," *The* [Cleveland] *Plain Dealer* (August 16, 1995), p. 2-C; "The Profits of Sin," *The Economist* (August 12, 1995), p. 23; George White, *Los Angeles Times,* reported in "Agents Raid Sweatshop That Detained Migrants," *The* [Cleveland] *Plain Dealer* (August 3, 1995), p. 4-A.

4. Adapted from John S. DeMott, "Product-Liability Reform . . . Maybe," *Nation's Business* (April 1995), p. 32.

5. Rushworth M. Kidder, *How Good People Make Tough Choices* (New York: William Morrow and Company, Inc., 1995), p. 48.

6. Ibid.

7. "Who Do You Trust?" *Entrepreneur* (September 1995), p. 18.

8. Comment made by Charles E. Wilson, former chairperson of General Motors, in testimony before the U.S. Senate Armed Services Committee in 1953. Taken from *The Oxford Dictionary of Quotations* (Oxford: Oxford University Press, 1980), p. 574.

9. Quoted in "Radical in the Boardroom," *Forbes* (May 15, 1972), pp. 61–62.

10. Quoted by Desmond M. Reilly, "Students View the Business Ethics Dilemma," *The Collegiate Forum* (Winter 1980), p. 10.

11. "Cause-Related Marketing That Works," *Inc.* (August 1994), p. 102.

12. Tom Peters, "Overachievers of the Decade," *On Achieving Excellence* (January 1995), p. 10; Marjorie Kelly and Craig Cox, "Interview: Anita Roddick," *Business Ethics* (September/October 1992), p. 27; Anita Roddick, *Body and Soul* (New York: Crown Publishers, 1992); Bo Burlingham, "This Woman Has Changed Business Forever," *Inc.* (June 1990), p. 34.

13. Author's interview with entrepreneur in Cleveland, Ohio (December 1, 1995).

14. Civil Rights Act, Title IV (1964).

15. Thomas S. Andrzejewski, "Idealist Untouchables Battle for Consumers," *The* [Cleveland] *Plain Dealer* (April 9, 1972), p. 1-AA.

16. Larry Barth, "Says Consumer Law Can Go Too Far," *The Cleveland Press* (September 26, 1974), p. 2-B.

Chapter 4

1. Harold Blancke, quoted by Marvin Bower, *The Will to Manage* (New York: McGraw-Hill, 1966), p. 46.

2. U.S. Small Business Administration, *Business Plan for Small Manufacturers* (Washington, D.C.: U.S. Government Printing Office, 1992), p. 2.

3. Herman Holtz, *The Business Plan Guide for Independent Consultants* (New York: John Wiley & Sons, 1994), p. 2.

4. Adapted from U.S. Small Business Administration, *Business Plan for Retailers* (Washington, D.C.: U.S. Government Printing Office, 1992), p. 1.

5. Adapted from Robert Townsend, *Up the Organization* (New York: Alfred A. Knopf, 1970), p. 129.

6. Arnold C. Cooper, *Entrepreneurship: Starting a New Business* (Washington, D.C.: National Federation of Independent Business, 1983), p. 4.

7. William Bridges, "A Nation of Owners," *Special Issue: The State of Small Business, Inc.* (1995), p. 89.

8. Lynn Beresford et al., "Homeward Bound," *Entrepreneur* (September 1995), p. 116.

9. Rebecca Freligh, "Women Working at Home," *The* [Cleveland] *Plain Dealer* (June 20, 1995), p. 1-I.

10. Stephanie Barlow, "Home Free!" *Entrepreneur* (March 1992), p. 76.

11. Deborah L. Jacobs, "How to Look Like a Million When You're Not," *The New York Times* (July 10, 1994), section 3, p. 5.
12. Marv Gisser, "Home Alone, Too," *COSE Update* (August 1993), p. 12.

Chapter 5

1. *Planning and Financing for the Entrepreneurial Company* (New York: Price Waterhouse, 1990), p. 3.
2. Adapted from Myles L. Mace and George G. Montgomery, *Management Problems of Corporate Acquisitions* (Boston: Division of Research, Harvard Business School, 1962), pp. 37–56.
3. Adapted from ibid., pp. 37–56.
4. Ibid., p. 184.
5. Charles A. Scharf, *Acquisitions, Mergers, Sales, and Takeovers* (Englewood Cliffs, N.J.: Prentice-Hall, 1981), p. 75.
6. David G. Rosenbaum, *Patents, Trademarks and Copyrights: Practical Strategies for Protecting Your Ideas and Inventions* (Hawthorne, N.J.: The Career Press, 1994), p. 4.
7. Adapted from Patent and Trademark Office, U.S. Department of Commerce, *Patents* (Washington, D.C.: U.S. Government Printing Office, 1988), pp. 3–22.
8. Directory available from the Superintendent of Documents of the U.S. Government Printing Office in Washington, D.C. (1995).
9. Patent and Trademark Office, *Patents,* p. 25.
10. David G. Rosenbaum, op. cit., p. 30.
11. Adapted from Thomas Field, U.S. Small Business Administration, *Avoiding Patent, Trademark and Copyright Problems* (Washington, D.C.: U.S. Government Printing Office, 1992), p. 2.

Chapter 6

1. Lynn Beresford, "New Horizons," *Entrepreneur Magazine's 1996 Buyer's Guide to Franchise and Business Opportunities* (1995), p. 2.
2. Nerilee Hing, "Franchise Satisfaction: Contributors and Consequences," *Journal of Small Business Management* (April 1995), p. 26.
3. Robert Justin and Richard Judd, *Franchising* (Cincinnati: Southwestern, 1989), pp. 42–44.
4. Lynn Beresford, op. cit., p. 8.
5. Ibid., p. 11.
6. Earl C. Gottschalk Jr., "Tax Shop? Gym? Finding a Franchise Without Losing Your Shirt," *The New York Times* (March 26, 1995), section 3, p. 12.
7. Ibid.
8. Timothy Bates, "Analysis of Survival Rates among Franchise and Independent Small Business Startups," *Journal of Small Business Management* (April 1995), p. 26.

9. Ibid.
10. Bank of America, NT&SA, "Franchising," *Small Business Reporter*, vol. 9, no. 9 (1978). This report is currently out of print.
11. Ibid., p. 3.
12. Andrew A. Caffee, "Understanding the UFOC," *Entrepreneur* (January 1995), p. 106.
13. U.S. Department of Commerce, *Franchise Opportunities Handbook* (Washington, D.C.: U.S. Government Printing Office, June 1991), p. x.
14. Committee on Small Business, U.S. House of Representatives, *Franchising in the U.S. Economy: Prospects and Problems* (Washington, D.C.: U.S. Government Printing Office, 1990), p. 55.
15. Barbara Marsh, "Pros and Cons of Being a Chain's First Franchisee," *Franchises and Business Opportunities Monthly* (October 9, 1992), p. B-6.
16. Robert M. Dias and Stanley I. Gurnick, *Franchising: The Investor's Complete Handbook* (New York: Hastings House, 1969), p. 89.
17. *Black Enterprise* magazine, quoted by Lisa Biank Fasig, "All About the Pin-Striped Arches," *Small Business News* (April 1995), p. 43.
18. U.S. Department of Commerce, *Franchise Opportunities Handbook*, p. 277.
19. Anita M. Samuels, "Here's a 'Mickey D' with Kente Cloth and Artists from Ellington to Jackson," *The New York Times* (October 18, 1992), section 3, p. 8.
20. Janean Huber, "Room to Grow," *Entrepreneur* (March 1995), p. 234.
21. Kerry A. Dolan, "Very Golden Arches," *Forbes* (January 1, 1996), p. 137.

Chapter 7

1. Adapted from Veronica M. Gray, "What Insiders Like and Dislike About Firms," *The National Law Journal* (July 25, 1994), p. C-2.
2. Patrick R. Liles, *New Business Ventures and the Entrepreneur* (Homewood, Ill.: Richard D. Irwin, 1984), p. 78.
3. Adapted from Antonio M. Olmi, U.S. Small Business Administration, *Selecting the Legal Structure for Your Firm*, MP 25 (Washington, D.C.: U.S. Government Printing Office, 1992), p. 2.
4. Adapted from Denis Clifford and Ralph Warner, *The Partnership Book* (Reading, Mass.: Addison-Wesley, 1982), p. 46.
5. Adapted from Antonio M. Olmi, op. cit., p. 2.
6. Adapted from Roger LeRoy Miller and Gaylord Jentz, *Business Law Today* (New York: West Publishing Company, 1994), p. 626.
7. *Choosing a Business Entity in the 1990s* (Washington, D.C.: Coopers & Lybrand L.L.P., 1994), p. 33.
8. Ripley Hotch, "A Liability Shield for Entrepreneurs," *Nation's Business* (August 1994), p. 36.
9. Adapted from U.S. Small Business Administration, *The Regulatory and Paperwork Maze: A Guide for Small Business* (Washington, D.C.: U.S. Government Printing Office, 1980), p. 8.

10. Susan M. Eckerly, ed., *A Citizen's Guide to Regulation* (Washington, D.C.: The Heritage Foundation, September 1994), p. 1.
11. Ibid., p. 31.
12. Brent Bowers, "FDA Regulatory Tide Swallows Up McCurdy Fish Company," *The Wall Street Journal* (May 18, 1993), p. B-2.
13. E. O. Schonsted, "Robber Reg Has Backfired," *The Washington Times* (February 16, 1993), p. B-5.
14. Zandra Burlak, "Why Should You Get Involved," *COSE Update* (October 1992), p. 12. Council of Smaller Enterprises, "Small Business Agenda." Reprinted by permission.
15. Tom Pitrone, Ibid., Council of Smaller Enterprises, "Small Business Agenda." Reprinted by permission.

Chapter 8

1. Updated to 1995 from original source: Robert F. Hartley, *Retailing* (Boston: Houghton Mifflin, 1984), p. 141.
2. Quoted by Berry Berman and Joel R. Evans, *Retail Management* (New York: Macmillan, 1989), p. 252.
3. Adapted from Maurice Fulton, "New Factors in Plant Location," *Harvard Business Review* (May–June 1971), p. 4.
4. Fred I. Weber, Jr., *Locating or Relocating Your Business* MA 2.002 (Washington, D.C.: U.S. Government Printing Office, 1992), p. 5.
5. Bill Lubinger, "The Making of a Mall," *The* [Cleveland] *Plain Dealer* (November 19, 1995), p. 1–J.
6. Cynthia E. Griffin et al., "25 Best Cities for Small Business," *Entrepreneur* (October 1994), p. 98.

Chapter 9

1. Bank of America, NT&SA, "Understanding Financial Statements," *Small Business Reporter,* vol. 14, no. 6 (1980), p. 1.
2. LaRue Tone Hosmer, U.S. Small Business Administration, *A Venture Capital Primer for Small Business,* FM 5 (Washington, D.C.: U.S. Government Printing Office, 1992), p. 3.
3. "How Venture Capitalists Share the Wealth," *Venture* (October 1980), p. 32.
4. Suzanne Oliver, "How to be an Angel," *Forbes* (June 19, 1995), p. 228.
5. Ibid.
6. U.S. Small Business Administration, *Financing . . . Short Term Needs* (Washington, D.C.: U.S. Government Printing Office, 1965), p. 33.
7. Reprinted by permission from the April, 1989 issue of *Changing Times Magazine.* Copyright © 1989 by The Kiplinger Washington Editors, Inc.
8. Reprinted by permission from the April, 1989 issue of *Changing Times* Magazine. Copyright © 1989 by the Kiplinger Washington Editors Inc.
9. *How to Talk to Your Banker,* Special Report N245 (Alexandria, Virginia: National Institute of Business Management, August 1995), p. 45.

Chapter 10

1. Peter F. Drucker, *Managing in a Time of Great Change* (New York: Truman Talley Books/Dutton, 1995), p. 87.
2. Marvin Bower, *The Will to Manage* (New York: McGraw-Hill, 1996), p. 153.
3. Adapted from Kristen Baird, "Be Up Front with Employees Who Lack Certain Social Skills," *Small Business News* (November 1994), p. 41.
4. U.S. Small Business Administration, *Delegating Work and Responsibility* (Washington, D.C.: U.S. Government Printing Office, 1983), p. 38.
5. Mark Henricks, "Quality Makes a Difference," *Small Business Reports* (December 1992), p. 29.
6. U.S. Office of Personnel Management, *How to Get Started Implementing Total Quality Management* (Washington, D.C.: U.S. Government Printing Office, 1991), p. 1.
7. "Sales Rep Braves Blizzard for an Unhappy Client," *On Achieving Excellence* (December 1992), p. 11.
8. Tom Peters, "P.S.," *On Achieving Excellence* (November 1991), p. 1.
9. Daniel C. Kielson, "A New Paradigm for Competition," *The Futurist* (November/December 1994), p. 64.
10. John L. Ward, *Creating Effective Boards for Private Enterprises* (San Francisco: Jossey-Bass Publishers, 1991), p. 5.
11. Ibid., p. 6.
12. Ibid.
13. Perrin Stryker, "What's Your Problem," *Fortune* (March 1953), p. 107.
14. Louis L. Allen, *Starting and Succeeding in Your Own Small Business* (New York: Grosset & Dunlap, 1968), p. 28.
15. *Small Business Success,* vol. 5. Copyright © 1992 by Pacific Bell Directory. Used with permission.
16. Reprinted by permission, Nation's Business, August 1992. Copyright © 1992, U.S. Chamber of Commerce.
17. Karen Moeller, "Could Your Start-Up Use a Hand? Uncle Sam is Ready to Help," *Business Start-ups* (December 1995), p. 24.
18. U.S. Small Business Administration, *Association Services for Small Business* (Washington, D.C.: U.S. Government Printing Office, 1990), p. 6.
19. Sanford L. Jacobs, "Women Chief Executives Help Each Other with Frank Advice," *The Wall Street Journal* (July 2, 1984), p. 17. Reprinted by permission of Dow Jones & Company. © 1984 Dow Jones & Company, Inc. All Rights Reserved Worldwide.
20. Quoted by Michael Selz, "Small Businesses Learn the Value of Pooling Resources," *The Wall Street Journal* (October 16, 1992), p. B-2.

Chapter 11

1. Walter J. Cross, letter to the editor, *The* [Montreal] *Gazette* (April 7, 1970). This material also appeared in *Reader's Digest,* p. 151. Reprinted with permission from the May 1973 *Reader's Digest, The Gazette,* and the author.

2. Adapted from Constance Pinney and Charles J. Woelful, *Budgeting for the Small Business,* U.S. Small Business Administration (Washington, D.C.: U.S. Government Printing Office, 1991), pp. 1, 5.

Chapter 12

1. Jacquelyn Lynn, "Year One," *Business Start-Ups* (December 1995), p. 76.
2. Brochure, "Customer Service Strategies Conference," *Inc.* (January 1996), p. 2.
3. "John Kotter's New Rules for Success," *Harvard Business School Bulletin* (June 1995), p. 4.
4. John Persico, Jr., "A Little Information May Help More than a Lot of Benchmarking," *The Quality Observer* (October/November 1995), p. 11.
5. "The Knowledge," *The Economist* (November 11, 1995), p. 63.
6. Adapted from Robert Townsend, *Up the Organization* (New York: Alfred A. Knopf, 1970), pp. 129–30.
7. Peter F. Drucker, *Managing for Results* (New York: Harper & Row, 1964), pp. 12, 13.
8. Quoted by H. Igor Ansoff, *Corporate Strategy* (New York: McGraw-Hill, 1965), p. 43.
9. Jacquelyn Lynn, op. cit., p. 76.
10. David W. Ewing, "Corporate Planning at a Crossroads," *Harvard Business Review* (July–August 1967), p. 86.
11. Douglas McGregor, *The Human Side of Enterprise* (New York: McGraw-Hill, 1960), p. 49.

Chapter 13

1. Quoted by Robert N. Anthony and James S. Reece, *Accounting* (Homewood, Ill.: Richard D. Irwin, 1989), p. 529.
2. Phil Nadel, "The True Value of Ratios," *Cash Flow Today* (Summer 1995), p. 2.
3. Adapted from Jessica Khouzam, "Business Solutions," *Small Business News* (August 1995), p. 5.

Chapter 14

1. From *Marketing Research*. Used with permission of the American Marketing Association.
2. Theodore Levitt, *Innovation Marketing* (New York: McGraw-Hill, 1962), p. 120.
3. For some of this discussion, the author is indebted to William M. Pride and O. C. Ferrell, *Marketing* (Boston: Houghton Mifflin, 1995).

Chapter 15

1. "Jody Wright & Prakesh Laufer—Motherware," *Co-op America Quarterly* (Spring 1996), p. 24.
2. Harvey C. Krentzman, U.S. Small Business Administration, *Managing for Profits* (Washington, D.C.: U.S. Government Printing Office, 1968), p. 6.
3. Adapted from "Doing Business Abroad," *Boardroom Reports* (December 1, 1980), p. 6.

Chapter 16

1. Editors, "The Computer in the 21st Century," *Scientific American: Special Issue* (1995), p. 4.
2. Culled by the author from comments about information technology made by more than a hundred entrepreneurs at a small business seminar held at Cuyahoga Community College (February 18, 1995).
3. Ibid.
4. National Federation of Independent Business Foundation, *Small Business Primer* (Washington, D.C., 1988), p. 27.
5. Ronald E. Anderson and David R. Sullivan, *World of Computing* (Boston: Houghton Mifflin Company, 1988), p. 9.
6. *Dictionary of Computer Words* (Boston: Houghton Mifflin Company, 1995), pp. 120, 48.
7. Adapted from Lan Patterson, "Industry-Specific Computer Applications," *COSE Update* (December 1992), p. 6. Used with permission.
8. Richard D. Helppie, "Programming Your Computer Guru," letter appearing in *The Wall Street Journal,* Midwest ed. (March 8, 1985), p. 25. Reprinted by permission of Dow Jones & Company.
9. Bank of America, NT&SA, "Business Computers from A to Z—A Layman's Guide to Computerization," *Small Business Reporter* (1986), p. 10.
10. Derek Van Pelt, "Diving into the Net," *COSE Update* (December 1995), p. 9.
11. "Perilous Time for Online Computer Services," *The* [Cleveland] *Plain Dealer* (February 22, 1996), p. 1-A.
12. Gary McWilliams, "Small Fry Go Online," *Business Week* (November 20, 1995), p. 158.
13. Thinh Nguyen, "The Internet Generation," *Harvard Magazine* (November/December 1995), p. 72.

Chapter 17

1. Fyodor Dostoyevsky, *The House of the Dead* (London: William Heineman, 1915), p. 20.
2. Charles Garfield, *Second to None* (New York: Avon Books, 1992), p. xv.
3. Nora McGillivray, "Managers and Employees Will Never Understand Each Other," *Business Ethics* (November/December 1995), p. 62.

4. Adapted by permission, *Nation's Business,* August 1992. Copyright 1992, U.S. Chamber of Commerce.

5. Cited by Barry L. Reece and Rhonda Brandt, *Effective Human Relations in Organizations* (Boston: Houghton Mifflin Company, 1996), p. 153.

6. Abraham H. Maslow, *Motivation and Personality* (New York: Harper & Row, 1970), pp. 35–47.

7. Douglas McGregor, *The Human Side of Enterprise* (New York: McGraw-Hill, 1960).

8. Adapted from U.S. Small Business Administration, *Human Factors in Small Business* (Washington, D.C.: U.S. Government Printing Office, 1965), p. 12.

9. Updated from William F. Buckley, Jr., "How to Stimulate Will to Work," *The* [Cleveland] *Plain Dealer* (November 18, 1972), p. 11-A.

10. Thomas Michaud et al., Wheeling Jesuit College, reported by Vicki Kratz, "Proactive Employee Relations," *Business Ethics* (September/October 1995), p. 16.

11. Adapted from Donald K. Clifford, Jr., and Richard E. Cavanagh, *The Winning Performance of the Midsized Growth Companies* (New York: McKinsey and Company, 1983).

12. *The Habit of Winning,* a film produced by the U.S. Small Business Administration (1972).

13. Mary C. Gentle, *Differences That Work* (Boston: Harvard Business School Publishing Corporation, 1994), p. xi.

14. Cited by Alfonso d'Emilia, "Americans Embrace Diversity and Create a New Unity," *The* [Cleveland] *Plain Dealer* (February 18, 1995), p. 11-B.

Chapter 18

1. Adapted from U.S. Small Business Administration, *Business Basics: Purchasing for Manufacturing Firms* (Washington, D.C.: U.S. Government Printing Office, 1985), p. 1.

2. Adapted from ibid.

3. John S. Gammon, *The Barclays Guide to Buying and Selling for the Small Business* (Oxford, England: Basic Blackwell Ltd, 1991), p. 9.

4. Adapted from U.S. Small Business Administration, *Business Basics: Retail Buying Function* (Washington, D.C.: U.S. Government Printing Office, 1985), pp. 6–7.

5. Harvey C. Krentzman, U.S. Small Business Administration, *Managing for Profits* (Washington, D.C.: U.S. Government Printing Office, 1968), pp. 112–13.

6. Dan Steinhoff and John F. Burgess, *Small Business Fundamentals* (New York: McGraw-Hill, 1986), p. 197.

7. Adapted from U.S. Small Business Administration, *Business Basics: Inventory Management* (Washington, D.C.: U.S. Government Printing Office, 1985), p. 25.

8. National Association of Purchasing Management, *The Purchasing Handbook* (New York: McGraw-Hill, 1993), p. 510.

Chapter 19

1. Oliver Wendell Holmes, *Compania de Tabacos v. Collector*, 275 U.S. 87, 100 (1904).
2. "Cover Story: Taxes: The Big Bite," *Time* (March 10, 1952), p. 27.
3. Robert J. Havel, "Vanik Sponsors Measure to Bare Firms' Tax Data," *The* [Cleveland] *Plain Dealer* (February 7, 1973), p. 1-B.
4. Quoted by Martin Kaplan and Naomi Weiss, *What the IRS Doesn't Want You to Know* (New York: Random House, 1995), p. 67.

Chapter 20

1. Debra Nussbaum, "Few Financial Walls Against the Floods," *The New York Times* (February 18, 1996), section 3, p. 7.
2. Herbert S. Denenberg et al., *Risk and Insurance* (Englewood Cliffs, N.J.: Prentice-Hall, 1974), p. 149.
3. George Bernard Shaw, "The Vice of Gambling and the Virtue of Insurance," *Everybody's Political What's What* (Edinburgh: R. & R. Clark, 1944), p. 112.
4. Denenberg et al., *Risk and Insurance*, pp. 137–138.
5. Adapted from U.S. Small Business Administration, *Business Basics: Risk Management and Insurance* (Washington, D.C.: U.S. Government Printing Office, 1985), p. 1.
6. Adapted from ibid.
7. Quoted by Ralph Nader and Kate Blackwell, *You and Your Pension* (New York: Grossman, 1973), p. 93.

INDEX